M000209742

Commentary
on the
Book of Mormon

Volume IV

Commentary on the Book of Mormon

VOLUME IV
THE BOOK OF ALMA—Chapters 27 through 44

The Ammonites in the Land of Jershon, and the instructions of Alma to his sons.

From the notes of:

GEORGE REYNOLDS
and
JANNE M. SJODAHL

Amplified and Arranged by

PHILIP C. REYNOLDS and DAVID SJODAHL KING

PUBLISHED BY
DESERET BOOK COMPANY
SALT LAKE CITY, UTAH
1977

COPYRIGHT
PHILIP C. REYNOLDS
1959

ISBN 0-87747-042-1

Lithographed by

DESERET PRESS

in the United States of America

GEORGE REYNOLDS

In a note near the close of his great contribution to L.D.S. Church literature, *New Witness for God*, President B. H. Roberts penned this remarkable tribute to the labors of Elder George Reynolds:

"It is a pleasure to note the work of this my brother, and fellow President in the First Council of the Seventies, in this field of Book of Mormon labor. I feel myself much indebted to him because of his great achievements in this field of research.

"First, for his excellent *Book of Mormon Chronological Table*, published now for many years in connection with the late Elder F. D. Richards' *Compendium*.

"Second, for his *Myth of the Manuscript Found*.

"Third, for his *Story of the Book of Mormon*.

"Fourth, for his *Dictionary of the Book of Mormon*.

"Fifth, for a series of articles appearing in the *Contributor*, Vol. 5, on the *History of the Book of Mormon*.

"Sixth, for a second series of articles in the *Contributor*, Vol. 17, under the title, *Evidences of the Book of Mormon; Some External Proofs of its Divinity*.

"Seventh, and last, and greatest achievement of all, I thank him for his *Complete Concordance of the Book of Mormon*. The amount of patient, painstaking labor required for the production of this magnificent work will never be known to the general reader. Only the close student of the Nephite Scriptures will ever appreciate it. What Cruden and Young have done for Bible students, Elder Reynolds has more abundantly done for Book of Mormon students. The Elders of the Church through all generations to come will, I am sure, feel deeply grateful to Elder Reynolds for his great work which will stand as a monument to his painstaking habits of thorough application to a task; but what is better still, the work will stand as a monument of his love for the Book of Mormon."

JANNE M. SJODAHL

An editorial published in the *Deseret News*, June 25, 1939, will serve to acquaint those who know little of the life and labors of the co-author of this *Commentary*.

"Physically frail but mentally energetic; of serious manner, studious volition and sedentary habit; Janne Mattson Sjodahl lived simply and labored faithfully beyond the eighty-fifth anniversary of his birth. A native of Sweden, he was educated in Stockholm and London, becoming identified in early manhood with the Scandinavian Baptist Union having headquarters in Trondhjem, Norway.

"At the age of 33 he came to the United States and was converted to Mormonism after his arrival in Utah over a half century ago. His ability as a writer, his faculty for research, his skill as a translator brought him instant recognition and a life-time of labor.

"As a writer and as an editor he had been connected with the *Deseret News*, the *Improvement Era*, the *Millennial Star* and various foreign language publications once circulated by his Church. He served on various missions to Palestine, Switzerland, England, and Sweden. In the latter country he presented a special edition of the Book of Mormon to the king, who received the Utah delegation at the Royal Palace.

"Mr. Sjodahl was the author of many ecclesiastical works and a prolific writer of pamphlets and special articles relating to the organization of which he was a distinguished member. He devoted his whole time, energy, ability, and thought to religious issues and inquiries. Absorbed in meditation almost to a point of asceticism, subjecting his vigor and vitality to constant exertion, he lived many years longer than his acquaintances believed possible for a tireless soul that occupied a frame so fragile."

With the late Elder Hyrum M. Smith, of the Council of Twelve Apostles, Elder Sjodahl was the author of, and the compiler of the *Doctrine and Covenants Commentary*.

Chronology -- Volume IV

B.C.   Signifies—Before the Birth of Christ.

N.A.   Signifies—Nephite Annals, or Years after Lehi's Departure from Jerusalem.

Y.J.   Signifies—Year of the Judges.

	B.C.	N.A.	Y.J.
Second massacre of the people of Anti-Nephi-Lehi.	79	522	13
The people of Anti-Nephi-Lehi arrive in the land of Zarahemla.	78	523	14
The people of Anti-Nephi-Lehi established in the land of Jershon. The Lamanites pursue the Ammonites; are defeated by the Nephites with great slaughter.	77	524	15
Korihor, the anti-Christ, struck dumb, and afterwards killed in a city of the Zoramites. Alma and others proceed to Antionum and minister among the Zoramite dissenters; the majority reject their words, and afterwards cast out their believing brethren. The latter flee to the Land of Jershon, while the unrepentant ally themselves with the Lamanites and prepare for war.	75	526	17
The Ammonites remove to Melek. The Zoramites become Lamanites; the united armies occupy Antionum and attempt to invade Manti. They are defeated by Moroni and Lehi near the Hill Riplah. The Lamanites make a covenant of peace and return to their own lands. The record of Alma closes.	74	527	18
Alma transfers the records to his son Helaman.	73	528	19

GRACE

A GENERAL DISCUSSION

The theological doctrine of *grace* is one of the greatly misunderstood doctrines of the Book of Mormon and the New Testament. The word is frequently used therein, but nowhere is it clearly defined.[1] The Scriptures, as we all realize, do not contain a glossary of their own terms. Authors who first used the word *grace* followed the example of a mother teaching her child a new word: rather than to define it, they merely used it in proper context, until, after much repetition, its meaning became clear. Implicit in the New Testament word *grace* is the connotation that God has done for us something which we could not do for ourselves. When God bestows *grace* upon His children, He goes beyond the requirements of justice. His love transcends the *quid pro quo*[2] which, under the law of the land, is the binding element in all legal contracts.

Nowhere can we find a more forceful nor more poetic expression of this principle than in Portia's famous plea, in which the word *mercy* may be considered roughly equivalent to the word grace:

> The quality of mercy is not strained,
> It droppeth as the gentle rain from Heaven
> Upon the place beneath; it is twice blessed;
> It blesseth him that gives and him that takes;
> 'Tis mightiest in the mightiest; it becomes
> The throned monarch better than his crown;
> His scepter shows the force of temporal power
> The attribute to awe and majesty,

---

[1]Those who would turn to an up-to-date dictionary for an authoritative explanation of the word *grace* are apt to be disappointed. This is particularly true if they are doing more than seeking a conventional explanation of the word's etymology. It must be remembered that the dictionary draws its meaning from current usage far more than does current usage draw its meanings from the dictionary. If usage, therefore, should succeed, over the years, in obscuring the original meaning of a theological term such as grace, the dictionary definition would naturally tend to embody that obscurity. The dictionary shows that the meaning of the word *grace* is derived from the Latin word *gratis*, which was derived from *gratus*, meaning beloved, or dear. Grace, in English, denotes kindness, favor, benignity, largesse, condescension. It suggests an outpouring of the love of God upon the heads of His children.

[2]*Quid pro quo* means literally "this for that." As every law student learns, early in his course in contracts, a contract must be supported by good and sufficient consideration, or quid pro quo. Each party to the contract must do, or promise to do something which he is not by law required to do, or to promise to do. The little which man gives to God, however, can in no sense be considered as *consideration* given in exchange for God's gift of *grace* to man.

Wherein doth sit the dread and fear of kings;
But mercy is above this sceptered sway,
It is enthroned in the hearts of kings,
It is an attribute to God Himself,
And earthly power doth then show likest God's
When mercy seasons justice. Therefore, Jew,
Though justice be thy plea, consider this,
That in the course of justice none of us
Should see salvation: we do pray for mercy,
And that same prayer doth teach us all to render the deeds of mercy.

—*Merchant of Venice,*
Act IV, Scene I

God's gift of grace includes the gift of life, and the gift of faith which leads to true repentance. Forgiveness of sin is an act of grace; and crowning all other gifts, of course, is the gift of immortality and Eternal Life, wrought by the Atonement of our Lord and Savior, Jesus Christ. To obtain the riches of this world, one need go no further than the market place; but to obtain the gifts of grace, one can only look beseechingly to Heaven, for these gifts are unobtainable from among the treasures of the Earth.

And of His fulness have all we received, and grace for grace. For the law was given by Moses, but grace and truth came by Jesus Christ. (John 1:16-17)

The scriptural doctrine of grace springs from the recognition that finite man is powerless to create the agencies of his own existence and Salvation. It is true that as a son of God he is heir to an infinity of powers and dignities. It is true that man is made "a little lower than the angels," and is crowned "with glory and honor." (Psalm 8:5) It is also true that man may eventually "overcome all things" (D. and C. 76:60), and become "gods, even the sons of God." (*Ibid.* 76:58)

All of this cannot obscure the fact, however, that during the course of mortal life the children of God are very finite. Their vision is circumscribed. Their powers are weak. Their capacities are limited. Men realize, with a shattering awareness, intensified in the experiences of every passing day, that without help they are impotent.

No mature, thinking person could question the wisdom of Isaiah's words:

For My thoughts are not your thoughts, neither are your ways My ways, saith the Lord. For as the Heavens are higher than the Earth, so are My ways higher than your ways, and My thoughts than your thoughts. (Isaiah 55:8-9)

Even the startling sixth verse of the 64th Chapter of Isaiah must be accepted as a poetic, but essentially accurate portrayal of the lowliness of man's existing mortal state:

> But we are all as an unclean thing, and all our righteousnesses are as filthy rags; and we all do fade as a leaf; and our iniquities, like the wind, have taken us away. (Isaiah 64:6)

It has been truly said that the greatest of all Christian sins is the sin of self-sufficiency. This is the sin of repudiating not only God, but the very need for God. It is the rejection of Christ's atoning Sacrifice for the human race. It is the impious affirmation of man's omnipotence. Such impudence can only lead the way to spiritual death, and does more than any other act to divest humanity of its heritage of divine grace.

At the heart of the Christian doctrine, therefore, and at the fountainhead of all spirituality, is an awareness of man's inherent limitations, and of his need for power greater than his own to effectuate his exaltation.

> Be it known unto you all, and to all the people of Israel, that by the name of Jesus Christ of Nazareth, Whom ye crucified, Whom God raised from the dead, even by Him doth this man stand here before you whole. This is the stone which was set at nought of you builders, which is become the head of the corner. Neither is there Salvation in any other: for there is none other Name under Heaven given among men, whereby we must be saved. (Acts 4:10-12)

This dependence of man is reaffirmed with great clarity by Jacob, the son of the Prophet Lehi:

> Nevertheless, the Lord God showeth us our weakness that we may know that it is by His grace, and His great condescensions unto the children of men, that we have power to do these things. (Jacob 4:7)

This same prophet also stresses the interrelationship between grace and works:

> And He suffereth this that the resurrection might pass upon all men, that all might stand before Him at the great and Judgment Day. And He commandeth all men that they must repent, and be baptized in His Name, having perfect faith in the Holy One of Israel, or they cannot be saved in the Kingdom of God. And if they will not repent and believe in His Name, and be baptized in His Name, and endure to the end, they must be damned; for the Lord God, the Holy One of Israel, has spoken it. (II Nephi 9:22-24)

On still another occasion, Jacob spoke of grace:

> Wherefore, my beloved brethren, reconcile yourselves to the will of God, and not to the will of the devil and the flesh; and remember, after ye are reconciled unto God, that it is only in and through the grace of God that ye are saved. (Ibid., 10:24)

In a reference to the gift of grace, the Prophet Moroni observed:

> Yea, come unto Christ, and be perfect in Him, and deny yourselves of all ungodliness; and if ye shall deny yourselves of all ungodliness and love God with

all your might, mind, and strength, then is His grace sufficient for you, that by His grace ye may be perfect in Christ; and if by the grace of God ye are perfect in Christ, ye can in no wise deny the power of God. (Moroni 10:32)

Some of the celebrated words of the Apostle Paul explain the saving grace of Christ:

But God, Who is rich in mercy, for His great love wherein He loved us, Even when we were dead in sins, hath quickened us together with Christ, (by grace ye are saved;) and hath raised us up together, and made us sit together in heavenly places in Christ Jesus; that in the ages to come He might shew the exceeding riches of His grace in His kindness toward us through Jesus Christ. For by grace are ye saved through faith; and that not of yourselves: it is the gift of God: not of works, lest any man should boast. For we are His workmanship, created in Christ Jesus unto good works, which God hath before ordained that we should walk in them. (Ephesians 2:4-10)

But now the righteousness of God without the law is manifested, being witnessed by the law and the prophets; Even the righteousness of God which is by faith of Jesus Christ unto all and upon all them that believe: for there is no difference: for all have sinned, and come short of the glory of God; being justified freely by His grace through the redemption that is in Christ Jesus: Whom God hath set forth to be a propitiation through faith in His blood, to declare His righteousness for the remission of sins that are past, through the forbearance of God; to declare, I say, at this time His righteousness: that He might be just, and the justifier of him which believeth in Jesus. (Romans 3:21-26)

Therefore being justified by faith, we have peace with God through our Lord Jesus Christ: by whom also we have access by faith into this grace wherein we stand, and rejoice in hope of the glory of God.

And not only so, but we glory in tribulation also; knowing that tribulation worketh patience; and patience, experience; and experience, hope; and hope maketh not ashamed; because the love of God is shed abroad in our hearts by the Holy Ghost which is given unto us.

For when we were yet without strength, in due time Christ died for the ungodly. For scarcely for a righteous man will one die: yet peradventure for a good man some would even dare to die. But God commendeth his love toward us, in that, while we were yet sinners, Christ died for us. Much more then, being now justified by his blood, we shall be saved from wrath through him. For if, when we were enemies we were reconciled to God by the death of his Son, much more, being reconciled, we shall be saved by his life.

And not only so, but we also joy in God through our Lord Jesus Christ, by whom we have now received the atonement.

Wherefore, as by one man sin entered into the world, and death by sin; and so death passed upon all men, for that all have sinned: (for until the law sin was in the world: but sin is not imputed when there is no law. Nevertheless death reigned from Adam to Moses, even over them that had not sinned after the similitude of Adam's transgression, who is the figure of Him that was to come. But not as the offence, so also is the free gift. For if through the offence of one many be dead, much more the grace of God, and the gift by grace, which is by one man, Jesus Christ, hath abounded unto many. And not as it was by one that sinned, so is the gift: for the judgment was by one to condemnation, but the free gift is of many offences unto justification.

For if by one man's offence death reigned by one; much more they which receive abundance of grace and of the gift of righteousness shall reign in life by one, Jesus Christ.)

Therefore as by the offence of one judgment came upon all men to condemnation; even so by the righteousness of one the free gift came upon all men unto justification of life. For as by one man's disobedience many were made sinners, so by the obedience of one shall many be made righteous. Moreover the law entered, that the offence might abound. But where sin abounded, grace did much more abound: that as sin hath reigned unto death, even so might grace reign through righteousness unto eternal life by Jesus Christ our Lord. (Romans 5)

The grace of God was manifested in providing a Savior and Redeemer, whose atoning Sacrifice gave immortality to all the human race. Through the Savior, God also gave mankind an opportunity to achieve individual exaltation through the exercise of faith (which includes works) and through obedience to other Gospel laws and ordinances.

The extent of the suffering which Jesus endured for us in His crucifixion is beyond the power of finite minds to comprehend.

For behold I, God, have suffered these things for all, that they might not suffer if they would repent; but if they would not repent they must suffer, even as I; which suffering caused myself, even God, the greatest of all, to tremble because of pain, and to bleed at every pore, and to suffer both body and spirit—and would that I might not drink the bitter cup, and shrink—nevertheless, glory be to the Father, and I partook and finished My preparations unto the children of men. (Doctrine and Covenants 19:18-19)

This was the supreme act of grace, the most impressive manifestation of pure love in all the history of mankind.

For God so loved the world, that He gave His only begotten Son, that whosoever believeth in Him should not perish, but have everlasting life. (John 3:16)

He that loveth not knoweth not God; for God is love. In this was manifested the love of God toward us, because that God sent His only begotten Son into the world, that we might live through Him. (I John 4:8-9)

To fail to understand the doctrine of grace is to fail to understand God's love and, therefore, to fail to understand God.

THE NECESSITY OF BOTH GRACE AND WORKS

Theological disputations over the relative role of *grace* and *works* in the process of man's Salvation have spanned the centuries of Christian history. From Augustine's agonized confessions to Luther's protestations, *works* were spurned by the lofty theologian, presumably with Paul's blessing,[3] while the lowly Christian masses,

---

[3]For by grace are ye saved through faith; and that not of yourselves; it is the gift of God; not of works, lest any man should boast. (Ephesians 2:8-9)

prodded along by a superstitious clergy, performed countless little acts of penance, designed to move both the depraved living and the deceased occupants of purgatory heavenward inch by inch. These lowly efforts supposedly found strong support in James' treatise on works.[4] This controversy has not yet ended. However, the *Reformation* brought a simplification of the forms of worship and an enduring emphasis on *grace*.

Could Paul possibly have intended, in his statement to the Ephesians on grace, to eliminate the need for personal righteousness (good works)? His admonitions to the Saints to live righteously dispel such a notion. His counsel to Titus characterizes these admonitions:

> In all things shewing thyself a pattern of good works: in doctrine shewing uncorruptness, gravity, sincerity . . . For the grace of God that bringeth Salvation hath appeared to all men, teaching us that, denying ungodliness and worldly lusts, we should live soberly, righteously, and godly, in this present world; looking for that blessed hope, and the glorious appearing of the great God and our Savior Jesus Christ; Who gave Himself for us, that He might redeem us from all iniquity, and purify unto Himself a peculiar people, zealous of good works. (Titus 2:7; 11-14)

Paul's encouraging words to faithful Hebrews make his position on this doctrine abundantly clear:

> For God is not unrighteous to forget your work and labor of love, which ye have shewed toward His Name, in that ye have ministered to the Saints, and do minister. (Hebrews 6:10)

In a search for the true position of James on this matter, it is well not to overlook the admonition which precedes James' aforementioned treatise on works:

> Do not err, my beloved brethren. Every good gift and every perfect gift is from above, and cometh down from the Father of lights, with Whom is no variableness, neither shadow of turning. (James 1:16-17)

James makes plain his belief that the grace of Christ is always available to man provided his attitude and deeds qualify him for this good gift:

> But He giveth more grace. Wherefore, He saith, God resisteth the proud, but giveth grace unto the humble. Submit yourselves therefore to God. Resist the devil, and he will flee from you. Draw nigh to God, and He will draw nigh to you. Cleanse your hands, ye sinners; and purify your hearts, ye double minded. (James 4:6-8)

Nowhere is the true relationship of grace to works more clearly and cogently stated than in the Book of Mormon:

> For we labor diligently to write, to persuade our children, and also our brethren,

---

[4]What doth it profit, my brethren, though a man say he hath faith, and have not works? can faith save him? (James 2:14; also verses 15-26)

to believe in Christ, and to be reconciled to God; for we know that it is by grace that we are saved, *after* all we can do. (II Nephi 25:23)

Latter-day restoration of the Gospel clarified the doctrine of exaltation, thus making it clear that obedience to the laws and ordinances of the Gospel (works) was not lost in the doctrine of grace. Unfortunately, however, this renewed concept of the place of works in the plan of salvation has not alone clarified the relationship of works and grace, but has also had a tendency to elevate works above grace in the minds of many believers. Moreover, some exponents of the latter-day word, after making clear allowance for both grace and works, have oversimplified the matter. They have limited grace to the free gift of resurrection, and have attributed to works alone the power to exalt man in the Celestial Kingdom of Glory. This conclusion is unsupported by written authority. Full recognition is given throughout the scriptures to the fact that man is incapable of fully living the Gospel in any of his stages of progress, without help from God. In His great doctrinal sermon, Jesus made clear that living His Gospel would be much more than the simple application of a clear-cut formula to the problems of life. Man's salvation would be achieved by keeping in touch — by asking and searching.

Ask, and it shall be given you; seek, and ye shall find; knock, and it shall be opened unto you. (Matthew 7:7)

He promised that the good gifts would be forthcoming to those who righteously searched and requested them.

For every one that asketh receiveth; and he that seeketh findeth; and to him that knocketh it shall be opened. Or what man is there of you, whom if his son ask bread, will he give him a stone? Or if he ask a fish, will he give him a serpent? If ye then, being evil, know how to give good gifts unto your children, how much more shall your Father which is in heaven give good things to them that ask him? (Matthew 7:8-11)

Thus we see that man's forward movement is aided by one gift after another, or as John has said: "grace for grace."[5]

A careful reading of the teachings of Jacob in the Book of Mormon dispels any notion that works alone have the power to exalt.

Wherefore, my beloved brethren, reconcile yourselves to the will of God, and not to the will of the devil and the flesh; and remember, after ye are reconciled unto God, that it is only in and through the grace of God that ye are saved. Wherefore, may God raise you from death by the power of the resurrection, and also from everlasting death by the power of the atonement, and that ye may be received into the eternal kingdom of God, that ye may praise him through grace divine. (II Nephi 10:24, 25)

---

[5]John 1:16

THE DOCTRINE OF GRACE IN A BROADER CONTEXT

Much has been said in recent years about the doctrine of eternal progression. This doctrine is filled with vitality and inspiration. Properly understood, it is both rational and scriptural.[6] It teaches that God's children may progress throughout the eternities, until they may reach the status and the glory of the Creator Himself. However, this doctrine requires qualification to render it entirely consistent with the Holy Scriptures.

Its exponents liken man's quest for eternal glory to climbing a flight of endless stairs. By mastering one more eternal principle, or conquering one more weakness of the flesh, the heaven-bent pilgrim mounts a new stair.

This analogy has merit, and suggests the vast and seemingly limitless possibilities for growth open to every mortal, as he pursues his quest for eternal glory. The analogy, however, as it stands, is deficient. It does not give sufficient recognition to the doctrine of grace. The analogy suggests that once man has found the endless staircase (which staircase presumably represents the Plan of Salvation), he becomes, thereafter, the means of his own salvation. Salvation becomes a matter of exerting the effort required to climb the stairs. In such a concept, our Heavenly Father's role becomes essentially that of an omniscient instructor, who is eternally urging His children to exert the effort to ascend to greater heights. This concept, however, fails to give full force and effect to the atoning Sacrifice of Jesus Christ.

If we must cling to the stairway analogy, we should modify it to include a huge and unbridgeable chasm somewhere along the stairs' upward course. When man reaches that chasm, he cannot cross it without aid. All the wisdom, righteousness, and brilliance of performance which mortal man may marshal in his own cause cannot transport him across the empty void ahead. Finite powers stand in helplessness before this impasse in infinity.

The Third Article of Faith reads: "We believe that through the atonement of Christ, all mankind may be saved, by obedience

---

[6]The doctrine of eternal progression is strongly inferred, among other places, in that portion of the celebrated 76th Section of the Doctrine and Covenants which deals with the qualifications for entry into the celestial kingdom, and particularly the following verses: "They are they into whose hands the Father has given all things—they are they who are priests and kings, who have received of his fulness and of his glory; and are priests of the most high, after the order of Melchizedek, which was after the order of Enoch, which was after the order of the Only Begotten Son. Wherefore, as it is written, they are Gods, even the sons of God. Wherefore, all things are theirs, whether life or death, or things present or things to come, all are theirs, and they are Christ's, and Christ is God's. And they shall overcome all things." (Doctrine and Covenants 76:55-60)

to the laws and ordinances of the gospel." In our analogy, obedience becomes the effort by which we ascend the endless stairs; it is the Atonement of Christ which carries us across the otherwise unbridgeable chasm. No mortal man has ever earned this Atonement for anything which he has done. It is not a stipend. It is not a reward. It is a gift of love beyond price. It is the grace of God.

To the above qualification to the stairway analogy we add another. Man may, from time to time, find himself without the strength to keep climbing; he also may become confused and find himself in danger of falling. But he has been told that he may ask for help. When that help comes, it is a gift or an outpouring of grace.

The restless mind, however, may find itself impelled to go behind and beyond the conclusions herein expressed, in search of causes and justifications more remote. "Why," it may ask, "was the Atonement of Our Savior necessary; Why did the Heavens decree this bloody orgy to be prerequisite to the throwing open of celestial gates which mark the entrance-way to Heaven's glory? Why this agony? these tears? this broken flesh, and flowing blood? Why did not this cup of sorrow pass by the only lips in all the world which had no obligation to drink?"

There are reasons. They are plainly perceptible even to those of limited discernment. The Atonement was an act of love. The Creation itself was an act of love. Christ's responses to our petitions are acts of love. Life is shaped and nourished and given meaning by countless acts of love. Without love expressed in human conduct, life would be bestial, anarchistic, and meaningless. Existence would degenerate into a dreary battle for survival.

The birth of a child is a baptism of pain and anguish to its mother. It is one of the most dramatic expressions of love in all of human experience. From birth until death, the human being lives and breathes and survives through countless acts of love. Tender hands and arms caress him, feed him, clean him, and rock him in his infancy. Loving parents give, and plan, and work, and suffer so his life might ripen and unfold in the fulfillment of his destiny. He goes to secular and to ecclesiastical schools to learn. He realizes that he would not be there — in fact there would be no schools at all — but for the sacrifices of hosts of scholars, teachers, saints, and martyrs whose impressive accumulation of knowledge and culture was often purchased at the cost of great effort, even of life itself.

So it is that the human being moves through life. He gives and he takes. He loves and is loved. His wife, his children, his friends and his neighbors sacrifice ten-thousand times for him, and he for them. He contributes willingly his time and money for the destitute whom he will never see. He spends his efforts on causes from which he will derive no apparent personal benefit. He gives up wealth and personal treasures that others might have opportunities. He goes into the temples of God, and there he spends long hours to help save others whom no then-living person has ever seen.

Why? How can we explain love? We can not! It is the ultimate justification of all else. We do not use a ruler to measure itself. Neither do we justify love in terms of other virtues. Love is its own justification.

How then could the plan of salvation ignore the basic principle of love? Without it, salvation would be no more than a self-centered, ugly spectacle.

Imagine, if you will, a plan of salvation without love expressed in some great sacrifice. What would you have? Millions of ambitious, jealous candidates for celestial glory, selfishly pushing themselves forward and upward along the road to Heaven.

It seems manifest that Salvation must embody more than a struggle for self perfection. True, it involves self perfection, but it involves much more. In any university one can see a host of students spending time and efforts perfecting themselves. This effort is no doubt commendable; progress would be impossible without education. Can anyone argue, however, that education alone represents the ultimate in human achievement? The world is full of intellectual giants who are selfish, egocentric, and spiritually dwarfed, who often compound rather than relieve human miseries. Intellect without love is cold and unproductive. Salvation is not exclusively individual, and cannot be. The human race is knit together by the ties of inter-dependence. No man is an island unto himself. His highest fulfillment is made possible through acts and thoughts of love.

In recognition of this transcendently glorious principle, God gave the world His greatest and most beloved possession: His Only Begotten Son. In this supreme act of love, the human race is brought into a closer union. A supremely perfect and divinely-ordained pattern of individual conduct is presented. God has given His sanction to, and has placed His seal of approval upon, all righteous sorrow and the agony of love. By this agony, man will be purified. By this grace, man will be saved.

REFERENCE TO VOLUME III

Volume III of the COMMENTARY ON THE BOOK OF MORMON commences with the first year of Alma's Reign as Chief Judge. Could our readers have taken a glimpse at the fair Capital of the Nephites at that time (91 B.C.), already rich in the rewards of human industry, combined with the lavish productions of nature in that much favored land, they might have noticed in the principal street, a portly, handsome man, manifesting in his carriage the evidence of great bodily strength, combined with vanity, self-sufficiency, and subtlety. They might have observed that his raiment was made of the finest fabrics that the looms of Zarahemla could produce, lavishly embroidered and ornamented with the labors of the cunning workman in silk, feathers, and the precious metals, while at his side hung a richly decorated sword. This man was no king, no governor, no general of the armies of Israel; he was simply Nehor, the successful religious charlatan of the hour, to whom the unstable listened and the weak-minded flocked. His teachings had at any rate the interest of novelty to the Nephites, yet some of his theories were older than Idumea. They had been rejected in the *Counsels of Heaven* before Lucifer, the Son of the Morning, fell. He would save all men in their sins and with their sins; he abolished Hell, established a paid order of priests, and taught doctrines so liberal that every man could be a member of his church and yet continue to gratify every vice his nature inclined to. For this liberality of doctrine, Nehor expected in return liberality of support for himself and assistants, in which anticipation he was not disappointed. Many adopted his heresies; his success fired his zeal and developed his vanity. He was so used to the sycophancy of his converts that he was restive under contradiction, and when Gideon, the aged patriot and teacher in the true Church, one day met him in the streets of Zarahemla and upbraided him for his wicked course, neither respecting his great age nor his many virtues, Nehor drew his sword and smote him until he died. For this wilfull and unprovoked crime, the murderer was tried, convicted, and afterward executed. His execution took place on a Hill called Manti, and, from the way his death is spoken of, we imagine that he was hanged.

Though Nehor's shameful life was thus ended, unfortunately his doctrine did not die with him. It was too pleasant to those who desired to gain Heaven without a life of righteousness. Consequently it spread widely through the teachings of his followers. In later years the traitorous Amlicites, the apostate Amalekites, the blood-thirsty

Amulonites and Ammonihahites, were all believers in his soul-destroying doctrines. The bloodshed, the misery produced, the treasure expended, the wickedness and folly of these base creatures cannot be computed.

The increase of these false teachers among the Nephites rapidly developed class distinctions and social divisions; their adherents being generally gathered from amongst those who loved the vain things of the world. Naturally, they became proud and overbearing, and bitter in their feelings towards the members of the true Church of Christ. Many of the latter received severe persecution at the hands of the dissenters and bore it without retaliation, while others returned insult for insult, and gave blow for blow.

The example of these self-appointed teachers produced a like spirit throughout their churches, and their members became idle and full of devices to enable them to live without honest toil. They gave way to sorcery and idolatry, to robbery and murder, and to all manner of wickedness, for which offences they were duly punished according to the law whenever conviction could be obtained, and when the intent of the law was not thwarted by their unholy combinations. This development of priestcraft also gave rise to another evil. Many belonging to the apostate churches, though not willing to openly plunder or murder for gain, were anxious for a monarchy to be established, that thereby they might be appointed office holders and fatten themselves at the public crib. Their hope and intention was to destroy the Church of God, and undoubtedly to despoil its members.

In the Fifth Year of the Judges, a willing instrument arose to effect their purposes. His name was Amlici, corrupt and ambitious, but cunning in the wisdom of the world. He was chosen by the enemies of the Commonwealth to be the king of the Nephites. The whole question was brought before the people at a general election, as provided by the Code of Mosiah. The monarchists were outvoted; the Republic and the Church were saved.

This should have ended the matter, but it did not; the turbulent minority, incited by Amlici, would not accept this constitutional decision. They assembled and crowned their favorite as king of the Nephites, and he at once began to prepare for war, that he might force the rest of the people to accept his government. Nor was Alma idle; he also made ready for the impending contest. He gathered his people and armed them with all the weapons known to Nephite warfare. The two armies of those who so short time before were brethren, met near a Hill called Amnihu, on the eastern bank of the River Sidon. There a bloody battle followed, in which Amlici's forces were disastrously defeated with a loss of 12,532 men, while the victors had to mourn the loss of 6,562 warriors slain.

After pursuing the defeated monarchists as far as he was able, Alma rested his troops in the Valley of Gideon which was named after the martyr slain by Nehor. There he took the precaution to send out four officers with their companies to watch the movements and learn the intentions of the retreating foe. These officers were named Zeram, Amnor, Manti, and Limher. On the morrow these scouts returned in great haste, and reported that the Amlicites had joined a vast host of Lamanites in the Land of Minon, where unitedly they were slaying the Nephite population and ravaging their possessions; at the same time they were pushing rapidly towards the Nephite Capital with the evident intent of capturing it before Alma's army could return. Alma, at once headed his soldiers for Zarahemla, and with all haste marched toward it. He reached the crossing of the Sidon without meeting the enemy, but while attempting to pass to the western bank of the river he was confronted by the allied armies.

A terrible battle ensued; the Nephites were taken somewhat at a disadvantage, but being men of faith, they fervently sought Heaven's aid, and in the increased valor this faith inspired, they hastened to the combat. With Alma at their head, the advance guard forded the river and broke upon the enemy who stood awaiting them. By the impetuosity of their charge they drove in the ranks of the enemy, and as they pushed onward they cleared the ground by throwing the bodies of their fallen foes into the Sidon, thus making an opening for the main body of the Nephite army to obtain a foothold. In this charge Alma met Amlici in personal combat and they fought desperately. In the midst of this hand-to-hand fighting, Alma lifted his heart On High, and prayed for renewed strength that he might not be overpowered, but live to do more good to his people. His prayers were answered, and thereby he gained new vigor to battle with and eventually slay Amlici. Amlici slain, Alma led the attack to where the king of the Lamanites fought. But that monarch retired before the impetuous valor of the High Priest and commanded his guards to close in upon his assailant. This order was promptly obeyed, but it did not succeed. Alma and his men bore down upon them with such fury that the few of the king's warriors who escaped their valiant charge made a hasty retreat. Pushing steadily on, Alma kept driving the allies before him until his whole army had crossed the Sidon. There the enemy, no longer able to withstand his well ordered advance, broke in all directions, and retreated into the wilderness that lay to the north and west. They were hotly pursued by the Nephites as long as the latter's strength permitted, and were met on all quarters by patriots who rallied to the call of the Commonwealth and who slew them by thousands. A remnant eventually reached that part of the wilderness known as Hermounts. There many died and their carcasses were devoured by the wild beasts and vultures with which that region abounded.

A few days after this battle, another Lamanite army appeared. This one advanced along the east bank of the Sidon. Alma, having been wounded, sent one of his officers, who met the hosts of the Lamanites, and drove them back to their own lands.

The great losses sustained by the Nephites in this war, not of warriors alone, but of women and children, together with the vast amount of their property which was destroyed, had the effect of humbling them and softening their wayward hearts, so that many thousands, during the next few years, were added to the Church by baptism. But the recollection of their former disasters was gradually worn away by time and prosperity. Three years later we find great inequality in the Church — some poor and some rich, the more powerful abusing and oppressing their weaker brethren. This course proved a great stumbling-block to those who were not numbered with the Church, as well as being the cause of much sorrow and ill-feeling among its members. Finding that no one man could properly attend to the duties of his many offices, Alma determined to resign the Chief Judgeship, and devote his entire time to his duties as the earthly head of the Church. Preparatory to his resignation, he selected one of the leading Elders of the Church, named Nephihah, to be his successor as Chief Judge. This choice was confirmed by the people (83 B.C.).

Alma now gave his entire attention to the duties of his calling as a preacher of righteousness. He commenced his labors in Zarahemla. Thence he went to the City of Gideon. After ministering there for some time, he returned for rest to his home in the Capital City.

The next year (82 B.C.), Alma turned his face westward. He visited the Land of Melek, where his labors were crowned with abundant blessings. Having satisfied himself with the good that he had accomplished, he traveled three days' journey on the north of the Land of Melek to a great City called Ammonihah. There he found a godless people filled with the falsehoods of Nehor, who were committing all manner of abominations without repentance, because they cherished the flattering lie, as the foundation of their religion, that all men would be saved. This city was in the hands of a corrupt clique of judges and lawyers, who stirred up sedition, tumult, and rioting, that they might make money out of the suits that followed such disturbances. Further than this, they were secretly plotting to overthrow the government, and rob the people of their highly prized liberties. Among such a people Alma labored in vain; none would listen, none would obey, none offered him rest and food. Scorn and mockery were his reward; and he was spat upon, maltreated and cast out of the city.

Weary in body and sick at heart because of the iniquity of the people, after many fruitless efforts, fervent prayers and long fastings, Alma sought some other people more worthy of Salvation's priceless gifts. He bent his way toward the City of Aaron; but as he journeyed, an angel of the Lord (that same angel that beforetime had been the agent of his conversion to God) stood before him and blessed him. He told Alma to lift up his heart and rejoice, for because of his faithfulness he had great cause to do so. The angel then directed Alma to return to the sin-cursed city he had just left, and proclaim unto its citizens the awful message that except they repented the Lord would destroy them.

Without delay the prophet obeyed the angel's words. By another road he drew near the doomed city, which he entered by its south gate. As he passed in he hungered, and asked a man whom he met, "Will ye give to an humble servant of God something to eat?" With joy the man (and strange though it may appear, he was a rich man) took him to his home, and fed, clothed, and lodged, him. Furthermore, Amulek, for such was his name, told Alma that he also had received a visit from a holy angel who had informed him of the High Priest's coming, and had directed him to receive him into his house. Then Alma blessed Amulek and all his household, and tarried with him and recruited his strength under the generous hospitality which their home afforded. But Alma's rest was not to be an extended one; the people waxed stronger in sin; the cup of their iniquity was nearly full. "Go," came the word of the Lord, "Go forth, and take with thee My servant Amulek, and prophesy unto this people, saying, Repent ye, for thus saith the Lord, Except ye repent, I will visit this people in Mine anger; yea, I will turn not My fierce anger way." Filled with the Holy Ghost, these servants of God went forth and valiantly delivered their terrible message. One of those who most bitterly opposed Alma and Amulek was a lawyer named Zeezrom. We find recorded at great length the details of the controversy that occurred between him and the two servants of the Lord. As a result we have handed down to us some of the plainest teachings regarding the Atonement, the Resurrection, the powers of the Priesthood, etc., that are had among mankind. No matter what Alma and his companion said, Zeezrom could twist it from its proper meaning; find blasphemy and heresy in the sublime truths of the Gospel, and extract treason from the simplest of God's laws. Zeezrom questioned and cross-questioned, he promised and threatened, he twisted and turned, he abused and vilified, but all to no purpose, he was caught in his own trap. His Heaven-inspired opponents made manifest his thoughts and intentions, they exposed his lying, they overthrew his sophistries, and with a power more than human, they exhibited the blackness of his heart. As Alma and Amulek proceeded, the power of God increased upon them, their words grew yet more forcible until Zeezrom, himself, felt their power. As his corruptions were laid bare before him, he began to tremble, first with rage, then with fear. Bad as he was, he was not the worst among his people, and when once he realized the power he was combating, his heart began to acknowledge its guilt.

With this feeling he commenced to inquire of Alma, not now in mockery, but in solemn earnestness, with regard to the Kingdom of God. The answers he received were like a two-edged sword, piercing to his inmost soul, bringing to him a terrible sense of his awful position before God, and encompassing him about with the pains of Hell. He realized that he had been a leader in iniquity, that his lyings and deceivings had greatly contributed to drag the people down to their existing corruption, and that he was among those most responsible for their hardness of heart.

In this frame of mind Zeezrom made an effort to plead with the people; he acknowledged his guilt, testified to the virtue and integrity of Alma and Amulek, and interceded in their behalf. But in vain. The degraded populace reviled him, they mocked at him, they said he was possessed of a devil, and further, they spat on him; then they cast stones at him, and ultimately, with some others, drove him out of their city; while the two prophets, with many who believed in their holy message, were thrown into prison, there to suffer all the indignities, persecutions, and annoyances that apostate hate could inflict. Nor was this the worst; these retrobates took the wives and babes of those believers whom they had driven away, with such as had accepted the truth who still remained in the city, and, gathering them in a body they mercilessly burned them to death in one great martyr's fire. Into the torturing flames they cast the records that contained the Holy Scriptures, as though, they imagined, in their blind fury, that they could thereby destroy the truths that were so odious to them.

In their devilish glee and savage exultation, they carried the two enchained prophets to the place of martyrdom, that they might harrow up their souls with a view of the sufferings of the perishing women and children. Amulek's brave and impetuous spirit could ill bear the fearful scene. The groans, the cries, and supplications of the tortured innocents carried untold agony to his soul. He begged Alma to exercise the power of God that was in them to save the martyrs. But the Holy Spirit revealed to Alma that this sacrifice was by Heaven's consent, and he replied, "The Spirit constraineth me that I must not stretch forth mine hand; for behold the Lord receiveth them up unto Himself, in glory; and He doth suffer that they may do this thing, or that the people may do this thing unto them, according to the hardness of their hearts, that the judgments which He shall exercise upon them in His wrath may be just; and that the blood of the innocent shall stand as a witness against them, yea, and cry mightily against them at the Last Day." Then Amulek said, "Perhaps they will burn us also." To which Alma responded, "Be it according to the will of the Lord. But, behold, our work is not finished; therefore they burn us not."

When the fire had burned low, and the precious fuel of human bodies and sacred records were consumed, the chief judge of the city came to the two prisoners as they stood bound, and mocked them. He smote them on the cheeks, and jeeringly asked them if they would preach again that his people should be cast into a lake of fire and brimstone, seeing that they had no power to save those who had been burned, neither had God exercised His power in their behalf. But neither answered him a word. Then the chief judge smote them again and remanded them to prison.

After the missionaries had been confined three days, they were visited by many judges and lawyers, priests and teachers, after the order of Nehor, who came to exult in the misery of their prisoners. They questioned and badgered them, but neither would reply. They came again the next day, and went through the same performance. They mocked at, smote and spat upon the two disciples. They tantalized them with blasphemous questions, such as pertaining to the nature of the faith their obedience inspired. "How shall we look when we are damned?" sneeringly asked these unbelievers in damnation.

Patiently and silently all this was borne. Day after day was it repeated. Harder and harder grew the hearts of the Ammonihahites towards their prisoners. Fiercer and stronger grew their hatred. They stripped Alma and Amulek, and, when naked, bound them with strong ropes. They withheld food and drink from them, and in various ways they tortured their bodies, and sought to aggravate and tantalize them and harrow up their minds. On the twelfth day of the tenth month of the tenth year of the Judges (82 B.C.), the Chief Judge of the city together with his followers again went to the prison. According to his usual custom, he smote the brethren, saying as he did so, "If ye have the power of God, deliver yourselves from these bonds, and then we will believe that the Lord will destroy this people according to your words." This impious challenge, the crowd, one by one, repeated as they passed by the prophets, and smote them in imitation of their leader. Thus each individual assumed the responsibility of the defiance cast at the Almighty, and virtually said, "Our blood be upon our own heads."

The hour of God's power had now come — the challenge had been accepted. The prophets, in the majesty of their calling, rose to their feet. They were endowed with the strength of Jehovah. Like burnt thread the cords that bound them were snapped asunder and they stood free and unshackled before the terror-stricken crowd. To rush from the prison was the first impulse of the God-defying followers of Nehor. In their fear some fell to the earth, others, impelled by the crowd behind them stumbled and fell over the prostrate bodies. They quickly became a confused mass of frightened mobsters, blocking each other's way; struggling, yelling, cursing, pleading, fighting; frantically, but vainly, endeavoring to reach the outer gate.

At this moment of supreme horror an earthquake rent the prison walls. They trembled, then tottered, then fell on the struggling mass of humanity below, burying in one vast, unconsecrated grave, rulers and judges, lawyers and officers, priests and teachers. Not one was left alive of all the impious mob, who a few minutes before defied Heaven and challenged Jehovah's might. But Alma and Amulek stood in the midst of the ruins unhurt. Straightway they left this scene of destruction, and went into the city. When the citizens saw the two servants of God, great fear fell upon them, and they fled, as a goat fleeth with her young from two lions.

Alma and Amulek were then ordered to leave the city. This they did, and went to the neighboring Town of Sidom. There they found those who had been cast out of Ammonihah, and in grief and sorrow they related the story of the burning of the wives and children of the fugitives, and also the history of their own miraculous deliverance.

While the fearful tragedy was being enacted in Ammonihah, Zeezrom — trembling, heart-sick and faint — wandered with the others to Sidom. The horrors of the damned took hold of him, until his body succumbed to the agony of his mind. He was scorched with a burning fever, which continually increased until the glad tidings reached his ears that Alma and Amulek were safe; for he had feared that through his iniquities they had been slain. No sooner did they reach Sidom than he sent for them, as his heart then began to take courage. They did not hesitate, but at once proceeded to where he lay. When they entered his presence, he stretched forth his hands and besought them to heal him. Alma questioned him regarding his faith in Christ, and finding that the good seed planted in his bosom had brought forth fruit, this mighty High Priest cried unto the Lord, "O Lord, our God, have mercy on this man, and heal him according to his faith which is in Christ." When Alma had said these words, Zeezrom leaped upon his feet and walked, to the great astonishment of all who witnessed it. Alma then baptized the repentant lawyer, who began from that time forth to preach the glorious message of Eternal Salvation. His energy, wisdom, learning, and talents were now used towards the upbuilding of the Kingdom of God. With as much zeal as he before time had labored for corruptible riches and worldly fame — for Zeezrom was a whole-souled, courageous man, he did nothing by halves — when he served the devil he was a profitable servant; when he turned to God, he did it with all his heart. From this time Zeezrom became a preacher of righteousness, laboring under the direction of Alma, and we next hear of him ministering with Amulek to the people in the Land of Melek.

Next year Ammonihah was destroyed. Less than four months had elapsed since the two inspired followers of the Lamb had left it to its fate, when the Lamanites fell upon it like a whirlwind in its suddenness, and as an avalanche in its utter destruction. The dark-skinned warriors of Laman swept over these murderers of the Saints like a tempest of fire, leaving neither young nor old, babe or grand-sire, to repeat the story of their woes. Not one of Ammonihah's boasting children was left to defy Heaven. Nor was the city itself spared; it, also, was given to the destroyer, and its palaces and temples, its homes and its workshops, were consumed by the devouring fire. For in one day the fierce flames consumed the walls and towers of Ammonihah. Their light illuumined the lurid skies, shone on the distant mountain tops, and lit the neighboring valleys. Then an uninhabitable desolation, stinking with the rotting carcasses of man and beast, only remained to mark the place where Ammonihah once stood. As the Desolation of Nehors, it was known and avoided by the Nephites for many succeeding years.

Emboldened by this signal triumph, the Lamanites entered the borders of the neighboring Land of Noah. There they continued their depredations, carrying off many Nephite captives into the wilderness. At this juncture the Nephite General, Zoram, with his two sons, Lehi and Aha, rallied their forces in the hope of intercepting the Lamanite armies on their return to the Land of Nephi, and of delivering the captives.

Before starting on their march, Zoram determined to inquire of the Lord. He and his sons knew that Alma was a prophet and revelator unto the nation. Wisely they went first to him and sought to know if it was the Lord's will for them to advance into the wilderness in search of their captive brethren.

Alma laid the matter before the Lord. The divine answer came: "Behold, the Lamanites will cross the River Sidon in the South Wilderness, away up beyond the Land of Manti. And behold there shall ye meet them, on the east of the River Sidon, and there the Lord will deliver unto thee thy brethren who have been taken captive by the Lamanites."

Obedient to these plain instructions, Zoram and his sons crossed over the River Sidon with their armies, and marched southward beyond the borders of the Land of Manti, into that part of the great southern wilderness which lay east of the River Sidon. There they came upon the enemy, as the Word of the Lord had declared, and there they joined in battle. The Lamanites were defeated, scattered and driven into the wilderness, and the Nephite captives were delivered. Great was the joy in the Land of Zarahemla when it was found that not one Nephite had been lost of all those taken prisoners; but every one, great and small, had escaped the horrors of slavery in the hands of the Lamanites, and they all returned in peace to possess their own lands. Here we have the happy result of seeking the Word of the Lord and then faithfully carrying out His instructions.

Again there was peace throughout the land, but the name of Zoram, the Nephite General, is no more mentioned in the Sacred Record.

During this period of peace, Alma and his fellow brethren preached God's Holy Word in the power and demonstration of the Spirit, and with much success. Great prosperity came to the Church throughout all the Lands of the Nephites. At this happy time there was no inequality among members of the Church. The Lord poured out His Spirit upon every part of the land where His people dwelt, as Alma supposed it was to prepare their hearts for the coming of the promised Savior. Like many others of the ancient prophets, he antedated that glorious event. He little knew of the wars and contentions, the apostasies and dissensions, the spiritual tribulations and material commotion, that would precede that blessed day. But, however, with the prospect of Christ's coming at no far distant time, he labored and rejoiced, preached, blessed, and prophesied; never tiring or failing in his energies, and feeling sorrowful only because of the hardheartedness and spiritual blindness of some of the people.

At the same time that Alma was ministering to the Saints throughout the Land of Zarahemla, and also in seasons parallel with the horrific scenes enacted in Ammonihah, the sons of King Mosiah and their brethren were laboring in the Land of Nephi on a perilous mission they had undertaken to convert the Lamanites to belief in the Everlasting Gospel of Christ.

The names of Mosiah's sons were Aaron, Ammon, Omner, and Himni; among their companions were Muloki and Ammah. These all took their journey into the southern wilderness during the last year of Mosiah's reign, or 91 B.C. They carried with them their bows and arrows and other weapons, not to wage war but to kill game for their food in the wilderness. Their journey was a tedious one; they lost their way and almost lost heart, and indeed were on the point of returning when they received Divine assurance of their ultimate success. Nerved by this assurance, and with much fasting and prayer, they continued their wanderings, and before long reached the borders of the Lamanites. Commending themselves to God they here separated, each one trusting to the Lord to guide him to the place where he could best accomplish the purposes of Heaven.

Ammon entered the Lamanite territory at a Land called Ishmael. Here Lamoni was the chief ruler under his father who was King of all the Lamanites. Ammon was no sooner discovered than he was taken, bound with cords, and conducted into the presence of Lamoni. It was the custom of the Lamanites to so use every Nephite they captured, and it rested with the king whether the captive should be slain, imprisoned, or sent out of the country. The king's will and pleasure was the only law on such matters. The king's whim was the captive's reward.

Through God's grace, Ammon found favor in the eyes of Lamoni, and, learning that it was Ammon's desire to reside among the Lamanites, the king offered him one of his daughters to wife. Ammon courteously declined this intended honor and begged to be accepted as one of the king's servants, which arrangement pleased Lamoni, and Ammon was placed in that part of the king's household that had charge of the monarch's flocks and herds.

Lamoni was rich in the possession of many cattle, probably the result of taxes he levied upon his people, but even the king's property was not secure from theft. Marauding bands of rustlers would watch for his numerous flocks and herds as they approached their watering places. Then with yelling and prolonged shouting they would stampede the frightened animals and drive away all they could beyond the reach of the king's servants. These would gather up what few cattle remained, if any they found, and return to the king in the full expectancy of being made to forfeit their lives in payment of the stolen domesticated beasts. They were seldom disappointed for Lamoni, or some one of his predecessors had established a somewhat unique criminal code with regard to stealing the royal cattle. They had adopted the idea that it was easier and cheaper to make the herdsmen responsible for the losses and to punish them therefore, than to hunt out and capture the thieves. It had at least one virtue, it prevented collusion between the robbers and the servants; but it produced much discontent among Lamoni's subjects.

On the third day of Ammon's service, one of these raids was made upon the king's cattle as they were being taken to the Waters of Sebus, the common watering place. The cattle fled in all directions, and the dispirited servants, with the fear of death before their eyes, sat down and wept instead of attempting to stop them. Ammon perceived that this was his opportunity. He first reasoned with the other servants, then he encouraged them, and having sufficiently aroused their feelings, he led them in the attempt to head off the flying herds. With much exertion he succeeded. The cattle were all gathered, but the robbers still watched and waited at the watering place to renew the attack when they drew near enough. Ammon perceiving this, placed the servants at various points on the outside of the flock and himself went forward to contend with the robbers. Though they were many, he knew he was more powerful than them all, for God was with him. The idea of one man withstanding so many was supremely ridiculous to the robbers. But as one after another fell before his unerring aim, they were astonished, and dreaded him as something more than human. Enraged at the loss of six of their number they rushed upon him in a body, determined to crush him with their clubs. Ammon, undaunted, drew his sword and awaited the onslaught. Their leader fell dead at his feet, and as one after another raised their clubs, Ammon struck off their arms until none dared to approach him, but, instead, retreated afar off.

It was a strange procession that returned to the palace of the king. The fears of the herdsmen had been turned into joy, and they marched in triumph into the presence of their royal master with the arms of the robbers as testimonies of the truth of the story of Ammon's prowess. Doubtless they did not diminish the telling points in the narrative; the numbers of the band, the courage of the Nephite, were each dilated upon with the vividness of superstitious imagination. When the king had heard their marvelous story his heart was troubled, and he came to the conclusion that Ammon must be the Great Spirit of whose existence he had an indistinct idea. He trembled at the thought that perhaps this Spirit had come to punish him because of the number of his servants whom he had slain for permitting his cattle to be stolen.

Notwithstanding his misgivings, Lamoni desired to see Ammon, who, acting as if nothing particular had happened, was preparing the king's horses and chariots, as the servants had been directed. When he entered the royal presence of the king, the king was too much filled with emotion to speak to him. More than once Ammon drew to the king's attention that he stood before him as he had been commanded, and wished to know what were the king's desires. But Ammon's inquiries elicited no response. At last, perceiving the monarch's thoughts, he began to question Lamoni regarding sacred things, and afterwards to expound to him the principles of Life and Salvation. Lamoni listened and believed. He was conscience-stricken, and with all the strength of his new-born faith, he humbly asked the Lord to show the same mercy on him and to his people that He had shown to the Nephites. Overcome with the intensity of his feelings the king sank to the earth as in a trance. In this state he was carried to his wife, who with her children anxiously watched over him for two days and two nights, awaiting his return to consciousness. There was great diversity of opinion among his retainers as to what troubled the king. Some said that the power of the Great Spirit was upon him, others said an evil spirit possessed him, yet still others asserted that he was dead, and with remarkable acuteness of smell affirmed, "he stinketh." At the end of this time they had resolved to lay him away in the sepulchre when the queen sent for Ammon and pled with him in her husband's behalf. Ammon gave her the joyful assurance, "He is not dead, but sleepeth in God, and tomorrow he shall rise again." Then Ammon added, "Believeth thou this?" She answered, "I have had no witness, save thy word and the word of our servants, nevertheless I believe it shall be according as thou hast said." Then Ammon blessed her and told her "there has not been so great faith among all the people of the Nephties."

So the queen continued her loving watch by the bedside of her husband until the appointed hour. Lamoni then arose, as Ammon had foretold. Lamoni's soul was filled with heavenly joy. His first words were of praise to God, his next were blessings upon his faithful wife whose constancy he felt or knew. He testified to the coming of the Redeemer, and of His greatness, glory, power, and mercy, of which he had learned while in the spirit. His body was too weak for the realities of Eternity that filled his heart. Again Lamoni sank overpowered to the earth, and the same spirit overcame his wife also. Ammon's rejoicing heart swelled within him as he heard and witnessed these things. He fell on his knees and poured out his soul in praise and thanksgiving to God until he could not contain the brightness of the glory, the completeness of the joy, that overwhelmed him. Unconscious of all earthly things he sank beside the royal pair. The same spirit of unmeasured joy then fell upon all present, and with the same results. There was but one exception, a Lamanitish woman named Abish, who many years before had been converted to the Lord, but kept the secret in her own bosom. She comprehended the why and wherefore of this strange scene. She saw the workings of the Almighty through which the untutored minds of the Lamanites could be brought to an understanding of the Plan of Salvation. From house to house she went, calling the people to witness what had occurred in the palace of the king. They gathered at her call, but as might be expected, their impressions were very conflicting. Some said one thing, some another; some argued for good, some for evil; to some, Ammon was a god, to others, a demon. One man, who had a brother killed at the Waters of Sebus, drew his sword and attempted to slay Ammon, but was struck dead by an unseen power before he could carry his rash intent into action. So fierce was the contention, so angry grew the controversy, that Abish, fearing greater trouble, by an inspiration took hold of the hand of the queen, who thereupon rose to her feet. The queen's first thought was of her husband. She took his hand and raised him up, and ere long all who had been reposing in the spirit stood upon their feet. The king, the queen, the servants, all rejoiced with an ecstasy unspeakable. They all bore testimony to God's abundant love and goodness, and some declared that holy angels had visited them. Still the contention was not entirely appeased until Lamoni stood forth and explained to them the divine mysteries of which they were so ignorant. Many believed, others did not, but Ammon had the indescribable happiness of shortly thereafter establishing a Church to the Lord in the midst of the people of the Land of Ishmael. Ammon's humility, faith, and patience were bringing forth their fruit; while his soul gathered faith and strength in the fulfillment of the promises of the great Jehovah in answer to the pleadings of his faithful, loving, father.

When the Church was satisfactorily established in the Land of Ishmael, Lamoni arranged to pay a visit to his father who was the great king of all the Land of Nephi, to whom Lamoni was desirous of introducing Ammon. However, the voice of the Lord warned Ammon not to go, but instead thereof to proceed to the Land of

Middoni where his brother Aaron and other of the missionaries were suffering in prison. When Lamoni heard of Ammon's intentions, and the causes thereof, he decided to accompany him. Lamoni felt that he could be more serviceable in releasing the prisoners than could Ammon alone, as Antiomno, the king of Middoni, was one of his personal friends and likely to grant any favor he might ask. They accordingly started on their errand of mercy, but on their way were surprised to meet Lamoni's father, who grew exceedingly angry when he found Ammon in the company of his son. All the hatred born and nurtured of false tradition boiled up in his breast. He listened impatiently to Lamoni's story of Ammon's visit and its fruits, and when it was finished he broke out in a torrent of abuse toward the Nephite "son of a liar," as he ungraciously styled Ammon, and ordered Lamoni to slay him. Lamoni, without hesitation, refused to become the murderer of his most loved friend, whereupon the old monarch, in the blind fury of his anger, turned upon his own son, and would have killed him if Ammon had not interposed. Little used to controversy, much less to direct opposition, the king was not softened by Ammon's interference. Savagely he turned upon Ammon, but youth, dexterity, and above all the protecting care of the Lord were with him, and he struck the king's sword arm so heavy a blow that it fell useless at his side. Realizing that he was now in the power of the man whom he had so foully abused, Lamoni's father made abundant promises, even to half of his kingdom, if his life was spared. This boon Ammon quickly granted, asking only favors for Lamoni and his own imprisoned brethren. The king, unused to such generosity and manly love, granted all Ammon's requests, and when he proceeded on his journey his mind was filled with reflections regarding Ammon's courage and great love for his son. He was also troubled in his heart concerning certain expressions of Ammon on doctrinal points, which opened up ideas that were entirely new to his mind.

Lamoni and Ammon continued their journey to Middoni, where by God's grace, they found favor in the eyes of King Antiomno, and by his command the prisoners were released from the horrors and inhumanities practiced upon them. When Ammon met his faithful brethren, he was greatly grieved because of their naked, wounded, starved, and otherwise wretched condition, but when they were delivered they enjoyed a season of grateful joy, thanksgiving, and mutual congratulation. After this Ammon returned to the Land of Ishmael to continue his labors.

It appears that when Ammon and his brethren separated on the borders of the Lamanites, Aaron took his journey towards a Land called Jerusalem, which was situated near the Waters of Mormon (*See* Mosiah 18:4-8). Here the Lamanites, the people of Amulon, and some others, had built a great city to which they gave the name of Jerusalem. In this great city the people, many of whom were Nephite apostates, were very wicked. They would not listen to his teachings so he left them and went to a Village called Ani-Anti. There Aaron found Muloki, Ammah, and others preaching the Word. But their efforts were fruitless; the people of this place would not receive the truth, therefore he left them and went over to the Land of Middoni. There they preached unto many though few believed in their words. Before long the wicked raised a rebellion against Aaron and his brethren, and some of them were cast into prison, while others fled to escape the hatred of the Lamanites into regions round about. In prison they were treated with great cruelty; they were bound with strong cords which cut into their flesh; they were deprived of proper food, drink, and clothing, and otherwise suffered nameless afflictions. There they remained until they were released through the intercession of Ammon and Lamoni.

Some time after Aaron and his fellow-prisoners were released, he, with some others, went to the Land of Nephi-Lehi, or as it is more often called *Nephi*. They were presented before the old king who was the father of Lamoni. When this monarch saw them he was greatly pleased, for his heart had been touched by the words and conduct of Ammon. At his request Aaron explained to him many of the things that related to the nature of God; for, though he recognized the power and might of the Great Spirit, he was altogether ignorant of things concerning the Deity.

Aaron, by degrees explained to him the principles of the Everlasting Gospel. He commenced with the creation of man, showed the aged king how Adam fell that man might be, and how the Plan of Salvation, or the Plan of Redemption, through the Savior's sufferings was devised before the world was, and how man, by obedience to the Gospel, would triumph over death, Hell, and the grave.

Aaron's words were gratefully received by the king, who besought him to teach him how he might obtain this Eternal Life of which Aaron spoke. Aaron instructed the king to bow down before the Lord in prayer, and then in faith ask for the blessings he desired.

The aged king did as Aaron had told him. He prostrated himself on the ground and cried mightily, saying, "O God, Aaron hath told me there is a God, and if there is a God, and if thou art God, wilt thou make Thyself known unto me, and I will give away all my sins to know Thee, and that I may be raised from the dead and be saved at the Last Day." So great was the king's emotion that when he had said these words, he was struck as if he were dead.

When the king thus fell his servants ran and told the queen what had happened. She at once came into the room where he lay, and seeing Aaron and his brethren standing by, she became very angry as she supposed that they were the cause of evil that had, in her estimation, befallen her husband. She, without hesitation, ordered the king's servants to take the missionaries and slay them; but the servants dared not for they feared the power which was in Aaron. The queen was also afraid, but she seemed to think that the best way to get rid of the trouble was to destroy those who she fancied brought it. As the king's servants refused to obey her command, she ordered them to go out onto the streets and call upon the people to come in and kill Aaron and his companions.

When Aaron saw the temper of the queen, he feared lest the multitude, in the hardness of their hearts, would raise a great commotion, and be a cause of hindering the work of God, which had so auspiciously commenced with the king. Therefore he put forth his hand and raised the monarch from the earth, and at the same time said to him, "Stand." The king at once received his strength and arose, at the sight of which the queen and the servants wondered greatly and were filled with fear.

Then the king began to explain to them what he had learned while in the spirit in regard to God and the Gospel. He spoke with such power that his whole household was converted, and the multitude also that had gathered at the call of the queen were pacified by his words. At last when the king saw that their hearts were softened he caused that Aaron and his brethren should teach them the Word of God. After the king was converted, he sent a proclamation throughout the land forbidding any and all from persecuting Ammon and his missionary companions, giving them liberty to preach anywhere and everywhere that they desired. Our readers may be sure that this privilege was not neglected. To use Ammon's own words, the missionaries entered into the houses of the people and taught them; they taught them in their temples and synagogues, in the open streets and on the lofty hills. But often they were cast out, spit upon, smitten, stoned, bound, cast into prison, and made to suffer all manner of afflictions, from which the Lord, in His mercy, delivered them, and from which the king's proclamation afterwards protected them. Nor was the result of Aaron's labors trifling, but glorious in the saving of many souls; for unto the Lord were converted the people of the Lamanites who dwelt in the lands of Ishmael, Middoni, Shemlon, and also in the cities of Nephi, Lemuel, and Shimnilon; and they became a righteous, peaceful, God-serving people; and from faithful obedience to His Law they never fell away. But the various bodies of Nephite apostates who dwelt among the Lamanites universally rejected the Gospel message, with the exception of one single Amalekite, and of what ultimately became of him we have no record.

History often repeats itself, but we have no recollection of any parallel to the events that followed this marvelous conversion. The Lamanite people now became two as distinct and separate bodies as they and the Nephites had beforetimes been. But with this strange complication, the apostate Nephites now occupied the place and did the work of the natural Lamanites, while the true descendants of Laman and Lemuel took the ground previously held by the righteous Nephites. So clearly defined did the division become that the supreme ruler (Lamoni's father), having turned from the traditions, habits, and customs of the Lamanites, was determined to also cast aside the old name. If they were Lamanites in name only they would cut that weak cord which alone held them to the past, and be as new in name as they were in spirits, feelings, hopes, loyalty, and religion. So, after advising with Ammon, and his fellow missionaries he gave to his people the name of Anti-Nephi-Lehies, and to his son, to whom he transferred the royal power, that of Anti-Nephi-Lehi.

The renegade Amalekites, Amulonites, and others, were not willing to be ruled by a Christian monarch. They had rejected Christianity altogether, and would not have it as the ruling power, either in Nephi or in Zarahemla. With the old sophistries and falsehoods they raised a mutiny in the hearts of their associate Lamanites and urged them on to rebellion against the rightful king and his believing subjects. But the converted Lamanites made no preparations to resist them; they felt that in times past with unholy hands they had spilt blood as water on the land; blood that they could never atone for, but they would do it no more. Passive non-resistance would for the future be their policy, but the blood of a fellow being they would never again shed no matter how great the peril, or how intense the aggravation. As a witness of the completeness of this resolve, they took their weapons of war and buried them deep in the earth with an oath and a covenant that they would never dig them up again. When the maddened hosts of their embittered brethren rushed upon them, they came forth unarmed, bowed down before their assailants, and submitted to their fate. With them, to live was Christ, to die was Salvation. The vengeful Nephite apostates led the inglorious charge and shed most of the blood that flowed that day, when 1005 unresisting martyrs glorified the Lamanite Race by the tribute of their lives to God and the truth. A thousand ransomed souls, washed white in the Blood of the Lamb, that day entered the *Gates of Heaven* to stand amongst the saviors on *Mount Zion* in the *Great Day of the Redeemed*. Nor was there joy alone in that bright *World Beyond*, but on Earth the Church of God was gladdened by fresh accessions to His cause. When many of the actual Lamanites — not apostate Nephites — witnessed the great change that had taken place in the hearts of their brethren, even that they would quietly, peacefully, joyously, lay down their lives, their consciences smote them; they stayed their hands, and rose in tumult against their Amalekite leaders, and refused more to be the murderers of their kin. *The blood of the martyrs* was indeed the seed of the Church, for there were more added to the *Fold of Christ* on that memorable day than all those who had passed away to the presence of their God.

Near the close of their glorious undertaking among the Lamanites in the Land of Nephi, Ammon and his brethren met in what developed to be a grand reunion where all rejoiced in the blessings which the Lord had bestowed upon them. Great was their happiness in the success which crowned their efforts, for had they not, they reasoned, brought literally thousands of their Lamanite brethren into Christ's Church? Ammon ended his *Song of Praise* with these words: "Now my brethren, we see that God is mindful of every people, whatsoever land they may be in; yea, He numbereth His people, and His bowels of mercy are over all the Earth. Now this is my joy, and my great thanksgiving; yea, and I will give thanks unto my God forever. Amen."

THE BOOK OF ALMA

CHAPTER 27

1. People of Anti-Nephi-Lehi seek safety in Zarahemla.

1. Now it came to pass that when those Lamanites who had gone to war against the Nephites had found, after their many struggles to destroy them, that it was in vain to seek their destruction, they returned again to the land of Nephi.

2. And it came to pass that the Amalekites, because of their loss, were exceeding angry. And when they saw that they could not seek revenge from the Nephites, they began to stir up the people in anger against their brethren, the people of Anti-Nephi-Lehi; therefore they began again to destroy them.

VERSE 1. *The Lamanites found it was impossible to destroy the Nephites.* When the Lamanite warriors who had gone down into the Land of Zarahemla intent upon the destruction of the Nephites saw that their intended victims were more than equal to the planned onslaught of their Amalekite commanders, they changed whatever plot they had designed and made a disorganized retreat to the Land of Nephi whence they had come. In vain the darkskinned hordes of Laman had struggled to impose the godless will of their apostate leaders upon the faithful and peaceful Nephites. In vain they had challenged the might of the Lord in preserving His people. Now defeated and confused the Lamanite army sought the seclusion of their homes in their own land.

VERSE 2. *The Amalekites were exceeding angry.* The great losses sustained by the Amalekites in their repeated assaults upon the beleagured Nephites so weakened their attacking forces that it was useless for them to attempt any further depredations. In their efforts they had faltered, then disbanded; there was One more powerful than they. The prayers of the righteous Nephites had prevailed on Him who reigns On High. They were delivered! It is enlightening to remember that of the many Lamanites who were slain by the Nephites in defense of their homes most of them were Amalekites and Amulonites.

Now it happened that because of their losses, not only in men and their equipment, but in morale as well, the Amalekites no longer held the firm grasp that they previously had upon their underling hosts. They sought for revenge that they imagined would repay the ruin that had come upon them. But they saw that to obtain it from the Nephites was a hazardous undertaking in which they had already failed. In their disappointed pride which grew more bitter and malignant as their

3. Now this people again refused to take their arms, and they suffered themselves to be slain according to the desires of their enemies.

4. Now when Ammon and his brethren saw this work of destruction among those whom they so dearly beloved, and among those who had so dearly beloved them—for they were treated as though they were angels sent from God to save them from everlasting destruction — therefore, when Ammon and his brethren saw this great work of destruction, they were moved with compassion, and they said unto the king:

5. Let us gather together this people of the Lord, and let us go down to the land of Zarahemla to our brethren the Nephites, and flee out of the hands of our enemies, that we be not destroyed.

---

defeat became more apparent, they began to incite the remaining part of their disorganized army to murder their brethren, the Anti-Nephi-Lehies, whom they said were friendly to the Nephites. The Sacred Record says: "Therefore they began to destroy them."

VERSE 3. *The Anti-Nephi-Lehies again refused to take their arms.* Notwithstanding what appeared to mean sure death in so doing, the Christian Lamanites refused again to use their implements of war even in defending themselves. Their almost passionate determination not to shed the blood of their fellow men stiffened the resolve they had made when they buried their swords deep in the earth (Alma 24:12-18). "They suffered themselves to be slain according to the desires of their enemies."

VERSE 4. *Ammon and his brethren were moved with compassion.* The slaughter of the Anti-Nephi-Lehies by their vengeful brethren, the unbelieving Lamanites, could not go unheeded by Ammon and his fellow missionaries who were filled with compassion for the defenseless believers in Christ. Because of their love for all His children, Ammon and his brethren had offered their lives upon the altar of service in God's Kingdom. They had forsaken all they held dear to proclaim the Gospel to the benighted Lamanites whom they knew to be a "wild and a hardened and a ferocious people." On the other hand, too, the Lamanites whom they, with the help of the Lord, had converted to His cause, looked upon the missionaries "as though they were angels sent from God to save them from everlasting destruction." The love of each, that is the missionaries and the converts they had made, was mutual, and in their distress which was also mutual, Ammon and his brethren sought ways and means to deliver the oppressed Anti-Nephi-Lehies from a fate so appalling that it made the strongest among them quake with despair and anguish.

To the end that the Anti-Nephi-Lehies should be freed from the prospect of annihilation the missionaries consulted with the king, whose name also was Anti-Nephi-Lehi. In the hope that justice would prevail, and that mercy from Heaven be given, the Nephite servants of God judged that the Lord, having so thoroughly tried the faith of this devoted people would provide some way of escape. With this thought in mind, "they said unto the king":

VERSE 5. *Let us flee out of the hands of our enemies.* Ammon and his brethren were not willing to have the new disciples continually harassed by their enemies and be ultimately exterminated. No doubt plan after plan to insure their safety had been devised and then laid aside as being unworkable. To return blow for

6. But the king said unto them: | and sins we have committeed
Behold, the Nephites will destroy | against them.
us, because of the many murders |

---

blow and injury for injury had not even entered their heads. At last they saw only
one way to escape the wrath and hatred of their erstwhile friends and neighbors.
That was in flight! To go some place and settle there where peace and liberty
prevailed was the objective of which they dreamed. That place was in the land of
the Nephites. There, if the Christian Lamanites could be transplanted, they would
be safe from the predatory assaults and the angry passions of their former countrymen.

"Let us gather together this people of the Lord, and let us go down to the
Land of Zarahemla to our brethren the Nephites, and flee out of the hands of our
enemies, that we be not destroyed," was the counsel the Lord's servants gave to
the king."

VERSE 6. *Behold, the Nephites will destroy us.* You will remember that the
king, Anti-Nephi-Lehi, was only recently born to a new life in Christ, and with
this new life came new ideals. He was now about to learn the meaning of just one
of those ideals. For centuries the Lamanites had been brought up in hatred of the
Nephites. On every hand they had sought to destroy what their white brethren had
laboriously made. Their spite of the Nephites was keen and inexhaustible. Murder,
robbery, rapine, and all manner of vicious crimes gave shape and form to the
method the Lamanites used to lay waste the peaceful pursuits of the Nephites.
Raid after raid, assault upon assault, especially in the outlying districts, kept the
Nephites in a constant dread of open warfare. True, many of the Christian Nephites
often resorted to reprisal. Ill will, and a desire to get even, guided their actions. Thus
we find retaliatory measures were used by both in seeking to subdue each other's
ambitions whether good or bad.

The king now came into direct opposition to this age-old practice. Ammon
and his brethren taught him the great truth that Christian people do not harbor
the idea of reprisal. Neither do they long remember the past. Forgiveness is a
Christian virtue. It was taught by the Lord, Himself, and was graven upon the
Brass Plates of Laban and therefore was familiar to Ammon and the other missionaries because King Mosiah, the father of four of the missionaries, had them in his
possession, and the study of them was the greatest part of his sons' education. The
Lord in remonstrating with His people, Israel, said through the prophet: ". . . thou
hast wearied Me with thine iniquities." But He continued, "I, even I, am He
that blotteth out thy transgressions for Mine own sake, and will not remember thy
sins." (Isaiah 43:24-25) This promise to ancient Israel included, we may be sure,
that branch of the tree that was transplanted in the Western Hemisphere.

The Nephites at this time were full of the spirit of forgiveness, they loved the
Lord and sought to do His bidding. Having taken upon themselves the Name of
Christ, and having truly repented of their sins, the Anti-Nephi-Lehies, nevertheless
thought that the Nephites would destroy them for past sins which they had committed
if they settled in their midst. This afforded a rare example to the king of Christian
forgiveness. He needed not to have expected the Christian Nephites to meet out to
his people the penalties of savage warfare, but, instead, the Christian Law of love
which both peoples had espoused. He was further assured that the Nephites would
not attempt to right a wrong by committing another wrong. Imbued with the Spirit
of Christ men do not return evil for evil. Neither do they fight error with evil
intentions. Therefore, King Anti-Nephi-Lehi was mistaken when he supposed that
the Nephites in Zarahemla would destroy his people because of deeds perpetrated
by them in the past, and of which they had now fully repented.

7. And Ammon said: I will go and inquire of the Lord, and if he say unto us, go down unto our brethren, will ye go?

8. And the king said unto him: Yea, if the Lord saith unto us go, we will go down unto our brethren, and we will be their slaves until we repair unto them the many murders and sins which we have committed against them.

9. But Ammon said unto him: It is against the law of our brethren, which was established by my father, that there should be any slaves among them; therefore let us go down and rely upon the mercies of our brethren.

10. But the king said unto him: Inquire of the Lord, and if he saith unto us go, we will go; otherwise we will perish in the land.

VERSES 7-10. *Ammon said: I will go and inquire of the Lord.* When Ammon and his fellow missionaries saw and realized that any plan of theirs to deliver their brethren from the hands of their enemies was beforehand doomed to failure, they, after much tribulation and searching of their souls, decided to place their problem directly before the Lord. They knew that He was wiser and more powerful than them all, and that He would not forsake them nor leave them in their grief. Confident that He would hear and answer their supplications, Ammon, in the strength of his faith, cried unto his brethren and to the king: "I will go and inquire of the Lord."

Ammon's solemn proposal found immediate acceptance in the king's heart. What before had appeared as an utterly unanswerable and dark mystery now became illumined with light and hope from Above. Despair gave way to gladness; the king *saw triumph in the Lord;* together with Ammon he affirmed the joyful prospect, "Yea, if the Lord saith unto us go, we will go down unto our brethren, and we will be their slaves until we repair unto them the many murders and sins which we have committed against them,"

Ammon thereupon explained another of the great Christian ideals to the king. It had been the habit of the Lamanites for many generations to make slaves of any Nephites who fell into their hands, this or slay them. But with the Nephites it was different. The Nephites, being of the House of Israel, could not observe the Law of Moses and enslave their brethren. (*See* Mosiah 2:13) Also according to the Code of Mosiah which was the supreme law of the Nephites it was unlawful to make slaves of human beings. Ammon knowing the hearts and the desires of the Nephites, their willingness to forgive and their anxiety to extend the Gospel of Christ unto all men, answered the king: "therefore let us go down and rely upon the mercies of our brethren."

The king, now more than ever, was anxious to rely on the wisdom of the Lord. Again he bade Ammon: "Inquire of the Lord, and if He saith unto us Go, we will go; otherwise we will perish in the land." With no thought of abandoning his new belief in Christ and His Gospel to gain respite from earthly tribulations, Anti-Nephi-Lehi was ready to obey the counsels of God, and in the event that the Lord said No, he was ready to pay the cost of his recently discovered faith with the sacrifice of his life.

11. And it came to pass that Ammon went and inquired of the Lord, and the Lord said unto him:

12. Get this people out of this land, that they perish not; for Satan has great hold on the hearts of the Amalekites, who do stir up the Lamanites to anger against their brethren to slay them; therefore get thee out of this land; and blessed are this people in this generation, for I will preserve them.

13. And now it came to pass that Ammon went and told the king all the words which the Lord had said unto him.

14. And they gathered together all their people, yea, all the people of the Lord, and did gather together all their flocks and herds, and departed out of the land, and came into the wilderness which divided the land of Nephi from the land of Zarahemla, and came over near the borders of the land.

15. And it came to pass that Ammon said unto them: Behold, I and my brethren will go forth into the land of Zarahemla, and ye shall remain here until we return and we will try the hearts of our brethren, whether they will that ye shall come into their land.

16. And it came to pass that as Ammon was going forth into the land, that he and his brethren met Alma, over in the place of which has been spoken; and behold, this was a joyful meeting.

17. Now the joy of Ammon was so great even that he was full; yea, he was swallowed up in the joy of his God, even to the exhausting of his strength; and he fell again to the earth.

18. Now was not this exceeding joy? Behold, this is joy which none receiveth save it be the truly penitent and humble seeker of happiness.

19. Now the joy of Alma in meeting his brethren was truly

VERSES 11-15. *Ammon went and inquired of the Lord.* We judge by the text that Ammon went by himself to place his petition before the Lord. Here in the solemnity of a Heavenly grace, and with no desire but to aid his fellow men, Ammon poured forth his unselfish soul to the great Giver of all Good. No doubt he reminded the Lord of the devotion of the Anti-Nephi-Lehies; of their integrity to righteous principles; of their loyalty to His servants, and of their trials and afflictions. To Ammon's fervent prayer the answer came. The Lord said unto him: "Get this people out of this land, that they perish not." (Verse 12) The Lord promised a blessing on them besides the instructions He gave unto Ammon. The Lord said: "Blessed are this people in this generation, for I will preserve them."

The Word of the Lord thus received was joyfully obeyed. The Anti-Nephi-Lehies gathered up their flocks and herds, and departed into the wilderness that lay between the lands of Nephi and Zarahemla. There they rested while Ammon and his brethren went forward and treated with the Nephites in behalf of the persecuted hosts they had left behind.

VERSES 16-19. *Ammon and his brethren meet Alma.* As Ammon and his fellow missionaries were on their way to the City of Zarahemla, they, in one most glorious event, had unspeakable joy. They met Alma, the companion of their youth

great, and also the joy of Aaron, of Omner, and Himni; but behold their joy was not that to exceed their strength.

20. And now it came to pass that Alma conducted his brethren back to the land of Zarahemla; even to his own house. And they went and told the chief judge all the things that had happened unto them in the land of Nephi, among their brethren, the Lamanites.

21. And it came to pass that the chief judge sent a proclamation throughout all the land, desiring the voice of the people concerning the admitting their brethren, who were the people of Anti-Nephi-Lehi.

22. And it came to pass that the voice of the people came, saying: Behold, we will give up the land of Jershon, which is on the east by the sea, which joins the land Bountiful, which is on the south of the land Bountiful; and this land Jershon is the land which we will give unto our brethren for an inheritance.

23. And behold, we will set our armies between the land Jershon and the land Nephi, that we may protect our brethren in the land Jershon; and this we do for our brethren, on account of their fear to take up arms against their brethren lest they should commit sin; and this their great fear came because of their sore repentance which they had, on account of their many murders and their awful wickedness.

24. And now behold, this will we do unto our brethren, that they may inherit the land Jershon; and we will guard them from their enemies with our armies, on condition that they will give us a portion of their substance to assist us that we may maintain our armies.

---

who was now the Presiding High Priest of God's Church. Alma was traveling south on one of his missionary journeys from the Land of Zarahemla to the Land Manti when the meeting occurred. Mutual rejoicing crowned the reunion. (*See* COMMENTARY ON THE BOOK OF MORMON, Volume III, p. 242 ff, also Alma 17:1-4) The joy that filled Ammon's bosom was more than his physical body could endure and he fell to the earth, his strength exhausted. (Read the 26th Chapter of Alma where Ammon's rejoicing in the Lord is more fully stated.)

VERSES 20-25. *Behold, we will give up the Land of Jershon.* The story of the plight of the Christian Lamanites was rehearsed to Alma, who on hearing it, returned with the missionaries to Zarahemla. There the condition of affairs among the Lamanites was unfolded to the Chief Judge, who thereupon laid the whole subject before the people, so that whatever was done in relation to the Anti-Nephi-Lehies might be done by common consent.

The Nephites decided to give the Land of Jershon to these people for an inheritance. And not only that, but because the people of Anti-Nephi-Lehi had foresworn any resort to arms, no matter how much they were provoked to do so, the Nephites also pledged their armies in the protection of the newcomers. "And behold, we will set our armies between the Land Jershon and the Land Nephi, that we may protect our brethren in the Land Jershon."

The Land Jershon was situated to the north of the City of Zarahemla, and

25. Now, it came to pass that when Ammon had heard this, he returned to the people of Anti-Nephi-Lehi, and also Alma with him, into the wilderness, where they had pitched their tents, and made known unto them all these things. And Alma also related unto them his conversion, with Ammon and Aaron, and his brethren.

2. *They are called the People of Ammon.*

3. *Land of Jershon given to them.*

26. And it came to pass that it did cause great joy among them. And they went down into the land of Jershon, and took possession of the land of Jershon; and they were called by the Nephites the people of Ammon; therefore they were distinguished by that name ever after.

27. And they were among the

---

was evidently chosen for the reason that the strength of the Nephite Nation would lie between the fugitives and their former countrymen, the Lamanites, who thirsted for their blood. It was bounded by the Caribbean Sea and the Land Bountiful on the north and east, and by the Land of Antionum on the south. Its western boundary is not defined, but we are inclined to believe, from the context, that it was the River Sidon. With regard to its southern boundary (Alma 31:3) Antionum lay to the south of it.

Jershon means the Land of the expelled, or of the strangers. We think it altogether probable that this significant name was given it at the time it was set off for the habitation of these expatriated Lamanites, as it defines their condition as exiles, and their relation to the Nephites as strangers. The name is not mentioned before this event, and would possibly be the only local name by which it was known to the compiler of the Book of Mormon. Before the date of the exodus of the Anti-Nephi-Lehies, it was, we think, considered a part of the Land of Zarahemla.

The only condition imposed on them by the Nephites upon giving up this vast area to the Christian Lamanites was that the newcomers should help maintain the army which was necessary to protect them by imparting a portion of their "substance" to assist in carrying on.

With this cheering news Ammon, accompanied by Alma, returned into the Southern Wilderness, to the place where his people were awaiting the decision of the Nephites. There the Anti-Nephi-Lehies were ministered to and comforted by Alma and others. After a short period of preparation in which both bodies and minds of the travelers were strengthened, they resumed their journey to the land set apart for their future abode.

VERSES 26-30. *And they went down into the Land of Jershon.* The Anti-Nephi-Lehies, after a further long journey to Jershon, occupied that land, and set to work making it another center of Nephite productiveness.

In honor of Ammon, who was their leader, the Anti-Nephi-Lehies took upon themselves his name, and thereafter were called the People of Ammon. Also from that time forth they were considered to be part of the Nephite Nation, and were numbered among the *"people who were of the Church of God."*

It was a requirement of the Saints then, as it is now, to have their names

people of Nephi, and also numbered among the people who were of the church of God. And they were also distinguished for their zeal towards God, and also toward men; for they were perfectly honest and upright in all things; and they were firm in the faith of Christ, even unto the end.

28. And they did look upon shedding the blood of their brethren with the greatest abhorrence; and they never could be prevailed upon to take up arms against their brethren; and they never did look upon death with any degree of terror, for their hope and views of Christ and the resurrection; therefore, death was swallowed up to them by the victory of Christ over it.

29. Therefore, they would suffer death in the most aggravating and distressing manner which could be inflicted by their brethren, before they would take the sword or cimeter to smite them.

30. And thus they were a zealous and beloved people, a highly favored people of the Lord.

---

written in the books of the Church. *Thus they were numbered among its members.* This was, we may be sure, an ancient Israelitic custom which was an inspired institution among them. The Nephites had inherited this custom from the Jews who were their ancestors. We read more often that names of transgressors were *blotted out.*[2] Their names were taken from the number of those who remained faithful, and in this manner a record was kept of all who continued in fellowship one with the others.

Moroni, the last writer in the Book of Mormon, describes fully the reasons for and the qualifications of those who by their actions proved themselves worthy of being numbered with the members of God's Church:

And now I speak concerning baptism. Behold, elders, priests, and teachers were baptized; and they were not baptized save they brought forth fruit meet that they were worthy of it.

Neither did they receive any unto baptism save they came forth with a broken heart and a contrite spirit, and witnessed unto the Church that they truly repented of all their sins.

And none were received unto baptism save they took upon them the Name of Christ, having a determination to serve Him to the end.

And after they had been received unto baptism, and were wrought upon and cleansed by the power of the Holy Ghost, *they were numbered among the people of the Church of Christ; and their names were taken,* that they might be remembered and nourished by the good Word of God, to keep them in the right way, to keep them continually watchful unto prayer, relying alone upon the merits of Christ, who was the Author and the Finisher of their faith. (Moroni 6:1-4)

Although the foregoing was written nearly 500 years after the account of the Ammonites was recorded, the words of Moroni, though he did not mention them therein, speak eloquently of the spiritual and moral qualities that imbued the Lamanite Saints of God in the days of Alma, the younger. We may be assured that the same requirements have been made of all those who have affiliated themselves with the Church of God in every generation of its adherents.

The Sacred Record says of the Ammonites, we presume it is a comment made by Mormon the abridger of Alma's record:

"And they were also distinguished for their zeal towards God, and also towards men; for they were perfectly honest and upright in all things; and they were firm in the faith of Christ, even unto the end."

The hardened ways of the Lamanites, their savage and ferocious nature, their bloodthirsty desires, upon which from childhood the Ammonites had been nurtured, were now all swallowed up in their *views and hopes* in Christ, for they saw in Him an everlasting and glorious victory over death. They neither flinched when death approached, nor did they fear it. Again the Sacred Record says that when threatened with death they awaited its coming calmly, and even joyously. (Read Alma 23-25) "They never did look upon death with any degree of terror."

Now, in this generation of mankind, when the world and the things of the world threaten to crowd all thoughts of God from our hearts, it seems to be the proper time to consider well the story of the Ammonites told in the Book of Mormon; their fidelity to God, and their integrity to righteous principles. "Too many of us, day by day, go our way forgetting His wisdom and guidance." The tasks and trials of life, its pursuits and pleasures, absorb us, and we have little time or thought for else than "What shall we eat, or what shall be drink, or wherewithall shall we be clothed?" However, the satisfaction of those demands is not the aim or the end of our actions. It is not the true objective of life! The real purpose of our existence, *the ideal life,* has been revealed by God to all His children everywhere. *That is a life in Christ.* None of His Children have been forgotten. He revealed to the Ammonites, through His Nephite servants, enough to establish in them the hope in Christ which they cherished and from which they never fell away. Their belief in Him was a great bulwark in their defense when the powers of Satan sought their destruction. *This is true and real life has also been revealed to us!* The birth of Christ, His death and resurrection, are revelations of divine love which we can no more ignore than we can the air we breathe. The Ammonites made this life of which we speak, their life.

David in his 23rd Psalm likens life unto a valley through which all must pass; death is its end. And that from birth the travelers there through are continually overshadowed by a coming woe which they cannot escape. Now what are our thoughts of death? If we thought of it at all, it was with fears, and tears, and trembling. Many think of death as a cold and dark chasm along the highway of life where despair and anguish take possession of our souls. This is a wrong conception of this wonderful experience. With Christ in our hearts, it should be the reverse. It is, notwithstanding the sorrow caused at passing, the brightest incident of life. For as we approach that land where the poet says, "All have gone and all must go," we see emblazoned upon the very portals of Eternal Life, the words of our Lord and Savior, Jesus of Nazareth: "I am the resurrection and the life: he that believeth in Me, though he were dead, yet shall he live: And whosoever liveth and believeth in Me shall never die." (John 11:25-26) No doubt Ammon and his fellow missionaries had taught this very same doctrine, though in different words, to the believing Lamanites.

"Therefore," the sacred historian says of the Ammonites, "They would suffer death in the most aggravating and distressing manner which could be inflicted by their brethren, before they would take the sword or cimeter to smite them. And thus they were a zealous and beloved people, a highly favored people of the Lord."

---

[1]*Anti.* There are several words in the Book of Mormon in which *anti* is one of the component parts, as for instance, *Ani-Anti,* the name of an Amalekite village in which Aaron, Muloki, and Ammah, preached the Gospel. (Alma 21:11) *Anti-Nephi-Lehi,* the name of a king and also of a people. (Alma 24:1-5) *Antion,* a piece of gold used as money. (Alma 11:19) *Antipas,* the name of a mountain. (Alma 47:7) All are instances, with others, that denote that the word was in common use among the people of Nephi.

The Indian word *Quichua* corresponding to *anti* is, we are assured, *anta*, which Garcilasso de la Vega tells us means *copper*. (Royal Commentaries, Book 5, Chapter 14)

From *anta* the magnificent mountain chain that forms the backbone of South America was called the *Andes*, possibly because of the abundance of metals, especially copper, found in these mountains.

In the Book of Mormon, *anti* means a mountain or hill. When it is used to denote a country it probably means a hilly or mountain country, and when the name is applied to a city, it may indicate its location in a mountain region. In the same way *Anti-Nephi-Lehies* may mean that they were located in a hilly or mountainous country. As applied to a piece of money, the word would indicate that they were made of an alloy in which copper formed a considerable part.

Anti appears in *Antisuyu,* the name given by the Peruvians to the eastern part of their vast domain; that is, to the part that is traversed by the loftiest ridges of the Andes Mountains. That proves, beyond question, that the Peruvians used the word exactly as we find it used in the Book of Mormon.

Antipas is a name of a mount or hill on the summit of which Lamanite armies on one occasion had gathered themselves for battle. (Alma 47:7)

This is a genuine Indian word. On the mountain slopes of the Cordilleras, in the upper Amazon Basin, there is, according to Dr. Brinton (The American Race, p. 284), a tribe of Indians, of the Jivaro linguistic stock, known as the *Antipas*. They are described as "rather tall, or light color, with thin lips, aquilline noses, straight eyes, prognatic jaws, hair black or with reddish tint."

---

[2]*Blottd out.* Following is a complete concordance of the term, as it is used in the sense that *there is something taken from;* it means to cancel, expunge, efface.

BOOK OF MORMON

Blotted out—

Mosiah	1:12	A name that shall never be b. out
	5:11	Name ... that never should be b. out
	11	The name be not b. out of your hearts
	26:36	And their names were b. out
Alma	1:24	And their names were b. out
	5:57	Their names shall be b. out
	6:3	And their names were b. out
Moroni	6:7	Confessed not, their names were b. out

DOCTRINE AND COVENANTS

Section	20:83	Their names may be b. out of the
	109:34	And let them be b. out forever

BIBLE

Exodus	32:32	Not b. me out of Thy book
	33	Whosoever sinned, will I b. out
Numbers	5:23	Shall b. them out with
Deut.	9:14	Me alone that I b. out
	25:19	B. out the remembrance of
	29:20	Lord shall b. out his name
2 Kings	14:27	He would b. out Israel
Psalms	51:1	Have mercy O God, b. out
	9	Hide my sins and b. out all
Revelation	3:5	I will not b. his name out
Psalm	109:13	Let their name be b. out

BOOK OF MORMON

Numbered—

1 Nephi	14:2	They shall be n. among the seed of
	2	They shall be n. among the House of Israel
2 Nephi	4:11	Thy seed shall be n. with his seed
	10:18	The Gentiles shall be ... n. among the house
	19	They who shall be n. thy seed
Mosiah	14:12	And He was n. among the transgressors
	18:9	Be n. with those of the first resurrection
	25:12	And be n. among those who are called
	13	People of Zarahemla were n. with the
	26:32	Shall not be n. among my people
	36	The same were not n. among the people of
Alma	5:57	The names of the wicked shall not be n.
	6:3	Their names were not n. among these
	27:27	People of Nephi, and also n. among the people
	45:13	Who are now n. among the people of
	13	Shall be no more n. among the people of
Helaman	15:13	True Shepherd, and be n. among His sheep
3 Nephi	2:14	United with the Nephites, were n. among
	16	Were n. among the Nephites, and were called
	3:14	All them who were n. among the Nephites
	15:24	Ye are n. among those whom the Father
	16:3	And shall be n. among My sheep
	13	They shall be n. among My people
	18:31	If he repent not, he shall be n. among
	31	I know My sheep, and they are n.
	21:6	That they may be n. among My people
	22	Be n. among this remnant of Jacob
	30:2	That ye may be n. with My people
Mormon	4:17	That they were not n. because of the greatness
	7:10	Ye are n. among the people of the firstborn
Ether	6:21	After that they had n. them, they did
	13:10	Who are n. among the remnant ... of Joseph
Moroni	6:4	Were n. among the people of the Church
	7	Were not n. among the people of Christ
	7:39	To be n. among the people of His Church

BIBLE

Numbered—

Genesis	13:16	Thy seed also be n.
Numbers	2:16	Were n. in camp of Reuben
	24	N. of Ephraim
	31	N. in camp of Dan
	3:16	Moses n. them
	4:45	These whom Moses and Aaron n.
	7:2	And over them that were n.
II Samuel	18:1	David n. the people
I Chronicles	21:17	The people to be n.
II Chronicles	2:17	Solomon n. all the

CHAPTER 28

1. *Lamanites Make War Upon Nephites*—2. *A Tremendous Battle*—3. *Lamanites Defeated*—4. *Deep Mourning.*

1. *Lamanites make war upon Nephites.*

1. And now it came to pass that after the people of Ammon were established in the land of Jershon, and a church also established in the land of Jershon, and the armies of the Nephites were set round about the land of Jershon, yea, in all the borders round about the land of Zarahemla; behold the armies of the Lamanites had followed their brethren into the wilderness.

2. And thus there was a tremendous battle; yea, even such an one as never had been known among all the people in the land from the time Lehi left Jerusalem; yea, and tens of thousands of the Lamanites were slain and scattered aboard.

VERSE 1. *The armies of the Lamanites had followed their brethren into the wilderness.* No sooner had the Ammonites taken up their refuge in the Land of Jershon, and had established a Church of God therein, and notwithstanding that the Nephite armies had ringed them about with protective strength, the armies of the Lamanites came upon the Ammonites intent upon destroying their former brethren who had escaped their wrath in the Land of Nephi. But the Nephites had been made ready. Not only were the forces of the Nephites deployed around the Ammonites' new home in Jershon, but the Nephites expecting a general assault by the Lamanites upon all their settlements both far and near, posted their warriors "in all the borders round about the Land of Zarahemla." The Nephites did this to anticipate any sudden raid by the Lamanite hordes in any district whatsoever, and to ready themselves for the coming conflict which promised to be fierce and decisive.

2. *A tremendous battle.*

VERSE 2. *Thus there was a tremendous battle.* The Nephites and the Lamanites joined battle. It was bloodthirsty and cruel. The Lamanites made furious charges to inspire terror within the ranks of their less malignant and menacing brethren. But the Nephites stood their ground. They did not falter or yield to their ferocious foes. Never before, even since the forefathers of their race had inhabited the land, had such a devastating and "tremendous battle" been fought between the enlightened descendants of Nephi and their dark skinned brethren, the savage Lamanites. In a general statement the Sacred Record says that "tens of thousands of the Lamanites were slain and scattered abroad."

3. *Lamanites Defeated.*

3. Yea, and also there was a tremendous slaughter among the people of Nephi; nevertheless, the Lamanites were driven and scattered, and the people of Nephi returned again to their land.

4. *Deep mourning.*

4. And now this was a time that there was a great mourning and lamentation heard throughout all the land, among all the people of Nephi—

5. Yea, the cry of widows mourning for their husbands, and also of fathers mourning for their sons, and the daughter for the brother, yea, the brother for the father; and thus the cry of mourning was heard among all of them, mourning for their kindred who had been slain.

6. And now surely this was a sorrowful day; yea, a time of solemnity, and a time of much fasting and prayer.

VERSE 3. *Yea, and also there was a tremendous slaughter among the people of Nephi.* Notwithstanding the gallant and successful defense of their homeland by the Nephites many of their men, women, and children, were destroyed by the inhuman tactics of the barbarous Lamanites. Yet in the end of hostilities the Lamanites were driven out of the Nephite lands, and as has been said, were scattered abroad, presumably into spent remnants of a once powerful host. The Nephites, then, when peace once more ruled their lives, returned to their own lands to again care for their flocks and herds, and again raise crops of corn and barley which was the greater part of their sustenance, and their main standard of value. Their money being valued by a measure of barley.

VERSES 4-6. *Now this was a time that there was a great mourning . . . among all the people of Nephi.* In spite of the fact that the Nephites were victorious in the dread conflict with the Lamanites, they were themselves sorely tried. Upon their return to the homes they had established throughout the Land of Zarahemla the Nephite defenders of their sod found many of their crops ruined, their flocks and herds scattered, and what was worse yet, that numbers of their loves ones and their neighbors had been slain by the hands of the wicked Lamanites. Not only that, but the returning warriors, in many cases, did not bring home with them a father, or a son, a husband or a brother, who had gone forth together in a band to defend their sacred religion and their home land which, too, was sacred to them.

Day after day as the widows and orphans awaited the return of their husbands and fathers who did not come, and parents their sons and sisters their brothers, whose existence only a short time previously had presaged for the Nephites a grand and glorious future, the realization that their loved ones would not come back turned their joy into sorrow and their laughter into mourning "for their kindred who had been slain." "Now this was a time that there was a great mourning and lamentation heard throughout all the land, among all the people of Nephi." (v. 4)

Mormon, the abridger of Alma's record, reasserts in verse six the sorrow that was almost universal among the Nephites at this time. He says it was a day of "solemnity," and we may judge for ourselves the suffering caused by the loss of

7. And thus endeth the fifteenth year of the reign of the judges over the people of Nephi;

8. And this is the account of Ammon and his brethren, their journeyings in the land of Nephi, their sufferings in the land, their sorrows, and their afflictions, and their incomprehensible joy, and the reception and safety of the brethren in the land of Jershon. And now may the Lord, the Redeemer of all men, bless their souls forever.

9. And this is the account of the wars and contentions among the Nephites, and also the wars between the Nephites and the Lamanites; and the fifteenth year of the reign of the judges is ended.

10. And from the first year to the fifteenth has brought to pass the destruction of many thousand lives; yea, it has brought to pass an awful scene of bloodshed.

11. And the bodies of many thousands are laid low in the

dear ones which loss left many women and children without adequate means of support. If it had not been for their reliance upon a merciful God in Whom they had been taught to trust they might have been overwhelmed. But in Him they lived, and by Him they were sustained. Almost as one they invoked His holy Name, and almost as one they received from Him succor according to the hour and power of their need. He did not forsake them, nor leave them in their grief. We shall see as we progress further in our study of this Branch of the House of Israel, that as long as Nephi's descendants kept the commandments of the Lord a Providential care enfolded them about, and by their enemies they were never overcome.

VERSE 7. *End of the Fifteenth Year.* Mormon here notes that the Judges had ruled the people of Nephi for a continuous period reaching back from when the Republic was founded by King Mosiah to the present time which then was 76 years Before Christ.

VERSE 8. *This is the account of Ammon and his brethren.* This verse is a resumé of the account previously given by Mormon, himself, of the mission to the Lamanites by the Sons of King Mosiah. In it he reiterates, or calls to our attention their vast travels in the Land of Nephi among the Lamanites; he notes the afflictions which they endured, the sorrows which no doubt purified and strengthened them, and their almost "incomprehensible joy" at the end of the mission which they, with the help of the Lord, had so gloriously performed. Mormon also notes "the reception and the safety" of the converted Lamanites in Jershon which was a land set aside by the Nephites as the Land of the Ammonites' inheritance. He ends this part of the summary he made with a prayer that the Lord, the Redeemer of all men, would bless the souls of the missionaries forever.

VERSES 9-12. *And the fifteenth year of the reign of the Judges is ended.* Mormon, the abridger, saw in retrospect the vast amount of suffering that had befallen the Nephites during the fifteen years that had transpired since King Mosiah had established a republic as the Nephite form of government. He saw in these years where the teachings and influence of Nehor had led many of his brethren to destruction. He saw where priestcraft had entered into the worship of Nehor's followers. He saw where brethren had been turned against brethren, and where strife and angry passion had mocked divine guidance. He also saw where the ambitions of Amlici had been frustrated, but not without the loss of many lives. Mormon, in making

earth, while the bodies of many thousands are moldering in heaps upon the face of the earth; yea, and many thousands are mourning for the loss of their kindred, because they have reason to fear, according to the promises of the Lord, that they are consigned to a state of endless wo.

12. While many thousands of others truly mourn for the loss of their kindred, yet they rejoice and exult in the hope, and even know, according to the promises of the Lord, that they are raised to dwell at the right hand of God, in a state of never-ending happiness.

13. And thus we see how great the inequality of man is because of sin and transgression, and the power of the devil, which comes by the cunning plans which he hath devised to ensnare the hearts of men.

---

the abridgment of Alma's record had read over and over again Alma's and Amulek's account of the wickedness that abounded in Ammonihah, and where that City with all its iniquitous people had been destroyed by the Lamanites. All in all he saw in the first fifteen years of the Reign of the Judges "an awful scene of bloodshed," and that therein those years had "brought to pass the destruction of many thousand lives." The annals of those times revealed to him the depravity into which some of the Nephites had fallen.

May we imagine the sorrow, and in fact, the indignation that filled Mormon's breast as he contemplated the appalling destruction that had taken place among his forebears, many of whose dead bodies, he read from the Larger Plates of Nephi, lay strewn about the battlefields on which they had fought and bled that righteousness should prevail, and that God alone should be their King. He saw in it all the awful penalties of disobedience to God's laws, wherein men had chosen to follow darkness instead of that which cometh from the light. Alma recorded, and Mormon thought it was important to include in his abridgment, that there were at least two important conclusions drawn by the Nephites of this period: First, that many of the dead, because of unbelief, had been "consigned to a state of endless wo." Therefore they feared for the future of their loved ones who had not kept God's commandments. They remembered the "promises of the Lord" in which the warning was given that all such ones would suffer as if tortured in a "lake of fire and brimstone." Then, too, there were the Lamanites who had refused to accept the light when it was placed before them. It must be kept in mind when studying the Nephite Records that the children of Nephi always regarded the Lamanites as brethren, and saw in them the victims of a corruption that had been foisted upon them by a wicked ancestry. The Nephites therefore truly mourned for the Lamanites who had been slain, they seeing no redemption for their fallen brethren. Secondly, according to the same promises that had been made to the wicked, those who had died in Christ were assured of a grand and glorious hereafter. The Sacred Record says, "Many thousands of others truly mourn for the loss of their kindred, yet they rejoice and exult in the hope, and even know, according to the promises of the Lord, that they are raised to dwell at the right hand of God, in a state of never-ending happiness."

VERSES 13-14. *And thus we see how great the inequality of man is because of sin and transgression.* No lesson presented in the Nephite Record is more vividly shown or as frequently given than the one here that Mormon emphasizes. He stresses the point that it is "sin and transgression, and the power of the devil" that

14. And thus we see the great call of diligence of men to labor in the vineyards of the Lord; and thus we see the great reason of sorrow, and also of rejoicing— sorrow because of death and destruction among men, and joy because of the light of Christ unto life.

---

divides men into class and class distinction. We may trace many Nephite woes to pride and self-anointed righteousness. The ambition of Amlici to be king of the Nephites is an example of what we mean. His desire to exercise unrighteous authority over his brethren started with pride which in turn had its beginning in the things of the world which he and his followers had accumulated. His wicked aim was to destroy the Republic which was God-inspired. Satan put it into Amlici's heart to aspire to kingship, and thereby overthrow the Work of the Lord. In this way the Nephites were divided into two classes: Those who hoped to profit by Amlici's wicked venture, and those who stood fast with Alma in upholding the law of the land. The evil intent of Amlici not only divided the Nephites into two great groups, but it resulted in open warfare in which internecine strife thousands of Nephites on both sides were slain. The "cunning plans" which Satan put into Amlici's heart failed to thwart the purposes of God. Mormon saw in the experiences of these fifteen years that God will not forsake His people, nor as the Psalmist says, "Leave them in their grief," when they earnestly seek to do His will. In other words, there is nothing that equalizes men more than does righteous behavior. We all stand before God as equals, save those who do and those who do not, obey His words. There is nothing that equalizes men more than by them walking together with the Lord. Again, how often this truth is made known to us when we study the Nephite Scriptures!

That righteousness abound and wickedness be brought to naught, that all His enemies be subdued and men dwell together in unity and peace, is the triumphant call that goes forth to every God-serving man to labor in the Lord's Vineyard that all the people of the Earth shall rejoice in the mercies of Christ, that in Him death is not the end, but only a narrow corridor which leads to a life that is eternal.

Mormon's rejoicing, even though sorrow for his forebear's folly dulled his song of triumph, gives us exceeding cause to exult with him "because of the light of Christ unto life."

CHAPTER 29

1. *Alma's yearning desire to cry repentance to all.*

1. O that I were an angel, and could have the wish of mine heart, that I might go forth and speak with the trump of God, with a voice to shake the earth, and cry repentance unto every people!

2. Yea, I would declare unto every soul, as with the voice of thunder, repentance and the plan of redemption, that they should repent and come unto our God, that there might not be more sorrow upon all the face of the earth.

VERSES 1-2. *O that I were an angel.* (In theology, an angel is a messenger of God.) This entire chapter (29) is a discourse made by Alma to himself, when in solitude, he contemplated the glory with which all mankind would be crowned when they yield to God's command to repent. It is a soliloquy which finds Alma talking to Alma when none but God was near. It is a song of praise in which he exults in God's goodness and mercy. It is an unselfish prayer for the welfare of each and all. In it Alma expresses the innermost desire of his heart: "To cry repentance unto every people." "O that I were an angel," he entreated, "that I might deliver this message to all the world." "O that my voice would be as the sound of God's trump"; that it be like thunder, the reverberations of which would shake the earth. Alma's burning desire was that the Gospel of Jesus Christ should be proclaimed to every nation under Heaven; that it should be preached in power to every kindred, tongue, and people. That he should be an instrument in God's hands to that end was the prayer he uttered.

It is the opinion of the authors hereof that when Mormon, the abridger of Alma's record, saw this prayer that Alma had engraved upon the Larger Plates of Nephi, he, after reading it time and time again, copied it word for word, or nearly so, in the abridgment of the Nephite Records he was making, and which translated is the Book of Mormon. Thus we have preserved to us what we believe to be a full copy of Alma's prayer.

In the 65th Section of the Book of Doctrine and Covenants is recorded another prayer which when read in conjunction with this one of Alma's will illumine much that we now see as through a glass darkly, and makes clear many things that seem distorted and confused because of the imperfect glass above mentioned.

Alma saw, in the bitter contentions that rise between the forces of evil and the righteousness of the righteous, a never ending source of sorrow which eventually, like a flood of water, would inundate all peoples, bond and free, good and bad, male and female, alike. If he had, for so he yearned, a voice of thunder, his words, he mused, would penetrate even the most formidable barriers, and would therein summon all men to "repent and come unto our God, that there might not be more sorrow upon all the face of the Earth."

Alma, imbued as he was with wisdom from On High, reasoned gently with himself that when all men should invoke God's Holy Name, sorrow would disappear, hatred would be no more, and peace, God's most precious gift, would cover the Earth. Happiness and peace would then take the place of sorrow and mourning. He thought of the words of Isaiah that Nephi had engraved upon his Smaller Plates: "And it shall come to pass in that day that the Lord shall give thee rest, from thy sorrow, and from thy fear. . ." (II Nephi 24:3) Other words of the Prophet Isaiah undoubtedly came to his mind, and in them Alma rejoiced for all the Nephites delighted in the Prophet's words. (See II Nephi 25:5) Thinking of the words of Isaiah he remembered that on an occasion the Lord, Himself, in comforting Israel referred to that day spoken of by Isaiah, and caused the Prophet to promise that then "all thy children shall be taught of the Lord; and great shall be the peace of thy children." (Isaiah 54:13) Alma, with bands stronger than iron, tied together peace and the *cause for which he hoped*: "no more sorrow upon all the face of the Earth." He also remembered the words of the Psalmist that were written upon the Brass Plates of Laban. In singing praises to the Creator, who was the King of all, David, Judah's king, exclaimed, "Great peace have they which love thy law. . ." (Psalm 119:165) *Peace and gladness*, Alma knew were inseparable as were *sorrow and travail*. He wanted peace that sorrow would be expelled. But not, we imagine, any and every peace. He wanted the peace of which King David spoke: Peace founded upon truth, upheld and sustained by righteousness. Any peace in opposition to this he profoundly meditated is, "Peace, peace, when there is no peace." (Jeremiah 6:14) The thought ran through his head: How can there be peace if sorrow prevails? And again, How can there be sorrow when peace is established? He thought of peace, and rest from sorrow through Christ, the Prince of Peace. He would enlist all men under His Royal Banners. Alma pondered over and over again that blessed day when sorrow would disappear, and hatred would be no more, and even its prospects brought him joy and gladness. Again he thought of sorrow and fear, also of the promised peace and rest. O what a gap between them! These last, Alma concluded were the marks of God's presence, His power, and His great purposes.

As Presiding High Priest of God's Church, Alma had in his possession the Smaller Plates of Nephi, and of their contents he was closely acquainted. About 500 years earlier than Alma's time, Nephi, the son of the Prophet Lehi, — when the plates of which we have spoken were quite new — engraved a remarkable statement made to him by an angel from Heaven. This explanation of what the Lord will do is of exceeding great importance to every Latter-day Saint as it was no doubt to Alma. In its fulfillment he saw the fruition of his hopes:

For the time cometh, saith the Lamb of God, that I will work a great and a marvelous work among the children of men; a work that shall be everlasting, either on the one hand or on the other—either to the convincing of them unto *peace and life eternal*, or unto the deliverance of them to the hardness of their hearts and the blindness of their minds unto their being brought down into captivity, and also into destruction, both temporally and spiritually, according to the captivity of the devil, of which I have spoken. (I Nephi 14:7)

Peace and Life Eternal go hand in hand.

All in all, Alma saw that by keeping the commandments of the Lord peace would be established, and Christ's Millennial reign will be begun. It is the work of righteousness, ever, to establish peace and eliminate all sorrow. Peace, the Lord's peace, is our portion. It is the source from whence springs our fulness of joy, and our gladness; our happiness and content; our love for God's law, and again we repeat the Psalmist: "Great peace have they which love Thy law."

And still again Alma thought of that day when sorrow shall disappear, and

3. But behold, I am a man, and do sin in my wish; for I ought to be content with the things which the Lord hath allotted unto me.

4. I ought not to harrow up in my desires, the firm decree of a just God, for I know that he granteth unto men according to their desire, whether it be unto death or unto life; yea, I know that he allotteth unto men according to their wills, whether they be unto salvation or unto destruction.

5. Yea, and I know that good and evil have come before all men; he that knoweth not good from evil is blameless; but he that knoweth good and evil, to him it is given according to his desires, whether he desireth good or evil, life or death, joy or remorse of conscience.

6. Now, seeing that I know these things, why should I desire more than to perform the work to which I have been called?

---

peace will cover the Earth. Silently Alma meditated long in prayer; fervently he inscribed these words upon the Larger Plates of which he was custodian:

"O that I were an angel, and could have the wish of mine heart, that I might go forth and speak with the trump of God, with a voice to shake the earth, and cry repentance unto every people."

This wish of Alma's had its inception in his own experience. In his conversion, when in gaiety he with the sons of King Mosiah went about persecuting the Saints of God, an angel from the *Courts of Glory* stopped them on their way, and with a voice of thunder which shook the earth upon which they stood, commanded them to no more follow the wicked course they then pursued, but to repent and serve the Lord thereafter. Alma remembered the awful sense of his guilt, and to save others from the fate to which he and his companions were headed, prayed for the same power as the angel's that he might lead all mankind to glorify the Name of the Eternal Father.

We need go no farther back than Alma's words recorded in the preceding chapter to sense the terrific anxiety for the welfare of God's Kingdom which imbued him, and caused him to write: "O that I were an angel, . . ."

And thus we see the great call of diligence of men to labor in the vineyards of the Lord; and thus we see the great reason of *sorrow*, and also of rejoicing — *sorrow* because of the death and destruction among men, and joy because of the light of Christ unto life. (Alma 28:14)

VERSES 3-6. *But behold, I am a man.* Almost immediately Alma saw and recognized the impropriety of his wish. The Lord of the Vineyard wherein Alma labored had in wisdom obtained a choice field, and it had produced much *good fruit.* Its Master had provided husbandmen to care for the trees and preserve them. To some was given the task of preparing the soil; to others to dig about the roots of the trees, and still others to water, and to nurture, and to gather in the precious crop when harvest time should come. A special commitment was given to every workman. Each one had a duty to perform. All worked together that the trees should abundantly bring forth good fruit. Alma was one of these workmen.

Its Owner had given to Alma particular charge of His Vineyard in Zarahemla. That sacred duty was a trust in which Alma delighted. The *Head Keeper* of the Vineyard had watched over Alma as if Alma, himself, was a watered garden. He

2. *God's word apportioned in wisdom.*

7. Why should I desire that I were an angel, that I could speak unto all the ends of the earth?

8. For behold, the Lord doth grant unto all nations, of their own nation and tongue, to teach his word, yea, in wisdom, all that he seeth fit that they should have; therefore we see that the Lord doth counsel in wisdom, according to that which is just and true.

9. I know that which the Lord hath commanded me, and I glory in it. I do not glory of myself, but I glory in that which the Lord hath commanded me; yea, and this is my glory, that perhaps I may be an instrument in the hands of God to bring some soul to repentance; and this is my joy.

had hedged Alma about; He had placed watchmen over him that none should despoil or ravage the tender flowers that blossomed in his heart. Angels from Heaven had ministered unto him. The Holy Spirit had sustained him in time of need. Knowledge from *On High* had guided his footsteps. Alma knew good and evil; he also had the power to choose right and wrong. Alma's mission was in Zarahemla. There, with his own people he cauld lead and counsel them. However, in spite of the great work God had allotted him, Alma sought world-wide service: "to cry repentance unto every people." But a sudden change came over Alma. To do well the work that God had assigned him was the thing he wanted most to do. To labor in that part of the Lord's Vineyard wherein he had been called became uppermost in his mind. "Now seeing that I know these things, why should I desire more than to perform the work to which I have been called?" In his mind he undoubtedly recalled the words of Jacob, the Prophet Nephi's brother, "Wherefore, brethren, seek not to counsel the Lord, but to take counsel from His hand. For behold, ye yourselves know that He counseleth in wisdom, and in justice, and in great mercy, over all His works." (Jacob 4:10)

VERSES 7-8. *Why should I desire that I were an angel?* Only in different words, a Jewish concept of Jacob's sentiment is expressed thusly: In every part of the Earth and in all ages of the World, God has raised up men and women to struggle and endure that His word should be preached to all people, that in the end every nation, kindred, tongue, and people should hear His voice.

To the thoughtful student of religious history especially as it is outlined in the written annals of the Restored Church of Jesus Christ (L.D.S.), the thoughts expressed by Alma are being borne out by factual experience. Except for a time when the Gospel was being introduced in the several nations of the Earth, men of that nation have been raised up to teach the word of the Lord in wisdom "all that He seeth fit that they should have." Thus we see, for example, the Lord is now raising up Chinese to declare His word among that people; Japanese are being prepared by Him to carry the Gospel Message to the Nipponese, and Polynesians to them that inhabit the Islands of the Pacific. "The Lord doth grant unto all nations, of their own nation and tongue, to teach His word."

VERSES 9-10. *I know that which the Lord hath commanded me, and I glory in it.* These words of Alma's bring to our minds similar words of his intrepid father when in the Land of Helam his followers clamored for him to be their king. The student will recall that Alma, the elder, was commanded of the Lord to gather up

10. And behold, when I see many of my brethren truly penitent, and coming to the Lord their God, then is my soul filled with joy; then do I remember what the Lord has done for me, yea, even that he hath heard my prayer; yea, then do I remember his merciful arm which he extended toward me.

---

the righteous in the Land of Nephi, where many Nephites had emigrated, that they might possess again the land of their father's first inheritance. Under their leader, Zeniff, they became a great and mighty people. Upon Zeniff's death, his son, Noah, became king, and the people were led by him into all manner of iniquities.

Alma's father did as he was commanded, and with him several hundred members of Christ's Church, which was established by him, escaped the clutches of wicked King Noah, and journeyed through the wilderness until they came to a suitable spot in which they set up a community that at length prospered far beyond that for which they had hoped. It was then they desired that the elder Alma should be their king. He refused their request, saying:

. . . Behold, it is not expedient that we should have a king; for thus saith the Lord: Ye shall not esteem one flesh above another, or one man shall not think himself above another; therefore I say unto you it is not expedient that ye should have a king.

Nevertheless, if it were possible that ye could always have just men to be your kings it would be well for you to have a king.

But remember the iniquity of King Noah and his priests; and I myself was caught in a snare, and did many things which were abominable in the sight of the Lord, which caused me sore repentance;

Nevertheless, after much tribulation, the Lord did hear my cries, and did answer my prayers, and has made me an instrument in His hands in bringing so many of you to a knowledge of His truth.

Nevertheless, in this I do not *glory* for I am unworthy to *glory* of myself. (Mosiah 23:7-11)

Alma's thoughts were like those expressed by Jeremiah who prophesied to the Jews about the same time Father Lehi left Jerusalem, and who, it appears, was personally acquainted with him:

Thus saith the LORD, Let not the wise man *glory* in his wisdom, neither let the mighty man *glory* in his might, let not the rich man *glory* in his riches:

But let him that glorieth *glory* in this, that he understandeth and knoweth me, that I am the Lord which exercise lovingkindness, judgment, and righteousness, in the earth: for in these things I delight, saith the LORD. (Jeremiah 9:23-24)

We need only turn back to the account of the mission performed by the sons of King Mosiah. At the conclusion thereof the joy experienced by Ammon and his brethren knew no bounds. Alma took great comfort in the words of Ammon:

Yea, I know that I am nothing; as to my strength I am weak; therefore I will not boast of myself, but I will boast of my God, for in His strength I can do all things; yea, behold, many mighty miracles we have wrought in this land, for which we will praise His Name forever.

Behold, how many thousands of our brethren has He loosed from the pains of hell; and they are brought to sing redeeming love, and this because of the power of His word which is in us, therefore have we not great reason to rejoice?

Yea, we have reason to praise Him forever, for He is the Most High God, and has loosed our brethren from the chains of hell.

11. Yea, and I also remember the captivity of my father; for I surely do know that the Lord did deliver them out of bondage, and by this did establish his church; yea, the Lord God, the God of Abraham, the God of Isaac, and the God of Jacob, did deliver them out of bondage.

12. Yea, I have always remembered the captivity of my father; and that same God who delivered them out of the hands of of the Egyptains did deliver them out of bondage.

13. Yea, and that same God did establish his church among them; yea, and that same God hath called me by a holy calling, to preach the word unto this people, and hath given me much success, in the which my joy is full.

Yea, they were encircled about with everlasting darkness and destruction; but behold, He has brought them into His everlasting light, yea, into everlasting Salvation; and they are encircled about with the matchless bounty of His love; yea, we have been instruments in His hands of doing this great and marvelous work.

Therefore, let us *glory*, yea, we will *glory* in the Lord; yea, we will rejoice, for our joy is full; yea, we will praise our God forever. Behold, who can *glory* too much in the Lord? Yea, who can say too much of His great power, and of His mercy, and of His long-suffering towards the children of men? Behold, I cannot say the smallest part which I feel. (Alma 26:12-16)

VERSES 11-13. *Yea, and I also remember the captivity of my fathers.* Directed by his thoughts which were guided by the Holy Spirit within him, Alma took a retrospect of his past life, and gloried in the God of all goodness Whom he served, and to Whom he offered praise and thanksgiving. Alma's joy was unbounded as he prayerfully contemplated the long-suffering of the Lord and His mercy.

Had not the Lord God, the Mighty Father of all men, Alma asked himself, delivered his earthly fathers from the sore bondage of the Lamanites in the Land of Nephi; also the righteous of his brethren from the wicked grasp of King Noah? Again Alma meditated on the power and the purposes of the Lord God, and saw in them the wisdom of a higher Judge than he to bring about the eternal Plan of Salvation. For, he knew it was by the grace of God alone that through his fathers' delivery from the bitter gall of afflication that His Church, "Yea," the Church of "the Lord God, the God of Abraham, the God of Isaac, and the God of Jacob," was established by his intrepid father.

Going back still further in the recesses of his mind, Alma remembered the Children of Israel, that they had been delivered from Egyptian bondage by the power of that same God Who had only recently severed the bands of Lamanitish serfdom that had held his fathers in its unyielding malignity. Alma's fathers, both far and near, had experienced the working of God's power, His glory and dominion, in their preservation. Now, in humility, Alma reasoned that the same God Who had worked such marvelous works among his fathers had also called him "to preach the word unto this people, and hath given me much success, in the which my joy is full." Alma's success in bringing souls to Christ reminds one that to do so is the greatest work of the angels in Heaven, or of men on Earth. Members of the Church of Jesus Christ of Latter-day Saints have a similar duty as did Alma. "The Lord has called us to His service, and has found us worthy to be His witness to the peoples of the Earth. May we receive grace to fulfill this mission with zeal tempered with wisdom and guided by a regard for other men's faith. May our lives prove the strength of our belief in the things we proclaim. May our bearing toward

3. *Alma rejoices over success of his brethren.*

14. But I do not joy in my own success alone, but my joy is more full because of the success of my brethren, who have been up to the land of Nephi.

15. Behold, they have labored exceedingly, and have brought forth much fruit; and how great shall be their reward!

16. Now, when I think of the success of these my brethren my soul is carried away, even to the separation of it from the body, as it were, so great is my joy.

17. And now may God grant unto these, my brethren, that they may sit down in the kingdom of God; yea, and also all those who are the fruit of their labors that they may go no more out, but that they may praise him forever. And may God grant that it may be done according to my words, even as I have spoken. Amen.

---

our neighbors, our constancy in defeat or triumph, our faithfulness in every sphere of duty, our compassion for the suffering, our patience under trial, show that He Whose laws we obey is the God of all goodness and the loving Father of all men; that to serve Him is our greatest freedom, and to worship Him the soul's purest happiness."

VERSES 14-17. *My joy is more full because of the success of my brethren, who have been up to the Land of Nephi.* Alma's joy in being in the service of the Lord was rendered even greater when he, almost in exultation, contemplated the marvelous work that was performed by the sons of King Mosiah and the other missionaries who went with them, and for fourteen years had labored among the Lamanites in the Land of Nephi preaching the Gospel of Jesus Christ.

Alma thought of the missionaries' faithfulness in every sphere of duty; of their patience under trial; of their compassion for their dark skinned brethren who then suffered in ignorance of the Plan of Salvation. He thought of the long years they had labored as husbandmen in the Lord's Vineyard, and we are constrained to say that their lives proved the strength of their belief in the things they proclaimed, and that the God Whom they served was indeed the loving Father of all men. (*See* Comments on previous verse.) Behold, Alma noted, they had labored exceeding, almost unceasingly, that when harvest time came round, and the field which was left in their care yielded its meat, the gathering thereof would be bounteous and its fruit good. "How great shall be their reward."

Alma now closed his humble prayer, which was a song of thanksgiving and praise to God for His mercy, with an added supplication to the Almighty Father that "these my brethren, that they may sit down in the Kingdom of God; yea, and also all those who are the fruit of their labors that they may go no more out, but that they may praise Him forever. And may God grant that it may be done according to my words, even as I have spoken. Amen."

A complete concordance of the word GLORY, or any of its modifications is hereby appended; also the word WISDOM:

Glorified—

I Nephi	21:3	My servant, O Israel, in whom I will be g.
III Nephi	9:15	In Me hath the Father g. His Name
	11:7	In whom I have g. My Name; hear ye
	11	Have g. the Father in taking upon Me
	19:29	Be one, that I may be g. in them
Ether	12:8	And g. the Name of the Father

Glorify—

II Nephi	6:4	And g. the Name of your God
Jacob	2:21	Keep His commandments and g. Him for
Helaman	11:18	The people did rejoice and g. God
III Nephi	12:16	See your good works and g. your Father
	23:9	The Father shall g. His Name in Me
Ether	3:21	That I shall g. My Name in the flesh
	12:4	In good works, being led to g. God

Glorious—

I Nephi	21:5	Israel be not gathered, yet shall I be g.
II Nephi	1:24	Brother, whose views have been g.
	9:46	Prepare your souls for that g. day
	14:2	Branch of the Lord be beautiful and g.
	21:10	Gentiles seek: and his rest shall be g.

Glory—

Glory of God—See Glory of God.

Great Glory—

I Nephi	11:28	Unto the people, in power and great g.
	14:14	And with the power of God in great g.
	22:24	And might, and power, and great g.
II Nephi	6:14	Manifest Himself unto them in . . . great g.
	33:11	Show unto you, with power and great g.
Ether	8:9	Did obtain kingdoms and great g.?
Moroni	7:35	With power and great g. in the last

His Glory—

II Nephi	1:15	I have beheld His g.
	2:4	And thou hast beheld in thy youth His g.
	12:21	The majesty of His g. shall smite them
	13:8	Against the Lord, to provoke the eyes of His g.
	16:3	The whole Earth is full of His g.
	18:7	The King of Assyria and all his g.
	20:16	Under His g. He shall kindle a burning
Jacob	4:4	We had a hope of His g. many hundreds
	4	Not only we ourselves had a hope of His g.
Alma	5:50	The Son of God cometh in His g.
	9:26	The Son of God shall come in His g.

	26	And His g. shall be the g. of the Only Begotten
	12:15	Come forth and stand before Him in His g.
	29	Who caused men to behold of His g.
	13:24	At the time of His coming in His g.
III Nephi	13:29	Solomon, in all his g., was not arrayed
	26:3	The time that He should come in His g.
Mormon	8:15	Be done with an eye single to His g.
Moroni	9:25	The hope of His g. and of Eternal Life

My Glory—

I Nephi	20:11	And I will not give my g. to another
Alma	29:9	This is My g., that perhaps I may be an
III Nephi	28:7	When I shall come in My g.

Glory—

I Nephi	19:13	And power and g. of the God of Israel
II Nephi	12:10	The g. of His majesty shall smite thee
	19	The g. of His majesty shall smite them
	14:5	Upon all the g. of Zion shall be a defence
	15:14	And their g., and their multitude
	20:3	And where will ye leave your g.
	12	King of Assyria, and the g. of his high
	18	And shall consume the g. of his forest
	23:19	And Babylon, the g. of kingdoms
	24:18	All of them, lie in g., every one
	27:16	Because of the g. of the world
	33:6	I g. in plainness; I g. in truth
	6	I glory in my Jesus, for He hath redeemed
Jacob	4:11	And obtained a good hope of g. in Him
	5:54	Yet have g. in the fruit of My vineyard
Mosiah	4:12	Grow in the knowledge of the g. of Him
	23:11	Nevertheless, in this I do not g., for
	11	I am unworthy to g. of myself
Alma	5:50	Behold the g. of the King of all the Earth
	14:11	Receiveth them up unto Himself, in g.
	22:14	Should be swallowed up in the hopes of g.
	26:16	Let us g., yea, we will g. in the Lord
	16	Who can g. too much in the Lord?
	29:9	I g. in it; I do not g. of myself
	9	But I g. in that which the Lord hath
	36:28	Will raise me up . . . to dwell with Him in g.
	48:16	Moroni, and his heart did g. in it
	60:32	Iniquity is for the cause of your love of g.?
Helaman	5:44	Joy which is unspeakable and full of g.
	7:5	That they might get gain and g. of the
	8:23	They gave unto him g., because of that
III Nephi	13:2	In the streets, that they may have g. of
	13	The power, and the g., for ever. Amen.
	20:9	With one voice, and gave g. to Jesus
	10	When they had all given g. unto Jesus
Ether	8:7	Set his heart . . . upon the g. of the world
	9:22	And did rejoice and g. in his day

Glory of God—

I Nephi	19:13	And power and g. of the God of Israel
II Nephi	1:25	But he hath sought the g. of God
	27:16	They say this, and not for the g. of God
Mosiah	4:11	Come to the knowledge of the g. of God
	27:22	See and know of the goodness and g. of God
Alma	19:6	Which was the light of the g. of God
	60:36	But for the g. of my God, and the freedom
Mormon	9:5	Be brought to see . . . the g. of God

WISDOM

I Nephi	3:19	It is w. in God that we should obtain
	5:22	It was w. in the Lord that we should
	11:35	Behold the world and the w. thereof
II Nephi	1:8	It is w. that this land should be kept
	2:12	Must needs destroy the w. of God
	24	All things have been done in the w. of God
	3:19	The words which are expedient in My w.
	9:8	O the w. of God! His mercy and grace!
	28	Their w. is foolishness, and it profiteth
	42	Who are puffed up . . . because of their w.
	20:13	By My w. have I done these things
	21:2	The spirit of w. and understanding
	26:20	Preach up unto themselves their own w.
	27:22	Until I shall see fit in Mine own w.
	26	For the w. of their wise . . . shall perish
	28:30	For they shall learn w.
Jacob	4:10	Know that He counseleth in w.
Mosiah	2:17	These things that ye may learn w.
	36	In you to guide you in w. paths
	4:6	God and His matchless power and His w.
	9	Believe that He has all w.
	27	See that all things are done in w.
	5:15	Through the w., and power, and justice
	8:20	Men; for they will not seek w.
	24:7	Wise people, as to the w. of the world
Alma	2:1	A wise man, as to the w. of the world
	22:33	Thus the Nephites in their w., with their
	34	This was w. in the Nephites, as the Lamanites
	26:11	In my own strength, or in my own w.
	29	Through the power and w. of God we
	35	God; for He has all power, all w.
	29:8	To teach His word; yea, in w. all things
	8	We see that the Lord doth counsel in w.
	31:35	Give unto us, O Lord, power and w.
	32:12	Be humble, that ye may learn w.
	12	It is necessary that ye should learn w.
	37:8	It has hitherto been w. in God that
	12	He doth counsel in w. over all His works
	35	My son, and learn w. in thy youth
	38:9	I have told you this that ye may learn w.
	11	See that ye do not boast in your own w.

	13	And to be praised for their w.
	39:2	Unto boasting in thy strength and thy w.
	49:5	Because of the w. of the Nephites in preparing
	15	This was w. in Moroni; for he had supposed
Helaman	1:16	With his great w., that by sending him
	12:5	Yea, how slow to walk in w. paths
	15:16	I will cause that in the day of my w.
	16:15	Began to depend . . . upon their own w.
III Nephi	21:4	For it is w. in the Father that they
	10	For I will show unto them that My w.
	26:2	It was w. in Him that they should be given
	28:29	When the Lord seeth fit in His w.
	29:1	When the Lord shall see fit in His w.
Mormon	5:13	The Lord, when He shall see fit in His w.
Ether	5:1	Except, by and by, it shall be w. in
	8:23	It is w. in God that these things should
Moroni	10:3	If it be w. in God that ye should read
	9	That ye may teach the word of w.

WISE

Wise purpose—See wise purpose.

Wise—

I Nephi	19:3	Also for other w. purposes, which purposes
II Nephi	9:28	Are learned, they think they are w.
	42	The w., and the learned, and they that
	43	But the things of the w. and the prudent
	15:21	Wo unto the w. in their own eyes
	27:26	For the wisdom of their w. . . . . shall perish
	28:15	O the w., and the learned, and the rich
Jacob	6:12	O be w.: what can I say more
Mosiah	12:27	Therefore, ye have not been w.
	24:7	A w. people, as to the wisdom of the world
	29:8	Let us be w. and consider these things
	10	Let us be w. and look forward to these
	11	We will appoint w. men to be judges
	19	The interposition of their all-w. Creator
Alma	2:1	A w. man, as to the wisdom of the world
	4:16	A w. man who was among the elders
	10:24	Our w. lawyers whom ye have selected
	18:22	Now Ammon being w., yet harmless, he
	30:20	They were more w. than many of the
	32:23	Children do have words . . . which confound the w.
	37:6	In many instances doth confound the w.
	7	Small means the Lord doth confound the w.
Helaman	16:14	Angels did appear unto men, w. men
III Nephi	14:24	I will liken him unto a w. man, who built his house
Mormon	9:28	Be w. in the days of your probation
	31	Ye may learn to be more w. than we have been

CHAPTER 30

1. *Korihor, the Anti-Christ.*

1. Behold, now it came to pass that after the people of Ammon were established in the land of Jershon, yea, and also after the Lamanites were driven out of the land, and their dead were buried by the people of the land—

2. Now their dead were not numbered because of the greatness of their numbers; neither were the dead of the Nephites numbered—but it came to pass after they had buried their dead, and also after the days of fasting, and mourning, and prayer, (and it was in the sixteenth year of the reign of the judges over the people of Nephi) there began to be continual peace throughout all the land.

3. Yea, and the people did observe to keep the commandments of the Lord; and they were strict in observing the ordinances of God, according to the law of Moses; for they were taught to keep the law of Moses until it should be fulfilled.

4. And thus the people did have no disturbance in all the sixteenth year of the reign of the judges over the people of Nephi.

5. And it came to pass in the seventeenth year of the reign of the judges, there was continual peace.

6. But it came to pass in the latter end of the seventeenth year, there came a man into the land of Zarahemla, and he was Anti-Christ, for he began to preach unto the people against the prophecies which had been spoken by the prophets, concerning the coming of Christ.

VERSES 1-6. *In the seventeenth year of the Reign of the Judges, there was continual peace.* For almost three years there was an unbroken peace among the Nephites, or from the beginning of the fifteenth year to nearly the end of the seventeenth year of the Reign of the Judges over that pepple.

Many of the scars inflicted on them during their recent conflict with the Lamanites were now healed. The great number of dead who were slain during that prolonged struggle were buried by the People of Zarahemla, who had driven the Lamanites out of their fair land. The dead of both the Nephites and the Lamanites were not counted because of their vast number.

Also, the People of Ammon, or the Christian Lamanites who had changed their name from Anti-Nephi-Lehies, were firmly established in their new home, the Land of Jershon, where they appeared to be safely ensconced.

Mormon comments that during this relatively short period of time "the people

7. Now there was no law against a man's belief; for it was strictly contrary to the commands of God that there should be a law which should bring men on to unequal grounds.

8. For thus saith the scripture: Choose ye this day, whom ye will serve.

9. Now if a man desired to serve God, it was his privilege; or rather, if he believed in God it was his privilege to serve him; but if he did not believe in him there was no law to punish him.

10. But if he murdered he was punished unto death; and if he robbed he was also punished; and if he stole he was also punished;

and if he committed adultery he was also punished; yea, for all this wickedness they were punished.

11. For there was a law that men should be judged according to their crimes. Nevertheless, there was no law against a man's belief; therefore, a man was punished only for the crimes which he had done; therefore all men were on equal grounds.

12. And this Anti-Christ, whose name was Korihor, (and the law could have no hold upon him) began to preach unto the people that there should be no Christ. And after this manner did he preach, saying:

13. O ye that are bound down

did observe to keep the commandments of the Lord." They were taught to abide strictly the laws and ordinances of the Gospel as provided in the Law of Moses until that time should come when it would be fulfilled with the coming of Christ. Thus the Nephites, a kindly and righteous people, passed away in peace the 75th and 74th years before the Savior's advent here upon the Earth.

But now it seems that the calm occasioned by their righteous behavior was disrupted by a form of priestcraft introduced by an eloquent propagandist who was violently Anti-Christ, "for he began to preach unto the people against the prophecies which had been spoken by the prophets, concerning the coming of Christ."

VERSES 7-11. *Choose ye this day, whom ye will serve.* The just laws provided by the Code of Mosiah, the governing rules of Nephite conduct, not only protected the innocent, but they ofttimes shielded the guilty in their iniquitous ways. There was no law which prohibited any man from teaching or practicing his beliefs, or in any way forbidding or restraining him from attempting to indoctrinate others with his private opinions no matter how false they were, just so long as he believed them himself. Therefore, it was left for every man to choose for himself in what he would believe. No let nor hindrance came to him from any governmental sources whatsoever. They remembered the words of the ancient prophet, and abided thereby: "Choose ye this day, whom ye shall serve." (Joshua 24:15)

All men appeared before the law upon equal grounds; there were none better than were others; the advocate of Christ, and the Anti-Christ, the follower of the Law of Moses and those who had fallen by the wayside; all were peers, and it was against the mind and will of God upon which the law was based, to afford more privilege to one than to the other.

VERSES 12-18. *And this Anti-Christ whose name was Korihor.* Now the name of this impostor was Korihor, and he went about declaring as false the finest traditions that had inspired and inspirited the Nephite Nation from the very first. The doctrines he advocated were of a kind that would gain ready adhesion from those who did not

THE BOOK OF ALMA

under a foolish and vain hope, why do ye yoke yourselves with such foolish things? Why do ye look for a Christ? For no man can know of anything which is to come.

14. Behold, these things which ye call prophecies, which ye say are handed down by holy prophets, behold, they are foolish traditions of your fathers.

15. How do ye know of their surety? Behold, ye cannot know of things which ye do not see; therefore ye cannot know that there shall be a Christ.

16. Ye look forward and say that ye see a remission of your sins. But behold, it is the effect of a frenzied mind; and this derangement of your minds comes because of the traditions of your fathers, which lead you away into a belief of things which are not so.

17. And many more such things did he say unto them, telling them that there could be no atonement made for the sins of men, but every man fared in this life according to the management of the creature; therefore every man prospered according to his genius, and that every man conquered according to his strength; and whatsoever a man did was no crime.

18. And thus he did preach unto them, leading away the hearts of many, causing them to lift up their heads in their wickedness, yea, leading away many women, and also men, to commit whoredoms—telling them that when a man was dead, that was the end thereof.

---

fervently love purity, truth and righteousness, as they flattered their vanity, and gave them liberty to follow the lead of their passions without fear of the judgment of, or condemnation of a Divine Being.

He denied the coming of the Messiah, and ridiculed prophecy and revelation. He asserted that it was impossible for men to know the future. Korihor also inveighed against the Atonement of the Redeemer as a foolish superstition, and taught, instead of the unchanging truths of the Everlasting Gospel, the theory that every man fared in this life according to the judicious use of the means at the "creature's" hands; a man, he said, prospered according to his genius, and conquered according to his strength. Further, he announced that whatsoever a man did was no crime, for that when a man was dead, there was an end thereof.

It is almost needless to say that those who accepted such dogmas gave way to all manner of evil doing. They became overbearing to others, exceedingly keen in business transactions, were full of covetousness, duplicity, and lasciviousness, and indulged in various wanton practices and pleasures. Their motto might be said to have been: "Let us eat, drink, and be merry, for tomorrow we die; and what we do here will not be brought against us hereafter."

Korihor also gained a strong hold among the discontented, for such are ever found where universal perfection does not dwell. He railed at the Holy Priesthood with fierce words of falsehood. He charged that they sought to keep the people down, that they encouraged ignorance in the masses, that they bound their minds with foolish traditions; all this and much more, that they might usurp power and authority, and glut themselves with the results of their victims' daily toil.

2. Expelled from Jershon and arrested at Gideon.

19. Now this man went over to the land of Jershon also, to preach these things among the people of Ammon, who were once the people of the Lamanites.

20. But behold they were more wise than many of the Nephites; for they took him, and bound him, and carried him before Ammon, who was a high priest over that people.

21. And it came to pass that he caused that he should be carried out. of the land. And he came over into the land of Gideon, and began to preach unto them also; and here he did not have much success, for he was taken and bound and carried before the high priest, and also the chief judge over the land.

22. And it came to pass that the high priest said unto him: Why do ye go about perverting the ways of the Lord? Why do ye teach this people that there shall be no Christ, to interrupt their rejoicings? Why do ye speak against all the prophecies of the holy prophets?

23. Now the high priest's name was Giddonah. And Korihor said unto him: Because I do not teach the foolish traditions of your fathers, and because I do not teach this people to bind themselves down under the foolish ordinances and performances which are laid down by ancient priests, to usurp power and authority over them, to keep them in ignorance, that they may not lift up their heads,

but be brought down according to thy words.

24. Ye say that this people is a free people. Behold, I say they are in bondage. Ye say that those ancient prophecies are true. Behold, I say that ye do not know that they are true.

25. Ye say that this people is a guilty and a fallen people, because of the transgression of a parent. Behold, I say that a child is not guilty because of its parents.

26. And ye also say that Christ shall come. But behold, I say that ye do not know that there shall be a Christ. And ye say also that he shall be slain for the sins of the world—

27. And thus ye lead away this people after the foolish traditions of your fathers, and according to your own desires; and ye keep them down, even as it were in bondage, that ye may glut yourselves with the labors of their hands, that they durst not look up with boldness, and that they durst not enjoy their rights and privileges.

28. Yea, they durst not make use of that which is their own lest they should offend their priests, who do yoke them according to their desires, and have brought them to believe, by their traditions and their dreams and their whims and their visions and their pretended mysteries, that they should, if they did not do according to their words, offend

some unknown being, who they say is God—a being who never has been seen or known, who never was nor ever will be.

29. Now when the high priest and the chief judge saw the hardness of his heart, yea, when they saw that he would revile even against God, they would not make any reply to his words; but they caused that he should be bound; and they delivered him up into the hands of the officers, and sent him to the land of Zarahemla, that he might be brought before Alma, and the chief judge who was governor over all the land.

3. Arraigned in Zarahemla.

30. And it came to pass that when he was brought before Alma and the chief judge, he did go on in the same manner as he did in the land of Gideon; yea, he went on to blaspheme.

31. And he did rise up in great swelling words before Alma, and did revile against the priests and teachers, accusing them of leading away the people after the silly traditions of their fathers, for the sake of glutting on the labors of the people.

32. Now Alma said unto him: Thou knowest that we do not glut ourselves upon the labors of this people; for behold I have labored even from the commencement of the reign of the judges until now, with mine own hands for my support, notwithstanding my many travels round about the land to declare the word of God unto my people.

33. And notwithstanding the many labors which I have performed in the church, I have

VERSES 19-29. *Now this man went over to the Land of Jershon.* As a propagandist, Korihor, for a short time, was a success. We first hear of him preaching his satanic doctrines in the Land of Zarahemla, and as he claimed to believe all he taught, the law could not touch him, as full religious liberty was guaranteed under the constitution and laws of the Nephite Commonwealth. From Zarahemla he went to the Land of Jershon to inoculate the Ammonites with his soul-destroying vagaries. But they were a wiser and more zealous people for the Gospel than were many of the Nephites. They took him, bound him, and carried him before Ammon (Son of King Mosiah), their High Priest. He directed that Korihor should be removed beyond the borders of their land, which command having been obeyed, we next find the unabashed imposter laboring among the people of the Land of Gideon. There he also met with rebuffs. He was arrested by the people and taken before the chief officers in that land. They found that they could do nothing with him that would be satisfactory, so they remanded him into the custody of the proper officers, with instructions to carry him before Alma and Nephihah, in Zarahemla.

When brought before these worthies — the highest dignitaries of the Church and the State — Korihor continued in his course of loud-mouthed blasphemy, defiant assumption, and willful falsehood.

VERSES 30-42. *When he was brought before Alma . . . he did go on in the same manner as he did in the Land of Gideon.* Korihor, when he was brought before Alma and the Chief Judge in Zarahemla continued to accuse the Priesthood bearers of

never received so much as even one senine for my labor; neither has any of my brethren, save it were in the judgment-seat; and then we have received only according to law for our time.

34. And now, if we do not receive anything for our labors in the church, what doth it profit us to labor in the church save it were to declare the truth, that we may have rejoicings in the joy of our brethren?

35. Then why sayest thou that we preach unto this people to get gain, when thou, of thyself, knowest that we receive no gain? And now, believest thou that we deceive this people, that causes such joy in their hearts?

36. And Korihor answered him, Yea.

37. And then Alma said unto him: Believest thou that there is a God?

38. And he answered, Nay.

39. Now Alma said unto him: Will ye deny again that there is a God, and also deny the Christ? For behold, I say unto you, I know there is a God, and also that Christ shall come.

40. And now what evidence have ye that there is no God, or that Christ cometh not? I say unto you that ye have none, save it be your word only.

41. But, behold I have all things as a testimony that these things are true; and ye also have all things as a testimony unto you that they are true; and will ye deny them? Believest thou that these things are true?

42. Behold, I know that thou believest, but thou art possessed with a lying spirit, and ye have put off the Spirit of God that it may have no place in you; but the devil has power over you, and he doth carry you about, working devices that he may destroy the children of God.

---

treachery toward the people and with great swelling words reviled the prophets as he had done in Gideon. He argued against the existence of the Father and the coming of His Only Begotten. Alma accused him of arguing against his convictions, but this Korihor stoutly denied.

In verse 31 it is noted the vehemence with which Korihor accused the Presiding High Priest, and his subordinate priests and teachers of "glutting on the labors of the people." This charge is a familiar complaint lodged against the leaders of the Saints in these Last Days. It is a favorite device of the devil so as to cause dissention among the people of God. It has been used by all servants of evil.

In Alma's answer to this charge we have a pleasing insight into his private life. He labored with his own hands to provide the necessities of life, and notwithstanding his personal burdens, he travelled "round about the land to declare the Word of God unto my people," and he notes "I have never received so much as even one senine for my labor; neither has any of my brethren, save it were in the Judgment Seat; and then we have received only according to law for our time."

Alma now asked Korihor the logical questions recorded in verses 34-35, to which Korihor answered in opposition to the truth. He knew the injustice of his claims, but there are none, it has been said, so blind as those who will not see, none so deaf as those who will not hear.

4. *He demands a sign and is stricken dumb.*

43. And now Korihor said unto Alma: If thou wilt show me a sign, that I may be convinced that there is a God, yea, show unto me that he hath power, and then will I be convinced of the truth of thy words.

44. But Alma said unto him: Thou hast had signs enough; will ye tempt your God? Will ye say, Show unto me a sign, when ye have the testimony of all these thy brethren, and also all the holy prophets? The scriptures are laid before thee, yea, and all things denote there is a God; yea, even the earth, and all things that are upon the face of it, yea, and its motion, yea, and also all the planets which move in their regular form do witness that there is a Supreme Creator.

45. And yet do ye go about, leading away the hearts of this people, testifying unto them there is no God? And yet will ye deny against all these witnesses? And he said: Yea, I will deny, except ye shall show me a sign.

46. And now it came to pass that Alma said unto him: Behold, I am grieved because of the hardness of your heart, yea, that ye will still resist the spirit of the truth, that thy soul may be destroyed.

47. But behold, it is better that thy soul should be lost than that thou shouldst be the means of bringing many souls down to destruction, by thy lying and by thy flattering words; therefore if thou shalt deny again, behold God shall smite thee, that thou shalt become dumb, that thou shalt never open thy mouth any more, that thou shalt not deceive this people any more.

48. Now Korihor said unto him: I do not deny the existence of a God, but I do not believe that there is a God; and I say also, that ye do not know that there is a God; and except ye show me a sign, I will not believe.

49. Now Alma said unto him: This will I give unto thee for a sign, that thou shalt be struck dumb, according to my words; and I say, that in the name of God, ye shall be struck dumb, that ye shall no more have utterance.

50. Now when Alma had said these words, Korihor was struck dumb, that he could not have utterance, according to the words of Alma.

51. And now when the chief judge saw this, he put forth his hand and wrote unto Korihor, saying: Art thou convinced of the power of God? In whom did ye desire that Alma should show forth his sign? Would ye that he should afflict others, to show unto thee a sign? Behold, he has showed unto you a sign; and now will ye dispute more?

52. And Korihor put forth his hand and wrote, saying: I know that I am dumb, for I cannot speak; and I know that nothing

save it were the power of God could bring this upon me; yea, and I also knew that there was a God.

53. But behold, the devil hath deceived me; for he appeared unto me in the form of an angel, and said unto me: Go and reclaim this people, for they have all gone astray after an unknown God. And he said unto me: There is no God; yea, and he taught me that which I should say. And I have taught his words; and I taught them because they were pleasing unto the carnal mind; and I taught them, even until I had much success, insomuch that I verily believed that they were true; and for this cause I withstood the truth, even until I have brought this great curse upon me.

54. Now when he had said this, he besought that Alma should pray unto God, that the curse might be taken from him.

55. But Alma said unto him: If this curse should be taken from

thee thou wouldst again lead away the hearts of this people; therefore, it shall be unto thee even as the Lord will.

56. And it came to pass that the curse was not taken off of Korihor; but he was cast out, and went about from house to house begging for his food.

57. Now the knowledge of what had happened unto Korihor was immediately p u b l i s h e d throughout all the land; yea, the proclamation was sent forth by the chief judge to all the people in the land, declaring unto those who had believed in the words of Korihor that they must speedily repent, lest the same judgments would come unto them.

58. And it came to pass that they were all convinced of the wickedness of Korihor; therefore they were all converted again unto the Lord; and this put an end to the iniquity after the manner of Korihor. And Korihor did go about from house to house, begging food for his support.

VERSES 43-58. *And now Korihor said unto Alma:* . . . *show me a sign.* Korihor demanded a sign be given him, as he pretended, that he might be convinced. Alma at length, wearied by his impious importunities, told him that God, as a sign, would smite him dumb. This terrible warning, though it caused the pretender some uneasiness, only resulted in an attempt on Korihor's part at prevarication. Korihor received the sign he asked for; Alma's words were fulfilled; the sign-seeker never more spoke on Earth. When the hand of the Lord fell upon him he recanted. By writing, as he could not speak, he confessed the power of God, and acknowledged that he had been led astray by Satan who had come to him as an angel of light. He begged that the curse might be removed, but Alma, knowing the baseness of his heart, refused to intercede before Heaven in his behalf lest when speech was restored to him he would again strive to deceive the people.

And it came to pass that the curse was not taken off Korihor; but he was cast out and went from house to house begging for his food.

A proclamation was next sent throughout all the land. In it the Chief Judge recited what had happened to Korihor, and called upon those who had believed in his words to speedily repent, lest the same judgments should come upon them.

5. Korihor's miserable death.

59. And it came to pass that as he went forth among the people, yea, among a people who had separated themselves from the Nephites and called themselves Zoramites, being led by a man whose name was Zoram — and as he went forth amongst them, behold, he was run upon and trodden down, even until he was dead.

60. And thus we see the end of him who perverteth the ways of the Lord; and thus we see that the devil will not support his children at the last day, but doth speedily drag them down to hell.

VERSES 59-60. *And thus we see the end of him who perverteth the ways of the Lord.* This proclamation put an end to the iniquity of Korihor, for his followers were all brought back again to the truth. But Korihor, deserted by the devil, a vagabond and a beggar, still continued to beg his way from town to town, from house to house; until one day in a city of the Zoramites, he was run over and trodden down. The injuries he received at this time were so great that he soon after died.

KORIHOR

An anti-Christ who appeared among the Nephites B.C. 75. He taught many of the heresies of Nehor, prominent among which were the denial of the coming of the Redeemer and of the efficacy of His Atonement. His doctrine was that every man fared in this life according to his management, prospered according to his shrewdness and conquered according to his strength. He proclaimed that whatsoever a man did was no crime for when a man was dead there was an end thereof.

As a missionary Korihor was, for a short time, a success. We first hear of him preaching his satanic doctrines in the Land of Zarahemla and as he claimed to fully believe all he taught, the law could not touch him, as full religious liberty was guaranteed under the constitution and laws of the Nephite Commonwealth. From Zarahemla he went to the Land of Jershon to inoculate the Ammonites with his soul-destroying vagaries. But they were a wiser and more zealous people for the Gospel than were many of the Nephites. They took him, bound him and carried him before Ammon, their High Priest. He directed that Korihor should be removed beyond the border of their land, which command having been obeyed, we next find the unabashed imposter laboring among the people of the Land of Gideon. There he also met with rebuffs. He was arrested by the people and taken before the chief officers in that land. They found they could do nothing that would be satisfactory with him so they remanded him into the custody of the proper officers with instructions to carry him before Alma and Nephihah, in Zarahemla. When brought before these worthies — the highest dignitaries of the Church and State — Korihor continued in his course of loud-mouthed blasphemy, defiant assumption and willful falsehood. He argued against the existence of the Father and the coming of His Only Begotten. Alma accused him of arguing against his convictions but this he stoutly denied and clamored for a sign to be given. Wearied of his impious importunities Alma told him that God, as a sign, would smite him dumb. This terrible warning, though it caused the pretender some uneasiness, only resulted in an attempt at prevarication. He said: I do not deny the existence of a God, but I do not believe there is a God; and I say also that ye do not know that there is a

God; and except ye show me a sign I will not believe. Then Alma answered: This will I give unto thee for a sign, that thou shalt be struck dumb, according to my words; and I say that, in the name of God, ye shall be struck dumb, that ye shall no more have utterance.

Korihor received his sign. Alma's words were fulfilled; the sign-seeker never more spoke on Earth. When the hand of the Lord fell on him he recanted. By writing, as he could not speak, he confessed the power of God and acknowledged that he had been led astray by Satan who had come to him in the form of an angel of light. He begged that the curse might be removed, but Alma, well knowing the baseness of his heart, refused to intercede before Heaven in his behalf lest when restored to speech he would again strive to deceive the people.

A proclamation was next sent throughout all the land. In it the Chief Judge recited what had happened to Korihor and called upon those who had believed in his words to speedily repent lest the same judgments should come upon them. This proclamation put an end to the iniquity of Korihor for his followers were all brought back again to the truth. But Korihor, deserted by the devil, a vagabond and a beggar, continued to beg his way from town to town, from house to house, until one day, in a city of the Zoramites he was run over and trodden down. The injuries that he received at this time were so great that he soon after died.

CHAPTER 31

1. *Alma heads a mission to reclaim the apostate Zoramites.*

1. Now it came to pass that after the end of Korihor, Alma having received tidings that the Zoramites were perverting the ways of the Lord, and that Zoram, who was their leader, was leading the hearts of the people to bow down to dumb idols, his heart again began to sicken because of the iniquity of the people.

2. For it was the cause of great sorrow to Alma to know of iniquity among his people; therefore his heart was exceeding sorrowful because of the separation of the Zoramites from the Nephites.

3. Now the Zoramites had gathered themselves together in a land which they called Antionum, which was east of the land of Zarahemla, which lay nearly bordering upon the seashore, which was south of the land of Jershon, which also bordered upon the wilderness south, which wilderness was full of the Lamanites.

4. Now the Nephites greatly feared that the Zoramites would enter into a correspondence with the Lamanites, and that it would be the means of great loss on the part of the Nephites.

5. And now, as the preaching of the word had a great tendency to lead the people to do that which was just—yea, it had had more powerful effect upon the minds of the people than the sword, or anything else, which had happened unto them—therefore Alma thought it was expedient that they should try the virtue of the word of God.

6. Therefore he took Ammon, and Aaron, and Omner; and Himni he did leave in the church in Zarahemla; but the former three he took with him, and also Amulek and Zeezrom, who were at Melek; and he also took two of his sons.

7. Now the eldest of his sons he took not with him, and his name was Helaman; but the

---

VERSES 1-11. *Alma received tiding that the Zoramites were perverting the Ways of the Lord.* In our last chapter we stated that Korihor, the Anti-Christ, was killed in a city of the Zoramites. Who was Zoram? and who were the Zoramites? are questions that now present themselves.

There are two distinct classes of people called Zoramites in the Book of Mormon. The first, the descendants of Zoram, the servant of Laban, who accompanied Nephi from Jerusalem. The second were followers of the Nephite apostate Zoram, whose defection and treason caused so much trouble and bloodshed in the Nephite Republic.

Of the last named Zoram and his individual life we have no history. We

names of those whom he took with him were Shiblon and Corianton; and these are the names of those who went with him among the Zoramites, to preach unto them the word.

8. Now the Zoramites were dissenters from the Nephites; therefore they had had the word of God preached unto them.

9. But they had fallen into great errors, for they would not observe to keep the commandments of God, and his statutes, according to the law of Moses.

10. Neither would they observe the performances of the church, to continue in prayer and supplication to God daily that they might not enter into temptation.

11. Yea, in fine, they did pervert the ways of the Lord in very many instances; therefore, for this cause, Alma and his brethren went into the land to preach the word unto them.

12. Now, when they had come into the land, behold, to their astonishment they found that the Zoramites had built synagogues, and that they did gather themselves together on one day of the week, which day they did call the day of the Lord; and they did worship after a manner which Alma and his brethren had never beheld;

13. For they had a place built up in the center of their synagogue, a place for standing, which was high above the head, and the top thereof would only admit one person.

14. Therefore, whosoever desired to worship must go forth and stand upon the top thereof, and stretch forth his hands towards heaven, and cry with a loud voice, saying:

15. Holy, holy God; we believe that thou art God, and we believe that thou art holy, and that thou wast a spirit, and that thou art a spirit, and that thou wilt be a spirit forever.

16. Holy God, we believe that thou hast separated us from our brethren; and we do not believe in the tradition of our brethren, which was handed down to them by the childishness of their fathers; but we believe that thou hast elected us to be thy holy children; and also thou hast made it known unto us that there shall be no Christ.

17. But thou art the same yesterday, today, and forever; and thou hast elected us that we shall be saved, whilst all around us are elected to be cast by thy wrath down to hell; for the which holiness, O God, we thank thee; and we also thank thee that thou hast

---

only know him through his pernicious teachings, and the sad results thereof. But it is altogether probable that before he started out as a religious reformer on his own account, he was a follower of Nehor, as a majority of his adherents appear to have been gathered from that sect and to have belonged to that order.

Zoram assembled his people in a region of the South American Continent which at that time was but a very thinly settled territory. It was called the Land of Antionum, and lay to the east of the River Sidon, while it stretched from the

elected us, that we may not be led away after the foolish traditions of our brethren, which doth bind them down to a belief of Christ, which doth lead their hearts to wander far from thee, our God.

18. And again we thank thee, O God, that we are a chosen and a holy people. Amen.

2. The Rameumptom or holy stand.

19. Now it came to pass that after Alma and his brethren and his sons had heard these prayers, they were astonished beyond all measure.

20. For behold, every man did

Land of Jershon on the north to the great southern wilderness which was infested with the more savage, wandering Lamanites. To this broad land the Zoramites gathered, and there built their cities, erected their synagogues, and grew in material wealth until, in the year 75 B.C., they had become an important, though an undesirable portion of the Nephite Commonwealth. As friends, they were unreliable, as enemies, formidable.

In the various apostasies, partial or total, that from time to time disgraced the Nephites, there was one characteristic feature that seems to be universal to them all, however much they may have differed in minor points. It was the denial of the coming of the Savior in the flesh, and the necessity of His Atonement for the sins of the world. This was the evil one's strong point in his efforts to mislead the ancient Nephites. Let him but to persuade any people to reject this, the foundation of the Gospel scheme, and little does he care what else they believe or disbelieve. For when this fundamental truth is rejected their spiritual enslavement is secured.

This was the case with the Zoramites. They claimed to be a chosen and a holy people, separate from their fellowmen, and elected of God to eternal Salvation, while all around were predestined to be cast down to Hell. This atrocious creed naturally resulted in its adherents and advocates being puffed up in vanity and consumed with pride. They became haughty, uncharitable, and tyrannical, and oppressors of their poorer neighbors. They covered their bodies with the finest apparel, and profusely adorned their persons with costly ornaments of gold and jewels. In their arrogance and self-righteousness they became the Pharisees of their age and country. But in other phases of iniquity they far exceeded their counterparts in the Holy Land. They bowed down to idols, denied the coming of Christ, declared the doctrine of the Atonement to be a foolish tradition, and, like many of the sects of modern Christendom, they misinterpreted the teachings of the Holy Scriptures with regard to the being of God. Their declaration of faith was: "Holy, holy God; we believe that Thou art God, and we believe that Thou art holy, and that Thou wast a spirit, and that Thou art a spirit, and that Thou wilt be a spirit forever."

This strange medley of ideas gave birth to corresponding vagaries of worship. They left off praying. Being chosen and elected to be God's holy children, they had no need of prayer. Once a week they assembled in their synagogues and went through an empty form, which was a little prayer, a little praise, and considerable self-glorification. Having done this, they never mentioned God or holy things again throughout the week. Indeed, it was a portion of their creed that in their synagogues were the only places in which is was lawful to talk, or even to think of religious matters.

go forth and offer up the same prayers.

21. Now the place was called by them Rameumptom, which, being interpreted, is the holy stand.

22. Now, from this stand they did offer up, every man, the self-same prayer unto God, thanking their God that they were chosen of him, and that he did not lead them away after the tradition of their brethren, and that their hearts were not stolen away to believe in things to come, which they knew nothing about.

23. Now, after the people had all offered up thanks after this manner, they returned to their homes, never speaking of their God again until they had assembled themselves together again to the holy stand, to offer up thanks after their manner.

3. *The Zoramite form of worship.*

24. Now when Alma saw this his heart was grieved; for he saw that they were a wicked and a perverse people; yea, he saw that their hearts were set upon gold, and upon silver, and upon all manner of fine goods.

25. Yea, and he also saw that their hearts were lifted up unto great boasting, in their pride.

26. And he lifted up his voice to heaven, and cried, saying: O, how long, O Lord, wilt thou suffer that thy servants shall dwell here below in the flesh, to behold such gross wickedness among the children of men?

27. Behold, O God, they cry unto thee, and yet their hearts are swallowed up in their pride. Behold, O God, they cry unto thee with their mouths, while they are puffed up, even to greatness, with the vain things of the world.

28. Behold, O my God, their costly apparel, and their ringlets, and their bracelets, and their ornaments of gold, and all their precious things which they are ornamented with; and behold, their hearts are set upon them, and yet they cry unto thee and say—We thank thee, O God, for we are a chosen people unto thee, while others shall perish.

29. Yea, and they say that thou

VERSES 19-23. *Now the place was called . . . Rameumptom.* The religious ceremonies of the Zoramites were as absurd as their creed. In the center of each of their synagogues was erected a holy stand, or pulpit, called by them, *Rameumptom,* which stood high above the congregation. From the slight description given of it in the Book of Alma we judge it may have been somewhat pyramidal in form, the top being only large enough for one person to stand upon. Each worshiper mounted to the top thereof, stretched out his hands toward Heaven, and, in a loud voice, repeated their set form of worship. Having done this, he descended and another took his place, and so on, until all who desired to go through this mummery had satisfied their conscience or gratified their pride.

VERSES 24-38. *Now when Alma saw this his heart was grieved.* The tidings of this defection having reached Alma, he selected several leading members among

hast made it known unto them that there shall be no Christ.

30. O Lord God, how long wilt thou suffer that such wickedness and iniquity shall be among this people? O Lord, wilt thou give me strength, that I may bear with mine infirmities. For I am infirm, and such wickedness among this people doth pain my soul.

31. O Lord, my heart is exceeding sorrowful; wilt thou comfort my soul in Christ. O Lord, wilt thou grant unto me that I may have strength, that I may suffer with patience these afflictions which shall come upon me, because of the iniquity of this people.

32. O Lord, wilt thou comfort my soul, and give unto me success, and also my fellow laborers who are with me—yea, Ammon, and Aaron, and Omner, and also Amulek and Zeezrom and also my two sons—yea, even all these wilt thou comfort, O Lord. Yea, wilt thou comfort their souls in Christ.

33. Wilt thou grant unto them that they may have strength, that they may bear their afflictions which shall come upon them because of the iniquities of this people.

34. O Lord, wilt thou grant unto us that we may have success in bringing them again unto thee in Christ.

35. Behold, O Lord, their souls are precious, and many of them are our brethren; therefore, give unto us, O Lord, power and wisdom that we may bring these, our brethren, again unto thee.

36. Now it came to pass that when Alma had said these words, that he clapped his hands upon all them who were with him. And behold, as he clapped his hands upon them, they were filled with the Holy Spirit.

37. And after that they did separate themselves one from another, taking no thought for themselves what they should eat, or what they should drink, or what they should put on.

38. And the Lord provided for them that they should hunger not, neither should they thirst; yea, and he also gave them strength, that they should suffer no manner of afflictions, save it were swallowed up in the joy of Christ. Now this was according to the prayer of Alma; and this because he prayed in fatih.

---

those holding the Holy Priesthood, and as soon as possible, proceeded to the Land of Antionum. Those who accompanied him were his two younger sons, three of the sons of King Mosiah, Amulek and Zeezrom. To his anxiety to bring these dissenters back from the error of their ways, and to avert Heaven's righteous wrath from falling upon them, was added the fear that if they remained in their wickedness they would join the Lamanites and bring trouble upon the more faithful Nephites by urging the renewal of war.

On the arrival of Alma and his fellow-laborers at the seat of the apostasy, they at once commenced their ministrations. They taught in the synagogues and preached in the streets. They visited the people from house to house, using every possible effort to bring these misguided dissenters to an understanding of their perilous condition. To these labors we are indebted for some of the plainest and most powerful Gospel teachings contained in the Book of Mormon, all of which will repay our perusal. Suffice it here to say that many of the poor and humble, those who were oppressed, abused and trodden down by their false priests and unrighteous rulers as well as by the wealthier portion of the community, received the words of Salvation, while a majority rejected them with contemptuous scorn. Some of the missionaries were maltreated. Shiblon, the son of Alma, was imprisoned and stoned for the truth's sake, while others fared but little better. Unfortunately the work of God was retarded by the misconduct of Corianton, the brother of Shiblon, who, for a time, deserted his ministerial duties for the company of a harlot. This folly caused Alma great sorrow, as it gave the ungodly a pretext for rejecting the Gospel, of which they were not slow to avail themselves.

Although his astonishment at the Zoramites' wickedness was almost more than Alma could bear, he was not overwhelmed by the prospect that faced him. To lead back into the right path those who had gone astray was the objective for which he labored, and the aim sought by all the missionaries who had accompanied him to Antionum. God was his helper, and on His help Alma relied. In the depths of affliction — for by their wickedness Alma was afflicted — he called upon the Lord in mighty prayer, saying: "Behold, O Lord, their souls are precious, and many of them are our brethren; therefore, give unto us, O Lord, power and wisdom that we may bring these, our brethren, again unto Thee." (v. 35)

In his prayer, Alma also reminded the Lord of the folly in which the Zoramites took pleasure, of their wicked ways, and the hypocrisy of their approach to His gracious throne. In none of these was Alma bitter in his denouncement; he only asked for strength, that grace might be given to himself and his fellow missionaries that they might fulfill with zeal, tempered with wisdom, the mission in which they had embarked.

When Alma had finished his unselfish supplication to the Almighty Father, Who is the loving Father of all men, and which Alma recognized, he placed his hands "upon all them who were with him," and behold, as he laid his hands upon their heads, blessing each one of them and setting them apart for the mission they were to perform, "they were filled with the Holy Spirit."

Taking no thought of what they should eat, or what they should drink, or what they should put on, the missionaries separated themselves from one another, and went forth in the power of the Priesthood to cry repentance unto their brethren, who, in the hardness of their hearts, had gone astray. This order of embarking on such a calling as theirs was Heaven-inspired, for this also was according to the instructions the Risen Redeemer gave unto the Nephites when He visited them about a hundred years later:

And now it came to pass that when Jesus had spoken these words He looked upon the twelve whom He had chosen, and said unto them: Remember the words which I have spoken. For behold, ye are they whom I have chosen to minister unto this people. Therefore I say unto you, take no thought for your life, what ye shall eat, or what ye shall drink; nor yet for your body, what ye shall put on. Is not the life more than meat, and the body than raiment?

Behold, the fowls of the air, for they sow not, neither do they reap nor gather into barns; yet your Heavenly Father feedeth them. Are ye not much better than they?

Which of you by taking thought can add one cubit unto his stature?

And why take ye thought for raiment? Consider the lilies of the field how they grow; they toil not, neither do they spin;

And yet I say unto you, that even Solomon, in all his glory, was not arrayed like one of these.

Wherefore, if God so clothe the grass of the field, which today is, and tomorrow is cast into the oven, even so will He clothe you, if ye are not of little faith.

Therefore take no thought, saying, What shall we eat? or, What shall we drink? or, Wherewithal shall we be clothed?

For your Heavenly Father knoweth that ye have need of all these things.

But seek ye first the Kingdom of God and His righteousness, and all these things shall be added unto you.

Take therefore no thought for the morrow, for the morrow shall take thought for the things of itself. Sufficient is the day unto the evil thereof. (III Nephi 13:25-34)

Alma's prayer, because he prayed in faith, was answered in blessings upon the heads of all the missionaries. Mormon notes that the Lord provided for their wants. They hungered not, neither did they thirst. Strength was given them that they overcame all afflictions, save at times for God's glory they suffered pain and anguish but even through their tears they saw His divine blessings and discerned His providential care.

ZORAM

A Nephite apostate of the time of the Republic. He was the founder of the sect of Zoramites, and established them in the Land of Antionum. Of his birth, death, or personal history, we are told nothing. He was alive at the time that Alma and his co-laborers visited and endeavored to reclaim his deluded followers (75 B.C.).

ZORAMITES

The Zoramites were an apostate sect of the Nephites who took their name from one Zoram, their leader. They occupied the Land of Antionum where they flourished 75 B.C.

In the various apostasies, partial or total, that from time to time disgraced the Nephites there is one characteristic that seems universal to them, however much they differed on minor points. It was the denial of the coming of the Savior in the flesh and of the necessity of His atonement for the sins of the world. This was the evil one's strong point in his efforts to mislead the ancient Nephites. Thus it was with the Zoramites. They bowed down to idols, denied the coming of Christ, declared the doctrine of the Atonement to be a foolish tradition and misinterpreted the teaching of Holy Scripture with regard to the being of God. Their declaration of faith was: "Holy, holy God; we believe that Thou art God, and we believe that Thou art holy, and that Thou wast a spirit, and that Thou art a spirit and that Thou wilt be a spirit forever." Moreover, they claimed to be a chosen and a holy people, separated from their fellowmen and elected of God to eternal salvation, while all around were predestined to be cast down to Hell. This creed naturally resulted in its adherents and advocates being puffed up in vanity and consumed with pride. They became haughty, uncharitable and tyrannical and oppressors of their poorer neighbors. Their strange medley of religious ideas gave birth to corresponding vagaries of worship. Being elected to be God's holy children they had not need of prayer. Once a week they assembled in their synagogues and went through an empty form, which was a little prayer, a little praise and considerable self-glorification. Having done this, they never mentioned God or holy things again throughout the week; indeed, it was a portion of their creed that their synagogues were the only places in which it was lawful to talk or think of religious matters.

Their ceremonies were as absurd as their creed. In the center of each of their synagogues was erected a holy stand, called Rameumptom, which stood high above the congregation; the top being only large enough for one person to stand upon. Each worshiper mounted to this top, stretched out his hands toward Heaven and in a loud voice, repeated their set form of worship. Having done this, he descended and another took his place, and so on, until all who desired to go through the mummery had satisfied their consciences or gratified their pride.

When the tidings of this defection reached Alma he proceeded to the Land Antionum. He was accompanied by his two younger sons, three of the sons of King Mosiah, also by Amulek and Zeezrom. To his anxiety to bring these dissenters back from the error of their ways was added the fear that if they remained in their wickedness they would join the Lamanites and bring trouble upon their more faithful fellow citizens by urging the renewal of war.

On the arrival of Alma and his fellow-laborers at the seat of this apostasy they at once commenced their ministrations. They taught in the synagogues and preached in the streets. They visited the people from house to house, using every possible effort to bring these misguided dissenters to an understanding of their perilous condition. Many of the poor and humble received the word of God while the majority rejected it with contemptuous scorn. Some of the missionaries were maltreated. Shiblon, the son of Alma, was imprisoned and stoned for the truth's sake while others fared but little better.

Having done all the good they cauld, the missionaries withdrew to Jershon, into which land the believing Zoramites were soon after driven by their unrepentant fellows. There they found a safe asylum among the Ammonites, who, regardless of the entreaties and afterwards the threats of those who remained in Antionum, shielded and comforted them. The Zoramites then affiliated with the Lamanites and an army of the latter race, commanded by Zerahemnah, entered Antionum and attempted to drive the Ammonites out of Jershon. In this they were not successful and eventually, after a most desperate conflict, they were forced back into their own lands. It appears that the Zoramites accompanied them as many of the Lamanite military leaders are afterwards spoken of as belonging to that sect.

LAND OF ANTIONUM

The Land of Antionum was a district of country eastward of the River Sidon, and was inhabited by the Zoramites. (75 B.C.) Thither Alma and his brethren repaired to convince them of their errors. The mission was not altogether successful. Those who believed Alma's words were driven out of the land, but found a refuge among the Ammonites in Jershon. The unconverted Zoramites joined the Lamanites, who, the next year occupied Antionum, while the Nephites prepared to meet them in the Land of Jershon. The Lamanites did not consider themselves equal to attacking the Nephites and changed the plan of their campaign. They retired from Antionum into the wilderness with the intention of invading Manti, in which purpose they were thwarted by Moroni and disastrously defeated by his soldiers. The Land of Antionum appears to have been of considerable extent, stretching from the great southern wilderness to Jershon on the north; the Land of Zarahemla formed its western border, while on the east it extended indefinitely into the great eastern wilderness.

RAMEUMPTOM

Rameumptom was the name given by the Zoramites to the elevated place in their synagogues whence they offered up their vain-glorious and hypocritical prayers. Alma states that the word means a holy stand. It resembles, in its roots, Hebrew and also Egyptian in a remarkable manner. *Ramoth*, high (as Ramoth Gilead), elevated, a place where one can see and be seen; or, in a figurative sense, sublime or exalted. *Mptom* has probably its roots in the Hebrew word translated threshold, as we are told that the Philistines' god, Dagon, has a threshold in Ashdod (*See* I Samuel 5:4-5). Words with this root are quite common in the Bible. Thus we see how Rameumptom means a high place to stand upon, *a holy stand.*

CHAPTER 32

1. *The poor hearken to message of Salvation.*

1. And it came to pass that they did go forth, and began to preach the word of God unto the people, entering into their synagogues, and into their houses; yea, and even they did preach the word in their streets.

2. And it came to pass that after much labor among them, they began to have success among the poor class of people; for behold, they were cast out of the synagogues because of the coarseness of their apparel—

3. Therefore they were not permitted to enter into their synagogues to worship God, being esteemed as filthiness; therefore they were poor; yea, they were esteemed by their brethren as dross; therefore they were poor as to things of the world; and also they were poor in heart.

4. Now, as Alma was teaching and speaking unto the people upon the hill Onidah, there came a great multitude unto him, who were those of whom we have been

---

VERSES 1-3. *They were poor as to the things of the world; and also were poor in heart.* In the last Chapter we noted that when Alma and his companions reached the principal city of the Zoramites, they lost no time, nor did they leave a thing undone that would hasten the return to the right path those of their brethren who had been led astray. They began their labors by entering into the Zoramites' synagogues to declare the divine message they bore, "and also into their houses, and even they did preach in their streets."

It was not long, but, however, not without great effort on their part, until the labors of the missionaries, acting as husbandmen in the stony soil of this part of the Lord's Vineyard, began to bear much fruit.

As unfailing is the case, Satan's plan in ensnaring the Zoramites was to implant disunion and discord in their hearts. One of his favorite devices is not only to stir up rebellion among his servants, but to infuse those who would do his bidding with a sense of superiority over their co-laborers. Thus he creates class distinction among those who serve him. The rich and the poor are with him as tools with which he carves out the pattern of every apostate movement. First he instills *ambition* into the hearts of men; they seek unrighteous dominion and conquest, and with flattering words would make followers of the weak and unwary. How often this course was followed by many Nephites. Strife, contention, and angry passions, were the legitimate children of their way of life. Among the Zoramites, the rich "esteemed the poor as filthiness" and had no truck with them. Because of the coarse clothing worn by the poor, the rich cast them out of their places of worship, and refused them any kind of communion as brethren. The Sacred Record says "therefore they were poor as to the things of the world; and also they were poor in heart."

speaking, of whom were poor in heart, because of their poverty as to the things of the world.

5. And they came unto Alma; and the one who was the foremost among them said unto him: Behold, what shall these my brethren do, for they are despised of all men because of their pov-erty, yea, and more especially by our priests; for they have cast us out of our synagogues which we have labored abundantly to build with our own hands; and they have cast us out because of our exceeding poverty; and we have no place to worship our God; and behold, what shall we do?

VERSES 4-5. *As Alma was teaching . . . a great multitude came unto him.* It was a custom of the Nephites to gather themselves together upon hills, or otherwise prominent places to preach and to teach any doctrines that were excluded from being taught in their houses of worship. Ammon and his brethren when on their famous mission to the Lamanites often resorted to this practise:

And now behold, we have come, and been forth amongst them; and we have been patient in our sufferings, and we have suffered every privation; yea, we have traveled from house to house, relying upon the mercies of the world—not upon the mercies of the world alone but upon the mercies of God.

And we have entered into their houses and taught them, and we have taught them in their streets; yea, and we have taught them *upon their hills;* and we have also entered into their temples and their synagogues and taught them; and we have been cast out, and mocked, and spit upon, and smote upon our cheeks; and we have been stoned, and taken and bound with strong cords, and cast into prison; and through the power and wisdom of God we have been delivered again. (Alma 26: 28-29)

It was on an occasion such as we have noted that as Alma was declaring God's Holy Word to a multitude of the apostate Zoramites that another multitude of the poorer class came unto him. "Because of their poverty as to the things of the world" they had been cast out of the synagogues which they themselves had greatly helped to build, but nevertheless they evinced a desire to know the truth. They sought not to harass the missionaries, but with hearts bowed down with humility, they hoped to get from Alma answers to many questions that had pained their hearts and perplexed their minds.

The leader of this great throng, he who was appointed by them to be their mouthpiece, approached Alma and inquired of him, "Behold, what shall these my brethren do, for they are despised of all men because of their poverty, and more especially by our priests; . . ." We have here an insight to what is a self-evident fact; that is when preaching the Gospel is made a craft, when ministering its precepts becomes a business, or when its blessings are known only to the rich, its mercies and its comforts flee and what is left is merely a sham, a make-believe in which there is no soul, no holy promptings.

This state of religion practised among the Zoramites recalls the words of the Prophet Nephi:

Behold, hath the Lord commanded any that they should not partake of His goodness? Behold, I say unto you, Nay; but all men are privileged the one like unto the other, and none are forbidden.

He commandeth that there shall be no priestcrafts; for, behold, priestcrafts are that men preach and set themselves up for a light unto the world, that they may get gain and praise of the world; but they seek not the welfare of Zion. (II Nephi 26:28-29)

2. *Alma's commendation and discourse.*

6. And now when Alma heard this he turned him about, his face immediately towards him, and he beheld with great joy; for he beheld that their afflictions had truly humbled them and that they were in a preparation to hear the word.

7. Therefore he did say no more to the other multitude; but he stretched forth his hand, and cried unto those whom he beheld, who were truly penitent, and said unto them:

Other words of Nephi are well to remember: But the laborer in Zion shall labor for Zion; for if they labor for money they shall perish. (II Nephi 26:31)

And mind you the words of Jacob, Nephi's brother: Come, my brethren, every one that thirsteth, come ye to the waters; and he that hath no money, come buy and eat; yea, come buy wine and milk without money and without price. (II Nephi 9:50)

Let us refer the reader to the following passages of Nephite Scripture which show the constancy and faithfulness with which the Nephites regarded the preaching of the Gospel without price, and the abhorence they felt at its opposite.

II Nephi	9:51	Do not spend money for that which is of no
Alma	1:5	Began to support him, and give him money
	20	One with another, without money and without
	11:20	That they might get money according to
Helaman	7:5	Wicked go unpunished, because of their money
	9:20	Here is money; and also we will grant unto
III Nephi	20:38	And ye shall be redeemed without money
Mormon	8:32	For your money you shall be forgiven of your sins
	8:37	Ye do love money, and your substances

Now, what pained the multitude of the poorer class most was that notwithstanding the labors they had spent in building their places of worship, they were deprived of its comforts and blessings by those who had arrogated to themselves, because of their riches, a superiority over them, or a plane more elevated in place or position than they. They therefore were not permitted to enter the synagogues, and "we have no place to worship our God; and behold, what shall we do?" asked their leader.

VERSES 6-7. *When Alma heard this . . . he beheld . . . that they were prepared to hear the Word.* When Alma heard their appeal he recognized that it came from brethren in distress. His soul was filled with joy for he saw and realized that the afflictions that had so plagued them had brought them down to the depths of despair, and of humility. They were in a proper condition to hear the Gospel preached, and to accept it. Alma, at this juncture, refused more to exhort the sullen Zoramites who with a feeling of self-righteousness mocked the servants of God standing before them. Not defeated by their coarse accusations and undismayed by their false charges, he turned himself about, directly facing his newly found friends; stretching forth his hand, apparently as a sign of brotherhood, Alma, moved by the sincere aspect which showed in their faces, began to commend the course they had begun to pursue.

8. I behold that ye are lowly in heart; and if so, blessed are ye.

9. Behold thy brother hath said, What shall we do?—for we are cast out of our synagogues, that we cannot worship our God.

10. Behold I say unto you, do ye suppose that ye cannot worship God save it be in your synagogues only?

11. And moreover, I would ask, do ye suppose that ye must not worship God only once in a week?

12. I say unto you, it is well that ye are cast out of your synagogues, that ye may be humble, and that ye may learn wisdom; for it is necessary that ye should learn wisdom; for it is because that ye are cast out, that ye are despised of your brethren because of your exceeding poverty, that ye are brought to a lowliness of heart; for ye are necessarily brought to be humble.

13. And now, because ye are compelled to be humble blessed are ye; for a man sometimes, if

---

VERSES 8-16. *Alma said unto them, I behold that ye are lowly in heart.* Alma commenced the answer to their problems by first mentioning with approbation his understanding of their conduct while heavily laden with the burdens their wealthier brethren had imposed on them. If their load was heavy and their hearts lowly, Alma implied, then would their burden be lightened. Alma softened the impact of their plight by the reassurance to them that it does not take a temple built with hands to provide a place in which to worship Almighty God. If they saw and recognized this great truth and if moreover they were humble and true, "blessed are ye," Alma cried.

"And moreover, I would ask, do ye suppose that ye must worship God only once a week?" Alma's question was prompted by the custom which prevailed among the Zoramites. It was just this:

Now it came to pass that after Alma and his brethren and his sons had heard these prayers, they were astonished beyond all measure.

For behold, every man did go forth and offer up the same prayers.

Now the place was called Rameumptom, which, being interpreted, is holy stand.

Now, from this stand they did offer up, every man, the self same prayer unto God, thanking their God that they were chosen of Him, and that He did not lead them away after the tradition of their brethren, and that their hearts were not stolen away to believe in things to come, which they knew nothing about.

Now, after the people had all offered up thanks after this manner, they returned to their homes, never speaking of their God again until they had assembled themselves together again to the holy stand, to offer up thanks after their manner. (Alma 31:19-23)

We will repeat what we have already said in the previous Chapter: The strange medley of their ideas gave birth to corresponding vagaries of worship. They left off praying. Being chosen and elected to be God's holy children, they had no need of prayer. Once a week they assembled in their synagogues and went through an empty form, which was a little prayer, a little praise, and considerable self-glorification. Having done this, they never mentioned God, or holy things throughout the week; indeed, it was a portion of their creed that their synagogues were the only places in which it was lawful to talk or think of sacred things.

he is compelled to be humble, seeketh repentance; and now surely, whosoever repenteth shall find mercy; and he that findeth mercy and endureth to the end the same shall be saved.

14. And now, as I said unto you, that because ye were compelled to be humble ye were blessed, do ye not suppose that they are more blessed who truly humble themselves because of the word?

15. Yea, he that truly humbleth himself, and repenteth of his sins, and endureth to the end, the same shall be blessed— yea, much more blessed than they who are compelled to be humble because of their exceeding poverty.

VERSES 12-15. *It is well that ye are cast out of your synagogues.* To learn the lesson of humility, Alma told the poor it was necessary that they should be cast out of their places of worship, and be despised of their brethren. One may note that to be looked down upon by one's own equals does not necessarily mean a mark of inferiority, but ofttimes such a one so looked down upon is lifted to heights never before dreamed of because the contempt showered upon one acts as a stimulus, or in other words, something that rouses the mind or spirits. It proved so with the poorer class of the Zoramites. It proved to be the only way in which they, under their circumstances, could learn about the true life. Wisdom and real humility, also uprightness of heart, are from above, but often it seems the lessons learned here below came penally and punishing. That is not true; they do not! God does not delight in punishing His children, but His children must accept His corrections as a "mark of His chastening love which comes to purify and strengthen" just as the refiner's fire comes to purify and strengthen precious metals.

Alma, realizing that the proper time had come, began to preach to the poor and lowly doctrines which they understood, and which they, notwithstanding their former freedom of restraint in matters religious, recognized as true. He commenced his sermon to them by showing unto them the urgent need of their being humble. Humility is a state of mind, indeed it does not connote self-effacement. In preaching the Words of Salvation, a man may be humble, yet bold in declaring his divine message. The burden of Alma's message was faith, the first principle of the Gospel of Jesus Christ. Time and time again he brought to their senses the fact that if it had not been for their miserable plight, they, in all probability, would not have taken the opportunity afforded them to hear his words. Only because they had been cast out from among their brethren, did they seek elsewhere the comforts of religious worship which communion one with another affords. "In this you are blessed," Alma told them. They were forced, possibly against their own desires, into humility. In spite of any motive they may have had, whatsoever it might have been, that impelled them to seek redress for the wrong their brethren did unto them, they found themselves bitterly opposed to the mandate of their oppressors.

Having been thus deprived of participation in religious association with those who delegated to themselves virtues of superior qualities, notably worldly goods, the under class, or poor in the things of the world, were rendered *lowly in spirit*. Alma reminded them that many others so situated and with like humility as they, had seen the errors which they had committed and had repented thereof. He assured them that if they like their repentant brethren should have a change of heart, and should continue steadfast to the end, then mercy would be shown them and they would be saved in God's Kingdom.

He also warned them, however, not to put off repentance until that day comes

16. Therefore, blessed are they who humble themselves without being compelled to be humble; or rather, in other words, blessed is he that believeth in the word of God, and is baptized without stubbornness of heart, yea, without being brought to know the word, or even compelled to know, before they will believe.

---

when despair and anguish would dull their desires for the higher things of life. He cautioned them against delay in so doing, noting that "they are more blessed who truly humble themselves because of the Word," and do not wait for changing conditions to alter the events of their lives. To obtain life's greatest blessings, *the will to do good* must come as a voluntary contribution. Heaven will then render it most for one's own good and greatest for the glory of God.

In verse thirteen, Alma teaches the same doctrine that Christ and all the holy prophets proclaimed, that is *whosoever endureth to the end shall be saved.*

And I heard a voice from the Father, saying: Yea, the words of My Beloved are true and faithful. He that *endureth to the end,* the same shall be saved.

And now, my beloved brethren, I know by this that unless a man shall *endure to the end,* in following the example of the Son of the living God, he cannot be saved. (II Nephi 31:15-16)

ENDURE—

I Nephi	13:37	If they e. unto the end, they shall be
	22:31	And e. to the end, ye shall be saved
II Nephi	9:24	And e. to the end, they must be damned
	31:16	Unless a man shall e. to the end
	20	The word of Christ and e. to the end
	33:4	To believe in Him, and e. to the end
Omni	1:26	In fastings and praying, and e. to the end
Mosiah	2:39	Doom is to e. a never-ending torment
	28:3	That any soul should e. endless torment
III Nephi	15:9	Look unto Me, and e. to the end
	28:8	Ye shall never e. the pains of death
Mormon	9:29	And if ye do this, and e. to the end

ENDURETH—

II Nephi	31:15	He that e. to the end, the same shall be
Alma	32:13	And e. to the end, the same shall be saved
	15	And e. to the end, the same shall be saved
	38:2	For blessed is he that e. to the end
III Nephi	15:9	For unto him that e. to the end
	27:6	E. to the end, the same shall be saved
	16	If he e. to the end, behold, him will I
	17	He that e. not to the end, the same is
Moroni	7:45	Hopeth all things, e. all things

VERSE 16. *Blessed is he who believeth in the Word of God.* Alma draws a distinction between one who is humble by choice, and one who may be forced by circumstances into humility of heart. The one may be blessed by bending himself to any righteous demands made of him, but not so greatly, Alma says, as one will be who receives the Word of God with gladness, and complies with its injunctions "without stubbornness of heart." Such a man accepts a Gospel requirement without it being proved to him that to comply with it is the will of the Lord.

17. Yea, there are many who do say: If thou wilt show unto us a sign from heaven, then we shall know of a surety; then we shall believe.

VERSE 17. *Show us a sign from Heaven*. In all places of the earth, and among all people, there have been those who disclaim *belief* in the supernatural without having a perfect knowledge of it. They clamor that a sign be given them that they may know for certain that God lives, and that He is all-powerful both in Heaven and upon Earth. In Nephite annals many unbelievers came unto the people who denied this great truth, and also that "Christ shall come." Sherem, in the days of Jacob, the Prophet Nephi's brother, was the first who is recorded in the Book of Mormon as asking for such a sign. (Jacob 7:1-19) Nehor, whose teachings and influence lasted down through the years even after the great mission of the sons of King Mosiah to the Lamanites, was a noted agitator. (Alma 1:1-15) Korihor who followed Nehor in the attempt to destroy the children of men, also asked for a sign. That sign was given to him.

And now Korihor said unto Alma: If thou wilt show me a sign, that I may be convinced that there is a God, yea, show unto me that He hath power, and then will I be convinced of the truth of thy words.

But Alma said unto him: Thou hast had signs enough; will ye tempt your God? Will ye say, Show unto me a sign, when ye have the testimony of all these my brethren, and also all the holy prophets? The Scriptures are laid before thee, yea, and all things denote there is a God; yea, even the Earth, and all things that are upon the face of it, yea, and its motion, yea, and also all the planets which move in their regular form do witness that there is a Supreme Creator.

And yet do ye go about, leading away the hearts of this people, testifying unto them there is no God? And yet will ye deny against all these witnesses? And he said: Yea, I will deny, except ye shall show me a sign. (Alma 30:43-45)

We will quote from Elder John Morgan who has assembled some pertinent scripture under the heading FAITH AND SIGNS. We often hear the same cry that greeted the ears of Jesus, "Master, we would see a sign from Thee. But He answered and said unto them, an evil and adulterous generation seeketh after a sign." (Matthew 12:38-39) What was true of the generation was true of the individual, and what was true then is true now, which places sign seekers in a most unenviable position, but doubtless where they justly belong. Faith is not produced by sign seeking, but in the words of Paul, "Faith cometh by hearing, and hearing by the word of God. (Romans 10:17)

After the death and resurrection of Jesus, He left this grand test of faith upon record, to serve as a guide for all future generations: "And these signs *shall follow them that believe* (that is, have faith); In My Name shall they cast out devils; they shall speak with new tongues; they shall take up serpents; and if they drink any deadly thing, it shall not hurt them; they shall lay hands on the sick, and they shall recover." (Mark 16:17-18) (John Morgan, PLAN OF SALVATION, p. 12)

To aid the reader to understand the meaning of the word, *sign*, every mention of it in the Book of Mormon, is herewith noted:

SIGN—

I Nephi	11:7	Shall be given unto thee for a sign
	19:10	Which should be a sign, given of His death
II Nephi	17:11	Ask thee a s. of the Lord thy God
	14	The Lord Himself shall give you a s.

18. Now I ask, is this faith? Behold, I say unto you, Nay; for if a man knoweth a thnig he hath no cause to believe, for he knoweth it.

19. And now, how much more cursed is he that knoweth the will of God and doeth it not, than he that only believeth, or only hath cause to believe, and falleth into transgression?

20. Now of this thing ye must judge. Behold, I say unto you, that it is on the one hand even as it is on the other; and it shall be unto every man according to his work.

21. And now as I said concerning faith—faith is not to have a perfect knowledge of things; therefore if ye have faith ye hope for things which are not seen, which are true.

22. And now, behold, I say

Jacob	7:13	Show me a s. by this power of the Holy Ghost
	14	Should tempt God to show unto thee a s.
	14	Let that be a s. unto thee that He has
Alma	30:43	Korihor said . . . If thou wilt show me a s.
	44	Will ye say, Show unto me a s., when
	45	I will deny, except you shall show me a s.
	48	Except ye show me a s., I will not believe
	49	This will I give unto thee for a s.
	51	Desire that Alma should show forth his s.?
	51	Should afflict others, to show unto thee a s.?
	51	It shall be a s. unto them, that they may know
	32:17	If thou wilt show unto us a s. from the
Helaman	2:7	Met Kishkumen, and he gave unto him a s.
	9:24	Because I showed unto you this s., ye
	25	I will show unto you another s.
	14:2	Behold, I give unto you a s.; for five days
	3	This will I give unto you for a s.
	4	And this shall be unto you for a s.
	5	And this also shall be a s. unto you
	14	Behold, again another s. I give unto you
	14	Yea, a s. of His death
	20	I said unto you concerning another s.
	20	A s. of His death, behold, in that day
III Nephi	1:9	Except the s. should come to pass which
	13	And on this night shall the s. be given
	14	And this night shall the s. be given
	18	The s. which had been given was already
	19	Because of the s. which had been given
	2:1	Began to be less and less astonished at a s.
	7	From the time when the s. was given
	8	From this period when the s. was given
	8:3	Began to look with great earnestness for the s.
	11:2	Christ, of Whom the s. had been given
	21:1	I give unto you a s., that ye may know
	2	The thing which I will give unto you for a s.
Moroni	10:1	Behold, He has showed unto you a s.
	7	Since the s. was given of the coming of

unto you, and I would that ye should remember, that God is merciful unto all who believe on his name; therefore he desireth, in the first place, that ye should believe, yea, even on his word.

23. And now, he imparteth his word by angels unto men, yea, not only men but women also. Now this is not all; little children do have words given unto them many times which confound the wise and the learned.

VERSES 18-23. *Now I ask, Is this faith?* One may ask, "What is faith?" Perfect faith is another condition of Salvation. The Apostle Paul (Hebrews 11:1-3) after quoting Habakkuk 2-4; "The just shall live by faith," explains what faith is: "The substance of things hoped for, the evidence of things not seen." The word *substance* means that which stands under, or, the underlying reality of things. It is that which sustains the creations of the mind, or the physical world (including all created existences). It is that which makes matter perceptible to us. For instance: here is an object. We examine it, and find that it has a certain weight. It has a peculiar color, and also that it is impervious to most acids. It readily amalgamates with mercury, and that for practical purposes, it forms valuable alloys with silver, or copper, etc., etc. We call it gold. Another object, with a different combination of qualities, we call silver, another we call copper. That which sustains all matter is its *substance*. What *substance* is in the material world, *faith* is in the spiritual world. It is the very foundation of the qualities—love, humility, peace, joy, benevolence, etc.—which are essential characteristics of the Christian character.

St. Paul further explains that "through faith we understand that the worlds were framed by the word of God, so that things that are seen were not made of things which do appear;" for no matter what scientists may assert, the beginning of things, their origins, being outside our sphere of experience or observation, can nevertheless be known through faith. Only through faith do we comprehend that the universe of which we are part is the Divine idea which received form in a material creation. Abel, Noah, Abraham, Sarah, Isaac, Jacob, Joseph, Moses, Joshua, Samuel, and many others, are mentioned as examples of what mortals can accomplish if they have the power that comes from faith in God. (*See* pp. 302 and 303, Vol. 1, COMMENTARY ON THE BOOK OF MORMON)

It is important to remember that *faith* means not only the conviction of the mind, but also that which is believed. That is, the Gospel or the creed, which in the mind of the Apostle is a long step in advance of the Law of Moses. (*See* Acts 6:7; 13:8; 14:22-27; Romans 1:5; 3:27; 10:8; Galatians 1:23; 2:16; 3:2, 5; Ephesians 2:8; Timothy 1:2; 4:1) When this is kept in mind, it is evident that there is no conflict between the views of Paul and James. For when it is argued that Salvation is by faith and not by works, as for instance in Galatians 3, it is not maintained that a Christian is without works of righteousness, but that it is the Gospel and not the Law of Moses that has *saved* him, and made him capable of living a righteous life.

When we left our Celestial Abode to dwell with mortals on the Earth, we left behind all memory of that happy, holy, home. There, it has been revealed to us, God was indeed our Father, and all men are our brothers. To the unenlightened and those who refuse to believe the Lord's words when He speaks through His Holy Prophets, such an abiding place is entirely within the realm of fantasy. Every suggestion of the reality of that pre-existent home has become obscure to the unbeliever in a maze of human denials, personal opinions, and selfish irresponsibilities. All such individuals, it may be said, have been drawn into a labyrinth of incon-

3. *Faith developed by desire to believe.*

24. And now, my beloved brethren, as ye have desired to know of me what ye shall do because ye are afflicted and cast out —now I do not desire that ye should suppose that I mean to judge you only according to that which is true—

25. For I do not mean that ye all of you have been compelled to humble yourselves; for I verily believe that there are some among you who would humble themselves, let them be in whatsoever circumstances they might.

26. Now, as I said concerning faith—that it was not a perfect knowledge—even so it is with my words. Ye cannot know of their surety at first, unto perfection, any more than faith is a perfect knowledge.

27. But behold, if ye will awake and arouse your faculties, even to an experiment upon my words, and exercise a particle of faith, yea, even if ye can no more than desire to believe, let this desire work in you, even until ye believe

sistent and opposing doctrine. Some students when considering the philosophy of life, reject the guidance offered them by the Word of the Lord and therefore sink deeper and deeper into the muck of unbelief where ignorance and superstition lead them to deny that which faith and good works impart to those who love the truth.

As we have stated *faith* is a Gospel requirement. Also we have pointed out that some men refuse to believe His Holy Word; they, in their peremptory manner, demand that they be given a sign which will dispel all uncertainty from their minds regarding God and His relationship to the human family. But, as Alma said to the Zoramites that if a man knoweth a thing "he hath no cause to believe, for he knoweth it." (v. 18) *Belief in God* is a motivating power which causes obedience to His laws, and it is easily understood when we consider the same incentive applied to other activities. Again, we quote from Elder Morgan, "To enable a man to perform any work whatever requires that he have faith in the ultimate result of his work. No farmer would plant unless he expected to reap; no builder build, unless he expected to inhabit; no speculator invest, unless he expected to increase his means; no journey would be attempted unless there existed the hope of reaching the destination. So, likewise, no commandment of God would be obeyed unless there existed faith that certain blessings would follow obedience. With this idea plainly before us we can comprehend the assertion of the Apostle Paul to the Hebrews: "But without faith it is impossible to please Him: for he that cometh to God must believe that He is, and that He is a rewarder of them that diligently seek Him." (Hebrews 11:6)

To impress upon the minds of his hearers that God is just and merciful, and that He requires no more than He provides for, Alma stressed the vast difference in responsibility between one who through faith alone — one who only believes in God — keeps the Lord's commandments, and one who notwithstanding greater knowledge, nevertheless "doeth it not." The one who knoweth the *will of God* and does not abide it is more cursed than he who merely has faith, or belief, and "falleth into transgression." "It," meaning the justice meted out, Alma said, "shall be unto every man according to his work." By the word *abide* we understand its meaning is to face or submit to a thing without shrinking.

in a manner that ye can give place for a portion of my words.

28. Now, we will compare the word unto a seed. Now, if ye give place, that a seed may be planted in your heart, behold, if it be a true seed, or a good seed, if ye do not cast it out by your unbelief, that ye will resist the Spirit of the Lord, behold, it will begin to swell within your breasts; and when you feel these swelling motions, ye will begin to say within yourselves—It must needs be that this is a good seed, or that the word is good, for it beginneth to enlarge my soul; yea, it beginneth to enlighten my understanding yea, it beginneth to be delicious to me.

29. Now behold, would not this increase your faith? I say unto you, Yea; nevertheless it hath not grown up to a perfect knowledge.

30. But behold, as the seed swelleth, and sprouteth, and beginneth to grow, then you must needs say that the seed is good; for behold it swelleth, and sprouteth, and beginneth to grow.

31. And now, behold are ye sure that this is a good seed? I

VERSE 26. *Faith is not a perfect knowledge — even so it is with my words.* Once more Alma noted that *faith* does not constitute a perfect knowledge. Even so, he concluded in his exhortations, that his words alone were not final in establishing the truth in their hearts. His mere stating of a truth, he implied, does not make it stable in their hearts, nor does it fix it immovably or firmly in the hearer's mind. In this verse, Alma in speaking of his words, notes: "Ye cannot know of their surety at first, unto perfection, any more than faith is a perfect knowledge."

VERSE 27. *Awake and arouse your faculties.* Alma now invited his listeners, one and all, to heed his words. (*Invite* means to ask courteously, or to request and urge politely that certain objectives be attempted.) He counseled them to give all due attention to what he said to them; if only as an *experiment* put a measure of trust in his words, that they being good, a desire would grow and grow within them, until, little by little, they could and would believe them all.

VERSE 28. *Now we will compare the word unto a seed.* If Alma's listeners hearkened to the plea he made and which is recorded in the previous verse, his words, he said, would be like unto a seed which is planted in fertile ground. He indicated that in their hearts could be found the proper soil in which to sow the seed, or cast his words. The seed so planted would eventually produce good fruit in abundance if unbelief did not smother its tender shoots. Let the Spirit of the Lord nurture every thought harbored by the seed, or fostered by his words; let it be a refuge, we imagine Alma saying, when doubt and drought assail the struggling seed, or the heart because of malnutrition begins to fail. If this is done Alma expressed indirectly to them, you will grow in grace and in the knowledge of God, or of that which is just and true. More directly he said that the seed so planted and cared for "Will begin to swell within your breasts; and when you feel these swelling motions, ye will begin to say within yourselves — "It must needs be that this is a good seed, or that the word is good, for it beginneth to enlarge my soul; yea, it beginneth to enlighten my understanding, yea, it beginneth to be delicious to me."

VERSES 29-41. *And now, behold, are ye sure that this is a good seed?* When the seed begins to swell in your hearts, and the *word* implanted therein starts to enlighten your minds, your *faith* will increase in the exact proportion as the diligence

say unto you, Yea; for every seed bringeth forth unto its own likeness.

32. Therefore, if a seed groweth it is good, but if it groweth not, behold it is not good, therefore it is cast away.

33. And now, behold, because ye have tried the experiment, and planted the seed, and it swelleth and sprouteth, and beginneth to grow, ye must needs know that the seed is good.

34. And now, behold, is your knowledge perfect? Yea, your knowledge is perfect in that thing, and your faith is dormant; and this because ye know, for ye know that the word hath swelled your souls, and ye also know that it hath sprouted up, that your understanding doth begin to be enlightened, and your mind doth begin to expand.

35. O then, is not this real? I say unto you, Yea, because it is light; and whatsoever is light, is good, because it is discernible, therefore ye must know that it is good; and now behold, after ye have tasted this light is your knowledge perfect?

36. Behold I say unto you, Nay; neither must ye lay aside your faith, for ye have only exercised your faith to plant the seed that ye might try the experiment to know if the seed was good.

37. And behold, as the tree beginneth to grow, ye will say: Let us nourish it with great care, that it may get root, that it may grow up, and bring forth fruit unto us. And now behold, if ye nourish it with much care it will get root, and grow up, and bring forth fruit.

38. But if ye neglect the tree, and take no thought for its nourishment, behold it will not get any root; and when the heat of the sun cometh and scorcheth it, because it hath no root it withers away, and ye pluck it up and cast it out.

39. Now, this is not because the seed was not good, neither is it because the fruit thereof would not be desirable; but it is because your ground is barren, and ye will not nourish the tree, therefore ye cannot have the fruit thereof.

40. And thus, if ye will not nourish the word, looking forward with an eye of faith to the fruit thereof, ye can never pluck of the fruit of the tree of life.

41. But if ye will nourish the word, yea, nourish the tree as it beginneth to grow, by your faith with great diligence, and with patience, looking forward to the fruit thereof, it shall take root; and behold it shall be a tree springing up unto everlasting life.

42. And because of your diligence and your faith and your patience with the word in nourishing it, that it may take root in you, behold, by and by ye shall

you show in caring for the seed, or obeying the word's holy promptings. Not at first, but gradually; not to begin with, but by steps or degrees, faith will be added upon faith, precept upon precept, until a mere belief becomes knowledge, and you begin to say that the seed is good; "for behold it swelleth and sprouteth, and

pluck the fruit thereof, which is most precious, which is sweet above all that is sweet, and which is white above all that is white, yea, and pure above all that is pure; and ye shall feast upon this fruit even until ye are filled, that ye hunger not, neither shall ye thirst.

43. Then, my brethren, ye shall reap the rewards of your faith, and diligence, and patience, and long-suffering, waiting for the tree to bring forth fruit unto you.

---

beginneth to grow." Any seed that fails to grow in soil that is prepared for it, is not good. But if it is good it brings forth, like unto itself, that which is also good.

FAITH—

Faith in Christ

I Nephi	10:17	Which power he received by f. on the
II Nephi	1:10	Power given them to do all things by f.
Ether	12:3	That by f. all things are fulfilled
	7	It was by f. that Christ showed Himself
	10	It was by f. that they of old were called
	11	By f., was the Law of Moses given
	11	And it was by f. that it has been fulfilled
	16	Wrought miracles, wrought them by f.
	17	It was by f. that the three disciples
	20	Which word he had obtained by f.
	21	The brother of Jared had obtained by f.
	22	It is by f. that my fathers have obtained
	23	Thou hast made us mighty in word by f.
Moroni	7:25	And thus by f. they did lay hold
	26	Men also were saved by f. on His Name
	26	And by f., they became the sons of God
	37	For it is by f. that miracles are wrought
	37	And it is by f. that angels appear
	8:25	And baptism cometh by f.

Exceeding Faith

II Nephi	3:24	With exceeding f., to work mighty miracles
Jacob	3:1	And pray unto Him with exceeding f.
Mosiah	4:3	Because of the exceeding f. which they
	26:15	Thou art blessed because of thy f. in the words
	16	Because of their exceeding f. in the word
Alma	13:3	On account of their exceeding f.
	10	It was on account of their exceeding f.
	19:10	Blessed art thou because of thy exceeding f.
	57:26	Because of their exceeding f. in that
	60:26	And this because of their exceeding f.
Ether	3:9	With such exceeding f. as thou hast

Great Faith

II Nephi	33:7	I . . . have great f. in Christ
Alma	13:3	And exercising exceeding great f.
	19:10	There has not been such great f. among

	58:11	And did grant unto us great f.
III Nephi	19:35	So great f. have I never seen among
Moroni	19:11	To another, exceeding great f.

Have Faith

Jarom	1:4	Many as are not stiffnecked and have f.
Alma	7:14	That ye may have f. on the Lamb of God
	24	See that ye have f., hope, and charity
	32:21	Therefore if ye have f., ye hope
Alma	34:15	That they may have f. unto repentance
Helaman	5:41	Even until ye shall have f. in Christ
Ether	12:9	Partakers of the gift, if ye will but have f.
	27	Have f. in Me, then will I make weak
	30	Thou workest after men have f.
Moroni	7:28	He claimeth all those who have f. in
	28	And they who have f. in Him, will cleave
	32	Residue of men may have f. in Christ
	33	If ye will have f. in Me, ye shall have
	34	And have f. in Me that ye may be saved
	38	Save they shall have f. in His Name
	39	For I judge that ye have f. in Christ
	42	If a man have f., he must needs have
	43	He cannot have f. and hope, save he shall
	10:23	If ye have f., ye can do all things

In Faith

I Nephi	15:11	Not harden your hearts and ask Me in f.
II Nephi	33:3	And I cry unto my God in f.
Enos	1:15	Whatsoever thing ye shall ask in f.
Mosiah	4:21	Whatsoever ye ask that is right, in f.
Alma	22:16	Before God, and call upon His Name in f.
	31:38	Alma; and this because he prayed in f.
Helaman	10:5	Word and in deed, in f. and in works
Moroni	7:26	In f., believing that ye shall receive

In the Faith

Jarom	1:7	Our leaders were mighty men in the f.
Mosiah	4:6	Continue in the f. even unto the end
	11	Standing steadfastly in the f. of that
	30	Continue in the f. of what ye have heard
Alma	1:25	To those that did stand fast in the f.
	27:27	And they were firm in the f. of Christ
	45:17	Those who should stand fast in the f.
	46:27	If we do not stand fast in the f. of Christ
	41	Those who died in the f. of Christ are
	48:13	Was a man who was firm in the f. of
Helaman	3:35	Did wax . . . firmer in the f. of Christ
	6:1	Firmness and their steadiness in the f.
	15:8	Are firm and steadfast in the f.

Our Faith

| II Nephi | 25:25 | Made alive in Christ, because of our f. |
| Jacob | 4:6 | And our f. becometh unshaken |

Alma	14:26	Give us strength according to our f.
	44:3	Because of our religion and our f. in
	3	Ye see that ye cannot destroy this our f.
	4	Are faithful unto Him, and unto our f.
	4	Fall into transgression and deny our f.
	5	Have gained power over you by our f.

Because of their Faith

I Nephi	1:20	He hath chosen, because of their f.
	12:10	Because of their f. in the Lamb of God
	11	Because of their f. in Him
II Nephi	3:21	Because of their f., their words shall
Helaman	15:9	Because of their f. in Christ
III Nephi	1:11	Destroyed because of their f. in the tradition
	9:20	Because of their f. in Me
	19:28	Chosen, because of their f.
	29	Out of the world, because of their f.
	27:19	Because of their f., and the repentance

According to their Faith

II Nephi	26:13	The children of men according to their f.
	27:23	I work not . . . save it be according to their f.
Enos	1:18	Be done unto them according to their f.
Jarom	1:4	Unto the children of men, according to their f.
Mosiah	27:14	Might be answered according to their f.
Alma	12:30	According to their f. and repentance
	14:28	According to their f. which was in Christ
	37:40	Did work . . . according to their f. in God
	57:21	According to their f. it was done unto them
III Nephi	5:14	Should be fulfilled according to their f.
Mormon	9:37	May be answered according to their f.
Ether	12:29	Children of men according to their f.

Their Faith

II Nephi	3:19	From the dust: for I know their f.
	21	Words will I make strong in their f.
Enos	1:18	For their f. was like unto Thine
Mosiah	23:21	He trieth their patience and their f.
	24:16	So great was their f. and their patience
	26:4	They were a separate people as to their f.
	27:33	Confirming their f., and exhorting them
Alma	9:20	According to their desires, and their f.
	13:4	This holy calling on account of their f.
	25:16	Serve to strengthen their f. in Christ
	33:1	They should begin to exercise their f.?
	37:33	With their f. on the Lord Jesus Christ
	41	Slothful, and forgot to exercise their f.
	48:15	This was their f., that by so doing, God
	58:40	Their f. is strong in the prophecies
III Nephi	1:8	Know that their f. had not been vain
	30	And began to decrease as to their f.
	26:9	They should have first, to try their f.
Mormon	8:24	And He knoweth their f.; for in His Name

Ether	12:12	He showed not Himself until after their f.
	17	Obtained not the promise until after their f.
	18	Wrought miracles until after their f.
Moroni	6:4	Was the Author and Finisher of their f.

Through Faith

Mosiah	3:9	Even through f. on His Name
	5:7	Hearts are changed through f. on His Name
	8:18	That man, through f., might work mighty miracles
Alma	9:27	Repentance, through f. on His Name
	22:14	Christ, atoneth for their sins, through f.
	25:16	Thus did they retain a hope through f.
III Nephi	7:16	Remission of sins through f. on His Name
	19:28	Purified in Me, through f. on their words
Mormon	9:37	Through f. on the Name of Jesus Christ

Thy Faith

I Nephi	2:19	Blessed art thou Nephi, because of thy f.
Enos	1:8	Because of thy f. in Christ, whom thou
	8	Go to, thy f. hath made thee whole
	12	According to thy desires, because of thy f.
Alma	14:15	Saved them, because they were of thy f.
	19:10	Blessed art thou because of thy f.
	23	It shall be unto him according to thy f.
Ether	3:9	Because of thy f. thou hast seen that I

Your Faith

Alma	7:17	And now because your f. is strong
	27	According to your f. and good works
	32:29	Would not this increase your f.?
	34	And your f. is dormant
	36	Neither must ye lay aside your f.
	36	For ye have only exercised your f.
	41	Nourish the tree . . . by your f.
	42	Because of your diligence, and your f.
	43	Ye shall reap the rewards of your f.
	33:23	Swell, even so nourish it by your f.
	34:17	Begin to exercise your f. unto repentance
	44:9	Behold, we are not of thy f.
Helaman	5:47	Because of your f. in My well Beloved Son
III Nephi	1:6	Therefore . . . your f. . . . hath been vain
	17:8	For I see that your f. is sufficient
	20	Blessed are ye because of your f.
Ether	12:6	No witness until after the trial of your f.
Moroni	7:41	And this because of your f. in Him

Faith

I Nephi	7:12	If it so be that they exercise f. in Him
	17	According to my f. which is in Thee
	16:28	They did work according to the f.
	29	According to the f. and diligence which
II Nephi	9:23	Having perfect f. in the Holy One of Israel
	31:19	Word of Christ, with unshaken f. in His

Jacob	1:5	For because of f. and great anxiety
	4:11	Having f., and obtained a good hope
	7:5	He had hope to shake me from the f.
Enos	1:11	My f. began to be unshaken in the Lord
	14	Vain in restoring them to the true f.
	16	I had f., and I did cry unto God
	20	To restore the Lamanites unto the true f. in God
Mosiah	3:12	Except it be through repentance and f.
	21	Through repentance and f. on the Name
	5:4	It is the f. which we have had on
	18:7	And redemption, and f. on the Lord
	20	Were redemption and f. on the Lord
	21	Having one f. and one baptism
	21:30	F. on the words which had been spoken
	25:15	Preaching unto the people . . . f. on the Lord
	22	Except it were repentance and f. in God
	27:14	For he has prayed with much f.
Alma	2:30	Being exercised with much f., cried
	5:12	According to his f. there was a mighty
	15	Do ye exercise f. in the redemption?
	15	Do you look forward with an eye of f.?
	7:6	With an everlasting f. which is to come
	13:18	Melchizedek having exercised mighty f.
	29	Having f. on the Lord
	14:16	This judge was after the . . . f. of Nehor
	15:10	According to his f. which is in Christ
	18:35	According to my f. and desires which
	26:22	He that repenteth and exerciseth f.
	32:18	Now I ask, Is this f.
	21	And now as I said concerning f.
	21	F., is not to have a perfect knowledge
	26	Now as I said concerning f.
	26	Any more than f. is a perfect knowledge
	27	And exercise a particle of f.
	40	Looking forward with an eye of f.
	34:3	And he hath exhorted you unto f.
	4	That ye would have so much f. as ever
	16	While he that exercises no f. unto repentance
	16	Only unto him that has f. unto repentance
	28	Are as hypocrites who do deny the f.
	37:33	Preach . . . f. on the Lord Jesus Christ
	40	If they had f. to believe that God
	44:4	Ye see that this is the true f. of God
	49:16	And this was the f. of Moroni
	57:27	This was the f. of those of whom I have
	61:17	According to the f. which is in us
Helaman	6:4	Did exhort them to f. and repentance
	8:15	Should look upon the Son of God with f.
	9:16	That he might convert us unto his f.
	13:6	Save it be repentance and f. on the Lord
	15:7	Which leadeth them to f. on the Lord
	7	Which f. and repentance bringeth a change

III Nephi	6:14	Who were converted unto the true f.
	7:18	So great was his f. on the Lord Jesus
	13:30	Clothe you, if ye are not of little f.
	26:11	Saying, I will try the f. of My people
Mormon	3:12	It was without f., because of the hardness
Ether	3:19	He had f. no longer, for he knew
	4:7	In that day that they shall exercise f.
	12:4	Which hope cometh of f.
	6	F. is things which are hoped for and not
	7	Until after they had f. in Him
	7	It must needs be that some had f. in Him
	8	But because of the f. of men
	12	If there be no f. among the children of men
	13	It was the f. of Alma and Amulek that
	14	It was the f. of Nephi and Lehi that wrought
	15	It was the f. of Ammon and his brethren
	19	Many whose f. was so exceeding strong
	19	Which they had beheld with an eye of f.
	20	For so great was his f. in God
	28	I will show unto them that f., hope
	30	If he had not had f., it would not have
	31	For after they had f., and did speak
Moroni	3:3	By the endurance of f. on His Name
	7:1	Mormon, which he spake concerning f.
	21	And now I come to that f. of which I
	30	Showing themselves unto them of strong f.
	38	Then has f. ceased also
	39	For if ye have not f. in Him, then ye are
	40	How is it that ye can attain unto f.?
	42	For without f. there cannot be any hope
	44	If so, his f. and hope is vain
	8:3	Through the endurance of f. on His Name
	14	For he hath not f., hope, nor charity
	10:7	According to the f. of the children of men
	20	Wherefore there must be f.
	20	And if there must be f., there must also
	21	In the Kingdom of God, if ye have not f.

Faithful—

I Nephi	2:1	And because thou hast been f.
	3:16	Wherefore let us be f. in keeping the commandments
	21	That they might be f. in keeping
	4:1	Let us be f. in keeping the commandments
	7:12	Wherefore let us be f. to Him
	13	And if it so be that we are f. to Him
	21:7	Because of the Lord that is f.
II Nephi	1:31	Wherefore, because thou hast been f.
	2:28	Be f. unto His words, and choose
	6:11	Because of the prayers of the f.
	18:2	And I took unto me f. witnesses
	26:15	The prayers of the f. shall be heard
	27:13	That the words of the f. should speak
	31:15	Words of My Beloved are true and f.

Mosiah	2:41	If they hold out f. to the end
	10:13	Because that Nephi was more f. in keeping
Alma	5:13	Behold, they were f. until the end
	8:15	Thou hast been f. in keeping the commandments
	18:10	That has been so f. as this man
	44:4	So long as we are f. unto Him
	46:15	Did belong to the Church were f.
	48:7	The people to be f. unto the Lord
	15	If they were f. in keeping the commandments
	50:22	Those who were f. in keeping the commandments
	52:10	He would be f. in maintaining that quarter of the land
Ether	1:38	Let us be f. unto the Lord
	4:19	Blessed is he who is found f.
	8:13	Will ye swear unto me that ye will be f.
	12:37	Thou hast been f.; wherefore thy garment
Moroni	9:25	My son, be f. in Christ

Faithfulness—

I Nephi	17:15	I did exhort my brethren to f.
II Nephi	21:5	And f. the girdle of his reins
	30:11	And f. the girdle of his reins.
Alma	18:2	He had learned the f. of Ammon
	10	Because of the f. of Ammon
	38:2	Because of your f. . . . unto God
	3	Because of thy f. and thy diligence
	39:1	Thy brother, his f., and his diligence
	62:1	Joy, because of the f. of Pahoran
III Nephi	27:19	And their f. unto the end

CHAPTER 33

1. *Alma's discourse continued.*

2. *True worship not confined to sanctuaries.*

1. And after Alma had spoken these words, they sent forth unto him desiring to know whether they should believe in one God, that they might obtain this fruit of which he had spoken, or how they should plant the seed, or the word of which he had spoken, which he said must be planted in their hearts; or in what manner they should begin to exercise their faith.

2. And Alma said unto them: Behold, ye have said that ye could not worship your God because ye are cast out of your synagogues. But behold, I say unto you, if ye suppose that ye cannot worship God, ye do greatly err, and ye ought to search the scriptures; if ye suppose that they have taught you this, ye do not understand them.

VERSES 1-2. *Behold, ye have said that ye could not worship your God because ye are cast out of your synagogues.* No doubt Alma paused for a moment's rest between portions of his lengthy sermon, of which rest the throng that had gathered there were quick to take advantage. Alma's message met with a deep response among them. It is true many did not understand the meaning of his words, but they nevertheless took them to be good. Some wanted to know more of God; their belief in Him and whether or not He was just one, or many different Beings. Alma had spoken to them of a certain kind of precious fruit which they might pluck from a tree planted as a seed in their hearts. Behold, he told them that if they would water and nurture such a seed, that it would swell and sprout, and that they would feel it grow, and then they "must needs know that the seed is good." By caring for the seed planted in their hearts, they would show by doing so that they had begun to exercise their faith. Concerning these things, and many others, they wanted Alma to speak further.

Reverting in his mind, Alma remembered the lament of one of their number, apparently their leader, who, in his anguish, had reached the depths of despair, because, not only he but also his fellows, had been cast out of their synagogues and therefore had no place in which to worship God. (Alma 32:5) They were poor in the things of the world, and could contribute little of earthly goods to the priests and leaders of the church. One is reminded of Jacob's words, the Prophet Nephi's brother: But wo unto the rich, who are rich as to the things of the world. For because they are rich they despise the poor, and they persecute the meek, and their hearts are upon their treasures; wherefore, their treasure is their God. And behold, their treasure shall perish with them also. (II Nephi 9:30) Thus the Zoramites regarded their poorer brethren.

3. *The Prophets Zenos and Zenock again cited.*

3. Do ye remember to have read what Zenos, the prophet of old, has said concerning prayer or worship?

4. For he said: Thou art merciful, O God, for thou hast heard my prayer, even when I was in the wilderness; yea, thou wast merciful when I prayed concerning those who were mine enemies, and thou didst turn them to me.

5. Yea, O God, and thou wast merciful unto me when I did cry unto thee in my field; when I did cry unto thee in my prayer, and thou didst hear me.

6. And again, O God, when I did turn to my house thou didst hear me in my prayer.

7. And when I did turn unto my closet, O Lord, and prayed unto thee, thou didst hear me.

8. Yea, thou art merciful unto thy children when they cry unto thee, to be heard of thee and not of men, and thou wilt hear them.

9. Yea, O God, thou hast been merciful unto me, and heard my cries in the midst of thy congregations.

10. Yea, and thou hast also heard me when I have been cast out and have been despised by mine enemies; yea, thou didst hear my cries, and wast angry with mine enemies, and thou didst visit them in thine anger with speedy destruction.

11. And thou didst hear me because of mine afflictions and my sincerity; and it is because of thy Son that thou hast been thus merciful unto me, therefore I will cry unto thee in all mine afflictions, for in thee is my joy; for thou hast turned thy judgments away from me, because of thy Son.

However, Alma, himself, was quick to carry home his message of forbearance. "Ye do greatly err," he said unto them, "if ye suppose that ye cannot worship God" without synagogues or sanctuaries. Search the Scriptures, it may be, perchance, ye have not understood them when they speak of houses of worship.

VERSES 3-11. *What Zenos, the prophet of old, has said concerning prayer or worship.* Copies of the Hebrew Scriptures were quite common among the Nephites, and Alma, taking foreknowledge of their wide distribution, called upon the throng standing before him to look for themselves in them and see what two of the ancient prophets said about prayer and worship. Alma cited Zenos and Zenock. He quoted Zenos. That they would find in the prophet's words a complete answer to the problem that perplexed them, Alma told them.

Alma read to them what Zenos said: Thou art merciful, O God, for Thou hast heard my prayer, even when I was in the wilderness; yea, Thou wast merciful when I prayed concerning those who were mine enemies, and Thou didst turn them to me. Yea, O God, and Thou wast merciful unto me when I did cry unto Thee in my field; when I did cry unto Thee in my prayer, and Thou didst hear me. And again, O God, when I did turn to my house Thou didst hear me in my prayer. And when I did turn unto my closet, O Lord, and prayed unto Thee, Thou didst hear me. Yea, Thou are merciful unto thy children when they call unto Thee, to be heard of Thee and not of men, and Thou wilt hear them. Yea, O God, Thou hast been merciful

12. And now Alma said unto them: Do ye believe those scriptures which have been written by them of old?

13. Behold, if ye do, ye must believe what Zenos said; for behold he said: Thou hast turned away thy judgments because of thy Son.

14. Now behold, my brethren, I would ask if ye have read the scriptures? If ye have, how can ye disbelieve on the Son of God?

15. For it is not written that Zenos alone spake of these things, but Zenock also spake of these things—

16. For behold, he said: Thou art angry, O Lord, with this people, because they will not understand thy mercies which thou hast bestowed upon them because of thy Son.

17. And now, my brethren, ye see that a second prophet of old has testified of the Son of God, and because the people would not understand his words they stoned him to death.

18. But behold, this is not all; these are not the only ones who have spoken concerning the Son of God.

19. Behold, he was spoken of by Moses; yea, and behold a type was raised up in the wilderness, that whosoever would look upon it might live. And many did look and live.

20. But few understood the

unto me, and heard my cries in the midst of Thy congregations. Yea, and Thou hast also heard me when I have been cast out and have been despised by mine enemies; yea, Thou didst hear my cries, and wast angry with mine enemies, and Thou didst visit them in Thine anger with speedy destruction. And Thou didst hear me because of mine afflictions and my sincerity; and it is because of Thy Son that Thou hast been thus merciful unto me, therefore I will cry unto Thee in all mine afflictions, for in Thee is my joy; for Thou hast turned Thy judgments away from me, because of Thy Son.

VERSES 12-16. *Do ye believe these scriptures which have been written of old?* After having read the words of Zenos, Alma not only was confident that the question which troubled the anxious multitude was therein answered, but furthermore, the message of Christ's Salvation was also made plain. "Thou hast turned away Thy judgments because of Thy Son," reveals to us that the entire meaning of the Plan of Life and Salvation was known to the worthies of old, as it is now understood by us. Besides Zenos, Zenock also prophesied concerning the coming of the Son of God to Redeem His people. Alma also read Zenock's words which were written on the Brass Plates of Laban: Thou art angry, O Lord, with this people, because they will not understand Thy mercies which Thou hast bestowed upon them because of Thy Son.

VERSES 17-18. *Zenos and Zenock were not the only ones who have spoken concerning the Son of God.* Alma gave the information that because Zenock testified of the Son of God, and further that the people among whom he prophesied would not "understand his words," they put him to death in a most ignominious manner. Besides these two already mentioned, Alma called forth other prophets to testify to the Son of God.

VERSES 19-22. *Behold, He was spoken of by Moses.* When Moses and the Children of Israel were wandering in the Wilderness of Arabia, the Plan of the Messiah

meaning of those things, and this because of the hardness of their hearts. But there were many who were so hardened that they would not look, therefore they perished. Now the reason they would not look is because they did not believe that it would heal them.

21. O my brethren, if ye could be healed by merely casting about your eyes that ye might be healed, would ye not behold quickly, or would ye rather harden your hearts in unbelief, and be slothful, that ye would not cast about your eyes, that ye might perish?

22. If so, wo shall come upon you; but if not so, then cast about your eyes and begin to believe in the Son of God, that he will come to redeem his people, and that he shall suffer and die to atone for their sins; and that he shall rise again from the dead, which shall bring to pass the resurrection, that all men shall stand before him, to be judged at the last and judgment day, according to their works.

---

was only rudely understood by all except the great leader, himself. To awaken them to a lively interest in things spiritual, and establish among them something to constantly remind them of the responsibility they bore as God's chosen people — at the same time bring them blessings that was part of their heritage — a type of the Messiah, or a thing regarded as a symbol of Him who was yet to come, was placed in the midst of Israel that all who *looked upon* It obtained the gifts and promises that come through obedience. *Look upon*, we believe to mean observe and keep the ordinances and testimonies of the Messiah, whom the type mentioned portrayed, or represented. "Many did look and live."

Because of "the hardness of their hearts" many of the Children of Israel did not understand what was meant by the *Type* established pertaining to what they looked forward. Others of them, more hardened than they, refused to abide by the laws God gave them through Moses. Some would not even look, because, Alma offered the explanation that their faith was insufficient to make themselves believe that they would be "healed" of their infirmities.

Alma, now made a direct appeal to the assembled throng. The first principle of the Gospel of Jesus Christ had been the theme of his sermon. Faith in Him was a simple, yet effective, measure which was to be taken by all who desired to know the mind and will of God. Some fifty years earlier than Alma's time, King Benjamin, in Zarahemla, taught faith in God as a necessary principle, and belief in His power of redemption as a saving grace for all mankind: Believe in God; believe that He is, and that He created all things, both in Heaven and in Earth; believe that He has all wisdom, and all power, both in Heaven and in Earth; believe that man doth not comprehend all the things the Lord can comprehend. And again, believe that ye must repent of your sins and forsake them, and humble yourselves before God; and ask in sincerity of heart that He would forgive you; and now, if you believe all these things see that ye do them. And again I say unto you as I have said before, that as ye have come to a knowledge of the glory of God, or if ye have known of His goodness and have tasted of His love, and have received a remission of your sins, which causes such exceeding great joy in your souls, even so I would that ye should remember, and always retain in remembrance, the greatness of God, and your own nothingness, and His goodness and long-suffering towards you, unworthy creatures, and humble yourselves even in the depths of humility, calling on the Name of the

23. And now, my brethren, I desire that ye shall plant this word in your hearts, and as it beginneth to swell even so nourish it by your faith. And behold, it will become a tree, springing up in you unto everlasting life. And then may God grant unto you that your burdens may be light, through the joy of his Son. And even all this can ye do if ye will. Amen.

Lord daily, and standing steadfastly in the faith of that which is to come, which was spoken by the mouth of the angel. And behold, I say unto you that if ye do this ye shall always rejoice, and be filled with the love of God, and always retain a remission of your sins; and ye shall grow in the knowledge of the glory of Him that created you, or in the knowledge of that which is just and true. (Mosiah 4:12)

If, Alma argued, all that is necessary is to cast your eyes about you, and see for yourselves the marvelous Salvation of the Lord as did the Children of Israel, would "ye not behold quickly, or would ye rather harden your hearts in unbelief?" Would ye rather be "slothful" or indolent, and too lazy, to "cast about your eyes" and therefore perish when all that is required of you is that you see and recognize the great Redemption of the Lord? Yet, it is as easy to believe on the Son of God and have faith in His *Atoning Blood*, that it "shall bring to pass the resurrection" of the dead and other great and marvelous works, as it was for the Children of Israel to "look" upon the "type" of the Messiah which was raised in their midst. Prepare now by believing in Him, for it is the proper time to make yourselves ready to stand, as all men must, before Him, "to be judged at the *Last and Judgment Day*, according to their works."

VERSE 23. *May God grant unto you that your burdens may be light, through the joy of His Son.* Alma had provided the Zoramites who had gathered about him with the *seed* which he invited them to plant in their hearts. That seed was the *Word of God!* If, when you receive that seed and feel it swell within you, then "even so nourish it by your faith," he counseled them. That little seed once it becomes imbedded within a sincere heart, will sprout and send its tender shoots into every part of the body, and will grow and grow until at last it will become a tree whose fruit will be good, and will in turn nourish its keeper, or in other words, will feed the one who has watched over it, guarded it, and maintained a care of it. It will continue to grow and develop into a tree, "Springing up in you unto Everlasting Life."

In closing his words which he delivered to them, Alma, always cognizant of the burdens carried by any of his people, prayed to God that the load these Zoramites bore would be made light through a belief in the Son of God, and that although they had no synagogue in which to worship Him, they would be enabled to do as did the Prophet Zenos: Worship Him in the wilderness; in their own fields of grain, in their closets at home, among their flocks and herds, and when they, as was he, cast out and was despised by his enemies. In the joy they would receive through obedience to God's will, Alma promised that they could do all these things, and ended his exhortations by a benediction, Amen.

CHAPTER 34

1. *Amulek's testimony.*

1. And now it came to pass that after Alma had spoken these words unto them he sat down upon the ground, and Amulek arose and began to teach them, saying:

2. My brethren, I think that it is impossible that ye should be ignorant of the things which have been spoken concerning the coming of Christ, who is taught by us to be the Son of God; yea, I know that these things were taught unto you bountifully before your dissension from among us.

3. And as ye have desired of my beloved brother that he should make known unto you what ye should do, because of your afflictions; and he hath spoken somewhat unto you to prepare your minds; yea, and he hath exhorted you unto faith and to patience—

4. Yea, even that ye would have so much faith as even to plant the word in your hearts, that ye may try the experiment of its goodness.

5. And we have beheld that the great question which is in your minds is whether the word be in the Son of God, or whether there shall be no Christ.

6. And ye also beheld that my brother has proved unto you, in many instances, that the word is in Christ unto salvation.

7. My brother has called upon the words of Zenos, that redemption cometh through the Son of God, and also upon the words of Zenock; and also he has appealed unto Moses, to prove that these things are true.

8. And now, behold, I will testify unto you of myself that these things are true. Behold, I say unto you, that I do know that Christ shall come among the children of men, to take upon him the transgressions of his people, and that he shall atone for the sins of the world; for the Lord God hath spoken it.

9. For it is expedient that an atonement should be made; for according to the great plan of the Eternal God there must be an

---

VERSES 1-9. *Amulek arose and began to teach them.* After Alma had concluded his address to the Zoramites, he sat down upon the ground, and Amulek commenced to speak to the congregation who likewise sat upon the hill before him.

Amulek immediately began his discourse by painstakingly reminding the Zoramites of Christ, Whom they, as well as he and his companions, knew as *the Son of God.* Of Christ, Amulek said that the Zoramites could not be ignorant. His coming,

atonement made, or else all mankind must unavoidably perish; yea, all are hardened: yea, all are fallen and are lost, and must perish except it be through the atonement which it is expedient should be made.

2. The great and last Sacrifice.

10. For it is expedient that there should be a great and last sacrifice; yea, not a sacrifice of man, neither of beast, neither of any manner of fowls; for it shall not be a human sacrifice; but it must be an infinite and eternal sacrifice.

11. Now there is not any man that can sacrifice his own blood which will atone for the sins of another. Now, if a man murdereth, behold will our law, which is just, take the life of his brother? I say unto you, Nay.

12. But the law requireth the life of him who hath murdered; therefore there can be nothing which is short of an infinite atonement which will suffice for the sins of the world.

13. Therefore, it is expedient that there shoulld be a great and

---

which was now proclaimed anew by the missionaries, had been taught freely unto them while yet they were numbered as members of God's Church in Zarahemla, and from which they had separated.

However, to impress upon the minds of those who had come to them for advice concerning a place to worship God now that they had been deprived of the use of their synagogue, Amulek noted to them that Alma "hath exhorted you unto faith and patience." Amulek continued to use Alma's metaphor concerning planting the "word in your hearts." The *word* as used here is *faith in Christ*. Like a *seed* it will swell and grow in your hearts, "*even so nourish it by your faith.*" Then "wait for the Lord," and you will see that it is good; that it will grow into a mighty tree "springing up in you unto everlasting life." (Alma 33:23)

Alma and Amulek were quick to see and realize that what perturbed the Zoramites most was whether faith was to be exercised in the Son of God, or its alternative, "there shall be no Christ." Amulek also noted to the Zoramites that Alma had proved unto them many times that *faith in Christ is unto Salvation*. Amulek cited, as Alma also had done before him, the Prophets Zenos, Zenock, and Moses, "to prove that these things are true."

Amulek, now that the proper time had come, joined his own testimony with that of the prophets of old, in declaring "that these things are true." "Behold, I say unto you, that I do know that Christ shall come among the children of men, to take upon Him the transgressions of His people, and that He shall atone for the sins of the world; for the Lord God hath spoken it."

To bring about the necessary Plan of Salvation which God had made that His children should be spared from the everlasting effects of Adam's Fall, and to accomplish His purposes that they should not forever be bound by the chains of hell and be held prisoners by the grave, an Atonement which is infinite must be made.

VERSES 10-15. *It is expedient that there should be a great and last Sacrifice.* To the end that all men should be delivered from the effects of the *Fall of Adam,* which

last sacrifice; and then shall there be, or it is expedient there should be, a stop to the shedding of blood; then shall the law of Moses be fulfilled; yea, it shall be all fulfilled, every jot and tittle, and none shall have passed away.

14. And behold, this is the whole meaning of the law, every whit pointing to that great and last sacrifice; and that great and last sacrifice will be the Son of God, yea, infinite and eternal.

15. And thus he shall bring salvation to all those who shall believe on his name; this being the intent of this last sacrifice, to bring about the bowels of mercy, which overpowereth justice, and bringeth about means unto men that they may have faith unto repentance.

Fall brought woe to all mankind, a Sacrifice is necessary which will atone for, and blot out, every vestige of Adam's Fall. All evil and its transgressions will be done away with by this great and last Sacrifice. Amulek contrasted this Sacrifice with the sacrifices enjoined by the Law of Moses. It will "not be a sacrifice of man, neither of beast, neither of any manner of fowl; for it shall not be a human sacrifice; but it must be an infinite and eternal Sacrifice." There is no man, Amulek argued, that can have his own blood shed, or "that can sacrifice" it to amend totally for the sins of another. A man can in no way expiate, or make complete satisfaction for — atone for — the offenses of others. There is among us, a law, he said, which is just; it requires that a man who murdereth, forfeit his own life in expiation therefore, but it will not demand in reconciliation of that offense the life of his brother. For that reason, and we may be sure for it alone, a sacrifice which is all-inclusive; that is, a sacrifice "which will suffice for the sins of the world."

VERSES 13-14. *It is expedient that there should be a stop to the shedding of blood.* The Zoramites, in spite of their apostasy from the Nephite Church of God, and notwithstanding their dissension and withdrawal from Zarahemla to another place of abode where they could carry on a form of worship to their own liking, took with them a belief in the Law of Moses which they had garbled, and which they evidently did not understand. The Law of Moses required the rendering of sacrifice wherein animals and "and manner of fowl" were offered in token of the "great and last Sacrifice" which "will be the Son of God, yea, infinite and eternal," Amulek said. That great and last Sacrifice of the Son of God wherein His blood will be spilled to atone for the sins of all men will put a "stop to the shedding of blood." "Then," Amulek proclaimed to them, "shall the Law of Moses be fulfilled, every jot and tittle, and none shall have passed away." To this end, that is the "great and last Sacrifice of the Son of God" every ordinance, performance, and sacrifice, of that Law was pointed. Every sacrifice offered, the blood of the animals slain, was but typical of the *Blood of Jesus* which would end all sacrifice, and fulfill all requirements of the Law of Moses. Thus, He Who is infinite and eternal will make a Sacrifice for all which, like Him, is infinite and eternal.

When the Risen Redeemer introduced Himself to the astonished Nephites gathered near the temple site in the Land Bountiful shortly after His resurrection, among other things He said of Himself were: I came unto My own, and My own received Me not. And the Scriptures concerning My coming are fulfilled. And as many as have received Me, to them have I given to become the sons of God; and even so will I to as many as shall believe on My Name, for behold, by Me redemption cometh, and in Me is the Law of Moses fulfilled. I am the life and light of

3. *How mercy satisfies justice.*

16. And thus mercy can satisfy the demands of justice, and encircle them in the arms of safety, while he that exercises no faith unto repentance is exposed to the whole law of the demands of justice; therefore only unto him that has faith unto repentance is brought about the great and eternal plan of redemption.

17. Therefore may God grant unto you my brethren, that ye may begin to exercise your faith unto repentance, that ye begin to call upon his holy name, that he would have mercy upon you;

---

the world. I am Alpha and Omega, the beginning and the end. And ye shall offer up unto Me no more the shedding of blood; yea, your sacrifices and your burnt offerings shall be done way, for I will accept none of your sacrifices and your burnt offerings.

VERSES 16-17. *May God grant unto you, my brethren, that ye may begin to exercise your faith unto repentance.* If justice alone should mark man's station in life, and his own merit prevail, he would be of all creatures most miserable, most deeply to be pitied. But mercy which is shown in the Sacrifice of the Son of God "can satisfy the demands of justice," and redeem all men in the arms of love.

About 75 years previously, or about 148 B.C., the Prophet Abinadi in declaring the coming of the Messiah to redeem mankind from the effects of Adam's Fall, said to the wicked priests of King Noah: And thus God breaketh the bands of death, having gained the victory over death; giving the Son power to make intercession for the children of men — Having ascended into Heaven, having the bowels of mercy; being filled with compassion towards the children of men; standing betwixt them and justice; having broken the bands of death, taken upon Himself their iniquity and their transgressions, having redeemed them, and satisfied the demands of justice.

To, which President John Taylor adds this beautiful thought: Is justice dishonored? No, it is satisfied, the debt is paid. Is righteousness departed from? No, this is a righteous act. All requirements are met. Is judgment violated? No, its demands are fulfilled. Is mercy triumphant? No, she simply claims her own. Justice, judgment, mercy, and truth all harmonize as the attributes of Deity. "Justice and truth have met together, righteousness and peace have kissed each other." Justice and judgment triumph as well as mercy and peace; all the attributes of Deity harmonize in this great, grand, momentous, just, equitable, merciful and meritorious act. (*Meditation and Atonement*)

The aim, or the intent of the great and last Sacrifice, which Amulek proclaimed, was that all men should be saved through belief on the Name of the Son of God. The way was by Him prepared, and thus the means provided, whereby Salvation might come to those who "have faith unto repentance." Faith in Jesus Christ which brings repentance, also brings about the great and eternal Plan of Redemption. While he who does not believe, and therefore has no repentance in Him, will not share the mercy which mitigates and satisfies the demands of justice.

A full concordance of the words, *Atone* and *Justice*, are herewith appended:

ATONE—

Alma	33:22	He shall suffer and die to a. for their sins
	34:8	He shall a. for the sins of the world
	11	Which will a. for the sins of another
	36:17	A Son of God, to a. for the sins of the

ATONEMENT—

Through the Atonement

Jacob	4:11	Unto him through the a. of Christ
Mosiah	3:15	Except it were through the a. of his
	19	A saint, through the a. of Christ
	4:7	Through the a. which was prepared
Alma	13:5	Through the a. of the only begotten Son
	34:9	Perish except it be through the a.
Moroni	7:41	Have hope through the a. of Christ

Atonement

2 Nephi	2:10	To answer the ends of the a.
	9:7	It must needs be an infinite a.
	7	Save it should be an infinite a.
	25	Have claim upon them, because of the a.
	26	The a. satisfieth the demands of his just
	10:25	Death by the power of the a.
	25:16	The a., which is infinite for all mankind
Jacob	4:12	For why not speak of the a. of Christ
	7:12	I know if there should be no a. made
Mosiah	4:6	The a. which has been prepared
	13:28	The a. which God Himself shall make
Alma	21:9	Of Christ, and the a. of his blood
	24:13	Shall be shed for the a. of our sins
	30:17	Telling them that there could be no a.
	34:9	Expedient that an a. should be made
	9	There must be an a. made
	12	Nothing which is short of an infinite a.
	42:15	Except an a. should be made
Alma	42:23	Mercy cometh because of the a.
	23	The a. bringeth to pass the resurrection
Moroni	8:20	Setteth at nought the a. of him

Atoneth

Mosiah	3:11	His blood a. for the sins of those
	16	The blood of Christ a. for their sins
Alma	22:14	The death of Christ, a. for their sins
	42:15	Therefore God Himself a. for the sins

Atoning

Mosiah	3:18	In and through the a. blood of Christ
	4:2	And apply the a. blood of Christ
Helaman	5:9	' Only through the a. blood of Jesust Christ

JUSTICE—

Justice of God

I Nephi	14:4	According to the j. of God
	15:30	The j. of God did also divide the wicked
II Nephi	2:12	Power, and the mercy, and the j. of God
Alma	41:2	Is requisite with the j. of God
	3	Is requisite with the j. of God

	42:1	Which is concerning the j. of God
	14	The j. of God, which consigned them
	30	Deny the j. of God no more
	30	By denying the j. of God
	30	But do you let the j. of God
	54:6	Concerning the j. of God, and the
	61:12	If it were requisite with the j. of God
I Nephi	12:18	The word of the j. of the eternal God
	15:35	Because of that j. of which I have spoken
2 Nephi	9:17	O the greatness and the j. of our God!
	26	Atonement satisfieth the demands of his j.
	46	Glorious day, when j. shall be administered
	11:5	Delighteth in his grace, and in his j.
	19:7	To establish it with judgment and with j.
Jacob	3:1	J. upon those who seek your destruction
	4:10	He counselleth in wisdom, and in j.
	6:10	And according to the power of j.
	10	For j. cannot be denied
Mosiah	2:38	The demands of divine j. doth awaken
	3:26	Which j. could no more deny unto them
	5:15	Through the wisdom, and power, and j.
	15:9	Standing betwixt them and j.
	9	And satisfieth the demands of j.
	27	For he cannot deny j. when it has its claim
Alma	10:21	With equity and j. in my hands
	12:18	Cannot be redeemed according to God's j.
	32	For the works of j. could not be destroyed
	26:19	Why did he not let the sword of his j.
	20	He did not exercise his j. upon us
	34:15	Bowels of mercy, which overpowereth j.
	16	Thus mercy can satisfy the demands of j.
	16	Exposed to the whole law of the demands of j.
	41:14	Ye shall have j. restored unto you again
	42:13	According to j., the plan of redemption
	13	Except it should destroy the work of j.
	13	Now the work of j. could not be destroyed
	14	In the grasp of j.; yea, the j. of God
	15	Mercy, to appease the demands of j.
	21	What could j. do, or mercy either
	22	Otherwise, j. claimeth the creature
	22	If not so, the works of j. would be destroyed
	23	Their works, according to the law and j.
	24	J. exerciseth all his demands
	25	Do ye suppose that mercy can rob j.?
	46:29	Doubtful concerning the j. of the cause
	50:39	And to bring the wicked to j.
	60:13	That his j. and judgment may come
	29	The sword of j. doth hang over you
Helaman	3:20	Helaman did fill the judgment seat with j.
	37	That he did fill the judgment seat with j.
	5:3	Could not be governed by the law nor j.

18. Yea, cry unto him for mercy; for he is mighty to save. | 19. Yea, humble yourselves, and continue in prayer unto him.

	7:4	Doing no j. unto the children of men
	13:5	The sword of j. hangeth over this people
	5	The sword of j. falleth upon this people
3 Nephi	6:4	Formed their laws according to . . . j.
	29	Guilty of murder from the grasp of j.
	20:20	The sword of my j. shall hang over them
	26:5	According to . . . the j. . . . which is in Christ
	27:17	Return, because of the j. of the Father
	28:35	Do ye suppose that ye can get rid of the j.?
	29:4	For the sword of his j. is in his right
Moroni	5:24	Lest he shall come out in j. against
	6:22	He doeth with you according to his j.
Ether	8:23	The sword of the j. of the eternal God
	10:11	And he did do j. unto the people

Justified

| 1 Nephi | 16:2 | And the righteous have I j. |
| 2 Nephi | 2:5 | And by the law, no flesh is j. |

Justifieth

2 Nephi	7:8	And the Lord is near, and he j. me
Jacob	2:14	Do ye suppose that God j. you?
Alma	41:15	Condemneth the sinner, and j. him not

Justify

2 Nephi	15:23	Who j. the wicked for reward!
	28:8	He will j. in committing a little sin
Mosiah	14:11	Knowledge shall my righteous servant j.

Justly

Alma	41:14	Deal j., judge righteously, and do good
	57:26	We do j. ascribe it to the miraculous
3 Nephi	26:19	Every man dealing j., one with another

VERSES 18-19. *Yea cry unto Him for mercy; for He is mighty to save.* The Nephites throughout all past generations had been a righteous and prayerful people. They had been taught, not only by precept, but by the example of their leaders, the efficacy of prayer, or its power to produce effects. The story contained within the Book of Mormon begins with a prayer. Prophets had been warning the people of Jerusalem that unless they repented from their evil ways, the great City of Jerusalem would be destroyed.

Lehi, the scholarly ancestor of the Nephites and the Lamanites, was considerably moved by these prophecies. Some of the men who foretold these dire happenings were his friends whom he knew were worthy of belief. One day as he went about his way contemplating upon the promised ruination of his fair city, and the destruction of its people, he "prayed unto the Lord, yea," the Sacred Record says, "even with all his heart, in behalf of his people." "As he prayed . . . there came a pillar of fire and dwelt upon a rock before him; and he saw and heard much; and because of the things which he saw and heard he did quake and tremble exceedingly."

Lehi's dream of the Tree, the river, and the Rod of Iron, is the record of another prayer which, not only was an answer to his supplications, but has remained since then a solution to much that without it, might be a mystery to us. The answer to his prayer was this: And it came to pass that I saw a man, and he was dressed in a white robe; and he came and stood before me. And it came to pass that he spake unto me, and bade me follow him. And it came to pass that as I followed him I beheld myself that I was in a dark and dreary waste. And after I had traveled for the space of many hours in darkness, I began to pray unto the Lord that He would have mercy on me according to the multitude of His tender mercies. And it came to pass after I had prayed unto the Lord I beheld a large and spacious field. And it came to pass that I beheld a tree, whose fruit was desirable to make one happy. And it came to pass that I did go forth and partake of the fruit thereof; and I beheld that it was most sweet, above all that I ever before tasted. Yea, and I beheld that the fruit thereof was white, to exceed all the whiteness that I had ever seen. And I partook of the fruit thereof and it filled my soul with exceeding great joy; wherefore, I began to be desirous that my family should partake of it also; for I knew that it was desirable above all other fruit. (I Nephi 8:5-12)

A study of Lehi's prayer and the answer thereto should be made by every student for it shows God's willingness to answer the prayers of His servants.

Another answer to prayer, this to the prayers of Nephi, the son of the Patriarch Lehi: And I, Nephi, did go into the mount oft, and I did pray oft unto the Lord; wherefore the Lord showed unto me great things. (I Nephi 18:3) And it came to pass after they had loosed me, behold, I took the compass, and it did work whither I desired it. And it came to pass that I prayed unto the Lord; and after I had prayed the winds did cease, and the storm did cease, and there was a great calm. (Ibid. 18:21)

Again: Behold, He hath heard my cry by day, and He hath given me knowledge by visions in the night-time. (II Nephi 4:23)

The annals of the Nephites disclose that they were indeed a people who continually called upon the Lord, not only did they do so when in trouble, but in times of praise and thanksgiving. Throughout their entire history, it shows that God heard their cries, and answered them with many blessings — for the "Lord does not hide his face from any generation of His children who seek after Him, who seek after Him in truth." We need always remember God's gracious promise to their fathers, many times repeated, that, inasmuch as ye will keep My commandments ye shall prosper in the land; and inasmuch as ye will not keep My commandments ye shall be cut off from My presence. (II Nephi 4:4) Wherein the Nephites loved and kept His Word, we can discern God's divine blessings bestowed on every hand, and see in all their outgoings and incomings proofs of His providential care. Therefore, Amulek's exhortations to the apostate Zoramites to repentance, that they begin to "call upon His holy Name, that He would have mercy upon you."

In these verses Amulek's admonition was not unlike the Prophet Zenos' song of praise which was read by Alma in his sermon to the Zoramites. It was another answer to their question which they propounded to the missionaries when first they sought their help. Amulek's exhortation was that they not only were to worship God in a place prepared by their own hands, but were to seek Him in their fields "that ye may prosper in them," "Cry unto Him in your houses, yea, over all your household," and "Cry unto Him against the devil," and against your enemies. Not only that, but ye must "pour out your souls in your closets, and your secret places, and in your wilderness." And when not actively engaged in crying to Him for special favors, "let your hearts be full, drawn out in prayer unto Him continually for your welfare, and also for the welfare of those who are around you."

MERCIES—

I Nephi	1:20	Will show unto you that the tender m.
	8:8	According to the multitude of his tender m.
II Nephi	1:2	The m. of God in sparing their lives
	9:25	The m. of the Holy One of Israel have
Alma	24:25	Relying upon the m. of those whose arms
	26:28	Relying upon the m. of the world
	28	Not upon the m. of the world alone
	28	But upon the m. of God
	27:9	Go down and rely upon the m. of our
	33:16	They will not understand of thy m. which
	34:38	For the many m. and blessings which
III Nephi	16:9	Because of the m. of the Father unto
	22:7	But with great m. will I gather thee
Mormon	2:12	Knowing the m. and the longsuffering
Ether	6:12	Because of the multitude of his tender m.
Moroni	8:19	Awful wickedness to deny the pure m.
	20	Children need baptism, denieth the m.
	23	Mockery before God, denying the m. of

MERCIFUL—

Merciful unto them

II Nephi	6:11	The Lord will be m. unto them
	28:32	I will be m. unto them, saith the Lord
Jacob	3:6	Destroy them but will be m. unto them
Jarom	1:3	God is exceeding m. unto them, and
Mosiah	24:21	Because he had been m. unto them
Alma	9:16	Therefore the Lord will be m. unto them
Helaman	7:24	The Lord will be m. unto them
	15:12	The Lord shall be m. unto them
Mormon	2:12	Supposing that he would be m. unto them

Merciful

I Nephi	1:14	Because thou art m., thou wilt not
	8:37	Perhaps the Lord would be m. to them
	13:33	I will be m. unto the Gentiles
	34	I will be m. unto the Gentiles
	19:20	For had not the Lord been m., to show
II Nephi	1:3	How m. the Lord had been in warning
	4:7	Wherefore, he will be m. unto you
	9:6	To fulfil the m. plan of the great Creator
	10:2	Nevertheless, God will be m. unto man
	20	Seeing that our m. God has given us
	23:22	Yea, for I will be m. unto my people
Jacob	6:4	And how m. is our God unto us
Alma	9:17	For the Lord will be m. unto all who
	12:15	That he is m. unto the children of men
	24:15	Oh how m. is our God!
	26:17	Our God would have been so m. as to?
	35	He is a m. Being, even unto salvation
	29:10	Then I do remember his m. arm which
	32:22	Remember that God is m. unto all who

	33:4	Thou art m., O God, for thou hast heard
	4	Thou wast m. when I prayed concerning
	5	Thou wast m. unto me when I did cry
	8	Thou art m. unto thy children when
	9	O God, thou hast been m. unto me
	11	That thou hast been thus m. unto me
	41:13	Which is just; m. for that which is m.
	14	See that ye are m. unto your brethren
	42:15	Be a perfect, just God, and a m. God
	50:19	How m. and just are all the dealings
Helaman	3:27	Thus we may see that the Lord is m.
III Nephi	5:21	And hath been m. unto the seed of Joseph
	12:7	Blessed are the m., for they shall obtain
Ether	3:3	Nevertheless, thou hast been m. unto
	9:2	Nevertheless, the Lord was m. unto
	13:7	That he might be m. unto the seed of
	7	Even as he was m. unto the father of
Moroni	10:3	Remember how m. the Lord hath been

MERCY—

Have Mercy

I Nephi	8:8	Unto the Lord that he would have m.
	21:13	And will have m. upon his afflicted
II Nephi	19:17	Neither shall have m. on their father!
	24:1	For the Lord will have m. on Jacob
Mosiah	4:2	Saying, O have m., and apply the atonement
Alma	2:30	Saying, O Lord, have m. and spare my
	3:14	That I may have m. upon them
	12:33	Then will I have m. upon you through
	15:10	O Lord our God, have m. on this man
	18:41	To cry unto the Lord, saying: O Lord, have m.
	19:29	O blessed God, have m. on this people
	34:17	That he would have m. upon you
	36:18	O Jesus, thou Son of God, have m. on
	41:14	Ye shall have m. restored to you again
III Nephi	22:8	Everlasting kindness will I have m. on
Ether	11:8	As they did, the Lord did have m. on

His Mercy

II Nephi	9:8	O the wisdom of God! his m. and grace
Alma	5:6	Sufficiently retained in remembrance his m.?
	9:11	If it had not been for . . . his m.
	24:14	In his m. he doth visit us by his angels
	26:16	Who can say too much of . . . his m.?
	42:30	Let the justice of God, and his m. and
Helaman	12:6	His great goodness and his m. towards
Moroni	8:19	They are all alive in him because of his m.
	9:25	May . . . his m. and long suffering . . . rest

Mercy

| I Nephi | 1:14 | M. are over all the inhabitants of the |
| | 21:10 | For he that hath m. on them shall |

II Nephi	2:8	Save it be through the merits, and m.
	12	Power, and the m., and the justice of
	4:26	Hath visited men in so much m.
	9:19	O the greatness of the m. of our God!
	53	Because of his greatness, and his . . . m.
	11:5	In his justice, and power, and m.
Jacob	4:10	Justice, and in great m., over all his
	6:5	While his arm of m. is extended toward
Mosiah	2:39	M. hath no claim on that man
	3:26	M. could have claim on them no more
	5:15	M. of him, who created all things, in
	13:14	Showing m. unto thousands of them that
	15:9	Having the bowels of m.; being filled
	16:12	While the arms of m. were extended
	12	For the arms of m. were extended toward
	27:28	The Lord in m. hath seen fit to snatch
	28:4	The Lord saw fit in his infinite m. to
	29:20	Extending the arm of m. towards them
Alma	5:4	King Noah, by the m. and power of
	33	The arms of m. are extended towards
	48	Begotten of the Father, full of grace, and m.
	7:2	And the Lord in much m. hath granted
	12	That his bowels may be filled with m.
	9:26	Full of patience, m., and long suffering
	12:34	He shall have claim on m. through
	18:41	According to thy abundant m. which
	24:14	And the great God has had m. on us
	26:20	But in his great m. hath brought us
	37	His bowels of m. are over all the earth
	32:13	Whosoever repenteth, shall find m.
	13	And he that findeth m. and endureth
	34:15	To bring about the bowels of m.
	16	Thus m. can satisfy the demands of
	18	Cry unto him for m.; for he is mighty
	38:7	The Lord in his great m. sent his angels
	8	Cry out unto the Lord Jesus Christ for m.
	14	And remember my brethren in m.
	42:13	M. could not take effect except it should
	15	The plan of m. could not be brought about
	15	To bring about the plan of m., to appear
	21	What could justice do, or m. either?
	22	Which repentance, m. claimeth; other
	23	And m. claimeth the penitent
	23	And m. cometh because of the atonement
	24	Also m. claimeth all which is her own
	25	Do ye suppose that m. can rob justice?
	31	That the great plan of m. may have
	55:23	Cast them at the feet of the N., pleading for m.
III Nephi	9:14	Mine arm of m. is extended towards
	12:7	Blessed are the merciful, for they shall obtain m.
	17:7	My bowels are filled with m.
	22:10	Saith the Lord that hath m. on thee

	26:5	According to the m. . . . which is in Christ
	29:7	Son of perdition, for whom there was no m.
Mormon	6:22	Doeth with you according to his justice and m.
Moroni	7:27	To claim of the Father his rights of m.
	9:18	They are without order and without m.

SAVED—

Can Be Saved

II Nephi	25:20	None other name . . . whereby man can be s.
	31:21	Name given . . . whereby man can be s.
Mosiah	4:8	Any condition whereby man can be s.
	16:13	Only in and through Christ ye can be s.
Alma	5:21	There can no man be s. except his garments
	11:37	How can ye be s., except ye inherit the
	38:9	No other . . . means whereby man can be s.
Helaman	5:9	No other way . . . whereby man can be s.
Moroni	7:38	No man can be s., according to the
	10:21	Ye can in no wise be s. in the kingdom
	21	Neither can ye be s. in the kingdom of

Cannot Be Saved

I Nephi	13:40	Come unto him, or they cannot be s.
II Nephi	9:23	Or they cannot be s. in the kingdom of
	31:16	The Son of the living God, he cannot be s.
Alma	5:21	Know at that day, that ye cannot be s.
	31	He must repent, or he cannot be s.
	11:37	Therefore, ye cannot be s. in your sins
Helaman	12:22	Will do iniquity, and he cannot be s.
Mormon	7:3	Come unto repentance or ye cannot be s.
Moroni	10:26	And they cannot be s. in the kingdom

Shall Be Saved

I Nephi	13:37	Shall be s., in the everlasting kingdom
	22:17	They shall be s., even if it so be as by
	31	Ye shall be s. at the last day
II Nephi	2:9	And they that believe in him shall be s.
	6:12	Not unite . . . abominable church, they shall be s.
	25:13	Shall be s. in the kingdom of God
	28:8	At last we shall be s. in the kingdom of
	31:15	Endureth to the end the same shall be s.
Jacob	6:4	Their hearts, shall be s. in the kingdom
Alma	22:6	Keep the commandments of God ye shall be s.
Mosiah	12:33	If ye will repent, ye shall be s.
	24:16	We shall go to our God and shall be s.
	31:17	Thou hast elected us, that we shall be s.
	32:13	Endureth to the end, the same shall be s.
Helaman	12:23	For these are they that shall be s.
III Nephi	11:33	Is baptized, the same shall be s.
	23:5	And is baptized, the same shall be s.
	27:6	The same shall be s. at the last day
Mormon	9:23	That believeth and is baptized shall be s.
Ether	4:18	That believeth and is baptized shall be s.
Moroni	8:10	Shall all be s. with their little children

Be Saved

I Nephi	6:4	Come unto ... the God of Jacob, and be s.
	8:3	And also many of their seed, will be s.
	15:14	Know how to come unto him and be s.
II Nephi	33:12	That many of us, if not all, may be s.
Omni	1:26	And as the Lord liveth, ye will be s.
Mosiah	3:16	Children could sin, they could not be s.
	13:32	There could not any man be s., except
Alma	1:4	All mankind should be s. at the last day
	9:17	Many of them will be s., for the Lord
	20:17	In thine anger, thy soul could not be s.
	22:18	Raised from the dead, and be s. at the
	41:8	Whosoever will, may walk therein, and be s.
Helaman	12:22	For this cause, that men might be s.
	25	And I would that all men might be s.
	13:39	And that ye would repent and be s.
	14:29	That whosoever will believe might be s.
III Nephi	9:22	Come unto me, ye ends of the earth, and be s.
Ether	8:26	Fountain of all righteousness and be s.
Moroni	7:34	And have faith in me that ye may be s.
	8:13	If little children could not be s. without
	9:22	I trust in Christ that thou wilt be s.
	10:21	Charity, ye can in no wise be s.
	21	Neither can ye be s. in the kingdom

Saved

II Nephi	10:24	Through the grace of God that ye are s.
	25:23	That it is by grace that we are s.
Mosiah	13:9	Whither I go, if it so be that I am s.
Alma	5:9	I say unto you, that they are s.
	10	On what conditions are they s.?
	13	Faithful unto the end; therefore they were s.
	20	Can ye think of being s., when you have
	9:22	Having been s. from famine, and from
	14:15	Neither has God s. them, because they
	19:29	O blessed Jesus, who has s. me from
	24:26	No reason to doubt but what they were s.
	42:24	Thus, none but the truly penitent are s.
	60:8	Have s. thousands of them from falling
Helaman	13:12	Because of those who are righteous, that it is s.
III Nephi	10:12	Righteous part of the people who were s.
	12:20	Therefore come unto me and be ye s.
Ether	15:34	If it so be that I am s. in the kingdom
Moroni	7:26	Men also were s. by faith in his name

SAVETH—

Moroni	8:15	That God s. one child because of baptism

SAVING

Alma	26:30	We might be the means of s. some soul
	30	If perhaps we could be the means of s.
	55:19	But he delighteth in the s. of his people

CRY—

Cry Unto Him

Enos	1:4	All the day long did I c. unto him
Alma	34:18	C. unto him for mercy; for he is mighty
	20	C. unto him when ye are in your fields
	21	C. unto him in your houses
	22	C. unto him against the power of your
	23	C. unto him against the devil
	24	C. unto him over the crops of your field
	38:8	I did c. unto him, and I did find peace
Ether	1:38	C. unto him whither we shall go
	8:22	Shall always c. unto him from the

They Did Cry

Mosiah	21:10	And they did c. mightily from day to
	14	And they did c. mightily to God
Helaman	5:42	They did c. even until the cloud of
	8:5	Therefore they did c. unto the people
III Nephi	4:32	They did c., Hosanna to the Most High
	32	And they did c., blessed be the name
	11:16	They did c. out with one accord, saying
	20:9	And they did c. out with one voice
Ether	6:7	They did c. unto the Lord, and he did

Did Cry

I Nephi	2:16	Wherefore I did c. unto the Lord
II Nephi	5:1	I, Nephi, did c. much unto the Lord
Enos	1:16	I did c. unto God that he would preserve
Mosiah	9:17	I and my people did c. mightily to the
Alma	33:5	When I did c. unto thee in my field
	5	When I did c. unto thee in my prayer
	37:30	Did c. unto the Lord their God for vengeance
	38:8	Until I did c. out unto the Lord Jesus
	8	I did c. unto him, and I did find peace
Helaman	5:37	This man did c. unto the multitude
	8:7	Some who did c. out, let this man alone
	9:16	Unto the people, and did c. out against
	11:3	Nephi did c. unto the Lord, saying
III Nephi	4:28	And did c. with a loud voice, saying
	7:23	Nephi did c. unto the people in the community
Mormon	3:3	I did c. unto this people, but it was in
Ether	1:35	The brother of Jared did c. unto the Lord
	37	The brother of Jared did c. unto the Lord
	39	The brother of Jared did c. unto the Lord
	12:3	For he did c. from the morning, even

Shall Cry

II Nephi	3:20	And they shall c. from the dust
	23:22	The wild beasts of the islands shall c.
	27:4	Wonder, for ye shall c. out, and cry,
	28:10	The blood of the saints shall c. from

Mosiah	11:24	When they shall c. unto me, I will be
Helaman	13:32	In the days of your poverty ye shall c.
Mormon	8:23	Who have possessed this land, shall c.;
	27	In a day when the blood of saints shall c.

They Cry

Mosiah	21:14	All the day long did they c. unto their
Alma	31:27	O God, they c. unto thee, and yet their
	27	O God, they c. unto thee with their mouths
Alma	31:28	Yet they c. unto thee, and say, we that
	33:8	When they c. unto thee to be heard of
Mormon	8:23	Even from the dust will they c. unto
Ether	8:24	For they c. from the dust for vengeance

CRY—

I Nephi	10:8	He should go forth and c. in the wilderness
II Nephi	3:20	Their c. shall go even according to the
	4:23	He hath heard me c. by day, and he
	30	Rejoice, O my heart, and c. unto the
	35	I will c. unto thee, my God, the rock of
	15:7	For righteousness, but behold a c.
	18:4	Not have knowledge to c., my father
	24:31	Howl, O gate; c., O city; thou, whole
	26:3	The c. of the blood of the saints shall
	7	But I must c. unto my God, thy ways
	25	Doth he c. unto any, saying, Depart from
	27:4	And wonder, for ye shall c. out and c.
	33:3	And I c. unto my God in faith
	3	And I know that he will hear my c.
Jacob	7:22	He had heard my c. and answered my
Mosiah	11:25	And c. mightily to the Lord their God
	21:15	The Lord was slow to hear their c.
	23:28	And began to c. unto the Lord
	24:10	They began to c. mightily to God
Alma	5:49	To c. unto them that they must repent
	7:9	C. unto this people, saying, Repent ye
	9:25	C. mightily unto this people, saying, Repent
	10:20	Well doth he c. unto his people
	21	Well doth he c., by the voice of his angel
	14:7	He began to c. unto the people, saying
	11	C. mightily against them at the last day
	16:1	Was a c. of war heard throughout the
	18:41	He began to c. unto the Lord, saying,
	19:15	They also began to c. unto God, for the
	20:18	His blood would c. from the ground
	28:5	The c. of the widows mourning for their
	5	The c. of mourning was heard among
	29:1	And c. repentance unto every people
	31:14	Towards heaven, and c. with a loud voice
	33:11	I will c. unto thee in all mine afflictions
	34:25	C. over the flocks of your fields, that the

	27	And when you do not c. unto the Lord
	37:36	And c. unto God for all thy support
	47:25	The servants of Amalickiah raised a c.
Helaman	5:41	You must repent, and c. unto the voice
	42	They all did begin to c. unto the voice
	9:6	Raising the c. of murder among them
	11:8	C. unto the Lord our God, that he turn
	13:32	In vain shall ye c., for your desolation
	14:9	C. unto this people, repent and prepare
III Nephi	3:12	He did cause that his people should c.
	15	Repent of all your iniquities, and c. unto
	4:30	They did rejoice and c. again with one
	8:24	In one place they were heard to c., saying
	25	In another place they were heard to c.
	9:11	Might not c. unto me from the ground
	20:41	Then shall a c. go forth, Depart ye, devils
	22:1	Break forth into singing, and c. aloud
Mormon	2:10	Began to c. even as had been prophesied
	3:2	C. unto this people repent ye, and come
	8:40	Blood of their fathers and their husbands to c.?
	9:6	C. mightily unto the Father in the name
Ether	1:34	C. unto the Lord, that he will not confuse
	36	Jared said unto his brother, C. again unto
	9:34	Repent of their iniquities, and c. unto
	14:18	A c. went forth throughout the land,

CRYING—

II Nephi	33:13	As the voice of one c. from the dust
Alma	9:29	Voice of the angel, c. unto the people
	16:18	C. that these things might not so to be
	46:19	Wrote upon the rent, and c. with a loud
Helaman	16:4	And preaching, c. repentance unto the
III Nephi	9:1	A voice heard . . . upon all . . . this land, c.
Ether	9:28	Prophets in the land again, c. repentance
Moroni	10:27	By this man, like as one c. from the

CRIED—

Cried again

Mosiah	27:13	He c. again, saying, Alma, arise!
Helaman	11:9	He c. again unto the Lord, saying
Ether	2:22	He c. again unto the Lord, saying
	3:1	And c. again unto the Lord, saying

Cried

I Nephi	2:18	I c. unto the Lord for them
	11:6	The Spirit c. with a loud voice, saying
	17:7	Went up into the mountain, and c. unto
II Nephi	3:19	As if the fruit of thy loins had c.
	16:3	And one c. unto another, and said, Holy
	4	Posts of the door moved at the voice of him that c.
Enos	1:4	And I c. unto him in mighty prayer
	15	I c. unto him continually for he had

Mosiah	4:2	They all c. aloud with one voice
	5:2	They all c. with one voice, saying
	17:14	Flames began to scorch him, he c.
	18:12	Stood forth in the water, and c.
	19:7	The king c. out in the anguish of his soul
	29:20	Because they c. mightily unto him
Alma	2:30	C., saying, O Lord, have mercy and
	10:24	Angry with Amulek; and they c. out
	25	C. the mightier unto them, saying
	28	The people c. out against him
	13:21	And c. with a mighty voice, saying
	14:26	Alma c., saying, How long shall we suffer
	15:10	Alma c. unto the Lord, saying, O Lord
	19:29	C. with a loud voice, saying, O blessed
	22:17	The king did bow down . . . and c. mightily
	31:26	Lifted up his voice to heaven, and c.
	32:7	And c. unto those whom he beheld
	36:18	I c. within my heart, O Jesus, thou Son
	43:49	They c. with one voice unto the Lord
	50	They c. unto the Lord for their freedom
	44:19	C. mightily unto Moroni, promising
	57:31	C. unto us, saying, Behold the armies
Helaman	8:1	Were angry, and they c. out against him
	13:4	Stretched forth his hand and c. with a
	16:6	They came unto their captains, saying,
III Nephi	1:11	Bowed himself . . . and c. mightily to his
	12	He c. mightily unto the Lord, all the
	12:1	C. unto them saying, Blessed are ye if
Mormon	6:16	Because of the slain of my people, and I c.
Ether	1:43	Because this long time have ye c. unto
	2:18	The brother of Jared c. unto the Lord
	11:20	And c. repentance unto the people

CRIES—

Their cries

Mosiah	11:24	I will be slow to hear their c.
	21:15	Nevertheless the Lord did hear their c.
	24:11	That they should stop their c.; and he
Alma	2:28	Therefore the Lord did hear their c.
	57:32	Our prisoners did hear their c.
	60:10	For known unto God were all their c.
III Nephi	4:8	Did lift their c. to the Lord their God
Mormon	8:41	For he will not suffer their c. any longer
Ether	15:16	So great were their c., their howlings
	17	They did rend the air with their c.

Cries

Jacob	2:32	The c. of the fair daughters of this people
Mosiah	9:18	God did hear our c. and did answer
	21:11	Their continual c. did stir up the remainder
	23:10	The Lord did hear my c., and did answer
Alma	9:26	Quick to hear the c. of his people

	33:9	Heard my c. in the midst of thy congregation
	10	Thou didst hear my c., and wast angry
Moroni	9:15	My heart c., Wo unto this people

CRIETH—

| II Nephi | 28:25 | Wo be unto him that c., All is well |
| Alma | 5:51 | C. unto me with a mighty voice, saying |

Prayed or Pray Unto Him

II Nephi	9:52	Pray unto h. continually by day
Jacob	3:1	Pray unto h. with exceeding faith
Enos	1:11	I prayed unto h. with many long struggles
III Nephi	19:24	Continue, without ceasing, to pray unto h.
	25	Jesus blessed them, as they did pray unto h.

PRAY—

I Pray

II Nephi	9:44	I p. the God of my salvation that he
	15:3	Judge, I p. you, betwixt me and my
	27:15	The learned, saying, Read this, I p. thee
	33:2	For I p. continually for them by day
	12	I p. the Father in the name of Christ
Mosiah	2:40	I p. that ye should awake to a remembrance
	20:17	I p. thee forbear, and do not search
Helaman	13:39	I p. that the anger of the Lord be turned
III Nephi	19:21	Father, I p. thee that thou wilt give
	23	Father, I p. unto thee for them
	28	Because of their faith, I p. for them
	29	Father, I p. not for the world, but for
Moroni	9:22	And I p. unto God that he would spare

Pray

I Nephi	7:21	Would p. unto the Lord . . . for forgiveness
	8:8	I began to p. unto the Lord that he would
	18:3	I, Nephi, did p. oft unto the Lord
II Nephi	32:8	The Spirit which teacheth a man to p.
	8	Ye would know that ye must p.; for
	8	The evil spirit teacheth not a man to p.
	8	But teacheth him that he must not p.
	9	I say unto you, that ye must p. always
	9	P. unto the Father in the name of Christ
W Mormon	11:1	I, Mormon, p. to God that they may be
Mosiah	26:39	Being commanded of God to p. without
	27:22	They began to fast and to p. to the Lord
Alma	13:28	Call on his holy name, and watch and p.
	30:54	He besought that Alma should p. unto
	38:13	Do not p. as the Zoramites do
	13	Ye have seen that they p. to be heard
	45:1	And they did fast and p. much
	62:51	Did p. unto the Lord their God continually
Helaman	3:35	Nevertheless they did fast and p. oft

III Nephi	3:20	People said unto Gidgiddoni, P. unto
	12:44	P. for them who despitefully use you
	13:5	As the hypocrites, for they love to p.
	6	When thou hast shut thy door, p. to thy
	7	But when ye p., use not vain repetitions
	9	After this manner therefore p. ye
	17:17	At the time we heard him p. for us
	18:15	Ye must watch and p. always, lest ye
	18	Even so shall ye p. in my church
III Nephi	18:16	Ye must watch and p. always
	19	Ye must always p. unto the Father in
	21	P. in your families unto the Father
	23	But ye shall p. for them, and shall not
	23	Ye shall p. for them unto the Father
	30	And shall p. for him unto the Father
	19:6	Should p. unto the Father in the name
	7	The disciples did p. unto the Father almost
	9	They did p. for that which they most
	17	Commanded his disciples that they should p.
	18	And behold, they began to p.
	18	And they did p. unto Jesus
	22	Thou hearest them, and they p. unto me
	22	And they p. unto me because I am with
	24	It was given unto them what they should p.
	26	And Jesus said unto them, p. on
	26	Nevertheless they did not cease to p.
	30	And behold they did p. steadfastly
	20:1	The multitude that they should cease to p.
	1	They should not cease to p. in their hearts
	31	And shall p. unto the Father in my name
	28:30	If they shall p. unto the Father in the
IV Nephi	1:12	Both to p. and to hear the word of the
Moroni	4:2	P. to the Father in the name of Christ
	6:5	Did meet together oft, to fast and to p.
	9	Whether to preach, or exhort, or to p.
	7:9	If he shall p., and not with real intent
	48	P. unto the Father with all the energy
	8:28	P. for them, my son, that repentance

PRAYED—

I Nephi	1:5	Lehi, as he went forth, p. unto the Lord
	6	As he p. unto the Lord, there came a
	7:17	I p. unto the Lord, saying, O Lord
	8:9	After I had p. unto the Lord, I beheld
	18:21	It came to pass that I p. unto the Lord
	21	And after I had p., the winds did cease
Enos	1:11	I p. unto him with many long strugglings
	12	After I had p., and labored with all diligence
Mosiah	27:4	He has p. with much faith concerning
	23	After they had fasted and p. .... two days
Alma	2:28	Having p. mightily to him that he would
	5:46	I have fasted and p. many days

	31:38	Alma, and this because he p. in faith
	33:4	Yea, thou wast merciful when I p.
	7	And p. unto thee thou didst hear me
	46:13	And he p. mightily unto his God
	16	Moroni p. that the cause of the Christian
III Nephi	17:15	And behold he p. unto the Father, and
	15	The things which he p. cannot be written
	21	And blessed them, and p. unto the Father
	18:16	As I have p. among you, even so shall
	24	Ye see that I have p. unto the Father
	19:8	They knelt again and p. to the Father
	10	And when they had thus p., they went
	24	When Jesus had thus p. unto the Father
	27	And he p. again unto the Father, saying
	31	A little way off, and p. unto the Father
	32	Tongue cannot speak the words which he p.
	32	Can be written by man the words which he p.
	33	Understand in their hearts the words which he p.
	34	So ... marvelous were the words which he p.
Ether	12:36	I p. unto the Lord that he would give
Moroni	3:2	After they had p. unto the Father in

PRAYER—

Mighty Prayer

II Nephi	4:24	By day have I waxed bold in mighty p.
Enos	1:4	I cried unto him in mighty p.
Alma	6:6	And join in fasting and mighty p.
	8:10	Wrestling with God in mighty p.
III Nephi	27:1	And were united in mighty p. and fasting
Moroni	2:2	Call on the Father in my name, in mighty p.

My Prayer

Jacob	7:22	For he had heard my cry and answered my p.
W Mormon	1:8	My p. to God is concerning my brethren
Alma	29:10	Yea, even that he hath heard my p.
Alma	33:4	Merciful, O God, for thou hast heard my p.
	5	When I did cry unto thee in my p.
	6	Thou didst hear me in my p.

Prayer

Alma	17:3	They had given themselves to much p.
	19:14	And began to pour out his soul in p.
	28:6	And a time of much fasting and p.
	30:2	After the days of fasting, and mourning, and p.
	31:10	To continue in p. and supplication to God
	22	Every man, the self same p. unto God
	38	Now this was according to the p. of Alma
	33:3	Zenos ... has said concerning p.?
	34:19	And continue in p. unto him
	27	Drawn out in p. unto him continually
	28	Your p. is vain, and availeth you nothing

	39	Be watchful unto p. continually
	58:10	We did pour out our souls in p. to God
IV Nephi	1:12	Continuing in fasting and p., and in
Mormon	3:12	And my soul has been poured out in p.
Moroni	6:4	To keep them continually watchful unto p.
	8:26	Which love endureth by diligence unto p.

PRAYERS—

I Nephi	18:19	My wife with her tears and p.
	26:15	And the p. of the faithful shall be heard
II Nephi	6:11	Not ... perish, because of the p. of the faithful
	33:4	God will consecrate my p., for the gain
Mosiah	3:4	For the Lord hath heard thy p.
	9:18	Hear our cries and did answer our p.
	10:13	For the Lord heard his p. and answered
	11:25	I will not hear their p.
	23:10	Did hear my cries, and did answer my p.
	27:14	The Lord hath heard the p. of his people
	14	And also the p. of his servant, Alma
	14	That the p. of his servants might be answered
	16	That their p. may be answered
Alma	9:20	According to their desires ... and p.
	26	Cries of his people and to answer their p.
	10:22	If it were not for the p. of the righteous
	23	But it is by the p. of the righteous
	19:14	Poured out according to his p. upon the
	25:17	Granted unto them according to their p.
	31:19	Brethren and his sons had heard these p.
	20	Every man did ... offer up the same p.
	62:40	Because of the p. of the righteous, they
III Nephi	3:25	And they did put up their p. unto the
	5:14	That the p. of those who have gone
Mormon	5:21	The Lord will remember the p. of the righteous
	8:24	He knoweth their p. that they were in
	25	Their p. were also in behalf of him that
	9:36	Is according to the p. of all the saints
	37	Christ grant that their p. may be answered
Moroni	8:3	I am mindful of you always in my p.

PRAYEST—

| III Nephi | 13:5 | When thou p., thou shalt not do as |
| | 6 | When thou p., enter into thy closet |

PRAYETH—

| Alma | 26:22 | And p. continually without ceasing |
| Moroni | 7:6 | If he offereth a gift, or p. unto God |

PRAYING

I Nephi	7:21	After they had done p. unto the Lord
Omni	1:26	Continue in fasting and p., and endure
Alma	15:17	Before the altar, watching and p. continually

20. Cry unto him when ye are in your fields, yea, over all your flocks.

21. Cry unto him in your houses, yea, over all your household, both morning, mid-day, and evening.

22. Yea, cry unto him against the power of your enemies.

23. Yea, cry unto him against the devil, who is an enemy to all righteousness.

24. Cry unto him over the crops of your fields, that ye may prosper in them.

25. Cry over the flocks of your fields, that they may increase.

26. But this is not all; ye must pour out your souls in your closets, and your secret places, and in your wilderness.

27. Yea, and when you do not cry unto the Lord, let your hearts be full, drawn out in prayer unto him continually for your welfare, and also for the welfare of those who are around you.

28. And now behold, my beloved brethren, I say unto you, do not suppose that this is all; for after ye have done all these things, if ye turn away the needy, and the naked, and visit not the sick and afflicted, and impart of your substance, if ye have, to those who stand in need—I say unto you, if ye do not any of these things, behold, your prayer is vain, and availeth you nothing, and ye are as hypocrites who do deny the faith.

29. Therefore, if ye do not remember to be charitable, ye are as dross, which the refiners do cast out. (it being of no worth) and is trodden under foot of men.

III Nephi	17:18	When Jesus had made an end of p.
	19:35	When Jesus had made an end of p.
	27:2	They were p. unto the Father in his name
Moroni	8:3	Continually p. unto God the Father in

VERSES 20-29. *Do not suppose that this is all.* A common fallacy in the thinking of many is to suppose that prayer to God is ended with the word, AMEN. Prayer, as some are inclined to believe, is an admixture of meaningless words, or a concoction of ideas that nobody ran digest. To them it is the expression of a frustration; a recitation to be forgotten when *Amen* is said. That is not so! Prayer should linger in the heart long after any words are uttered. "And when you do not cry unto the Lord," Amulek said, "let your hearts be full, drawn out in prayer unto Him continually for your welfare, and also for the welfare of those who are around you." However, let us always remember that to bring about the end or conditions for which we pray, it is necessary to accompany our prayers with good works. And when we cry unto the Lord let us remember also that "only by obedience to His commandments, by faithfulness to our duties, by the goodness of our deeds," can we make our prayers heard by Him.

Amulek went a step further than only to declare prayer, its necessity and its hallowing effects upon the individual, but he also pointed out to the Zoramites that "if ye turn away the needy, and the naked, and visit not the sick and afflicted, and impart of your substance, if ye have, to those who stand in need . . . your prayer is vain, and availeth you nothing, and ye are as hypocrites who do deny the faith."

The same doctrine preached by Amulek to the Zoramites regarding prayer was also preached by King Benjamin to the Saints in Zarahemla almost fifty years before:

And again I say unto you as I have said before, that as ye have come to the knowledge of the glory of God, or if ye have known of His goodness and have tasted of His love, and have received a remission of your sins, which causeth such exceeding great joy in your souls, even so I would that ye should remember, and always retain in remembrance, the greatness of God, and your own nothingness, and His goodness and long-suffering towards you, unworthy creatures, and humble yourselves even in the depths of humility, calling on the Name of the Lord daily, and standing steadfastly in the faith of that which is to come, which was spoken by the mouth of the angel.

And behold, I say unto you that if ye do this ye shall always rejoice, and be filled with the love of God, and always retain a remission of your sins; and ye shall grow in the knowledge of the glory of Him that created you, or in the knowledge of that which is just and true.

And ye will not have a mind to injure one another, but to live peaceably, and to render to every man according to that which is his due.

And ye will not suffer your children that they go hungry, or naked; neither will ye suffer that they transgress the laws of God, and fight and quarrel one with another, and serve the devil, who is the master of sin, or who is the evil spirit which hath been spoken of by our fathers, he being an enemy to all righteousness.

But ye will teach them to walk in the ways of truth and soberness; ye will teach them to love one another, and to serve one another.

And also, ye yourselves will succor those that stand in need of your succor; ye will administer of your substance unto him that standeth in need; and ye will not suffer that the beggar putteth up his petition to you in vain, and turn him out to perish.

Perhaps thou shalt say: The man has brought upon himself his misery; therefore I will stay my hand, and will not give unto him of my food, nor impart unto him of my substance that he may not suffer, for his punishments are just—

But I say unto you, O man, whosoever doeth this the same hath great cause to repent; and except he repenteth of that which he hath done he perisheth forever, and hath no interest in the Kingdom of God.

For behold, are we not all beggars? Do we not all depend upon the same Being, even God, for all the substance which we have, for both food and raiment, and for gold and for silver, and for all the riches which we have of every kind?

And behold, even at this time, ye have been calling on His Name, and begging for a remission of your sins. And has He suffered that ye have begged in vain? Nay; He has poured out His Spirit upon you, and has caused that your hearts should be filled with joy, and has caused that your mouths should be stopped that ye could not find utterance, so exceeding great was your joy.

And now, if God, Who has created you, on Whom you are dependent for your lives and for all that ye have and are, doth grant unto you whatsoever ye ask that is right, in faith, believing that ye shall receive, O then, how ye ought to impart of the substance that ye have one to another.

And if ye judge the man who putteth up his petition to you for your substance that he perish not, and condemn him, how much more just will be your condemnation for withholding your substance, which does not belong to you but to God to Whom also your life belongeth; and yet ye put up no petition, nor repent of the thing which thou hast done.

I say unto you, wo be unto that man, for his substance shall perish with him;

and now, I say these things unto those who are rich as pertaining to the things of this world.

And again, I say unto the poor, ye who have not and yet have sufficient, that ye remain from day to day; I mean all you who deny the beggar, because ye have not; I would that ye say in your hearts that: I give not because I have not, but if I had I would give.

And now, if ye say this in your hearts ye remain guiltless, otherwise ye are condemned; and your condemnation is just for ye covet that which ye have not received.

And now, for the sake of these things which I have spoken unto you — that is, for the sake of retaining a remission of your sins from day to day, that ye may walk guiltless before God — I would that ye should impart of your substance to the poor, every man according to that which he hath, such as feeding the hungry, clothing the naked, visiting the sick and administering to their relief, both spiritually and temporally, according to their wants.

And see that all these things are done in wisdom and order; for it is not requisite that a man should run faster than he has strength. And again, it is expedient that he should be diligent, that thereby he might win the prize; therefore, all things must be done in order. (Mosiah 4:11-27)

In all the religious observances of the Nephites it is plain to be seen that the lesson of *service to others* was deeply impressed on them as part of their belief. We today, members of Christ's Church, have reached the same conclusion as did they. It is not to be escaped: that we serve God best by sharing with the needy the gifts we receive from His bounteous hands; by showing compassion for the distressed, by upholding the falling, by loosing the bound. Truly, we can ennoble our lives no more graciously than by serving God with deeds of loving-kindness to our fellow men.

A complete commentary on Amulek's and King Benjamin's words is found in a sermon preached by Jacob, the brother of Nephi, and who was also the son of the Prophet Lehi: But wo unto the rich, who are rich as to the things of the world. For because they are rich they despise the poor, and they persecute the meek, and their hearts are upon their treasure; wherefore, their treasure is their God. And behold, their treasure shall perish with them also. (II Nephi 9:30)

Sharing with others the gifts we receive at God's hands renders us more unselfish, and like Him, more longsuffering, and too, doing so, adds comfort to our hearts when we are faint. It awakens within us a love for His children, and at the same time helps us "to use our powers for the benefit of our fellow men, so that the hearts of His children may be gladdened by" the service we therein perform. It helps us put to the highest use the gifts He continually bestowes upon us.

The Psalmist cites God's blessings on the charitable man in these words: Blessed is he that considereth the poor: the Lord will deliver him in time of trouble. The Lord will preserve him, and keep him alive; and he shall be blessed upon the earth: . . . The Lord will strengthen him upon the bed of languishing: thou wilt make his bed in his sickness. (Psalm 41:1) We can show by our actions that we truly are His children and that He is the loving Father of all.

It is indisputable that "feeding the hungry, clothing the naked, visiting the sick and afflicted and administering to their relief, both spiritually and temporally," makes us more obedient to God's laws. Serving God's children is a sacrifice when in offering it we put our trust in the Lord. There is no surer way to remember the Lord, His goodness and mercy, than to serve His children who want and have not. It is a sacrifice on our part in which the Lord delights.

4. *Repentance not to be procrastinated.*

30. And now, my brethren, I would that, after ye have received so many witnesses, seeing that the holy scriptures testify of these things, ye come forth and bring fruit unto repentance.

31. Yea, I would that ye would come forth and harden not your hearts any longer; for behold, now is the time and the day of your salvation; and therefore, if ye will repent and harden not your hearts, immediately shall the great plan of redemption be brought about unto you.

32. For behold, this life is the time for men to prepare to meet God; yea, behold the day of this life is the day for men to perform their labors.

33. And now, as I said unto you before, as ye have had so many witnesses, therefore, I beseech of you that ye do not procrastinate the day of your repentance until the end; for after this day of life, which is given us to prepare for eternity, behold, if we do not improve our time while in this life, then cometh the night of darkness wherein there can be no labor performed.

34. Ye cannot say, when ye are brought to that awful crisis, that I will repent, that I will return to my God. Nay, ye cannot say this; for that same spirit which doth possess your bodies at the time that ye go out of this life, that same spirit will have power to possess your body in that eternal world.

35. For behold, if ye have procrastinated the day of your repentance even until death, behold, ye have become subjected to the spirit of the devil, and he doth seal you his; therefore, the Spirit of the Lord hath withdrawn from you, and hath no place in you, and the devil hath all power over you; and this is the final state of the wicked.

36. And this I know, because the Lord hath said he dwelleth not in unholy temples, but in the hearts of the righteous doth he dwell; yea, and he has also said that the righteous shall sit down in his kingdom, to go no more out; but their garments should be made white through the blood of the Lamb.

37. And now, my beloved brethren, I desire that ye should remember these things, and that ye should work out your salvation with fear before God, and that ye should no more deny the coming of Christ;

38. That ye contend no more against the Holy Ghost, but that ye receive it, and take upon you the name of Christ; that ye hum-

---

Ye that fear the Lord, trust in the Lord. Pour out your heart before Him: God is a refuge for us. (See Psalm 62:8)

VERSES 30-41. *If ye have procrastinated the day of your repentance even until death, behold, ye have become subjected to the spirit of the devil.* Procrastinate means to put off from day to day; to defer; postpone. Amulek closed his powerful

ble yourselves even to the dust, and worship God, in whatsoever place ye may be in, in spirit and in truth; and that ye live in thanksgiving daily, for the many mercies and blessings which he doth bestow upon you.

39. Yea, and I also exhort you, my brethren, that ye be watchful unto prayer continually, that ye may not be led away by the temptation of the devil, that he may not overpower you, that ye may not become his subjects at the last day; for behold, he rewardeth you no good thing.

40. And now my beloved brethren, I would exhort you to have patience, and that ye bear with all manner of afflictions; that ye do not revile against those who do cast you out because of your exceeding poverty, lest ye become sinners like unto them;

41. But that ye have patience, and bear with those afflictions, with a firm hope that ye shall one day rest from all your afflictions.

---

and provocative address to the Zoramites with an appeal to them not to procrastinate the day of their repentance, or not put off from day to day, even unto the end, a resolve to return to God from Whom they had strayed.

CHAPTER 35

1. *Nephite missionaries retire to Land of Jershon.*

2. *Their Zoramite converts.*

1. Now it came to pass that after Amulek had made an end of these words, they withdrew themselves from the multitude and came over into the land of Jershon.

2. Yea, and the rest of the brethren, after they had preached the word unto the Zoramites, also came over into the land of Jershon.

3. And it came to pass that after the more popular part of the Zoramites had consulted together concerning the words which had been preached unto them, they were angry because of the word, for it did destroy their craft; therefore they would not hearken unto the words.

4. And they sent and gathered together throughout all the land all the people, and consulted with them concerning the words which had been spoken.

5. Now their rulers and their priests and their teachers did not let the people know concerning their desires; therefore they found out privily the minds of all the people.

6. And it came to pass that after they had found out the minds of all the people, those who were in favor of the words which had been spoken by Alma and his brethren were cast out of the land; and they were many; and they came over also into the land of Jershon.

7. And it came to pass that Alma and his brethren did minister unto them.

VERSES 1-2. *The missionaries withdrew themselves . . . and came over to the Land of Jershon.* When Amulek had finished his address to the multitude, and in the opinion of Alma the missionaries had done all the good that seemed possible, they, including those who labored elsewhere, withdrew from the Land of Antionum and "came over to the Land of Jershon," thus leaving the apostate Zoramites to tread their own devious way.

VERSES 3-7. *The Zoramites were angry because of the word.* No sooner had the missionaries left than the more crafty of the Zoramites devised a plan to discover the feelings of the community. They gathered the people together throughout the land and consulted with them concerning that which they had heard preachea. In this way they quickly found out those who favored the missionaries' message, and those who rejected it. Finding that the poor and uninfluential were those who received it, they resorted to persecution and plunder. They drove the believers from their homes and out of the land. Most of these fled to the Land of Jershon, whither Alma and his associates had preceded them.

8. Now the people of the Zoramites were angry with the people of Ammon who were in Jershon, and the chief ruler of the Zoramites, being a very wicked man, sent over unto the people of Ammon desiring them that they should cast out of their land all those who came over from them into their land.

9. And he breathed out many threatenings against them. And now the people of Ammon did not fear their words; therefore they did not cast them out, but they did receive all the poor of the Zoramites that came over unto them; and they did nourish them, and did clothe them, and did give unto them lands for their inheritance; and they did administer unto them according to their wants.

10. Now this did stir up the Zoramites to anger against the people of Ammon, and they began to mix with the Lamanites and to stir them up also to anger against them.

11. And thus the Zoramites and the Lamanites began to make preparations for war against the people of Ammon, and also against the Nephites.

12. And thus ended the seventeenth year of the reign of the judges over the people of Nephi.

13. And the people of Ammon departed out of the land of Jershon, and came over into the land of Melek, and gave place in the land of Jershon for the armies of the Nephites, that they might contend with the armies of the Lamanites and the armies of the Zoramites; and thus commenced a war betwixt the Lamanites and the Nephites, in the eighteenth year of the reign of the judges; and an account shall be given of their wars hereafter.

The Land of Jershon was inhabited by the People of Ammon. They also had left home and country for truth's sake, and now that others were suffering from the same cause, they received them with open arms as it were. They fed and clothed them, and gave them lands whereon they might build up new homes.

VERSE: 8-13. *The Zoramites were angry with the people of Ammon.* When the wicked Zoramites heard of the kind reception their injured fellow-citizens had received in Jershon they were greatly angered. They were not content to spoil them themselves, but they wanted to make them fugitives and vagabonds on the face of the whole earth. Their leader, a very wicked man, sent messengers to the Ammonites, desiring them to expel the refugees, adding many threats of what would follow should his cruel demand not be complied with. But the Ammonites were a brave people; they had already suffered unto death for the cause of God; and they were not of the kind to desert their afflicted brethren.

The refusal of the Ammonites to drive them out, or to force the converted Zoramites to abandon their newly found homes in their midst, further angered their haughty antagonists from the south to all kinds of depredations. The hatred of the apostate Zoramites knew no bounds. They began to incite the cruel Lamanites to again make war on the peaceful Ammonites. Nevertheless, the Ammonites remained firm in their resolve not to bow to the demands made of them to be unfaithful to their trust. Rather than do so, they would again forsake their homes and find in

3. *Preparations for war.*

14. And Alma, and Ammon, and their brethren, and also the two sons of Alma returned to the land of Zarahemla, after having been instruments in the hands of God of bringing many of the Zoramites to repentance; and as many as were brought to repentance were driven out of their land; but they have lands for their inheritance in the land of Jershon, and they have taken up arms to defend themselves, and their wives, and children, and their lands.

15. Now Alma, being grieved for the iniquity of his people, yea for the wars, and the bloodsheds, and the contentions which were among them; and having been to declare the word, or sent to declare the word, among all the people in every city; and seeing that the hearts of the people began to wax hard, and that they began to be offended because of the strictness of the word, his heart was exceeding sorrowful.

16. Therefore, he caused that his sons should be gathered together, that he might give unto them every one his charge, separately, concerning the things pertaining u n t o righteousness. And we have an account of his commandments, which he gave unto them according to his own record.

---

some other region a land of peace: for we must remind our readers that the Ammonites had entered into covenant with God never again to bend the bow, or draw the sword to take human life. They therefore withdrew to the Land of Melek, and the armies of the Nephites occupied the Land of Jershon that they might better contend against the combined forces of the Lamanites and the wicked Zoramites.

VERSES 14-16. *Alma . . . returned to the Land of Zarahemla.* After ministering to the needs of the Ammonites in the Land of Jershon, Alma and Ammon and their fellow missionaries, returned to their homes in Zarahemla. The results of their labors were indeed great, for they had carried the Gospel Message to a great many of the Zoramites who had accepted it, and had in every way complied with its requirements.

Wishing not to be disrupted in their desire to continue on in their easy-going way of life, the leaders and the priests of the apostate Zoramites resolved that to be rid of the believing ones among them would be the simplest way to carry on their nefarious, or impiously wicked, teachings without any hindrance whatsoever. Those who accepted the truth and repented of the folly that had ensnared them in the fowlers' net, were driven "out of their land," but, however, in the Land of Jershon they were made welcome and given lands which under their religious laws — the Law of Moses — were to be theirs for a permanent inheritance. The new homes they established in Jershon made it their homeland, and to defend it from attack by any erstwhile friends now turned enemies became an obligation to their wives and children that quickly turned peaceful adverents of the Gospel into warlike avengers of the atrocities that had been perpetrated upon them.

Alma's mission whereunto he had been called to preach the Gospel was not ended when he returned to Zarahemla. Instead, it seems to have been the reverse.

With a doubled zeal he went to every city and among all people and declared to all who would listen to his words the great truths of Life Eternal. But gradually, we conceive, with a heart bowed down with anxiety for God's cause, he became aware that the people were not observing the Law as they had been taught. Prosperity had again hardened their hearts and again it was enfeebling their efforts in the advancement of God's Kingdom. He sought new ways to infuse fresh efforts in the attempt to stop the decline in the rapidly deteriorating moral and spiritual fibre of the Nephite people which to him was apparent.

As before time was done by many of the prophets and teachers of old, he called his sons to him and charged them concerning the things of righteousness. Separately, one by one, he admonished them pertaining to what the Lord required of them, and with a father's blessing on each, he solemnly pronounced the Lord's blessings.

CHAPTER 36
THE COMMANDMENTS OF ALMA TO HIS SON, HELAMAN

1. *Alma Recounts His Sinful Past, His Miraculous Conversion, and His Subsequent Zeal in the Ministry.*

1. *Alma recounts his sinful past, his miraculous conversion, and his subsequent zeal in the ministry.*

Alma was now growing old. Notwithstanding his unceasing efforts and fervent prayers, the Nephites were again backsliding into iniquity. To every Nephite city, and to every Nephite land, he went or sent, to revive the Gospel fires in the souls of the inhabitants. But many became offended because of the strictness of the Gospel's laws, which forbade not only sin itself, but the very appearance of sin. As this feeling grew, Alma's heart became exceedingly sorrowful, and he mourned the depravity of his people.

Like many of the ancient patriarchs, when they felt their mortal career was drawing to its close, he called his sons to him, and gave them his last charge and blessing, speaking to each as the spirit of instruction and prophecy inspired. To Helaman, the eldest, he transferred the custody of the sacred plates, and with many words of warning and caution he advised on how they were to be kept. With hearts strengthened and renewed by the inspiration of his fervent admonitions, his sons went forth among the people; nor could Alma himself rest while there was a soul to save or a wrong made right. Alma also went forth once again in the spirit of his holy calling, and raised his voice once more in advocacy of the principles of the Everlasting Gospel.

It was in the nineteenth year of the Judges (73 B.C.), that Alma took his beloved son, Helaman, and after having ascertained, through divers questions, the strength and integrity of his faith, he prophesied to him of many important events that would occur in the distant future, especially with regard to the destruction of the Nephite people. This prophecy Alma commanded Helaman to record on the plates he had placed in Helaman's hands, but not to reveal it to anyone. Alma then blessed Helaman, also his other sons; indeed Alma blessed all who should stand firm in the truth of Christ's Gospel from that time forth. Shortly after this, Alma departed out of the Land of Zarahemla as if to go to the Land of Melek, and was never heard of more in this life. Of Alma's death and burial no men were witnesses. Then the saying went abroad throughout the Church that the Lord had taken him as He had beforetime taken Moses. This event occurred exactly one hundred years from the time of the elder Alma's birth.

After the departure of Alma we learn no more of the life of his associate missionary, Zeezrom, though Zeezrom's name and teachings are more than once referred to by latter servants of God. We also read of a city called Zeezrom, and, as it was the custom among the Nephites to name their cities and villages after whoever founded them, it is highly probable that, in the colonization of the country so vigorously carried on in the age that these men lived, he commenced the building of this place, and it would not be unreasonable to believe that he dwelt in the midst of its citizens as their High Priest, or Chief Judge.

Alma's son, Helaman, appears to have succeeded his father as the Presiding High Priest of the whole Church. After Alma's departure from this earth, Helaman and others went through the cities of the Nephites and regulated the affairs of the Church. Owing to the pride of many who would not give heed to the instructions which were given them, nor walk uprightly, dissensions arose which in after years led to numerous evils, among the greatest of which was a long continued war, or series of wars, between the faithful Nephites on the one hand and the apostate Nephites and soon after the Lamanites on the other. Still for four years, Helaman and his associate members of the Priesthood were enabled by God's providential care to maintain order in the Church. Many died in full faith of the Gospel Plan of Redemption, and in joyous hope of its never-ending rewards; indeed, during that period there was much peace and great prosperity enjoyed by those who remained faithful to the covenants they had made.

1. My son, give ear to my words; for I swear unto you, that inasmuch as ye shall keep the commandments of God ye shall prosper in the land.

2. I would that ye should do as I have done, in remembering the captivity of our fathers; for they were in bondage, and none could deliver them except it was the God of Abraham, and the God of Isaac, and the God of Jacob; and he surely did deliver them in their afflictions.

VERSE: 1-2. *My son, give ear to my words.* A father's anxiety for the future welfare of his son was evident in Alma's appeal to Helaman to always keep the Lord's commandments. He saw that in so doing, Helaman would place himself among the great throng of those who in times past had prospered according to God's promises:

And He hath said that: Inasmuch as ye shall keep My commandments ye shall prosper in the land; but inasmuch as ye will not keep My commandments ye shall be cut off from My presence. (II Nephi 1:20)

And thus being prepared to meet the Lamanites, they did not prosper against us. But the word of the Lord was verified, which He spake unto our fathers, saying that: Inasmuch as ye will keep My commandments ye shall prosper in the land. (Jarom 9)

For the Lord would not suffer, after He had led them out of Jerusalem and kept and preserved them from falling into the hands of their enemies, yea, He would not suffer that the words should not be verified, which He spake unto our fathers, saying that: Inasmuch as ye will not keep My commandments ye shall not prosper in the land. (Omni 6)

And now, my sons, I would that ye should remember to search them diligently, that ye may profit thereby; and I would that ye should keep the commandments of God, that ye may prosper in the land according to the promises which the Lord made unto our fathers. (Mosiah 1:6)

And behold, all that He requires of you is to keep His commandments; and He has promised you that if ye would keep His commandments ye should prosper in the land; and He never doth vary from that which He hath said; therefore, if ye do keep His commandments He doth bless you and prosper you. (Mosiah 2:22)

Behold, do ye not remember the words which He spake unto Lehi, saying that: Inasmuch as ye shall keep My commandments, ye shall prosper in the land? And again it is said that: Inasmuch as ye will not keep My commandments ye shall be cut off from the presence of the Lord. (Alma 9:13)

Alma took an oath, swearing to Helaman that the promise of the Lord is true.

3. And now, O my son, Helaman, behold, thou art in thy youth, and therefore, I beseech of thee that thou wilt hear my words and learn of me; for I do know that whosoever shall put their trust in God shall be supported in their trials, and their troubles, and their afflictions, and shall be lifted up at the last day.

4. And I would not that ye think that I know of myself—not of the temporal but of the spiritual, not of the carnal mind but of God.

---

and that by keeping His commandments the blessings of the Lord would follow him always.

Alma reminded Helaman of the bondage in which his fathers, the Children of Israel, were held in Egypt, and that none but the God Whom they, themselves, served, even the God of Abraham, and of Isaac and Jacob, could deliver them from its awful perils. Always keep in mind the power and the might of that One Who is powerful to save "for He surely did deliver them in their afflictions," he warned Helaman.

VERSES 3-4. *I know . . . not of the temporal but of the spiritual, not of the carnal mind but of God.* Alma's plea to Helaman was a gentle appeal as one might expect a loving father to make to a son of tender years. It reminds us of the first verse of the fifth Proverb: My son, attend unto my wisdom, and bow thine ear to my understanding. The word *wisdom* is used in both the Book of Mormon and the Bible to denote learning, and spiritual insight. So when Alma asks Helaman to *hear my words and learn of me* he desires to impart to Helaman the wisdom and understanding that has accumulated in his heart and head for, lo, the many years of his ministry and even before that. For by experience Alma knew that whosoever puts their trust in God, the same shall not be overcome by the adversary. "Thou wilt not forsake me, nor leave me in my grief" is an old Jewish proverb, much older than Alma. (For the Lord thy God is a merciful God;) he will not forsake thee, neither destroy thee, nor forget the covenant of thy fathers which He sware unto them. (Deut. 4:31) These passages, and many others, of the ancient Hebrew Scriptures were widely known to Alma. They were written upon the Brass Plates of Laban which had been in his possession for a considerable time, and the study of them was a great part of Nephite learning.

Other portions of the Hebrew Scriptures were known to Alma, and they undoubtedly influenced, giving shape and form to many of his conclusions, when in love and tenderness he bade Helaman "hear my words, and learn of me."

Happy is the man that findeth wisdom, and the man that obtaineth understanding.

Behold, the fear of the Lord, that is wisdom, and to depart from evil is understanding.

The possession thereof is better than silver, and rather to be sought than fine gold.

Treasures of wickedness profit nothing: the Lord will not suffer the soul of the righteous to famish.

The blessing of the Lord, it maketh rich; and no sorrow is added thereto.

Let not kindness and truth forsake thee; bind them about thy neck, write them upon the table of thy heart.

So shalt thou find grace and good favor in the sight of God and man.

Trust in the Lord with all thy heart, and lean not upon thine own understanding.

Wait for the Lord; be strong and let thy heart take courage; yea, wait thou for the Lord.

Alma's instructions to Helaman included, we suppose, all these, and more too, but Alma's testimony of God's goodness and mercy to those who put their trust in Him revived in Helaman his youthful zeal. It imparted courage and strength to his tired frame, which we feel likely had become a little weary and worn with the toils he had undergone among the Zoramites when on a mission among them to advance his Master's cause.

VERSE 4. *I would not that ye think that I know of myself.* Alma reinforced his personal testimony to Helaman by impressing upon Helaman's youthful mind the fact that he (Alma) had received an overwhelming knowledge of its truthfulness from sources sent down to him from On High. Manifestations of God's power were his constant guide, and Celestial visitors were his companions. Angels had ministered to him; beings from the Courts of Glory had shielded him from destruction. Alma dwelt, as it were, in a realm of heavenly light where only God's Holy Spirit shines, and where His Word is known and recognized by all.

VERSES 4-24. *If I had not been born of God I should not have known these things.* Helaman had no doubt heard somewhat concerning his father's miraculous conversion. (*See* COMMENTARY ON THE BOOK OF MORMON, Vol. II: p. 274 ff.) But, evidently, never before from his father's own lips. In relating this experience to his son, Alma went into great detail. He gave Helaman to understand that by no wisdom of his own did he know these things, but that God, Himself, had vouchsafed to him many wonderful blessings that culminated in his firmness and steadfast devotion. Alma knew whereof he spoke, "not of the temporal but of the spiritual, not of the carnal mind but of God."

Alma remembered the words of Jacob, the younger brother of the Prophet Nephi, which were written upon the Smaller Plates:

O, my beloved brethren, remember the awfulness in transgressing against that Holy God, and also the awfulness of yielding to the enticings of that cunning one. Remember, to be carnally-minded is death, and to be spiritually-minded is Life Eternal. (II Nephi 9:30)

Not of the carnal mind . . . The word *carnal* is used in the Book of Mormon to distinguish between that of the flesh and that of the spirit. It does not necessarily infer sin, but when it is contrasted with spirit it sometimes is so intended. It comes from the Latin *carnis,* which means flesh.

A better understanding of its use and meaning is to be had by studying its employment in both the Book of Mormon and the Bible.

BOOK OF MORMON

Carnal—

II Nephi	29:21	And lull them away into c. security
Mosiah	4:2	Viewed themselves in their own c. state
	16:3	For they are c. and devilish
	3	Was the cause of all mankind becoming c.
	5	He that persists in his own c. nature
	12	Gone according to their own c. wills
	26:4	Even in their c. and sinful state
	27:25	Changed from their c. and fallen state
Alma	22:13	Laying . . . before him, and their c. state
	30:53	They were pleasing unto the c. mind

	36:4	Not of the c. mind, but of God
	41:11	In a c. state, are in the gall of bitterness
	13	Evil for evil, or c. for c., or devilish
	42:10	As they had become c., sensual

Carnally—

| II Nephi | 9:39 | Remember, to be c. minded is death |

BIBLE

Carnal—

Romans	7:14	Spiritual, but I am c.
	8:7	The c. mind is enmity against
	15:27	Duty to minister to them in c.
I Corinthians	3:1	As unto c. even to babes
	3	For ye are yet c.
	4	Are ye not yet c.?
	9:11	Thing if we reap c. things
II Cor.	10:4	Of our warfare not c.
Hebrews	7:16	Not after the law of a c.
	9:10	Which stood in c. ordinances

Carnally—

Leviticus	18:20	Shalt not lie c. with thy
	19:20	Lieth c. with a bond-maid
Numbers	5:13	A man lie with her c.
Romans	8:6	For to be c. minded is death; but to be spiritually minded is life and peace

(Compare II Nephi 9:39 with Romans 8:6)

In spite of my own unworthiness, Alma confided to Helaman, the Lord made me aware by the mouth of His holy angel that these things whereof I speak are true. Beginning with the underlying reason therefor, Alma recounted his sinful past; that with the sons of King Mosiah he went about molesting the Saints of God, thereby seeking to destroy His Church. One day as they went about seeking to employ their impiously devised plans on the faithful and true, "God sent His holy angel," Alma said to Helaman, "to stop us by the way." Alma related in quite some detail that never-to-be-forgotten rebuke given them by the angel from God's presence. In a voice like thunder, the reverberations of which shook the earth upon which they stood, Alma was commanded to arise from the ground onto which he had fallen and to stand forth.

We repeat what we have said of this marvelous incident in our comments, previously referred to, on Chapter 27, Book of Mosiah, Volume II, COMMENTARY ON THE BOOK OF MORMON.

One day as Alma and his company were going about persecuting the members of the Church, an holy angel descended in a cloud and stopped them in the way. When the angel spoke, his voice was as thunder that caused the earth under their feet to tremble. Naturally, this manifestation of God's power spread terror and dismay in the hearts of those who witnessed it. They fell to the ground, and so confused and terrified were they that they failed to understand the words of the holy messenger.

"Alma, arise and stand forth," he cried. And when Alma arose, his eyes were opened to see who stood before him. It was an angel sent down from Heaven. He had a divine mission to perform —— to rebuke Alma and his companions.

The earth continued to shake as the angel spoke to them; the ground around them seemed ready to come apart. Again, they fell to the ground. We can understand their thoughts more forcefully if the words of the Psalmist are remembered: "Fearlessness and trembling are come upon me, and horror hath overwhelmed me." (Psalm 55:5)

"Why persecuteth thou the Church of God?" the angel asked of Alma. Knowest thou not, "that the Lord hath said, This is My Church, and I will establish it." Further the Lord sayeth, "Nothing shall overthrow it, save it is the transgression of My people."

Besides these things, the angel spoke to Alma of his father's captivity in the Lands of Helam and Nephi, and of their miraculous deliverance therefrom. But Alma heard nothing of these latter sayings because of the terrors of the first salutation that had overpowered him.

Even if thou wilt of thyself be cast off. This warning to Alma undoubtedly means, "Even if thou will not thyself be cast out of God's presence."

When the angel departed, Alma was dismayed and overcome; soul stricken, he sank to the ground. His companions gathered around him, and found he could not move, neither could he speak. Outwardly, he was dead to the world. The torments of the damned had taken hold of his soul, and, in the most bitter pain and mental anguish he. lay racked with the remembrance of all his past sins. The thought of standing before the *Bar of God* to be judged for his iniquities overwhelmed him with dread. He desired to become extinct, both body and spirit, so that he could not be brought before his creator. Thus for three days and three nights he suffered the pains of Hell. (*See* Alma 36:16.) (According to the author of the Book of Mosiah, Alma's father and other Church members fasted and prayed for the younger Alma for two days and two nights. We have no way of telling how much time was consumed by Alma's companions in carrying him to his father. The difference between two and three days may have been used in so doing.) Whichever it may have been, in his racked conscience, it must have seemed an eternity.

Alma became dumb, and his companions carried him to his father. When his companions found that Alma could neither speak nor move his limbs, they carried him to his father and related to him all that had happened. Strange as it must have appeared to them, the elder Alma's heart was filled with joy, and he praised God when he saw the apparently dead body of his much-loved son, for he realized it was the Lord's power that had brought this manifestation, and that his long-continued prayers had now been answered.

In his joy, Alma's father gathered the people together so that they might witness this great showing of the goodness and power of God. He assembled the priests, sought their cooperation, and unitedly they fasted and prayed for the stricken youth.

If we would recall the parable told by Jesus concerning another son who chose to do evil and thereby brought misery to his devoted father, we can understand, somewhat more fully, the joy that flowed from the elder Alma's heart when he beheld his own son lying unconscious before him.

Jesus told of a father who had two sons, the younger of whom asked that he be given his portion of his father's estate. When he had gathered it all together, he went to a distant land "and there wasted his substance in riotous living. And when he had spent all, there arose a mighty famine in that land; and he began to be in want. And he went and joined himself to a citizen of that country; and he sent him into his fields to feed swine," a labor thought by the Jews to be contemptible.

The son grew hungry and no one *gave unto him,* whereupon he was glad to eat the food prepared for the swine.

One day as he meditated his lot, the Prodigal son, for by this name is he known, thought of his home with his father. He remembered the fine clothes he there wore, and the abundance of good food there. Even his father's servants had more to eat than what they needed "and I perish with hunger," he said.

5. Now, behold, I say unto you, if I had not been born of God I should not have known these things; but God has, by the mouth of his holy angel, made these things known unto me, not of any worthiness of myself;

6. For I went about with the sons of Mosiah, seeking to destroy the church of God; but behold, God sent his holy angel to stop us by the way.

7. And behold, he spake unto us, as it were the voice of thunder, and the whole earth did tremble beneath our feet; and we all fell to the earth, for the fear of the Lord came upon us.

8. But behold, the voice said unto me: Arise. And I arose and stood up, and beheld the angel.

9. And he said unto me: If thou wilt of thyself be destroyed, seek no more to destroy the church of God.

10. And it came to pass that I fell to the earth; and it was for the space of three days and three nights that I could not open my mouth, neither had I the use of my limbs.

11. And the angel spake more things unto me, which were heard by my brethren, but I did not hear them; for when I heard the words—If thou wilt be destroyed of thyself, seek no more to destroy the church of God—I was struck with such great fear and amazement lest perhaps I should be destroyed, that I fell to the earth and I did hear no more.

12. But I was racked with eternal torment, for my soul was harrowed up to the greatest degree and racked with all my sins.

13. Yea, I did remember all my sins and iniquities, for which I was tormented with the pains of hell; yea, I saw that I had rebelled against my God, and that I had not kept his holy commandments.

14. Yea, and I had murdered many of his children, or rather led them away unto destruction; yea, and in fine so great had been my iniquities, that the very thought of coming into the presence of my God did rack my soul with inexpressible horror.

15. Oh, thought I, that I could be banished and become extinct

---

The poor *Prodigal* was afar off, serving a strange master in a strange land, feeding on husks.

"I will arise and go to my father, and will say unto him, "Father I have sinned against Heaven, and before thee!"

His father in the meantime had all along expected his son to return, and when he saw him coming, he was yet a long way off. However, the father prepared for his son, the ring for his withered finger, the robe for his naked body, the shoes for his sore feet; and the father called to his servants to prepare the fatted calf which he always had in readiness for the time when his son should come home. Not only that did the father do, but he sent his servants to ask his neighbors to come and rejoice and make merry, for he said, "For this my son was dead, and is alive again; he was lost, and is found. And they began to be merry." (Luke 15:11-24)

Also, let us hear the Prophet Habakkuk. The East Wind had sowed destruction broadcast throughout the land. The fig tree did not blossom, there was no fruit on the vines, the labor of the olive failed, and the field yielded no meat. The flock

both soul and body, that I might not be brought to stand in the presence of my God, to be judged of my deeds.

16. And now, for three days and for three nights was I racked, even with the pains of a damned soul.

17. And it came to pass that as I was thus racked with torment, while I was harrowed up by the memory of my many sins, behold, I remembered also to have heard my father prophesy unto the people concerning the coming of one Jesus Christ, a Son of God, to atone for the sins of the world.

18. Now, as my mind caught hold upon this thought, I cried within my heart: O Jesus, thou Son of God, have mercy on me, who am in the gall of bitterness, and am encircled about by the everlasting chains of death.

19. And now, behold, when I thought this, I could remember my pains no more; yea, I was harrowed up by the memory of my sins no more.

20. And oh, what joy, and what marvelous light I did behold; yea, my soul was filled with joy as exceeding as was my pain!

21. Yea, I say unto you, my son, that there could be nothing so exquisite and so bitter as were my pains. Yea, and again I say unto you, my son, that on the other hand, there can be nothing so exquisite and sweet as was my joy.

22. Yea, me thought I saw, even as our father Lehi saw, God sitting upon his throne, surrounded with numberless concourses of angels, in the attitude of singing and praising their God; yea, and my soul did long to be there.

23. But behold, my limbs did receive their strength again, and I stood upon my feet, and did manifest unto the people that I had been born of God.

24. Yea, and from that time even until now, I have labored without ceasing, that I might bring souls unto repentance; that I might bring them to taste of the exceeding joy of which I did taste; that they might also be born of God, and be filled with the Holy Ghost.

---

was cut off from the fold, and there was no herd in the stalls; "Yet," said the prophet, "I will rejoice in the Lord, I will joy in the God of my salvation." (Habakkuk 3:17)

This some exultant cry left the heart of the elder Alma as he beheld his son, for he "knew it was the power of God."

For two days they continued their supplications to Heaven. In the 27th Chapter of the Book of Mosiah, verses 23-31 is an account of what Alma said upon regaining consciousness:

And it came to pass after they had fasted and prayed for the space of two days and two nights, the limbs of Alma received their strength, and he stood up and began to speak unto them, bidding them to be of good comfort:

For, said he, I have repented of my sins, and have been redeemed of the Lord; behold I am born of the Spirit.

And the Lord said unto me: Marvel not that all mankind, yea, men and women, all nations, kindreds, tongues, and people, must be born again; yea, born of God,

THE BOOK OF ALMA

25. Yea, and now behold, O my son, the Lord doth give me exceeding great joy in the fruit of my labors;

26. For because of the word which he has imparted unto me, behold, many have been born of God, and have tasted as I have tasted, and have seen eye to eye as I have seen; therefore they do know of these things of which I have spoken, as I do know; and the knowledge which I have is of God.

27. And I have been supported under trials and troubles of every kind, yea, and in all manner of afflictions; yea, God has delivered me from prison, and from bonds, and from death; yea, and I do put my trust in him, and he will still deliver me.

---

changed from their carnal and fallen state, to a state of righteousness, being redeemed of God, becoming His sons and daughters;

And thus they become new creatures; and unless they do this, they can in nowise inherit the Kingdom of God.

I say unto you, unless this be the case, they must be cast off; and this I know, because I was like to be cast off.

Nevertheless, after wandering through much tribulation, repenting nigh unto death, the Lord in mercy hath seen fit to snatch me out of an everlasting burning, and I am born of God.

My soul hath been redeemed from the gall of bitterness and bonds of iniquity. I was in the darkest abyss; but now I behold the marvelous light of God. My soul was racked with eternal torment; but I am snatched, and my soul is pained no more.

I rejected my Redeemer, and denied that which had been spoken by our fathers; but now that they may foresee that He will come, and that He remembereth every creature of His creating, He will make Himself manifest unto all.

Yea, every knee shall bow, and every tongue confess before Him. Yea, even at the last day, when all men shall stand to be judged of Him, then shall they confess that He is God; then shall they confess, who live without God in the world, that the judgment of an everlasting punishment is just upon them; and they shall quake, and tremble, and shrink beneath the glance of His all-searching eye.

From then on to the end of his mortal career, Alma labored without ceasing to bring souls to Christ, and to guide his fellowmen in the Paths of Salvation.

It is well to note the effect this heavenly visit had upon the sons of King Mosiah. From that moment they were changed men. When the vioce of the angel reached their astonished ears, the understanding of divinity entered their souls. They knew, they felt, they realized there was a God, and that they had been fighting against Him. The sense of their own unworthiness filled their hearts; remorse and anguish reigned supreme therein, and they condemned themselves as the vilest of sinners.

Finally, the bitterness of their remorse was swallowed up in their faith in the coming of Christ, and they determined that, with the help of the Lord, they would undo the evil that their previous course had wrought. These resolutions they faithfully carried out. If they had been energetic in their wrongdoings, they would in the future be doubly active in works of restitution. They journeyed from city to city, from land to land, and everywhere bore triumphant testimony of their miraculous conversion. And in no equivocal tones they proclaimed the glorious Gospel of Christ, the love of God, and the Salvation of Mankind.

VERSES 25-30. *The Lord doth give me exceeding great joy in the fruit of my labors.* After relating to Helaman the details of his miraculous conversion, Alma continued on by bringing to his son's attention the many fruits that this remarkable incident had brought forth unto him. Not only was he, himself, carried to great

28. And I know that he will raise me up at the last day, to dwell with him in glory; yea, and I will praise him forever, for he has brought our fathers out of Egypt, and he has swallowed up the Egyptians in the Red Sea; and he led them by his power into the promised land; yea, and he has delivered them out of bondage and captivity from time to time.

29. Yea, and he has also brought our fathers out of the land of Jerusalem; and he has also, by his everlasting power, delivered them out of bondage and captivity, from time to time even down to the present day; and I have always retained in remembrance their captivity; yea, and ye also ought to retain in remembrance, as I have done, their captivity

30. But behold, my son, this is not all; for ye ought to know as I do know, that inasmuch as ye shall keep the commandments of God ye shall prosper in the land; and ye ought to know also, that inasmuch as ye will not keep the commandments of God ye shall be cut off from his presence. Now this is according to his word.

---

heights of joy and gladness, but Alma had, because of God's holy Word that had been imparted unto him, been able to share with others the tasty fruit his labors had borne. With him, the converted ones now enjoyed the savory morsels of divine love which were set before them. They saw eye to eye with Alma; their united purpose was God's glory; their joy was serving Him, their gladness lay in His praise. Their praise was doing His will.

Those to whom Alma had imparted God's holy Word rejoiced with him that to God all honor and glory were due because He had in mercy delivered them from evil. In spite of troubles and trials of *every kind,* even possible death, and *all manner of afflictions,* Alma had trusted in the Lord. His thoughts were not unlike those of the Psalmist when the sweet singer of Israel cried:

Let all those that put their trust in Thee rejoice: let them ever shout for joy . . let them also that love Thy Name be joyful in Thee. (Psalm 5:11)

Let them shout for joy, and be glad, that favor My righteous cause: yea, let them say continually, Let the LORD be magnified, which hath pleasure in the prosperity of His servant. (*Ibid.* 35:27)

In darkness as in light, in joy as in sorrow, let us trust in the Lord, as did Alma, that even through our tears we may discern His divine blessings, and see all about us the proofs of His providential care over us. As in the past, so in the future, Alma affirmed to Helaman, "I will put my trust in Him, and He will still deliver me."

Alma again impressed upon Helaman the power and might of the Great Jehovah. How in His wisdom and strength He brought "our fathers out of Egypt" and "swallowed up the Egyptians in the Red Sea." Time and time again, Alma had read upon the *Plates of Laban* how their forefathers had been oppressed by Egyptian taskmasters, and how God in His mercy had ended their affliction. He also read of God's command to Pharaoh, "Let my people go, that they may serve me." (See Exodus 7:16) Of this the Jews, in great thanksgiving and gratitude, note, "With mighty hand and outstreched arm didst God deliver them that they might become a kingdom of priests and a holy people." Not only that but He appointed them "a light unto the nations, so that in time the Earth might be filled with the knowledge of the Lord, even as the waters cover the sea." The work of the Lord is endless. Alma remembered the bondage of his own ancestors who lived in the Land of Lehi-

Nephi, and how the Lord delivered them from Lamanite servitude, as also from the grasp of wicked King Noah. The Lord, he reminisced, brought Lehi and his little company out of Jerusalem, thereby saving them from captivity and pagan servitude in Babylon, and in His watchful care has delivered them from such restraints "from time to time even down to the present day." Alma always kept in his mind a recollection of God's power manifest in these things, and urged Helaman do "as I have done." The great lesson that Alma wanted to implant in Helaman's heart, and also in his head, seems to have been: Ye that fear the Lord, trust in the Lord! He will bless them that fear Him, both small and great.

HELAMAN, SON OF ALMA

We have no account of the date or place of birth of this prophet and general of the Nephites, but as his father's permanent residence was in the City of Zarahemla it is not unreasonable to suppose that it was there that he first saw the light of day. He is not introduced to the reader of the Book of Mormon until he arrived at the age of manhood (75 B.C.) when it is stated that Alma took his two younger sons with him on his mission to the Zoramites, while Helaman was left in Zarahemla, most probably to take charge of the interests of the Church in that land during the absence of the Presiding High Priest, his father.

When Alma returned home from this mission he called his three sons to him and gave to each his blessing and instructions. His admonitions to Helaman are recorded in great length in the inspired pages. Alma therein reviews his own life and the history of the Nephites, prophesying many things with regard to the future of that people. He also exhorts Helaman to be diligent as a preacher of God's holy word and to lead an individual life of righteousness as an example to the Church. At this time he likewise gave him a strict charge with regard to the keeping of the records, to continue the annals of the nation thereon, to preserve them sacred and to prevent certain portions (containing the secret oaths, covenants and other works of darkness of the Jaredites), being published to the world, lest others be ensnared by the same abominations.

After receiving their separate instructions, Helaman, as also his two brothers and their father, went forth among the Nephites declaring the word according to the spirit of prophecy and revelation and they preached after the Holy Order of God, by which they were called.

In the year following, the Lord took Alma, as he had previously taken Moses. The prophet, being doubtless aware of his speedy departure from this dwelling-place of humanity, took his son Helaman and having received the latter's confession of faith in the coming of Christ, he blessed him and prophesied of things that should occur even until the people of Nephi should become extinct. Having done this, he blessed the Church and its faithful members and departed out of the land, never by mortal eyes to be seen again. His son Helaman and others then went through the cities of the Nephites and regulated the affairs of the Church; but owing to the pride of many who would not give heed to the instructions given them, nor walk uprightly, dissension arose, which in after years led to numerous evils, among the greatest of which was a long-continued war, or series of wars between the faithful Nephites on one side, and the apostates and afterwards the Lamanites, on the other. Still, for four years, Helaman and his associate priesthood were enabled to maintain order in the Church and many died in full faith of the Gospel and the joyous hope of its never-ending rewards; indeed, during that period there was much peace and great prosperity enjoyed by those who remained faithful.

The leader of those who apostatized from the true faith and commenced to wage war against their former brethren was named Amalickiah. Being defeated by Moroni, the Nephite commander and his army crushed (73 B.C.) he went over to the Lamanites and stirred them up to anger against the race to which he belonged. For some time he was unsuccessful in this attempt, as the Lamanites had too lately received severe defeats to be anxious to try the fortunes of war. By this craft, however, he removed every obstacle until he was acknowledged the king of the descendants of Laman. Towards the end of the year his armies advanced into the Land of Ammonihah and from that time the war was carried on with slight intermissions and with varying success, for about thirteen year (to 60 B.C.) when the Lamanites had been driven out of the possessions of the Nephites and peace was restored. Owing to the utter prostration of the Lamanites hostilities were not resumed until the year 53 B.C. when they again made on incursion into the Nephite territory but were speedily driven back to their own lands, suffering great loss. It was during this thirteen years' war that Helaman appears most prominently in the record of his nation and in the annals of his life is contained one of the sublimest and sweetest episodes in Nephite history.

The war (66 B.C.) had been working disastrously to the Nephites, when the people of Ammon, feeling that they were a burden rather than a help to their benefactors, though indeed they were not, desired to be released from their oath and covenant "never again to take up deadly weapons against their fellows." They desired in this hour of extreme peril to take up arms in defense of the liberties of their adopted country. From this rash step Helaman and his brethren dissuaded them lest by so doing they should imperil their eternal salvation. But they had sons that had grown far towards manhood who had not entered into this covenant and consequently were not shut off from participating in the dangers and glories of the war. So with their fathers' and mothers' consent, faith, prayers and words of encouragement two thousand of these youths were mustered into the Nephite army. These striplings were all men of truth, faith, soberness and integrity and were conspicuous for their courage, strength and activity. Being organized, they desired that Helaman, for whom they had great love and respect, should be their leader. He consented and at their head marched to the relief of the forces of the Republic that were struggling against considerable odds on the southern borders of the Nephites' dominions, from the shores of the Pacific Ocean eastward.

Helaman found the Nephite forces, numbering about six thousand warriors, in a somewhat deplorable condition. The Lamanites, in the strength of greatly superior numbers, had captured the cities of Manti, Cumeni, Zeezrom and Antiparah and held possession of the country round about. These cities had not been taken without much bloodshed on both sides. The Nephites had especially lost large numbers in prisoners, who were generally put to death by their captors, except the superior officers who were sent to the Land of Nephi. Antipus, the Nephite commander, was blocked up in the City of Judea, where dispirited and weakened by excessive toil and fighting his troops were making a desperate and painful effort to fortify the city. The arrival of Helaman and his corps brought hope and joy again to their hearts and renewed vigor to their endeavors.

King Ammoron, learning that reinforcements had reached the defenders of Judea, ordered all active operations to be suspended for a season. The suspension was most providential to the soldiers of Antipus as it gave them time to finish the work of fortifying the beleaguered city and also to recruit their health and energies. By the commencement of the following year the works of defense were completed and the Nephites became anxious for the onslaught they had so greatly dreaded a few months previous. But they were disappointed. The Lamanites did not feel sufficiently strong to renew aggressive movements. They contented themselves with occupying the Nephite cities they had already captured. In the second month of this year (65 B.C.) a convoy of two thousand additional warriors arrived from the Land of Zarahemla with abundant provisions. The Nephites in the City of Judea were now ten thousand strong and they were anxious for a forward movement in order, if possible, to retake some of their cities which were in the hands of the enemy.

Antipus and Helaman resolved on a ruse to entice the Lamanites from behind their fortifications. It was decided that Helaman and his command should march out of Judea with the apparent intention of carrying supplies to one of the cities in the hands of the Nephites, that was built near the sea shore. In executing this maneuver they purposely passed at no great distance from the City of Antiparah, in which was stationed the most numerous of the Lamanite armies, in the hope that the Lamanites would notice that their numbers were few and thus be led to attack them. The strategem proved successful. The garrison of Antiparah issued forth in pursuit of Helaman who with all haste, retreated into the wilderness north- ward, his intent being to draw his pursuers as far as possible from Antiparah. When the Lamanites had started in pursuit of Helaman, Antipus, with a considerable portion of his army, marched out of the City of Judea and fell on the Lamanite's rear. The retreat soon became a race. The Lamanites crowded forward with all possible expedition in the endeavor to reach Helaman before Antipus caught them. Helaman, on the other hand, used his utmost energy to keep out of their clutches. Neither of the three bodies turned to the right or to the left but kept straight on in the effort to out march their foes. Night came and went and on the morrow the double pursuit was still kept up. Another night fell but not one dared turn from his course.

On the third morning the race for life and victory was again renewed but before long the Lamanites, concluding they could not overtake Helaman, suddenly stopped and awaited the coming of Antipus and his weary soldiers, whom they unexpectedly attacked with great fury, slew Antipus and several of his captains, threw the Nephite troops into great confusion and forced them to commence a retreat. In the meantime Helaman discovered that he was no longer pursued and not knowing the reason, was in doubt what course to take. He called a hasty council of war at which it was determined to return at once and risk the chances of being caught in a trap by the crafty Lamanites. The statement which Helaman makes regarding the conduct of his young soldiers at this council is very interesting. After he had explained the situation to them, he inquired, "What say ye, my sons, will ye go against them in battle?" Without hesitancy they answered in the affirmative, saying: "Father, behold our God is with us, and he will not suffer that we shall fall; then let us go forth; we would not slay our brethren if they would let us alone; therefore let us go lest they should overpower the army of Antipus." Here Helaman remarks: "Now they never had fought, yet they did not fear death; and they did think more of the liberty of their fathers than they did upon their lives; yea, they had been taught by their mothers that, if they did not doubt, God would deliver them. And they rehearsed unto me the words of their mothers, saying, we do not doubt our mothers knew it."

Helaman and his sons arrived none too soon on the field of battle. The soldiers of Antipus were already fleeing before their more numerous foes but the valor and impetuosity of the youthful Ammonites were irresistible. They fell on the Lamanite rear with a daring and miraculous strength possessed only by men who put their whole trust in God. Thus attacked in the rear the Lamanites immediately halted, changed front and threw their whole force against the Ammonites. The surviving officers of Antipus' army, finding that Helaman had come to their rescue, stopped their retreat, reorganized their scattered bands and renewed the attack. The Lamanites were compelled to succumb; they could not resist the desperate courage of the Nephites that was driving them in at both front and rear. Their legions all surrendered and by Helaman's orders were sent as prisoners of war to Zarahemla.

And what about the young warriors of Ammon? So great was their faith, so potent its workings, that when, after the battle, Helaman called the roll of his youthful heroes and not one was missing. The faith sown by their mothers' words had borne fruit — they were all preserved. To their undaunted prowess, for they fought as if with the strength of God, the Nephites unhesitatingly accorded the glory of the day.

Still the hardly contested war continued. Six thousand men with provisions, reached Helaman from Zarahemla and the region round about (63 B.C.), besides sixty more young Ammonites who had grown sufficiently vigorous to assume the hardships of military life. The City of Cumeni shortly afterwards capitulated through the want of provisions, its supplies having been continuously cut off by Helaman's troops. This surrender threw so many prisoners on the hands of the Nephites that they were unable to guard or feed them. An officer named Gid, with a sufficient force, was detailed to convoy them to Zarahemla, but on their way, passing near an invading body of Lamanites the prisoners made a desperate attempt to escape. A few succeeded in getting away but the greater number were slain by their guards. Gid and the escort having no further occasion to go on to Zarahemla returned to Helaman.

His arrival was most inopportune for Ammoran, he having received large reinforcements, suddenly attacked the Nephites and were driving all their corps from their positions, except the youthful Ammonites who stood firm as a rock, when the arrival of Gid and his company turned the tide of battle. The young warriors again received the warm praise of the father and general. They had remained firm and undaunted through all the perils of fight, obeying and performing every command with the exactness and coolness of veterans. In the hottest of the encounter they never forgot their mothers' words nor their Heavenly Father's protecting blessing. Though in this fierce conflict, wherein they undauntedly bore the brunt of the enemy's savage onslaughts, every one was wounded, even that two hundred fainted for loss of blood, yet not one was slain and their preservation was marvelous in the eyes of their fellow-soldiers.

After this battle the Nephites retained the City of Cumeni while the Lamanites retreated eastward to Manti which was situated on the upper waters of the Sidon. Nor was it for several months that that city could be taken, as owing to internal dissensions at the Nephite capital and the attempt on the part of some of the people to overthrow the Republic and establish a monarchy, Pahoran, the Chief Judge, was unable to supply the necessary provisions and reinforcements.

In this strait Helaman and his fellow-officers called on the Lord in fervent prayer which was not unanswered. They received assurances of deliverance and victory. These blessed assurances inspired fresh faith and infused renewed courage in the war-weary hearts of those not given over to the love of carnage. Fired with the determination by God's grace, to conquer, they entered on a campaign against the City of Manti, which by strategy they captured before the end of the year (63 B.C.). The moral effect of this victory was so great that the Lamanites retreated into the wilderness, evacuating the whole of the Nephite territory on the west but unfortunately taking with them as prisoners, many women and children. Such was the condition of affairs when Helaman wrote to Moroni, the Nephite commander-in-chief, who was directing the campaign on the eastern side of the continent and it is from this letter that the above details of the war on the Pacific slope are condensed.

For more than a year Moroni could not send the needed help to Helaman.

The rebels in Zarahemla had driven the Chief Judge out of the city and he had taken refuge in Gideon. From there he wrote to Moroni to come to his assistance, which that officer did at the earliest possible moment, leaving the armies in the northeast under the command of Lehi and Teancum. As he advanced he rallied the people on his line of march to the defense of the liberties of the Republic and was so successful that, after having joined the Chief Judge, Pahoran, he succeeded in overthrowing the "king men," killing their leader, Pachus and completely crushing the rebellion. This being accomplished he sent 6,000 men with the necessary provisions to reinforce Helaman·(61 B.C.).

The campaign during this year, along the Atlantic coast was a decisive one. The Lamanites, in many stubborn battles, were driven from city to city until they were forced out of every one that they had captured, during the progress of the war, from the Nephites. On the west coast they do not appear to have renewed hostilities. The consequence was that in the next year peace was established in all the land, not a Lamanite warrior remaining on Nephite soil. Then Pahoran returned to his judgment seat and Helaman recommenced his labors in the ministry (60 B.C.).

The long continued and savage war just closed had brought various evils to the Church, in many parts of the land it may be said to have been disorganized. The occupancy of so many of the Nephite cities by the unbelieving Lamanites had produced numerous demoralizing effects; murders, contentions, dissensions and all manner of iniquity had become rife and the hearts of the people became hardened, yet not altogether so, for there were some who acknowledged the hand of the Lord in their afflictions and these humbled themselves in the depths of humility and because of the prayers of these righteous ones, the people were spared.

Such was the state of affairs when Helaman went forth to call the people to repentance and set the Church in order. In this blessed work he had much success and with the help of his brethren he again established the Church of God throughout all the land. These labors he continued until the time of his death and his joy therein was greatly increased by the continued faithfulness of the people, who notwithstanding their abundant prosperity, which, as ever, followed their repentance, they remained humble, fervent in prayer and diligent in works of righteousness. Such was the happy condition of the people of Nephi when Helaman died (57 B.C.), he having survived his illustrious father sixteen years. And Shiblon, his brother, "took possession of the sacred things that had been delivered unto Helaman by Alma."

CHAPTER 37

1. *Helaman entrusted with the Records and other sacred relics.*

1. And now, my son Helaman, I command you that ye take the records which have been entrusted with me;

2. And I also command you that ye keep a record of this people, according as I have done, upon the plates of Nephi, and keep all these things sacred which I have kept, even as I have kept them; for it is for a wise purpose that they are kept.

3. And these plates of brass, which contain these engravings, which have the records of the holy scriptures upon them, which have the genealogy of our forefathers, even from the beginning—

4. Behold, it has been prophesied by our fathers, that they should be kept and handed down from one generation to another, and be kept and preserved by the hand of the Lord until they should go forth unto every nation, kindred, tongue, and people, that they shall know of the mysteries contained thereon.

VERSES 1-4. *I command you that ye take the records.* Alma knew the steadfast spirit of his son, Helaman, and in the confidence he had of Helaman's integrity, he enjoined him to take charge of the Sacred Records and the Plates of Laban on which were inscribed the Holy Scriptures of the Jews and also the genealogy of the Nephites' forefathers who had come out of Jerusalem, the sacred city of the Jews.

Alma had received from King Mosiah all the plates upon which a record had been kept of the Nephites' history, also the Brass Plates and other sacred things which the Lord had commanded should be preserved. This was about 125 years Before Christ. The abridger of the Nephite records, Mormon, summed up many incidents connected with this transaction in a very few words:

And now, as I said unto you, that after King Mosiah had done these things, he took up the Plates of Brass, and all the things which he had kept, and conferred them upon Alma, who was the son of Alma; yea, all the records, and also the interpreters, and conferred them upon him, and commanded him that he should keep and preserve them and also to keep a record of the people, handing them down from one generation to another, even as they had been handed down from the time that Lehi left Jerusalem. (Mosiah 28:20)

King Mosiah had been entrusted with them by his father, King Benjamin, who in turn had received them from other kings of the Nephites who had preceeded him. King Benjamin cared for these sacred things from 200 years Before Christ, to 125 years of that same era. Also he received from Amaleki, the last one to write upon Nephi's Smaller Plates, their custodianship, and putting them with the Larger Plates brought together in a single record, the religious and political accounts of the people.

And it came to pass that I began to be old; and, having no seed, and knowing

King Benjamin to be a just man before the Lord, wherefore, I shall deliver up these plates unto him . . . (Amaleki, *Omni* 25)

Wherefore, it came to pass that after Amaleki had delivered up these plates into the hands of King Benjamin, he took them and put them with the other plates, which contained records which had been handed down by the kings, from generation to generation until the days of King Benjamin.

And they were handed down from King Benjamin, from generation to generation until they have fallen into my hands . . . (Words of Mormon 10-11)

Alma commanded Helaman to continue as he, himself, had done, to inscribe upon the Plates which Nephi had made at the Lord's bidding over 500 years previously, a record of his people and their actions during Helaman's own days. Also, Alma cautioned his son to keep sacred all the things which were then being entrusted into Helaman's care. "For it is for a wise purpose that they are kept." (*See* vv. 12; 14; 18)

In speaking of the plates which the Lord had instructed him to prepare, Nephi, about 600 years Before Christ, wrote what is the full purpose of doing so — it being for a wise purpose in God:

And all these things did my father see, and hear, and speak, as he dwelt in a tent, in the valley of Lemuel, and also a great many more things, which cannot be written upon these plates.

And now, as I have spoken concerning these plates, behold they are not the plates upon which I make a full account of the history of my people; for the plates upon which I make a full account of my people I have given the name of Nephi; wherefore, they are called the plates of Nephi, after mine own name; and these plates also are called the plates of Nephi.

Nevertheless, I have received a commandment of the Lord that I should make these plates, for the special purpose that there should be an account engraven of the ministry of my people.

Upon the other plates should be engraven an account of the reign of the kings, and the wars and contentions of my people; wherefore these plates are for the more part of the ministry; and the other plates are for the more part of the reign of kings and the wars and contentions of my people.

Wherefore, the Lord hath commanded me to make these plates for a wise purpose in him, which purpose I know not.

But the Lord knoweth all things from the beginning; wherefore, he prepareth a way to accomplish all his works among the children of men; for behold, he hath all power unto the fulfilling of all his words. And thus it is. Amen. (I Nephi 3-6)

Mormon, in a similar vein, explained the reason why he regarded both sets of plates as being sacred:

And now, I speak somewhat concerning that which I have written; for after I had made an abridgment from the plates of Nephi, down to the reign of this king Benjamin, of whom Amaleki spake, I searched among the records which had been delivered into my hands, and I found these plates, which contained this small account of the prophets, from Jacob down to the reign of this king Benjamin, and also many of the words of Nephi.

And the things which are upon these plates pleasing me, because of the prophecies of the coming of Christ; and my fathers knowing that many of them have been fulfilled; yea, and I also know that as many things as have been prophesied concerning us down to this day have been fulfilled, and as many as go beyond this day must surely come to pass—

Wherefore, I chose these things, to finish my record upon them, which remainder of my record I shall take from the plates of Nephi; and I cannot write the hundreth part of the things of my people.

But behold, I shall take these plates, which contain these prophesyings and

5. And now behold, if they are kept they must retain their brightness; yea, and they will retain their brightness; yea, and also shall all the plates which do contain that which is holy writ.

6. Now ye may suppose that this is foolishness in me; but behold I say unto you, that by small and simple things are great things brought to pass; and small means in many instances doth confound the wise.

7. And the Lord God doth work by means to bring about his great and eternal purposes; and by very small means the Lord doth confound the wise and bringeth about the salvation of many souls.

---

revelations, and put them with the remainder of my record, for they are choice unto me; and I know they will be choice unto my brethren.

And I do this for a wise purpose; for thus it whispereth me, according to the workings of the Spirit of the Lord which is in me. And now, I do not know all things; but the Lord knoweth all things which are to come; wherefore, he worketh in me to do according to his will.

And my prayer to God is concerning my brethren, that they may once again come to the knowledge of God, yea, the redemption of Christ; that they may once again be a delightsome people. (Words of Mormon 3-8)

Alma also impressed upon Helaman's mind the importance of keeping inviolable, or secure from profanation, corruption, destruction, and violence, the Brass Plates of Laban. Upon them was engraved "the genealogy of our forefathers, even from the beginning," Alma assured his son. Not only that, but equally of great consequence to their well being the Holy Scriptures of the Jews were contained thereon.

It seems that the self-evident consequences of keeping secure these Brass Plates were noted by their fathers, both near and far, who emphasized their worth as spiritual guides and moral instructors by prophesying of their future: "That they should be kept and handed down from one generation to another, and be kept and preserved by the hand of the Lord until they should go forth unto every nation, kindred, tongue, and people," that all men should know of God's goodness, and of His great purposes which without these Plates would not be to the understanding of men.

VERSE 5. *If they are kept they must retain their brightness.* We assume this means physical brightness, and we imagine that the custodians of the Plates maintained a watchful care over them. Brass, as it is known today, an alloy of copper and zinc, is not meant by the term used in the Bible or Book of Mormon, as zinc was not then known. The word means *copper,* and in some places in the Bible it is used to signify a simple metal, such as bronze, an alloy of copper and tin. We judge that the Plates of Laban being made of *brass,* were largely copper, and as copper has a tendency to corrode, or to wear away gradually, as by the action of strong acid, we believe the Brass Plates were in need of constant care. The same result is found when oxygen which is in the air we breathe comes into contact with copper as with iron, it causes the iron to corrode or rust away. Therefore, the necessity of keeping clean "all the plates which do contain that which is Holy Writ" so that in the end after passing through the hands of many keepers, they will remain bright as when they were new.

VERSE: 6-7. *By small and simple things are great things brought to pass.* Alma feared that Helaman might regard his anxiety over the future of the plates as a groundless worry, or that it was "foolishness in" him. But often we discern God's

8. And now, it has hitherto been wisdom in God that these things should be preserved; for behold, they have enlarged the memory of this people, yea, and convinced many of the error of their ways, and brought them to the knowledge of their God unto the salvation of their souls.

9. Yea, I say unto you, were it not for these things that these records do contain, which are on these plates, Ammon and his brethren could not have convinced so many thousands of the Lamanites of the incorrect tradi-tion of their fathers; yea, these records and their words brought them unto repentance; that is, they brought them to the knowledge of the Lord their God, and to rejoice in Jesus Christ their Redeemer.

10. And who knoweth but what they will be the means of bringing many thousands of them, yea, and also many thousands of our stiffnecked brethren, the Nephites, who are now hardening their hearts in sin and iniquities, to the knowledge of their Redeemer?

---

blessings come by simple means, and His providential care is manifest to us in small beginnings. Thus, the wise and those who rely upon their own understanding are confused and confounded. Truth needs no scholarly defense, but by abiding the Holy Spirit's promptings we are able to know the truth and accept its admonitions. If the plates, Alma suggested to Helaman, were constantly kept free from contamination, or the elements kept from befouling that which ought to be kept clean, pure, or sacred, the plates would live on forever; indeed a small *means* "to bring about His great and eternal purposes," and "the Salvation of many souls." This is a suitable place to repeat the words of Nephi:

O that cunning plan of the evil one! O the vainness, and the frailties, and the foolishness of men! When they are learned they think they are wise, and they hearken not unto the counsel of God, for they set it aside, supposing they know of themselves, wherefore, their wisdom is foolishness and it profiteth them not. And they shall perish.

But to be learned is good if they hearken unto the counsels of God. (II Nephi 9:28-29)

VERSES 8-10. *It has hitherto been wisdom in God that these things should be preserved.* At the time when Alma included in his writing the incidence of him giving Helaman the blessing herein recorded (73 B.C.), it was the same then as it always had been, the Brass Plates of Laban, the Larger and the Smaller Plates of Nephi, and many other precious things which were dear to the hearts of the Nephites and which reposed in Alma's custody, the Sacred Record tells us their possession was continually sought after by Nephite apostates and the Lamanites both of whom considered such objects as plunder of war.

Also, Alma recorded of them that careless handling would impair their usefulness, and corruption mar the purpose for which they were made. Therefore, God, in His wisdom, caused that constant vigilance for their safety and well-being be exercised that none of the sacred things should become the prey of wicked men, nor their divine aim be thwarted by the heedless elements.

Because of constant watchful care, and by painstaking methods of concealment, the Lord, through His servants, preserved them from generation to generation, and now as He has in the past, entrusted them into the safe keeping of good and

11. Now these mysteries are not yet fully made known unto me; therefore I shall forbear.

12. And it may suffice if I only say they are preserved for a wise purpose, which purpose is known unto God; for he doth counsel in wisdom over all his works, and his paths are straight, and his course is one eternal round.

righteous men who in addition to keeping them free from theft and contamination, have kept a faithful record of Nephite history which included an account of God's dealings with them. Now, because the Lord has preserved them, they are available to all who then as now desire to know the mind and will of God. Their use, and service, and profit, are testified to by Alma, who records: For behold, they have enlarged the memory of this people, yea, and convinced many of the error of their ways, and brought them to the knowledge of their God unto the salvation of their souls. Yea, I say unto you, were it not for these things that these records do contain, which are upon these plates, Ammon and his brethren could not have convinced so many thousands of the Lamanites of the incorrect tradition of their fathers; yea, these records and their words brought them unto repentance; that is, they brought them to the knowledge of the Lord their God, and to rejoice in Jesus Christ their Redeemer.

As in the past, they have proved their worth in bringing many souls to Christ, Alma, in the spirit of prophecy, declared these plates, together with the other sacred things in his keeping would bring many more of the Lamanites, and "also many thousands of our stiffnecked brethren, the Nephites, who are now hardening their hearts in sin and iniquities, to the knowledge of their Redeemer?"

VERSES 11-12. *They are preserved for a wise purpose.* The proper understanding of these verses is better had by searching out the use of the words, *wisdom* and *wise purpose* when they are used elsewhere in the Sacred Record. We refer the student to the following:

WISDOM—

I Nephi	3:19	It is w. in God that we should obtain
	5:22	It was w. in the Lord that we should
	11:35	Behold the world and the w. thereof
II Nephi	1:8	It is w. that this land should be kept
	2:12	Must needs destroy the w. of God
	24	All things have been done in the w. of
	3:19	The words which are expedient in My w.
II Nephi	9:8	O the w. of God! his mercy and grace!
	28	Their w. is foolishness, and it profiteth
	42	Who are puffed up because of . . . their w.
	20:13	By my w. have I done these things
	21:2	The spirit of w. and understanding
	26:20	Preach up unto themselves their own w.
	27:22	Until I shall see fit in mine own w.
	26	For the w. of their wise . . . shall perish
	28:30	For they shall learn w.
Jacob	4:10	Know that he counseleth in w.
Mosiah	2:17	These things that ye may learn w.
	36	In you to guide you in w. paths
	4:6	God and his matchless power and his w.
	9	Believe that he has all w.
	27	See that all these things are done in w.

	5:15	Through the w., and power, and justice
	8:20	Men; for they will not seek w.
	24:7	Wise people, as to the w. of the world
Alma	2:1	A wise man, as to the w. of the world
	22:33	Thus the Nephites in their w., with their
	34	This was w. in the Nephites; as the Lamanites were
	26:11	In my own strength, or in my own w.
	29	Through the power and w. of God we
	35	God; for he has all power, all w.
	29:8	To teach his word; yea, in w., all that
	8	We see that the Lord doth counsel in w.
	31:35	Give unto us, O Lord, power and w.
	32:12	Be humble, that ye may learn w.
	12	It is necessary that ye should learn w.
	37:8	It has hitherto been w. in God that
	12	He doth counsel in w. over all his
	35	My son, and learn w. in thy youth
	38:9	I have told you this that ye may learn w.
	11	See that ye do not boast in your own w.
	13	And to be praised for their w.
	39:2	Unto boasting in thy strength and thy w.
	49:5	Because of the w. of the Nephites in preparing
	15	This was w. in Moroni; for he had supposed
Helaman	1:16	With his great w., that by sending him
	12:5	Yea, how slow to walk in w. paths
	15:16	I will cause that in the day of my w.
	16:15	Began to depend . . . upon their own w.
III Nephi	21:4	For it is w. in the Father that they
	10	For I will show unto them that my w.
	26:2	It was w. in him that they should be
	28:29	When the Lord seeth fit in his w., that
	29:1	When the Lord shall see fit in his w.
Mormon	5:13	The Lord, when he shall see fit, in his w.
Ether	5:1	Except, by and by, it shall be w. in
	8:23	It is w. in God that these things should
Moroni	10:3	If it be w. in God that ye should read
	9	That he may teach the word of w.

WISE PURPOSE—

I Nephi	9:5	Make these plates for a wise p. in him
W Mormon	1:7	And I do this for a wise p.
Alma	37:2	It is for a wise p. that they are kept
	12	They are preserved for a wise p.
	14	Preserve for a wise p. in him
	18	Reserve these things for a wise p. in
I Nephi	9:3	Make these plates for the special p.
	5	Which p. I know not
II Nephi	2:12	Been no p. in the end of its creation
	24:26	This is the p. that is purposed upon
	25:18	Be given them for the p. of convincing
Jacob	5:36	For mine own p. I have preserved them
	53	Preserve . . . the roots thereof for mine own p.
	54	Preserve them also for mine own p.

Mosiah	7:22	For the sole p. of bringing this people
	8:19	Prepared for the p. of unfolding
	27:14	For this p. have I come to convince the
	28:14	For the p. of interpreting languages
Alma	11:20	It was for the sole p. to get gain
	13:24	For the p. of preparing the hearts
	19:1	Made for the p. of burying their dead
	24:20	For the p. of destroying the king
	37:12	Which p. is known unto God
	19	One p. hath he fulfilled, even to the
	55:2	Ammaron, save he will withdraw his p.
	56:43	For the p. that we should come against
	50	They would have obtained their p.
Mormon	5:14	His great and eternal p., in restoring

Purpose

No wise

II Nephi	25:29	If ye do this ye shall in no w. be cast
Mosiah	27:26	They can in no w. inherit the kingdom
Alma	5:51	Except ye repent ye can in no w. inherit
	9:12	Ye can in no w. inherit the kingdom of
	39:9	Ye can in no w. inherit the kingdom of
III Nephi	3:15	They would in no w. be delivered out
	11:37	Or ye can in no w. receive these things
	38	Ye can in no w. inherit the kingdom of
Mormon	9:29	Endure to the end, ye will in no w. be
Moroni	10:21	Ye can in no w. be saved in the kingdom
	32	Ye can in no w. deny the power of God

On (or in) this wise

Jacob	7:6	On this w. did he speak unto me, saying
Mosiah	7:18	He spake unto them in this w., saying
Alma	12:2	And he [Alma] spake on this w.
	56:30	The Lamanites began to grow uneasy on this w.
III Nephi	11 Hd	On this w. did he show himself unto
	22	On this w. shall be baptize
	23	On this w. shall ye baptize them
Ether	1:6	And on this w. do I give the account
Moroni	8:1	And on this w. did he write unto me

Wise

I Nephi	19:3	Also for other w. purposes, which purposes
II Nephi	9:28	Are learned, they think they are w.
	42	The w., and the learned, and they that
	43	But the things of the w. and the prudent
	15:21	Wo unto the w. in their own eyes!
	27:26	For the wisdom of their w. . . . . shall perish
	28:15	O the w., and the learned, and the rich
Jacob	6:12	O be w.: what can I say more?
Mosiah	12:27	Therefore, ye have not been w.
	24:7	A w. people, as to the wisdom of the
	29:8	Let us be w. and consider these things

13. O remember, remember, my son Helaman, how strict are the commandments of God. And he said: If ye will keep my commandments ye shall prosper in the land—but if ye keep not his commandments ye shall be cut off from his presence.

	10	Let us be w. and look forward to these
	11	We will appoint w. men to be judges
	19	The interposition of their all-w. Creator
Alma	2:1	A w. man, as to the wisdom of the world
	4:16	A w. man who was among the elders
	10:24	Our w. lawyers whom we have selected
	18:22	Now Ammon being w., yet harmless, he
	30:20	They were more w. than many of the
	32:23	Children do have words ... which confound the w.
	37:6	In many instances doth confound the w.
	7	Small means the Lord doth confound the w.
Helaman	16:14	Angels did appear unto men, w. men
III Nephi	14:24	I will liken him unto a w. man, who
Mormon	9:28	Be w. in the days of your probation
	31	Ye may learn to be more w. than we

COUNSEL—

II Nephi	9:28	They hearken not unto the c. of God
	15:19	Let the c. of the Holy One of Israel draw nigh
	17:5	Have taken evil c. against thee, saying
	18:10	Take c. together, and it shall come to naught
	21:2	The spirit of c. and might
	27:27	They seek deep to hide their c. from the
	28:30	And lend an ear unto My c.
	10	Brethren, seek not to c. the Lord
Jacob	4:10	But to take c. from His hand
	5:22	C. Me not; I knew that it was a poor spot of
Alma	29:8	We see that the Lord doth c. in wisdom
	37:12	For He doth c. in wisdom over all His works
	37	C. with the Lord in all thy doings
	39:10	C. with your elder brothers in your undertakings
	10	And give heed to their c.

COUNSELS—

I Nephi	19:7	And hearken not to the voice of His c.
II Nephi	9:29	If they hearken unto the c. of God
	28:9	Seek deep to hide their c. from the Lord
Helaman	12:5	And to give ear unto His c.
	6	And they set at naught His c.

ONE ETERNAL ROUND—

I Nephi	10:19	The course of the Lord is one eternal round
Alma	7:20	Therefore, His course is one eternal round
	37:12	And His course is one eternal round

VERSES 13-20. *And now remember, my son, that God has entrusted you with these things.* In the 29th chapter of Mosiah, the 20th verse, we read: And now, as

14. And now remember, my son, that God has entrusted you with these things, which are sacred, which he has kept sacred, and also which he will keep and preserve for a wise purpose in him, that he may show forth his power unto future generations.

15. And now behold, I tell you by the spirit of prophecy, that if ye transgress the commandments of God, behold, these things which are sacred shall be taken away from you by the power of God, and ye shall be delivered up unto Satan, that he may sift you as chaff before the wind.

16. But if ye keep the commandments of God, and do with these things which are sacred according to that which the Lord doth command you, (for you must appeal unto the Lord for all things whatsoever ye m u s t do with them) behold, no power of earth or hell can take them from you,

for, God is powerful to the fulfilling of all his words.

17. For he will fulfil all his promises which he shall make unto you, for he has fulfilled his promises which he has made unto our fathers.

18. For he promised unto them that he would reserve these things for a wise purpose in him, that he might show forth his power unto future generations.

19. And now behold, one purpose hath he fulfilled, even to the restoration of many thousands of the Lamanites to the knowledge of the truth; and he hath shown forth his power in them, and he will also still show forth his power in them unto future generations; therefore they shall be preserved.

20. Therefore I command you, my son Helaman, that ye be diligent in fulfilling all my words, and that ye be diligent in keeping ,the commandments of God as they are written.

I said unto you, that after King Mosiah had done these things, he took the Plates of Brass, and all the things which he had kept, and conferred them upon Alma, who was the son of Alma; yea, all the records, and also the interpreters, and conferred them upon him, and commanded him that he should keep and preserve them, and also keep a record of the people, handing them down from one generation to another, even as they had been handed down from the time that Lehi left Jerusalem.

When King Mosiah had, at length, finished the work of translating the twenty-four Gold Plates which King Limhi had brought with him from the Land of Nephi, he took all the sacred articles which had been given him by his father, King Benjamin, and in turn gave them into the keeping of Alma as has been stated. King Mosiah also instructed Alma as to the manner in which they were to be preserved by him. Mosiah made it a special obligation on Alma's part, to hand them down to whomsoever was appointed to be his successor, and thereby continue the custom that had been begun by Nephi when Lehi, his father, together with his father's family, departed out of Jerusalem.

We also refer the reader to the 11th verse of *The Words of Mormon*: And they (meaning the Plates of Nephi) were handed down from King Benjamin, from generation to generation until they have fallen into my hands. And I, Mormon, pray to God that they may be preserved from this time henceforth. And I know that they will be preserved; for there are great things written upon them, out of which my people and their brethren shall be judged at the great and last day, according to the word of God which is written.

A complete history of the custodianship of the Plates of Nephi is herewith given that will give great light upon the course taken by the Church and the political government — both the Monarchy and the Republic.

The Smaller Plates of Nephi containing the sacred annals of Nephi's people were not entirely filled with engravings until about 200 years before Christ. They were started by Nephi between 570-560 B.C. But the history they contain goes back to the time when Lehi left Jerusalem, or 600 B.C. So in reality they contain the history of God's dealings with that branch of the House of Israel for about four hundred years.

When Nephi died, he transferred these sacred records to the care of his brother, Jacob. From then until Moroni finally hid them in the Hill Cumorah, they continued in the hands of four families, who had charge of them as near as can be told from the abridgment. We may summarize as follows: Jacob and his descendants held them from 546 B.C. to about 200 B.C., when they were transferred to King Benjamin. He, with his son, Mosiah, held them until 91 B.C., at which time they were given into the care of Alma, the Chief Judge. Alma and his posterity retained them until 320 years after the advent of the Messiah. After these, Mormon and Moroni were the custodians until the close of the record in the year A.D. 420.

Here are the facts concerning the custodianship of the sacred plates from the foregoing statement of the Prophet Mormon. Beginning with Amaleki, he gave the plates to King Benjamin about 200 B.C. Of King Benjamin, we read ". . . that when King Benjamin had made an end of all these things, he had consecrated his son Mosiah to be a ruler and a king over his people, and he had given him all the charges concerning the kingdom . . ." (Mosiah 6:3) Which "charges" we may declare, was to be the keeper of the sacred things, including the plates. We read further in the account of Mosiah's reign, "He took the plates of brass, and all the things which he had kept, and conferred them upon Alma, who was the son of Alma; yea, all the records, . . ." (Mosiah 28:20) This was in 91 B.C.

Alma, about seventeen year later, entrusted the plates to his son, Helaman. It is recorded in the Book of Alma, 37:1-2, "And now, my son Helaman, I command you that ye take the records which have been entrusted with me; And I also command you that you keep a record of this people, according as I have done, upon the Plates of Nephi, and keep all these things sacred which I have kept, even as I have kept them; for it is for a wise purpose that they are kept."

In the year 544 of the Nephite Annals, or fifty-seven years before the birth of Christ, Helaman died, and Shiblon, his brother, we are told, ". . . took possession of these sacred things which had been delivered unto Helaman by Alma." (Alma 63:1)

Four years later, or 53 B.C., Shiblon died, and, "It became expedient for Shiblon to confer those sacred things, before his death, upon the son of Helaman, being called after the name of his father." (Alma 63:11)

In 39 B.C., "Helaman died, and his eldest son Nephi began to reign in his stead." (Helaman 3:37) Of him it is written:

And Nephi, the son of Helaman, had departed out of the land of Zarahemla, giving charge to his son Nephi, who was his eldest son, concerning the plates of brass, and all the records which had been kept, and all those things which had been kept sacred from the departure of Lehi out of Jerusalem. Then he departed out of the land, and whither he went, no man knoweth; and his son Nephi did keep the records in his stead, yea, the record of this people. (III Nephi 1:2-3)

Nephi, the son of Nephi and the grandson of Helaman, thus, shortly before the birth of the Savior in Bethlehem of Judea, received the Sacred Records with instructions as to their care. This second Nephi was chosen by the Risen Redeemer to be a member of the Twelve whom He named. Nephi, the second, kept the plates in his possession until after the glorious appearing of the Savior, when he gave them into the care of his son, who was also named Nephi. He, presumably, was a young man at that time, for he kept them seventy-six years, or until A.D. 110, when a son, named Amos received them. "And he kept it eighty and four years," . . . "and he kept it upon the plates of Nephi also." (IV Nephi 20, 19)

And it came to pass that Amos died also (and it was an hundred and ninety and four years from the coming of Christ) and his son Amos kept the record in his stead; and he also kept the record upon the plates of Nephi; . . . (IV Nephi 21)

And it came to pass that after three hundred and five years had passed away, (and the people did still remain in wickedness) Amos died; and his brother, Ammaron, did keep the records in his stead. (IV Nephi 47)

Ammaron hid up all the plates in the Hill Shim. (IV Nephi 48-49)

Ammaron gave them to Mormon. (Mormon 1:2-3)

Mormon obtained the plates as Ammaron had directed. (Mormon 4:23)

Mormon hid all the records in the Hill Cumorah, save the abridged ones, which he gave to his son, Moroni. (Mormon 6:6)

Moroni said, "I am the son of Mormon. . . . And I am the same who hideth up this record unto the Lord; . . ." (Mormon 8:14) And I seal up these records, . . ." (Moroni 10:2)

The following are the names of the Nephite historians, with the times during which they held the plates. Where a blank space is noted, the information is not given in the Book of Mormon, and therefore can only be guessed at, which we choose not to do.

Nephi, from .... to 546 B.C.	Helaman, the Elder, from 73 to 57.
Jacob, from 546 to	Shiblon, from 57 to 53.
Enos, from .... to 422.	Helaman, the Younger, from 53 to 39.
Jarom, from 422 to 362.	Nephi, from 39 to 1.
Omni, from 362 to 318.	Nephi, the Disciple, from 1 to A.D. 34.
Amaron, from 318 to 280.	Nephi, the son of the Disciple, 34 to 110.
Chemish, from 280 to	Amos, from 110 to 194.
Abinadom, from .... to	Amos, the Younger, from 194 to 306.
Amaleki, from .... to 200 (circa).	Ammaron, from 306 to 320.
King Benjamin, from 200 to 125.	Mormon, from 320 to 385.
King Mosiah, from 125 to 91.	Moroni, from 385 to 420. Record closes.
Alma, the Younger, from 91 to 73.	

In these verses (13-20) Alma emphatically declared to Helaman that if he is faithful in keeping the commandments of the Lord, he will always retain the plates and other sacred things, and that there is no power of earth or hell that can take them from him.

That the Lord, Alma reiterated, has promised our fathers "that He would reserve these things for a wise purpose in Him, that He might show forth His power unto future generations."

Now remember, my son, Helaman, Alma again insisted that the injunction to be obedient to God's commands was of preeminent value or importance, for the Lord has entrusted into your care those things which are sacred, those things which throughout many generations He has kept sacred, and which He will still keep sacred that the promises He has made to our fathers will be fulfilled. The Lord, Alma continued, has already fulfilled one of these promises He made, "Even

21. And now, I will speak unto you concerning those twenty-four plates, that ye keep them, that the mysteries and the works of darkness, and their secret works, or the secret works of those people who have been destroyed, may be made manifest unto this people; yea, all their murders, and robbings, and their plunderings, and all their wickedness and abominations, may be made manifest unto this people; yea, and that ye preserve these interpreters.

2. Gazelem.

22. For behold, the Lord saw that his people began to work in darkness, yea, work secret murders and abominations; therefore the Lord said, if they did not repent they should be destroyed from off the face of the earth.

23. And the Lord said: I will prepare unto my servant, Gazelem, a stone, which shall shine forth in darkness unto light, that I may discover unto my people who serve me, that I may discover unto them the works of their brethren, yea, their secret works, their works of darkness, and their wickedness and abominations.

---

to the restoration of many thousands of the Lamanites to the knowledge of the truth; and He hath shown forth His power in them, and He will also still show forth His power in them unto future generations; therefore they shall be preserved." It is well for us to remember that because of the Nephite Records, a copy of which was carried on their mission to the Lamanites, Ammon and his brethren were able to convince them of their folly and corruption. We repeat, word for word, the 20th verse: Therefore I command you, my son, Helaman, that ye be diligent in fulfilling all my words, and that ye be diligent in keeping the commandments of God as they are written.

VERSE 21. *And now, I wi'l speak unto you concerning those twenty-four plates.* Among the sacred things which Alma entrusted into the care and keeping of Helaman were twenty-four plates of gold which King Limhi had in his possession before they were submitted by him to King Mosiah for translation.

Upon the translation of them which was made by King Mosiah it was discovered that these twenty-four gold plates contained the history of a great people who lived in the Land of America many years before. They are known to us as Jaredites, being named after one of their great leaders, and who were destroyed in battle by God's edict because of their continual wickedness from which they would not repent. Alma, with the authority of his office as Presiding High Priest, commanded Helaman "keep them, that the mysteries and the works of darkness, and their secret works, or the secret works of those people who have been destroyed, may be made manifest unto this people."

VERSE 23. *And the Lord said: I will prepare unto my servant Gazalem, a stone* . . By the power of God, which is shown in the *Interpreters* rendering old and forgotten writings understandable to later generations, thereby bringing to light all the "secrets and abominations," which brought destruction upon the nation herein described, fulfilled the promise of the Lord "that I may discover unto My people who serve Me . . . the works of their brethren, yea, their secret works, their works

24. And now, my son, these interpreters were prepared that the word of God might be fulfilled, which he spake, saying:

25. I will bring forth out of darkness unto light all their secret works and their abominations; and except they repent I will destroy them from off the face of the earth; and I will bring to light all their secrets and abominations, unto every nation that shall hereafter possess the land.

26. And now, my son, we see that they did not repent; therefore they have been destroyed, and thus far the word of God has been fulfilled; yea, their secret abominations have been brought out of darkness and made known unto us.

27. And now, my son, I command you that ye retain all their oaths, and their covenants, and their agreements in their secret abominations; yea, and all their signs and their wonders ye shall keep from this people, that they know them not, lest peradventure they should fall into darkness also and be destroyed.

28. For behold, there is a curse upon all this land, that destruction shall come upon all those workers of darkness, according to the power of God, when they are fully ripe; therefore I desire that this people might not be destroyed.

29. Therefore ye shall keep these secret plans of their oaths and their covenants from this people, and only their wickedness and their murders and their abominations shall ye make known unto them; and ye shall teach them to abhor such wickedness and abominations and murders; and ye shall also teach them that these people were destroyed on account of their wickedness and abominations and their murders.

30. For behold, they murdered all the prophets of the Lord who came among them to declare unto

---

of darkness, and their wickedness and abominations." The Lord promised to prepare a *stone* "unto My servant *Gazalem* . . . which shall shine forth in darkness unto light." We understand this statement to mean that this promised *stone* will cause that knowledge and understanding shall come forth where before only ignorance prevailed.

GAZALEM is a name given to a servant of God. The word appears to have its roots in Gaz — a stone, and Aleim, a name of God as a revelator, or the interposer in the affairs of men. If this suggestion is correct, its roots admirably agree with its apparent meaning — a seer.

VERSES 27-31. *And now, my son, I command you that ye retain all their oaths* . . . That his people, the Nephites, should in no way learn of the secret oaths, "and their covenants, and their agreements in their secret abominations," all the signs and wonders of the Jaredites wherein they brought destruction upon themselves, Alma forbade Helaman to make them known unto them that his people should not fall into "darkness also and be destroyed," as were the Jaredites.

Alma feared that his people upon learning such oaths and signs as were administered to each other among the Jaredites, would like them fall into all kinds

them concerning their iniquities; and the blood of those whom they murdered did cry unto the Lord their God for vengeance upon those who were their murderers; and thus the judgments of God did come upon these workers of darkness and secret combinations.

31. Yea, and cursed be the land forever and ever unto those workers of darkness and secret combinations, even unto destruction, except they repent before they are fully ripe.

---

of iniquity and therein encourage wickedness among them. He knew that a curse had been placed by the Lord upon all the Land of America "that destruction shall come upon all those workers of darkness, according to the power of God, when they are fully ripe; therefore I desire that this people might not be destroyed."

These Gold Plates were found by subjects of Limhi who had gone in search of help from their brethren in Zarahemla who did not know of the perilous condition of Limhi's people who were in bondage to the Lamanites in the Land of Nephi, and who were sore afflicted by their masters. This is the inspired account.

It was about 121 B.C. Continual peace for a number of years in Mosiah's realm caused many of his subjects to wonder more and more about the fate of those who had returned to their old homes in the Land of Lehi-Nephi. The Sacred Record says, "They wearied him with their teasings," for they had heard nothing of them for many years, not since they had left Zarahemla to re-establish their homes in that land.

Under King Mosiah's direction, sixteen strong and presumably young men were provisioned and made ready to proceed to the Land of Lehi-Nephi, or to the City of Lehi-Nephi, to ascertain the fate of their brethren. Not knowing the course they should travel, these men, headed by Ammon, took forty days to reach a hill north of Lehi-Nephi, but for a while they were lost in the wilderness, and roamed about not knowning just where to go. The ruler of these expatriates from Zarahemla was Limhi, a grandson of Zeniff, who led the malcontents to their former homes.

Ammon made what he thought were adequate and proper arrangements to fulfill his mission. He chose three of their number to accompany him, "and they went down into the Land of Nephi." King Limhi's guards, fancying Ammon and his men were spies, put them into prison. After two days incarceration in the vilest of goals, they were brought forth and made to stand before the king. The bands that held them tightly were released, or, at least loosened. Ammon was then commanded to answer any question the king might ask. Ammon's life and the lives of his companions were solely in the hands of the king.

Ammon was given the privilege of speaking thereby explaining the peculiar circumstances of being in Lehi-Nephi.

With due regard for the courtesies due one of royal station, Ammon paid obeisance to his regal captor. He recounted, after praising God for the privilege of speaking, his own birth and how he had come from Zarahemla to bring succor if it were needed, and thereby learn of the circumstances surrounding the condition of their brethren whom Zeniff had "brought up out of the land."

The Nephites, who under King Limhi dwelt in the Land of Lehi-Nephi, like their brethren in Zarahemla, had heard nothing of the others since they parted many years before. At one time they all lived in that great city which was their capital, but restive souls among them, urged many to unite and return to Lehi-Nephi where it was hoped they could re-establish homes in the land which under the Mosaic Law they believed was the land of their inheritance. Many who departed with Zeniff and also many who remained in Zarahemla felt bereft of the association of friends and loved ones from whom they hoped to hear.

The uncertainty of the fate of the others preyed heavily upon them. They wished to know what had become of one another. They grew insistent to the extent that King Mosiah, who lived in Zarahemla, ordered a party of strong men to go search them out. After forty days wandering in the wilderness Ammon found their ill-fated brethren existing in a most grievous manner. He learned that they were horribly abused, spied upon, and were watched continually by the Lamanites, who had imposed taxes upon them which were beyond any measure of need. In fact, they were in bondage.

King Limhi, though sorely burdened, rejoiced because now that their brethren in Zarahemla would soon know of their oppression, they would be delivered. In his hour of thankfulness, the king even expressed the willingness of his people to be slaves of their brethren if they so desired. But, however, this thing could not be done. The Law of Moses, which they practiced, prohibited brethren from enslaving brethren. In any event, Limhi, the wretched overseer — for he was only nominally a king — determined, that, if possible, his people would no longer pay tribute to the Lamanite king. "I will rejoice," he said, "and on the morrow I will cause that my people shall rejoice also."

King Limhi then bid his soldiers to release Ammon and his friends, and to take such help to the others of Ammon's companions that he had left at the camping place near Shilom, for they, doubtless, were weary and worn with the toils of a long journey in which they had "suffered hunger, thirst, and fatigue."

It was the custom among the Nephites to meet at the call of their ruler at some common place where they could receive any message the king wished to give. Jacob had imparted the word of the Lord to the Nephites from the Temple his brother, Nephi, had caused to be erected; King Benjamin sent heralds throughout all the land to proclaim a conference at the Temple in Zarahemla; in similar manner King Limhi now ordered his people to present themselves at the temple in Lehi-Nephi where they "would hear the words he should speak to them."

The people gathered as King Limhi had commanded, and he spoke words of comfort and courage to them. He told them that the time was coming and "it is not far distant," when with joy they would cease to be tyrannized by their enemies, and that in spite of the many vain struggles they had made to escape their oppressive bondsmen, they now would be delivered, and that they would be set free from being slaves of the Lamanites.

Limhi also told his people about his brethren in Zarahemla. In the abdrigment he had made of the great number of plates in his possession, Mormon notes that after King Limhi had finished speaking to his distraught and greatly distressed people, he told them all the things Ammon had previously made known unto him concerning "their brethren in Zarahemla." But, by way of interpolation, Mormon also notes that only a few of the things King Limhi said in addressing his people were written by the abridger, himself, "in this book."

King Limhi caused that Ammon should speak. The second-hand account which King Limhi gave to his people concerning their brethren in Zarahemla was verified by Ammon, who stood before the multitude that had gathered there and rehearsed to them the many things that had happened in Zarahemla under the reign of King Benjamin, or from the time Zeniff and his followers left their own capital city up until "the time that he, himself, came up out of the land."

Ammon told the assembled throng of the peaceful reign of King Benjamin, and of the growth of the people there in both numbers and material. He told them of the righteous desires of Benjamin for his people, and of the examples he set for them to follow. He recounted how King Benjamin had "labored with his own hands" that his people should not be burdened with taxes which might become oppressive, and, also, that Benjamin desired no recompense for his service to them, save that they serve God by ministering to each others' wants.

Many other of King Benjamin's teachings were explained to Limhi's people by Ammon. How great, they thought, was the difference under which they, themselves, had been forced to live by wicked King Noah and the unselfish rule of King Benjamin in Zarahemla. It is worthy of note to remember that for many years Limhi's people had not been taught Gospel principles. Noah's priests had explained none of them to the people of Lehi-Nephi, but rather had led them into transgression. They were confused by Ammon's remarks concerning the angel's visit to Benjamin, and the wonderful things the angel had said to him. Ammon, with great care, explained to them the coming of Christ, His Atoning Sacrifice and the Salvation prepared for the children of men. He pointed out, so that they might understand, the fulfillment of the Law of Moses in the coming of the Messiah, which, he noted to them, according to the words of King Benjamin "was not far distant."

When Ammon had finished telling King Limhi's people the wonderful story about Benjamin and his people in Zarahemla, Limhi dismissed the eager throng that had listened to Ammon's recital. As they each went to their own houses, we may imagine the anguish that every memory of King Noah and his wicked priests produced in their aching hearts.

Limhi had the records of his people brought before Ammon to read. The Nephites dwelling in Lehi-Nephi, notwithstanding their many faults, had kept a record of their doings from the time of Zeniff to when Ammon came among them. The plates upon which this record was kept were brought before him that Ammon might read them.

The ease with which Ammon read of Limhi's people astonished Limhi; his evident understanding of many obscure writings therein, and his knowledge of different races and nations of men, including the Jews and other contemporary peoples, prompted Limhi to inquire of Ammon, "If he could interpret languages?" "Ammon told him that he could not." We presume that Ammon had become acquainted with Jewish history by intently reading the Hebrew Scriptures, which you remember were written upon the Brass Plates of Laban.

King Limhi sent an expedition to find Zarahemla. In the hope that they would get help in their efforts to escape Lamanite bondage, King Limhi told Ammon that, in dire distress, he had chosen forty-three of "my people" to go to Zarahemla and seek assistance to that end.

The men Limhi selected became lost in the surrounding wilderness; they did not know the proper way to travel, nor the distance between Lehi-Nephi and Zarahemla. They only knew it was far to the north, and traveled for many days in that direction. At last they reached a land of "many waters."

In this land they found the remains of a great people. There they discovered the ruins of many buildings. Scattered among the broken arches and displaced columns of a strange architecture they came across the dry bones of great numbers of men who had evidently fallen in battle. The Sacred Record describes them as "a people who were as numerous as the hosts of Israel."

To prove to Limhi that the discovery they had made was true, and that their supposition was correct in which they supposed that their brethren in Zarahemla were all destroyed in battle, they brought back with them many relics of these dead people.

Among the proofs of their surmise were many artifacts used by their supposed brethren. They carried back to King Limhi in Lehi-Nephi copper breastplates which were undamaged by age and were yet sound; they also brought back swords whose hilts were decayed and gone, and the blades thereof were corroded with rust.

But by far the most important of their finds was a set of twenty-four *gold plates,* which they brought with them on their return. These gold plates were filled with engravings written in a strange language which no one in King Limhi's domain could translate. Again and again, he sought their interpretation; he felt that in them was hidden a great mystery. The anxiety to learn what this mystery was, greatly induced Limhi to ask Ammon, "Canst thou translate?"

Knowest thou of any one that can translate? King Limhi proceeded to question Ammon further concerning the translation of the plates that had fallen into his hands. He made no mention of their probable worth, they being made of gold, but talked to Ammon only of the great store of knowledge and understanding which he felt was hidden behind the faces of innumerable and to him, incomprehensible glyphs. Ammon listened to Limhi's words as the king intently explained to him the reasons why he desires that they be translated "into our language." Perhaps, he ventured, they may tell us of those people who were destroyed, and the causes therefore. Now, I ask you again, "Knowest thou of any one that can translate?"

I can assuredly tell thee, O king, of a man that can translate the records. Ammon answered the king and said that there is a man in Zarahemla who has a gift from God, who can translate all records of ancient peoples. He has "wherewith that he can look" and by the power of God can translate writings belonging to ages now long past dead. The *wherewith* of which Ammon spoke, he said "are called interpreters," and that no man could look into them and receive the blessings they imparted unless he was commanded by the Lord so to do. Whosoever the Lord commanded "to look in them," Ammon said, "is called seer."

The Presiding High Priest in Zarahemla, who also is king of that land, Ammon continued, is he who is commanded by the Lord to "do these things, and who has this high gift from God."

King Limhi then observed that a "seer is greater than a prophet," to which Ammon explained to the king the many different gifts had by each. A seer, he said, is a revelator and a prophet, too, and no gift is greater than, by the power of God, to reveal the history of any nation in the undecipherable writings of their prophets and wise men.

Not only, Ammon went on to explain, does a seer know the history of peoples now long forgotten, but also of things to come. By them all things are made known; hidden things are brought to light, and secret things are made manifest. Things "that otherwise could not be known" are made known by a seer. He is both *prophet and seer.*

Thus God had provided a means. Ever mindful of the needs of His children, the Lord, in His watchful care over them, has provided the means whereby they can obtain great knowledge and understanding; this *means,* also, through faith, is a lamp unto their feet and an unending source of spiritual help in time of need.

Limhi was filled with joy as he heard Ammon discourse on the gift of God which He had endowed King Mosiah with. Limhi's great hope regarding these twenty-four gold plates would now be fulfilled. For a moment he forgot all plans to escape the bondage his people were in; with great reason he proclaimed the *majesty of God,* and thanked the Giver of all good for His mercy and kindness to

His children. He was persuaded that a great mystery was contained in these plates, and from it his own people would learn many lessons. It was but natural that King Limhi, abounding in the new faith and hope Ammon's visit had inspired, interposed his heartfelt conclusion, "These interpreters were doubtless prepared for the purpose of unfolding all such mysteries to the children of men."

The twenty-four plates are called *The Book of Ether* (Ether 1:2). Their discovery was not an accident. For, when Ether had finished his record, "He hid them in a manner that the people of Limhi did find them." (Ether 15:33)

GENERAL NOTES

Before the Jaredites left Moriancumer, their camp in the old country, the Brother of Jared was given indescribable visions on Mount Shelem. The Lord instructed him not to make them public during his lifetime, but to place them on record before his death, in the language commonly spoken by all before the building of the Towel of Babel, but a tongue no longer known by later generations. This record was to be sealed. He also received *two stones,* prepared so as to *magnify,* or make clear "the things which ye shall write." These were also to be sealed. (Ether 3:21-24, 27, 28)

From the information given by Moroni, we know that King Mosiah, the son of Benjamin, had the writings of the Brother of Jared, and that he kept them in case the time for their publication should come. We also know that those writings, together with "the interpretation thereof"—the translation by Mosiah—had come into his (Moroni's) possession, as also the interpreters. (Ether 4:1-5)

There is, then, no doubt that Mosiah, the son of Benjamin, was the custodian in his day of the Jaredite records and the stones of interpretation. (Mosiah 28:11-16)

The Jaredite record was part of the twenty-four plates of Ether which came providentially, into the hands of Mosiah through the expedition of Limhi. In all probability he received the interpreters from his father, Benjamin, who may have received them from Mosiah the First, his father.

Amaleki, the son of Abinadom, gives, in the Book of Omni, what is, perhaps, the correct clue to the question, how the stones of interpretation, originally given to the Brother of Jared, came into the hands of the kings in Zarahemla. He says that a large stone, possibly a monumental pillar or stele, was brought to King Mosiah the First, who interpreted the engravings by the "gift and power of God." We may, perhaps, infer that this means that he had the interpreters. By this power it was found that the stone contained an account of Coriantumr and the slain of his people. (Omni 20:22) Undoubtedly, Coriantumr had brought this information to Zarahemla. May he not have carried with him the interpreters also? It must be remembered that this survivor after the battle of Ramah had usurped the highest ecclesiastical as well as the political offices, and that he, therefore, may have had the sacred instrument in his possession, although it was useless to him. Ether prophesied that he would not fall in war, but that he would live, to be buried by another people. The inference is not far-fetched that he was spared for the very purpose of bringing to the Nephites the story of the dealings of God with the Jaredites.

The records preserved. At the proper time, Alma gave his son, Helaman, charge of the sacred treasures entrusted to him by Mosiah. (Alma 37:1-4) By such transfers they were preserved from generation to generation. About the year 320 of our era, Ammaron, having received them from his brother Amos, prompted by the Spirit, did "hide them unto the Lord, that they might come again unto the remnant of the House of Jacob." (4 Nephi 48-49; *Comp.* Words of Mormon 10:11; Alma 37:4)

Mormon instructed concerning the records. The great Nephite commander and leader, Mormon, relates that, when he was about ten years old, Ammaron charged him to go to the Hill Shim, in the Land of Antum, when he should reach the age of about twenty-four years. The sacred writings had been deposited there, Ammon said. He instructed Mormon to take the Plates of Nephi and complete the records from his own observations. The other plates and articles were to be left in the hill. (Mormon 1:14; 2:17, 18)

Cumorah, the final place of safety. Mormon carried out his instructions. Later, he again went to the hill and "did take up all the records which Ammon had hid up unto the Lord." (Mormon 4:23) He finally, hid them in the Hill Cumorah, having first furnished his son, Moroni, with the entire story of the Plates of Nephi, in a greatly abridged form. (Mormon 6:6)

Moroni finished the tragic chapter of the final battle of Cumorah and then hide "up the records in the earth," (Mormon 8:4) presumably in the Hill Cumorah. But he also predicted that they would be found and come to light at some future day, (Mormon 8:14-16) a prophecy fulfilled through the instrumentality of the Prophet Joseph Smith.

Moroni gives one final reference to the miraculous interpreters, when he says: "But the Lord knoweth . . . that none other people knoweth our language; therefore he hath prepared *means* for the interpretation thereof." (Mormon 9:34) This *means* was the very crystals prepared for, and presented to the Brother of Jared on the mount. (D. & C. 17:1)

Only two Miraculous Interpreters. History knows of only two sacred instruments of this kind, also known as the Urim and Thummim, meaning *"lights and perfections."* One was given to Abraham in the City of Ur of the Chaldees. (Pearl of Great Price, Abraham 3:1) This was, probably, handed over by Moses to Aaron, the High Priest, who carried it in his "breastplate of judgment," an important part of his ecclesiastical equipment. (Exodus 28:30) It was finally lost sight of.

The other was given to the Brother of Jared. It was this that the Prophet Joseph had in his possession for some time.

"Urim and Thummim: According to the Hebrew, Exodus 28:30, the literal signification of these two words is *lights and perfections, or the shining and the perfect.* According to St. Jerome, *doctrine and judgment.* According to the Septuagint, *declaration* or *manifestation and truth.* They were worn in or attached to the breastplate of the high priest when inquiring of God." (Cruden's *Concordance of the Bible*)

Exodus	28:30	Breastplate of judgment, the U. and T.
Numbers	27:21	Counsel after the judgment of U.
Leviticus	8:8	Put in the breastplate the U. and T.
Deuteronomy	33:8	Let thy T. and U. be with thy holy
Ezra	2:63	Stood up priest with U. and T.
Nehemiah	7:65	Stood up priest with U. and T.
I Samuel	28:6	The Lord answered him not, neither by dreams, nor by U.

During the Millennial reign of the Son of God, when the great temples shall adorn the Old and New Jerusalem, they may again be needed for new revelations; for then "Out of Zion shall go forth the law, and the word of the Lord from Jerusalem." (Isaiah 2:30)

Hundreds of years later than the events herein recorded, the last of the Nephite prophets, Moroni, in commenting on this particular subject which was included in the history of the Jaredites written on the twenty-four plates of gold, said, And it came to pass that the Lord said unto the Brother of Jared: Behold, thou shalt not suffer these things which ye have seen and heard to go forth unto the world, until the time cometh that I shall glorify My Name in the flesh; wherefore, ye shall treasure up the things which ye have seen and heard, and show it to no man.

And behold, when ye shall come unto me, ye shall write them and shall seal them up, that no one can interpret them; for ye shall write them in a language that they cannot read.

And behold, these two stones will I give unto thee, and ye shall seal them up also with the things which ye shall write.

For behold, the language which ye shall write I have confounded; wherefore I will cause in my own due time that these stones shall magnify to the eyes of men these things which ye shall write.

And when the Lord had said these words, he showed unto the brother of Jared all the inhabitants of the earth which had been, and also all that would be; and he withheld them not from his sight, even unto the ends of the earth.

For he had said unto him in times before, that if he would believe in him that he could show unto him all things—it should be shown unto him; therefore the Lord could not withhold anything from him, for he knew that the Lord could show him all things.

And the Lord said unto him: Write these things and seal them up; and I will show them in mine own due time unto the children of men.

And it came to pass that the Lord commanded him that he should seal up the two stones which he had received, and show them not, until the Lord should show them unto the children of men. (Ether 3:21-28)

And the Lord commanded the brother of Jared to go down out of the mount from the presence of the Lord, and write the things which he had seen; and they were forbidden to come unto the children of men until after that he should be lifted up upon the cross; and for this cause did king Mosiah keep them, that they should not come unto the world until after Christ should show himself unto his people.

And after Christ truly had showed himself unto his people he commanded that they should be made manifest.

And now, after that, they have all dwindled in unbelief, and there is none save it be the Lamanites, and they have rejected the gospel of Christ; therefore I am commanded that I should hide them up again in the earth.

Behold, I have written upon these plates the very things which the brother of Jared saw; and there never were greater things made manifest than those which were made manifest unto the brother of Jared.

Wherefore the Lord hath commanded me to write them; and I have written them. And he commanded me that I should seal them up; and he also hath commanded that I should seal up the interpretation thereof: wherefore I have sealed up the interpreters, according to the commandment of the Lord. (Ether 4:1-5)

For this cause did King Mosiah keep them. (Ether 4:1) This Mosiah, the son of King Benjamin, was the last of the kings of Zarahemla, preceding the judges. He was the translator of the contents of the twenty-four plates of gold, which were delivered to him by King Limhi. The translation was made by "the means of two stones which were fastened into the two rims of a bow." The stones, we read in the Book of Mosiah, were "prepared from the beginning, and were handed down from generation to generation, for the purpose of interpreting languages." (Mosiah 28:11-14) They were in all probability, the stones which were given to Moriancumr and, later, to the Prophet Joseph by the resurrected prophet of the Nephites, Moroni.

How did King Mosiah get them? We turn to the Book of Omni. We read there that during the reign of the first Mosiah, the father of King Benjamin, a large stone with engravings thereon was brought to Zarahemla, to the king. He translated the text "by the gift and power of God," and found that it contained an "account of one Coriantumr and the slain of his people." The chronicler (Amaleki) adds the explanation that Coriantumr had been found by the people of Zarahemla—perhaps by hunters—and that he had lived in that country the last nine moons—months—of his life.

Coriantumr was the last king of the Jaredites of whom we have any historical record, as Ether was the last of their prophets. He fought his savage enemy, Shiz, at Ramah, until both their armies were annihilated. Then he ended the life of his antagonist. He, himself, lay on the battlefield, apparently lifeless. But he recovered, and began his pilgrimage which eventually ended in Zarahemla. As the head of the Jaredite government, or knigdom, Coriantumr may have had charge of the *Interpreters,* although they were useless to him, and brought them with him to Zarahemla where they were later given into the custody of King Mosiah, the father of Benjamin.

If the conversation between Limhi and Ammon recording the *Interpreters* refers to the Urim and Thummim, as it undoubtedly does, it is evident that the two stones were no part of Limhi's treasure. Limhi had the plates, there is no doubt about that, and King Mosiah had the *Interpreters* long before he received the plates to interpret.

All dwindled in unbelief. Moroni also informs us that the Nephites had dwindled in unbelief and the Lamanites had rejected the Gospel, therefore he had been commanded to hide the sacred relics in the earth to come forth again at some future time. These relics were the account of Moriancumr of his visions on the mount as he wrote it and sealed it up until the appearance of Christ on this continent. There were also the Plates of Brass, the Plates of Nephi, the translation of the twenty-four plates, the plates themselves, and the Interpreters, all of which sacred objects had been used by the Church of Christ on this continent. (*Compare* Mosiah 28:11-13) All these the Prophet Moroni entrusted to the bosom of motherly earth, there to rest until the Gentiles would repent and exercise faith in the Lord. (Ether 4:7)

The Two Stones. These two stones, which are also known as the *Interpreters* (Ether 4:5; Mosiah 28:20) were, as we read here, entrusted to the care of Moriancumr before he descended from the ever memorable scene of his vision and revelations. They were delivered to him with the admonition that they be sealed up, together with the sacred records that were kept, and thus hidden from the eyes of the world until they, in the due time of the Lord, were to come forth. Their purpose is stated to be to "magnify," that is to say, to make clear, "the things which ye shall write." (Ether 4:7)

According to the Doctrine and Covenants (17:1) the sacred instrument that was deposited in the Hill Cumorah and delivered to the Prophet Joseph Smith, was the *Urim and Thummim** which was received by the Brother of Jared while on the mount. When the Prophet Joseph received the *stones,* Sept. 22, 1827, they were framed in silver bows and fastened to a *breastplate.* (Pearl of Great Price, Joseph Smith 2:35)

From the Doctrine and Covenants 130:8-9, where God is said to dwell on a globe which is a *Urim and Thummim,* the name by which we know the *Interpreters,* we learn that the earth is to be sanctified and made immortal—"made like a *crystal* and will be a *Urim and Thummim* to the inhabitants thereon." We conclude from that statement, that the *two stones* were *crystals.* The Prophet Joseph, further, adds to our information that the "white stone" mentioned in Revelation 2:17 "will become a *Urim and Thummim* to each who receives one, and that "a white stone" will be given to everyone who is privileged to come into the Celestial Kingdom. On the *stone* a new name will be written. By that means "things pertaining to a higher order of kingdoms, even all kingdoms, will be made known."

---

*Meaning, *Lights and perfections.*

All the inhabitants of the earth. When Moriancumr had received the *Urim and Thummim*, the Lord opened his vision, possibly by means of these *stones*, and he was shown the human race, past and future, passing as if in panorama.

Enoch had a similar view of "many generations" upon Mt. Simeon (Pearl of Great Price, Moses 7:2-6, 22-69). Abraham, who received the *Urim and Thummim* while he was in Ur, of the Chaldees, (Abraham 3:1) had marvelous visions and revelations concerning the creation of the universe and the intelligences that were organized "before the world was." (Abraham 1:28 and Chapters 4 and 5) He was thus prepared for his mission to Egypt. (Abraham 3:15) Moses, too, who may have had in his possession the same *Urim and Thummim* that had been given to Abraham, had similar visions. (Moses 1:1ff) He "beheld the earth, yea, even all of it; and there was not a particle of it which he did not behold. . . . And he beheld also the inhabitants thereof, and there was not a soul which he beheld not; and he discerned them by the Spirit of God. . . . And he beheld many lands; and each land was called earth, and there were inhabitants on the face thereof." (Moses 1:27-29)

JAREDITES

The contemporary nations on the eastern continent — Egypt, Chaldea, and Babylonia — were insignificant when compared with the vast extent of territory held and filled by the Jaredites; they were the sole rulers of the whole western hemisphere, and possibly the originals, whence arose the stories of the greatness and grandeur of the fabled Atlantis; for we have no account in the sacred records that God shut them off from the knowledge of the rest of mankind when he planted them in America, as he afterwards did the Nephites; and later research has shown that geographical knowledge of the ancients was much greater in the earlier ages than at the time of the Savior.

According to the Book of Ether, a colony, some time shortly after the attempt to build the famous Tower of Babel, came to America from the region occupied by the tower builders.

Very little is known about these colonists and their descendants, but we may suppose that their migration was part of a general movement in all directions, which took place at that time, from the land of Shinar, afterwards called Chaldea.

A general migration from Babylon. That such a general migratory movement actually took place can hardly be doubted. Josephus, who drew information from both Hebrew and Greek sources, says:

"After this they were dispersed abroad, on account of their languages, and went out by colonies everywhere, and each colony took possession of that land which they lit upon and unto which God led them; so that the whole continent was filled with them, both the inland and the maritime countries. There were some, also who passed over the sea in ships and inhabited the islands."[1]

In a much more recent work we read:[2]

"All history demonstrates that from that central focus (Babylon) nations were propelled over the globe with an extraordinary degree of energy and geographical enterprise."

A Chinese tradition is mentioned by Dr. Fisher of Yale, thus:

"The nucleus of the Chinese nation is thought to have been a band of immigrants, who are supposed by some to have started from the region southeast of the Caspian

---

[1]*Antiquities of the Jews,* Book 1, Chapter 5.
[2]Schoolcraft, *Hist. and Statis. Information,* Vol. 1, p. 14; Philadelphia, 1852.

Sea, and to have crossed the headwaters of the Oxus. They followed the course of the Hoang Ho, or Yellow, river, having entered the country of their adoption from the northwest, and they planted themselves in the present province of Shan-se." (*Improvement Era*, Feb., 1927, p. 314.)

It is not impossible that others of the Jaredite race followed the pioneers of the Book of Ether, and remained at the sea shore, laying the foundation of the Chinese empire. The annual pilgrimage of Chinese to the top of their sacred mount just at the point of the peninsula of Shantung confirms this supposition.

Date of the Jaredite Migration. According to the chronology of Bishop Usher, which appears in English versions of the Bible, the building of the Tower was undertaken about 2,200 B.C. Dr. Joseph Angus, in his *Bible Handbook*, suggests 2,247. According to Babylonian tradition the City of Babel was founded about the year 2,230 B.C. But as early as 2,000 B.C., there were in the Babylonian library clay tablets, now preserved in the British Museum, containing the story of the Tower-building. It must have been ancient history already at that time. Everything considered, the great dispersion can hardly have taken place much later than 2,500 B.C.

Location of the Tower. Near a place called Hillah on the east bank of the Euphrates, ·there is a splendid ruin, known as *Birs Nimrud,* standing like a watch-tower on a vast plain. It is in the shape of a pyramid and is 150 feet high. On its top there is a solid mass of vitrified bricks. From inscriptions Sir Henry Rawlinson found its name to be *The Temple of the Seven Planets*.[3] This ruin has been supposed to be what is left of the Tower of Babel.

The Jaredites at Moriancumer. According to the Book of Ether[4] the Jaredites began their journey by going northward into the Valley of Nimrod. In the course of their journey from this valley, they crossed many waters, — lakes and rivers — and eventually they came to "that great sea which divideth the lands," and there they pitched their tents and called the place Moriancumer (Ether 2:13) — probably after the brother of Jared, who was the head of the little colony. Here they remained for four years.

Jaredite Civilization. The Jaredites were far from being savages, or even barbarians, as those terms are used by modern writers. They were agriculturists familiar with "seeds of every kind" (Ether 2:3), and they also had "flocks of every kind" (Ether 2:1). They were hunters and trappers and bee-keepers,[5] and they understood how to utilize the food supply in the rivers and lakes, for, as part of their equipment for the journey into the wilderness "where there never had man been," they made a vessel "in which they did carry with them the fish of the waters." (Ether 2:2) All this indicates a civilization farther advanced than we generally give the people of the so-called stone age credit for. A people cultivating the soil, taking care of flocks, keeping bees, hunting and fishing and constructing boats (Ether 2:6) must have known a great variety of industries.[6]

But, as a further evidence of the high intellectual and spiritual level attained by the Jaredites, their records tell us that they had revelations of the most exalting

---

[3] *Assyrian Discoveries,* p. 59.
[4] Ether 1:42; 2:1.
[5] Their name for honey bee was *deseret,* a word which seems to have survived to our day in the Arabian *aseleth,* which also means "honey."
[6] According to Berosus it was the "fish god" Oannes who brought civilization to the Chaldeans out of the sea; which in modern language simply means that the discovery of the vast food resources of the sea was a long step forward on the high road to progress. Fish, and especially shell fish, were very abundant in the early ages, which is evident in the numerous shell heaps that are found both in the Old and the New World.

truths concerning God and man (Ether 3:15-20) which presupposes a high degree of intellectual and spiritual advancement.

Building Barges. At Moriancumer the Jaredites constructed eight barges, or vessels, in which they crossed the ocean. (Ether 2:16-21)

Let us note one remarkable circumstance connected with the building of these vessels. When they were completed, the question of illumination presented itself. The barges had no windows, and the travelers were not permitted to make a fire. The brother of Jared, consequently, prompted by the most sublime, childlike faith, presented the difficulty before the Lord. But the divine Architect, instead of giving his faithful servant direct instructions on the matter, referred the question back to him: "What will ye that I should do?" The ingenuity of the brother of Jared thus being put to the test, this great leader of men went up on a mountain, and there he did "molten" out of a rock sixteen small stones, clear and transparent. These he presented before the Lord, and asked him to make them luminous. God did so. He touched them with his finger, and they became light-bearers.[7]

Settlement in the Land of Promise. The first country settled in the Land of Promise was called Moron.[8] Where that country was, we know not, except that it was near the land which was called *Desolation*, by the Nephites. (Ether 7:6) From this center the Jaredites spread out in different directions, and became so numerous that there was no greater nation "upon all the face of the earth," according to the word of the Lord. (Ether 8:2)

Orson Pratt was of the opinion that "the [Jaredite] colony, . . . landed on the western coast of Mexico, and extended their settlements over all the North American portion of the continent, where they dwelt until about six centuries before Christ, when, because of wickedness they were all destroyed." (*Mill. Star*, Vol. 38, p. 693)

Very early in their history, the people made Orihah, the youngest son of Jared, their "king." He walked humbly before the Lord, exercised his judicial functions in righteousness, and lived a happy domestic life, being the father of thirty-one children.

Omer, the fourth successor of Jared, had a rebellious son, whom he had named Jared, and who left the country of Moron and established himself in the land of Heth. (Ether 8:2)

Omer, being warned in a dream to leave his country because of the secret combinations, "traveled many days and came over and passed by the Hill Shim, and came over by the place where the Nephites were destroyed, and from thence eastward, and came to a place which was called *Ablom*" (Ether 9:3), possibly after Abel. Here, Omer was joined, later, by Nimrah and his followers.

During a season of drought and famine, in the days of Heth, the eighth from Jared, many of the Jaredites fled "towards the land southward, which was called by the Nephites Zarahemla," and many perished, being attacked by poisonous serpents: nevertheless, "there were some who fled into the land southward." (Ether 9:30-33)

---

[7]It should be noted here that some scholars are of the opinion that the "window" which God commanded Noah to make for the ark, was just such a luminous stone. The word in the original is *tsohar*, which is said to mean something "bright," or "clear," and Jonathan Ben Uzziel understands it to mean a precious luminous stone, which Noah, by divine command, took from a certain river and carried into the ark. If this is correct, the brother of Jared merely asked that the Lord would do for him what he had done for that famous ancestor of the race.

[8]This name is in all probability akin to the name *Meron* (Josh. 12:20), now known as *Marun*. It may also be akin to *Maran* (Cor. 16:22), where it means "Our Lord." In passing it may be observed that "Maranatha," should be written "Marana tha," and be rendered, "Come, O our Lord." For it is, no doubt, the same expression which we find in the Rev. 22:20: "Come, Lord."

These were separated from the rest of the people, for the "Lord caused the serpents . . . that they should hedge the way that the people could not pass." (Ether 9:33)

Although the history of the Jaredites in the Book of Ether is merely a faint outline, it makes it clear that, while Moron was the center of interest to the historian, the people had spread from there in various directions. (Ether 6:18)

The first king of Moron was Orihah, the son of Jared.[9]

Shule was one of the great rulers of the Jaredites. His reign was exceedingly stormy, with wars and rebellions, and he fought with varying success, until he had overcome his enemies and given his people peace. He was a righteous judge and a wise law-giver, as well as a mighty warrior. But the spirit of prophecy had departed from the high office he held, and, consequently, when the Lord had a message to be delivered, he raised up somebody from the people to deliver it. (Ether 7:23)

The success of Shule as a warrior is attributed to his superior arms. The historian notes: "Wherefore, he came to the hill Ephraim, and he did molten out of the hill, and made swords out of steel for those whom he had drawn with him." (Ether 7:9)

Steel! The Jaredites, in all probability, did not know iron in the particular form which we call "steel," but from the earliest days of history the people had a metal which in the Old Testament Hebrew is called *nechushah* and *nechushet,* and which our Bible translators have rendered "steel" in four places, and "brass" twice. In Gen. 4:22 we read that Tubal-cain, a descendant of Cain, was an expert in "brass" (nechushah), and Job says of this metal that it is "molten" out of the stone, using an expression almost identical with that of Ether. In 2 Sam. 32:35, Job 20:24, Ps. 18:34 and Jer. 15:12 the same word has been rendered "steel." It means, in fact, neither. According to Gesenius it means copper, "mostly as hardened and tempered in the manner of steel and used for arms and other cutting instruments." That was the kind of "steel" that Tubal-cain converted into implements, and may also have been the kind that Shule used in making swords.[10]

The question of as to what extent hardened metal tools were used among the ancient Americans is not settled by scientists. Mr. Earl H. Morris, who has spent many years in archaeological research in New Mexico and Southern Colorado, in a letter to the author, dated Aztec, N. M., Dec. 27, 1920, kindly answers an inquiry thus:

"I have found but three examples of worked metal. These were small sub-spherical copper hawk bells such as were in common use among certain Old Mexican tribes in pre-Columbian periods. These bells undoubtedly were brought by trade together with parrot and macaw feathers from the distant south. Objects of iron, hammered or cast, have not been found in any ruins upon our continent. The aborigines of the area in which I have worked used hematite and similar oxides of iron for ornaments and for pigments. In the manufacture of the former, the natural

---

[9]The following list of rulers is given in the Book of Ether:

Orihah	Com	Levi	Aaron	Ahah
Kib	Heth	Corom	Amnigaddah	Ethem
Shule	Shez	Kish	Coriantum	Moron
Omer	Riplakish	Lib	Com	Coriantor
Emer	Morianton	Hearthom	Shiblon	
Coriantum	Kim	Heth	Seth	

The last ruler, the contemporary of Ether, the prophet, was Corianthumr. (Ether 12:1)

[10]This narrative takes us back to the beginning of the bronze age. How far back the use of iron can be traced in this country is another question. J. W. Foster says that in shell heaps at Grand Lake on the Teche have been found "unique specimens of axes of hematite iron ore," and that they were found in mounds covered with soil in which large oaks were growing and had been growing for centuries. (*Prehis. Races of the United States,* p. 159)

pebble was reduced to the desired form by abrasion, a gritty sandstone being the usual abrading implement employed.

"I recall that two or three copper beads were also found in the great ruin at this place—Aztec, N. Mex."

On the other hand, Mr. A. Hyatt Verrill, who is connected with the Museum of the American Indian, Heye Foundation, New York, and who has discovered remarkable ruins in Panama, reports in an article in *World's Work* for January, 1927, that he is convinced that the people who built there, as well as many other prehistoric races, possessed iron or steel tools. How, he asks, can one explain the evidence of tool marks on much of the stone work? Not the irregular indentations which have been, and very likely were, made by pecking with a stone hammer, but clearly cut, delicate lines and chisel marks?

He further says:

"Indeed, less than two years ago, I was scoffed at for suggesting that an entirely new and unknown culture of great antiquity had existed in Panama, but we now have undeniable proofs of the fact. Moreover, at a depth of five and one-half feet below the surface, at the temple site, among broken pottery and embedded in charcoal, I found a steel or hardened iron implement. The greater portion is almost completely destroyed by corrosion, but the chisel-shaped end is in good condition. It is so hard that it is scarcely touched by a file and will scratch glass, and with such an implement it would be a simple matter to cut and carve the hardest stone."

We can, it seems to me, safely accept the statements in the Book of Mormon on this subject and wait for further scientific discoveries.

Coriantumr. The last king of Moron was Coriantumr. In his day the country was the scene of incessant warfare. It was invaded by Shared, by Gilead, a brother of Shared; by Lib, and by Shiz, his brother, in succession, and so fierce were the conflicts during these invasions that two million men and many women and children perished. (Ether 15:2) Coriantumr, appalled at the loss of life, made overtures for peace, but in vain. The opposing armies then took up strong positions near the hill Ramah. For four years Coriantumr and Shiz prepared themselves for a decisive battle. Each gathered together his followers, "that they might get all who were upon the face of the land, and that they might receive all the strength which it was possible that they could receive." (Ether 15:14) Even women and children were conscripted (v. 15), as in our first and second world wars. The outcome of that battle was that both armies were annihilated. (Ether 15:15-32) Shiz was slain. Coriantumr escaped and eventually reached the country of Zarahemla. (Omni 21)

All Jaredites not slain. The general understanding, we believe, is that the entire Jaredite race was exterminated in this sanguinary battle, with the exception of Coriantumr. It is, of course, possible that the narrative is to be so understood, but the probability is that the prophet only refers to the annihilation of the two armies and the end of the monarchial form of government.

At the time of the battle of Ramah there must have been probably millions of Jaredites in this hemisphere; that is evident from the fact that two million souls had perished four years before that battle. But it would be absurd to suppose that every Jaredite, man, woman, and child, old and young, sick, and cripples, as well as strong and well-informed individuals, were enlisted in the armies and encamped around the hill. It would, furthermore, be contrary to human experience to suppose that there were no desertions from the armies during the long and deadly encounters. It is much more probable that some escaped and, when missing, were counted as dead. Again, is it improbable that some of the wounded recovered and survived, without any record being made of their recovery? We know, from Ether 9:32, that some Jaredites escaped into the "land southward," during the famine in the days of King Heth, and they must also have become numerous, and, possibly, were not directly interested in the war between Shiz and Coriantumr.

It is very customary to speak of an entire nation when we mean only the more important part of it. We say, for instance, that the kingdom of Judah was carried away into captivity, when, as a matter of fact, only a small portion, though an important one, was transported to Babylon. Thus, in the first captivity, 598 B.C., the Babylonians carried away 3,023 souls, leaving the common people in their homes. Ten years later, 832 captives, and in 584 B.C., 745 more were expatriated— 4,600 in all;[11] or, if these figures give only the number of men, say 15,000, including women and children. In the same way we speak of the return of the captives, when, as a matter of fact, only half of them, 31,629, according to one estimate, and 42,360, according to another, left the land of captivity.[12]

Furthermore, it seems to me that some Indian traditions regarding the migration of their forefathers, some of their religious ideas, especially the place of the heavenly bodies and the serpents in their symbolism, and many linguistic peculiarities point to a Jaredite origin, which cannot be explained on the supposition that the entire race perished.

Destruction does not always mean extermination. We speak of the destruction of Jerusalem and of the Jews (1 Nephi 10:3), but they still exist. Compare 2 Nephi 25:9 where the Jews are said to have been destroyed "from generation to generation."

If we set Bishop Usher's chronolgy aside as too short,[13] and assume that the building of the Tower and the dispersion took place about 2,500 B.C., and if the battle of Ramah took place not long after the arrival of the Mulekites in America, the history of the Jaredites in the book of Ether covers a period of about nineteen centuries. During all that time the people built cities, cultivated the ground, engaged in arts, industries, and trade; they lived, loved, and died, until, because of moral degeneration, their governments were broken up and their countries made desolate, through famine, pestilence, and war.

Jaredites had time to increase. Nineteen centuries may not be a long period in the history of the earth, but what a multitude of events are crowded into 1900 years of human records! Or even much less time than that! Here is an illustration.

In 1865 one of the famous big trees in Calaveras County, Cal., was cut down. Edgar de la Rue calculated that it began to grow about 620 A.D. Then he went over history to see what had happened during the lifetime of that venerable tree. His article found its way into print, in the form of a dispatch dated Red Bluff, Cal., Feb. 4, 1922.

The tree was born about the time Mohammedanism began to take root, and we may add, when papacy was established by the imperial decree of Emperor Phocas,[14] in A.D. 607. It was 110 years old when the battle of Tours was fought. Figuratively speaking, the tree saw the introduction of Christianity in Scandinavia in 830; the beginning of the reign of Alfred the Great in England; the crusades; the signing of the Magna Charta in 1220; and the conquest of Wales in 1280. The tree was growing

---

[11]Flinders Petri, *Egypt and Israel,* p. 81.

[12]Ezra 2:6-65; Nehemiah 7:6-67.

[13]Short correctly observes that the authors of the Bible do not profess to give a complete chronolgy or even to furnish data for an infallible system. Their accounts are condensed. In their genealogies they leave out several generations, which can be seen if we compare the genealogy of our Lord as given in the Gospels with those of the Old Testament. Their purpose was not to give a complete list of descendants, but to prove descent through a certain line, and their condensed lists serve that purpose only. (*See* Short's *North Americans of Antiquity,* p. 199)

32. And now, my son, remember the words which I have spoken unto you; trust not those secret plans unto this people, but teach them an everlasting hatred against sin and iniquity.

33. Preach unto them repentance, and faith on the Lord Jesus Christ; teach them to humble themselves and to be meek and lowly in heart; teach them to withstand every temptation of the devil, with their faith on the Lord Jesus Christ.

34. Teach them to never be weary of good works, but to be meek and lowly in heart; for such shall find rest to their souls.

35. O, remember, my son, and learn wisdom in thy youth; yea, learn in thy youth to keep the commandments of God.

36. Yea, and cry unto God for all thy support; yea, let all thy doings be unto the Lord, and whithersoever thou goest let it be in the Lord; yea, let thy thoughts be directed unto the Lord; yea, let the affections of thy heart be placed upon the Lord forever.

37. Counsel with the Lord in all thy doings, and he will direct thee for good; yea, when thou liest down at night lie down unto the Lord, that he may watch over you in your sleep; and when thou risest in the morning let thy heart be full of thanks unto God; and if ye do these things, ye shall be lifted up at the last day.

---

and developing when Columbus discovered America, in 1492, and when Balboa, in 1520, first viewed the Pacific Ocean. The tree was 1030 years old when Oliver Cromwell was made Protector; and had reached the age of 1,156 years when America's Declaration of Independence was signed, in 1776. It was, finally, 1,244 years old at the close of the Civil War, in 1865, when it was cut down. If to this age of a tree we add six or seven centuries for the history of the Jaredites, we can form an idea of the immensity and infinite diversity of the contents of that history, of which only a fraction, and that in mere outline, has been handed down to us.

Consider, also, that it is about 1900 years since the Christian religion, itself, was revealed. Think for yourself, the things that have happened since that event.

VERSES 32-37. *Counsel with the Lord in all thy doings, and He will direct thee for good.* In these verses Alma in exhorting Helaman to ever be faithful to the truths "which I have spoken unto you," is Solomon-like in his advice to his son. We are reminded of the wise old Hebrew king: My son, forget not my law; but let thine heart keep my commandments. (Proverbs 3:1) Never mind telling our people what the "secret plans" of the Jaredites were; burden the Nephites not with the story of their folly, but "teach them an everlasting hatred against sin and iniquity." "Preach repentance, and faith on the Lord Jesus Christ," were among the instructions Alma gave. Counsel with the Lord in all thy doings, and He will direct thee for good. Another of King Solomon's Proverbs comes to our minds: In all thy ways acknowl-

---

14Boniface III was a deacon of the Roman church, who in 603 was sent to Constantinople by Gregory the Great as a legate (*apocrissarius*). There he supported Phocas, an usurper of the throne of the vilest character, and in return when Boniface had been elected pope, in 607, Phocas issued, at his request, a decree against Cyriacus, bishop of Constantinople, in which it was ordained that "the see of blessed Peter, the apostle, should be the head of all the churches," and that the title "universal bishop" belonged exclusively to the bishop of Rome. And this was, evidntly, the keystone in the arch of apostasy.

edge Him, and He shall direct thy paths. (Proverbs 3:6) The counsel of the Lord is with them that fear Him, and we must not forget to quote again: Ye that fear the Lord, trust in the Lord.

3. The Liahona a type of the Word of Christ.

38. And now, my son, I have somewhat to say concerning the thing which our fathers call a ball, or director—or our fathers called it Liahona, which is, being interpreted, a compass; and the Lord prepared it.

39. And behold, there cannot any man work after the manner of so curious a workmanship. And behold, it was prepared to show unto our fathers the course which they should travel in the wilderness.

40. And it did work for them according to their faith in God; therefore, if they had faith to be-

lieve that God could cause that those spindles should point the way they should go, behold, it was done; therefore they had this miracle, and also many other miracles wrought by the power of God, day by day.

41. Nevertheless, because those miracles were worked by small means it did show unto them marvelous works. They were slothful, and forgot to exercise their faith and diligence and then those marvelous works ceased, and they did not progress in their journey;

VERSES 38-46. *And now, my son, I have somewhat to say concerning the thing which our fathers call a ball, or director, or our fathers called it Liahona —.*

LIAHONA. This interesting word is Hebrew with an Egyptian ending. It is the name which Lehi gave to the ball or director he found outside his tent the very day he began his long journey through the "wilderness," after his little company had rested for some time in the Valley of Lemuel. (I Nephi 16:10; Alma 37:88)

L is a Hebrew preposition meaning "to," and sometimes used to express the possessive case. *Iah* is a Hebrew abbreviated form of "Jehovah," common in Hebrew names. *On* is the Hebrew name of the Egyptian "City of the Sun," also known as Memphis and Heliopolis. *L-iah-on* means, therefore, literally, "To God is Light"; or, "of God is Light." That is to say, God gives light, as does the Sun. The final *a* reminds us that the Egyptian form of the Hebrew name *On* is *Annu*,* and that seems to be the form Lehi used.

Lehi had just received the divine command to begin his perilous journey. The question uppermost in his mind, after having received that call, must have been how to find the way. That must have been quite a problem. But he arose early in the morning, determined to carry out the command given. Undoubtedly he had prayed all night for light and guidance. And now, standing in the opening of the tent, perhaps as the first rays of the sun broke through the morning mists, his attention is attracted by a metal ball "of curious workmanship." He picks it up and examines it. And then, as he realizes that it is the guide for which he had been praying, he exclaims in ecstacy, *L-iah-on-a!* Which is as much as to say, This is

---

*Dr. E. A. Wallis Budge, *Gods of the Egyptians*, Vol. 1, p. 100.

God's delight; it has come from him! And that became the name of the curious instrument. This was not a compass. It was a miraculously formed instrument which served both as compass and actant.

Now, the fact is that this manner of giving names was an ancient Semitic custom. Hagar, when her son was perishing in the wilderness and she beheld the angel by the life-giving spring, exclaimed, *Beer-lachai-roi!* which means, literally, "Well, to live, to see." That is to say, "the well of him that liveth and seeth me," for that was the thought that came to her mind. (Gen. 16:13-14) And that became the name of the well. In the same way, Abraham called the place where he had offered Isaac on the altar, *Jehovah-jireh,* "the Lord will provide"; because the Lord did provide for himself a ram instead of Isaac, as Abraham had assured his son the Lord would do. (Gen. 27:7-8) And that became the name of the Mount "to this day."

Lehi gave the metal ball a name commemorative of one of the great experiences of his life, just as these Old Testament worthies had done. And, furthermore, he gave it a name that no one but a devout Hebrew influenced by Egyptian culture would have thought of. Is that not the strongest possible evidence of the truth of the historic part of the Book of Mormon?

VERSE 39. *And behold, it was prepared to show unto our fathers the course which they should travel in the wilderness.* The Prophet Nephi in recording the events connected with the acquisition of this ball of "curious workmanship," says: And thus my father had fulfilled all the commandments of the Lord which had been given him. And also, I, Nephi, had been blessed of the Lord exceedingly. And it came to pass that the voice of the Lord spake unto my father by night, and commanded him that on the morrow he should take his journey into the wilderness. And it came to pass that as my father arose in the morning, and went forth to the tent door, to his great astonishment he beheld upon the ground a round ball of curious workmanship; and it was of fine brass. And within the ball were two spindles; and the one pointed the way whither we should go into the wilderness. (I Nephi 16:8-10)

Lehi had received a command to start on his journey on the morrow. Naturally, his great concern was how to find the road through the wilderness, and how to avoid encounters with those who might prove enemies. Ezra, in leading a large company of his countrymen from Babylon to Jerusalem, was confronted with a similar problem. He could have obtained an armed escort from the king, but because he had told the ruler that the Lord would protect them, he was, as he says, ashamed to ask the king for a band of soldiers, thereby proving that his faith in Jehovah had no practical value. Ezra gathered his company, instead, at the River Ahavah, and for three days they fasted and prayed for guidance and protection. Then they set out on their perilous journey. "And the hand of our God," Ezra says, "was upon us, and He delivered us from the hand of the enemy, and of such as lay in wait by the way." (Ezra 9:15-23, 31-32) As for Lehi the problem of guidance and protection from robbers was solved in a most remarkable way. He was up early in the morning. As he stood by the opening of his tent, undoubtedly wondering what course to take in his journey, he perceived a ball lying on the ground before the tent door. He picked it up and found, on examining it, that it contained two spindles, one of which pointed the way "whither we should go." That solved the problem. The spindle indicated the general direction, and also where to go to find food and safety from robber bands.

VERSES 40-41. *And it did work for them according to their faith in God.* Lehi's journey was thus continued for a long time. The company would travel for a few days, then rest and hunt, then again take up their directed course as the compass indicated. It generally guided them through the most fertile portions of the great desert. Their journeys appear to be frequently disturbed by the actions of Laman and Lemuel and of those who would heed them.

An incident of this recurring mutiny led by Nephi's older brothers is recorded in Chapter 16, I Nephi, beginning with the 18th verse. There it is stated that Nephi broke his bow which was made of fine steel. His brothers became angry with him because of it; a scarcity of food and subsequent famine threatened the camp.

Presently, Laman and Lemuel began an agitation against their brother. They were joined by the sons of Ishmael, and also by Father Lehi. Even a prophet of the Lord may make mistakes. The dissatisfaction towards Nephi soon became open rebellion against God (I Nephi 16:22). This brought Nephi out in defense of the Lord. "I, Nephi, spoke much unto my brethren, because they had hardened their hearts again." Note that Nephi did not rebuke his father.

The next step of Nephi was to make a bow of wood, and to prepare a sling and to gather suitable stones. Thus equipped, he asked his father for instructions as to where to go to find game. Nephi recognized the authority of his father as head of the family.

Lehi now truly repentant for his rash actions in criticizing with others conditions unfortunately brought about, sought the Lord in this time of trouble. He went before his Maker in all humility, with sorrow in his heart.

Arrows and slings. At the time of Lehi, the Jews were not, generally speaking, great hunters. In the early days, the pursuit of wild beasts either for the protection of the domestic animals and the cultivated fields, or for food, was a common occupation, both necessary and dangerous. We read of Nimrod, the "mighty hunter before the Lord" (Gen. 10:8, 9); Esau was a "cunning hunter," a man of the field (Gen. 25:27), skilled in the use of the bow (Gen. 27:3). But generally the Hebrews in later times did not practise archery for hunting or for sport. The bow and the arrow became weapons of war, the playthings of soldiers and rulers in times of peace. To use either the bow or the sling successfully, it was necessary to possess great strength and long practice.

These facts account for the predicament of Nephi and his brothers. They were not really skilled archers. Or, their bows may not have been of the best material, or make. Or, they may not have understood how to take good care of them, since they were out of commission at this early stage of the journey.

At all events, Nephi was inspired to come to the rescue. The Lord could use him as his instrument. The older brothers, who ought to have had the knowledge and experience necessary to overcome the difficulty, proved their weakness by their inactivity and grumbling. Nephi proved his strength by his activity.

Slings. These were also effective weapons in the hands of a youth, like Nephi. The story of David and Goliath was well known by these boys. (I Sam. 17:32-53)

At the time of the Judges, the men of the tribe of Benjamin were celebrated for their skill as stone slingers. "Among all this people there were seven hundred chosen men lefthanded; every one could sling stones at an hairbreadth and not miss." (Judges 20:16)

God's answer. Nephi had asked his father for instructions as to where to go to find game. Lehi presented the matter before the Lord. God then dirted him to look upon the ball. Just what was written is not stated, but it had the effect of causing Lehi, his older sons, the sons of Ishmael, and the women to fear exceedingly. They were evidently unnerved by that emotion.

Nephi, then looked and discovered (1) that the pointers worked according to the faith and diligence and heed which were given unto them; (2) that the Lord would instruct them from time to time by means of the pointers concerning His ways; and (3) that the instructions asked for, as where to go to find food, were given.

Nephi did not linger now. He immediately followed the directions that were given. The result was that he obtained the needed provisions, and there was joy in the camp. Peace was again established; the necessary foodstuffs prepared for cartage, and Lehi's little company continued its journey "for the space of many days."

Another instance of Divine disfavor is recorded in I Nephi 18:1-22. After eight years of traveling in which they were delayed many times by the faithlessness of some of their numbers, Lehi's company came to the open sea. They named it *Irreantum*, which name means many waters. The land on its shores they called *Bountiful*, because of its much fruit and wild honey. While they rested upon the sea shore the Lord gave Nephi a new command. It was that he should build a ship to carry the company across the ocean. As we may suppose, Nephi's brothers made light of the undertaking when they found he was about to try building a ship. But this did not deter him in commencing such a task. He knew that God never told a man to do a thing but that He gave him power so to do. It was so in this case. The Lord revealed to Nephi all that was necessary, and the building of the ship was commenced.

At first Nephi's brothers would not help him in the least. They treated him as the people did Noah when he was building the ark. They called him a fool, and mocked him, and then threatened to throw him into the sea. But the power of God was so strong upon Nephi that had they attempted to carry out their rash purpose they would have withered before him like a dried reed. As it was, when he stretched forth his hand towards them, they felt a shock which made their whole frames quake. This convinced them that God was with their brother, for no man could have such power unless God was with him. After this they went to work and helped Nephi build the ship; and a good ship it was for the Lord had directed the way in which it should be fashioned.

When the vessel was finished the Lord told Lehi and his people to go on board. They took with them fruit, meat, honey, and other food in abundance, with many other things needful for their comfort; also seeds to plant in the soil of the new Promised Land. Then they all embarked — men, women, and children — beginning at the eldest down to the last. A favorable wind sprang up and they were swiftly carried towards their goal.

But on the voyage they had another of those ever-recurring outbreaks. Laman and Lemuel together with some of Ishmael's sons and others, at one time grew very merry. By and by they became boisterous and rude. They danced and sang and talked improperly. Nephi reproved them. This opened the old sore. They said that they would not have him for their ruler, but would do as they pleased. Then they seized and bound him, hands and feet, so tightly that it caused him much pain. The result was that the Lord was angry and the compass ceased to work. A heavy storm arose, a head wind drove them back upon the waters, the waves threatened to engulf them, and they were all in danger of being drowned. For three days the rebels continued stubborn in their anger and merrymaking; during that time they would not release Nephi from his bonds, and every one that pled for him or spoke in his favor was threatened with like tortures. At last, however, the danger grew so threatening that they released him; but his legs and arms had swollen so greatly by reason of the way in which he had been tied that he could scarcely use them. Notwithstanding his great weakness and suffering, as soon as he was loosed and took the compass in his hands, it began to work. Then the wind

42. Therefore, they tarried in the wilderness, or did not travel a direct course, and were afflicted with hunger and thirst, because of their transgressions.

43. And now, my son, I would that ye should understand that these things are not without a shadow; for as our fathers were slothful to give heed to this compass (now these things were temporal) they did not prosper; even so it is with things which are spiritual.

---

fell, the storm ceased, and there came a great calm. And Nephi took charge of the ship and guided it without further trouble to the Promised Land.

The "compass" is the round ball of curious workmanship described in I Nephi 16:10. Some have assumed that the term was meant to convey the idea that Lehi, more than 500 years B. C. had the mariners' instrument which is supposed to have been unknown in the western world until the 12th century A. D., and that "compass" therefore, is an anachronism which furnishes evidence of the very human origin of the Book of Mormon. But that reasoning disregards two facts: First, that the "compass" in question was not the magnetic instrument of the mariner, but a special contrivance which pointed the way they were to go, and that only in response to the faith of the sailor; secondly, that the word "compass" is a good English word, meaning not only the mariners' instrument but a circle or a globe in general, a round, a circuit. In Numbers 34:5 and Joshua 15:13, it refers to the bend in the southern boundary line of the land of Israel, "from Azmon unto the river of Egypt" and from there to the sea. Luke, in Acts 28:13 uses the term for the course steered by the ship from Syracuse to Rhegium. In Exodus 27:5 and 38:4, it means the inside rim of the altar to which a metal net, or grate, was fastened, evidently in order to protect the wood work of the altar. In 2 Samuel 5:23 and 2 Kings 3:9, to "fetch a compass" means to surround a portion of the army of an enemy. In Proverbs 8:23, "compass" refers to the circular horizons, and in Isaiah 44:13 to the compasses of a sculptor. It is clear from these references that the term as applied in the Book of Mormon to the little round ball of Lehi is correct. It is not an anachronism.

VERSES 42-43. These things are not without a shadow. In the journey of Lehi's company during the eight years that elapsed between the time when it left Jerusalem until it reached Irreantum, its members spent much of that period needlessly in delays caused by transgressions. The compass, or Liahona, simply would not work, nor would it show those who depended upon its instructions, which way to go in their further travels. Delay after delay, because of Laman's and Lemuel's truculence, lengthened out the time of the already arduous trek across the Arabian Desert. Time and time once more, they set their own feelings above God's commands. Again and again, they kindled their wrath against their righteous father and brother because of their righteousness. Their actions hindered the progress of the little company both spiritually and temporally. But, in spite of it all, the Lord preserved them, showing His loving-kindness and watchful care, even to those who disobeyed Him, providing them with food and water when needed, but always protecting those who served Him.

Alma saw a resemblance in following the Lord, thereby doing His will, to the

---

Some amusing anachronisms are on record. Shakespeare furnishes a few. For instance, he makes a "clock" in "Julius Caesar" strike three, long before anyone had heard of a striking clock. In Thackeray's "Esmond," in 1712 a book published in 1750 is mentioned. Schiller, in Piccolomini, has a lightning rod 150 years before it was invented.

44. For behold, it is as easy to give heed to the word of Christ, which will point to you a straight course to eternal bliss, as it was for our fathers to give heed to this compass, which would point unto them a straight course to the promised land.

45. And now I say, is there not a type in this thing? For just as surely as this director did bring our fathers, by following its course, to the promised land, shall the words of Christ, if we follow their course, carry us beyond this vale of sorrow into a far better land of promise.

46. O my son, do not let us be slothful because of the easiness of the way; for so was it with our fathers; for so was it prepared for them, that if they would look they might live; even so it is with us. The way is prepared, and if we will look we may live forever.

47. And now, my son, see that ye take care of these sacred things, yea, see that ye look to God and live. Go unto this people and declare the word, and be sober. My son, farewell.

Compass or Director which showed unto Lehi the way to go in his exodus from Jerusalem. He impressed upon Helaman the idea that temporal blessings came to their fathers when they yielded obedience to the directions upon the ball. They guided Lehi's colony to the Promised Land, and that by the shortest route. Even so, spiritual blessings may be had, he solemnly promised Helaman, if obedience were given to the Lord's commands. "For," he said, "as our fathers were slothful to give heed to this compass (now these things were temporal) they did not prosper; even so it is with things which are spiritual."

VERSES 44-45. *It is as easy to give heed to the word of Christ, . . . as it was for our fathers to give heed to this compass.* Alma, in speaking to his son, Helaman, drew this remarkable conclusion that in the same manner as Lehi and his followers were obedient in carrying out the instructions that were written on the Liahona, just so it is in obeying the words of Christ. They, by doing as told, were led to the Promised Land. We, by following the course offered by God's commands, it shall 'carry us beyond this vale of sorrow into a far better land of promise."

VERSES 46-47. *Do not let us be slothful because of the easiness of the way.* As it was with our fathers, the Children of Israel, in their great exodus from Egypt, a *Serpent*, representing God, was raised up in their midst that whomsoever should look with faith in His coming would be saved. Now, Alma implied, to follow Christ's words is as easy for us to do as it was for them to offer that bit of reverence. A *Way* is prepared for us, just as a way was prepared for them, "and if we will look we may live forever."

In ending his instructions to Helaman, Alma enjoined him to take care of 'these sacred things," and do as the Children of Israel did, "look to God and live." Preach the word of God unto the people, and be sober, which we may understand to mean, be longsuffering, be just, be patient, showing loving-kindness to all, be prayerful and diligent in every way.

CHAPTER 38

THE COMMANDMENTS OF ALMA TO HIS SON, SHIBLON

1. *Commended for Faithfulness, and Counseled to Observe Meekness and Self-control.*

1. *Commended for faithfulness, and counseled to observe meekness and self-control.*

1. My son, give ear to my words, for I say unto you, even as I said unto Helaman, that inasmuch as ye shall keep the commandments of God ye shall prosper in the land; and inasmuch as ye will not keep the commandments of God ye shall be cast off from his presence.

2. And now, my son, I trust that I shall have great joy in you, because of your steadiness and your faithfulness unto God; for as you have commenced in your youth to look to the Lord your God, even so I hope that you will continue in keeping his commandments; for blessed is he that endureth to the end.

3. I say unto you, my son, that I have had great joy in thee already, because of thy faithfulness and thy diligence, and thy patience and thy long-suffering among the people of the Zoramites.

VERSES 1-3. *I say unto you, even as I said unto Helaman.* In blessing his son, Shiblon, Alma repeated what he beforetime had promised Helaman when that worthy pronounced a father's blessing upon the head of his eldest son. To bless his sons, when age made uncertain the length of time a patriarch would dwell with his children here below, was a sacred rite which had been inherited by the Nephites from their forefathers, the Israelites who dwelt in the Land of Jerusalem. This promised blessing was first made by the Lord, Himself, to the Prophet Nephi and to all those who would keep the commandments of God, and it was oft repeated by His servants. It was that "inasmuch as ye shall keep the commandments of God ye shall prosper in the land; and inasmuch as ye will not keep the commandments of God ye shall be cast off from My presence." (Jarom 9; Omni 6; Mosiah 1-7)

The aged Alma, feeling that his time upon Earth was getting short, took delight, and great satisfaction in acknowledging to Shiblon that *his integrity and faithfulness unto God* brought his father unmeasurable joy. Shiblon was yet very young, but notwithstanding his youth, he evinced remarkable steadiness. His devotion to duty, his bearing toward those among whom he labored, his compassion for the afflicted, his patience under trial, his long-suffering when persecution threatened to rob him of his faith in God and in his calling, filled his father's heart with gladness. That Shiblon would always remain faithful in keeping the Lord's commandments was Alma's heartfelt desire, for he said, "Blessed is he that endureth to the end." Alma, a short time before this *father-son* episode, took Shiblon to Antionum to preach the Gospel of Christ to the Zoramites, and there he had seen manifest the rather uncommon qualities in Shiblon's character that made of him a great preacher of righteousness.

4. For I know that thou wast in bonds; yea, and I also know that thou wast stoned for the word's sake; and thou didst bear all these things with patience because the Lord was with thee; and now thou knowest that the Lord did deliver thee.

5. And now my son, Shiblon, I would that ye should remember, that as much as ye shall put your trust in God even so much ye shall be delivered out of your trials, and your troubles, and your afflictions, and ye shall be lifted up at the last day.

6. Now, my son, I would not that ye should think that I know these things of myself, but it is the Spirit of God which is in me which maketh these things known unto me; for if I had not been born of God I should not have known these things.

7. But behold, the Lord in his great mercy sent his angel to declare unto me that I must stop the work of destruction among his people; yea, and I have seen an angel face to face, and he spake with me, and his voice was as thunder, and it shook the whole earth.

8. And it came to pass that I was three days and three nights in the most bitter pain and anguish of soul; and never, until I did cry out unto the Lord Jesus Christ for mercy, did I receive a remission of my sins. But behold, I did cry unto him and I did find peace to my soul.

VERSE 4. *I know that thou wast in bonds.* What seemed to crown with God's favor, Shiblon's determination to serve the Lord completely, was Shiblon's fixed conclusion to walk undaunted in the path of duty and fidelity to his Maker even though it might cost him all that was near and dear to him. Imprisonment could not deter him in the fulfillment of his commitment to declare the Word of the Lord; and when stoned because of his testimony of Christ, he bore all obloquy with patience and never, in spite of threats, retracted his words. When Shiblon's mission among the apostate Zoramites was ended, and he, in retrospect, viewed again the scenes of his travail among them, he rendered thanks unto God, his Preserver, for he knew that no power but the Lord's kept and delivered him from the hatred of such blood-thirsty men as those who had forsaken the truth, and now were seeking to destroy the Church of God.

VERSE 5. *Put your trust in God.* As He had in the past, so in the future, God will deliver you out of your trials if you put your trust in Him. Just as in the exact ratio of the fear of Him that animates your being, just so will be the help and strength you will receive at His hands. "Ye that fear the Lord, trust in Him," is an old Jewish proverb, "He will not forsake you, nor leave you in your grief." This thought Alma impressed upon the youthful mind of Shiblon, and promised that whatsoever might come upon him the Spirit and power of God would deliver him and lead him "out of your trials, and your troubles, and your afflictions, and ye shall be lifted up at the Last Day."

VERSES 6-8. *It is the Spirit of God . . . which maketh these things known to me.* Not of himself, but by the Holy Spirit of God which was in him, and therein guided him into all truth, Alma emphasized, did he know these things. The old and perhaps well-known account of his father's miraculous conversion was again

9. And now, my son, I have told you this that ye may learn wisdom, that ye may learn of me that there is no other way or means whereby man can be saved, only in and through Christ. Behold, he is the life and the light of the world. Behold, he is the word of truth and righteousness.

10. And now, as ye have begun to teach the word even so I would that ye should continue to teach; and I would that ye would be diligent and temperate in all things.

11. See that ye are not lifted up unto pride; yea, see that ye do not boast in your own wisdom, nor of your much strength.

12. Use boldness, but not overbearance; and also see that ye bridle all your passions, that ye may be filled with love; see that ye refrain from idleness.

13. Do not pray as the Zoramites do, for ye have seen that they pray to be heard of men, and to be praised for their wisdom.

14. Do not say: O God, I thank thee that we are better than our brethren; but rather say: O Lord, forgive my unworthiness, and remember my brethren in mercy— yea, acknowledge your unworthiness before God at all times.

15. And may the Lord bless your soul, and receive you at the last day into his kingdom, to sit down in peace. Now go, my son, and teach the word unto this people. Be sober. My son, farewell.

---

cited by Alma to his son, Shiblon. It was this: a dramatic change had suddenly come into Alma's life. When before he had been rebellious, had rejected the truth, and even persecuted the righteous because of their righteousness, now all was changed. There was a change without, therefore there was a change within. The things Alma before had loved, he now hated, and what he once despised he now drew close to his bosom. Alma now loved the Lord, and sought with all his might to do His bidding. He was a different man, a new man. If he had been energetic in his wrong-doing, he was yet more active in his works of restitution. He testified to Shiblon "for if I had not been born of God I should not have known these things." (*See* Chapter 36:5-24, Book of Alma)

VERSE 9. *There is no other way or means whereby man can be saved, only in and through Christ.* Alma, personally, as father to son, testified to Shiblon the great truth that only through Christ, can man's salvation be wrought. "He is the life and the light of the world. Behold, He is the Word of Truth and Righteousness," he said, painting a vivid picture in Shiblon's mind of the greatness and the majesty of the Lord, thereby connoting, stirring, arousing, inspiriting and inspiring thoughts that all through life would lead Shiblon along wisdom's way. "That ye may learn of me" shows the intense confidence each (that is father and son) had in the word of the other.

VERSE 10. *I would that ye continue to teach.* Shiblon's decorum in the mission field among the Zoramites was ample proof to his father that Shiblon was prepared to continue the work of the ministry in teaching and admonishing unto righteousness. "Be diligent and temperate in all things"; by that Alma meant be zealous in your work, but temper your fervor in the things you proclaim with wisdom, "and be guided by regard for other men's faith."

VERSES 11-15. *See that ye are not lifted up in pride.* Alma's exhortations to

Shiblon recorded in these next verses were based upon instructions Alma was prepared to give to Corianton, one of his other sons. Many of Corianton's failings are here noted, not as faults in Corianton's behavior, but as things of such as Shiblon should beware. (*See* Chapter 39:1-2)

SHIBLON, SON OF ALMA

Shiblon "was a just man, and he did walk uprightly before God, and he did observe to do good continually, to keep the commandments of the Lord his God." Such is the high encomium passed upon the character of this son of Alma by the sacred historian of the Book of Mormon.

Shiblon, like his brothers Helaman and Corianton, is first mentioned in the sacred pages of the Book of Mormon in connection with the Zoramite mission of his father. Of his birth and his childhood we know nothing, but he was yet in his youth when his father called him to be one of the missionaries to the Land of Antionum. (75 B.C.)

Like the rest of his fellow-servants of the Lord, he received the Holy Spirit under the hands of his father, and then went forth in the spirit and might of his calling to proclaim the Gospel to the misguided and stiff-necked Zoramites. He labored in their midst with energy, faith, and patience, much to the joy of his father, Alma, who in the commandments he afterwards gave to his sons, commended Shiblon's course in the following language: "I say unto you, my son, that I have had great joy in thee already because of thy faithfulness and thy diligence, and thy patience, and thy long-suffering among the people of the Zoramites. For I know that thou wast in bonds; yea, and I also knew that thou wast stoned for the Word's sake; and thou didst bear all these things in patience, because the Lord was with thee; and now thou knowest that the Lord did deliver thee." These words of Alma are the only intimation that we have of the persecutions and sufferings endured by Shiblon at the hands of the followers of Zoram. The life of Shiblon appears to have been almost constantly occupied with the duties of his Priesthood. We do not read of him acting in any secular capacity, though it is presumable that like his father and the rest of his brethren, he labored with his hands to sustain himself during the short periods that intervened between his numerous missions. After the death of his father he was intimately associated with his elder brother Helaman and appears to have stood next to him in authority in the Church. We have no account of his taking part as a military officer (as did Helaman in the long-continued war that succeeded the apostasy of Amalickiah, but after the war was ended (60 B.C.) he ably seconded Helaman's efforts to re-establish the Church and set it in order. At Helaman's death Shiblon took possession of the "sacred things" (57 B.C.). These he held until his death which happened four years afterwards (53 B.C.), shortly before which event he conferred them upon his nephew Helaman, the son of his older brother.

The four years preceding Shiblon's death are principally noteworthy for the commencement of the Nephite migration to the northern continent. It was during this period that Hagoth established his ship-building yards on the borders of the Land Bountiful.

In the year that Shiblon died the Lamanites made another incursion into the lands of the Nephites but were quickly driven back to their own country after suffering great loss.

Shiblon must have died a comparatively young man. He was styled a youth when he went with his father to labor among the Zoramites and died twenty-two years after.

CHAPTER 39

THE COMMANDMENTS OF ALMA TO HIS SON, CORIANTON

1. *Corianton Reproved for Harlotry*—2. *His Sinful Conduct Had Affected the Faith of the Zoramites*—3. *Christ's Redemption Retroactive.*

1. *Corianton reproved for harlotry.*

1. And now, my son, I have somewhat more to say unto thee than what I said unto thy brother; for behold, have ye not observed the steadiness of thy brother, his faithfulness, and his diligence in keeping the commandments of God? Behold, has he not set a good example for thee?

2. For thou didst not give so much heed unto my words as did thy brother, among the people of the Zoramites. Now this is what I have against thee; thou didst go on unto boasting in thy strength and thy wisdom.

3. And this is not all, my son. Thou didst do that which was grievous unto me; for thou didst forsake the ministry, and did go over into the land of Siron, among the borders of the Lamanites, after the harlot Isabel.

4. Yea, she did steal away the hearts of many; but this was no excuse for thee, my son. Thou shouldst have tended to the ministry wherewith thou wast entrusted.

5. Know ye not, my son, that these things are an abomination in the sight of the Lord; yea, most abominable above all sins save it be the shedding of innocent blood or denying the Holy Ghost?

6. For behold, if ye deny the Holy Ghost when it once has had place in you, and ye know that ye deny it, behold, this is a sin which is unpardonable; yea, and whosoever murdereth against the light and knowledge of God, it is not easy for him to obtain forgiveness; yea, I say unto you, my son, that it is not easy for him to obtain a forgiveness.

VERSES 1-8. *And now, my son, I have somewhat more to say unto thee than what I said unto thy brother.* Corianton, Alma's youngest son, had been sent on a mission to the apostate Zoramites along with several others including his father and older brother, Shiblon, and had been led into abandoning his obligations there as one of God's servants to follow the meretricious charms of a harlot named Isabel who lived in the Land of Siron on the borders of the Lamanites.

He had left his field of labor in spite of the "good example" set him by his brother, who proved by his actions to be a steadfast and a faithful worker in that part of the Lord's Vineyard, and who also manifest the integrity of his heart by keeping the Lord's commandments.

We may seek to excuse and palliate Corianton's behavior in doing so by hiding the facts, and by offering apologies and pretexts which we may reinforce with arguments of his youth, but, nevertheless, the impetuosity of youth does not lead us

7. And now, my son, I would to God that ye had not been guilty of so great a crime. I would not dwell upon your crimes, to harrow up your soul, if it were not for your good.

8. But behold, ye cannot hide your crimes from God; and except ye repent they will stand as a testimony against you at the last day.

---

to believe that his years is anything but a pretext to cloak the real condition of his mind. Corianton, not only erred, but boasted in doing so. In the strength of his youth he went about exaggerating his prowess, and sought to impress others with his wisdom. All the time Corianton was thus indulging in self-heroics, Shiblon was undoubtedly taking care of the work of the ministry, humbly and unselfishly.

2. *His sinful conduct had affected the faith of the Zoramites.*

Corianton's infidelity not only brought infamy to himself, but public disgrace to his father and his missionary companions. The Zoramites, among whom they labored, were quick to grasp any and every reason to excuse their own actions, and therefore they seized upon his illicit relations with a prostitute as a ground on which to disclaim and deny his father's words. This attitude of the Zoramites toward his message caused great sorrow in Alma's heart, and in all likelihood hastened the missionaries' withdrawal from among them.

The enormity of Corianton's moral offense was pictured to him by his father who spared no words in impressing upon his youthful mind the extent to which he had been misguided. "Know ye not," Alma said to him, "that these things are an abomination in the sight of the Lord; yea, most abominable above all sins save it be the shedding of innocent blood or denying the Holy Ghost?"

When once the Holy Ghost has had place in you, or has imbued one with the knowledge of Its divine powers, it is unpardonable to deny those same powers. After that great Spirit has witnessed in the heart of man that *Jesus is Christ*, the knowledge of His divinity cannot wilfully be denied. That conviction, born of the *Third Member of the God-head* will remain forever a testimony, even to the humblest, that He, who was born in Bethlehem of Judea was, indeed, the Savior and the Redeemer of the world. To deny the truth after such a Witness has given evidence of it, makes one a liar, and the truth is not in him; a liar cannot enter the Kingdom of Heaven, therefore the sin is unpardonable.

And, again, whosoever may commit murder wherein one slays another, and does so despite the light and understanding of God which he has received through God's Spirit, can be forgiven only by Him Who is the Creator of the life he has taken. Murder, wherein innocent blood is shed, and sinning against the Holy Ghost, are sins not surpassed in enormity, or in exceeding wickedness, by any other transgression of God's laws. Next to those two offenses in greatly exceeding all bounds of iniquity is the occasion of Corianton's sin. It is most abominable in God's sight, and like *murder,* it is a child of hell.

A father's love for his children, even though the child concerned was at the present time wayward and loathe to take instruction, or prone not to accept wisdom, those divine qualities of tenderness and long-suffering evinced by most fathers are very deeply to be seen in this dialogue between the father, Alma, and his son, Corianton. There is no doubt that as Alma understood and realized the import of God's laws, and that they could not be broken with impunity, his sensibilities regarding any infraction of them were keen, and his feelings most poignant. "I would to God that ye had not been guilty of so great a crime," father Alma expressed his sorrowing

9. Now my son, I would that ye should repent and forsake your sins, and go no more after the lusts of your eyes, but cross yourself in all these things; for except ye do this ye can in nowise inherit the kingdom of God. Oh, remember, and take it upon you, and cross yourself in these things.

10. And I command you to take it upon you to counsel with your elder brothers in your undertakings; for behold, thou art in thy youth, and ye stand in need to be nourished by your brothers. And give heed to their counsel.

11. Suffer not yourself to be led away by any vain or foolish thing; suffer not the devil to lead away your heart again after those wicked harlots. Behold, O my son, how great iniquity ye brought upon the Zoramites; for when they saw your conduct they would not believe in my words.

12. And now the Spirit of the Lord doth say unto me: Command thy children to do good, lest they lead away the hearts of many people to destruction; therefore I command you, my son, in

---

judgment of Corianton's waywardness, but made a solemn promise to his son that only would he *dwell* upon his sins, not to (harry) persecute him by constant repetition or ill-treatment and annoyance, but would, for Corianton's own good, impress upon him the utter folly of the vain things he had sought. As many do today, Corianton evidently hoped to keep his actions secret, and by so doing withhold from the Great Judge at the Last Day all knowledge of his wrongdoing. "But, behold, ye cannot hide your crimes from God," Alma insisted to imprint upon Corianton's mind; your deeds are all known to Him, and unless a sincere repentance of them is made, they will stand as a witness against you when on that Judgment Day you shall appear before the Bar of God to be judged of Him for all you did while here on Earth.

VERSES 9-11. *Now my son, I would that ye should repent and forsake your sins.* The thought that Corianton's youth excused his actions found no place in Alma's heart, so he called upon his son to exercise the knowledge of good and evil he had received and thereafter choose the good. Repent and forsake sin, he entreated Corianton; follow no more "the lusts of your eyes," deny yourself the spurious joys and the follies of life. Seek happiness by doing the will of the Lord. "For except ye do this ye can in no wise inherit the Kingdom of God."

Alma also urgently petitioned Corianton to seek the counsel of "your elder brothers in your undertakings." Rely not upon your own wisdom and understanding; boast no more of thy strength for it is weakness when compared with God's. The experiences of his youth, his father implied, have been insufficient to make Corianton stand alone, but sustained by his elder brothers his weakness would become strength, and his understanding great. Therefore, Alma said, "Give heed to their counsel."

VERSES 12-14. *Command thy children to do good.* Alma being the Presiding High Priest of God's Church in Zarahemla, his children were looked upon to lead others in serving the Lord and keeping His commandments. The infidelity of which Corianton was guilty brought some of the Nephites to a place where they excused themselves in doing much wrong, and where they offered many pretexts in so doing.

3. Christ's redemption retroactive.

In speaking to Corianton of this unjustified departure from Church discipline Alma

the fear of God, that ye refrain from your iniquities;

13. That ye turn to the Lord with all your mind, might, and strength; that ye lead away the hearts of no more to do wickedly; but rather return unto them, and acknowledge your faults and that wrong which ye have done.

14. Seek not after riches nor the vain things of this world; for behold, you cannot carry them with you.

15. And now, my son, I would say somewhat unto you concern-ing the coming of Christ. Behold, I say unto you, that it is he that surely shall come to take away the sins of the world; yea, he cometh to declare glad tidings of salvation unto his people.

16. And now, my son, this was the ministry unto which ye were called, to declare these glad tidings unto this people, to prepare their minds; or rather that salvation might come unto them, that they may prepare the minds of their children to hear the word at the time of his coming.

---

warned his son that by committing whoredoms and other grievous sins, he had caused the Zoramites to reject his message. To quote Alma exactly: For when they saw your conduct they would not believe my words.

The sorrow in Alma's heart caused by Corianton's wilful behavior in its turn brought him comfort from above. How to meet this painful and perplexing problem had been a matter of prayer, and in answer to them the answer came to Alma: Command thy children to do good lest they lead away the hearts of many people to destruction. In obedience to God's command Alma ordered Corianton thusly: Therefore I command you, my son, in the fear of God, that ye refrain from your iniquities; That ye turn to the Lord with all your mind, might, and strength; that ye lead away the hearts of no more to do wickedly; but rather return unto them, and acknowledge your faults and that wrong which ye have done. Seek not after riches nor the vain things of this world; for behold, you cannot carry them with you.

VERSES 15-16. *And now, my son, I would say somewhat unto you concerning the coming of Christ.* At this period of his life Corianton appears to have been afflicted with a failing somewhat common to youth. He had an inflated idea of his own worth, an inordinate estimate of his strength and wisdom. Along with these weak-nesses, he was inclnied to scepticism, if not infidelity. He was a doubter of every-thing except his own supposed abilities. He marveled that the assurance of the coming of the Messiah should be given to men so long before His advent. His mind was worried concerning the resurrection of the dead, the restoration of all things, the eternal punishment of the sinner and other points of Gospel doctrine. He denied the justice of God in the condemnation of the evil doer, and sought to justify himself in sinning, on the plea of God's mercy.

Seeking to enlighten Corianton's mind concerning these things, Alma began a comprehensive explanation of them. He, first of all, spoke to Corianton of Christ: One who should surely come "to take away the sins of the world; yea, He cometh to declare glad tidings of Salvation unto His people."

Alma stressed upon Corianton's mind that to declare these *glad tidings* to the Zoramites was the ministry unto which he with his brothers had been called. His mission was to declare Christ's coming so that the people there would be prepared for that great event, and that their children also should be made ready "to hear the word at the time of His coming."

17. And now I will ease your mind somewhat on this subject. Behold, you marvel why these things should be known so long beforehand. Behold, I say unto you, is not a soul at this time as precious unto God as a soul will be at the time of his coming?

18. Is it not as necessary that the plan of redemption should be made known unto this people as well as unto their children?

19. Is it not as easy at this time for the Lord to send his angel to declare these glad tidings unto us as unto our children, or as after the time of his coming?

VERSES 17-19. *And now I will ease your mind somewhat on this subject.* The words contained in these verses are so plain that they need no comments. We will only say what we have said before that the Saints living before His advent looked forward to Christ's coming. We look backward. Both visions are equally efficacious.

CORIANTON, SON OF ALMA

Of Corianton's birth and death we have no record. With his brothers, he is first mentioned in the Book of Mormon at the time of the Zoramite apostasy, when, though young and inexperienced, his father took him on a mission to that people. At this period of his life Corianton appears to have been afflicted with a failing common to youth — an inordinate estimate of his own strength and wisdom and an inclination to scepticism, if not infidelity. He was a doubter of everything except his own supposed abilities. He marveled that the assurance of the coming of the Messiah should be given to men so long before his advent. His mind was worried concerning the resurrection of the dead, the restoration of all things, the eternal punishment of the sinner and other points of doctrine. He denied the justice of God in the condemnation of the evil doer and sought to justify himself in sinning, on the plea of God's mercy. Possessed of such a frame of mind as this, no wonder that he sinned. Notwithstanding that, Alma had imparted the Holy Spirit to him, like unto the rest of the brethren, when they started out to reclaim the Zoramites from their sin-satisfying apostasy, he deserted his field of labor and went over to the borders of the Lamanites to enjoy the sinful embraces of Isabel, of Siron, a harlot, whose meretricious charms had led many away from the paths of virtue. As might reasonably be expected this iniquitous conduct of Corianton placed a stumbling block in the way of his fellow laborers and caused many of the Zoramites to reject the light of the Gospel. Alma, in his "commandments" to Corianton, severely chided him for his sinful conduct, pointed out the awful criminality of his course and entered into a lengthy explanation of the doctrines Corianton doubted or denied.

From the tenor of Corianton's after life we judge that he sincerely repented of his youthful follies and unbelief. We find that during his father's lifetime he accompanied him on his missionary travels, and after Alma's death he labored under the direction of his brother Helaman. He survived both his elder brothers and at the time of Shiblon's death (53 B.C.) was in North America, whither he had gone in a ship to carry provisions to the settlers. This is the last time his name is mentioned in the sacred pages.

We infer from the manner in which the statement is made, that if Corianton had been in Zarahemla at the time of Shiblon's death, the latter would have transferred the records and other sacred things to his charge, instead of to their nephew, Helaman; if this be so, it is evident that by his later life he had proved himself worthy of such a high honor.

CHAPTER 40

1. *Alma to Corianton continued.*

2. *Resurrection universal.*

1. Now my son, here is somewhat more I would say unto thee; for I perceive that thy mind is worried concerning the resurrection of the dead.

2. Behold, I say unto you, that there is no resurrection—or, I would say, in other words, that this mortal does not put on immortality, this corruption does not put on incorruption — until after the coming of Christ.

VERSE 1. *I perceive thy mind is worried concerning the resurrection of the dead.* Among the many teachings of the Gospel of Jesus Christ which we bear to the world, there are none that have created more speculation, or we might say, that have caused men to ponder a subject in its different aspects and relations, as much as has the doctrine of the resurrection of the dead. The fact that there is a resurrection of the dead is plainly noted by every believer in Christ, but the metaphysics of how our bodies will be raised from the grave has brought forth many arguments both pro and con. Skeptics delight to twist and turn every promise made to us concerning the certainty of this grand and remarkable experience. Believers exultingly proclaim it, the incredulous, with equal fervor, deny it. We may imagine that Paul in preaching it to the Corinthians introduced his paean in praise to God for this great triumph over death by declaring it thusly: You may wonder at it, ye sophists of Greece and you incredulous of Rome, but this poor body that you see, with all its certain traces of death, shall be swallowed up in everlasting and glorious victory. "O death," he said, "where is thy sting? O grave, where is thy victory?" And then, in a most triumphant voice, he shouted, "Thanks be to God, which giveth us the victory through our Lord Jesus Christ." (Corinthians 15:55-57) (*See* COMMENTARY ON THE BOOK OF MORMON, Vol. III, p. 179 ff.)

We imagine that there was in the time of Alma, as there is today, a group of individuals who deny and deride everything that is not discernible by the senses which they limit to five.

We may be pardoned if we quote from the above reference:

Among the many teachings of the Savior's Gospel which modern Christian philosophy has surrounded with mysticism is the resurrection of man's mortal body from the grave. Men do not agree on even the most fundamental reasoning. One say one thing, another something else; what one denies, others affirm most emphatically. And so on, until at present, all who listen to the pros and cons of debate are drawn into a labyrinth of inconsistent and opposing doctrine. The confusion caused by these divergent opinions, and the perplexity of mind this disunity creates, are affected by men who refuse to accept the truths set forth in their own Bibles. They wrest each passage of scripture to suit their personal ideas. They give theory superiority over fact, and allow supposition to dominate eternal truth. Of such a course there can be but one general result. The late President Brigham H. Roberts of the First Council of the Seventy, in his book, *The Gospel*, points to it: "Death to belief in the Bible; death to it as the inspired and revealed word of God."

Many of the critics of Christian doctrines are professional skeptics, or hypocrites, who love to find fault with our established beliefs and doctrines. They attack our most sacred heritage. To dignify their diatribes they say that if we explain to them the several questions which they, themselves, have created, then they will believe our dogmas; that then they will regard the doctrine of Christ's Atonement, which encompasses the doctrine of the resurrection of the dead, as acceptable to them.

What they ask us to do — we who believe by *faith* — they, themselves, cannot do in their religion which, they boast, is founded upon *sight*.

Before they demand from us a complete analysis of our beliefs, let them, first, explain to us many of the phenomena that abound today in natural religion of any kind. Let them explain, "What is life." There are manifestations that it exists all about us. We experience it; we see its effects; we hope for it. Yet, what it is, we do not know. Perhaps they will tell us, "What is death?" or, explain that little corridor that divides the living from the dead. Perhaps, too, they will explain why it is that two plants placed side by side in a field, each produce, the one wheat, the other barley. Their roots intermingle in the same coarse sand; the same raindrops refresh the parched earth in which they grow; the same sunbeams warm the delicate leaves of both. Yet, one produces wheat, the other barley. How is it? Again, we do not know. But we would think it strange; we would think him deranged who would refuse to eat the beautiful white loaf, because, forsooth, he does not understand why that plant should eventually make a wheatcake instead of a barley loaf.

But that is just what the skeptic desires. He asks us to reject the doctrine of the resurrection because we cannot explain completely, its workings. He asks for what he does not offer. Truly, we cannot explain how the resurrection will take place; neither can we explain the metaphysics of how God forgives us our transgressions, nor can we say how He answers our prayers. Yet we know He does! To reject the fact would be foolishness; and to deny it would be folly. The skeptic, however, urges us so to do. He forgets that there is a power beyond our *ken* in which men are lifted to heights where things merely hoped for, become realities. It is so with our belief in the *resurrection of the dead*.

Notwithstanding our inability to prove the idea of man's coming forth from the tomb — for proof is a mental conclusion — we are aided by many who have suggested, what to us is an unanswerable argument — "We can reason from analogy!" They say, "When poison has been taken into the system, and ended in death, the chemist is able, through his knowledge of chemical reactions, to separate every element of that poison no matter how it may have been mixed with a thousand different ingredients, and bring it out and place it before a court of justice." The logical conclusion to this noteworthy comparison is the question we ask, "Is it presumption to suppose that the great *Chemist of the Universe* can separate every atom of my scattered dust and reconstruct it into a perfectness of such as, perhaps, we at this time, have very little idea?"

We can sum it all up in these words, "There is enough in revealed and natural religion to establish beyond any doubt, the hope in Christ which we cherish, and we can leave the solution of the mystery to that day when the things we know not now, we shall know hereafter." (See John 13:7) "We can trust in a wisdom we cannot fathom, and we can lean upon an omnipotence we cannot grasp."

There is no doubt in our minds that Corianton, to whom Alma addressed these words, was of a brilliant mind. He, however, pondered only briefly the things

3. Behold, he bringeth to pass the resurrection of the dead. But behold, my son, the resurrection is not yet. Now, I unfold unto you a mystery; nevertheless, there are many mysteries which are kept, that no one knoweth them save God himself. But I show unto you one thing which I have inquired diligently of God that I might know—that is concerning the resurrection.

4. Behold, there is a time appointed that all shall come forth from the dead. Now when this time cometh no one knows; but God knoweth the time which is appointed.

5. Now, whether there shall be one time, or a second time, or a third time, that men shall come forth from the dead, it mattereth not; for God knoweth all these things; and it sufficeth me to know that this is the case—that there is a time appointed that all shall rise from the dead.

---

he proclaimed, but after his father had thus talked to him, his life proved the strength of his belief in them. But now, tossed about by the opinions of those who "were worldly wise," and relying on his own wisdom which in his youth he thought was great, he became afflicted with an inordinate estimate of his own strength and wisdom, and an inclination to skepticism, if not infidelity. He was a doubter of everything but his own supposed abilities. He marvelled that the assurance of the coming of the Messiah should be given to men so long before His advent. His mind was worried concerning the resurrection of the dead, the restoration of all things, the eternal punishment of the sinner, and many other points of doctrine. His father, Alma, perceiving this, sought to bring peace and stability to Corianton's troubled mind.

VERSES 2-8. *No resurrection . . . until after the coming of Christ.* Corianton lived with his father and brothers in Zarahemla about 73 B.C. The doctrine of the Resurrection of man from the dead had been proclaimed by all the holy prophets, both Nephite and Jewish, and in their ecstasy Alma's people looked forward to it but, however, they did not know when it would take place.

For many generations the people of the Earth had been told that the bodies of all the dead would be raised from the grave; that in this great event, which they called the Resurrection, their bodies would put on immortality, and they would no more see corruption. The day by prophets long foretold would be a happy one; no more pain, and to the righteous, no more sorrow. The coming of that day had been long deferred. Waiting for it, and it not coming, caused a sort of disappointed pride in the hearts of many who mourned the loss of loved ones. Delay, anxiety and uncertainty, had filled them with despair. Hopelessness began to mock the words of the prophets. This manner of thought imbued Corianton. Therefore, and in the spirit of prophecy, Alma, sensing the need of greater enlightenment in Corianton's mind concerning the Resurrection, had gone before the Lord in mighty prayer, seeking knowledge of its truth that he, himself, might know of a surety whereof he spoke; that in the process of making the doctrine clear to his understanding, only God-inspired verities should be presented to Corianton's comprehension.

The Lord answered Alma's prayer! There shall be no resurrection "until after the coming of Christ." It is through Christ, Alma noted, that men will be resurrected, and through Him only will it come to pass. And Alma offered Corianton

6. Now there must needs be a space betwixt the time of death and the time of the resurrection.

7. And now I would inquire what becometh of the souls of men from this time of death to the time appointed for the resurrection?

8. Now whether there is more than one time appointed for men to rise it mattereth not; for all do not die at once, and this mattereth not; all is as one day with God, and time only is measured unto men.

9. Therefore, there is a time appointed unto men that they shall rise from the dead; and there is a space between the time of death and the resurrection. And now, concerning this space of time, what becometh of the souls of men is the thing which I have inquired diligently of the Lord to know; and this is the thing of which I do know.

10. And when the time cometh when all shall rise, then shall they know that God knoweth all the times which are appointed unto man.

11. Now, concerning the state

---

the definite assurance "the Resurrection is not yet." Christ is the first fruit of the Resurrection, or the first of all men to come forth from the tomb. Until then all those who have lived and died before Him, must await that glorious victory which He, as the Redeemer of mankind, shall bring about.

Many mysteries, known only to God, Alma told Corianton, surround the facts that have been revealed to man concerning the Resurrection. When it shall be, at that time which was about three-quarters of a century before Christ, only God knew, but Alma said that all men shall rise from the dead.

VERSES 6-8. *Now there must needs be a space betwixt the time of death and the time of the Resurrection.* Even as all men are not born and die at the same time, it makes no difference whether they are raised from the dead all at once. There is a period of time which begins when the body of flesh and blood is separated from man's spirit that lasts down until they are reunited again in the Resurrection. In verse six a fact is noted which undoubtedly perplexed Corianton. But Alma's explanation is easily apprehended: *All is as one day with God, and time only is measured unto man.*

That Alma understood there is only one resurrection may be judged from the explanations he offered his son. Corianton had no doubt listened to many discussions concerning the Resurrection, its extent and its effect upon mankind. But the arguments given to sustain the different views therein stated served only to give him further reign to his doubts and passions.

In God's Plan of Redemption there is only one Resurrection, but the Resurrection itself may extend over what is to us a long dispensation the continuity of which seems broken by relatively long periods of time, thus in the minds of many, making of one thing several integral parts or portions. Alma, however, was sure that a time was appointed by God for man to be raised from the dead. Now, he interposed, "Whether there is more than one time appointed for man to rise it mattereth not," and his logical conclusion heretofore stated: *all is as one day with God . . .* is a complete commentary thereon.

VERSES 9-11. *Now, concerning the state of the soul between death and the resurrection.* The time when all men shall rise from the dead is known only to

of the soul between death and the resurrection—Behold, it has been made known unto me by an angel, that the spirits of all men, as soon as they are departed from this mortal body, yea, the spirits of all men, whether they be good or evil, are taken home to that God who gave them life.

3. *Separate states of righteous and wicked ...*

12. And then shall it come to pass, that the spirits of those who are righteous are received into a state of happiness, which is called paradise, a state of rest, a state of peace, where they shall rest from all their troubles and from all care, and sorrow.

13. And then shall it come to pass, that the spirits of the wicked, yea, who are evil—for behold, they have no part nor portion of the Spirit of the Lord; for behold, they chose evil works rather than good; therefore the spirit of the devil did enter into them, and take possession of their house— and these shall be cast out into outer darkness; there shall be weeping, and wailing, and gnashing of teeth, and this because of their own iniquity, being led captive by the will of the devil.

14. Now this is the state of the souls of the wicked, yea, in darkness, and a state of awful, fearful looking for the fiery indignation of the wrath of God upon them; thus they remain in this state, as well as the righteous in paradise, until the time of their resurrection.

God Who has appointed it, and there is a space of time between death and the Resurrection are facts which have been established by Alma. Now, he asked, during that "space of time, what becometh of the souls of men." Alma informed Corianton that he had inquired *diligently* of the Lord to know, and the Lord answered his prayer, "and this is the thing which I do know."

An angel from the *Courts of Glory* had visited him in answer to his prayers, and had made it known to him, Alma said, "that the spirits of all men, as soon as they are departed from this mortal body, yea, the spirits of all men, whether they be good or evil, are taken home to that God Who gave them life." They return to that place whence they came, not to God's actual presence, but to that home in the world of spirits where they once dwelt and where they grew from their spirit birth to when in God's wisdom they developed and progressed enough to become mortals.

VERSES 12-14. *The spirits of those who are righteous are received into a state of happiness.* There, as it is here, the righteous find no pleasure in mingling with the wicked, and in justice will not be forced to. The righteous and the wicked are segregated; the righteous, because of their righteousness, seek companionship with the righteous, and a place is provided for them called *Paradise* where they can mingle with their own kind, those who, too, are righteous. Paradise, according to Alma, is "a state of rest, a state of peace, where they shall rest from all their troubles and from all care, and sorrow."

The wicked, also, have a place prepared for them. It is a place where spiritual

15. Now, there are some that have understood that this state of happiness and this state of misery of the soul, before the resurrection, was a first resurrection. Yea, I admit it may be termed a resurrection, the raising of the spirit or the soul and their consignation to happiness or misery, according to the words which have been spoken.

16. And behold, again it hath been spoken, that there is a first resurrection, a resurrection of all those who have been, or who are, or who shall be, down to the resurrection of Christ from the dead.

17. Now, we do not suppose that this first resurrection, which is spoken of in this manner, can be the resurrection of the souls and their consignation to happiness or misery. Ye cannot suppose that this is what it meaneth.

18. Behold, I say unto you, Nay; but it meaneth the reuniting of the soul with the body, of those from the days of Adam down to the resurrection of Christ.

---

darkness prevails, because the inhabitants thereof "have no part nor portion of the Spirit of the Lord; for behold, they chose evil works rather than good; therefore the spirit of the devil did enter into them, and take possession of their house — and these shall be cast out into outer darkness." The wicked there await the "fiery indignation of the wrath of God" to be executed upon them because of their iniquity. A fearful expectation, or an awful looking forward for a just punishment, is continually before them, and "thus they remain in this state, as well as the righteous in Paradise, until the time of their resurrection."

VERSES 15-18. *And behold, again it hath been spoken, that there is a first resurrection.* . . . In the uncertainty caused by the lack of revealed word, many personal ideas became the special points of discussion among the Nephites. Some supposed one thing, others something else. There were a number who understood that the segregation of the righteous from the wicked was "a first resurrection"; the spirits of the righteous being raised to a pre-eminent condition of peace, rest, and happiness, while those of the wicked were consigned to a state of misery and wretched expectancy. Alma admitted to his son that this "may be termed a resurrection," but such is not the Resurrection of which all the holy prophets had spoken. Alma's expression *may be termed a resurrection* shows the various meanings a word may have. The word resurrection as used in this sense was almost meaningless to Alma's introspection, and its true prophetic meaning — the coming forth of men from the grave — was lost to him in a maze of uninspired thinking. By twisting and turning its evident sense the word was used by the advocates of that idea to designate the rising of the soul, the righteous to higher levels of peace and tranquility, and the spirits of the wicked to greater misery and unhappiness. This, they contended, was really a resurrection. Of this usage, Alma said, "It may be termed a resurrection," but, he continued, the resurrection "of the souls and their consignation to happiness or misery. Ye cannot suppose that this is what it meaneth," when the resurrection was spoken of by the holy prophets.

Now, those who understand that the rising of the spirits of the dead — the righteous to a state of happiness and the wicked to a state of misery — before their resurrection from the grave, were misguided in their thinking that it was a "first resurrection." It was not! If and when we speak of a *first resurrection*, thus implying a second or a third, etc., we divide the Resurrection into parts, and make

19. Now, whether the souls and the bodies of those of whom has been spoken shall all be reunited at once, the wicked as well as the righteous, I do not say; let it suffice, that I say that they all come forth; or in other words, their resurrection cometh to pass before the resurrection of those who die after the resurrection of Christ.

20. Now, my son, I do not say that their resurrection cometh at the resurrection of Christ; but behold, I give it as my opinion, that the souls and the bodies are reunited, of the righteous, at the resurrection of Christ, and his ascension into heaven.

21. But whether it be at his resurrection or after, I do not say; but this much I say, that there is a space between death and the resurrection of the body, and a state of the soul in happiness or in misery until the time which is appointed of God that the dead shall come fotrh, and be reunited, both soul and body, and be brought to stand before God, and be judged according to their works.

---

the gift of God a series of occurrences. We do as man does when he divides the day of twenty-four hours into A.M. and P.M. It, nevertheless, remains the same day. There are first hours of the day, but their continuity extends over them all. It is as one day with the Lord. The Resurrection began with Christ coming forth from the tomb. It will continue until all men are raised by the power of the Resurrection.

VERSES 19-21. *Now, whether the souls and the bodies of those of whom has been spoken shall all be reunited at once, the wicked as well as the righteous, I do not say.* Alma was careful not to imply that the wicked as well as the righteous would come forth from the grave at the same time. He spoke of those who died before the Resurrection of Christ.

The Prophet Abinadi who ministered to the People of Zeniff in the Land of Nephi and whose words were recorded by Alma, the father of Alma who later became the Presiding High Priest of God's Church, and whose occupancy of that position we are now discussing: But behold, the bands of death shall be broken, and the Son reigneth, and hath power over the dead; therefore, He bringeth to pass the resurrection of the dead.

And there cometh a resurrection, even a first resurrection; yea, even a resurrection of those that have been, and who are, and who shall be, even until the resurrection of Christ — for so shall He be called.

And now, the resurrection of all the prophets, and all those that have believed in their words, or all those that have kept the commandments of God, shall come forth in the first resurrection; therefore, they are the first resurrection.

They are raised to dwell with God Who has redeemed them; thus they have Eternal Life through Christ, Who has broken the bands of death.

And these are those who have part in the first resurrection; and these are they that have died before Christ came, in their ignorance, not having Salvation declared unto them. And thus the Lord bringeth about the resurrection of these; and they have a part in the first resurrection, or have Eternal Life, being redeemed by the Lord. (Mosiah 15:20-24)

In verse 20, Alma gives as his opinion that only the spirits of the righteous shall be resurrected at the time when Christ, Himself, shall rise from the dead, and shall ascend into Heaven.

When we speak of a *first resurrection* it is best not to imagine that the term refers to a separate and distinct period of time in which some who are chosen will come forth from the dead. Unless the chosen are the righteous ones, the words, themselves, provoke misconceptions in considering the prophetic understanding of the Resurrection as a definite continuous period during which all men will be raised from the dead. *First resurrection* is better understood as not referring principally to time, but as a reward for righteous living. *First resurrection* is a resurrection of the just. "The resurrection of Christ and of the righteous who died before His coming is not, however, all that is meant by the "first resurrection" as indicated by the promises which are yet being made to the living. Moroni, who lived long after the time of Christ, was nevertheless of the "first resurrection." The problem is somewhat clarified if we use the terms "resurrection of the just" and "resurrection of the unjust." The resurrection of the just, whenever it may occur precedes the resurrection of the unjust and is hence a "first resurrection." So resurrections of the righteous, yet to take place, are a "first resurrection" as contrasted with the last resurrection which shall take place at the end of the Millennium. The promise is repeatedly found in Scripture that, at the second coming of Christ, the righteous dead who have not previously been resurrected, will arise from their graves and dwell on the earth during the Millennium. This resurrection, being definitely a resurrection of the "just," is also a "first resurrection," and it is the promise of this resurrection which is used in temple ordinances and patriarchal blessings in our day. (William E. Berrett, *Teachings of the Book of Mormon,* p. 58)

And again we bear record — for we saw and heard, and this is the testimony of the gospel of Christ concerning them who shall come forth in the resurrection of the just —

They are they who received the testimony of Jesus, and believed on his name and were baptized after the manner of his burial, being buried in the water in his name, and this according to the commandment which he has given —

That by keeping the commandments they might be washed and cleansed from all their sins, and receive the Holy Spirit by the laying on of the hands of him who is ordained and sealed unto this power;

And who overcome by faith, and are sealed by the Holy Spirit of promise, which the Father sheds forth upon all those who are just and true.

They are they who are the church of the Firstborn.

They are they into whose hands the Father has given all things —

They are they who are priests and kings, who have received of his fulness, and of his glory;

And are priests of the Most High, after the order of Melchizedek, which was after the order of Enoch, which was after the order of the Only Begotten Son.

Wherefore, as it is written, they are gods, even the sons of God —

Wherefore, all things are theirs, whether life or death, or things present, or things to come, all are theirs and they are Christ's, and Christ is God's.

And they shall overcome all things.

Wherefore, let no man glory in man, but rather let him glory in God, who shall subdue all enemies under his feet.

These shall dwell in the presence of God and his Christ forever and ever.

These are they whom he shall bring with him, when he shall come in the clouds of heaven to reign on the earth over his people.

These are they who shall have part in the first resurrection.

These are they who shall come forth in the resurrection of the just.

These are they who are come unto Mount Zion, and unto the city of the living God, the heavenly place, the holiest of all.

These are they who have come to an innumerable company of angels, to the general assembly and church of Enoch, and of the Firstborn.

These are they whose names are written in heaven, where God and Christ are the judge of all.

These are they who are just men made perfect through Jesus the mediator of the new covenant, who wrought out this perfect atonement through the shedding of his own blood.

These are they whose bodies are celestial, whose glory is that of the sun, even the glory of God, the highest of all, whose glory the sun of the firmament is written of as being typical. (Doctrine and Covenants, Section 76:50-70)

RESURRECTION—

Mosiah	15:21	Evil until the r. of Christ
Alma	40:16	Down to the r. of Christ
	18	From the days of Adam, down to the r. of Christ
	19	Who die after the r. of Christ
	20	Cometh at the r. of Christ
	20	The r. of Christ, and his ascension
	41:2	The power and r. of Christ
Helaman	14:17	The r. of Christ redeemeth mankind
III Nephi	6:20	Or in other words, the r. of Christ

Resurrection of the dead—

II Nephi	2:8	Bring to pass the r. of the dead
Mosiah	13:35	Bring to pass the r. of the dead
	15:20	He bringeth to pass the r. of the dead
	18:2	Concerning the r. of the dead
	26:2	Concerning the r. of the dead
Alma	4:14	Because of the r. of the dead
	12:8	Concerning the r. of the dead
	24	Is after the r. of the dead
	25	Could have been no r. of the dead
	25	Bring to pass the r. of the dead
	16:19	And also the r. of the dead
	21:9	Concerning the r. of the dead
	40:1	Worried concerning the r. of the dead
	3	Bringeth to pass the r. of the dead
	3	That is concerning the r.
	42:23	Bringeth to pass the r. of the dead
	23	And the r. of the dead bringeth back man into the presence
Helaman	14:15	He dieth, to bring to pass the r. of
Mormon	7:6	He bringeth to pass the r. of the dead
Alma	11:45	Concerning the r. of the mortal body

First resurrection—

Mosiah	15:21	Cometh a r., even a first r.
	22	Shall come forth in the first r.
	22	Therefore, they are the first r.
	24	Are those who have a part in the first r.
	24	And they have a part in the first r.
	26	That have no part in the first r.
	18:9	Numbered with those of the first r.

22. Yea, this bringeth about the restoration of those things of which has been spoken by the mouths of the prophets.

23. The soul shall be restored to the body, and the body to the soul; yea, and every limb and joint shall be restored to its body; yea, even a hair of the head shall not be lost; but all things shall be restored to their proper and perfect frame.

24. And now, my son, this is the restoration of which has been spoken by the mouths of the prophets—

25. And then shall the righteous shine forth in the kingdom of God.

26. But behold, an awful death cometh upon the wicked; for they die as to things pertaining to things of righteousness; for they are unclean, and no unclean thing can inherit the kingdom of God; but they are cast out, and consigned to partake of the fruits of their labors or their works, which have been evil; and they drink the dregs of a bitter cup.

Alma	40:15	Before the r., was a first r.
	16	There is a first r.; a r. of all those
	17	We do not suppose that this first r.

Of the resurrection—

II Nephi	9:12	It is by the power of the r. of the Holy One
	10:25	From death by the power of the r.
Jacob	4:11	According to the power of the r.
Alma	4:14	Joy, because of the r. of the dead

Resurrection—

II Nephi	9:6	Must needs be a power of r.
	6	And the r. must needs come unto man by reason of the fall
	22	That the r. might pass upon all
	26:3	Birth, and also of his death and r.
Jacob	4:11	That ye may obtain a r.
	12	To attain to a knowledge of a r.?
	6:9	And the r. which is in Christ
Mosiah	15:21	And there cometh a r.
	21	Even a r. of those that have been
	22	The r. of all the prophets, and all
	16:7	There could have been no r.
	8	But there is a r., therefore the grave
	11	If they be good, to a r. of endless
	11	If they be evil, to a r. of endless

4. A literal restoration.

VERSES 22-24. *Yea, this bringeth about the restoration . . .* The Resurrection with its universal benefits to man, bringeth to pass every promise made by the holy prophets that the bodies of all men should be raised from the dead. The spirits of men, once separated from their tabernacles of flesh and blood, shall again be restored one to the other as it was in mortality. Every limb, every joint, even every hair of the head, shall be restored as it was in the beginning to "their proper and perfect frame." Every particle of our scattered dust, no matter how through the years it may have been mixed with a thousand different ingredients will be raised in the Resurrection to a beauty and perfectness, of such as, perhaps, we, at this time, have very little idea.

VERSES 25. *And then shall the righteous shine forth in the Kingdom of God.* Here we will only quote two passages from the Scriptures: First from Matthew: The Son of Man shall send forth His angels, and they shall gather out of His Kingdom all things that offend, and them which do iniquity; And shall cast them into a furnace of fire . . . *And then shall the righteous shine forth as the Sun in the Kingdom of their Father.* (Matthew 13:41-43) Again: And many of them that sleep in the dust of the Earth shall awake, some to Everlasting Life, and some to shame and everlasting contempt. *And they that be wise shall shine as the brightness of the firmament: and they that turn many to righteousness as the stars for ever and ever.* (Daniel 12:3)

VERSE 26. *An awful death cometh upon the wicked.* Notwithstanding God's mercy and His long-suffering, the wicked have no place in His Kingdom. Their deeds while on Earth were evil, therefore, they "have no part nor portion" of His Spirit with them. They prefer darkness to light in the hope that their actions are obscured; their hope is in vain because darkness does not abide where God lives. "They are unclean," Alma noted, "and no unclean thing can inherit the Kingdom of God. They are cast out, and consigned to partake of the fruits of their labors or their works, which have been evil; and they drink the dregs of a bitter cup."

CHAPTER 41

1. *Alma to Corianton Continued*—2. *What Restoration Signifies*—3. *Men to be Judged According to Their Deeds and Desires*—4. *Self-judgment.*

1. *Alma to Corianton Continued.*

2. *What restoration signifies.*

1. And now, my son, I have somewhat to say concerning the restoration of which has been spoken; for behold, some have wrested the scriptures, and have gone far astray because of this thing. And I perceive that thy mind has been worried also concerning this thing. But behold, I will explain it unto thee.

2. I say unto thee, my son, that the plan of restoration is requisite with the justice of God; for it is requisite that all things should be restored to their proper order. Behold, it is requisite and just, according to the power and resurrection of Christ, that the soul of man should be restored to its body, and that every part of the body should be restored to itself.

VERSES 1-2. *And now my son, I have somewhat to say concerning the restoration of which has been spoken.* Restoration means the act of re-establishing, or putting back to its original state, a former thing or condition, unimpaired. Also, it sometimes means to bring back to a healthy state, or to reinstate in a former favorable position something that has been abused or degraded. To give back again, as in Genesis 20:14; Judges 11:13. To bring back to the first state or condition, Genesis 40:13; Isaiah 1:13; Acts 1:6. To recover, or get again, II Kings 14:25. To heal or cure, Matthew 12:13.

But to begin the discussion of the term, *restoratoin,* let us not limit its meaning to a dictionary definition, nor confine its objective to the prescribed area of material things. It has a deep significance in the spiritual world if but seen by us and accepted will make known to us many things that otherwise we would see only "as through a glass darkly."

Since the very first, opposition to His righteousness has endured in the hearts of some of God's children. In every generation and among all peoples there have been those who preferred the pseudo-joys and follies of the world to keeping His laws and testimonies. They have sought for the world's goods instead for that "which maketh truly rich." They have not searched for their Father's Kingdom, but instead have bartered away their birthright for *husks* which are given to swine. Some have wandered far, and are in a strange land.

Their Father, in the meantime, has prepared for them, the rings, the robes, the shoes, and has sent His messengers looking for them that they might be found and their heritage renewed. The holy prophets are His messengers. Likewise, in every age of the world, even before *Israel* was established as the Lord's Chosen People, the Lord God repeatedly sent His holy servants to proclaim forgiveness, and the restoration of all the blessings which had been promised the righteous since the world began. The Nephites had a record of these promises written upon the Brass Plates of Laban which they had brought out of Jerusalem when first they left the Land of their father's inheritance. What were these promises? In spite of the plainness with which God speaks to His children, and notwithstanding His mercy and His grace, many among the Nephites twisted and turned the plainest of His teachings into misshapen and conflicting statements which could not be understood by even the wisest. Like many others, they excused themselves in doing that which was most to be eschewed. They offered pretexts and apologies for the things they did, knowing all the time that their actions needed defending because they were contrary to the *Word of the Lord.*

In order that we may approach the subject under discussion — restoration — in a proper frame of mind, let us refer the student to several passages of both Nephite, Hebrew, and Latter-day Saint Scriptures. In the first place, a description of those who *wrest* the Scriptures: They wear stiff necks and high heads; yea, and because of pride, and wickedness, and abominations, and whoredoms, they have all gone astray save it be a few, who are the humble followers of Christ; nevertheless, they are led, that in many instances they do err because they are taught by the precepts of men. (II Nephi 28:14) And also, O the wise, and the learned, and the rich, that are puffed up in the pride of their hearts, and all those who preach false doctrines, and all those who commit whoredoms, and pervert the right way of the Lord, wo, wo, wo be unto them, saith the Lord God Almighty, for they shall be thrust down to hell. (*Ibid.* 28:15) Again: And there shall also be many which shall say: Eat, drink, and be merry; nevertheless fear God—He will justify in committing a little sin, yea, lie a little, take the advantage of one because of his words, dig a pit for thy neighbor; there is no harm in this; and do all these things, for tomorrow we die; and if it so be that we are guilty, God will beat us with a few stripes, and at last we shall be saved in the Kingdom of God. Yea, and there shall be many which shall teach after this manner, false and vain and foolish doctrines, and shall be puffed up in their hearts, and shall seek deep to hide their counsels from the Lord; and their works shall be in the dark. (*Ibid.* 28:7-9)

Now, listen to David, King of the Jews:

Have mercy upon me, O God, according to Thy loving-kindness: according unto the multitude of Thy tender mercies blot out my transgressions.

Wash me thoroughly from mine iniquity, and cleanse me from my sin.

For I acknowledge my transgressions: and my sin is ever before me.

Against Thee, Thee only, have I sinned, and done this evil in Thy sight: that Thou mightest be justified when Thou speakest, and be clear when Thou judgest.

Behold, I was shapen in iniquity; and in sin did my mother conceive me.

Behold, Thou desireth truth in the inward parts: and in the hidden part Thou shalt make me know wisdom.

Purge me with hyssop, and I shall be clean! wash me, and I shall be whiter than snow.

Make me to hear joy and gladness; that the bones which Thou hast broken may rejoice.

Hide Thy face from my sins, and blot out all mine iniquities.

Create in me a clean heart, O God; and renew a right spirit within me.

Cast me not away from Thy presence; and take not Thy holy Spirit from me.

Restore unto me the joy of Thy salvation; and uphold me with Thy free Spirit. (Psalm 51)

In our own generation the Lord has said through the Prophet Joseph Smith:

This is wisdom in Me; wherefore, marvel not, for the hour cometh that I will drink of the fruit of the vine with you on the Earth, and with Moroni, whom I have sent unto you to reveal the Book of Mormon, containing the fulness of My everlasting Gospel, to whom I have committed the keys of the record of the Stick of Ephraim;

And also Elias, to whom I have committed the keys of bringing to pass the restoration of all things spoken by the mouth of all the holy prophets since the world began, concerning the last days. (Doctrine and Covenants 27:5-6)

Now, among the Nephites, there were many who believed, as many among us now believe, that for His glory God will look with forbearance upon evil, or will refrain from enforcement of His laws and commandments. That is not true; He will not, and cannot. He is merciful and long-suffering, but to any evil, however little we may conceive it to be, He stands adamant. His Kingdom is founded upon obedience to His commands; it is upheld and ustained by the righteousness of His children everywhere. Evil is the enemy of all truth and of that which is just. God, whom we worship, is the Father of truth and justice, and until all evil and error are conquered and brought into subjection to Him, His Kingdom will not fill the Earth, and in just the same ratio His will done in Heaven will not be done here below. May we in all humility insert here the full prayer offered by the Prophet Joseph Smith at Hiram, Ohio, October 1831. *"The Prophet designates this revelation as a prayer.—Commitment of the keys of the Kingdom of God unto man.—The Kingdom of God and the Kingdom of Heaven named separately.—Supplication that the Kingdom of God, already on Earth, may go forth that the Kingdom of Heaven may come."* (Heading)

Hearken, and lo, a voice as of one sent down from On High, Who is mighty and powerful, whose going forth is unto the ends of the Earth, yea, Whose voice is unto men—Prepare ye the Way of the Lord, make His paths straight.

The keys of the Kingdom of God are committed unto man on Earth, and from thence shall the Gospel roll forth unto the ends of the Earth, as the stone which is cut out of the mountain without hands shall roll forth, until it has filled the whole Earth.

Yea, a voice crying—Prepare ye the Way of the Lord, prepare ye the supper of the Lamb, make ready for the Bridegroom.

Pray unto the Lord, call upon His Holy Name, make known His wonderful works among the people.

Call upon the Lord, that His Kingdom may go forth upon the Earth, that the inhabitants thereof may receive it, and be prepared for the days to come, in the which the Son of Man shall come down in Heaven, clothed in the brightness of His glory, to meet the Kingdom of God which is set up on the Earth.

Wherefore, may the Kingdom of God go forth, that the Kingdom of Heaven may come, that Thou, O God, mayest be glorified in Heaven so on Earth, that Thine enemies may be subdued; for Thine is the honor, power and glory, forever and ever. Amen. (Doctrine and Covenants, Section 65)

Alma recognized the evil existing among the Nephites — that in spite of the inspired teachings of the prophets who had ministered among their forefathers, and notwithstanding that now they were guided by men who were sent of God, many well-meaning and righteous people "had gone astray" because of false teachings. Some of their teachers and leaders had put into the Scriptures, by *wresting* them, otherwise by twisting and turning them, meanings that were not true. Corianton's mind had become perplexed along with others because "of this thing." Errors and foolishness had dulled his gifts and abilities to discern the truth. His father, Alma, perceived in Corianton's demeanor that he was also influenced by this "loose thinking." But, Alma said, "I will explain it unto thee," he meaning the *restoration* of all things.

God, who is just in all His Ways, has decreed that all things here below shall return to their normal state in the which they were in their very beginning. Justice requires it so to be. If it were not so, then repentance and forgiveness, for example, would consitute an empty show of faith; a sacrifice with no meaning; a scale having

3. *Men to be judged according to their deeds and desires.*

3. And it is requisite with the justice of God that men should be judged according to their works; and if their works were good in this life, and the desires of their hearts were good, that they should also, at the last day, be restored unto that which is good.

4. And if their works are evil they shall be restored unto them for evil. Therefore, all things shall be restored to their proper frame—mortality raised to immortality, corruption to incorruption—raised to endless happiness to inherit the kingdom of God, or to endless misery to inherit the kingdom of the devil, the one on one hand, the other on the other—

5. The one raised to happiness according to his desires of happiness, or good according to his desires of good; and the other to evil according to his desires of evil; for as he has desired to do evil all the day long even so shall he have his reward of evil when the night cometh.

---

no harmony. These Gospel principles — repentance and forgiveness — would have no place in God's Plan of Life and Salvation. His divine purposes would be "as a mill without a miller, continually grinding and grinding, but grinding out no meal for His hungry children." It is *requisite* to the promise He has made — that the Earth shall be renewed and receive its paradisiacal glory. "The Earth is the Lord's, and the fulness thereof," . . . and we are readily assured that before He claims it as His own, its goodness and its purity will be restored as it was when He created it. Restoration "to their proper order" is something required by the very nature of things; it is necessary, or a thing demanded to bring to pass the end of His work which He has in view. And as long as one soul, or a thing, remains an enemy of His, or its desires are unrighteous, His work will not be finished. Through the power of Christ's resurrection not only will the mortal body and the spirit of man be restored one to the other, but also it made possible that all things, both good and bad, evil and righteous, should return to their place of origin, or to where they were born. It is impossible for such opposites to dwell together eternally. Goodness will be restored to the good, and evil to the realm of Satan.

VERSES 3-5. *It is requisite with the justice of God that men should be judged according to their works.* God's justice, which is an attribute of His divinity, demands that all things created by Him perform their allotted tasks. We were placed upon the earth by the Lord Jehovah, and appointed to do His bidding. Often times we forget His wisdom and guidance and go our way day after day relying upon our own understanding. "All thoughts of God are crowded from our hearts." The world and the things of the world are idols to which we bow down and worship. We have no time or thought for else than "What shall we eat? or, What shall we drink? or, Wherewithal shall we be clothed?" (III Nephi 13:31) When these questions present themselves to our minds, it is then we should remember the words of the Savior, "Man shall not live by bread alone, but by every word that proceedeth out of the mouth of God." (Matthew 4:4) By His words our thirst is slaked, and we hunger no more. They are meat and drink to our souls; they feed us with knowledge and understanding from above, and the words of His servants, whether they be of Abraham, or of Joseph, who was sold into Egypt, or of Moses, the great leader of Israel, or of the Hebrew prophets, or of the Nephite servants of God in this land, or the apostolic message of the Twelve, "Jesus is the Son of God, or the fulness of the Gospel of Jesus Christ as proclaimed by the Prophet Joseph Smith in our generation, we must remember that Jesus Christ said, "For I am He Who speaketh." (Ether 4:8) Christ's words and the words of His servants reveal a vivid picture of our Father's Plan of Salvation, and, too, have a permanent authority about them that all may· recognize who desire to know the mind and will of God.

It is requisite with the Justice of God that men should be judged according to their works. We are given discernment by which we know good and evil and also the power to choose right or wrong. In every dispensation of the Gospel, the Lord God has, through the prophets of old and the seers of our own time, made known what is required of men that they may be saved at the Last Day and be exalted in the Kingdom of Heaven. The *Way* has been made known and the *Path* marked out. Some men are more steadfast in keeping the commandments of the Lord than are others; some pursue the Path of righteousness with greater diligence than do their brethren. "The *Light* which lighteth every man that cometh into the world" burns more brightly in some than in others. In other words, among men there are different degrees of integrity as shown by obedience to righteous principles just as there are different degrees of glory for which the righteous strive. David, the Psalmist, had this fact in his mind when he exclaimed: Teach me, O Lord, the way of Thy statutes and I will keep it at every step. Give me understanding that I keep Thy law and observe it with my whole heart. Make me to tread in the path of Thy commandments; for therein do I delight. Incline my heart unto Thine testimonies, and not to covetousness. Turn away mine eyes from beholding vanity, and quicken me in Thy ways. Confirm unto Thy servant Thy word, which pertaineth unto the fear of Thee. Turn away my reproach which I dread, for Thine ordinances are good. Behold, I have longed after Thy precepts; quicken me in Thy righteousness . . . (Psalm 119. Jewish Rendition)

Those whose *works* were good in mortal life and who also desired that goodness and purity should prevail by keeping God's commandments shall mingle only with those, who like themselves, sought the Kingdom of God and its righteousness. They will be put beyond the reach of all evil, which is Eternal Salvation. It is Everlasting Life in the Kingdom of our Father, where all that is good and just and pure, enter unrestrained, and where joy and gladness reign supreme. Unto us, in the Kingdom of Heaven, there will be re-established or renewed our highest ideals, and their satisfaction will there be known to us. In our goodness and purity the things we once loved when "nurtured by His side," and perhaps now have forgotten, will be restored unto us again.

"On the one hand as on the other" those whose works were evil, and who sought not that justice and righteousness prevail, shall inherit "the kingdom of the devil." In Satan's dominion they will find that for which they strived on Earth to obtain. You cannot with any measure of justice place the wicked, or those who love evil, in a place of contentment and happiness, or with the just, the pure in heart, and with those who love the Lord. That will not be done! The little corridor that divides the living and the dead does not make in a single night, a saint of a sinner, neither does it instill in the sinner's heart a desire to walk in the right path. Evil seeks evil, and the heart that yearns for evil will find it ensconced in the realm of the evil one. By choice that is where he will go, and there he will dwell eternally with the devil and his angels. In the Day of Judgment, Justice demands that those who do wickedly and those who have been righteous shall be rewarded according to their works; the righteous shall be righteous still, and the wicked cast out to dwell with him whom they served. Men will be rewarded in the same ratio as have been their righteous endeavors. If their actions here below have been good, their reward will

6. And so it is on the other hand. If he hath repented of his sins, and desired righteousness until the end of his days, even so he shall be rewarded unto righteousness.

---

be good, and transversely so, if their deeds were evil, their reward will be evil, or it will be relatively less according to their hardness of heart. In other words, men will be punished for their own transgressions; if they reject the truth, truth will not abide in them; if they love not the pure, then impurity is their standard. Guile, envy, and pride, are the motives that fixed their earthly desires. Worldly goods they cannot take with them, but what follows them and remains to constitute their station in the *life to come* are the qualities that guided them here on Earth. What we do here conditions us for the life to come. The wicked who on Earth sought for evil, or sowed it, shall reap that which they planted, while the righteous will have restored to them the beautiful harmonies of the Gospel of Jesus Christ which are peace, contentment, freedom from fear and sorrow, joy and gladness, and above all else, the love of Jesus Christ will be in their hearts.

Concerning this very subject, it is well to note what the Prophet Abinadi proclaimed to the Nephites about 150 years before the birth of the Savior in Bethlehem of Judea:

He is the Light and the Life of the world; yea, a light that is endless, that can never be darkened; yea, and also a life which is endless, that there can be no more death.

Even this mortal shall put on immortality, and this corruption shall put on incorruption, and shall be brought to stand before the Bar of God, to be judged of Him according to their works whether they be good or whether they be evil—

If they be good, to the resurrection of endless life and happiness; and if they be evil, to the resurrection of endless damnation, being delivered up to the devil, who hath subjected them, which is damnation—

Having gone according to their own carnal wills and desires; having never called upon the Lord while the arms of mercy were extended towards them; for the arms of mercy were extended towards them, and they would not; they being warned of their iniquities and yet they would not depart from them; and they were commanded to repent and yet they would not repent. (Mosiah 16:9-12)

Almost six hundred years before the advent of the Savior, Lehi, who led his little colony to the Promised Land which the Lord had promised him, in blessing his son, Jacob, said:

Wherefore, how great the importance to make these things known unto the inhabitants of the Earth, that they may know that there is no flesh that can dwell in the presence of God, save it be through the merits, and mercy, and grace of the holy Messiah, who layeth down His life according to the flesh, and taketh it again by the power of the Spirit, that He may bring to pass the resurrection of the dead, being the first that should rise.

Wherefore, He is the firstfruits unto God, inasmuch as He shall make intercession for all the children of men; and they that believe in Him shall be saved.

And because of the intercession for all, all men come unto God; wherefore, they stand in the presence of Him to be judged of Him according to the truth and holiness which is in Him. Wherefore, the ends of the law which the Holy One hath given, unto the inflicting of the punishment which is affixed, which punishment that is affixed is in opposition to that of the happiness which is affixed, to answer the ends of the Atonement—

For it must needs be, that there is an opposition in all things. If not so, my first born in the wilderness, righteousness could not be brought to pass, neither wickedness, neither holiness or misery, neither good nor bad. Wherefore, all things must needs be a compound in one; wherefore, if it should be one body it must needs remain as dead, having no life neither death, nor corruption nor incorruption, happiness nor misery, neither sense nor insensibility.

Wherefore, it must needs have been created for a thing of naught; wherefore there would have been no purpose in the end of its creation. Wherefore, this thing must needs destroy the wisdom of God and His eternal purposes, and also the power, and the mercy, and the justice of God. (II Nephi 2:2-12)

Almost half a century after his father's blessing, Jacob, whose inspired understanding brought into our vision many of the most sublime teachings of the Gospel of Jesus Christ, declared to his brethren:

Yea, I know that ye know that in the body He shall show Himself unto those at Jerusalem, from whence we came; for it is expedient that it should be among them; for it behooveth the great Creator that He suffereth Himself to become subject unto man in the flesh, and die for all men, that all men might become subject to Him.

For as death hath passed upon all men, to fulfil the merciful plan of the great Creator, there must needs be a power of resurrection, and the resurrection must needs come unto man by reason of the Fall; and the Fall came by reason of transgression; and because man became fallen they were cut off from the presence of the Lord.

Wherefore, it must needs be an infinite Atonement — save it should be an infinite Atonement this corruption could not put on incorruption. Wherefore, the first judgment which came upon man must needs have remained to an endless duration. And if so, this flesh must have laid down to rot and to crumble to its mother earth, to rise no more.

O the wisdom of God, His mercy and grace! For behold, if the flesh should rise no more our spirits must become subject to that angel who fell from before the presence of the Eternal God, and became the devil, to rise no more.

And our spirits must have become like unto him, and we become devils, angels to a devil, to be shut out from the presence of our God, and to remain with the father of lies, in misery, like unto himself; yea, to that being who beguiled our first parents, who transformeth himself nigh unto an angel of light, and stirreth up the children of men unto secret combinations of murder and all manner of secret works of darkness.

O how great the goodness of our God, Who prepareth a way for our escape from the grasp of this awful monster; yea, that monster death and hell, which I call the death of the body, and also the death of the spirit.

And because of the way of deliverance of our God, the Holy One of Israel, this death, of which I have spoken, which is the temporal, shall deliver up its dead; which death is the grave.

And this death of which I have spoken, which is the spiritual death, shall deliver up its dead; which spiritual death is hell; wherefore, death and hell must deliver up its captive spirits, and the grave must deliver up its captive bodies, and the bodies and spirits of men will be restored one to the other; and it is by the power of the resurrection of the Holy One of Israel.

O how great the plan of our God! For on the other hand, the paradise of God must deliver up the spirits of the righteous, and the grave must deliver up the body of the righteous; and the spirit and the body is restored to itself again, and all men become incorruptible, and immortal, and they are living souls, having a perfect knowledge like unto us in the flesh, save it be that our knowledge shall be perfect.

Wherefore, we shall have a perfect knowledge of all our guilt, and our uncleanness, and our nakedness; and the righteous shall have a perfect knowledge of their enjoyment, and their righteousness, being clothed with purity, yea, even with the robe of righteousness.

And it shall come to pass that when all men shall have passed from this first death unto life, insomuch as they have become immortal, they must appear before the judgment-seat of the Holy One of Israel; and then cometh the judgment, and then must they be judged according to the holy judgment of God.

And assuredly, as the Lord liveth, for the Lord God hath spoken it, and it is His eternal word, which cannot pass away, that they who are righteous shall be righteous still, and they who are filthy shall be filthy still; wherefore, they who are filthy are the devil and his angels; and they shall go away into everlasting fire; prepared for them; and their torment is as a lake of fire and brimstone, whose flame ascendeth up forever and ever and has no end. (II Nephi 9:5-16)

Alma, who was the Presiding High Priest of the Church of God, said unto the Saints residing in their Capital City of Zarahemla:

And now behold, I ask of you, my brethren of the Church, have ye been spiritually born of God? Have ye received His image in your countenances? Have ye experienced this mighty change in your hearts?

Do ye exercise faith in the redemption of Him Who created you? Do ye look forward with an eye of faith, and view this mortal body raised in immortality, and this corruption raised in incorruption, to stand before God to be judged according to the deeds which have been done in the mortal body? (Alma 5:15)

As Alma's missionary companion to the wicked Ammonihahites, Amulek in preaching to them gave some of the most easily understood instructions regarding the reunion, or the restoration, of the spirit and the body:

And He shall come into the world to redeem His people; and He shall take upon Him the transgressions of those who believe on His name; and these are they that shall have Eternal Life, and Salvation cometh to none else.

Therefore the wicked remain as though there had been no redemption made, except it be the loosing of the bands of death; for behold, the day cometh that all shall rise from the dead and stand before God, and be judged according to their works.

Now, there is a death which is called a temporal death; and the death of Christ shall loose the bands of this temporal death, that all shall be raised from this temporal death.

And the spirit and the body shall be reunited again in its perfect form; both limb and joint shall be restored to its proper frame, even as we now are at this time; and we shall stand before God, knowing even as we know now, and have a bright recollection of all our guilt.

Now, this restoration shall come to all, both old and young, both bond and free, both male and female, both the wicked and the righteous; and even there shall not so much as a hair of their heads be lost, but everything shall be restored to its perfect frame, as it is now, or in the body, and shall be brought and be arraigned before the Bar of Christ the Son, and God the Father, and the Holy Ghost, which is one Eternal God, to be judged according to their works, whether they be good or whether they be evil.

Now, behold, I have spoken unto you concerning the death of the mortal body, and also concerning the resurrection of the mortal body. I say unto you that this mortal body is raised to an immortal body, that is from death, even from the first death unto life, that they can die no more; their spirits uniting with their bodies, never to be divided; thus the whole becoming spiritual and immortal, that they can no more see corruption. (Alma 11:40-45)

The Prophet Mormon, near the close of a life which was dedicated to the welfare of his people who were sometimes very slothful in keeping the commandments of God, and who towards the end of their national existence grew exceedingly wicked, wrote to them hoping that someday they might read his words:

O ye fair sons and daughters, ye fathers and mothers, ye husbands and wives, ye fair ones, how is it that ye could have fallen?

But behold, ye are gone, and my sorrows cannot bring your return.

And the day soon cometh that your mortal must put on immortality, and these bodies which are now moldering in corruption must soon become incorruptible

4. Self-judgment.

7. These are they that are redeemed of the Lord; yea, these are they that are taken out, that are delivered from that endless night of darkness; and thus they stand or fall; for behold, they are their own judges, whether to do good or do evil.

8. Now, the decrees of God are unalterable; therefore, the way is prepared that whosoever will may walk therein and be saved.

9. And now behold, my son, do not risk one more offense against your God upon those points of doctrine, which ye have hitherto risked to commit sin.

10. Do not suppose, because it has been spoken concerning restoration, that ye shall be restored from sin to happiness. Behold, I say unto you, wickedness never was happiness.

---

bodies; and then must stand before the Judgment-seat of Christ to be judged according to your works; and if it so be that ye are righteous, then are ye blessed with your fathers who have gone before you.

O that ye had repented before this great destruction had come upon you. But behold, ye are gone, and the Father, yea, the Eternal Father of Heaven, knoweth your state; and He doeth with you according to His justice and mercy. (Mormon 6:19-22)

In the light of day when man can work, if he works for happiness, so will his happiness be when day is ended; and if in that day his desires were for good, he will be raised to that which is good. On the other hand, if man chooses to do evil all his days and does not repent, and furthermore, desires that evil be his portion, when the night comes and he cannot work, "he will be raised to evil according to his desires for evil." In the Resurrection the righteous shall be raised to everlasting happiness proportionately as they served the Lord, and the wicked and those who chose to do evil to "endless misery to inherit the kingdom of the devil," where all that is evil abides. There they will be with their kind, to dwell with those whom they loved and with those whom they served.

VERSE 7. *These are they that are redeemed of the Lord.* Those who walked in the *right path,* and, also, those who saw their faults and follies and repented thereof with sincere hearts, are those who are redeemed of the Lord. *Repent with a sincere heart* means that thereafter the life of a man will prove the strength of his determination to keep God's commandments and hate instead of love evil. "These are they," the Sacred Record says, "Who are taken out." Out of what? Out of the prison that has held them bound with the bands of death and the chains of hell. In other words, *hell and the grave.* They are *The Redeemed of the Lord* who are delivered from "that endless night of darkness" which enshroud the wicked because they, and only they, refuse to come forth into the light. We can always remember that they who may have been wicked, as soon as they repent of their sins and serve the Lord, "Light will come forth unto them out of darkness." Man, when he stands before the great *Judge* at the Last Day, will be his own accuser; he will stand before Him, naked, without a thing to hide his actions here below. He will assist in the judicial decree handed down by the *High Tribunal* before which he will stand. He will be his own judge whether his actions were good or evil. "Therefore, let us walk in the light of the Lord," for "In Thy light do we see light."

VERSES 8-10. *The decrees of God are unalterable.* Men are not to be judged by a capricious God, or by One who may change His requirements to obtain Life Eternal in His Kingdom to suit a whim or a fanciful notion. What He demands from one, He will demand from all, the same yesterday, today, and forever. *He will not change!* The *edicts* of God do not vary; He will not change them into something else. Their meanings are plain so that all may understand.

Alma cautioned his son, Corianton, not to make the mistake of thinking that God, in His mercy, will overlook and not visit with a penalty any infraction of divine law. Or will He look with any degree of tolerance upon the continued course of evil. In the end, when all is said and done, wickedness will be its own paymaster, and its pay will be after the manner of the service rendered, misery for the wicked. *Restoration* implies that all things shall be returned to their former state, or their natural state; good unto good, and evil unto evil, misery unto misery, and happiness unto happiness. But a sinful person whose actions have brought him only misery, will not have happiness restored to him in his evil desires.

VERSE 10. *Wickedness never was happiness.* Alma's conclusion, "wickedness never was happiness," was based upon his understanding of men's weaknesses, and their mental and moral choices which were exhibited in the history of the preceding 4,000 years.

Alma had in his possession the *Brass Plates of Laban.* He had read them and re-read them. They contained the Hebrew Scriptures. He had read therein of the Fall of Man, and of the sorrow and misery Adam's transgression brought upon all his sons and daughters. Alma also read how the descendants of Patriarch Jacob were made slaves by the Egyptians and were forced to do the bidding of relentless taskmasters.

Moreover, a history of the Jews down to the reign of King Zedekiah was engraved upon these plates. In reading it Alma became acquainted with the many follies and faults of the Jews. He learned how prone they were to heed the adversary. Time and time again, they had rejected God's holy Word which was proclaimed to them by the holy prophets. Wickedness had dulled their sense of what was just and true. To the prophets the Jews gave little heed.

The Jews were God's Chosen People, but in that lofty height they had fallen. They preferred "darkness rather than light because their deeds were evil." (John 3:19) Wickedness weakened them and they became the prey of other powerful nations. Coalitions were formed against them and allied armies came upon them. We may assume, and rightly so, that because of their waywardness and backsliding, God did not quickly deliver them from the predatory assaults of their ambitious neighbors.

It appears that the Jews could not long dwell in peace. "There is no peace, saith the Lord, unto the wicked." (Isaiah 48:22) However, the relatively short periods of peace which the Jews enjoyed, coupled with their rich heritage and the geographical location of their Sacred City, Jerusalem, brought them great material wealth. To the Jews the Lord gave much and much was expected, yet, they became proud and stiffnecked. They forgot God who had delivered their fathers from cruel bondage, and besides, they did not hesitate to change the requirements of the Torah (Law) to excuse the wicked designs of willful and evil-minded men.

As a nation they plowed and sowed iniquity and they reaped sorrow. "They drank deeply of the cup of bitterness and ate the bread of tears." To the Jews, it seemed to be unending that they were the victims of foreign oppression and the servants of foes who showed no pity.

We, like Alma, must conclude that neglect of God's laws and failure to abide them are unfailing signs that mark bitter servitude — the slavery of men's souls.

By the expression *souls,* we mean the body which we can see and the spirit that inhabits it. There is no happiness to be had in wickedness. These departures from the paths of holiness constitute man's greatest weakness and his utmost folly. It was ever so. Alma knew it, and therefore he sought to impress it upon the mind of his son, Corianton.

The Prophet Jeremiah, who lived in Jerusalem at the same time as did the Prophet Lehi, the scholarly ancestor of both the Nephites and the Lamanites, exclaimed, "How long shall the land mourn . . . for the wickedness of them that dwell therein?" (Jeremiah 12:4) Also, he said, "Judah mourneth, and the gates thereof languish . . . and the cry of Jerusalem is gone up." (Jeremiah 14:2) In spite of the *words of warning* uttered ceaselessly by the prophets, the Jews spasmodically continued in wickedness. At length the anger of the Lord was inflamed against them, and again His voice came to them through His holy prophets, "Thou hast forsaken Me . . . thou art gone backward: therefore will I stretch out My hand against thee, and destroy thee; I am weary with repenting." (Jeremiah 15:6) In another place the Lord said, "I will not pity, nor spare, nor have mercy." (*Ibid.* 13:14)

When the Lord said, "I am weary with repenting," He meant just this: Often He had stayed His hand in punishing His Chosen People because they promised to turn from their wicked ways and seek Him. Just as often their promises were vain. They continued in the wicked course they pursued. Now the Lord had proved their perfidy and now He refused longer to withhold His anger. His patience with them was exhausted.

Alma saw in all these things the sorrow which each imposed, but he still had further proof that *wickedness never was happiness* in the experiences of his own people. He had also in his possession the *Record of Zeniff.* Although he was, at that time, very young, he remembered the words of his intrepid father as he told of the wickedness of King Noah. Noah who was the son of Zeniff was king of the Nephites who lived in the Land of Lehi-Nephi. The record of Zeniff's people told how wicked King Noah led his subjects into all manner of sin. Noah's wanton practices became examples for his people to follow. Although at first the debaucheries of his court brought seeming pleasure to many of his followers, they ended in sorrow, in fierce bondage to the Lamanites in which murder, pillage, rapine, theft, and every cruelty which the ingenuity of their masters could suggest or evil power achieve was made part. The story of Zeniff's people under King Noah is one of the blackest pages in Book of Mormon history. Its whole nature is a composite of crime and cruelty. It is a mystery. We cannot understand it. Alma's argument is unanswerable. The experience of ages proves it true — *wickedness never was happiness.*

Many people have the idea that to get the most *happiness* out of life they must feed the hunger caused within them by "foolish and extravagent passions." They feel that they should satisfy every fleshly desire. They plunge deeply into "the pseudo-joys and follies of the world." They are quickly submerged in the unclean waters of iniquity. They mire knee-deep in the muck left by others who believed as they do. Yet a little while and their dreams of *happiness* are ended. Their laughter is turned into mourning, their joy into sorrow. They "sought for *happiness* in doing iniquity." (Helaman 13:38) They shall never find it!

Listen to the words of Nephi, the son of Nephi, who was one of the Disciples of Christ:

And it came to pass that there was no contention in the land, because of the love of God which did dwell in the hearts of the people.

And there were no envyings, nor strifes, nor tumults, nor whoredoms, nor lyings, nor murders, nor any manner of lasciviousness; and surely there could not be a *happier* people among all the people who had been created by the hand of God. (IV Nephi 15-16)

We recall what David, the father of King Solomon, said, "Yea, *happy* is that people, whose God is the LORD." (Psalm 144:15) and there comes to our minds more of the Holy Scriptures: "*Happy* are they that are upright in the way, who walk in the law of the Lord." "*Happy* are they that keep His testimonies, that seek Him with the whole heart." "*Happy* are they that keep justice, that do righteousness at all times." "*Happy* is everyone that feareth the Lord, that walketh in His ways." "*Happy* is he that hath the God of Jacob for his help, whose hope is in the LORD his God." (Psalm 146:5)

Always let us think of the words of the Prophet Lehi to his son, Jacob, spoken nearly 600 years before the advent of our Lord: "And if there be no righteousness there be no *happiness*." (II Nephi 2:13)

Let us conclude as did Alma, "Wickedness never was happiness."

Also, as did Paul, "The wages of sin is death." (Romans 6:23) And remember, too, that in that death, which is the death of the spiritual man, there is no *happiness*.

And moreover, I would desire that ye should consider on the blessed and *happy* state of those that keep the commandments of God. For behold, they are blessed in all things, both temporal and spiritual; and if they hold out faithful to the end they are received into heaven, that thereby they may dwell with God in a state of never-ending *happiness*. O remember, remember that these things are true; for the Lord God hath spoken it. (*King Benjamin*, Mosiah 2:41)

Although the comparison we make is very imperfect, we bring our comments upon this verse to an end by quoting poems written by two of England's greatly loved men. The first was written by Lord Byron, a man of whom it has been said, "was blessed beyond measure in genius, but destitute more than many of grace." Upon the very verge of the tomb he told in his own beautiful but *unhappy* words, the experiences of his life:

> *Though gay companions o'er the bowl*
> *Dispel awhile the sense of ill,*
> *Though pleasure fill the maddening soul,*
> *The heart, the heart is lonely still.*
>
> *Ay, but to die, and go, alas!*
> *Where all have gone, and all must go,*
> *To be the nothing that I was*
> *Ere born to life and living woe.*
>
> *Count o'er the joys thine hours have seen,*
> *Count o'er thy days from anguish free*
> *And know, whatever thou hast been,*
> *'Tis something better not to be.*
>
> *Nay, for myself, so dark my fate*
> *Through every turn of life hath been,*
> *Man and this world so much I hate,*
> *I care not when I quit the scene.*

Contrast this "bitter sarcasm" with the following description of a poor, but *happy*, peasant woman, who loves God, lives rightly, and does justly; O what a gap between them! The one shows *waywardness*, the other, *happiness*.

11. And now, my son, all men that are in a state of nature, or I would say, in a carnal state, are in the gall of bitterness and in the bonds of iniquity; they are without God in the world, and they have gone contrary to the nature of God; therefore, they are in a state contrary to the nature of happiness.

12. And now behold, is the meaning of the word restoration to take a thing of a natural state and place it in an unnatural state, or to place it in a state opposite to its nature?

Yon cottager, who weaves at her own door,
Pillow and bobbins all her little store,
Content though mean, and cheerful if not gay,
Shuffling her threads about the livelong day,
Just earns a scanty pittance, and at night
Lies down secure, her heart and pocket light;
She, for her humble sphere by Nature fit,
Has little understanding, and no wit,
Receives no praise, but though her lot be such
(Toilsome and indigent), she renders much;
Just knows, and knows no more, her Bible true—
A truth the brilliant Frenchman never knew,
And in that Charter reads with sparkling eyes
Her title to a treasure in the skies.
O HAPPY peasant!   O UNHAPPY bard!
His the mere tinsel, hers the rich reward;
He praised, perhaps, for ages yet to come,
She never heard of half a mile from home:
He lost in errors his vain heart prefers,
She safe in the simplicity of hers.

—Unidentified

VERSE 11. *All men that are in a state of nature, or . . . in a carnal state, are in the gall of bitterness.* The nature of God is *immortality* and happiness; "He is the light and the life of the world; yea, a light that is endless, that can never be darkened; yea, and also a life which is endless, that there can be no more death." Mosiah 18:9) But, by the Fall of Adam, man's nature became carnal, that is subject to death, the opposite to God's nature. Man became mortal, or subject to the flesh. The *Fall of Adam,* often called *the Fall of Man,* is the fall from a higher plane to one of lower estate. It represents a descent from immortality to mortality; from a never-ending life where there is no death, to the bitterness and gall of a certain destruction. Being guided by fleshy desires, and being prone to suffer temptation, man in this carnal state is bound with bands strong as iron. They represent what we sometimes regard as the joys of everyday life, but they more often are the foolishness and follies of men. They bind with ever-increasing severity. Man's nature while on Earth is directly opposite to the nature of God, "and never the twain shall meet." Therefore, mortal man is without God while he endures this earthly estate. By the *Fall* man went contrary to "the nature of God," which nature is *happiness;* or went into a nature incompatible with happiness.

VERSES 12-15. *What is the meaning of the word restoration?* Alma explains to Corianton that *restoration* does not mean that what is evil will be received into the good, or that a thing will be placed "in a state opposite to its nature." To restore good where once it dwelt, or "bring back again" to man, his desire and his opportunity to live it; to justify him in seeking heavenly rewards or treasures, and to

THE BOOK OF ALMA

13. O, my son, this is not the case; but the meaning of the word restoration is to bring back again evil for evil, or carnal for carnal, or devilish for devilish—good for that which is good; righteous for that which is righteous; just for that which is just; merciful for that which is merciful.

14. Therefore, my son, see that you are merciful unto your brethren; deal justly, judge righteously, and do good continually; and if ye do all these things then shall ye receive your reward; yea, ye shall have mercy restored unto you again; ye shall have justice restored unto you again; ye shall have a righteous judgment restored unto you again; and ye shall have good rewarded unto you again.

15. For that which ye do send out shall return unto you again, and be restored; therefore, the word restoration more fully condemneth the sinner, and justifieth him not at all.

---

place the Earth in the Celestial glory it once, when first created, was, is the correct meaning of *Restoration*.

The great lesson of man's bearing to his neighbor was placed before Corianton to impress on him the necessity of being just, merciful, and kind, to all others. Corianton had been enormously provocative in his morals, and to give further reign to his debased nature, he abandoned the missionfield and followed after the charms of a harlot. He repented of his sin, and sought to make amends. His father, by using the same qualities as he hoped to find Corianton develop, urged his son "to be merciful unto your brethren; deal justly, judge righteously, and do good continually." In so doing he promised that mercy would be shown unto him again, and that justice would be renewed unto him again; or that he would be forgiven of his sins, and all that was good would be restored again unto what would be a new man. Corianton's reward would be great as was his desires for righteousness. "What you do unto others shall be done unto you," or "What you meet out unto others shall be meeted out again to you." "Bread cast upon the waters shall return unto you again." "Forgive and ye shall be forgiven." These and other familiar sayings express what is meant by *restoration* when used to relate to the individual. Therefore, if forgiveness comes to one who forgives another, then we may say that he has restored unto him the innocence that was his before a sin was committed; also that when forgiveness is so easy to obtain, then it condemneth the sinner not to obtain it.

CHAPTER 42

1. *Alma to Corianton continued.*

2. *Justice and mercy expounded.*

3. *The Tree of Life.*

1. And now, my son, I perceive there is somewhat more which doth worry your mind, which ye cannot understand—which is concerning the justice of God in the punishment of the sinner; for ye do try to suppose that it is injustice that the sinner should be consigned to a state of misery.

2. Now behold, my son, I will explain this thing unto thee. For behold, after the Lord God sent our first parents forth from the garden of Eden, to till the ground, from whence they were taken—yea, he drew out the man, and he placed at the east end of the garden of Eden, cherubim, and a flaming sword which turned every way, to keep the tree of life—

3. Now, we see that the man had become as God, knowing good and evil; and lest he should put forth his hand, and take also of the tree of life, and eat and live forever, the Lord God placed cherubim and the flaming sword, that he should not partake of the fruit—

VERSES 1-3. *The justice of God in the punishment of the sinner.* Alma perceived that there was still more in Corianton's behavior that his son seemed unable to understand, or that he was unwilling to admit even unto himself. Corianton had violated his missionary covenant by forsaking the ministry and going over to the Land of Siron after a harlot named Isabel. Corianton realized his mistake in so doing, but, nevertheless, he was inclined to excuse his actions by supposing that God, in keeping with all the facts, was unjust in consigning sinners to an everlasting state of misery. We may well conceive that Corianton's conclusions were based upon his own misconduct. (*See* v. 30)

Corianton's father, sensing his son's desire to repent, was quick in the attempt to smooth out any troubled apprehensions that perplexed Corianton's heart and mind. Let us not forget in discussing Corianton's misadventures that it is two of Satan's greatest devices to imbue transgressors with the idea that God is not just, and also that too much sin has already been committed by the transgressor that repentance and the forgiveness of sin is a forlorn hope. Notwithstanding Corianton's frame of mind, Alma, as a good and loving father, "offered to explain" these things unto him.

The Tree of Life.

Beginning at the first, or with the Fall of Adam, Alma rehearsed to Corianton

4. *Mortality, a period of probation.*

5. *Spiritual and temporal death.*

4. And thus we see, that there | repent, yea, a probationary time, was a time granted unto man to | a time to repent and serve God.

---

the Lord's Plan of Salvation which would bring Eternal Life to all God's children if they obeyed His commandments. In a few words Alma reminded Corianton that Adam fell by partaking of the *Forbidden Fruit.* The fruit which God had commanded Adam not to eat of, grew in the Garden of Eden. Eating thereof was Adam's great transgression, and for so doing he was driven forth from the Garden wherein all was peace and plenty. Nearby, also in the Garden of Eden, grew the *Tree of Life.* When God commanded Adam not to eat of the fruit *of the Tree of the Knowledge of Good and Evil,* He added to His admonition, "for in the day that thou eatest thereof thou shalt surely die." (Genesis 3:17) Adam was in a quandry. He had partaken of that which under penalty was forbidden. He had brought upon himself, suffering and death. If Adam now should partake of the Fruit of the Tree of Life, he would live forever in his fallen state.

God promised death to the transgressor; the Tree of Life offered one who would partake of its fruit a never-ending existence. If Adam did partake, he would live forever in his sins, subject to pain, sweat, and tears, and all the infirmities that attend mankind, except he could not escape them through death because for him there would be no death. The penalty pronounced by God upon Adam if he ate of the fruit which He forbade was that "thou shalt surely die." That promise seemed to conflict with the inviting assurance of the Tree of Life, "thou shalt live forever." To prevent Adam and his wife, Eve, from returning into the Garden and partaking of its fruit, which in so doing they would live eternally in their fallen, mortal condition, the Lord put guards between Adam and the Tree. (*See,* COMMENTARY ON THE BOOK OF MORMON, Vol. III, p. 193)

We may not fully understand all that the account in Genesis of the Fall of Man conveys to the reader, but we do realize that it is not a myth. It is history. "Adam fell that man might be; and men are that they might have joy." (Alma 2:25) "Adam did fall by the partaking of the forbidden fruit, according to the word of God; and thus we see, that by his fall, all mankind became a lost and fallen people." (*Ibid.* 12:22) "Now we see that the man had become as God, knowing good and evil; and lest he should put forth his hand and take also of the Tree of Life, and eat and live forever, the Lord God placed cherubim and the flaming sword, that he should not partake of the fruit."

From the moral point of view, we learn in this narrative that our first parents were free moral agents, capable of choosing for themselves a course of action, and therefore responsible for their acts. We also learn that sin is the transgression of divine law, the result of which is death.

The Mosaic story of the Fall conveys another important truth. It shows us that man was not sent out upon the uninhabited places of the Earth before he was fully equipped for the struggle before him. How long a time he had developed in Paradise under Divine tuition, we do not know. But we know that in the Garden, God had taught him the value of plants and trees, and how to take care of them. (Genesis 2:15) He had become so familiar with the animal kingdom that he could name the animals according to their characteristics. (*Ibid* 19) He was undoubtedly familiar with astronomy, for otherwise the Sun, the planets, the stars, could not have been to him for signs, and for seasons, and for days and for years. (*Ibid* 1:14)

5. For behold, if Adam had put forth his hand immediately, and partaken of the tree of life, he would have lived forever, according to the word of God, having no space for repentance; yea, and also the word of God would have been void, and the great plan of salvation would have been frustrated.

6. But behold, it was appointed unto man to die—therefore, as they were cut off from the tree of life they should be cut off from the face of the earth—and man became lost forever, yea, they became fallen man.

7. And now, ye see by this that our first parents were cut off both temporally and spiritually from the presence of the Lord; and thus we see they became subjects to follow after their own will.

8. Now behold, it was not expedient that man should be reclaimed from this temporal death, for that would destroy the great plan of happiness.

9. Therefore, as the soul could never die, and the fall had brought upon all mankind a spiritual death as well as a temporal, that is, they were cut off from the presence of the Lord, it was expedient that mankind should be reclaimed from this spiritual death.

VERSES 4-15. *And thus we see, that there was a time granted unto man to repent, yea, a probationary time to repent and serve God.* Had Adam been permitted by the Lord to partake of the *Tree of Life,* he then would have lived forever in his mortal condition; a life brought about by partaking of the fruit of another tree, the *Tree of the Knowledge of Good and Evil.* Indeed, Adam was a man who had fallen from a higher plane; he was without hope, certainly without any means whatsoever of his own to regain his former position in God's grand Creation. *A Higher than he must intercede.*

God, knowing that Adam would fall into sin, therefore, even before the incidence of his transgression, made plans to rehabilitate him, and redeem him from the consequences of his guilt.

Redeem means, (1) To buy again something that has been sold, by paying back the price that bought it. (Lev. 25:25; 27:20) (2) To deliver and bring out of bondage those who were kept prisoner by their enemies. (Deut. 7:5; 32:6) By sin came death; sin, the violation of divine law, it may be said, purchased it. God's Plan of Redemption provided that the price which was paid for it be given back. What was that price? When it was paid, demand would be made by the one who paid the price for death to deliver up all those who were in its bondage, or held in its relentless grasp. The ransom was high; only God, Himself, could pay it. He, alone, could meet the prescribed terms! The Redeemer's Plan of Salvation provided beforehand that He would pay the price, even with His own life, to loose the bands of death. That price was paid, the ransom met. He died, the Great Redeemer died.

There is more meaning to the great Sacrifice the Redeemer made than giving us the victory over death. It provides also that all men, no matter who, may be saved by giving heed to, and obeying the requirements enjoined upon them in His great *Plan of Salvation* which was adopted by the *Council in Heaven* even before the world was. The *Plan of Salvation* is the Gospel Plan. Note that one of those requirements which are made of men is *repentance.* God commands all men to repent. It is not optional in any case. He who will not repent, believe, and be baptized, "must be damned." Note also that repentance is not only a doctrine. It is

THE BOOK OF ALMA

10. Therefore, as they had become carnal, sensual, and devilish, by nautre, this probationary state became a state for them to prepare; it became a preparatory state.

11. And now remember, my son, if it were not for the plan of redemption, (laying it aside) as soon as they were dead their souls were miserable, being cut off from the presence of the Lord.

12. And now, there was no means to reclaim men from this fallen state, which man had brought upon himself because of his own disobedience;

13. Therefore, according to justice, the plan of redemption could not be brought about, only on conditions of repentance of men in this probationary state,

yea, this preparatory state; for except it were for these conditions, mercy could not take effect except it should destroy the work of justice. Now the work of justice could not be destroyed; if so, God would cease to be God.

14. And thus we see that all mankind were fallen, and they were in the grasp of justice; yea, the justice of God, which consigned them forever to be cut off from his presence.

15. And now, the plan of mercy could not be brought about except an atonement should be made; therefore God himself atoneth for the sins of the world, to bring about the plan of mercy, to appease the demands of justice, that God might be a perfect, just God, and a merciful God also.

---

the main manifestation of a *new life* which those who accept the Gospel Plan and have been "born again," make obvious to the understanding of their fellows. Genuine repentance brings forgiveness, and that was the special point Alma sought to impress upon Corianton's mind. (Mosiah 26:31; Alma 5:49, 51, 54, 56; 9:30. Also *see* Doctrine and Covenants 64:10-14)

Repentance means to amend, or resolve to amend one's life as a result of contrition for one's sins. (*Webster's New Collegiate Dictionary*) Broken down by sorrow for sin, and humbly and thoroughly penitent, the repentant one is in a fit condition to be forgiven. Repentance of things that he did which should not have been done, and of things left undone that should have been done, could not, in our opinion, have been required of Adam, if he had eaten of the fruit of the Tree of Life because repentance of sin would not have changed his lot in any way. However, repentance was a must. In Adam's mortal existence since partaking of the Forbidden Fruit, such another misadventure as eating of the *Fruit of the Tree of Life*, besides urging him further along the path of disobedience, would have accorded him no needed time to repent. And man's repentance being a necessary part of the Plan of Salvation, God's purposes therein, and His promise of Eternal Life would have come to naught. And too, His word would have been rendered void, "and the great Plan of Salvation would have been frustrated." *Repentance is vital to that Plan.*

But behold, it was appointed unto man to die. Notwithstanding the pleasing assurance of the Tree of Life that he would live forever if he ate of its fruit, it was fixed, or established by God, as if by decree, that man was destined to die, or in the words of the Sacred Record, "cut off from the face of the earth." Through death, or the separation of the body of flesh and blood from man's immortal spirit, which that phrase signifies, man became an unclothed spirit, which but for the grace of God, he ever would remain.

We hereby note that Adam brought sin into the world by breaking God's command. He, and all mankind, Alma noted, "had become carnal, sensual, and devilish, by nature." That state all men have inherited to a greater or lesser degree. And as revealed, no evil or unclean thing can dwell in the presence of God, Adam was therefore "cut off" from His presence. Thus spiritually, Adam was dead, he being subject to the wiles of Satan, was driven forth from the Garden of Eden. Now, Adam having brought death to himself, and thus to all his children as pertaining to this earthly life, and also being deprived of God's presence and guidance, he became both spiritually, and in prospect, temporally dead. For this cause Adam and his wife, Eve, were driven forth from the Garden of Eden to roam the earth at will, and thus they became free agents " to follow after their own will," and as we have said, "being responsible for their own actions."

In Adam's Fall, we can see the beguiling allurements of Satan, made manifest, but he understood not the mind of God, and notwithstanding his evil designs, the Plan of God triumphed. Lucifer, the arch enemy of Christ and all that is good, struggled vainly to bring the purpose of God to naught. He sought to frustrate God's Plan of Salvation. In tempting Adam and Eve, now as mortals, to eat of the fruit of the Tree of Life and thereby live forever in their sins, he hoped that all God's children would eke out such an existence in misery, therein being subject to the will of the devil. In spite of Satan's cunning the purposes of God rolled on. God's mind and will did not fail.

And so, death came upon all mankind. God decreed that after death and the resurrection therefrom, all men must stand before Him, and there answer for what they did while on Earth, or when in that *probationary state* of which Alma spoke to his son, Corianton.

After God had appointed that death should come to all mankind, and that, likewise, a resurrection of the bodies of men held captive by the grave, He decreed a Day of Judgment in the which we, in our resurrected condition, must give an account as before stated. So that man should be fully informed concerning God's purposes in establishing death, the Resurrection, and a Day of Judgment, He saw, in His wisdom, that it was wise for them to know the reasons therefore, and sent His holy servants to converse with men.

These heavenly messengers, sent from God's presence, were commissioned by Him to minister unto the children of men, making known to them the power and authority of God, the Plan of Salvation, and His great love. From then on men began to see the greatness of God, the glorious majesty of His presence, and the wisdom of His word. Wherefore, Alma had previously told the Ammonihahites when he and Amulek were on their famous mission to that people, *God gave commandments to men.* Man having transgressed the Laws of God by partaking of the Forbidden Fruit thereby became as Gods "knowing good from evil." They were empowered by committing that same act to tell right from wrong and to choose good or evil. Discretion to this end increased within them. Not only did they see and recognize the truth, but they had power given them to act "according to their wills and pleasures, whether to do evil or to do good."

God, seeing men's mental and moral growth, as we have said, gave unto them commandments with which they were bidden to comply. Obedience to them brought forth the blessings of Heaven, neglect or refusal to obey them, the wrath of God. Gradually, that man who chooses to do iniquity, or to do evil without repentance, looses the firm grasp he once had upon things righteous. Slowly, but surely, he finds it gets easier to choose the evil. He becomes oblivious to God's commands, and therein sees darkness where there is light. The penalty of such willful disobedience is *death*. Not death to the body of flesh and blood, for that came by Adam's partaking of the Forbidden Fruit, but death, a *second death*, "which was an everlasting death as to things pertaining to righteousness." Such a man prefers darkness to light, because his deeds are evil. No evil can enter the presence of God, and the doer thereof is likewise banned. Of him who refuses to repent there is no redemption, the justice of God cannot be thus violated. The supreme goodness and mercy of God cannot be made an excuse for evil. His promise of forgiveness is entirely predicated upon repentance with first a belief on His Only Begotten Son. Through Him, and Him alone, He said, "will I have mercy upon you." Repentance is, we repeat, vital in the Plan of Redemption. "All them that repent, having a sincere heart and a steadfast spirit, can claim and will receive mercy through Mine Only Begotten Son, and will find rest with Me in My Kingdom, thus saith the Lord who is God over all the Earth."

In this we see that man was given a time to repent, and also we can find in it a complete answer to the query of Corianton, that he who repents will receive of God's mercy when after the resurrection he stands before God to be judged of his works while on Earth. With the righteous he will enter a state of happiness, while he who refuses to cast aside his wicked ways, and thereafter worship God, will be consigned to a place where misery prevails and where despair and anguish take possession of his soul.

Thus, to summarize, death came into the world by transgression. It held fast in its clutches the inevitable decree, "Thou shalt surely die." (Genesis 2:17) Man was helpless; of himself, he could do nothing. He was cast out from God's presence, "For they are carnal, and devilish, and the devil has power over them." (Mosiah 16:3) Evil, in no form, can dwell in God's Kingdom. A way must be found in which God's children can regain the place they once had—a home with Him in the Celestial Abode.

That Way has been found, The Lord God, Himself, has prepared it. That Plan or Way, is the Gospel of Jesus Christ. His great Sacrifice on Calvary paved the way for man's return to glory; the resurrection of Christ from the dead broke the shackles of the grave that held man in its inexorable grasp. Through His Atonement we shall live again, and because of His resurrection we, too, will be raised to Immortality and Eternal Life, never to die again. The Sacrifice and Resurrection of Christ broke, by God's power and mercy, the bands of death that otherwise would have held men forever in their state as spirits. Christ's triumphant Resurrection gave Him power to intercede for us; thus through Him all men will be resurrected and placed beyond the power of hell and the grave. The Prophet Abinadi, in preaching the Gospel of Jesus Christ to the wicked priests of King Noah, therein extolled the loving-kindness in which Christ would suffer and die for men, of His patience in serving them, and of His compassion for their helpless condition in their fallen state. Christ, Abinadi declared, stood between men and their just punishment, He took "upon Himself their iniquities and their transgressions." (Mosiah 15:9) "Surely our afflictions He hath borne, and our sorrows he carrieth them." (See Mosiah 14:4)

Amulek, Alma's missionary companion, in declaring the great and last Sacrifice which would be made by Jesus Christ, said to the apostate Zoramites in the Land of Antionum: "And thus He shall bring Salvation to all those who shall believe on His Name; this being the intent of this last Sacrifice, to bring about the bowels of mercy, which overpowereth justice, and bringeth about means unto men that they may have faith unto repentance. And thus mercy can satisfy the demands of justice, and encircles them in the arms of safety, while he that exercises no faith unto repentance is exposed to the whole law of the demands of justice; therefore only unto him that has faith unto repentance is brought about the great and eternal Plan of Redemption."

Now that man had cut himself off from the presence of God, and by disobedience to His law had rendered service to Satan, thereby giving the devil victory over Christ, a just punishment awaited all mankind. In God's justice His children were "forever to be cut off from His presence." Mankind had become carnal, subject to the demands of the flesh. He had became devilish, often serving evil. To bring mankind back to God's presence an atonement for the sins of the world must be made; in His justice His anger must be appeased, His wrath must be reconciled. Otherwise man and his Creator must be forever separated. God, Himself, brought about this great atonement, thereby proving His love and long-suffering for His children. He tempered justice with mercy "that God might be a perfect God, and a merciful God also."

One, in contemplating the full demands of justice, may see in the *Plan of Mercy* a miscarriage of that same justice which rules the universe. But justice does not exclude mercy. Sometimes what we call *justice* may be rank injustice, because we do never know for certain what mitigating circumstances due to heredity or environment, are responsible in a case of transgression. Sometimes mercy is justice. In the Old Dispensation the *Tables of Law* were covered by the *Mercy Seat*, a wonderful type of the *Government of God*, Who has said: I, the Lord, will forgive whom I will forgive, but of you it is required to forgive all men. (Doctrine and Covenants 64:10)

In this regard, we print again President John Taylor's comments on the Justice of God: Is justice dishonored? No; it is satisfied, the debt is paid. Is righteousness departed from? No; this is a righteous act. All requirements are met. Is judgment violated? No; its demands are fulfilled. Is mercy triumphant? No; she simply claims her own. Justice, judgment, mercy and truth all harmonize as the attributes of Diety. "Justice and truth have met together, righteousness and peace have kissed each other." Justice and judgment triumph as well as mercy and peace; all the attributes of Deity harmonize in this great, grand, momentous, just, equitable, merciful and meritorious act. (Mediation and Atonement)

When Alma and Amulek were preaching the Gospel of Jesus Christ to the Ammonihahites (Alma 9-15), Amulek noted that the temporal body of man is destroyed by death. Death is the separation of the body of flesh and blood from the spirit of man. Before that separation occurs, there is a time appointed wherein men can prepare to meet their God. That time, he said, is now! This mortal life is a probationary state during which man can make himself ready to enjoy a life of happiness in the presence of God, or be cast into outer darkness where the Holy Spirit never dwells. These extremes are those *endless states* of happiness and misery of which Alma informed Corianton. Those *endless states* come after the resurrection of man, or after the reuniting of the soul has taken place.

About eight years after the notable mission of Alma and Amulek to the Ammonihahites, they again went on another tour of duty, this time to the Zoramites, there to proclaim to that apostate group the *Name of Christ*. As before they had preached to the Ammonihahites that now is the time for repentance, and that this life of mortality is the appointed season in which to prepare oneself to enter God's presence, so they in like manner declared it to the Zoramites.

And now, my brethren, I would that, after ye have received so many witnesses, seeing that the holy scriptures testify of these things, ye come forth and bring fruit unto repentance.

6. *Repentance, atonement, law, punishment, all necessary.*

16. Now, repentance could not come unto men except there were a punishment, which also was eternal as the life of the soul should be, affixed opposite to the plan of happiness, which was as eternal also as the life of the soul.

17. Now, how could a man repent except he should sin? How could he sin if there was no law? How could there be a law save there was a punishment?

18. Now, there was a punishment affixed, and a just law given, which brought remorse of conscience unto man.

19. Now, if there was no law given—if a man murdered he should die—would he be afraid he would die if he should murder?

20. And also, if there was no law given against sin men would not be afraid to sin.

21. And if there was no law given, if men sinned what could justice do, or mercy either, for they would have no claim upon the creature?

Yea, I would that ye would come forth and harden not your hearts any longer; for behold, now is the time and the day of your salvation; and therefore, if ye will repent and harden not your hearts, immediately shall the great plan of redemption be brought about unto you.

For behold, this life is the time for men to prepare to meet God; yea, behold the day of this life is the day for men to perform their labors.

And now, as I said unto you before, as ye have had so many witnesses, therefore, I beseech of you that ye do not procrastinate the day of your repentance until the end; for after this day of life, which is given us to prepare for eternity, behold, if we do not improve our time while in this life, then cometh the night of darkness wherein there can be no labor performed.

Ye cannot say, when ye are brought to that awful crisis, that I will repent, that I will return to my God. Nay, ye cannot say this; for that same spirit which doth possess your bodies at the time that ye go out of this life, that same spirit will have power to possess your body in that eternal world.

For behold, if ye have procrastinated the day of your repentance even until death, behold, ye have become subjected to the spirit of the devil, and he doth seal you his; therefore, the Spirit of the Lord hath withdrawn from you, and hath no place in you, and the devil hath all power over you; and this is the final state of the wicked. (Alma 34:30-35)

VERSES 16-28. *There is a law given, and a punishment affixed, and a repentance granted.* As we have noted, God saw that His children had become capable in and of themselves to tell right from wrong, and good and evil. The Sacred Record says, "Man had become as God, knowing good and evil." Our first parents, now alone out in the world, were free agents to act "according to their wills and pleasures, whether to do evil or to do good." To the end that men should prove themselves worthy of God's blessings, just laws and divine commandments were given unto them by Heaven's gracious plan. Thus a choice was placed before them. The alternative, to obey the laws and commandments or not, was their sacred right. We also noted that to these laws were affixed two opposites — happiness and misery. Happiness to those who obeyed them, and misery to those that through neglect or a refusal to obey, ignored them. A just punishment awaited all who disobeyed.

We again draw attention to our previous statement: that sin is the transgression of divine law. Punishment for sin is certain. The penalty that is exacted of the sinner is firm and steadfast. It is immovable. It provides that the same punishment for the same offense be equal no matter when or where the certain transgression was committed. God does not vary. He is not capricious, measuring out to one that which He demands not from another. It is well to remember that God is the same yesterday, today, and forever. Also remember that to each law or commandment God gave, there was attached thereto the same blessings to the penitent, and to the unrepentant, the same penalties were provided. For example: "And He hath said that: Inasmuch as ye shall keep My commandments ye shall prosper in the land; but inasmuch as ye will not keep My commandments ye shall be cut off from My presence." (II Nephi 1:20)

Now, the punishments for infraction of divine law were eternal, not subject to change. They were everlasting, of infinite duration, even "as the life of the soul should be." They were "affixed opposite to the *Plan of Happiness,* which was as eternal also as the life of the soul," which is never ending. To escape the punishment which God had decreed for disobedience, men were urged to repentance. The fear of punishment made alive in men a continuing impulse for good, but without the fear that they would be punished for sin there would be no repentance, because there would be no punishment to fear. In this dispensation the Lord has said through the Prophet Joseph Smith: "Eternal punishment is God's punishment. Endless punishment is God's punishment." In explanation of these terms, He also said: "Wherefore, I revoke not the judgments which I shall pass . . . nevertheless, it is not written that there shall be no end to this torment, but it is written *endless torment.* . . . For, behold, I am endless, and the punishment which is given from My hand is endless punishment, for *Endless is my Name.*" (Doctrine and Covenants, Section 19) We can see clearly in this that when Christ preached to the spirits in prison, he went to the prison-house to loose them from the bands that held them, and end their punishment. He brought them forth from the prison-house, but the law that affixed their punishment was in itself endless.

We refer the reader to the following passages of Nephite Scripture:

Punishment—

II Nephi	2:10	The inflicting of the p. which is affixed
	10	Which p. that is affixed is in opposition
	13	There be no p. nor misery
	26	Save it be by the p. of the law
	9:25	Where there is no law given, there is no p.

Endless Torment—

II Nephi	9:10	Fire and brimstone, which is endless t.
	26	Fire and brimstone, which is endless t.
	28:23	Fire and brimstone, which is endless t.
Jacob	6:10	Lake of fire and brimstone, is endless t.
Mosiah	3:25	Into a state of misery and endless t.
	28:3	That any soul should endure endless t.
Moroni	8:21	Danger of death, hell, and an endless t.

Never ending Torment—

| Mosiah | 2:39 | Doom is to endure a never ending t. |
| | 5:5 | Bring upon ourselves a never ending t. |

22. But there is a law given, and a punishment affixed, and a repentance granted; which repentance mercy claimeth; otherwise, justice claimeth the creature and executeth the law, and the law inflicteth the punishment; if not so, the works of justice would be destroyed, and God would cease to be God.

23. But God ceaseth not to be God, and mercy claimeth the penitent, and mercy cometh because of the atonement; and the atonement bringeth to pass the resurrection of the dead; and the resurrection of the dead bringeth back men into the presence of God; and thus they are restored into his presence, to be judged according to their works, according to the law and justice.

24. For behold, justice exerciseth all his demands, and also mercy claimeth all which is her own; and thus, none but the truly penitent are saved.

25. What, do ye suppose that mercy can rob justice? I say unto you, Nay; not one whit. If so, God would cease to be God.

26. And thus God bringeth about his great and eternal purposes, which were prepared from the foundation of the world. And thus cometh about the salvation and the redemption of men, and also their destruction and misery.

27. Therefore, O my son, whosoever will come may come and partake of the waters of life freely; and whosoever will not come the same is not compelled to come; but in the last day it shall be restored unto him according to his deeds.

28. If he has desired to do evil, and has not repented in his days, behold, evil shall be done unto him, according to the restoration of God.

Eternal Torment—

| Mosiah | 27:29 | My soul was racked with eternal t. |
| | 36:12 | But I was racked with eternal t. |

Endless—

II Nephi	9:7	Needs have remained to an e. duration
Mosiah	16:9	A light that is e.
	9	Also a life that is e.
Alma	9:11	Consigned to a state of e. misery
	12:24	A time to prepare for that e. state
	28:11	Are consigned to a state of e. wo
	41:4	Raised to e. happiness, to inherit the
	4	Or to e. misery, to inherit the kingdom
	7	Delivered from that e. night of darkness
Helaman	5:12	Down to the gulf of misery and e. wo
	7:16	Down to everlasting misery, and e. wo
	12:26	Be consigned to a state of e. misery
Mormon	8:38	Greater is the value of an e. happiness
	9:13	A redemption from an e. sleep
Moroni	8:13	These must have gone to an e. hell

29. And now, my son, I desire that ye should let these things trouble you no more, and only let your sins trouble you, with that trouble which shall bring you down unto repentance.

30. O my son, I desire that ye should deny the justice of God no more. Do not endeavor to excuse yourself in the least point because of your sins, by denying the justice of God; but do you let the justice of God, and his mercy, and his long-suffering have full sway in your heart; and let it bring you down to the dust in humility.

31. And now, O my son, ye are called of God to preach the word unto this people. And now, my son, go thy way, declare the word with truth and soberness, that mercy may have claim upon thou mayest bring souls unto repentance, that the great plan of them. And may God grant unto you even according to my words. Amen.

VERSES 29-31. *My son, let these things trouble you no more, and only let your sins trouble you* . . . Alma ended his instructions and his explanations of God's justice and mercy to Corianton with an exhortation that his son would no more harrow up his soul with thoughts of divine injustice. But instead, live so that past sins shall be forgiven. Worry only about the sins you have committed, not about the administration of justice in return for good or evil.

CHAPTER 43

1. *Another Lamanite invasion.*

1. And now it came to pass that the sons of Alma did go forth among the people, to declare the word unto them. And Alma, also, himself, could not rest, and he also went forth.

2. Now we shall say no more concerning their preaching, except that they preached the word, and the truth, according to the spirit of prophecy and revelation; and they preached after the holy order of God by which they were called.

3. And now I return to an account of the wars between the Nephites and the Lamanites, in the eighteenth year of the reign of the judges.

4. For behold, it came to pass that the Zoramites became Lamanites; therefore, in the commencement of the eighteenth year the people of the Nephites saw that the Lamanites were coming upon them; therefore they made preparations for war; yea, they gathered together their armies in the land of Jershon.

5. And it came to pass that the Lamanites came with their thousands; and they came into the land of Antionum, which is the land of the Zoramites; and a man by the name of Zerahemnah was their leader.

6. And now, as the Amalekites were of a more wicked and murderous disposition than the Lamanites were, in and of themselves, therefore, Zerahemnah appointed chief captains over the Lamanites, and they were all Amalekites and Zoramites.

VERSES 1-3. *And now I return to an account of the wars between the Nephites and the Lamanites.* The Abridger of the Nephite records, Mormon, diverged from an account of the year by year happenings among the Nephite people to give us a rather complete compendium of Alma's instructions to his sons, Helaman, Shiblon, and Corianton. He now resumed his digest of the political events that molded Nephite history for a long time to come.

It was now about 73 years before the birth of Christ in far away Judea, the land of their forefathers. Alma and his sons could not rest from the active preaching of the Lord's word, and so they went throughout the whole Land of Zarahemla and wherever they found listeners they declared the Gospel of Christ to them. They were imbued with the spirit of revelation and prophecy, and imparted to one and all the message of Christ's Redemption as the spirit of their office and calling inspired.

VERSES 4-21. *The Nephites gathered together their armies in the Land of Jershon.* Mormon says no more about the ministrations of Alma and his sons, but notes that it was at the end of the seventeenth year of the Reign of the Judges over the people

7. Now this he did that he might preserve their hatred towards the Nephites, that he might bring them into subjection to the accomplishment of his designs.

8. For behold, his designs were to stir up the Lamanites to anger against the Nephites; this he did that he might usurp great power over them, and also that he might gain power over the Nephites by bringing them into bondage.

9. And now the design of the Nephites was to support their lands, and their houses, and their wives, and their children, that they might preserve them from the hands of their enemies; and also that they might preserve their rights and their privileges, yea, and also their liberty, that they might worship God according to their desires.

10. For they knew that if they should fall into the hands of the Lamanites, that whosoever should worship God in spirit and in truth, the true and the living God, the Lamanites would destroy.

11. Yea, and they also knew the extreme hatred of the Lamanites toward their brethren, who were the people of Anti-Nephi-Lehi, who were called the people of Ammon—and they would not take up arms, yea, they had entered into a covenant and they would not break it—therefore, if they should fall into the hands of the Lamanites they would be destroyed.

12. And the Nephites would not suffer that they should be destroyed; therefore they gave them lands for their inheritance.

13. And the people of Ammon did give unto the Nephites a large portion of their substance to support their armies; and thus the Nephites were compelled, alone, to withstand against the Lamanites, who were a compound of Laman and Lemuel, and the sons of Ishmael, and all those who had dissented from the Nephites, who were Amalekites and Zoramites, and the descendants of the priests of Noah.

14. Now those descendants were as numerous, nearly, as were the Nephites; and thus the Nephites were obliged to contend with their brethren, even unto bloodshed.

---

of Nephi that the Zoramites allied with the Lamanites began to prepare for war against the Nephites. The Sacred Record says:

And the people of Ammon departed out of the Land of Jershon, and came over into the Land of Melek, and gave place in the Land of Jershon for the armies of the Nephites. (Alma 35:13)

The cause that led the Nephite armies to occupy Jershon was that the Zoramites, finding that their haughty and unjust demands would not be complied with, had excited the Lamanites to invade the territory of the Nephites. The Lamanite forces which were commanded almost entirely by Nephite apostates, on account of their fierce hatred of their former associates, marched first into the Land of Antionum where they were joined by the Zoramites. Then the whole of the invading hosts, under a man named Zerahemnah, advanced northward towards the Land of Jershon.

15. And it came to pass as the armies of the Lamanites had gathered together in the land of Antionum, behold, the armies of the Nephites were prepared to meet them in the land of Jershon.

16. Now, the leader of the Nephites, or the man who had been appointed to be the chief captain over the Nephites—now the chief captain took the command of all the armies of the Nephites—and his name was Moroni;

17. And Moroni took all the command, and the government of their wars. And he was only twenty and five years old when he was appointed chief captain over the armies of the Nephites.

18. And it came to pass that he met the Lamanites in the borders of Jershon, and his people were armed with swords, and with cimeters, and all manner of weapons of war.

19. And when the armies of the Lamanites saw that the people of Nephi, or that Moroni, had prepared his people with breastplates and with arm-shields, yea, and also shields to defend their heads, and also they were dressed with thick clothing—

20. Now the army of Zerahemnah was not prepared with any such thing; they had only their swords and their cimeters, their bows and their arrows, their stones and their slings; and they were naked, save it were a skin which was girded about their loins; yea, all were naked, save it were the Zoramites and the Amalekites;

21. But they were not armed with breastplates, nor shields—therefore, they were exceedingly afraid of the armies of the Nephites because of their armor, notwithstanding their number being so much greater than the Nephites.

This was a day of peril for the Nephites. Their enemies were much more numerous than they, and were filled with a savage thirst for blood, which was especially felt against those who were of their own race and kindred who had bowed in obedience to Heaven's command. At this juncture the Lord raised up one of the greatest heroes ever born on American soil. He was not only a military leader, but a priest and prophet, and by his inspiration and devoted courage the Nephites were for many years led to uninterrupted victory. Such was Moroni, who now, though only twenty-five years old, took the chief command of the armies of his nation.

Though the forces of the combined Lamanites and the Zoramites were much more numerous, nearly all other advantages were on the side of the Nephites. The discipline of the Nephites was better by far; the bodies of their soldiers were protected by armor, breastplates, helmets, shields, etc., and they were fighting for the sacred cause of their religion and their country, their altars and their firesides, their wives and little ones. Inspired by the justness of their cause and the extremity of their circumstances, they fought with a courage and a desperation never exceeded in all their annals.

The Lamanites, on the other hand, had no such holy impulses to nerve their arms for the combat. They were the aggressors, and were hasting to shed the blood of their brethren. Insane and infernal hatred alone inspired them for the conflict. Besides, they were ill-prepared to meet the Nephites, who had such a tactician as

22. Behold, now it came to pass that they durst not come against the Nephites in the borders of Jershon; therefore they departed out of the land of Antionum into the wilderness, and took their journey round about in the wilderness, away by the head of the river Sidon, that they might come into the land of Manti and take possession of the land; for they did not suppose that the armies of Moroni would know whither they had gone.

23. But it came to pass, as soon as they had departed into the wilderness Moroni sent spies into the wilderness to watch their camp; and Moroni, also, knowing of the prophecies of Alma, sent certain men unto him, desiring him that he should inquire of the Lord whither the armies of the Nephites should go to defend themselves against the Lamanites.

24. And it came to pass that the word of the Lord came unto Alma, and Alma informed the messengers of Moroni, that the armies of the Lamanites were marching round about in the wilderness, that they might come over into the land of Manti, that they might commence an attack upon the weaker part of the people. And those messengers went and delivered the message unto Moroni.

25. Now Moroni, leaving a part of his army in the land of Jershon, lest by any means a part of the Lamanites should come into that land and take possession of the city, took the remaining part of his army and marched over into the land of Manti.

26. And he caused that all the people in that quarter of the land should gather themselves together to battle against the Lamanites, to defend their lands and their country, their rights and their liberties; therefore they were prepared against the time of the coming of the Lamanites.

Moroni for their Commander-in-Chief. The descendants of Laman were simply armed with swords and cimeters, bows and arrows, slings and stones. Their bodies were naked with the exception of a skin wrapped about their loins. The Zoramites and other dissenters from the Nephites were better clothed; in dress they followed the fashion of the people from whom they sprang.

VERSES 22-26. *The Lamanites durst not come against the Nephites in the borders of Jershon.* The Lamanites, finding that Moroni was too well prepared for their attack on the Land of Jershon, retired through Antionum into the wilderness, where they changed direction and marched towards the headwaters of the River Sidon, with the intention of taking possession of the Land of Manti.

But Moroni, suspecting their motives, was too vigilant to allow his enemies to slip away without knowing what had become of them. He had his spies watch the movements of Zerahemnah's forces, and in the meantime sent to Alma to inquire the mind and will of the Lord in regard to his future course. The Word of the Lord was given to Alma, and he informed Moroni's messengers of the movements of the Lamanites. The young general, with becoming prudence, then divided his army. One corps he left to protect Jershon, and with the remainder he advanced

2. *Armies of Moroni and Lehi surround and overpower the enemy.*

27. And it came to pass that Moroni caused that his army should be secreted in the valley which was near the bank of the river Sidon, which was on the west of the river Sidon in the wilderness.

28. And Moroni placed spies round about, that he might know when the camp of the Lamanites should come.

29. And now, as Moroni knew the intention of the Lamanites, that it was their intention to destroy their brethren, or to subject them and bring them into bondage that they might establish a kingdom unto themselves over all the land;

30. And he also knowing that it was the only desire of the Nephites to preserve their lands, and their liberty, and their church, therefore he thought it no sin that he should defend them by stratagem; therefore, he found by his spies which course the Lamanites were to take.

31. Therefore, he divided his army and brought a part over into the valley, and concealed them on the east, and on the south of the hill Riplah;

32. And the remainder he concealed in the west valley, on the west of the river Sidon, and so down into the borders of the land Manti.

33. And thus having placed his army according to his desire, he was prepared to meet them.

34. And it came to pass that the Lamanites came up on the north of the hill, where a part of the army of Moroni was concealed.

35. And as the Lamanites had passed the hill Riplah, and came into the valley, and began to cross the river Sidon, the army which was concealed on the south of the hill, which was led by a man whose name was Lehi, and he led his army forth and encircled the Lamanites about on the east in their rear.

36. And it came to pass that the Lamanites, when they saw the Nephites coming upon them in their rear, turned them about and began to contend with the army of Lehi.

37. And the work of death commenced on both sides, but it was more dreadful on the part of the Lamanites, for their nakedness was exposed to the heavy blows of the Nephites with their swords and their cimeters, which brought death almost at every stroke.

38. While on the other hand,

by rapid marches toward Manti, by the most direct route. On his arrival there he at once mustered all the men who could bear arms into his forces to help in the defense of their rights and their liberties against the advancing foe. So rapid had been his movements and so prompt had been the response to his calls that when the Lamanites reached the neighborhood of the Sidon, Moroni was prepared for their coming.

there was now and then a man fell among the Nephites, by their swords and the loss of blood, they being shielded from the more vital parts of the body, or the more vital parts of the body being shielded from the strokes of the Lamanites, by their breastplates, and their arm-shields, and their head-plates; and thus the Nephites did carry on the work of death among the Lamanites.

39. And it came to pass that the Lamanites became frightened, because of the great destruction among them, even until they began to flee towards the river Sidon.

40. And they were pursued by Lehi and his men; and they were driven by Lehi into the waters of Sidon, and they crossed the waters of Sidon. And Lehi retained his armies upon the bank of the river Sidon that they should not cross.

41. And it came to pass that Moroni and his army met the Lamanites in the valley, on the other side of the river Sidon, and began to fall upon them and to slay them.

42. And the Lamanites did flee again before them, towards the land of Manti; and they were met again by the armies of Moroni.

43. Now in this case the Lamanites did fight exceedingly; yea, never had the Lamanites been known to fight with such exceeding great strength and courage, no, not even from the beginning.

44. And they were inspired by the Zoramites and the Amalekites, who were their chief captains and leaders, and by Zerahemnah, who was their chief captain, or their chief leader and commander; yea, they did fight like dragons, and many of the Nephites were slain by their hands, yea, for they did smite in two many of their head-plates, and they did pierce many of their breastplates, and they did smite off many of their arms; and thus the Lamanites did smite in their fierce anger.

45. Nevertheless, the Nephites were inspired by a better cause, for they were not fighting for monarchy nor power but they were fighting for their homes and their liberties, their wives and their children, and their all, yea, for their rites of worship and their church.

46. And they were doing that which they felt was the duty which they owed to their God; for the Lord had said unto them, and also unto their fathers, that: Inasmuch as ye are not guilty of the first offense, neither the second, ye shall not suffer yourselves to be slain by the hands of your enemies.

47. And again, the Lord has said that: Ye shall defend your families even unto bloodshed. Therefore for this cause were the Nephites contending with the Lamanites, to defend themselves, and their families, and their lands, their country, and their rights, and their religion.

48. And it came to pass that when the men of Moroni saw the

fierceness and the anger of the Lamanites, they were about to shrink and flee from them. And Moroni, perceiving their intent, sent forth and inspired their hearts with these thoughts—yea, the thoughts of their lands, their liberty, yea, their freedom from bondage.

49. And it came to pass that they turned upon the Lamanites, and they cried with one voice unto the Lord their God, for their liberty and their freedom from bondage.

50. And they began to stand against the Lamanites with power; and in that selfsame hour that they cried unto the Lord for their freedom, the Lamanites began to flee before them; and they fled even to the waters of Sidon.

51. Now, the Lamanites were more numerous, yea, by more than double the number of the Nephites; nevertheless, they were driven insomuch that they were gathered together in one body in the valley, upon the bank by the river Sidon.

2. Therefore the armies of Moroni encircled them about, yea, even on both sides of the river, for behold, on the east were the men of Lehi.

53. Therefore when Zerahemnah saw the men of Lehi on the east of the river Sidon, and the armies of Moroni on the west of the river Sidon, that they were encircled about by the Nephites, they were struck with terror.

54. Now Moroni, when he saw their terror, commanded his men that they should stop shedding their blood.

VERSES 27-54. *The armies of Moroni encircled them about.* The battle that was fought when the opposing armies met was one of the most stubborn and bloody in Nephite history. Never from the beginning had the Lamanites been known to fight with such exceedingly great strength and courage. Time after time their hosts rushed upon the well-ordered ranks of the Nephites, and notwithstanding the latter's armor, they crushed in their heads and cut off their arms.

But the cost to their own numbers of these charges was terrible. The battle began at a hill called Riplah, and afterwards extended to both sides of the River Sidon. At one time a lull took place in the carnage, and Moroni, who had no pleasure in the shedding of blood, ordered his men to stop the carnage.

MORONI

Moroni was one of the greatest Nephite prophets and military commanders. He was born in Zarahemla about the year 100 B.C. At the age of twenty-five years he had risen to the supreme command of the forces of the Commonwealth. At that time an army of the Lamanites, commanded by a man named Zerahemnah (75 B.C.) was threatening the Land of Jershon, having, by the invitation of the apostate Zoramites, occupied the Land of Antionum. Moroni sent to Alma, the High Priest and President of the Church, to inquire the mind and will of the Lord concerning the proper course to take in regard to combating the Lamanites. Having received that word, Moroni carried it out, or into effect. The Lamanites, having found out that Moroni was too well prepared for them, retreated southward towards the Land of Manti. Moroni left a portion of his forces to protect Jershon, and with the rest proceeded towards Manti by the most direct route. The opposing armies met near the River Sidon; one of the most obstinately contested battles in Nephite history was fought, and Zerahemnah was disastrously defeated. After this battle there was a short period of peace, but soon internal dissensions, caused by the intrigues of royalists and apostates led by one Amalickiah, convulsed the Nephite community. Moroni rose to greatness with the peril of the hour. By his patriotic appeal he roused the whole Nephite Nation.

He tore off a portion of his coat, and naming it the "Title of Liberty," sent it far and wide through all the land, into all the cities of his countrymen, that they might see the appeal he had inscribed thereon. It read, "In memory of our God, our religion and freedom and our peace, our wives and our children."

The call was not in vain. The hosts of the patriots rallied to his standard. Amalickiah, hearing the news of this great awakening, faltered in his purpose, his followers lost heart and retreat was deemed the fittest show of wisdom and discretion the better part of valor. By Moroni's vigilance their retreat was cut off, the rebels surrendered, Amalickiah fled for safety to the Lamanites, and the "Title of Liberty" continued to float uninterruptedly from the Atlantic to the Pacific shores as far as Nephi's children ruled, or Nephite homes were found.

Amalickiah retired to the court of the king of the Lamanites, and with the cunning and ingenuity of a demon, worked himself onto that throne, while at the same time he was plotting an invasion of the Nephite country. Moroni in the meantime was not idle. He reorganized the Nephite armies, compelled more stringent discipline, introduced new tactics, inaugurated a greatly superior system of fortifications, built towers and citadels, and altogether placed the defensive powers of the Commonwealth on a new and stronger footing.

The Lamanites, who appear to have developed no capacity for originating any means of defense but were apt in copying also, in course of time, adopted armor, and when they captured a weak Nephite city, they frequently made it a stronghold by surrounding it with ditches and walls after the system introduced and put in effect by Moroni.

The foundation of Moroni's system of fortifications was earthworks encircling the place to be defended. The earth was dug from the outside by means of which a ditch was formed. Sometimes walls of stone were erected. On the top of the earthworks strong defenses of wood, sometimes breastworks, in some cases to the full height of a man, were raised. Above these a stockade of strong pickets was built to arrest the flight of the stones and arrows of the attackers. Behind these walls towers were raised at various convenient points, from which observations of the movements of the enemy were taken, and wherein corps of archers and slingers were stationed during actual continuance of battle. From their elevated and commanding positions these bodies of soldiers could do great injury to the attacking forces.

In 73 B.C., Amalickiah commenced active hostilities. He raised an immense army and placing it under the direction of Zoramite commanders, ordered its advance into the western possessions of the Nephites, in which region stood the cities of Noah and Ammonihah. When the invaders reached the last named city they found it too strongly fortified to be taken by assault. They therefore retired to the City of Noah, originally a very weak place, but now, through Moroni's foresight and energy, made stronger than Ammonihah. The Zoramite officers well knew that to return home without having attempted something would be most disastrous. They, therefore, though with little hope, made an assault upon Noah. This step resulted in throwing away a thousand lives outside its walls while its well-protected defenders had but fifty men wounded. After this disastrous attempt to capture the city the Lamanites returned to their homes. Great was the anger of Amalickiah at the miscarriage of his schemes, he cursed God and swore he would yet drink the blood of Moroni.

During the next year the armies of Moroni drove the Lamanites out of that portion of the East Wilderness bordering on the Land of Zarahemla into their own lands. The northern line, or boundary of the latter ran in a straight line from the sea east to the sea west. The Lamanites having been driven from north of the dividing line, colonies of Nephites were sent to occupy the country and build cities on their southern border, even to the Atlantic Coast. To protect the new settlers Moroni placed troops all along this line and caused them to erect fortifications for the better defense of the frontier. This fortified line ran from the west sea (Pacific Ocean) by the head of the River Sidon (the Magdalena) eastward along the northern edge of the wilderness.

A few years of peace followed, disturbed only by a serious local quarrel between the people inhabiting the cities of Morianton and Lehi (68 B.C.).

In the following year (67 B.C.) Amalickiah commenced a devastating invasion of the Atlantic provinces of the Nephites. Commencing at Moroni, on the extreme southeast, he gradually advanced northward, capturing and garrisoning all the Nephite cities until he reached the Land of Bountiful. There a stop was put to his progress by the forces of the Commonwealth, and he, himself, was slain by Teancum. His advance corps then retired a short distance to the south and garrisoned the neighboring City of Mulek. In this condition matters remained for some time, but in 64 B.C., Moroni, with the assistance of his lieutenants, defeated the Lamanites commanded by Jacob, and recaptured the City of Mulek, which victory was slowly followed by the reconquest of all the cities and lands on the Atlantic Seaboard.

In the southwest, matters had also gone disastrously for the Nephites, and the forces of the Republic stationed in that region were greatly hampered for lack of provisions and the nonarrival of expected reinforcements. Affairs were complicated at that time by a royalist uprising in the City of Zarahemla under a leader named Pachus. Pahoran, the Chief Judge, was driven out of the capital, and besides a communication was opened up by them with the Lamanites. At the request of Pahoran, Moroni with a portion of his forces went to the aid of the government at the earliest possible moment, leaving the armies in the northeast under the command of Lehi and Teancum. As he advanced, he rallied the people on his line of march to the defense of the liberties of the Republic, and was so successful that, after having joined Pahoran, he succeeded in overthrowing the "King-men" killing their leader, Pachus, and completely crushing the rebellion. This being accomplished, Moroni sent 6,000 men, with the necessary provisions, to reinforce Helaman in the southwest. (61 B.C.)

The campaign during this year, along the Atlantic Coast, was a decisive one. At last the Lamanites were driven out of Omner, Morianton, Gid, Lehi, Nephihah, Moroni, and every other Nephite city on that Seaboard and the lands of the Nephites were free from the foot of the foe. A long-continued peace followed, for both nations were exhausted.

THE NAME MORONI

In 56 B.C., the valiant Moroni, one of the greatest and most virtuous of God's sons, passed away from this state of mortality to the glories of Eternity at the age of forty-three years. Some time before his death he had given the chief command of the Nephites to his son, Moronihah, who, from the history of later years, we judge him to have been a worthy son of so illustrious a sire.

Moroni, as is well known, is the name of the last of the Book of Mormon prophets. He finished the records of his father, Mormon, added his own abridgment of the plates of the Jaredites, and deposited the complete volume in the Hill Cumorah, about A.D. 421. In this same hill, Mormon had also deposited the original plates that had been entrusted to his care, from which he had compiled his briefer history.

And it came to pass that when we had gathered in all our people in one to the Land of Cumorah, behold, I, Mormon, began to be old; and knowing it to be the last struggle of my people, and having been commanded of the Lord that I should not suffer the records which had been handed down by our fathers, which were sacred, to fall into the hands of the Lamanites (for the Lamanites would destroy them) therefore I made this record out of the Plates of Nephi, and hid up in the Hill Cumorah all the records which had been entrusted to me by the hand of the Lord, save it were these few plates which I gave unto my son Moroni. (Mormon 6:6)

Moroni was also the name of the great Nephite general who was the first to proclaim the American Continents, the *Land of Liberty,* or, as we would say, "The Land of the Free." (Alma 46:11-17)

There was a City of Moroni on the East Sea, *on the south by the line of the possessions of the Lamanites;* (Alma 50:13) and a Land of Moroni, on the borders by the sea shore. (*Ibid.* 51:22; 62:25)

The word is Semetic. At the beginning of our era it had found its way into the Syriac spoken in Palestine, and was so generally understood that Paul used it in his first letter to the Corinthians (Corinthians 16:22); although that document was written in Greek, it still found favor with him when Paul used it, "If any man love not the Lord Jesus Christ, let him be Anathema Maranatha."

The word *Maranatha* has puzzled commentators, and various interpretations have been suggested, such as "In the coming of our Lord"; or, "Our Lord has come"; or, "Our Lord will come." Some read the word as two different words, *Marana tha,* which would mean, "Come, Lord," and is the very prayer that closes the Revelation by John, *erchou, Kyvie Iesou.* (Rev. 22:20) It was, in all probability, a conventionalized expression of pious sentiment, somewhat similar to the old, "Peace be with you," or our own, "Adieu," or "Goodbye," which if spelled out, would, of course be, "God be with you." But all agree that *Marana,* or as the word is transliterated in the Book of Mormon, *Moroni* means Our Lord. We have also, in the Book of Mormon, a longer form of the same word, *Moronihah,* which we take to mean, "Jehovah is my Lord," which gives us a meaning almost identical with that of the name *Elijah,* "Jehovah is my God."

This name, Marana, or Moroni, has been preserved in the name *Maranon,* which is the name by which the mighty Amazon River is known when it first begins its course towards the Atlantic Ocean.[1]

In the valley of the Maranon, remains of cyclopean buildings have been found, proving that the region was inhabited in prehistoric times.

In 1840, a remarkable sculptured stone was found there, now known as the Chavin Stone, named after the locality where it was discovered. It is 25 feet long by 2 feet 4 inches, and represents either some mighty ruler, or some divine personage, standing under a number of rays of light, each ending in a serpent's head, reminding one of an Egyptian pharaoh under the so-called Aten Rays.

Dr. Brinton, in *The American Race,* page 282, gives the name of a *Morona* Tribe of Indians among the *Zaparo* linguistic stock, in the upper Amazon valley.[2]

On the east coast of South America is a river called after the great name. The

---

[1]The chain of the Eastern Andes is penetrated by five great rivers, which unite to form the mighty Orellana. The first is *Maranon,* and, being the most western and distant in its source in the Andean Lake of Lauricocha, is considered to be the source of the Amazon.
—Sir Clements Markham, *The Incas of Peru,* p. 193.

[2]*The American Race,* p. 282.

Maroni River[3] flows from the Tumakurak Range and forms the frontier line between French and Dutch Guiana, and, after a course of about 380 miles, reaches the Atlantic.

The name *Moroni* is found even in Peruvian literature. The Peruvians had a drama, called *Apu Ollantay*, composed about the year 1470, long before the arrival of the Spaniards, (the Pizarros entered Caxamarca in the year 1532) and committed to writing in 1770. Sir Clements Markham has published an elegant translation of it. Von Tschudi, in his work on the Quichua language, also gives it in full.

The first act is supposed to depict something that happened at the end of the 14th century of our era. The other two acts cover the first ten or twelve years of the 15th century. The hero is the great chief Ollanta, and the story is about his love for Cusi Coyllur, a daughter of the proud Inca Pachacutec at a time when such a venture might have cost the lives of both. The first scene of the third act of this drama is laid in a street in Cusco called *Pampa Moroni*.[4]

We do not know how far back this name as a street name in Cusco goes. Montesinos says the fifth king, *Inti Capac Yupanqui* divided Cusco into districts, *Upper* and *Lower*, and the first was also divided into streets to which he gave names. If it was this Inca who gave the street or square referred to, the name of *Moroni*, that name must have been so well known in Indian tradition, in the first half of the 5th century A. D., as to suggest the propriety of naming a public place in the *Holy City* of the Peruvians in his honor.

LEHI

Lehi was one of the greatest of Nephite military commanders, and the associate of Moroni and Teancum, both of whom he survived for many years. It is not evident from the holy record, but we think it is highly probable that this Lehi was the same person as was Lehi, the son of Zoram (Alma 16:5), that young man being then (81 B.C.) a distinguished officer under his father. Lehi first prominently appears in the Nephite annals in the great battle fought (74 B.C.) with the Lamanites under Zerahemnah on the banks of the River Sidon, not far from Manti. Moroni was commander-in-chief of the Nephite forces, while Lehi commanded an army corps. Before the battle commenced, Moroni skillfully concealed his troops on both sides of the river and permitted the Lamanites to pass between.

Lehi's men, who had been massed on the east of the river, on the south slope of a hill named Riplah, closed in on the rear of the Lamanites when the latter faced about and gave battle. The fight soon grew fast and furious. The Lamanites perceiving that Moroni was attacking them on both sides fought with desperation, but with immense loss and in a short time they fled before Lehi, and were driven by him into the waters of the river. Lehi did not cross the Sidon in pursuit, but halted his soldiers on the eastern side while the troops more directly commanded by Moroni drove the enemy before them on the western banks. The day ended by a complete victory for the Nephites. When the devastating wars which Amalickiah inaugurated were begun we again find Lehi in high command. He was chief captain in the City of Noah, and when the Lamanites attacked it, his name alone added to their discomfiture, for as we are told "they feared Lehi exceedingly." (Alma 49:17) Lehi's cautious but resolute defense, combined with the highly efficient fortifications built around the city by Moroni, caused the Lamanites to throw away more than one thousand men and all their chief captains in the futile attempt to carry the city by storm. (73 B.C.)

Lehi continued to be actively engaged during the next war, and appears to

---

[3]*See*, for instance, Joyce's *South American Archaeology*.
[4]Markham, *The Incas of Peru*, p. 379. The spelling on this page is, letter for letter, as in the Book of Mormon. On page 337 the spelling is *Maroni*. But even so, the word cannot be mistaken.

have been second in command to Moroni over the army of the northeast. His next conspicuous recorded exploit was assisting in the defeat of Jacob between Bountiful and Mulek, and the recapture of the latter city (64 B.C.). Moroni placed Lehi in command of the captured city. When in 62 B.C. the revolt of the King-men under Pachus took place, Moroni, under the suggestion of Pahoran, the Chief Judge, hastened to the aid of the government at Zarahemla, and left Lehi and Teancum in charge of the armies in the northeast, that were then reduced by years of continued fighting and sadly in need of provisions. The next year Moroni sent them a reinforcement of 6,000 men and a sufficient supply of food which was followed by a brilliant campaign, in which Moroni, Lehi, and Teancum, by prearranged plans and simultaneous movements drove the Lamanites beyond the Nephite territory, and ended the long-continued and exhausting series of wars. (61 B.C.) When Moroni died (56 B.C.) he was succeeded by his son Moronihah as Commander-in-Chief of the armies of the Republic, and Lehi, now getting up in years, appears to have stood in the same position as second in command as he did to Moronihah's father.

In the calamitous invasion of the Land of Zarahemla by the Lamanites, under Coriantumr (51 B.C.), Lehi was the first to stay their victorious and devastating march northward. He met them somewhere between Zarahemla and Bountiful, and drove them back towards the former city. Their retreat was cut off by Moronihah and two other Nephite generals, one in front and one in the rear, signally defeating the invaders, and making prisoners all who were not slain.

It is in this campaign that Lehi's name is last mentioned in the Book of Mormon. In character, we are told by the sacred historian, that Lehi "was a man like unto Moroni," God-fearing, wise, prudent, and brave. "They were beloved by all the people of Nephi." (Alma 53:2)

ZERAHEMNAH

Zerahemnah was a Lamanite general who commanded the forces of that people and who at the request of the apostate Zoramites occupied Antionum with the intention of attacking the Ammonites in the Land of Jershon. Like most of the commanding officers of the Lamanite Armies at that age were like he, a Nephite dissenter. (74 B.C.)

Zerahemnah, finding that Moroni, the Nephite commander, was too well prepared for their attack on the Land of Jershon, retired through Antionum into the wilderness where they changed direction and marched towards the headwaters of the River Sidon with the intention of taking possession of the Land of Manti. But Moroni was too vigilant to allow his enemies to slip away without knowing what had become of them. He had his spies watch the movements of Zerahemnah's forces, and in the meantime sent to Alma to inquire the mind and will of the Lord with regard to his future course. The word of the Lord was given to Alma and he informed Moroni's messengers of the movements of the Lamanites. The young general then divided his army. One corps he left to protect Jershon, and with the other he advanced with rapid marches towards Manti by the most direct route. On his arrival he at once mustered all the men who could bear arms into his forces to protect their liberties against the advancing foe. So rapid had been his movements, and so completely and prompt had been the response to his call that when the Lamanites reached the neighborhood of the Sidon, he was ready for their coming.

The battle which was fought when the opposing armies met was one of the most stubborn and bloody in Nephite history. Never from the beginning had the Lamanites been known to fight with such exceeding great strength and courage. Time after time their hosts rushed upon the well-ordered ranks of the Nephites, and notwithstanding the latter's armor, they clove in their heads and cut off their arms. But the cost of these charges to their own numbers was terrible. The battle began at a hill called Riplah, and afterwards extended to both banks of the River Sidon. At one time a lull took place in the carnage, and Moroni, who had no pleasure in shedding blood, made an offer of such terms of surrender as he considered the circumstances warranted. But Zerahemnah and other captains of the Lamanites rejected the offer and urged their warriors to renewed resistance. So the battle recommenced with unabated fury. At last, however, Zerahemnah himself, to prevent the total annihilation of his armies, consented to the proposed terms of surrender and entered into the required covenant of peace with Moroni. So great were the losses on both sides that the dead were not counted. After this fearful battle, we read no more of Zerahemnah.

CHAPTER 44

1. *Moroni's Magnanimity.*

1. And it came to pass that they did stop and withdrew a pace from them. And Moroni said unto Zerahemnah: Behold, Zerahemnah, that we do not desire to be men of blood. Ye know that ye are in our hands, yet we do not desire to slay you.

2. Behold, we have not come out to battle against you that we might shed your blood for power; neither do we desire to bring any one to the yoke of bondage. But this is the very cause for which ye have come against us; yea, and ye are angry with us because of our religion.

3. But now, ye behold that the Lord is with us; and ye behold that he has delivered you into our hands. And now I would that ye should understand that this is done unto us because of our religion and our faith in Christ. And now ye see that ye cannot destroy this our faith.

4. Now ye see that this is the true faith of God; yea, ye see that God will support, and keep, and preserve us, so long as we are faithful unto him, and unto our faith, and our religion; and never will the Lord suffer that we shall be destroyed except we should fall into transgression and deny our faith.

5. And now, Zerahemnah, I command you, in the name of that all-powerful God, who has strengthened our arms that we have gained power over you, by our faith, by our religion, and by our rites of worship, and by our church, and by the sacred support which we owe to our wives and our children, by that liberty which binds us to our lands and our country; yea, and also by the maintenance of the sacred word of God, to which we owe all our happiness; and by all that is most dear unto us—

6. Yea, and this is not all; I command you by all the desires which ye have for life, that ye deliver up your weapons of war unto us, and we will seek not your blood, but we will spare your lives, if ye will go your way and come not again to war against us.

7. And now, if ye do not this, behold, ye are in our hands, and

---

VERSE 1. *We do not desire to be men of blood.* That they were brothers always permeated the thinking of the Nephites when the Lamanites were considered by them in a practical way. They both had the same ancestor, the venerable Lehi, and both therefore were of the House of Israel. Lehi was of the Tribe of Manasseh, but had

I will command my men that they shall fall upon you, and inflict the wounds of death in your bodies, that ye may become extinct; and then we will see who shall have power over this people; yea, we will see who shall be brought into bondage.

2. Zerahemnah rejects his offer of peace, but is compelled to accept terms.

8. And now it came to pass that when Zerahemnah had heard these sayings he came forth and delivered up his sword and his cimeter, and his bow into the hands of Moroni, and said unto him: Behold, here are our weapons of war; we will deliver them up unto you, but we will not suffer ourselves to take an oath

---

dwelt in Jerusalem all his days. That was a tie that bound them, and the righteous Nephites of every generation considered it such. Time and time again the Nephites refused to destroy the Lamanites although to do so would have been a simple end to many problems that perplexed them. The greatest of these was the fear of the Lamanite incursions into outlying communities when in their savage glee they murdered and debauched the peaceful Nephites. The Nephite Armies by destroying the Lamanite Armies could thereby enfeeble their barbarous tactics.

Moroni was true to this high ideal. When he saw the confusion among the armies of the Lamanites and the terror that struck them, he withdrew his soldiers from the face to face conflict that engulfed them. Seeking out Zerahemnah, their leader, he proposed terms of surrender to him after reminding this self-same commander that in coming to battle with him, his (Moroni's) purpose was not to gain power by shedding blood, as was Zerahemnah's, nor to put into bondage those who were overcome by any treachery or strategem. "Ye know," Moroni warned Zerahemnah, "that ye are in our hands, yet we do not desire to slay you." Not only was Zerahemnah ambitious to obtain the former of these things, but he was also imbued with the hatred that usually fills the hearts of apostates. Zerahemnah was a member of that apostate group who called themselves Zoramites, after their founder, Zoram, and who hated Christianity, the religion of the Nephites.

It is good that in our hearts we can note the difference between the ideals which God inspired in Moroni, and those which hatred and selfishness infused in the soldiers of Zerahemnah. He and his warriors sought power by purchasing it with blood; they hoped that with victory to enslave their opponents. On the other hand, Moroni denied that he nor his men were anxious for reprisal. The triumph of their arms was not an accident, but solely *a gift of God.* Our faith in Him and our sacred religion has delivered us from the snare you set to destroy us, and what is still more, "Ye see that God will support, and keep, and preserve us, so long as we are faithful unto Him, and unto our faith, and our religion; and never will the Lord suffer that we shall be destroyed except we should fall into transgression and deny our faith." Moroni now commanded Zerahemnah to cease his wicked ways, and deliver up to Moroni's men all his "weapons of war" and promise not to come again "to war against us." This command was given to Zerahemnah in the Name of God Who had preserved Moroni's armies, and "in the sacred support which "We owe," Moroni said, "to our wives and children, by that liberty which binds us to our lands and our country; yea, and also by the maintenance of the sacred *Word of God,* to which we owe all our happiness; and all that is most dear to us."

unto you, which we know that we shall break, and also our children; but take our weapons of war, and suffer that we may depart into the wilderness; otherwise we will retain our swords, and we will perish or conquer.

9. Behold, we are not of your faith; we do not believe that it is God that has delivered us into your hands; but we believe that it is your cunning that has preserved you from our swords. Behold, it is your breastplates and your shields that have preserved you.

10. And now when Zerahemnah had made an end of speaking these words, Moroni returned the sword and the weapons of war, which he had received, unto Zerahemnah, saying: Behold, we will end the conflict.

11. Now I cannot recall the words which I have spoken, therefore as the Lord liveth, ye shall not depart except ye depart with an oath that ye will not return again against us to war. Now as ye are in our hands we will spill your blood upon the ground, or ye shall submit to the conditions which I have proposed.

12. And now when Moroni had said these words, Zerahemnah retained his sword, and he was angry with Moroni, and he rushed forward that he might slay Moroni; but as he raised his sword, behold, one of Moroni's soldiers smote it even to the earth, and it broke by the hilt; and he also

---

VERSES 8-9. *We do not believe that it is God that has delivered us into your hands.* Zerahemnah, cruel, relentless, and hardhearted, without a human sympathy, and that certainly without a divine one, listened impatiently to Moroni's words, and agreed only in part to them. He readily offered to surrender his sword and cimeter, his bows and arrows, as a token of surrender to Moroni, but he declined to take an oath unto Moroni, Zerahemnah said, "Which we know that we shall break." But he was willing to deliver up his weapons of war providing that his warriors were allowed to depart "into the wilderness, otherwise we will retain our swords, and we will perish or conquer."

The haughtiness which Zerahemnah displayed in answering Moroni's appeal for peace was characteristic of the victor, not the vanquished. He appeared contemptuously proud, or disdainful of the battle's outcome. He abjured the faith of the Nephites, and disclaimed Moroni's declaration that God "has delivered you into our hands." But your cunning in battle and your shields and breastplates have kept you from injury and destruction by us, he boldly asserted.

VERSES 10-11. *Behold, we will end the conflict.* Whereupon Moroni seeing Zerahemnah's stubbornness, that the Lamanite leader would not accept the defeat that had come upon him although he was completely vanquished, resolved to end the conflict then and there. Moroni returned to Zerahemnah his personal armaments warning the commander of the combined forces of Zoramites and Lamanites that "Now as ye are in our hands we will spill your blood upon the ground, or ye shall submit to the conditions which I have proposed."

VERSES 12-15. *Zerahemnah was angry with Moroni.* Zerahemnah saw that Moroni was not equivocal and therefore would not bend himself to the selfish demands made of him by the Lamanites. Zerahemnah became very angry with his opponent,

smote Zerahemnah that he took off his scalp and it fell to the earth. And Zerahemnah withdrew from before them into the midst of his soldiers.

13. And it came to pass that the soldier who stood by, who smote off the scalp of Zerahemnah, took up the scalp from off the ground by the hair, and laid it upon the point of his sword, and stretched it forth unto them, saying unto them with a loud voice:

14. Even as this scalp has fallen to the earth, which is the scalp of your chief, so shall ye fall to the earth except ye will deliver up your weapons of war and depart with a covenant of peace.

15. Now there were many when they heard these words and saw the scalp which was upon the sword, that were struck with fear; and many came forth and threw down their weapons of war at the feet of Moroni, and entered into a covenant of peace. And as many as entered into a covenant they suffered to depart into the wilderness.

16. Now it came to pass that Zerahemnah was exceeding wroth, and he did stir up the remainder of his soldiers to anger, to contend more powerfully against the Nephites.

17. And now Moroni was angry, because of the stubbornness of the Lamanites; therefore he commanded his people that they should fall upon them and slay them. And it came to pass that

---

and attempted to kill him. He rushed forward and with his sword raised in angry protest, sought Moroni's life. "But as he raised his sword, behold, one of Moroni's soldiers smote it even to the earth, and it broke by the hilt." We can imagine that many of the Nephite soldiers rushed to Moroni's defense, but this one in particular trained in the strength of battle, was more than equal to the savage attack of Zerahemnah. He also, with one blow, struck off Zerahemnah's scalp and it fell to the earth." Zerahemnah thereupon made a hasty retreat to where his soldiers were gathered en masse.

Almost prophetic was this soldier of Moroni's as he cried to Zerahemnah's men; picking up Zerahemnah's scalp by the long blood-matted hair and placing it upon the point of his sharp sword, shouted, "Even as this scalp has fallen to the earth, which is the scalp of your chief, so shall ye fall to the earth except ye will deliver up your weapons of war and depart with a covenant of peace."

When the Lamanites saw what had taken place, and heard the warning of one of Moroni's bodyguards that they, too, would meet a like fate as did Zerahemnah's scalp if they failed to comply with Moroni's demands, many of them came forward and threw their weapons down at Moroni's feet, and at the same time covenanted with him that they no more would come to battle against his forces as he required that the treaty of peace should provide.

VERSES 16-18. *Zerahemnah was exceeding wroth; and Moroni, too, was angry because of the stubbornness of the Lamanites.* Both commanders of the opposing forces, Nephite and Lamanite, waxed increasingly angry, the one because of disappointed pride, which of all the passions that occupy the human heart, is the most bitter and malignant. The other commander, Moroni, grew angry "because of the

they began to slay them; yea, and the Lamanites did contend with their swords and their might.

18. But behold, their naked skins and their bare heads were exposed to the sharp swords of the Nephites; yea, behold they were pierced and smitten, yea and did fall exceedingly fast before the swords of the Nephites; and they began to be swept down, even as the soldier of Moroni had prophesied.

3. Lamanites make a covenant of peace.

19. Now Zerahemnah, when he saw that they were all about to be destroyed, cried mightily unto Moroni, promising that he would covenant and also his people with them, if they would spare the remainder of their lives, that they never would come to war again against them.

20. And it came to pass that Moroni caused that the work of death should cease again among the people. And he took the weapons of war from the Lamanites; and after they had entered into a covenant with him of peace they were suffered to depart into the wilderness.

21. Now the number of their dead was not numbered because of the greatness of the number; yea, the number of their dead was exceeding great, both on the Nephites and on the Lamanites.

22. And it came to pass that they did cast their dead into the waters of Sidon, and they have gone forth and are buried in the depths of the sea.

23. And the armies of the Nephites, or of Moroni, returned and came to their houses and their lands.

24. And thus ended the eighteenth year of the reign of the judges over the people of Nephi. And thus ended the record of Alma, which was written upon the plates of Nephi.

---

stubbornness of the Lamanites." After all attempts for a peaceful settlement were discarded; and when all else had failed to accomplish that result, Moroni commanded his men to "fall upon them and slay them."

4. End of Alma's record.

Verses 19-24. And thus ended the eighteenth year of the reign of the Judges over the People of Nephi. Now Zerahemnah and some of the other captains of the Lamanites urged their warriors to renewed resistance. So the battle recommenced with unabated fury. At last the faith and valor of the Nephites prevailed; many of the Lamanites surrendered and when they did so they entered into a covenant of peace as Moroni had demanded of them. Even Zerahemnah, himself, wounded and scalped, to prevent the total annihilation of his armies, at last consented to the proposed terms and entered that binding agreement. So great were the losses on both sides, especially of the Lamanites, that the dead were not counted.

Thus ended the war, but not the Zoramite heresy, for we read in the history of later wars between the two nations, of certain Lamanite captains being of the Zoramites. Foiled in their attempts to destroy their former brethren and to overthrow the Church of God, they still adhered to their false faith, and in every way and on every possible occasion, made manifest their undying hatred to those whose only offense was that they would not join them in their crimes nor consent to the destruction of the liberties of the people.

"And thus ended the eighteenth year of the Reign of the Judges over the people of Nephi. And thus ended the record of Alma, which was written upon the Plates of Nephi."

THE WOMEN OF THE BOOK OF MORMON

It is somewhat noticeable how little prominence is given to womenkind in the historical narrative of the Book of Mormon, and unfortunately when mention is made of them it too frequently grows out of man's sins and their misfortunes. Of all the descendants of Lehi and Sariah, but two women are mentioned by name; one, Abish, a converted waiting woman to a queen of the Lamanites; the other, Isabel, a harlot of the Land of Siron whose meretricious charms seduced Corianton, the son of Alma, from the work of the ministry among the Zoramites.

Although we have but few individual characters standing out in relief from the historical background, yet from many incidental references to women as the story of the Nephites is unfolded, we are led to the conclusion that women among the Book of Mormon peoples enjoyed a much greater degree of liberty and wielded a more powerful influence than women did among contemporary Gentile nations on the Eastern Continents — say in Babylon, Persia, or Greece. We deem it mainly to two causes, first, the Israelitic origin of the race; and again, the power and grace with which the principles of the Gospel were preached by a long succession of prophets, who almost uninterruptedly ministered to the seed of Nephi. That this later cause had much to do with women's pleasing condition among that people is evident, for we find out from the historical narrative that whenever they turned from the Lord it was then that tribulation and oppression came upon their wives and daughters, and they suffered from the iniquities of their husbands and the fury of their enemies. With regard to the first named cause, it is generally admitted that the Hebrew women of antiquity enjoyed greater liberty and possessed more privileges than did those of the surrounding pagan nations of the same period. Let the Bible and the history of contemporary nations be compared and the difference is therein apparent.

The Nephites lived in a dispensation when women were bound to sterner requirements than they are today. They observed the Law of Moses, to which was added the higher code of the Gospel of Christ. Our readers know how well both these standards protect the rights of women, and how sacredly they guard the marriage covenant. Infidelity to that sacred bond of union being regarded, whether in the man or in the woman, as a most heinous offense, and worthy of the severest penalties.

At the commencement of the Nephite national life, when they were few in numbers, they seem for a time to have been tainted with some of the social vices of the degenerate people from whom the Lord had separated them. They committed great immoralities and took wives for utterly unworthy purposes, and without the fear of the Lord before their eyes. After they had taken them, they frequently abused them or neglected them, until their suffering cries came up before the Eternal One, and therefore Heaven forbade any man among them taking more than one wife, but added this proviso: "For if I will, saith the Lord of Hosts, rise up seed unto Me, I will command My people; otherwise they shall hearken to these things." This injunction, we are of the opinion, was afterwards removed, and the foreshadowed command given, as it is evident from the later history of the Nephites that in a better era of their national life polygamy was sanctioned by the law and was practiced among them, and that, indeed, by the men most favored of God. As an example, we will cite the Prophet Amulek, the devoted friend of Alma, the younger, and his zealous fellowlaborer in the mission field. Amulek was the only man in the vast City of Ammonihah unto whom an angel was sent, and in whose behalf mighty miracles were wrought. In giving the wicked Ammonihahites an account of his conversion (Alma 10:11), Amulek specifically mentions his women, and as he expressly does so he places them next to himself and before his children, his father and all his other kinsfolk and kindred, and nowhere does he use the word wife or wives, it is evident that his wives were meant and not serving-women. No one, surely, would argue that he would give to the latter the place of honor in his address to his fellow-citizens, before his parents and his children. As another instance, the great number of Chief Judge Pahoran's sons is incidently mentioned.

It was during the brighter days of the rule of the Judges that women, more than at any time before the appearance of the *Messiah* on this Continent, seem to have been most highly regarded and esteemed. The Nephites were then living under that excellent code of laws drawn up by the inspired King Mosiah, which bear evidence of having been most admirably adapted to a people worthy of a large amount of liberty. This age was adorned with the presence of such men as Alma, Moroni (the prophet-general of the Nephite armies), Ammon and the other sons of King Mosiah, Helaman, Amulek, and others conspicuous for their devotion to the laws of God and the rights and liberties of the people. General Moroni, than whom a more devoted man to the cause of truth and humanity never lived, is especially conspicuous in his untiring efforts for the safety and happiness of the wives and little ones of his people. On the standard to which he rallied the patriot warriors of the Republic, which he named the *Title of Liberty*, he inscribed, "In memory of our God, our religion and freedom, and our peace, our wives and our children." This seems to have been his watchword throughout the long and sanguinary succeeding campaigns in which he defended the Nephites from the savage onslaughts of their Lamanitish foes. Again and again we find him rallying the hosts of Nephi with the soul-stirring cry, and under the ardor it wrought in their hearts it carried triumph to their banners and freedom to their land.

One series of events that occurred during this long war sheds a most pleasing light upon the inner life of the faithful among the Nephites. It is found in the story of Helaman and his 2000 striplings, who, very young, were so full of faith implanted in their hearts by the wise counsels of their loving and God-fearing mothers, that in the might of Jehovah they went forth against the enemies of their adopted country (for they were Lamanites by birth), and no power could withstand them. Their mother's teachings and their mother's prayers were weapons of destruction to their foes and shields of defense to themselves. They went forth conquering and to conquer, and only the All-seeing One knows how much the teachings of those saintly women effected towards the preservation of the Nephite Commonwealth from imminent destruction.

And what shall we say of the condition of women in that blessed Sabbatic era succeeding the glorious appearing of the Redeemer on this western land, when for nearly 200 years this continent enjoyed undisturbed and heavenly peace; when all men devoutly worshiped the Lord, and dealt justly with their fellows — men or women. It was an age in which no woman was wronged, no deserted children pined in the streets, no abused wives mourned in secret, or lifted their sorrowing hearts in anguish to the Great Father of all mankind. No brazen courtesans flaunted their wares on the broad highways, or ruined maidens hid their sorrow and shame wherever seclusion was the most profound. The inspired historian tells us that if ever there was a happy people on this earth, there they were found. And most happy must have been the gentler ones who bear in the stubborn battles of life so large a share of its sorrows and misfortunes.

But this golden age was soon followed by its opposite, when every virtue seems to have been supplanted by a vice, and all good was turned into evil. At almost lightning speed, the people having once taken the downward track, the nation rushed to ruin, until this continent became one vast field of carnage, rapine, and misery, over which devils gloated and hell enlarged itself. Indeed, the whole land seemed peopled with a race of demons who perpetrated cruelties that could alone be conceived in the hearts of the damned. During these lengthened years of untold horrors the fair daughters of the land suffered unspeakable barbarities. Life, virtue, everything was the plaything of the victor, be he Nephite or Lamanite, until in the hate of a revenge that never was satisfied and the fury of despair, they joined their leaders on the battlefield, and with their husbands, sons, and brothers, dyed their hands in the blood of the foe. Nor did they alone arm themselves, but they put weapons into the hands of their children, and inflamed their young minds with the savage love of slaughter. The war was not one of supremacy alone; it was one for national and individual existence. In the midst of carnage, unparalleled on any land save ours, the Nephite Nation was swept out of existence, leaving scarcely a trace behind, a most terrible instance of divine mercy scorned and divine laws abused.

DOMESTIC LIFE AMONG THE NEPHITES

From the casual references found in the historic portions of the Book of Mormon, we are led to infer that the domestic life of the Nephites was patterned, as it very naturally would be, after the manners and customs of their forefathers in the Land of Jerusalem, modified, of course, by time and their surroundings. The changed material conditions, the absence of older though co-existent people and powers, the new and sometimes strange animal and vegetable productions, etc., all had an influence in the formation and growth of their civilization; trivial, perhaps, when considered separately, but when taken together, and working for centuries, had a marked effect on their public polity and home life.

It is, however, necessary to explain that the details of the latter are very meager, and only obtained incidently, as they may form a link in the chain of some historic narrative, or be introduced as an illustration in some doctrinal or prophetic warning.

In the midst of a people guided or reproved through their entire national life by an almost continuous succession of inspired teachers, it is but reasonable to conclude that the domestic virtues were assiduously cultivated, and all departures therefrom severely rebuked. Industry, economy, thrift, prudence, and moderation in dress, were evidently as much the subject of the prophet's condemnation then as in these latter days. Zeniff and others directly refer to the labors and toils of the Nephite women in spinning and making the material with which they clothed themselves and their households; and the same fabrics which delight the modern daughters of Israel also appear to have pleased the eyes of their Nephite sisters in the long ago. We must, however, say to the praise of these ancient worthies, the mothers of Mosiah, Alma, Moroni, Helaman, and of the 2000 striplings who loved to call Helaman *father*, that the beauty of their apparel was the workmanship of their own hands. Electric looms, spinning jennys, and their like, were unknown, so far as we can learn, to the enterprising, vigorous, God-blessed race that for nearly a thousand years filled the American Continent with the favored seed of Jacob's much-loved son.

The materials of which the clothing of this race were made are frequently mentioned in the inspired record. Fine silks, fine twined or twisted linen, and cloth of every kind are often spoken of. In one place good homely cloth is mentioned. By the word *homely,* we must not understand the writer to mean ugly. The word as used in the Book of Mormon is evidently applied in its original significance as it is used today in England for homelike or fit for home. Such material as was suited to the every day life of an industrious, hard-working people.

The love for ornaments has ever been a characteristic of Abraham's chosen race. The golden earrings and bracelets that gladdened the eyes of Rebecca when she was sought as the wife of the patriarch's son, have had their counterpart in many a modern instance. It was so with Sariah's myriad daughters. Time again we have read of pride and vanity entering the hearts of the people, and of their affections being set upon their costly apparel and their ornaments of gold, of silver, of pearls, of precious things (gems), their bracelets, ringlets, etc.

Nor would it be just to convey the idea that the gentler sex were alone guilty of these extravagances. The Sacred Record admits of no such conclusion. We cannot judge by the sober drabs, greys, and browns, with which the civilized gentlemen of today clothes himself, of the colors, the styles, or the fashions of the raiment of the Nephite beaux. The only safe conclusion that can be drawn is that they probably copied to some extent the gorgeousness of tropical nature by which they were surrounded. Nor is it reasonable to suppose that a single description would apply to the styles in the days of Lehi, of Benjamin, and of Mormon, any more than the varied fashions of the days of Williams, the Edwards, the James, and the Georges of English history could all be condensed into one sentence. It is not conceivable that dress, or anything else, remained entirely unchanged throughout a thousand years, though it is quite possible that those changes were nothing like so sudden, or so radical as have been those that have taken place among the leading nations of western Europe. On these points, however, so far as the record of Mormon is concerned, we can simply surmise, as the military accoutrements, armor, etc., of the warriors are the only habiliments with regard to which he gives any particular details. It is this poverty of information on this and kindred subjects that makes it so difficult for our artists to illustrate with any assurance of approximate correctness, scenes, and incidents from Book of Mormon history.

Nor can we learn much more with regard to their residences than we can concerning their dress. The most detailed account given of any man's home is that of Nephi, the son of Helaman. His house was situated on the main highway which led to the chief market place of the City of Zarahemla. In front of his house was a garden, and near the gate opening upon the highway was a tower, upon the top of which the prophet was accustomed to pray. These towers, from the numerous references made of them, either as private property or attached to their places of worship, as watch towers, or as a part of their system of fortifications, must have formed quite a conspicuous feature in the Nephite landscape.

The residences of the rich were elegant and spacious, adorned with exceedingly fine woodwork, carvings, etc., and with ornaments of gold, silver, copper, steel, and other metals. From the importance attached to the fact that but little timber existed in the northern continent when the Nephites began to spread over it, and consequently that the immigrants had to build their houses of cement, it is presumable that wood entered largely into the composition of the buildings. This idea is strengthened by the frequently mentioned skill with which the artisans in woodworking had developed, and also the excellence they had attained in refining the ores and the manufacturing of metal ornaments for their houses and persons. Regarding one monarch it is written: King Noah built many elegant and spacious buildings: and he ornamented them with fine works of wood, and of all manner of precious things, of gold, and of silver, and of iron, and of brass, and of ziff, and of copper; and he also built him a spacious palace and a throne in the midst thereof, all of which was of fine wood, and was ornamented with gold and silver, and with precious things. And he also caused that his workmen should work all manner of fine work within the walls of the temple, of fine wood, and of copper, and of brass, etc. This was in the Land of Nephi.

We next turn to the food of this people. Here also we are without definite information, but we can measurably judge of their staple articles of diet by noticing the grains they cultivated most extensively: to wit, wheat, corn, and barley, the latter appearing to have been the standard by which they gauged the price of other commodities. Great attention was also given to the planting of fruit trees and grape vines. From the fruit of the grape abundance of wine was manufactured of which (we think that we do the Nephites no injustice by saying it) they were as fond of it as were the generality of mankind. They were not as attached to a meat diet as were the Lamanites who were great meat-eaters, but they apparently kept large flocks and herds as a food supply, as well as for wool, leather, etc., and to provide for the numerous sacrifices enjoined by the Law of Moses, which they carefully observed until the offering of that greatest of all sacrifices on Mount Calvary, of which all the rest were but types and shadows.

Thus we may conclude that bread made from corn, wheat or barley, the flesh of their flocks and herds, together with that of wild animals caught in the chase, fruit, wine, milk and honey, formed the basis of their daily food, differing no doubt in details according to the location, climate, and other circumstances.

Their method of locomotion and modes of transportation are not described in the Book of Mormn. They were very rich in the ownership of horses, and doubtless made use of them as beasts of burden. The fact that large bodies of this people made extensive journeys in their various migrations and colonizings, is beyond dispute. From one family they filled a continent, or more properly, two continents. The use of ships is not mentioned until the middle of the last century before the Christian Era. These were then used for conveying immigrants, lumber, provisions, etc., to the northern continent; the first ship-building, of which we have an account, having been done at the settlements near the Isthmus of Panama, to which good roads had by that time been constructed. In the earlier history of the Nephites it is probable that most of their material was transported on pack animals, as is done today in the regions then inhabited by them. In the dense tropical vegetation of the wilderness, and along the mountain slopes of the Andes, road-making was difficult and expensive, and packing on the backs of animals was the most convenient way of transportation for a comparatively poor and small people. Chariots are mentioned but seldom. The Lamanite monarch, Lamoni, had his horses and chariots, to which reference is more than once made; and in after years, when the Nephites gathered all they possessed into one place to defend themselves against the Gadianton Robbers (A.D. 17), they removed their provisions, grain, etc., by means of vehicles called chariots. These are the only instances which the writers remember where vehicles of any kind are mentioned in the Book of Mormon in connection with the inhabitants of this continent.

SCIENCE AND LITERATURE AMONG THE NEPHITES

The Nephites were unusually happy in having, as the founders of their nation, men who were not only wise in the ways of the Lord, but also learned in the knowledge of the world. Most nations that have made a mark in the history of bygone centuries have had to grope their way from darkness to light, from ignorance to knowledge. Little by little such races have advanced in the path of civilization, falling into manifold errors and committing grievous blunders. With Lehi and his posterity it was not so. They were taken from among a people who were surrounded by the most powerful and refined nations of antiquity, with whose wisdom and learning Lehi was undoubtedly well acquainted. We can readily conceive that the Lord in planting this mighty and vigorous offshoot of the House of Joseph on the richest and most favored land of all the earth would not only choose one of His most faithful, but also one of His most intelligent servants to commence His work. Indeed, on the very first page of the Book of Mormon, Nephi incidentally refers to the learning of his father; which learning, we infer from many passages in the Sacred Record, was obtained by Lehi in Egypt, as well as in Palestine; the association between the inhabitants of these two countries being, in his day, very close, and the inter-communication very frequent.

As the foundation of their literature, Lehi and his little colony carried with them a copy of the sacred Scriptures, which contained not only an account of God's dealings with mankind from the Creation to the age of Jeremiah, but also the only complete history in existence of the people who lived before the Deluge. The Egyptians, Chaldeans, and other nations had mangled, mythic, and jumbled-up accounts of man's history from the Creation to the Flood; but the Nephites possessed the details of this epoch in much greater completeness than even Christendom does today. These Scriptures — historical and doctrinal — being numerously reproduced and scattered among the people, formed the basis of Nephite literature, giving them the immense advantage over all others of possessing the unpolluted Word of God in every age then past, supplemented by a correct and undisputed history of the results to the world of man's obedience or disobedience to these heavenly messages. How much more complete were these Scriptures than the Bible of Christendom is shown by the numerous references to the lives and quotations from the teachings of ancient worthies, Melchizedek, Jacob, Joseph, and others. Also to the acts and infamies of Cain, etc., not found in the Bible, as well as by lengthy quotations from ancient prophets whose names —

Zenos, Neum, Ezias — are not even mentioned in its pages. How much modern Christianity has lost by these omissions may be partly inferred from the beauty and grandeur of the extracts of their prophecies and writings given in the Book of Mormon by even Zenos alone. Take as a single instance his parable of *The Wild and Tame Olive Trees* given in the Book of Jacob; no more important, no more sublime prophecy can be found in the whole contents of the Holy Scriptures.

The connection of Lehi with Egypt, whose language he appears to have adopted, doubtless gave him a practical knowledge of the condition of the whole civilized world in his day, when the glories of Chaldea had departed, and those of Assyria and Egypt were passing away; when Babylon was at the zenith of its power, and the growing strength of Persia and Greece was as yet scarcely felt. To this personal information he, like Moses, added an acquaintance with the learning of the Egyptians, a people wise above all other uninspired races in the numerous branches of science and art in which they excelled. With this knowledge, combined with the information of immeasurable value contained on the sacred plates, the foundation was laid for a stable civilization, guided, as he was, by past revelation and present inspiration; to which was added the experience of other nations as beacon lights to warn the Nephites of the dangers to which all communities are subject, and to guide them to havens of governmental and political safety.

The Nephites, then, from their earliest day had at least all the important historical and geographical knowledge possessed by the great and most favored communities of the eastern hemisphere, with as much more as it pleased Heaven to reveal. They had one advantage over the peoples they had left — they were well acquainted with them and their condition; but of the Nephites, the dwellers in the old world knew nothing. In regard to the knowledge received through revelation, it is evident, from several incidental expressions scattered through the record, that the Lord did give to His faithful servants information with regard to historical and geographical matters. We cite one instance: Jacob, the brother of Nephi, in one of his impressive exhortations, while encouraging his brethren (often downcast on account of their lonely condition, so far from the rest of mankind), remarks: "We have been led to a better land, for the Lord has made the sea our path, and we are upon an isle of the sea. But great are the promises of the Lord unto them who are upon the isles of the sea. Wherefore, as it says *isles*, there must needs be more than this, and they are inhabited also by our brethren."

How could Jacob have known except by revelation that the vast continent which the Nephites inhabited was entirely surrounded by the waters of the great oceans? He and his companions had, but a few short years before, first landed on its shores, and had now explored but a very small portion of its wide extent, and there were no others in communication with them who could supply the information that North and South America were one immense island. Evidently the Lord had revealed this fact to them. And, by the way, this simple statement is strong testimony of the divine authenticity of the Book of Mormon. At the time this portion of the plates was translated (A.D. 1827-28), or even when the whole book was published and the Church of Jesus Christ was organized (1830), it was not known to modern science that the American Continent was indeed an island. Joseph Smith could not have received of this fact, so unhesitatingly affirmed, from any learned geographer or practical navigator. The hope of centuries in Europe had been to discover a north-west passage to India, but to that date all attempts had met with disastrous failure, so far as the chief objective was concerned. Little, or nothing was known of the North American coast west of the Hudson Bay. It was not until after repeated expeditions, that in May, 1847, the truth of the statement of Jacob could be confirmed from actual knowledge of the geographical features of the country. It was not until 1854 that the first crew of any ship (that of Captain McClure), which ever sailed across the Arctic Ocean from the Pacific to the Atlantic along the northern coast of America, returned from their perilous voyage. We thus find that human geographical knowledge could not have aided the Prophet Joseph Smith in making this statement had it originated with him instead of the son of Lehi.

While ancient Greek and other philosophers were groping among the fallacies of the absurd system of astronomy given to the world by Ptolemy, and teaching that the sun with all the stars revolved around the Earth, the Nephites were in possession of the true knowledge with regard to the heavenly bodies, etc. Possibly they were the only people of their age that were blessed with a true comprehension of these sublime truths. It is altogether probable that among their scriptures were copies of the Book of Abraham, from which they could acquaint themselves with the beauties and harmonies of celestial mechanism. They undoubtedly had the writings of Joseph, the son of Jacob, as these are quoted in the Book of Mormon. And as the Prophet Joseph Smith found the writings of Abraham and Joseph together in the Egyptian mummies, it is far from improbable that the Nephites, as well as the early Egyptians possessed both. To show the astronomical knowledge possessed by the Nephites, we will draw attention to the words of two of their prophets. The first extract is from the reply of Alma to Korihor, the anti-Christ (75 B.C.), when the latter asked for a sign to prove the existence of God. His words were: Thou hast had signs enough; will ye tempt your God? Will ye say, Show me a sign, when ye have the testimony of all these thy brethren, and also the holy prophets? The Scriptures are laid before thee, yea, and all things denote there is a God; yea, even the Earth, and all things that are upon the face of it, yea, and its motion; yea, and also the planets which move in their regular form, doth witness that there is a Supreme Creator. (Alma 30:44) The next quotation is from the reflections of one of God's servants, probably Mormon, who inserted it into the Nephite record probably about 500 years after the quotation above mentioned was made by Alma, the younger. The writer, whoever he may have been, was speaking of the greatness and goodness of God, and among other things declared: Yea, by the power of His voice doth the whole Earth shake; by the power of His voice doth the foundations rock, even to the very center; yea, and if He say unto the Earth, Move, it is moved; yea, if He say unto the Earth, Thou shalt go back, that it lengthen out the day for many hours, it is done; and thus according to His word, the Earth goeth back; and it appeareth unto man that the Sun standeth still; yea, and behold, this is so; for surely it is the Earth that moveth, and not the Sun. Thus we find that in these points, the astronomical knowledge of the Nephites was, at least equal to that of the moderns.

NOTES ON STRIKING PASSAGES IN THE
BOOK OF MORMON

I make a record in the language of my father, which consists of the learning of the Jews and the language of the Egyptians. (I Nephi 1:12)

Language of my father. Nephi here tells us that his father was well versed in the Hebrew literature, and understood the Egyptian mode of writing, probably both the hieroglyphic and the hieratic. The expression, "language of my father," should be noted. Why did not Nephi say "the Hebrew language"? Because that term was not, in his day, applied to the language spoken by the Hebrews. The Assyrians called it "The Tongue of the West Country." In 2 Kings 18:26 it is called "The Jews' Language." Isaiah calls it "The Language of Canaan." The name "HEBREW" was not applied to the language until the days of the Son of Sirach, about 130, B. C., and then it did not mean the Hebrew but the Syro-Aramean. Josephus, it is thought, was the first to apply the name Hebrew to the *old* language of the Jews. In the targums it is called "The Holy Tongue." Christian writers soon adopted the name.[1] The prophet Moroni, in the 4th century of our era, applied the term to the Hebrew alphabet, as Josephus had applied it to the old Hebrew writings, both language and characters.[2]

It is certain that, if this verse had been penned by a modern impostor, he would have written, not "the language of my father," but "Hebrew," because that is the term now always used to denote the language spoken and recorded by the Jews at the time of Lehi. But Nephi did not know it under that name. The expression used is, therefore, unmistakable evidence of the genuineness of the book.

THE FIVE BOOKS OF MOSES

And he beheld that they did contain the five books of Moses, which gave an account of the creation of the world, and also of Adam and Eve, who were our first parents. (I Nephi 5:11)

Nephi is speaking of his father Lehi and the brass plates of Laban.

This is an unequivocal testimony to the Mosaic authorship of the books known as the Pentateuch. It shows us that the books mentioned were in existence before the Babylonian exile, and that they were accepted as the work of Moses before the days of Ezra.

The Mosaic authorship of those books was accepted by the translators of the Septuagint (completed probably about 285 B.C.);

---

[1] Joseph Angus, *Bible Handbook*, p. 13.
[2] Mormon 9:33.

also by Jewish and Christian early writers, such as Josephus, the authors of the Talmud, Jerome, Origen, etc. It was, above all, accepted by our Lord, who always refers to the Law (the *Torah*) as written by Moses. (*Compare* Matthew 8:4; 19:18; Mark 7:10; Luke 16:31; 24:27 and 44; John 5:45-47; 7:19, 22, and 23.) The first doubt expressed of the Mosaic authorship, in England, was by Hobbes, a philosopher, in the year 1650, at least three thousand years after Moses, and he may have taken his clue from an obscure writer of the 13th century, who is said to have been the first in this field of skepticism.[3]

In 1670, Spinosa, the Dutch philosopher, suggested that the Pentateuch may have been compiled by Ezra. Simon, a French priest, argued that what he regarded as variety of style indicated so many different authors. Astruc started the theories known as Jehovistic and Elohistic, claiming that the two divine names proved that there once existed two original, independent documents.

Later, German scholarship took the matter up. Eichhorn, whose *Old Testament Introduction* was published in 1780, molded Astruc's conjectures into some sort of scientific shape and paved the way for what has become known as "higher criticism." He was followed by De Wette, Ewald, Graf, and many others. Kuenen, the Leyden, Holland, professor, discovered that the Book of Joshua belongs to the Mosaic collection, which, therefore, really is a *Hexateuch* and not a *Pentateuch*, he alleged.

Then came the British-American scholars, who modified the German radicalism, to make it acceptable to Anglo-Saxon reverence for the Word of God. Among these, Dr. Samuel Davidson, Dr. S. R. Driver, and Dr. C. A. Briggs, at one time connected with Union Theological Seminary, New York, should be mentioned.

The present position of "higher critics" is, that the Hexateuch, as they call it, is composed of, at least, four independent documents: The Yahwist, the Elohist, the Deuteronomist, and the Priestly Code, which, for the sake of brevity, they call J, E. D, and P, respectively. The Yahwist and the Elohist documents may, they think, have been written some time between 800 and 700 B.C. The Deuteronomist they assign to some year between 650 and 625 B.C. The date of the Priestly Code they give as any time between 525 and 425 B.C. Some of the critics hold, however, that the entire Pentateuch belongs to some time after the Babylonian exile. The five books of Moses were, accordingly, not written by Moses, but by authors who lived much later, and by editors who pieced their work together the best they could. There were a number of such editors. Wellhausen found traces of 22, but Kuenen thought 16 would answer the purpose.

[3]Joseph Angus, *Bible Handbook*, p. 380.

Nephi refers to the five books in question as "the Books of Moses." That is his testimony to a skeptical world. Thus, the Book of Mormon confirms the Bible "at a time when so-called higher critics are doing all in their power to destroy the belief in the divine authority of the Scriptures. It is a 'new witness' as President B. H. Roberts so aptly has called it, for the authenticity of the Bible. It claims no other position in sacred literature. It is the 'stick of Ephraim,' joined to the 'stick of Judah,' according to the word of the Lord. (Ezekiel 37:15-19)"[4]

THE FOUNTAIN OF FILTH

Behold the fountain of filthy water which thy father saw; yea, even the river of which he spake; and the depths thereof are the depths of hell. (I Nephi 12:16)

Lehi had a remarkable vision.[5] He saw a large field. In this field was a tree, the fruit of which was delicious. There was also a river running by the tree and dividing his family. Sariah, Sam, and Nephi stood by the head thereof, and they came to Lehi, as soon as he beckoned to them. Laman and Lemuel were by themselves, and they refused to come to their father. Lehi also saw a rod of iron extending along the bank of the river and leading to the tree. Along the iron rod there was a straight and narrow path which led to the tree, but which branched off into a large field. Multitudes were walking along this path, to reach the tree. But a thick mist arose, and in the darkness many lost their way. Others reached the tree by clinging to the iron rod, but when they saw people on the other side of the river, occupying a large building, mocking them, they were ashamed and wandered away and were lost. Others who tried to reach the tree were drowned in the river.

The explanation of this vision is given.[6] The tree is the tree of life, from which we may conclude that the fruit is the legitimate enjoyments of life, which always are sweet and delicious. The rod of iron is the word of God, and in this connection is may be recalled that the *Koran* is called "The sure *cord* of God," which seems to convey an idea similar to this of the iron rod.[7] The mist is temptation. The large, magnificent building is the vanity of the world, and the river is a representation of hell itself.

Special attention should be given to the river in the vision. Nephi beheld his descendants and those of his brethren arrayed against each other in deadly battle, and as he gazed upon this scene of carnage, the angel said to him: "Behold the fountain of filthy water which thy father saw; yea, even the river of which he spake."

---

[4]Doctrine and Covenants 10:52; *Commentary,* p. 88.
[5]I Nephi 8:9-33.
[6]I Nephi 12:15-18; 15:21-28.
[7]*Koran,* chapter 3, p. 48, translated by George Sale, London, 1865.

War and its concomitants can best be likened to a filthy river having its source in hell. Has not even a modern warrior been credited with just such a remark about war? Yes, "war is hell." That is what the angel tells Nephi. War originated with the rebellion of Lucifer in heaven, but he was cast out from there. When will his policy and methods be driven off the earth? The angel told Nephi that the Lamanites would dwindle in unbelief and then become "a dark and loathsome and a filthy people, full of idleness and all manner of abominations." This has been literally fulfilled. Those are always the awful results of protracted wars.

OUT OF THE MOUTH OF A JEW

And he said, Behold it proceedeth out of the mouth of a Jew: and I, Nephi, beheld it. (I Nephi 13:23)

The prophet is here speaking of the Old Testament, as it was to appear through the labors of Ezra and his associates and successors.

When Lehi left Jerusalem, the so-called canon of the Old Testament, as we know it, was not yet completed. The five books of Moses, undoubtedly, had been collected and written on one roll, numerous copies of which must have been in existence. The writings of the prophets, such as Joshua, the Judges, Samuel, Kings down to the reign of Zedekiah, and the prophecies of Isaiah, Hosea, Amos, Micah, and parts of Jeremiah, and their contemporaries, Joel, Amos and Jonah, must have existed in separate volumes, and individual collectors may have owned more or less complete sets. The Book of Job, some of the Psalms, the Proverbs, the Song of Solomon, and Ecclesiastes were also known, even if not generally accepted as sacred scripture. There were also books by authors whose names are mentioned in the Bible, but whose writings have not come down to us. The collection of Laban, known in the Book of Mormon as the Brass Plates, must have been unusually complete, judging from the contents. It must have been a very valuable library.[8] Such libraries must have been owned by prominent individuals.

Ezra undertook the work of collecting all the sacred writings that existed at his time. This work included not only the discovery of copies in various places, the rejection of those that were not authentic and the copying of manuscripts the contents of which could not otherwise be secured, but also the correction of the text, after careful examination of the variations that must have been found.[9]

---

[8]Laban's collection contained The Five Books of Moses: Testimonies concerning a Remnant of the Seed of Joseph; Genealogies from the Beginning, possibly documents from which the Chronicles were compiled; and, finally prophecies by all the prophets down to Jeremiah. (Omni 14; I Nephi 5:11-13; II Nephi 4:2; Alma 37:3; III Nephi 10:17.)

[9]In Hebrew manuscripts examined by modern scholars some 80,000 various readings, not including vowel points occur. See Stuart, Crit. Hist. and Defense Old Test. Canon, p. 192.

It was this work that was shown to Nephi in his vision of the Old Testament, and therefore, he, very properly, says he beheld it coming "out of the mouth of a Jew."

This expression appears still more significant when we recall the fact that Ezra, after the completion of the Pentateuch, gathered the people and read it to them and expounded it for seven days, and submitted it to them for their acceptance. (Nehemiah 8:1-18; 9:3) Then it, literally, proceeded out of the mouth of a Jew. This took place about 445 B.C., about 150 years after the exodus of Lehi.

The canon was gradually completed by the addition of the writings of Ezra, Nehemiah, and the prophets who lived during and after the exile, Ezekiel, Daniel, Obadiah, Habakkuk, Zephaniah, Haggai, Zechariah, and Malachi. The canon as thus completed was accepted by our Lord Himself, and it is, in this remarkable vision, called, on that account, "The Book of the Lamb of God." (I Nephi 13:38)

In this vision, "they bear record" refers to the New Testament (v. 24); "these things" (v. 25) means The Old and The New Testament;[10] in verses 34-42 a prophecy is given concerning the Book of Mormon, and in the next chapter, vv. 18-27, further particulars are found regarding the Bible, and particularly the writings of John.

THE WORLD WAR PREDICTED

And when the day cometh that the wrath of God is poured out upon the mother of harlots * * * then, at that day, the work of the Father shall commence, in preparing the way for the fulfilling of his covenants, which he hath made to his people who are of the house of Israel. (I Nephi 14:15-17)

The prediction is here made that the time would come, when the whole world would be involved in war, and that the countries identified with "the great and abominable church" would be particularly affected; and that, when that war came, then "the work of the Father shall commence, in preparing the way" for the fulfilling of his covenants with Israel.

We have lived to see that war. On July 28, 1914, the Austrian archduke, Ferdinand, and his morganatic wife were killed by a Serbian student, at Sarajevo, Bosnia, where the archduke had gone to attend military maneuvers, and a month later Austria declared war on Serbia. That was the beginning. Then, as impelled by an

[10]According to Jewish tradition, Moses wrote his book, the Baalam section, and Job. Joshua wrote his book and eight verses of the law. (Deut. 34:5-12.) Samuel wrote his book, Judges and Ruth. David wrote Psalms for the elders. Jeremiah wrote his books, Kings, and Lamentations. Hezekiah and his company wrote Isaiah, Proverbs, the Song, and Ecclesiastes. The men of the Great synagogue wrote Ezekiel, the Twelve, Daniel, and Esther. Ezra wrote his book and the genealogies of the Chronicles up to his time. But "wrote" in this tradition must be understood to mean *copied* and *edited* and not composed.

invisible power, Germany, August 3, invaded French territory and, the next day, hurled defiance at Russia. Then Great Britain declared war on Germany. Soon war raged in Europe in all its fury, and every nation on earth was affected by it.

This war was poured out upon the great church of the world, for Austria was the main political support of that church. Its effects were felt most heavily there, since Austria was entirely broken up by it. Russia, too, the nearest relative of Rome, from an ecclesiastical point of view, suffered total collapse. The mighty German empire, more than half Catholic, suffered and was shaken on its foundations. It certainly was a war in which the so-called Christian world was involved.

But at that time, as stated by the angel, the Father began preparations for the gathering of the children of Israel. On Dec. 9, 1917, General Allenby took possession of Jerusalem, and on Nov. 2. the same year, Balfour issued his famous letter to Baron Rothschild, in which he stated that, "His Majesty's government view with favor the establishment in Palestine of a national home for the Jewish people." Ten nations, including the United States, gave official endorsement to that policy. And from that day earnest efforts have been made, with great success, to build up Palestine. The barren soil has been covered with trees, and herds and flocks have found feed on the hill sides. (Isaiah 41:18-20)

So this prophecy in the Book of Mormon has been literally fulfilled in our day and generation.

THE SPIRIT OF THE LORD

For I spake unto him as a man speaketh; for I beheld that he was in the form of a man; yet, nevertheless, I knew that it was the Spirit of the Lord. (I Nephi 11:11)

How can the Spirit of the Lord be in the form of a man and yet be imparted by the laying on of hands? The late President Joseph F. Smith says:

"The terms [The Holy Ghost and The Spirit of God] are frequently used synonymously. We often say The Spirit of God when we mean The Holy Ghost; we likewise say The Holy Ghost when we mean The Spirit of God. The Holy Ghost is a personage in the Godhead, and is not that which lighteth every man that comes into the world."[11]

It is not the third person of the Godhead that is imparted by the laying on of hands, but the Spirit that fills the universe. Speaking of The Holy Ghost, the divine person, President Heber C. Kimball says:

"Let me tell you, The Holy Ghost is a man; he is one of the sons of our Father

---

[11]*Doctrine and Covenants Commentary*, p. 240.

and our God; and he is that man that stood next to Jesus Christ, just as I stand by Brother Brigham."[12]

FIERY-FLYING SERPENTS

He sent fiery-flying serpents among them and after they were bitten, he prepared a way that they might be healed. (I Nephi 17:41)

In Numbers 21:6, where the incident referred to is related, Moses says the Lord sent "fiery serpents" — not "fiery-flying" — among the people. The same expression occurs in Deut. 8:15. It is clear, therefore, that Nephi did not copy this from Moses.

Isaiah (14:29) likens King Hezekiah to (comp. 2 Kings 18:8) a "fiery-flying serpent," and Nephi was familiar with this portion of the Old Testament. (See II Nephi 24) The inference is that he followed Isaiah, in his version of the occurrence, adopting the term used by the prophet as the one that furnishes the more detailed explanation.

Moses was commanded to make a "fiery serpent" and so he made a "serpent of brass" and raised it upon a pole. (Num. 21:8, 9) This brass serpent was preserved for perhaps seven centuries and was finally broken up by King Hezekiah, because the people burnt incense to it. Isaiah had seen that brazen serpent before it was destroyed, and he must have had some reason for using the term "flying" in addition to "fiery" or "brazen," in comparing Hezekiah to it. Is it not probable that it was the image of a serpent with wings, such as the Egyptians made?

In Egypt, where the Israelites as a nation were cradled and where Moses had received his first education, the sacred serpent was the symbol of divine power and wisdom. When Egyptians would express the conception that Egypt was "God's country" enjoying his special care and protection, they drew a picture of two flying serpents of the *uroeus* species, one wearing the crown of upper, and the other that of lower Egypt. In this picture divine power, wisdom, and protection were visualized, very much as we symbolize national power and other admirable characteristics, as we perceive them with the eye of patriotism, by an Eagle or a Lion, or a Dragon, etc. What has been called the Egyptian national emblem was the solar disc between two serpents, the latter probably representing the eastern and western horizon of the sky, where the sun apparently rises and sets. Wings are extending on either side.

The image of the sacred serpent occurs as one of the ornaments of most of the Egyptian divine personages. It is part of the crowns of Osiris, Isis, and Horus. When Moses, therefore, was commanded

---

[12]*Journal of Discourses*, Vol. 5, p. 179. *Compare* Alma 7:10 and 9:44.

to make a *seraph*,[13] he was, in all probability, instructed to make not an imitation of the venomous reptile crawling in the dust, but of the glorious personages serving before the thrones of God — the seraphs which Isaiah and other prophets saw in visions; the same personages which were represented in golden statues upon the mercy seat of the Ark of the Covenants, and embroidered upon the curtains in the most holy place,[14] also called *cherubim*.

This view is supported by strong considerations.

Just what kind of reptiles the serpents that the Lord sent among the Israelites were is not known. Moses calls them "seraphim serpents" (*hanechashim haseraphim*), either because their poison was very deadly, or because they were God's messengers of death.[15] But it is certain that the brazen serpent, which Isaiah seems to have referred to as a "flying" serpent, was a type of our Lord who is the source and giver of life; for so we read in John 3:14-15, where our Lord Himself says:

"And as Moses lifted up the serpent in the wilderness, even so must the Son of man be lifted up: That whosoever believeth in him should not perish, but have eternal life."

That was the great lesson of the serpent which Moses lifted up in the wilderness. Made of brass, the image must have appeared as fire in the rays of the desert sun, and suspended from a pole it was properly likened to a flying animal.

The prophecy in Isaiah 14:29 helps us to understand the symbolism of the winged serpent. "Him that smote thee" is understood to refer to Uzziah, king of Judah, who "smote" the Philistines. (2 Chron. 26:6, 7) That "rod" was broken by his death, and during the reign of Ahaz, the Philistines invaded Judah and took possession of some of the southern cities. Isaiah, therefore, tells them that they had better not rejoice, because of this success. It was only temporary, for out of the "broken rod," should come forth a "cockatrice" or "adder," referring to Hezekiah, the son of Ahaz, and great-grandson of Uzziah, a more terrible enemy than Uzziah. (2 Kings 18:8)

But Dr. Clarke informs us (*Com.* on Isa. 14:29) that the *Targum* renders the 29th and 30th verses thus: "For, from the sons of Jesse shall come forth the Messiah; and his works among you shall be as the flying serpent. And the poor of the people shall he feed, and the humble shall dwell with famine, and the remnant of thy people shall he slay."

13"Fiery serpent."

14Exodus 25:18; 26:1.

15For a description of seraphim see Ezekiel 1:5-21, where the prophet relates his vision of "four living creatures." Also Isaiah 6:2-8 and Rev. 4:6-11. In the Book of Enoch, 61:10 and 70:7 the "wheels" (*ophannim*) stand next to the cherubim and seraphim in the presence of God.

This may be, as Dr. Clarke remarks, a "singular" interpretation, but it shows that the Hebrew conception of the reign of the Messiah is expressed by the image of a "flying" or "winged" serpent. The word used by Isa. 14:29 is *saraph* which may be familiar to us in its plural form *seraphim* which we read "seraphs," and understand to mean a high order of angels attending the Lord. (Isa. 6:2, 6) They are represented as having six wings; such is the swiftness of their service. Winds are angels. (Heb. 1:7) They are princes, nobles, in heaven. But, says Gesenius, "If any one chooses to follow the Hebrew *usus loquendi,* in which *seraph is serpent,* he may indeed here render it [seraphim] by *winged serpents;* since the serpent both among the ancient Hebrews and Egyptians was the symbol of wisdom and of the healing art. See Numbers 21:8; 2 Kings 18:4.

The serpent appears in every conceivable form in ancient Egyptian theology. Sometimes it has a human body. It is a symbol of majesty, and as such has wings and a crown. Winged serpents represented the divine protectors of upper and lower Egypt. (*Light on the Land of the Sphinx,* Chapt. 9, by H. Forbes Witherby, London, 1896)

Now, the strange fact is that the winged serpent, or the feathered serpent, plays a prominent part also in the religious concepts of the American Indians, and in their traditions. Among the ancient Mexicans, one of the divinities was known as "the feathered" or "plumed serpent," *Quetzalcoatl,* which name corresponds to the "flying serpent" of the Hebrews. Quetzalcoatl among the Mexicans was what the brazen serpent was to the Hebrews — the representative of the healing, life-giving power, as Esculapius was among the Phœnicians.

Among the Nahuas Quetzalcoatl was revered as a God. At Cholula he was considered the chief God, somewhat like Jehovah among the Hebrews. He was regarded as the son of *Camaxtli,* the protector of hunters and fishers, but probably the same as the *Pachacamac,* the Creator, of the Peruvians.

But Quetzalcoatl also became a man. As such he was born of Chimalma, the wife of Camaxtli, who conceived him miraculously. He taught men the arts of civilization, and preached morality, penitence, and peace.

As a man he visited Cholula, remaining there for twenty years. He taught the people to work in silver, prohibited blood sacrifices, and showed them the way to happiness through virtue and peace. After his mission was finished, he left for the sea shore, where he bid his companions farewell and promised that, some time, in the future he would return.

One of the opponents of Quetzalcoatl was Tezcatlipoca, a personage of divine origin and great power, but evil, bent upon bringing calamities and misfortunes upon the people.

The ecclesiastical officer next in rank to the pontiff, or high priest, was called Quetzalcoatl, in honor of the great national hero, and there were, therefore, a great many quetzalcoatls, and the probability is that the traditions relating to the divine reformer and his successors have been so mixed as to preclude the possibility of a clear and perfect understanding of what the ancient Mexicans really did believe, but what is here stated seems to be the essence of it.

The Mexicans kept a sacred fire burning perpetually, as did the Hebrews, and by that fire they waited patiently for the return of Quetzalcoatl. It is claimed that the Pueblo Indians had a similar custom in their kivas, for a similar reason.[16]

"Amongst the semi-civilized nations of America, from Mexico southward, as also amongst many nations of the Old World, the serpent was a prominent religious symbol, beneath which was concealed the profoundest significance. Under many of its aspects it coincided with the sun, or was the symbol of the Supreme Divinity of the heathens, of which the sun was one of the most obvious emblems. In the instance before us, the plumed, sacred serpent of the aborigines was artfully depicted so as to combine both symbols in one." (E. G. Squire, Nicaragua, Vol. 1, p. 406.)

Whence could these Indians have their concept of a divine-human savior symbolized by a feathered or flying serpent, if not through traditions from ancestors to whom the contents of the Book of Mormon were known?

NO KING AGAINST THE LORD

For he that raiseth up a king against me shall perish, for I, the Lord, the king of heaven, will be their king. (II Nephi 10:14)

These are given us as the words of the Lord through Jacob, the son of Lehi. The prophet tells us, that the Jews will be restored to the land of their fathers, while his descendants and those of his brethren will inherit America. And then he says that this land shall be a land of liberty to the gentiles as well, and that he that fighteth against this land — Zion — shall perish; also that he who raiseth up a king here against the Lord, shall perish, for the Lord Himself will be the "king" of this country.

When reading this really remarkable prediction, one cannot but remember Montezuma II, the head of the Aztec confederacy at the time of the arrival of Cortez in the Valley of Mexico. True, he was not a "king" in name, but he was a despot of the worst kind.

---

[16]On a dit que la coutume singuliere de conserver perpetuellement un feu sacre pres duquel les anciens Mexicains attendaient le retour du dieu Quetzalcoatl, existe aussi chez les Pueblos." For an extensive presentation of the subject see Bancroft, Native Races, Vol. 1, p. 554; and Vol. 3, pp. 248-87, 449-56, and other places in the same work.

His predecessors had succeeded in forming an alliance with Tezcuco and Tlacopan, for the purpose of plundering and killing the neighbors who refused to pay tribute. Like the Lamanites of old, his forces sallied forth from their strongholds, the chief of which was Tenochtitlan, and carried off whatever they could lay their hands on, and especially human beings needed for sacrifices. Montezuma was the head of this plunderbund. When the Spaniards came, it had extended its sway over thirty or more cities and was threatening the outlying settlements in every direction. But the time had come for the fulfilment of this prophecy. Montezuma was captured by the Spaniards, deposed by his own people, and then killed in a battle, probably by being struck down by a stone thrown by an Aztec soldier. In 1520 his rule of blood came to an ignoble end.

The Aztec version of the death of this unfortunate ruler is somewhat different. According to this source of information, Montezuma was a prisoner. He had trusted in the good faith of the Spaniards. But when the final trial of strength came between the Indians and the Spaniards, Montezuma was true to his blood. He refused to bend to the Spaniard's demand. So they killed him. They killed him by a sword thrust that was so directed as to render his death agonizing beyond comprehension and degrading to a man of royal blood, and when the king at last was dead the conqueror threw his naked body into the street.

"There is your king," they cried to his royal subjects.

It was then that the fifty Spanish captives were sacrificed. Their furious comrades saw them led to the summit of the pyramid that then occupied the center of what is now the plaza in front of the national palace. On its summit was the altar to the Sun god. The Spaniards, from the buildings they used as a fort, could see their friends led up the steps of the pyramid. They saw their naked bodies flash white in the sun. One after another they were thrust down upon the stone of sacrifice, and the priests made the ritual slashes in their breast and held the palpitating hearts up toward the sun.

But even according to this version, the word of the Lord was wonderfully fulfilled in the tragic end of Montezuma.

The Incas of Peru were less brutal in their military operations, than the Aztecs. They made war, not to obtain human victims for their altars; nor, even, for the sake of plunder. Like the followers of Mohammed, or the soldiers of the medieval "defenders of the faith," they went out to fight in the interest of a more humane religion and a further advanced civilization than their neighbors had. But they were, nevertheless, despots, and their government soon developed into absolute despotism. It, naturally, created class dis-

tinction of the worst kind, a condition against which the history of
the ancient Americans contains a solemn warning.[17] For themselves,
the Incas claimed divinity, as *the* sons of the sun — that is, as they
understood it, of God; and they exacted submission to their word as
if it had been a divine decree. They had not learned — or, if they
had, they had put aside and forgotten — the fundamental principle
of true religion which our Lord stated in these words:

"The kings of the gentiles exercise lordship over them; and they that exercise
authority upon them are called benefactors. But ye shall not be so; but he that is
greatest among you, let him be as the younger; and he that is chief, as he that doth
serve." (Luke 22:25, 26)

Having no regard for this great law, the Incas created a wide
gulf between themselves and the people, no less impassable because
it was imaginary. For themselves they claimed every privilege that
almost unlimited wealth and power could procure; to produce this
wealth was the chief end and purpose for which the people existed.
They were part of the assets of the Incas, just as were the beasts on
the hill sides, and fishes in the brooks, the trees in the valleys, the
grain in the fields and the store houses, and the metals in the mountains. To be sure, under good and wise rulers, the subjects were well
cared for; and so were the beasts of burden and the birds and other
animals; but, though human beings, they were, strictly speaking,
nothing but "property." This was the condition of about eight
million human beings under the Incas in this "land of liberty," at
the time of the arrival of the Spaniards. It was put to an end with
the assassination of Inca Huascar at Cuzco and the pretender Atahualpa at Caxamarca, in 1533.

Atahualpa, as is well known, was promised his liberty, if he
would pay a large ransom. He did pay, but the Spaniards, fearing to
set him free, decided to take his life as well as the ransom. They
proposed to strangle him instead of burning him to death, if he would
let them baptize him first. Having obtained his consent to this,
they "baptized" him and then choked him to death.

"The treatment of Atahualpa," says Prescott, "forms undoubtedly one of the darkest chapters in Spanish colonial history. There
may have been massacres on a more extended scale, and executions
accompanied with greater refinement of cruelty. But the blood-stained
annals of the Conquest affords us no such example of cold-hearted
and systematic presentation, not of an enemy, but of one whose whole
deportment had been that of a friend and a benefactor."

For the murderous, perfidious conduct of the Spaniards both in
Mexico and in Peru, there can be nothing but condemnation. At

[17]Alma 32:2; IV Nephi 25, 26.

the same time, the history of their exploits is the record of the fulfilment of a remarkable prophetic utterance in the Book of Mormon.

This prediction has also been verified in later times.

In May, 1822, Augustus Iturbide proclaimed himself emperor of Mexico, and was crowned the following July under the name of Augustin I. His empire included, in addition to the Mexico of today, large portions of the United States and the Central American countries. But the Mexicans soon drove him from the throne into exile. The country treated him liberally, in recognition of former patriotic service. An allowance of $25,000 a year was voted for him, provided he would remain abroad. But some power seemed to prompt him to return. He arrived in Mexico in 1824, and was killed as an enemy of the country on July 19, that year.

Those who were engaged in the efforts to establish Archduke Maximilian, or Hapsburg, a brother of the late Emperor Francis Joseph, of Austria-Hungary, on a Mexican imperial throne, fared no better. The proposition, in all probability, came, with the consent of the pope, from Napoleon III, who, at any rate, furnished the military force for the enterprise. Marshal Bazaine was the commander of those troops. The outcome of it was one of the great tragedies of history. Maximilian, abandoned by Napoleon and betrayed by some of his generals, was captured and shot to death, June, 1867. His wife, Princess Carlotte, a sister of King Leopold, of Belgium, became insane. Napoleon early in the war with Germany, 1870-71, was captured at Sedan and died in exile. Bazaine was captured with a force of 173,000 men, and he was, subsequently, tried by a court martial and condemned to degradation and death, although the death sentence was commuted to life imprisonment. Verily, "he that raiseth up a king against me"—in this land of liberty—"shall perish."

There is, perhaps, no more tragic experience in all history than that of Maximilian and Carlotte. When Louis Napoleon III of France in 1863, decided to step into the imbroglio in Mexico, a committee of Mexican nobles went to Miramir and asked Maximilian to become their emperor. He hesitated, and Carlotte is said to have made the decision for him. They entered Vera Cruz harbor in 1864 on a French cruiser and were well received. The United States, having emerged from its Civil War troubles, made a vigorous restatement of the Monroe Doctrine, and Louis Napoleon hurriedly withdrew his troops. Bereft of his patron's support, Maximilian saw the scattered bands of guerillas become a united army, directed against his throne. Carlotte, foreseeing doom, fled to France to plead with Napoleon to return his troops and support her husband.

How she humbled her pride before the French sovereign and subsequently pleaded in vain for aid from the Vatican form the most dramatic episodes of her long life. Her interview with Napoleon was held secret, but at its close an attendant heard her shriek: "I ought never to have forgotten what I am and what you are! I ought not to have forgotten that there is Bourbon blood in my veins! I should not have disgraced my descent by lowering myself before a Bonaparte and being led away by an adventurer!"

Louis Napoleon left in the midst of her tirade, and attendants found her swooning on the floor. Some accounts have it that her mind failed her then, but the fact remains that her will drove her to the Vatican, where she also created a scene.

After this fruitless appeal in her husband's behalf, she is said to have been found wandering the streets of Rome, washing her hands in the fountains and babbling incoherently. Accounts differ as to whether Carlotte ever knew that Maximilian was betrayed and captured, or that he died with her name on his lips before a firing squad at Queretaro, on June 19, 1867.

Such is some of the testimony of secular history to the truth of the Book of Mormon.

GOLD AND SILVER

And we * * * became exceedingly rich in gold, and in silver * * * and also in iron and copper. (Jarom 8)

That some of the Indians knew both gold and silver, iron and copper, is clear from this statement of Dr. Brinton, referring to the culture of the Cakchiquels:

"Gold and silver were classed under the general name *puvak*, and distinguished as white and yellow (puvak); iron and copper were both known as *chich*,[18] and distinguished also by their color. The metals formed an important element of their riches, and are constantly referred to as part of the tribute paid to the rulers."[19]

This is really a notable gloss on the passage quoted from Jarom, although, of course, the learned and gifted author, to whom students of the pre-historic races of America owe so much, never intended it as such. Dr. Brinton practically says of the Cakchiquels what Jarom tells us regarding the Nephites.

The Hebrews, too, classed copper, brass, and bronze as one metal, *nechosheth*,[20] a word that has also been translated "steel."[21] In all probability the Cakchiquel "chic" or "khikh" is a close relative of the Hebrew "ne-*chosh*-eth."

---

[18]As near as the word can be rendered in English letters. The "ch" is described as a sound between hard "c" and "k," combined with a hard aspirant.
[19]Brinton, *Libr. of Abor. Amer. Liter.*, Vol. 6, p. 19.
[20]From *nachash*, "to be hard," or "firm," said of metals.

HONEY

And they did also carry with them deseret, which by interpretation, is a honey bee. (Ether 2:3)

In Guatemala, as in Yucatan, bees were domesticated for the wax as well as the honey.[22] That would seem to indicate the influence of Jaredite civilization.

ISLE OF THE SEA

"And we are upon an isle of the sea. (II Nephi 10:20)

Elder George Reynolds remarks:

"How could Jacob have known, except by revelation, that the vast continent which the Nephites inhabited was entirely surrounded by the waters of the great oceans? * * * And by the way, this simple statement is strong testimony of the authenticity of the Book of Mormon. At the time that this portion of the sacred plates was translated * * * it was not known to modern science that the American continent was indeed an island. Joseph Smith could not have received knowledge of this fact, so unhesitatingly affirmed, from any learned geographer or practical navigator. * * * It was not, until repeated expeditions, that in May, 1847, the truth of the statement of Jacob could be affirmed from actual knowledge of the geographical features of the country, as at that date the explorations and surveys by land and sea, from east to west, were brought sufficiently near to leave the matter without a doubt. It was not until 1854 that the first ship's crew (that of Captain McClure), which ever sailed across the Arctic Ocean from the Pacific to the Atlantic, along the northern coast of America, returned from their perilous voyage. We thus find that human geographical knowledge could not have aided the prophet Joseph Smith in making this statement, had it originated with him and not with the son of Lehi."[23]

Dr. Brinton has this to say:

"The Indians almost universally believed the dry land they knew, to be part of a great island, everywhere surrounded by wide waters whose limits were unknown. Many tribes had vague myths of a journey from beyond this sea; many placed beyond it the home of the sun and of light, and the happy hunting grounds of the departed souls."[24]

Where, may we ask, could the Indians have received their information, if not from the same source from which Jacob, the brother of Nephi, derived his knowledge?

WHITE AND DELIGHTSOME

And many generations shall not pass away among them save they shall be a white and delightsome people. (II Nephi 30:6)

This remarkable prophecy was literally fulfilled when the Lamanites in the Land of Nephi were converted through the instrumentality of Aaron and his brethren; for then the curse was re-

---

[21]*Nechushah;* 2 Samuel 22:35; Job 20:24; Psalm 18:34.
[22]See Brinton, *Libr. of Abor. Amer. Literature,* Vol. 6, p. 15.
[23]*Story of the Book of Mormon,* p. 253, fifth edition.
[24]*Library of Abor. Amer. Literature,* Vol. 5, p. 134.

moved. (Alma 23:18) The same happened twenty or thirty years later, when some Lamanites joined the Nephites. "Their curse was taken from them and their skin became white like unto the Nephites." (III Nephi 2:15)

The prophecy in II Nephi 30:6 should be compared with Words of Mormon, v. 8, where the inspired author says he prays that his brethren may again "be a delightsome people"; also with Mormon 5:17, where it is said that the Lamanites "were once a delightsome people," and with Moroni 9:12, where the prophet says they had once been a "civil and a delightsome people." For these passages, by not mentioning the color of the skin, prove that the principal thought in the expression "white and delightsome" is centered in the change of disposition, as well as in the complexion.

There is abundant evidence that the Indians have the race characteristics necessary to make them, under proper conditions, a "white and delightsome people." The weaving art of the Navajos has become famous, and American girls have not disdained to wear "sweaters" blazing in Navajo colors, red, green, yellow, white and black, with typical Indian designs. In the *Literary Digest* for May 6, 1922, there are reproductions of water colors, the originals being drawn by Ta-e, a Pueblo Indian, showing the spontaneous budding of a new art among the Indians. According to Leopold Godowsky, the pianist, as reported in the press, Oct. 14, 1921, many of the Mexican Indians are excellent musicians. The conductor of the symphony orchestra in the City of Mexico was at that time a full-blood Indian, and Mr. Godowsky said he was "a man of high musical attainments and broad education, who had studied much in the musical centers of Europe." The war record of the American Indians is simply wonderful. Of 17,313 registered by the draft boards only 228 asked for deferred classification or exemption. Eight thousand entered the military service, and 6,000 of these were volunteers. The following from a report by Brigadier General Enoch H. Crowder to the President, speaks volumes for the Indians:[25]

"It was the Prussian Guard against the American Indian on the morning of October 8 in the hills of Champagne. When it was all over, the Prussian Guards were farther on their way back toward the Aisne, and warriors of thirteen Indian tribes looked down on the town of St. Etienne. The Indians—one company of them— were fighting with the Thirty-sixth division, made up of Texas and Oklahoma rangers and oil men, for the most part."

In 1922, according to reliable statistics, there were about 350,000 Indians in the United States, scattered over 48 states. They belonged to 189 tribes. On October 18, 1922, representatives of the Society

---

[25]*Salt Lake Tribune,* Feb. 16, 1922.

of Indians, in session at Kansas City, Mo., passed a resolution demanding the right of franchise and all the other privileges that belong to American citizenship. Students of the American aborigines place them very high in the scale of intelligence.[26] They have every characteristic necessary to enable them to become a "white and delightsome people," and this fact, now generally recognized, was first pointed out in the Book of Mormon.

According to figures presented to Congress during the 1922-23 session, by Commissioner of Indian Affairs Charles H. Burke, the Indians are rapidly becoming independent. One-third are no longer under the supervision of the Indian Bureau. Nearly one million acres of land are being farmed by about 43,000 Indians, and 50,000 families are living in permanent houses. The total wealth of the Indians in the United States is estimated at one billion dollars, which would be almost $3,000 per capita. The Osages are the wealthiest, because of the value of their oil land in Oklahoma. Mr. Philip Howell, editor of *The American Indian Weekly,* himself an educated Indian, is of the opinion that the destiny of his people is to be assimilated with the white race. Government figures, he points out, show there are only 9,000 full blooded Indians left in the country, while the mixed Indian and white population totals 350,000. He also gives the information that the Indians have found tremendous interest in the Latter-day Saints' belief concerning their origin because of their numerous traditions which coincide with the Bible. This is especially true of Indian traditions of the flood, of which all Indians have vivid tales, says Mr. Howell. (*Deseret News,* July 28, 1927)

"NEPHI" AS A TITLE

And whoso should reign in his stead were called by the people, second Nephi, third Nephi, and so forth, according to the reigns of the kings. (Jacob 1:11)

The word *nephi* is the Hebrew *nevi* (or, perhaps, more correctly, *nebhi*), which means, *prophet.* But "prophet" is the official title of one who is authorized to "speak for," or instead of, God. As a "seer" his mind is opened to see visions and to receive revelations; as a prophet he communicates to the people that which he has thus received.

The "kings" in this choice land of promise were not to be kings in the sense of the Greek *basilevs* or the Roman *rex;* still less in the sense of the despots of the middle ages. They were to be the representatives of God, and exercise the functions of their office as his stewards. David was such a king. He was also a prophet (Acts 2:30), and as such a "man after God's own heart," although that can not be said of him in his private life, or conduct, at all times. The rulers in this country were to hold a position similar to that of Samuel in Israel, anciently, or of Moses, the greatest of all the prophets (*nebhiim*) of old.[27]

---

[26]See Dr. Brinton's *The American Race,* pp. 41-43.
[27]"Nephis" in 1 Esdras 5:21 is the "children of Nebo" in Ezra 2:29. Nebo is reasonably conjectured to be connected with the Hebrew *nebhi,* "prophet," for Nebo was the god of letters. —Smith's *Bible Dictionary.* Isaiah 46:1; Jeremiah 48:1.

DAVID AND SOLOMON

Behold, David and Solomon truly had many wives and concubines, which thing was abominable before me, saith the Lord; * * * wherefore, my brethren, hear me, and hearken to the word of the Lord for there shall not any man among you have save it be one wife; and concubines he shall have none; for I, the Lord God, delighteth in the chastity of women. And whoredoms are an abomination before me; thus saith the Lord of Hosts. (Jacob 2:24-28)

Different opinions concerning the true meaning of this text have been expressed by readers of the Book of Mormon. The reference to David and Solomon shows clearly *what* the Lord censured, and *why*.

In the case of David, the Lord said through the prophet Nathan:

"Thus saith the Lord God of Israel, I anointed thee king over Israel, and I delivered thee out of the hand of Saul; and I gave thee thy master's house, and thy master's wives into thy bosom, and gave thee the house of Israel and Judah; and if that had been too little, I would moreover have given unto thee such and such things. Wherefore hast thou despised the commandment of the Lord, to do evil in his sight? Thou hast killed Uriah the Hittite with the sword, and hast taken his wife to be thy wife, and hast slain him with the sword of the children of Ammon."[28]

That was David's awful sin. He had not only taken a wife without divine sanction — another man's wife at that — but he had committed foul murder, in order to get possession of her. I fancy his sin would have been as great, had he committed murder, to come in possession of houses or land, or even, as Nathan expressed it, "one little ewe lamb." Ahab and Jezebel were both sentenced to death, through the mouth of the prophet Elijah, for the murder of Naboth for the sake of his vineyard.[29]

In the case of Solomon we read:

"But King Solomon loved many strange women, together with the daughter of Pharaoh, women of the Moabites, Ammonites, Edomites, Zidonians, and Hittites; of the nations concerning which the Lord said to the children of Israel, Ye shall not go in to them, neither shall they come in to you: for surely they will turn away your heart after their gods: Solomon clave unto these in love. * * * For it came to pass, when Solomon was old, that his wives turned away his heart after other gods: and his heart was not perfect with Lord his God, as was the heart of David his father."[30]

Solomon, as is here shown, sinned in making social alliances with idolaters, contrary to the commandment of God, and in adopting features of their worship. It was this that kindled the anger of the Lord against him.[31]

Now it appears that the Nephites, shortly after the death of Nephi began to yield to the desires of their depraved hearts, and

---

[28]2 Samuel 12:7-9.
[29]1 Kings 21:17-24.
[30]1 Kings 11:1-4.
[31]*Ibid.*, vv. 5-11.

sought to justify their carnal practices by what is recorded of David and Solomon. The prophet Jacob, who had succeeded Nephi, was, therefore, directed by the Lord to explain to them the awful consequences of sexual indulgences outside the sacred precincts of divine sanction, as exemplified in the expreiences of those two kings of the Jews, and to command them to have only one wife and no concubines, unless the Lord for some special purpose, should give them a different law. See Jacob 2:30.

The American Indians, at the time of the conquest, were quite generally practicing plural marriage.

Among the Apaches, he who could support a number of wives was greatly honored, and the Apache women are said to have been remarkably chaste. A Pericui was permitted to take as many wives as he desired. The Mexicans practiced plurality of wives, and some had concubines as part of the family circle. The Chichimecs, however, had only one wife at a time, but frequent divorces. Protitution was tolerated and regulated. The Mayas generally acknowledged only one woman as wife, but the lords and chiefs had concubines. The Lacandones practiced polygamy, each wife having her own house. In Honduras the women had a reputation for chastity, but plurality of wives was the rule. The Carib who had several wives, provided a home for each. On the Isthmus the caciques married as many women as they could support, but only the first was *the* wife. Some of the natives were notorious for licentiousness. The Moquis, it is said, had periodical festivals which ended in drunkenness and promiscuous indulgence.[32] The Peruvians, according to all accounts, practiced polygamy on a large scale. The ruling Inca had thousands of "virgins of the sun" at his disposal, though he had only one Coya, or queen, and she was always his sister. The great lords and nobles were also permitted a plurality of wives, but the common mortals had only one wife, possibly for economic reasons.[33]

As is clear from the text at the head of this note, the moral status of the Nephites began to decline, shortly after the death of Nephi, and it became necessary to abolish an institution which they abused to their own injury and condemnation. It is equally clear, from secular history, that the descendants of Nephi did not generally keep the law as given through Jacob, though it must be admitted that among many of the Indians chastity was a precious and highly valued jewel.

THE CHOIRS ABOVE

And my immortal spirit may join the choirs above in singing the praises of a just God. (Mosiah 2:28)

---

[32]Bancroft, *Native Races*, Vol. 1, pp. 512-14, 551, 633, 703, 729, 731, 772; Vol. 2, pp. 266, 671.
[33]Prescott, *Conquest of Peru*, Vol. 1, pp. 98-100.

This is an extract from the farewell address of King Benjamin to his people.[34] He expresses the desire to be fully prepared to "join the choirs above." Compare Mormon 7:7, where we are told that those who are found guiltless will have the privilege of dwelling in the presence of God and singing "ceaseless praises with the choirs above."

Does it seem improbable that there are "choirs" in the realms inhabited by the redeemed? The ability to sing and to compose and to play music is a divine gift, if there ever was one. The very purpose of it is to enable us to praise the Lord and to glorify his name. There is no music so inspiring, so elevating, so refining as religious music, and it is a great question whether any other kind, especially so-called martial music, is not best characterized as a poor imitation, absolutely worthless.

We know that John, the beloved, on several occasions, in his Apocalyptic visions became aware of singing and music of heavenly origin. (Rev. 5:9; 14:3; 15:3) We also know that, at the time of the birth of our Lord, a heavenly host sang praise to God, audibly to mortal ear. (Luke 2:13, 14)

And here, let me, J. M. Sjodahl, in all humility, place on record that to my own personal knowledge singing and music were heard in the Manti Temple at the time of the dedication of that sacred building. On two separate occasions I had the privilege of hearing the super-earthly harmonies. The first was just before the beginning of the services on the day I attended. It sounded as a very distant organ music, for a brief moment, as if a door had been opened, through which the harmony reached us, and then almost immediately closed. The second occasion was a few days later, when I was preparing for work for some of my friends on the other side. It sounded as the singing of male voices, also for a brief moment, and came as from a distance. There were other manifestations during those days, never to be forgotten. During the services I noticed that some of the Twelve, notably Elder Heber J. Grant, the late President of the Church, and the late John W. Taylor, were surrounded by rays of light, re-

---

[34]This address of King Benjamin might well be compared with an address which the Nahua high priest delivered when their kings were anointed.

The High Priest:	King Benjamin:
"Consider well, sire, the great honor which your subjects have conferred upon you, and remember, now that you are king, that it is your duty to watch over your people with great care, to look upon them as your children, to preserve them from suffering, and to protect the weak from the oppression of the strong," etc.—Bancroft, *Native Races*, Vol. 2, p. 146.	"I have not sought gold nor silver; neither have I suffered that ye should be confined in dungeons, nor that ye should make slaves of one another * * * and even I, myself, have labored with my own hands, that I might serve you, and that ye should not be laden with taxes, and that there should nothing come upon you which was grievous to be born," etc.

sembling the colors of the rainbow but softer. These manifestations were recorded at the time by the press.

Yes, there are choirs on the other side, and bands, and John describes their performances as "the voice of many waters, and as the voice of a great thunder: * * * and the voice of harpers harping with their harps." (Rev. 14:2)

THE EAST WIND

If my people shall sow filthiness, they shall reap the east wind, which bringeth immediate destruction. (Mosiah 7:31; 12:6)

The reference to the "east wind" as an agent of destruction shows that the author of these texts was influenced by a mode of thinking that obtained in Palestine, anciently. In that country the east wind is very hurtful to vegetation. In the winter it is dry and cold, and in the summer dry and hot. It carries off the moisture of the leaves rapidly, and withers them. On the Mediterranean it is known as a "levanter" and is dangerous to the sailors. It was in such a storm that Paul was shipwrecked and, with all the crew and passengers, stranded on the island of Malta. See Acts 27:14-44.

DEATH BY FIRE

And now, when Abinadi had said these words, he fell, having suffered death by fire. (Mosiah 17:20)

Abinadi was consigned to the flames for his testimony of Jesus, among the people of Lehi-Nephi, under the reign of the wicked King Noah. King Noah, himself, suffered a similar fate, when he fell into the hands of his enemies. (Mosiah 19:20) Later on, many of the Lamanites were put to death by fire. (25:5) Some of the disciples of our Lord were cast into furnaces of fire, although they were miraculously rescued, as were the three Hebrew children in Babylon. (IV Nephi 32) From all of which it appears that the people in this western world, at the time covered by the Book of Mormon history, were in the habit of consigning captives to the flames.

Burning of prisoners was extensively practiced by natives at the time of the arrival in this country by the Spaniards. The Apaches used to put prisoners to death by fire.[35] In Tezcuco the punishment for certain unnatural crimes was torture and burning at the stake.[36] At the festival in honor of Xiuhtecutli, the god of fire, the people raised a "May pole," elaborately decorated. At the appointed time, the officiating priests hurled a number of prisoners, stripped of clothing and bound hand and foot, upon a great heap of smouldering coals, where they suffered untold agony, until raked out and slaughtered on

[35]Bancroft, *Native Races,* Vol. 1, p. 498.
[36]*Ibid.,* Vol. 2, p. 467.

the altar, whereupon the people enjoyed themselves singing and dancing around the pole.[37] At the termination of an age — a cycle of 52
years was so called — the sacred fires were permitted to go out, and
a new fire was kindled by friction of sticks placed on the wounded
breast of a captive provided for that purpose. The flame was soon
communicated to a funeral pyre on which the victim was consumed.[38]
Is there no historical connection between the flames of persecution
of which we read in the Book of Mormon and the cruelties practiced,
sometimes in behalf of "justice" and sometimes as religion, by the
later occupants of American soil?

That the Jews in Palestine burned human victims in honor of
Moloch is clear from Isaiah 30:33 and Ezekiel 20:26, and other
passages.

THE FATHER AND THE SON

The Father, because he was conceived by the power of God; and the Son,
because of the flesh; thus becoming the Father and the son. (Mosiah 15:2)

Abinadi here teaches us that our Redeemer is a divine person
who came among the children of men, and that He is called "the Son
of God," because He dwelt in a tabernacle of flesh, although, as conceived by the power of God, He is called "the Father." This is a
very clear statement of the doctrine of the two-fold nature of Christ.
He is not only a teacher, a prophet, a reformer; He is God and man.
He is both the Father and the Son.

"Jesus Christ is the Son of Elohim, both as spiritual and bodily offspring; that
is to say, Elohim is literally the Father of the spirit of Jesus Christ, and also of the
body in which Jesus Christ performed his mission in the flesh, and which body died
on the cross, and was afterwards taken up by the process of resurrection, and is now
the immortalized tabernacle of the eternal spirit of our Lord and Savior." (From
The Father and the Son, a doctrinal exposition by the First Presidency and the
Twelve; Mill. Star, Vol. 78, pp. 482-500; Doc. and Cov. Commentary, p. 556.

THE WRITING ON THE WALL

Aminadi who interpreted the writing which was upon the wall of the temple,
which was written by the finger of God. (Alma 10:2)

We know no more about this writing than what is stated here.
But the fact to note is that the ancient Americans, as the ancient
Egyptians, recorded important historical events on the walls of their
public buildings. At some time the Lord Himself had written something on a temple wall erected by Nephites, presumably, and Aminadi
had been given the gift of interpretation. Is it impossible that this
miraculous writing was the starting point of the strange American
hieroglyphs, which were developed gradually and which survived

[37]Ibid., Vol. 2, p. 329.
[38]Prescott, Conquest of Mexico, Vol. 3, p. 129.

after the records of the Nephites had been hidden and their alphabet and speech forgotten?

GOLD, SILVER, AND BARLEY

A senum of silver was equal to a senine of gold; and either for a measure of barley, and also for a measure of every kind of grain. (Alma 11:7)

In this verse and the context (vv. 4-19) information is given regarding the currency and standard of value as established by Mosiah II, who became ruler in Zarahemla about 125 B.C.

GOLD	SILVER
Senine is the Unit.	Senum is the Unit.
2 Senines equal 1 Seon.	2 Senums equal 1 Amnor
4 Senines equal 1 Shum	4 Senums equal 1 Ezrom
7 Senines equal 1 Limnah	7 Senums equal 1 Onti

A gold senine was equal in value to a silver senum, and a certain measure of barley or any other grain was equal in value to either.

The smaller pieces were:

1 Shiblon was equal to half a Senum or a Senine.
1 Shiblum was equal to a quarter of a Senum or a Senine.
1 Leah was equal to one eighth of a Senum or a Senine.

These were, probably, silver pieces. An *antion* was a gold piece equal in value to 3 Shiblons or one senine and a half.

It is not to be supposed that these metal pieces were stamped coins, such as we have. Coins were used in Greece perhaps as early as the 8th century, B.C., but in the Old Testament there is no mention of coins until after the Babylonian captivity. According to 1 Macc., Simon Maccabæus received permission to coin money, from Antiochus II, about 140 B.C. Previous to that time, silver was the main currency, and it was generally weighed. *Shekel* means a "weight." The "pieces of money" Jacob paid for a parcel of land are called *kesitah*, "lambs." It is possible that they were so called because the weights used to determine their value were formed in imitation of a lamb's head.[39] Such weights were used in Egypt very early, as well as imitations of ox heads, birds, etc. Gold was used very early as currency, generally in the shape of rings. The "gold out of the bag" mentioned by Isaiah (46:6) was probably rings. Lehi was familiar with this kind of currency.

Elder George Reynolds, in his *Story of the Book of Mormon*, calls attention to the fact that the Nephite names for their money were either identical with, or derived from, names of places or persons, analogous with our "Napoleons," "Louis d'ors," "sovereigns," etc. *Limnah*, however, may be related to the Hebrew *maneh*, "num-

---

[39]Or the picture of a lamb may have been scratched on them.

ber," "portion," "weight," with a performative "l," "for." *Maneh*
is the *mina* of the ancient Greeks, and our "money," "mint," and
their derivatives. *Seon* may be from the Hebrew *seah*, a corn measure.
(Gen. 18:6) *Shum* seems to be the Hebrew *shum*, to "value." *Shiblcn*
and *shiblum* may be related to the Hebrew *shibolim*, "ears of corn,"
since grain, among the Nephites, was the standard of value.

Among the Mexican and Central American Indians, at the
time of the conquest, cacao beans were extensively used as a medium
of exchange, as grain was among the Nephites. The Nahuas kept
beans in sacks, 24,000 to a sack, for larger transactions. In addition,
they used gold dust in quills, and copper pieces in the form of a T.
Among the Mayas, beans were valuable. A hundred of them would
pay for a slave. The Mayas also had copper bells, precious stones,
and copper hatches as circulating media. The Peruvians, it has been
asserted, had no currency, but Mr. Sqier, in his Peru,[40] says that
small, thin pieces of gold, silver, and copper, round and square, each
pierced with a small hole as if intended to be strung like a coin of
the Chinese, have been found at Chimu. Rafinesque in *The American
Nations*,[41] says, "Metallic coins were little known except in Central
America; but bits of silver, gold, tin, iron, were used as such. The
other mediums of exchange were skins, mats, nuts, cacao, shells,
beads, etc." Garcia, quoted by Mrs. Simon,[42] declares that iron money
in the shape of the skull of a tortoise was in use in Paraguay. In
mounds in the Mississippi valley bits of metal have been found,
which, it has been thought, the Mound Builders used as money.[43]

Special interest attaches to the statement that the Nahuas used
copper pieces in the form of a T. The Hebrew "T" (tav) means a
"mark," and especially a "signature." It was the "brand" that marked
a human being as somebody's property. In the early Hebrew the *tav*
was written as a cross, and a metal piece in the same form would be
a particularly appropriate representation of property value. But where
did the Nahuas get the idea, if not from a Nephite ancestry?

In the *Deseret News* for Dec. 12 and 19, 1860, and the *Millennial
Star*, Vol. 23, p. 93, there is an account of an old copper coin, which
was exhibited at the *News'* office by Hon. George Peacock, of Manti,
Utah, and which had been found by an explorer along the Colorado
River. The coin was shown to Prof. W. W. Phelps, who gave the
following interpretation of the characters on it:

On the observe: *"The king Hagagadoniah over the kingdom
near the sea sends to all greeting: One senine."*

[40]Page 172.
[41]Page 55.
[42]*The Ten Tribes*, p. 13.
[43]See Bancroft, *Native Races*, Vol. 2, pp. 382 and 737.

On the reverse: "In the 95th year of the Kingdom of Christ, 9th year of my reign: Peace and life."

Motto: "Weapon to Weapon; Life for Life."

The opinion is expressed that the coin is 1,765 years old, and that it is a Nephite senine, or farthing, as mentioned in III Nephi, chapter 12:26.

The item is mentioned here for what it is worth. The senine of the Book of Mormon is a gold coin, equal in value to a certain measure of grain, and also one day's wages of a judge. (Alma 11:3-7) From this passage it will be seen that a senine, in the days of Alma was a gold piece, but it is not impossible that later a small copper coin may have been in use and been known as a "senine." Of that there is no strong evidence, so far.

RESURRECTION OF THE BODY

I say unto you that this mortal body is raised to an immortal body; that is from death; even from the first death unto life, that they can die no more. (Alma 11:45)

The following comments on this all-important subject will be read with interest:

"We understand that when we are unclothed in the present state, then we are prepared to be clothed upon with immortality. These bodies will return to dust, but our hope and faith are that we will receive these bodies again from the elements— that we will receive the very organization that we have here, and that if we are faithful to the principles of freedom, we shall then be prepared to endure eternally. Can the wicked be brought forth to endure? No, they will be destroyed." (Brigham Young, July 19, 1857; Journal of Discourses, Vol. 5, p. 53)

"I expect, by the power of the resurrection and the quickening power of the celestial glory, that my memory will be perfected, and that I will be able to remember all the acts, duties, and doings of my own life. I will also remember, most correctly and perfectly, every act of benevolence that has ever been done to me in the name of the Lord and because of my calling." (Parley P. Pratt, Sept. 7, 1856; Journal of Discourses, Vol. 5, p. 196)

"So far as we are concerned, we were taken from the earth, and we may expect to return to it again; and that portion of me which is pure, after the dross of this mortality is separated from it, I expect will be Brother Heber. It is that which will be resurrected; but all that is not pure will remain; that is, it will not go back into any body again; and if there are ten parts out of the hundred which are dross and corruption, they will remain in the earth. I do not expect to take that up again, but I expect to take up the purified element that will endure for ever." (Heber C. Kimball, Journal of Discourses, Vol. 5, p. 107.

"The old Book talks about a city called the New Jerusalem. The passage I refer to is in the Revelations by John, 21:8-11: 'But the fearful and unbelieving and the abominable and murderers and whoremongers and sorcerers and idolaters and all liars shall have their part in the lake which burneth with fire and brimstone, which is the second death.'" (Geo. A. Smith, July 26, 1857; Journal of Discourses, Vol. 5, p. 61)

"The resurrection of mortal bodies, on earth, began with Jesus, who on the third day rose from the grave, and after his sojourn among the children of men, took his body with him into heaven. This was the first fruit of the resurrection. Since that time, the resurrection of man may have continued, and no doubt will continue, in the future; for many spirits have laid down their earthly bodies, and all must be raised from the grave. In the resurrection, order and law will prevail, and the just deserts of men will be kept in mind." (*Rational Theology*, Dr. John A. Widtsoe)

AMERICA THE LAND OF LIBERTY

When he had poured out his soul to God, he named all the land which was south of the land Desolation, yea, and in fine, all the land, both on the north and on the south—a chosen land, and the land of liberty. (Alma 46:17)

Lehi prophesied (II Nephi 1:7) that America would be "a land of liberty" to all whom God should bring here, provided they would keep the commandments of God; otherwise they would be "scattered and smitten" (v. 11). Moroni again dedicated the country to the cause of liberty. He tore his coat, or cloak, selected a suitable piece on which he wrote an impressive "slogan," and made this his standard. The coat was torn in remembrance of the rent coat of Joseph, and round this standard the friends of liberty gathered themselves. (Alma 46:12-27)

The Indians, as found by the Europeans, were great on carrying flags, or standards. They carried them in processions at religious festivals, at funerals, in war, etc. The Nahuas had flags of paper, or cloth, on which black bars were printed, which must have given them the appearance of having been torn. Others were decorated with feathers.[44]

These men dedicated the entire American continents to the cause of liberty, and not for their own benefit alone, but for all men, whom the Lord should lead to come here, and who would serve Him under the ensign of liberty.

"It is true, this is Zion—North and South America are Zion, and the land where the Lord commenced his work, and where he commenced he will finish. This is the land of Zion; but we are not yet prepared to go and establish the Center stake of Zion. The Lord tried that in the first place * * *Now it is for you and me to prepare to return back" (Brigham Young, *Journal of Discourses,* Vol. 11, p. 324)

"When we contemplate the designs of the country, and its influence, we contemplate not merely our own liberty, happiness, and progress, nationally and individually, but we contemplate the emancipation of the world, the flowing of the nations to this fountain, and to the occupation of these elements, blending together in one common brotherhood. They will thus seek deliverance from oppression, not in the style of revolution, but by voluntarily emerging into freedom and the free occupation of the elements of life." (Parley P. Pratt, Oration, July 4, 1853; *Journal of Discourses,* Vol. 1, p. 141)

Garcilasso de la Vega tells us that the Peruvians had no word

---

[44]Bancroft, *Native Races,* Vol. 2, pp. 323, 405; Vol. 3, p. 405.

for "king," but that their equivalent for that title was *Hatun Apu*, "great lord." The same remark, probably, applies to all the prehistoric Indians. They had "chiefs" and "great lords" and "melechs" in the ancient, Semitic meaning of that word, "providers." But they had no "kings" in the modern sense of the title. However, the Incas in Peru and the "Chief-of-men" of the Aztecs had become veritable despots before they were destroyed.

"These Colonies (Jaredites, Lehites, Mulekites) were located in the southern part of North America, in Central America, and in the northern part of South America. And all this land, as well as that into which they migrated to the north and the south, was designated by the Lord as the Land of Promise." (George F. Richards, Oct. 7, 1922; *Conference Report*, p. 81)

IN THE MORNING

And it was in the morning, and the darkness dispersed from off the face of the land. (III Nephi 10:9)

Orson Pratt calls attention to the fact that, making an allowance of 7½ hours for the difference in longitude between Palestine and the Land Bountiful, the three days of darkness at the latter place must have begun and ended at 7:30 a.m., and that the time of the death of our Savior must have been that hour in Bountiful. He comments as follows:

"This book, the Book of Mormon, informs us that the time of day at which Jesus was crucified, I mean the time of day in America, was in the morning; the New Testament tells us that Jesus was crucified in the afternoon, between the 6th and 9th hour according to the Jews' reckoning. They commenced their reckoning at six o'clock in the morning, and consequently, the sixth hour would be 12 o'clock at noon, and the ninth hour 3 o'clock in the afternoon. Jesus, from the sixth to the ninth hour, or in other words, from 12 o'clock to 3, was hanging on the cross. Now, the Book of Mormon, or the historians whose records it contains, when relating the incidents that transpired at the time of the crucifixion—the darkness that was spread over the face of the land, the earthquakes, the rending of rocks, the sinking of the cities, and the whirlwinds—say these events occurred in the morning; they also say that darkness was spread over the face of the land for the space of three days. In Jerusalem it was only three hours. But the Lord gave them a special sign in this country, and the darkness lasted three days, and at the expiration of three days and three nights of darkness it cleared off, and it was in the morning. That shows that, according to the time in this country, the crucifixion must have taken place in the morning.

"Says one, 'Is not this a contradiction between the Book of Mormon and the New Testament?' To an unlearned person it would really be a contradiction. * * * 'But,' says one, 'how do you account for it?' * * * Simply by the difference in longitude. This would make a difference of time of several hours; for when it would be 12 at noon in Jerusalem it would only be half past four in the morning * * * where the Book of Mormon was then being written. * * * If the Book of Mormon had said that the crucifixion took place in the afternoon we should have known at once that it could not be true."[45]

---

[45]*Journal of Discourses*, Vol. 13, p. 128.

This is evidence that can not be refuted. If the Book of Mormon had been fiction, written by an unlearned author, the difference in time would not have been even thought of.

OUR LORD APPEARS IN BOUNTIFUL

Behold, I am Jesus Christ, whom the prophets testified shall come into the world. (III Nephi 11:10)

The portion of the Book of Mormon from which this text is taken contains the account of the appearance of the resurrected Savior in the Land of Bountiful, and His teachings and instructions. (See III Nephi 11-26)

Is there, outside the Book of Mormon, any evidence whatever of the truth of this wonderful story?

Perhaps this question is best answered by a brief statement of what Father Remesel relates in his History. He affirms that when Bishop B. Las Casas came to his bishopric in 1545, he instructed an ecclesiastic in Campeche, whose name was Francisco Hernandez, to visit the Indians and inform them of the principal doctrines of the faith of the Spaniards. Some time afterwards this ecclesiastic informed Las Casas that he had met a chief who had explained the religious beliefs of the Indians to him. The Indians, he said, believed in the Father, the Son, and the Holy Spirit. They called the Father, *Yezona;* the Son, *Bahab;* and the Holy Spirit, *Ec-Ruach.* The Son was born of a virgin called, *Chiribrias,* whose mother was *Yxchel.* The Son, they said, was crowned with thorns and put to death by being placed on a beam of wood. On the third day he rose, and immediately afterwards the Holy Spirit came and filled the earth with whatsoever it stood in need of. Being questioned about how the Indians had obtained this information, he answered that the lords had instructed their sons, and that these instructions had come down from generation to generation.[46]

I am, of course, aware of the existing disposition to discredit the early historians, whenever they relate something for which modern research can, as yet, offer no acceptable explanation. But, is it fair to stamp them all as falsifiers or dupes because they tell us what seems marvelous?

I can understand that the early explorers and missionaries might sometimes have been misled, and that they read into the stories related to them a meaning which was not there. But, after every reasonable allowance for misunderstandings, the fact remains that there must have been some solid, tangible basis for a report like that of Father Hernandez to Las Casas, and many similar accounts.

[46]Cogullodo, *Historia de Yutikan* (sic!), Lib. IV, Chap. VI; in Kingsbourough's *Antiq. Mex.,* quoted by Mrs. Simon, *The Ten Tribes,* p. 219.

Whence, then, did the Indians get that basis on which their marvelous traditions rested? Whence came to them the fundamental principles of their religion, no nearly like those proclaimed by our Lord, that many held, as some yet claim, that the gospel had been preached here by one of the first Apostles of our Lord?

Is there any satisfactory answer to that question except that given in the Book of Mormon?

IF THE GOSPEL IS REJECTED

When the gentiles shall sin against my gospel, and shall be lifted up in the pride of their hearts above all nations, and above all the people of the whole earth, and shall be filled with all manner of lyings, and of deceits, and of mischiefs, and all manner of hypocrisy, and murders, and priestcrafts, and whoredoms, and of secret abominations; and if they shall do all those things, and shall reject the fulness of my gospel, behold, saith the Father, I will bring the fulness of my gospel from among them. (III Nephi 16:10)

Elder Orson Pratt[47] considers that this prediction, was fulfilled, when, beginning with the year 1847, the Lord removed the Church to the so-called American Desert, a thousand miles from the boundaries of civilization. The gospel was rejected and the prophet slain, and the Church was brought "from among" the gentiles as predicted by Nephi. "God," says Orson Pratt, "who can foresee all events among the children of men, had his eye fixed on the gathering of his children before the Church was organized, and he predicted that they should come out of every nation under heaven; not only from the settled portions of the gentile nation, but they should be brought forth out of the midst of that gentile nation, just as we have been."

SHINE FORTH IN DARKNESS

Touch these stones, O Lord, with thy finger, and prepare them that they may shine forth in darkness. (Ether 3:4; 6:3)

Noah, it will be remembered, was according to the English Bible translation, commanded to make a "window" to the ark. But it is pretty well agreed that the translation of the word rendered "window" is not good. The word means literally a shining object, and rabbinical tradition has it that the shining object was really a stone which the Patriarch had found in the River Pison and which was made luminous.[48] If this tradition is based on fact, the Brother of Jared must have known it, and that would account for his prayer and the miraculous answer that he obtained.

That precious stones can be made to shine seems to have been demonstrated by scientific experiments. In June, 1920, Dr. T. Coke

[47]*Journal of Discourses*, Vol. 13, p. 133.
[48]See Dr. Clarke's *Commentary.*

Squance, of Sunderland, England, was reported to have succeeded in changing a sapphire of faint pink hue into a beautiful ruby, by means of the action of radium. "During the process," the report said, "the lustre was increased to such an extent that the stone had almost the brilliance of a diamond." Later reports had it that experiments conducted at the United States Bureau of Mines, at Reno, Nevada, had given equally startling results. "Colorless Colorado topazes," it was reported, "have been given a rich yellow tinting." It seems, then, that the Brother of Jared, when praying the Lord to touch the stones and make them luminant, was in possession, by some means, of a knowledge that scientists of today are just beginning to dip into.

A scientific invention was announced in Philadelphia on Oct. 20, 1926, by W. D. Coolidge before the Franklin Institute. It consisted of a new cathode ray tube. According to the accounts, cathode rays in a darkened room became visible as a purple glow, and a crystal of calcite placed in these rays became glowing, as if red hot, although it was perfectly cold, and continued to glow for some time. Granite also became luminous.[49] It might, therefore, not be unreasonable to suppose that God could make the stones in the barges luminous.

THE BODY OF MY SPIRIT

This body, which ye now behold, is the body of my spirit; and man have I created after the body of my spirit. (Ether 3:16)

This is given to us as the word of the Lord to the brother of Jared, explaining to him what the meaning is of the expression, "Men were created, in the beginning, after mine own image." Orson Pratt, in a sermon, April 13, 1856, observes:

"This is the only place in the Book of Mormon where the pre-existence of man is clearly spoken of, and this was revealed before the organization of the Church, and is a doctrine which was not in possession of the Christian world; hence, it shows that it was dictated by a Spirit capable of revealing a doctrine unknown to the Christian World—the pre-existence of man."[50]

---

[49]*Juvenile Instructor*, Dec. 1926, p. 691.
[50]*Journal of Discourses*, Vol. 3, p. 352.

SOME PROPHECIES CONCERNING
THE BOOK OF MORMON

"I remember hearing related Brother Parley P. Pratt's first interview with the Saints at Fayette, Seneca County, where the Church was organized. * * * On that occasion he was called upon to speak. * * * He brought forth from the prophecies of Isaiah, Jeremiah, Ezekiel, and other prophets abundant proofs concerning the work which the Lord had established through his servant Joseph. A great many of the Latter-day Saints were surprised that there were so many evidences in the Bible concerning this work." (George Q. Cannon; *Jour. of Dis.*, Vol. 19, p. 105)

A student of the Scriptures, naturally, asks whether there is anything in the Bible, any prophetic utterance, which points to the coming of the Book of Mormon in the latter days. That is a legitimate question that should have due consideration.

ARIEL. Possibly one of the best known Old Testament prophecies concerning the Book of Mormon is that of Isaiah, 29:1-14: "Woe to Ariel, to Ariel, the city where David dwelt! * * * Yet will I distress Ariel, and there shall be heaviness and sorrow: and it shall be unto me as Ariel."

Two Ariels are here mentioned. One is the city where David dwelt; that is to say, Jerusalem in Palestine. The Lord, through the prophet, says this Ariel, this "lion of the Lord," should pass through heaviness and sorrow and, finally, become, in the sight of the Lord, as another Ariel: "It [the first-mentioned Ariel] shall be *unto me* as Ariel [the second]."

The prophet goes on to state in what respect the fate of Ariel, where David dwelt, should resemble that of the other Ariel: "Thou shalt be brought down, and shalt speak out of the ground," etc. That, then, must have happened to another Ariel; otherwise there would be no point of resemblance.

If we remember that the Lamanites, about 100 B.C., built a city which they called Jerusalem (Alma 21:2),[1] which was destroyed at the time of the crucifixion (III Nephi 9:7), the prophecy of Isaiah becomes clear. It says in plain language that, as the Lamanite city

---

[1]The Nahua city of *Cholula* (also spelled *Chorula*), it has been thought, was so named after the City of Jerusalem. If so, it may have been named in memory of the Jerusalem which is mentioned in the Book of Mormon and which was submerged. Bancroft (*Native Races*, Vol. 5, p. 200), says the pyramid of Cholula was erected under the direction of a chief named Xelhua, and that the occasion was connected in some way with a flood, either as a memorial of a former flood or as a place of refuge in case another deluge should come.

In referring the motto of Cortez (*Judicium Domini Apprehendit Eos*) to the destruction of Jerusalem, we must suppose, says Lord Kingsbourough, that he recognized in Mexico a *second Jerusalem,* and in his own conquests a triumph over the Hebrews of the New World, as Titus had before vanquished those of the Old. (From *Mex. Ant.*, quoted by Mrs. Simon, *The Ten Tribes,* p. 65.) No matter what value we may place on the stupendous work of which that of Mrs. Simon is but a partial copy, we must admit that this statement is a confirmation, from an outside source, of the view taken by Latter-day Saint writers on the passage of Isaiah on the two Ariels, or Jerusalems.

was wiped out, so would the city of David be destroyed, as actually happened about 40 years later, or in the year A.D. 70.

The prophet says: "Thou shalt be brought down and shalt speak out of the ground * * * and thy speech shall whisper out of the dust." That refers, literally, to the cities, which were destroyed. They spoke "out of the dust" through their records that were deposited in the Hill Cumorah. How could a nation, after it had become almost extinct, speak out of the ground or "whisper out of the dust," if not through some record deposited, as was the Book of Mormon?

Isaiah makes the meaning of this vision so clear that it need not be misunderstood. He speaks of a book, or rather *the* book, for the Hebrew text has the definite article, to which the translators have not given the full force; he speaks of *the* book that was sealed, "which men deliver to one that is learned, saying, Read this, I pray thee: and he saith, I cannot, for it is sealed." This book was also, as the prophet says, "delivered to him that is not learned," and he could not read it.[2] Therefore, "Behold," saith the Lord, "I will proceed to do a marvelous work among this people; even a marvelous work and a wonder; for the wisdom of the wise men shall perish, and the understanding of their prudent men shall be hid." (v. 14) And in that day, we read further, "shall the deaf hear the words of the book, and the eyes of the blind shall see * * * the meek also shall increase their joy in the Lord, and the poor among men shall rejoice in the Holy One in Israel." (vv. 18, 19)

"In that day shall the deaf hear the words of the book." What do you mean, Isaiah? He means the book he had just been speaking about in the 11th-14th verses. "And the vision * * * men shall be hid." Here we perceive the nature of the book that he mentions in the 18th verse, and we learn something about the way that it was to be brought forth; that the words of the book, not the plates themselves, not the original, but the transcript, a copy of the words, the words of the book would be delivered to the learned, requesting them to read it." (Orson Pratt, July 18, 1875; *Jour. of Dis.*, Vol. 4, p. 163)

THE TWO STICKS. The Prophet Ezekiel is commanded to take one stick and write upon it, "For Judah," and another and write upon it, "For Joseph," and join them together; and, when asked for the meaning of this symbolical act, he was to say: "Thus saith the Lord God, Behold, I will take the stick of Joseph, which is in the hand of Ephraim, and the tribes of Israel, his fellows, and will put them with him, even with the stick of Judah, and make them one

---

[2]Some tell us that "the book" does not mean a particular book but any book, or rather letter. But that is absurd. Even an illiterate individual would not ask a scholarly friend to read a sealed letter, and he would certainly not afterwards ask one who, like himself, had never mastered the art of reading, to read the letter which the scholar could not read. If the prophecy does not refer to some such event as the coming forth of the Book of Mormon and the presentation of the characters to the two scholars, it has no known fulfilment whatever.

stick, and they shall be one in my hand. * * * Behold, I will take the children of Israel from among the heathen, whither they be gone, and will gather them on every side, and bring them into their own land: And I will make them one nation in the land upon the mountains of Israel." (Ezekiel 37:15-28)

The prophet here predicts the final union of the "whole house of Israel" — Judah and Ephraim — and the establishment of the everlasting covenant of peace, and says this restoration is to be preceded by the joining together of the records of the two divisions of the people. The Old Testament is the record of Judah. It came to us through the efforts of the Jews. The Book of Mormon is, more particularly, the record of Israel. In the coming forth of the Book of Mormon the prediction is fulfilled.

"Now, my friends, you may go to work, with all your Christian benevolent societies, to gather the Jews from the nations; you may combine all the wisdom and learning of Christendom, and put all the funds they can rake and scrape together from the two hemispheres of the earth, and after all, you never can accomplish the gathering and restitution of Israel until the Lord does it in his own way, by uniting the records of Judah and Joseph to accomplish this work. Then, and not till then, will the house of Jacob rejoice in the Holy One of Israel, and no more be ashamed." (Orson Pratt, Jan. 7, 1855; Jour. of Dis., Vol. 2, p. 291)

A LITTLE BOOK OPEN. Turning, now, to the great prophetic book of the New Testament, the Revelation by John, we pause at the tenth chapter.

In the preceding chapter John saw the countries where the church of our Lord was first established swept as with a besom of destruction, because of the general apostasy. The children of men were destroyed by the terrible weapons of the invading hordes, but the rest of the men, which were not killed, "yet repented not," but continued to worship "idols of gold, and silver, and brass, and stone, and of wood." Naturally, the question arose in the mind of the seer, What about the church? Is this the end of it? Was the glorious structure that was filled with the Spirit of God on the day of Pentecost to be destroyed in a flood of apostasy and carnage? In answer to such questions, John received the wonderful vision recorded in chapter ten.

In this vision, John saw a mighty angel, or messenger,[3] come from heaven. This messenger was clothed with a cloud. A *cloud* was, in the Mosaic dispensation, the visible sign of the presence of God, as on Mount Sinai. John, therefore, by this symbol, was given to understand that the messenger he saw was surrounded by the divine influence, as was Moses on the Mount. There was a rainbow upon or over his head. That was the visible symbol of the covenant

---

[3]The word *angel* means "messenger."

of God with Noah. His face was, as it were, the sun. Christ is the "sun of righteousness," and his glory was reflected in the countenance of the messenger, as was the glory of Jehovah in the face of Moses, when he came from the divine presence. His feet were as "pillars of fire." This is, most probably, an allusion to the temple service. Outside the temple of Solomon there were two pillars, called Boaz and Jachin,[4] from each of which chains, in all probability, extended into the interior of the temple, if that is what Paul alludes to (Heb. 6:19), when he speaks of our hope as an "anchor," or chain, which "entereth into that within the veil." This messenger, therefore, comes with the power and authority of all the dispensations of former ages — that of Noah, the Mosaic, and that of the meridian of time, and, in addition, the last dispensation with its temple service.

Furthermore, this messenger had in his hand a "little book open." Fortunately, the explanation of this prophetic language is given in the Doctrine and Covenants. We read:

"What are we to understand by the little book which was eaten by John, as mentioned in the tenth chapter of Revelation? We are to understand that it was a mission and an ordinance for him to gather the tribes of Israel; behold, this is Elias, who, as it is written, must come and restore all things." (Sec. 77:14)

According to this, the messenger John saw, was, or represented, the Elias who was to come and restore all things, and Parley P. Pratt, in his *Key to Theology*, p. 70, tells us that the Prophet Joseph was the Elias, the Restorer, the Presiding Messenger, holding the keys of the dispensation of the fulness of times * * * to prepare the way of the Lord. If, then, the Prophet Joseph was the messenger described in the vision of John, and the little book was his "mission and ordinance" to gather the tribes of Israel, which mission was committed to him by Moses in the Kirtland Temple (Doc. and Cov. 110-11), the great latter-day work of which the coming forth of the Book of Mormon was the beginning, is foretold in this chapter with all the clearness that prophetic language can convey. There is no clearer prophecy in all the Bible.

In a communication to a Rochester paper, dated Jan. 4, 1833, the Prophet Joseph, speaking of the Book of Mormon, says in part:

"By it we learn that our Western Indians are descendants of that Joseph who was sold into Egypt, and that the land of America is a promised land unto them, and unto it all the tribes of Israel will come, with as many of the Gentiles as shall comply with the requirements of the new covenants. But the tribes of Judah will return to old Jerusalem. The city of Zion, spoken of by David in the 102nd Psalm, will be built upon the land of America, 'and the ransomed of the Lord shall return and come to Zion with songs of everlasting joy upon their heads' (Isa. 35:10), and then they will be delivered from the overflowing scourge that shall pass through the

---

[4] 1 Kings 7:21; 2 Chron. 3:17. *Jachin* means "strength," and *Boaz*, "stability."

land. But Judah shall obtain deliverance at Jerusalem. See Joel 2:32; Isa. 26:20-1; Jer. 31:12; Psalm 1:5; Ezek. 34:11-13." (*Hist. of the Church*, Vol. 1, p. 315)

From which it is clear that the Book of Mormon is very much a book of gathering of the children of Israel.

The messenger with his little book "set his right foot upon the sea, and his left foot on the earth." Remember that in the days of John the geography of the world was not what it is today. At that time it was thought that all beyond the western coast of the Old World was water. That the messenger was standing upon the sea and the earth means, in modern language, that he was standing on both hemispheres, the eastern and the western; that is, in other words, he was delivering a message in which all the world was concerned. That his right foot was on the sea and his left on the earth may indicate that he came from the western hemisphere, or that his message was first heard there.

John heard the message this angel had to deliver. It was that there should be no more "time" now; that is, no more delay, but that, as soon as the seventh angel begins to sound, "the mystery of God shall be finished, as he hath declared to his servants, the prophets." (vv. 5-7) That is, his message was that the time has now come for the completion of the plan of salvation — God's mystery (1 Cor. 2:7; 15:51; Eph. 5:32; Col. 1:26; 1 Tim. 3:16) — by the establishment of the kingdom of God, as promised through the holy prophets.

At the time this messenger appeared, seven thunders were heard (v. 14) John was not permitted to write what they uttered, but that they were messages concerning wars and other calamities is more than likely. These thunders, in all probability, began rolling with our own Civil War. Such calamities we certainly are led to expect as signs or indications that the second advent is near at hand.

John was told (v. 9) to "eat," that is to say, to read, or, as we should say, to "digest" the contents of, the little book. He did so, and found it sweet in his mouth. But the sweetness was mixed with bitterness (v. 10), which expression may indicate that the seer was given to understand that the acceptance of the Message of the angel would be accompanied by bitter struggles, and even martyrdom, among the faithful Saints.

The chapter closes with the assurance that the coming of that mighty messenger begins a new prophetic era in the history of the world; for that is the evident purport of the words of the angel: "Thou must prophesy again before many peoples, and nations, and tongues, and kings."

Every detail in this prophetic pen-picture is easily recognized in the life-work of the Prophet Joseph and the coming forth of the Book of Mormon. It is as plain as if the name itself had been written across the sacred page.

THE EVERLASTING GOSPEL. We now pause a moment at the familiar prediction in Rev. 14:6: "And I saw another angel fly in the midst of heaven, having the everlasting gospel to preach unto them that dwell on the earth, and to every nation, and kindred, and tongue, and people." This was fulfilled when the angel revealed the Book of Mormon and the Church was restored, with the administration of the ordinances and the proclamation of the truths of the gospel in its fulness. That there might be no doubt on this point, John tells us what the message of the everlasting gospel is: "Fear God, and give glory to him; for the hour of his judgment is come: and worship him that made heaven, and earth, and the sea, and the fountains of water." (v. 7) In this solemn message the very foundations of "Mormonism" are clearly seen. (1) Fear God! Repent! The hour of judgment has come? (2) Worship him who has made the world! Worship God, as revealed in the story of the creation; God, in whose image man was made, and not statues or pictures, nor the incomprehensible being created by the authors of the Athanasian creed! Worship the God of Abraham, Isaac, and Jacob! This message, which John the Revelator heard sounding in the midst of heaven, as the voice of rolling thunder, is the very message which the Prophet Joseph was commissioned to proclaim to the world.

In view of such prophetic evidence, we may well say, with Orson Pratt: "Never had mankind more prophetic evidence in confirmation of a revelation than they have for the Book of Mormon."

A LEAF FROM PERUVIAN HISTORY

MANY FEATURES INDICATING NEPHITE INFLUENCE

"We may reasonably conclude that there existed a race advanced in civilization before the time of the Incas; and, in conformity with nearly every tradition, we may derive this race from the neighborhood of Lake Titicaca; a conclusion strongly confirmed by the imposing architectural remains which still endure."—*Prescott.*

The South American Pacific coast has some topographical peculiarities. From Panama to the Straits the Andes mountains form a gigantic continental backbone — a mountain system with its greatest elevation between 15 and 17 degrees south latitude, in the region where Lake Titicaca, 12,500 feet above sea level, like an immense eye, gazes up into the blue sky and where the stupendous peaks, Nevada de Sorata and Illimani, lift their snow-capped heads to a height of 25,500 and 24,300 feet, respectively.[1] From this region the continent slopes in all directions. A traveler starting from the valley of Lake Titicaca in Bolivia, or from the Valley of Cuzco in Peru is going "down," literally, just as is one who is going from Jerusalem, in the hills of Judea, towards Jaffa on the Mediterranean, or Jericho in the Jordan valley. At the entrance to the Isthmus the mountain chain consists of mere hills.

The strip of land bathed by the Pacific seems to be rising slowly out of the Ocean. This land, from twenty to sixty miles in width, is largely a sandy desert, rainless, except for a mist that during the months of May-October often condenses into a drizzling down-pour. During this part of the year the ground is, as by magic, covered with grass and wild flowers, for a short season. At other times the only vegetation is the yucca plant, which yields edible roots, and some species of cactus.

At intervals this desert land is crossed by little rivers and creeks which come from the mountain sides, and, on their way to the Ocean, form fertile, verdant valleys. Sir Clements Markham tells us that there are fourty-four such valleys along the Peruvian seaboard of 1,400 miles, and he divides them, for historical purposes, into three districts. The northern twenty valleys formed the territory of the Grand Chimu. The central valleys, twelve in number, were occupied by the Chincha confederacy, and the remaining twelve were peopled by military colonists, the so-called *mitimaes.*

Densely Populated. One might be inclined to suppose that a country answering to this description would not be suitable for human occupation. But the fact is that the entire region was, even in pre-

---

[1]Prescott, *Conquest of Peru,* Vol. 1, p. 28.

historic times, rather densely populated, as is proved by the monuments still extant. On the plateaus and in the mountain valleys cities, towns, and hamlets nestled among the well irrigated orchards and gardens, and on the mountain slopes shepherds took care of their flocks in idyllic happiness. For so wonderful is the intelligence of the spirit that dwells in man, and so great are the powers with which that spirit is endowed, that, in a short time, a few generations at most, it is able so to form and fashion the entire body that it fits perfectly into its environment. And so it happens that the Peruvians can walk and work and carry burdens in their mountain valleys at an altitude where others find it difficult to breathe. The following observation by Thomas A. Joyce[2] on South American culture seems to be well taken:

"The only environment suitable to be the birthplace of a civilization are the fertile valleys of the Andes, where the temperature of the Tropics is tempered by the elevation, the soil is fertile, and the water supply constant. Here man provides himself with means of subsistence; not indeed with the fatal facility of the Tropics elsewhere, which seems to discourage all enterprise, but without having to expend the whole of his energies on providing the necessary food supply, and so being left with no leisure to apply to the perfection of arts and crafts. And, in fact, it is just in this region that South American culture reached its zenith."

A Great Country. At the time of the Spanish conquest the Peru of the Incas extended along the coast from about 2 or 3 degrees northern, to about 37 degrees southern latitude. Just how far it reached towards the east is not clear, but in some places it overlapped the mountains considerably. The entire area under Inca government has been estimated at from 800,000 to 1,000,000 square miles. That is to say, it covered an area equal to that of the United States between the Mississippi and the Atlantic. It took in part of Ecuador, Peru, Bolivia, and a large part of Chile. It has been compared to the combined areas of Austria, Hungary, Spain, France and the late German empire.[3] The census taken by order of King Philip II showed a total population of 8,280,000 souls.[4]

If we regard past generations of God's children as greatly inferior to ourselves in intelligence, as well as in achievement, we shall fail to understand how it was possible for the Incas to maintain a social structure, as complex as theirs and built on so vast a scale, long before there were railroads or telegraph lines. But they did.

Lines of Communication. Communication between the different parts of the vast domain was kept up by means of roads, constructed with great engineering skill and labor. One of these highways stretched along the plateau. In some places it passed over sierras

---

[2]*South American Archaeology,* Putnam & Sons, New York, p. 5.
[3]John Fiske, *Discovery of America,* Vol. 2, p. 325.
[4]Nadaillac, *Prehistoric America,* p. 389.

buried in snow. Dugways were cut in the solid rock, where necessary, and suspension bridges connected the banks of rivers and chasms. In some places were stairways, and in other places ravines were filled up with masonry. The road was, generally, twenty feet wide, and paved with heavy flags of free stone, and, in some parts covered with bituminous cement, which, it is said, time has made harder than the stone itself. The length of this road is variously given as from 1,200 to 2,000 miles. Another road followed the coast for a distance of 1,600 miles. This was laid on an embankment of earth, and guarded on either side by a wall of masonry. "Mile stone" at intervals of about a league marked the distance traveled. Trees and shrubs lined the road, where possible, and where the loose sand made road building impracticable, piles were driven into the ground, to mark the direction in which to travel. Inns, called *tambos*, were erected at regular intervals, and barracks and forts offered accommodation to the armies on the march. Numerous shorter roads intersected these main highways. To show the efficiency of this net of lines of communication, Garcilasso de la Vega tells us that when Inca Yupanqui sent 50,000 men into Chile, to annex the southern part of that region, that great army was as well provided for, 2,000 miles from headquarters, as if it had been quartered within the city of Cuzco, and the Inca, he says, received prompt intelligence of "all matters that succeeded."[5] And these roads, which Humboldt compares with the cause-ways of the Romans, were built in America at a time when, as Nadaillac observes, there were no roads in Europe.

Postal Service. To facilitate communication still further, the Incas had an admirable postal service. Little huts were built along the roads, about five miles apart, or less, in which runners, trained in speed and endurance, were stationed, whose business it was to forward government dispatches without delay. These *chasquis*, as they were called, would take verbal messages, or the knotted cords, *quipus*, which were their records, or even small packages. It is claimed that they could carry dispatches at the rate of 150 miles a day, and deliver fish, caught in the ocean, fresh in Cuzco. And this institution was known both in Peru and Mexico long before the "civilized" nations of Europe had a postal service.[6]

The Incas. At the time of the Spanish conquest, Peru was governed by Incas. Who were they? Whence did they come?

As the Peruvians, as far as known, had no written records, our

---

[5]*Roy. Com.*, Book VII, Chap. 19. Unlike Napoleon, he did not want to hear any bad news, seemingly.

[6]Prescott, *Peru*, Vol. 1, p. 70.

scholars have only tradition to guide them in their search for historical facts beyond a century and a half before the conquest.[7]

Beginning of History. Peruvian history begins with a tradition according to which the country was inhabited by four principal tribes, the Quichuas at the headwaters of the Apurimac; the Incas in the upper Yucay valley; and the Canas and Cauchis in the mountains between the Titicaca basin and the valley of Cuzco. Just how far back tradition takes us is, by no means, agreed on, Prof. Fiske[8] is of the opinion that "if the whole story of the semi-civilization of the Incas were accessible, it would carry us much farther into the past than anything to be found in Mexico." And he, further, calculates, from data furnished by Sir Clements Markham, that the so-called Pirua dynasty must have begun in the *fifth century,* B.C., which might be nearly two centuries after the landing of Lehi.

The list of Peruvian rulers, as obtained by Montesinos, begins with the name of the Deity, as does St. Luke's genealogy of our Lord.[9] The name referred to is, *Illa Tici Vira Cocha,* and it means, as has been explained in another place, "the Creator, the Infinite God."

Pirua Dynasty. The first human ruler on the list is, Pirua Pacari Manco. "Pirua" is supposed to be the title, as the Egyptian "pharaoh," and from that title the first eighteen rulers are called the Pirua dynasty.

Amautas or Recorders. The following forty-six heads of the government are known as the Amauta dynasty, because the first thirteen were amautas; that is to say, they were learned men, record keepers; just such men as Nephi, Jacob, Enos, Jarom, Omni, Mormon and Moroni, who figure in the history of the Book of Mormon. The Amauta dynasty evidently began a new form of government, different from that of the Pirua government, analogous to the reign of judges at the end of the reign of King Mosiah in Zarahemla.[11]

---

[7]There are certain ornaments on artifacts of pre-Incan origin, which seem to suggest writing of some kind. Such are the figures on the gateway at Tiahuanacu, the ornamentation on vases from various coast sites, certain carvings on rocks, and on the "breast plate" described by Sir Clements Markham. And Montesinos asserts that in the reign of Toca Corca Apu Capac, the fortieth Peruvian king, "there were letters and characters on parchment and on the leaves of trees, until all this was lost for a period of four hundred years."—*Antiguas Historiales del Peru,* Hukluyt Society, London, 1920, p. 53.

Undoubtedly, this is what Montesinos had been told, and there is nothing incredible in the tradition. But at the time of the conquest the only records the Peruvians had were the quipus. These consisted of strings of different lengths and colors with artistically tied knots, each with a meaning of its own. This contrivance served many purposes admirably—more so than we, with our elaborate system of writing can imagine—but as historical records the strings were not satisfactory. The early history of the Peruvians, aside from the light shed upon it by the Book of Mormon, is lost in myths and conjectures.

[8]*Discovery of America,* Vol. 2, pp. 302-3.

[9]"Adam, which was the son of God. (Luke 3:38)

[10]Mosiah 29:11 and 44. Markham is of the opinion that the Piruas and Amautas may

Titu Yupanqui Pachacuti. During the administration of Titu Yupanqui Pachacuti word came that armies consisting of fierce warriors were approaching from the mountains, and also from the coast. The provincial governors were unable to resist them. They devastated the fields and took possession of villages and towns on their march. Titu Yupanqui gathered his armies and sent strong forces to the threatened places. He, himself, with the main body of the army, took up a position in the mountains, which was called Pucara, where he fortified himself and laid up a vast amount of supplies. The whole stronghold formed a cone, and the entire army was within the walls. For some unknown reason, Titu Yupanqui, decided to meet the enemy in the open field, and this proved disastrous. The battle was long and fierce. Both armies were almost annihilated, and the dead remained unburied. The remnant of the invading army, 500 men, retreated into the Andes mountains. Titu Yupanqui was slain. And thus was the Amauta government overthrown. The remaining followers of the last Amauta retired into the mountain fastness and established themselves at Tamputocco, while a state of anarchy and chaos ensued in the country. This epoch-making battle, the description of which in some respects reminds one of the battle of Cumorah, is by some thought to have been fought about the year 900 of our era. Sir Clements Markham estimates that the state of anarchy lasted for about four centuries.

Centuries of Anarchy. During this time some of the people retained a measure of civilization, while others sank almost to the level of beasts. Many lived, scattered all over the valleys, in small huts, or in caves, and even in hollow trees. They robbed and killed each other, and had no higher ambition than the gratification of their animal cravings. Those who had any religious needs revered stones, animals, rivers, as the Egyptians did. They worshiped a multitude of objects, and sacrificed in their honor llamas, partridges, maize, herbs, etc., and even human beings, whose flesh they ate. Some drew blood from their own bodies and sprinkled it on their sacrifices.[11]

---

represent the megalitic empire, the decline and fall of which were followed by centuries of barbarism, so that the people had almost forgotten its existence, while the tribes of the Colloa were probably of another "race," the descendants of invaders.—*Incas of Peru,* p. 46.

[11]There is nothing improbable in the description of degradation given by Garcilasso de la Vega and others, into which the natives fell. Ezekiel lived to see Israel similarly debased. (Ez. 8:3-18) He saw the people worshiping idols in the temple, and burning incense to abominable beasts depicted on the temple walls. He saw the women "weeping for Tammuz" (Venus), and men worshiping the sun with their backs to the holy house of the Lord. And as a climax of abominations, "they put the branch to their nose"—an expression which Hebrew commentators have understood to conceal some shockingly obscene rite. (*Century Bible,* Ezek., p. 101) It is not strange, therefore, to find the American aborigines in this condition after a long period of social chaos, although they had at one time occupied the lofty position of which we read in the Book of Mormon. Easy, indeed, is the descent to Avernus.

The state of anarchy and degeneracy here referred to is said to have lasted till about four hundred years before the Spanish conquest. John Fiske believes three centuries come nearer the truth. He regards 1250 as the probable year of deliverance.

Manco Capac. About that time Manco Capac and his wife, Mamma Oello, came into the valley of Cuzco and established themselves there. Manco Capac gathered the scattered people into colonies of from 25 to 100 families, and taught them to till the ground, and gather, "the more gentle cattle, which ran dispersed through the woods and fields," into flocks. Mamma Oello taught the women to spin and weave, and to make garments.[12] And, above all, they taught the people to worship the Creator and Preserver of the world, of whom the sun and the moon are, as they conceived it, the visible and most glorious symbols.[13]

Manco Capac, the leader of these immigrants, was an Inca, and many of his followers were, undoubtedly, of that tribe. But nine other tribes were represented among them. The Quichuas must have preserved their common language in its greatest purity, for their dialect was adopted as the general vernacular, while the offices were held or controlled by the Incas,[14] and the chief rulers adopted their tribal name as their title. George Squier, in his *Peru*, says vague traditions point to Tiahuanacu as the locality, where the trek of Manco Capac began, but he regards a "sacred" island in the Lake Titicaca as the place of origin of the Inca culture. Be that as it may,

---

[12]Mr. M. D. C. Crawford, of the American Museum of Natural History, has an instructive article on "The Master Weavers of the Desert Empire," in *Harper's Monthly* for July, 1916. He asserts that, if perfection in textile art were the measure of a people's culture, ancient Peru would rank with the great civilizations of antiquity. For, he says, whether we judge by fineness of texture, purity of design, or harmony of color, her great art is rivaled only by the highest standards of Asia, and her technique of fabric construction, comprising, as it does, every method elsewhere known and certain crafts apparently unique, is in advance of the textile science and any single people. They worked in cotton, wool, hair, and maguey (hemp), and they carried spinning to the highest degree of perfection. They made rough sleeping mats, gossamer veils, and exquisite tapestry.

[13]That the common people actually worshipped the sun and other heavenly bodies is, probably, true. But there is no doubt that the educated, thinking classes saw in these luminaries only the visible manifestation, the glory, of the visible God whom they worshiped. There is a remarkable saying of Inca Rocca quoted by Garcilasso de la Vega after Blas Valera (*Royal Com.*, Book 4, Chap. 19), which proves this. The Inca, as quoted, said: "If the heaven be so glorious, which is the throne and seat of Pachacamac how much more powerful, glittering, and resplendent must his person and majesty be, who was the maker and creator of them all!" This is a purely Hebrew conception. David sings: "The heavens declare the glory of God; and the firmament sheweth his handiwork." (Ps. 19:1) The heavens are God's "garment." (Ps. 102:25-27) The "Lord God is a sun and shield." (Ps. 84:11) The Lord is also "the sun of righteousness." (Mal. 4:2) In the Christian language our Lord is the "dayspring from on high" (Luke 1:78), the "daystar" (2 Peter 1:19), and the "true light" (John 1:9), and his Church is clothed with the "sun." We should, in all probability, interpret the terms used in ancient Peruvian theology by the same rules that we apply to them when we use them ourselves.

[14]According to Sir Clements Markham, the color of the skin of the Incas was several shades lighter than that of their subjects, or their descendants; they had high foreheads, aquiline noses, and a refined, majestic, and intellectual bearing.

their progress towards the Cuzco valley was made in slow stages. They stopped in places, to raise crops. And, according to tradition handed down among the Incas, themselves, as told to Garcilasso de la Vega by his uncle, Manco Capac had a marvelous golden staff, half a yard long and two fingers thick, with which he tested the depth of the soil, with the understanding that where it sank down its entire length without great exertion on his part, there they should remain. This happened at Cuzco, and there they raised their standard. He also had a sacred bird with him, probably a symbol of God, as the sparrow hawk was among the Egyptians; but whether the bird was alive or stuffed, we are not told.

Migrations from Where? There can be no doubt that this tradition records the story of the wanderings of the ancestors of the founders of the Peruvian Incariate; but whether it relates to some very remote exodus, as, for instance, that of Lehi from Jerusalem, or of his journey from the point of landing in America to the place of his first permanent settlement; or whether it relates, in the form of a legend, the first separation of Nephi from his brethren, or the exodus under Mosiah to Zarahemla; or whether it tells the story of some notable migratory movement that took place after the close of the Book-of-Mormon record — and there must have been many such — we may not be able to decide. There are features in it that remind one of all of these journeys, and it is not improbable that in the legend they are all epitomized and made into one, without regard to chronological order of time, or perspective arrangement of localities, as is generally the case in myth and legend.

Manco Capac and His Wife, Reformers. As has already been stated, Manco Capac and his wife, who also was his sister, gathered up the scattered people and taught them the first principles of religion and civilization. But civilization made slow progress. More than a century after the first settlement the moral condition was as bad as ever. Then there appeared on the stage the great Peruvian woman, Siuyacu, the mother of Inca Rocca, who gave to the reformatory movement a new impetus. She persuaded her son to assume despotic powers. By the aid of her sister and son she convinced the people that he was a special representative of God, and they agreed to obey him as a divinely inspired son of God.[15]

The estimable ladies were well-intentioned. They reasoned that power thus obtained could be used for the benefit of the people, and they had no other purpose. But it is a grave mistake to resort to a fraud even for the furtherance of a laudable object. Inca Rocca at

---

[15]It appears that his mother had made for him a robe so richly ornamented with gold that when he stood, clothed in it, on the hill dominating Cuzco, at sunrise, he appeared to the people below to be all ablaze in glory. This was to them a miracle.

once assumed autocratic powers and made the people the slaves of militarism. He did the very thing against which the ancient prophets of America warned the people when they declared that, "There shall be no kings upon the land" (II Nephi 10:11; Comp. Mos. 29:16, 17, 31; III Nephi 6:30); also, when they taught that war and strife between brethren are "the fountain of filthy water," the source of which is "the depths of hell" (I Nephi 12:15, 16). Inca Rocca established both autocracy and militarism in this land of liberty. Autocracy soon became despotism. Inca Huascar, who was murdered by his own brother, Atahualpa, and the latter, who is generally referred to as the "last Inca" and who, after having been "baptized" was strangled by the order of Pizarro, in the public square of Caxamarca, Aug. 29, 1533, having been convicted of various crimes, including idolatry and polygamy — these Incas paid the penalty for the mistakes of their predecessors.[16]

Four Provinces. For administrative purposes the vast territory of the Incas was divided into four main provinces: *Chinchasuyu* to the north; *Sollasuyu* to the south; *Antisuyu* to the east, and *Cuntisuyu* to the west. A governor or viceroy ruled in each of these provinces, under the Inca. The entire country was called *Tavantisuyu,* or, as Markham spells it, *Tahuantn-suya,* a word which means either, "The Four Parts of the World," or, according to Markham, "The Four Combined Provinces." That was the native name of the old Peruvian domain.

Organization of the People. The people were divided into *chuncas,* consisting of ten families each. Ten chuncas, a hundred families, formed a *Pachaca.* Ten pachacas formed a *huaranca,* and ten huarancas, 10,000 families, was a *hunu.* A hunu, consequently, if we count five persons to a family, consisted of 50,000 individuals. Each of these divisions had its own presiding officers. The duty of the presidents of the Pachacas was to see that every family had seed to sow and material of which to make clothes, etc. They were also responsible for the morals of the people under them, and had to report acts of law-breaking to the higher officers, whose duty it was to punish the offenders. An overseer was at the head of each four hunus, and his duty was to see to it that the administration of the government worked with regularity and efficiency, and it appears that if an offender escaped merited punishment through the neglect

---

[16]The historic period of Peru begins with the eighth Inca, after Manco Capac, Viracocha, about A.D. 1380. If we can judge by the name, the Incas, at this time, were not satisfied with the title of Son of God, but assumed one of the names of the invisible God, himself. The tenth Inca, Inca Yupanchi, also called Pachacutec, "the changer of the world," was a truly great man. When he died the Incariate extended from the Lake Titicaca basin to the equator and from the Andes mountains to the Pacific. His successors extended the conquest until the arrival of the Spaniards.

of an officer, the latter was liable to receive the punishment the offender had escaped.

United Order. Socialism, or, as we may prefer to call it, the principles of the united order were applied in this commonwealth on a large scale. Land was held in trust by the chunca, and each married couple was entitled to the use of three *tupus* — enough to supply its wants. When a child was born, one tupu was added for a boy, and half a tupu for a girl.

The division of the population into chuncas, pachacas, huarancas, and hunus reminds one of the division of the twelve tribes of Israel into tens, fifties, hundreds, and thousands, with "rulers" over each division (Ex. 18:21; Deut. 1:15; and perhaps Lev. 26:26, where it appears that ten families used to share one oven). Prescott calls attention to the fact that the land law was a near approach to the agrarian law in Palestine, where, on the recurrence of the year of jubilee, estates reverted to their original owners.[17] Only, in Peru the tenant could not sell the land at any time. But as there was no law against allotting the same piece of ground to the same tenant every year, he practically owned the farm as long as he was able to cultivate it. And in case of old age or sickness, he was still entitled to his share of the produce, not as a matter of charity, but by right.

Division of the Products. The produce of the land was divided into three equal shares, one for the Inca, one for the religious service, and one for the producer. Laborers in the service of Inca were maintained out of his share, and those working for the priesthood were kept on the portion belonging to the temples. Any surplus was stored up for the benefit of the people, and if one portion of the country suffered from war, earthquake, pestilence, or any calamity, other portions were assessed for the benefit of the sufferers.

All Things Held in Common. Land was not the only kind of property held in common. Whenever a province accepted the Inca rule, all the assets — land, forests, lakes, rivers, animals, were turned over to the Inca. But as he was regarded as, and claimed to be, the representative of the Creator, the property, we may feel sure, was considered as "dedicated to the Lord," to use a modern expression. Then it was allotted to the people according to the need of each. The proceeding was a perfect application of the principle of what we call "The United Order."

The Organization of the Family. For industrial purposes the family was divided into ten classes, according to age. The age of accountability began with the eighth year. All between that age

[17]*Peru*, New York, 1898, Vol. 1, p. 57.

and sixty were given some kind of work, unless exempt because of sickness or temple service. From these classes a certain number were drawn every year for the public service. They were required to give two months, or at most three, each year, to public works, and while so employed, they were furnished with tools and material, and maintained out of the public funds.[18]

It is generally conceded that this masterly organization was not a new creation by the later Incas, but that these only applied on a large scale the institutions they had received from their forebears. From remote times, Markham tells us, the people of the Andean region had communities consisting of related families, which they called *Ayllus*. These communities allotted the arable land, *the marca*, to the heads of families, while they held pasture and woodland in common. The Incas built on this ancient foundation. But what was the origin of it in this country, if not the united order, which was established by the followers of our Savior in this land in the year A. D. 36, and of which we read: "And they had all things common among them; therefore there were not rich and poor, bond or free?" (4 Nephi 3) That was literally, the condition in Peru. "If no man," Prescott says,[19] "could become rich in Peru, no man could become poor."

Marriage Regulated. Under this order of society, marriage, as well as everything else, was regulated. On a certain day in the year all persons of marriageable age and fit for married life were called together on the public squares and paired off. A curaca — the chief of the village — joined the hands of the respective couples and declared them husband and wife. The Inca performed the same ceremony for the young folks of his own kin. In all probability, the parents had something to do with the selection of wives, as in Palestine and other Oriental countries, before the curaca tied the knot. Each couple was provided with a home and some land. The ceremony was followed by feasting and gayeties that sometimes lasted for many days, which proves that the Peruvians were a happy people. The nobility were permitted to have several wives. The Inca, who could do no wrong, for the simple reason that whatever *he* did was right, had numerous wives, as King Solomon, and also many concubines.[20] *The* wife of the Inca was always his sister. But there was also a sisterhood known as The Virgins of the Sun, or The Elect, consisting of a number of young maidens, dedicated to the service of the sun.

---

[18]Sir Clements Markham, *The Incas of Peru*, New York, 1910, p. 161.

[19]*Peru*, Vol. 1, p. 65.

[20]The moral condition among the high-caste Indians of early American historic times helps us to understand why it was necessary for the Lord to command the observance of chastity, through the prophet Jacob, the brother of Nephi. (Jacob 2:23-31)

They lived in convents under the watchcare of older women, who taught them their various duties. If any of them were detected in an intrigue she was buried alive, and her lover was strangled, and the town or village from which he came was razed to the ground. But the Inca, as the son of the sun, had free access to these maidens. There were fifteen hundred of them in the establishment of Cuzco, all of royal blood, and there were others, of inferior rank, in the provinces. It was also lawful for the Inca to select wives outside the convents, and every woman in the land considered it the highest possible honor to receive the attention of the "divine" ruler. As a consequence of this system of marriage, the Incas generally had very large families. According to Garcilasso de la Vega, his great grandfather, Tupac Yupanqui, had two hundred children, and Huayna Capac had between two and three hundred. Men of the common people were confined to one wife and smaller families. But all of marriageable age and sound in mind and body were by law required to marry, and no one was allowed to go outside his own community or kindred for a wife. In this respect they observed the law of Abraham, Isaac, and Jacob. (Gen. 24:4; 28:2)

Religious Conceptions. The religious conceptions of the Peruvians is a subject of intense interest. As far back as tradition takes us they believed in God, the Creator and Sustainer of the universe. They called him, as we have already seen, *Illa Tici Vira Cocha*, the meaning of which, according to Sir Clements Markham,[21] is *Illa*, "Light"; *Tici*, "Beginning," or "Foundation of Things"; *Vira*, "Storehouse of Creation"; *Cocha*, "Abyss," "Profundity." He suggests the following translations: "The Splendor, the Foundation, the Creator, the Infinite God."

This is certainly a sublime conception of the great Author of the universe, and one is naturally lost in wonder as to the source of it. A closer study of those words reveal the still more wonderful fact that they are in meaning, identical with the words that begin the story of the creation in Genesis. Moses says, "In the *Beginning God Created* [the heavens and the earth * * * and there was darkness upon the * * *] *Deep*." Note the four principal words in this quotation, which I have italicized, and compare them with the meaning of the Peruvian words, as given by Sir Clements. *Illa* is, undoubtedly, the same as the *Elohim* of Genesis, a word which in one form or another is found in all Semitic languages. "Illa Tici Vira Cocha" can, therefore, be paraphrased as "God who in the Beginning laid the Foundation of the Creation in the Deep,"—an almost literal quotation from Genesis. If we accept the Book of Mormon this is no mystery; if not, it will remain to us an unsolvable riddle forever.

---

[21]*The Incas of Peru*, New York, 1910, p. 41.

Conceptions of God. God was also known in ancient Peru as *Pachacamac,* which is said to mean, "He who sustains or gives life to the universe." It was this Divine Being which the Incas taught the people to worship. The sun, the lightning, and the thunder were the symbols of his glory and power. (Comp. Ex. 19:16; Ps. 77:18; and Rev. 4:5, where the presence of God is similarly manifested.) The rainbow also, which in the days of Noah was made the emblem of God's covenant with man, was venerated by the Peruvians. (Comp. Gen. 9:12-17; Ezek. 1:28; Rev. 4:3.) They also knew that there is a female element in the Godhead, as seems to be taught in Genesis 1:27; 5:1, 2; Comp. 1 Cor. 11:11, 12. And so they revered the moon as the abode of the sister-wife of God. The wind, the earth, the ocean, the rivers, the mountains; anything grand and sublime, was venerated as coming from God.

Schlegel[22] observes:

"The more I search into the ancient history of the world, the more I am convinced that the cultivated nations commenced with a purer worship of the Supreme Being; that the magic influence of nature upon the imaginations of the human race afterwards produced polytheism, and at length entirely obscured the spiritual conceptions of religion in the belief of the people, while the wise men alone preserved the primitive secrets in the sanctuary. Hence the mythology appears to me to be the latest developed, and the most fluctuating part of the ancient religion."

Causes of Spiritual Degeneration. Something like this happened all over America. The original inhabitants, as we know from the Book of Mormon, had pure conceptions of God. Then came a time of war, bloodshed, and anarchy. The people sank gradually down into savagery and brutality. In that condition they forgot a religion which they could no longer understand, and, like their forefathers, they worshiped created things instead of the Creator. Sun worship, with the attendant worship of the moon and the planets, had been made popular in Palestine during the reign of King Manasseh,[23] some time before the migration of Lehi from Jerusalem, and it was but natural for the Lamanites in rebellion against the servants of God to turn to the sun. However, the later sun worship under the Incas must be regarded as a reformatory movement, an endeavor to lift the people up from crass fetichism and idolatry to the original, higher conceptions of God. It served its purpose for a time. When it became useless, it was removed.

Temples Erected. Numerous temples were erected to the sun and other deities. The most magnificent of them was located at Cuzco. It consisted of a main building and many smaller chapels. The interior was a veritable gold mine. On the west wall was an enormous

---

[22]Quoted by Alex. W. Bradford, *American Antiquities,* p. 343; New York, 1843.
[23]2 Kings 23:5-11.

plate of massive gold, set with emeralds and other costly stones. It represented the sun. Every part of the building was aglow with precious metals and stones, and every utensil was of solid gold or silver. Sun temples were erected in almost every town and village, and everywhere sacrifices were offered among which were "burnt offerings," reminding one of the Mosaic law, because, as Dr. McCullo observes, this form of sacrifice was peculiar to the Peruvians, in this hemisphere. Twelve vases of silver, filled with grain, as an offering from the people, stood on the floor of the main hall, as the twelve tables with shewbread were placed in the temple at Jerusalem. (Lev. 24:5-7)

At the ancient city of Pachacamac, on the coast, there was a very sacred temple dedicated to Pachacamac. This was much older than the incariate.

The Loss of the Sabbath. From the Book of Mormon we know that the Nephites originally kept the law of Moses (II Nephi 26:24), and, therefore, also the Mosaic Sabbath. But during the centuries of war and anarchy that followed the schism between Nephites and Lamanites the observance of the day of rest was, naturally, at first, neglected and, ultimately, forgotten. This would be all the more certain because they had no names for the days — only numbers — except the seventh, which they called *shabbath.*[24] Even in our day, if it were not for calendars, diaries, newspapers, etc., the regular succession of days and dates would soon be lost track of irretrievably. That must have happened among the ancient Americans. And then, when the time came again that they felt the need of keeping anew a record of events, they constructed a calendar anew with the aid of such traditions or recollections as still lingered in the memory of their "wise men."

Sun Year and Moon Year. By that aid they studied the movements of the sun, and by and by, obtained a solar year consisting of twelve months of thirty days each, to which they added five days, to complete the year. They had also a lunar year, consisting of 354 days, to which they added eleven days to make it correspond with the solar year. This year began the 22nd of June, after the harvest, and was inaugurated with a festival called *Intip Raymi,* where sacrifices were offered and the people banqueted.

There is an extraordinary resemblance between this lunar year of the Peruvians and the sacred year of the Hebrews. The latter also had 354 days and a month added every third year. It began shortly

---

[24]The seven-day division of time was introduced in the Roman world during the two first centuries of our era. The week days were named in honor of the sun, the moon, Mercury, Venus, Jupiter, Mars, and Saturn, which the Egyptians called the seven planets. The Hebrews did not adopt this, to them, objectionable nomenclature.

after the first grain was ripe, and was inaugurated with a festival, the so-called feast of ingathering when sacrifices were offered and the people feasted. (Ex. 23:16; Lev. 23:9; Deut. 26:10) It would take a great deal of credulity to believe that this resemblance is due to chance only.[25]

The Priest Class. The religion of the Peruvians required a class of numerous priests to attend to the services. At their head stood the high priest, called *Villac Vmu* or, as Markham spells it, *Villa Uma*, which is said to mean, "The Head which Counsels." He was second in authority to the Inca, being a scion of the "royal" family. He was to the Inca what Aaron was to Moses: "He (Aaron) shall be thy spokesman to the people: and he shall be, even he shall be to thee instead of a mouth, and thou shalt be to him instead of God."[26] The high priest was learned in all matters pertaining to religion, but he was also an Amauta, and as such he had supervision and charge of the records of the country. Under him there were a great many priests of various degrees. Some attended to the sacrifices; others were "sooth-sayers," interpreting the portent of the flight of birds and peculiarities in the entrails of the sacrificed animals, like the Roman augurs. Some were hermits, and some received confessions. The high priest, it is said, never ate meat, and always drank only water.

The costume of the high Peruvian priest, when officiating, consisted of a robe which reached to the ankles. His tunic was without sleeves and reached to the ground. Over this he wore a pelisse, trimmed with red, which came down to the knees. His head dress was a kind of tiara richly adorned with gold and jewels, including a massive gold disc, representing the sun. It was also adorned with brilliantly colored feathers.

Priestly Robes Compared with those of Aaron. If we compare this priestly uniform with that of Aaron, we find a striking resemblance in some features. Josephus says the Hebrew high priest wore a close-fitting cassock of fine linen, white with a diamond-shaped pattern, and this garment reached almost to his feet. The girdle was white, embroidered with scarlet, blue and purple flowers. On his head he wore a cap in the shape of a flower.[27] Both the Hebrew and the Peruvian priests wore the peculiar uniform only when they officiated. It was their temple clothes.

National Festivals. Like the Hebrews, the Peruvians had yearly

[25]They (the Peruvians) had, also, weeks, but of what length, whether of seven, nine, or ten days, is uncertain." (Prescott, *Peru*, Vol. 1, p. 108)

[26]Exodus 4:16.

[27]Comp. Josephus, *Ant.* 3, 7. Ex. 29:5, 6; Lev. 8:7-9. Aaron, it will be noted, had an ephod and a breastplate with the urim and thummim, in addition to the other garments.

national festivals. At one of these, the *Situa*, the ceremonies symbolized the purification of the entire nation, by baptism. On that occasion, after opening prayers, four companies, one hundred men in each, were formed. They represented all ranks of the people. When everything was ready these companies set out from the temple square and marched toward the four cardinal points. As each company of men arrived at a certain river, they immersed themselves, in the belief that the running water would carry sin and sickness into the ocean. The people spent the night in prayer and dancing. Nor was the element of *fire* absent from this ceremony. The people passed burning torches from one to another, and when morning came, they immersed themselves in rivers or springs. Cakes of coarsely ground corn meal were prepared in every house, and the people applied these to their faces and to the lintels of the doors.[28]

The Raymi festival was observed at the time of the summer solstice, when the sun, after having touched the southern extremity of his course, returned to bless the people.[29] The festivities began with a three days' fast. As the rays of the sun gilded the tops of the buildings and mountains, the assembled multitudes burst out in song. Higher and higher rose the joyful chords. Sacrifices were offered. A fire was kindled by the sun, by means of a mirror, and this sacred flame was given over to the care of the maidens in the convent. High and low were banqueted. Fine bread was placed on the tables of the Incas and the nobles, and they gave to each guest a piece of this sacred bread, which was preserved by the recipient as a precious relic.

Meaning of Raymi. Sir Clements Markham tells us that the word *Raymi* has no meaning in the Quichua language. It must, therefore, be of foreign origin. It is supposed that the originator of the festival gave to it his own name. In Montesino's list of "kings," there are three Raymis, Capac Raymi Amauta, Titu Raymi Cozque, and Paullu Raymi. I believe the origin of the word may be found in the very root from which the Hebrew *Ramah*, "high," or the Egyptian *Ram-ses*,[30] meaning, "the son of the sun," are derived. The Incas claimed to be *the* children of the sun, the *Ra* of the Egyptians.

---

[28]Comp. Ex. 12:22 and 13:9, where Israel is commanded to apply the blood of the lamb to the lintels, and to eat unleavened bread in memory of the exodus: "It shall be for a sign unto thee upon thine hand, and for a memorial between thine eyes." It may be of interest to recall the fact that the "shew bread" of the Hebrews is sometimes called in the Scriptures *Lechem panim*, literally "bread of faces" (Ex. 25:30); or even *panim*, "faces," meaning, "presence"; that is, the presence of the Lord. (Ex. 39:36; Num. 4:7) The making of this bread and the weekly renewal of it was in ancient Israel part of the temple service. (Lev. 24:5-9) The meaning of it was that Israel acknowledged the presence of God as their source of life, as the candlestick signified that God was the light and giver of light; while the incense typified the prayers, through which we receive both life and light. See Edersheim, *The Temple*, p. 157.

[29]Prescott, *Peru*, Vol. 1, p. 94.

[30]Ramses, c'est-a-dire *enfant du soleil*, nom porte par treize rois qui appartiennent a la XIXe et a la XXe dynastie." (Paul Pierret, *Dictionnaire D'Archeologie Egyptienne*, p. 473)

Life after Death. The Peruvians believed in the existence of man after death, and the resurrection of the body. They had a conception of a "heaven" for the good, and another place for the wicked, which they located in the center of the earth, as the Hebrews did their *Sheol.* They also believed in the existence of an evil spirit, Cupay, and they believed that life after this was very much like the present, wherefore they buried with their loved ones their utensils and treasures, and, like the Egyptians, they preserved the bodies of their kings and princes.

Wonderful Buildings. The intelligence and energy of the ancient Peruvians are shown in their buildings and the products of their various industries.

On the Lake Titicaca plateau a number of monoliths and extensive ruins still testify to the existence there, at one time, of a civilization, "the most ancient and the most brilliant in South America."[31] The great city of Tiahuanaco had buildings which Garcilasso de la Vega refers to as "mountains of prodigious height made by the hand of man." The so-called "fortress" is really a pyramid, one hundred and fifty feet high, similar to those found in Mexico and Yucatan. The "temple" is a paralellogram, four hundred and forty-five feet by three hundred and eighty-eight. The so-called "hall of justice" was at one time an immense building. A doorway made of a single stone and ornamented with a frieze of human faces in relief gives evidence of wonderful workmanship.

Were they Nahuas? Nadaillac[32] connects the builders of these now ruined structures with the Nahuas. He says:

"History and tradition are alike mute on the relations which may connect the builders of Tiahuanaco with the Quichuas. We are no less ignorant of those which existed between the former and the Amayras. It is probable, although we cannot possibly assert it, that both sprang from Nahua races, and that they came from the north, perhaps even from the prolific table land of Anahuac. One thing we think certain: Such monuments cannot be the remains of a civilization of local growth, nor can a race, unaided, have developed from its own genius such architectural knowledge. We share the conclusion of Angrand, that the civilization of which the remaining ruins bear the impress, could not have taken its rise on the frozen table lands. Man must have arrived upon them sufficiently armed for the struggle, by previous experience of social life."

Leaving the question whether the founders of the Titicaca empire came from the north or south out of consideration, we may safely accept the rest of this important paragraph as absolutely true.

Titicaca. In the lake there is an island, also called Titicaca,[33]

---

[31]Nadaillac, *Prehistoric America,* p. 401.
[32]*Ibid.,* p. 405.
[33]The word is said to mean "Tiger Rock."

which the ancient Peruvians considered sacred. Tradition has it that Manco Capac and his sister-wife were born there. The island is covered with monuments of a great past, indicating that a people far advanced in civilization had found refuge there, possibly pursued by more savage enemies. The sacred rock was covered with tapestries and ornamented with gold and silver. There, the Peruvians say, the sun had reappeared after an eclipse that lasted several days. It was, therefore, so sacred that none but priests could approach close to it. Pilgrims worshiped from afar, as Israel by Mount Sinai.

Saxahuaman. The valley of Cuzco is overlooked by the Saxahuaman, a fortress built on a perpendicular rock. Squier classes it among such world's wonders as the pyramids, the Stonehenge, and the Coliseum. It is supposed to have been undertaken by the Incas of the 15th century in emulation of the buildings at Tiahuanaco, and it is said that it was still unfinished when the Spaniards arrived. Other public structures were temples, palaces, aqueducts, and smaller fortresses in sundry places, probably works of defense against the savage Chinchas who inhabited the dense forests. In the Valley of Yucay there is a tower on the outside of which a sculptured serpent is found and, above the door, the Egyptian *Tau*, the same as at Palenque.[34]

Pachacamac, situated on the coast, twenty miles from Lima, was once a large city, attracting pilgrims from far and near. There was a fortress, five hundred feet above sea level, on a rock. There was a temple in which there was an image of the Creator, kept in a dark recess, like the ark of covenant of the Hebrews. The image was destroyed and the temple plundered by the Spaniards under Hernandez.

Chimus from the North. According to Garcilasso de la Vega, the entire coast from Truxillo to Tumbez, more than 650 miles, was inhabited by a people called Chimus. Tradition has it that these strangers came by way of the sea, and that they brought the inhabitants between the sea and the mountains into submission. Their capital, also called Chimu, extended over an area of more than sixty square miles, over which explorers have found ruins of solid walls, huacas or sepulchers, palaces, aqueducts, water reservoirs, and granaries. Nadaillac[35] thinks their huacas resemble the teacallis of Mexico and Central America, and that "such resemblance cannot be accidental."

A Remarkable Government. The government of the Incas was

---

[34]Nadaillac, *Prehistoric America,* p. 417.
[35]*Prehistoric America,* p. 395.

one of the most extraordinary experiments in a united order ever attempted since the end of the Millennial conditions among the Nephites (IV Nephi 25), about A.D. 201. It united under one guiding hand a disunited population, very largely sunk to the moral level of brutes, and lifted them up from a condition of laziness, poverty, and bloodthirst, to one of industrious habits, plenty, and peace, internal if not external. It solved the great problems of unemployment and poverty, and it pointed the way to temporal happiness. Its great mistake was the class distinction it established, when it made the Incas gods, to be worshiped by all the rest. This unnatural chasm between the upper and the lower classes led to despotism. The Incas undertook to regulate everything for everybody. The people worshiped by command, married by command, danced and enjoyed themselves by command. And over all hovered militarism as the monster on the shoulders of Sinbad, the sailor. The Incariate came to an ignoble end, when the last native ruler, Tupac Amaru, was put to death at Cuzco, by Francisco de Toledo, in 1571, although he was merely a lad, innocent of wrongdoing.

The closer one studies the principle of government enunciated by the Prophet Joseph Smith: "I teach them correct principles and they govern themselves," the more admirable it appears. For history teaches us clearly that government in accordance with correct principles but without free agency, is as disastrous as self-government without correct principles.

MAYAS, NAHUAS, TOLTECS, AND AZTECS

From South America and the adjacent part of the Isthmus, our cursory survey of prehistoric American races takes us to the countries once inhabited by Mayas, Nahuas, and kindred peoples, and especially to Yucatan and Mexico.

In the Mexican Valley. In the Valley of Mexico and nearby countries there was found, at the time of the Spanish Conquest, a degree of civilization in some respects superior to that of the Peruvians under the Incas. It covered an area of about forty thousand square miles, from 125 miles north of the present City of Mexico to a line near southern Honduras, and from the Pacific to the Atlantic.

Foundation of the City of Mexico. The year A.D. 1325 is generally regarded as the beginning of the historic era of that region, that being the year in which Tenochtitlan, the present City of Mexico, was founded. The accounts of what happened before that time contain a liberal element of fiction. Mr. Bancroft,[1] however, thinks that the annals of Anahuac take us back to the 6th century, "by traditions sufficiently definite to be considered as historic records." At that time, according to Mr. Bancroft:

"We find the Nahua civilization and institutions established on the table land occupied by them, as at every subsequent time, by many tribes more or less distant from each other. And there this culture remained without intermixture of essentially foreign elements down to the 16th century."

The brilliant historian quoted goes still farther. Following such authorities as Bradford, Squier, Tylor, Villet-le-Duc, Bartlett, Mueller, and Brasseur de Bourbourg, he endeavors to draw an outline of the history of the region before the 6th century.[2] It should be noted, in parenthesis, that Mr. Bancroft, although fully aware of the defects of Brasseur's work, from a scientific point of view, expresses the opinion that the researches of the learned Abbe have "done more than those of all other writers combined to throw light on primitive American history."

Old Maya Empire. According to the authorities mentioned, for some centuries before the beginning of our era and the first two or three hundred years, A. D., there existed in the Usumacinta valley an old Maya empire, known to its neighbors as *Xibalba*. The inhabitants were called Chanes, from Chan, an ancestor of Votan, the founder of the empire. They were also known as Colhuas, or "Serpents."[3] and their capital was in Chiapas, at or near Palenque. This

[1]*Native Races,* Vol. 2, p. 96.
[2]*Native Races,* Vol. 5, pp. 230-236.
[3]May it not be that their country was the "Snakeland" of Indian traditions?

empire grew northwestward towards Anahuac, where the Quinames, or "Giants," lived; and northeastward into Yucatan, where Zamna, or Itzamna, is said to have led a colony of Cocones and Itzas.

Quinames or Giants. The Quinames or "Giants"[4] seem to have been among the early inhabitants of many parts of America. Torquemada identifies them with the "giants" of the Peruvian tradition, which were destroyed by fire on account of their wickedness. Ixtlilxochitl thinks they were the survivors of an ante-deluvian race. He, possibly, has in mind the "giants" of Gen. 6:4; but the word translated "giants" in that passage should rather be "apostates," from *naphal*, "to fall." Veytia says they subsisted on the raw meat of birds and other animals, and that they were, in many respects like brutes.

Meaning of Xibalba. The meaning of the word *Xibalba* is, according to Ximenes, "Inferno." He says it was the Quiche name for what we call "hell." It is also said to mean, "He Who Disappears," — the Maya name for an evil spirit. Whatever the meaning of the word is, it was the name given to the great empire of the Chans, or "Snake" Indians, and also to their metropolis, later called Palenque or Otolum. The name *Xhembobel Moyos*[5] "seems sometimes to have been used by the natives in connection with Palenque," and *Xibalba* might be an abbreviated form of that name.

The Earliest Dates Recorded. Here it should be mentioned that Dr. H. J. Spinden, of the Peabody Museum, Harvard University, has traced the Maya chronology back to Aug. 6, 613 B. C., and Dec. 10, 580 B. C. The material for his elaborate calculations he found mostly at Copan, Tikal and Palenque. On the first mentioned date Maya astronomers began observations for the purpose of perfecting a calendar, and on the second date, the calendar was completed, and it is stated that the work was so well done that the calendar functioned for 2,000 years without the loss of a day.

[4]These giants, by the way, were, according to a tradition related by Ixtlilovchitl, the descendants of some who had survived the destruction of the world by a flood. This tradition, if authentic, would point to a Jaredite origin. They are represented as "brutes" but that may not have to be accepted without explanation.

[5]Bancroft, *Native Races*, Vol. 4, p. 295.

It may, perhaps, be stated here that Palenque is not the name of the famous ancient city, but of a modern, small village, near the old ruins. The name is of Spanish origin and means a "stockade." Xhembobel Moyos, which seems to be the ancient name, may possibly be composed of three familiar words, *Shem, Babel,* and *Mayim,* the last meaning "waters." If this is the origin of the word, it might indicate that the builders of the Xibalba capital endeavored to embody in one word, easily remembered, some important facts of their history, viz., their Shemitic lineage, their escape from the tower of Babel, and their crossing of the waters. Or, it might point to a Mulekite rule of the Xibalba empire and capital. And be it remembered that the Mulekites, when found by Mosiah, though they had lost both their language and their religion, had by some means preserved the recollection of their lineage, the flight from Jerusalem, and their miraculous voyage. (Omni 14-16) The ancient traditions of the Mayas tell us that the founders of the empire originally came from "a land of shadow beyond the seas." (Nadaillac, *Prehistoric America*, p. 264)

It will be noticed that this calendar reform was commenced about 13 years before the Prophet Lehi left Jerusalem. It must, therefore, have been the work of people who preceded Lehi, and the Jaredites are the only ones of that class, of whom we have a reliable account.

Another and later date is of equal importance. According to Dr. Spinden, in the year A.D. 392, two monuments were set up on hills in the Valley of Copan, about four or five miles apart. A person at a certain spot in the city could see the sun set behind the western monument two times every year, viz., April 9 and Sept. 2. These dates were thus marked for the benefit of the farmers, indicating the times for sowing the first and second crops. The year 392 is, as is well known, about 7 years after the last battle of Cumorah. Then, in the year A. D. 503, there seems to have been another congress of astronomers.

Peace in the Maya Empire. About the end of the second century of our era, what is known as the Maya civilization was in a flourishing condition. This corresponds well with the condition of peace and prosperity depicted in the Book of Mormon (IV Nephi 18-21) as enjoyed by the Nephites at that time. The Nephites, we read, were blessed and prospered until an hundred and ten years had passed away * * * and there was no contention in all the land. At that time, among the Mayas, city after city sprang into prominence in the southern part of the territory; that is to say, in what is now Chiapas, Guatemala, and Honduras. This, says Mr. Silvanus Griswold Morley,[6] was a time of "extraordinary development" all along the line, as is evidenced in what has survived of monuments, and it lasted upward of four hundred years. That was the "golden age" of the Mayas. During this time Palenque and Yaxchilan in southern Mexico; Piedras Negras, Seibal, Tikal, Naranjo, and Quirigua in Guatemala, and Copan in Honduras rose to prominence.

Long before this time the descendants of Lehi had invaded this region and assimilated with the people preceding them. They became Mayas, as inhabitants of the Maya empire.

Migration Northward. About the sixth century, or ninth cycle of Maya chronology, there is, we are further told, a sudden cessation of dates in all these cities. What happened at that time is not known. But, presently, Chichen Itza in the northern part of Yucatan became prominent. There had, evidently, been a migration. Several colonies were founded in that barren region, where a long struggle for a bare existence must have ensued. The arts were then, necessarily, neglected. The settlers seem to have met with varying success. Bakhalal was occupied for sixty years and then abandoned. Chichen Itza was

---

[6]*Intorduction to the Study of the Maya Hieroglyphics,* Bull. 57, Bur. Am. Enth., p. 2.

inhabited for about a hundred years. Chakanputun flourished for two hundred and sixty years, until it was destroyed by fire.

Cities Founded. At the beginning of the 11th century[7] Chichen Itza was again occupied, and the cities of Mayapan and Uxmal were founded. Then architecture and sculpture were revived and several cities were built, among which were Merida, Izamal, Kabah, and Labna.

Civil War. In the 13th century civil war between the chiefs of the leading cities broke out. Mayapan was attacked by the rulers of Chichen Itza, whereupon that city or pueblo, called in the Nahuas in Mexico to their aid. Chichen Itza was destroyed, and the Nahuas eventually established themselves in Mayapan and kept the people under subjection until the Maya nobles combined their forces, sacked the city, and killed the tyrant. However, the Mayas were divided and weakened by civil war, famine, and pestilence, and that was their condition when the Spaniards, like destroying angels from another world, appeared upon the scene. The sterling character of the Mayas was then shown in the fact that they fought for their homes and liberty for fifteen years against the invaders, before they were finally defeated.

Personal Appearance. The Maya Indians, as described by the early Spanish historians, were tall, active, and strong. They must have had peculiar ideas of personal beauty, for they flattened the heads of their infants and deliberately made them squint-eyed, and when grown up, they disfigured themselves with scars. Tattooing and adornment with red paint were demanded by their fashionable set; on the other hand, chastity was highly praised among them. An adulterer was tied to a stake and left to the mercy of the injured party. The adulteress was generally cast adrift by the husband.

Farmers and Hunters. Agriculture and hunting were carried on by cooperation. To that extent the idea of a united order survived among them. Bands of twenty, or more, passed from field to field and did the sowing, harvesting, or whatever was needed. Fifty, or more, frequently formed hunting parties, and the hunters divided the food procured.

Extensive Trade Connection. The Maya traded in salt, cloth, slaves, etc., and they are said to have extended their trading expeditions as far north as Tabasco, and even to Cuba, across the water. As media of exchange they used cocoa, stone counters, and rare red shells.

Their Music. The musical instruments of the Mayas consisted of drums, rattles, reed flutes, wooden horns, and bone whistles. They

---

[7]When Leif Ericson and the Narthmen were exploring North American coasts.

enjoyed comedies, dances, and social parties. They entertained their friends on vegetables, roasts, fish, corn cakes, cocoa, and intoxicants, and each guest generally received a present. The meals were spread on mats on the floor.

Military Organization. Their military organization was well developed. At the head of the army the Mayas had two generals. The office of one was hereditary; the other was elected for a term of three years. A certain number of men in each village were taken into the army, by popular vote, and they formed the nucleus of the fighting forces. They were supported by the community. Their weapons were bows and arrows, lances, and copper axes. The arrows and lances were tipped with obsidian. The protective armor consisted of wicker shields and quilted cotton coats. The officers wore helmets with brilliant plumes, and cloaks of tiger skins, possibly to inspire fear. After a battle the slain were often mutilated, the jaw bones used for ornaments, and prisoners were made slaves, unless they were chiefs. These were frequently sacrificed.

Duties of the Chief Priesthood. The chief priest of the Mayas was called *Ahau can Mai.* The priests were supposed to educate the children of the lords and nobles in the computation of time, in fetes and ceremonies, in the administration of the sacraments, in divination, healing, history, reading and writing, as far as these arts were practiced. Genealogies were carefully kept. He who had a genealogical record was an *Ah kaba* — "a man with a name"; if he had no such record, he was "nameless."

The Name of Their God. The chief deity of the Mayas was *Itzamna.* He was regarded as the father of the gods and the creator. The Mayas, as the Peruvians, saw in the rising sun a glorious manifestation of the Deity. He was also regarded as the founder of the Maya civilization, and must therefore, at some time have appeared among the people as a divine leader and teacher. Next to him in importance was *Kukulcan,* the "feathered serpent," who was the founder of cities and the framer of laws. They also had a god of harvest, *Yum Kaax;* a god of death, *Apuch,* and a god of war; also a "black captain,"*Ek Ahau,* and many other deities.

Complicated Calendar System. The calendar system of the Mayas mentioned in a previous paragraph was very complicated. They had a period of 260 days, which has come to be known by the Aztec name *Tonalamatl,* because the Maya name is not known. *Kin Katun* has been suggested by Prof. Seler, but Dr. Morley doubts the correctness of that suggestion.[8] The tonalamatl has been called "the sacred year,"

---

[8]*Introduction to the Study of the Maya Hieroglyphics,* p. 43.

because it was divided into parts with special reference to festivals and religious observances. The priests studied the tonalamatl in order to ascertain which days were propitious for offering sacrifices, making confessions, etc.

They had also a solar year. This was called *Haab*. This year consisted of 365 days, divided into 18 *uinals,* or months, of 20 days each, with the addition of an extra 5 days at the end of the year. Each month had its own name, as had each day, except the last five, which were, therefore, the *xma kaba kin,* or "days without a name." They were considered the unlucky days. By an ingenious combination of the *tonalamatl* and the *haab* the Mayas obtained a cycle of 18,980 days, or 52 solar years, which have been called the "calendar round" for want of a better name. By calculation it was found that the precise order of the 260 days of the tonalamatl, with reference to the 365 positions each could occupy in the *haab,* repeated itself in 52 years, as the order of our week days does in seven years. By fixing an "initial date" which they called *4 ahau 8 cumbu,* and by dividing time into kins, uinals, tuns, katuns, cycles, great cycles, etc.,[9] they could fix any date within a period of 374,000 years.

Someone has well said: "Maya was the name of a powerful nation between the Isthmus of Tehuantepec and Darien. It was as well known among the ancients as France or England is today."

At Chichen Itza. Among recent explorations in Yucatan should be mentioned that of Edward H. Thompson, who conceived the idea of dredging the sacred well of the Itzas, and to examine the bottom in diving costume. This unique work was continued for two years, and it seems that it yielded many finds. The theory of the explorer is that maidens were sacrificed in the well, as messengers to the snake god, and that objects of value, of gold, copper and jade, were thrown after them, by the mourners. The Mayas, he further believes, were one branch of a race that at one time inhabited most of Central America, and even lived as far north as New Mexico and Arizona.

An Observatory. Dr. John C. Merriam, president of the Carnegie Institution, some time ago told of the finding of an ancient astronomical observatory, "probably the first ever built on this continent." The ruins were found at Chichen Itza by Dr. Sylvanus G. Morley. The discovery, deep under a temple already excavated, of the ruins of another and more beautiful temple is supposed to indicate that middle-American civilization is even older than archaeologists have believed.

The throne of the rulers of Chichen Itza has also been found

---

[9]Morley, *Introduction to the Study of the Maya Hieroglyphics,* p. 58. The day was called *kin.* 20 kins was a *uinal;* 18 uinals, a *tun;* 20 tuns, a *katun;* 20 katuns, a *cycle;* 20 cycles, a *great cycle.* The cycle, then, was equal to 144,000 days, and the great cycle to 2,880,000 days.

in recent years. It is thirteen feet wide, seven feet deep and three feet high, laborately and beautifully sculptured.

Four Cultures Meet. Recent explorations in the valley of Mexico have indicated the influence there of Mongolian, Egyptian, and Chaldean as well as Indian culture. The Book of Mormon accounts sufficiently for the Chaldean and Egyptian influences. And if tradition is reliable, we are supposed to believe that in the year 499, Hwui Shan, a Buddhist missionary, in company with five priests, found a land many miles to the eastward of China which he named Fusang. They sailed along the Chinese coast to Kamchatka and thence along the Aleutian islands to Alaska. From Alaska, which they called Great Han, they sailed along the coast to Fusang. Hwui Shan describes the dwellings made of blocks of sun-dried mud, which housed many people, a description which fits the pueblos and ancient America. He mentions a plant used in making cordage and paper, which afforded vegetable milk and which yielded tender edible sprouts. The maguey plant answers this description.

A few years ago the Chinese government directed its historians to make a search of the imperial records, and from them came the foregoing story. That would account for the Mongolian influence, and it is not impossible that the Chinese tradition relates to the colonization of the Jaredites.

The find of a "Mongolian library," as it has been called, seems to corroborate the accounts of an incursion from China. The library was unearthed in 1924, by Prof. Wm. Niven and Dr. J. H. Cornyn, from a thick layer of volcanic ashes. The offered explanation is that the entire valley once upon a time was a great volcanic cone with fifty active volcanic mountains, and at least three of these constantly in action, and streams of lava and ashes inundated the region like a great flood. This, they say, happened from seven to ten thousand years ago — a date which undoubtedly is too high. The library consists of stone tablets containing easily recognized characters or symbols. Among these are the symbol of the moon, the symbol of fire, the earth mother, water, lightning, the sun's rays, the symbol of the volcano god, the symbols of morning and evening, the symbols of the various stars and heavenly bodies. Many of the books of the Mongoloid library are books on the stars.

A former Chinese minister to Mexico, M. L. Tao, is quoted as having said, that there are definite accounts of an emigration from China across the Pacific about the years 2500 to 2000 B.C. That is important, for the immigrants are said to have been highly cultured even at that time.

The Egyptian influence is seen in the pyramids and in the various sculptured articles unearthed.

Lubaantum. One of the recent discoveries in Yucatan is what remains of an ancient city, which has been called Lubaantum. These ruins were discovered in the very heart of British Honduras, by the English archæologist, Dr. Gann, and his companion, Mitchell Hedges. The two explorers, with their attendants, were proceeding up the Rio Grande, when their boat was upset, and they had to swim to the shore. It was while trying to cut their way through the almost impenetrable jungle that they came upon the ruins. They found a gigantic pyramid of earth, surrounded by large columns of lime rock, or sandstone. Father into the jungle they discovered terraces leading up to an immense table land, where six pyramids of stone had been erected. There were also the remnants of a burial chamber of stone, which had caved in. According to Dr. Gann, all these structures were the resting places of kings and priests, who may belong to the time of the first dynasty of the Maya kingdom. Excavations are being made, and the hope is entertained that light will be shed on the beginning of the remarkable Maya culture.

The Nahuas. Writers on prehistoric America tell us that a people called *Nahuas* flourished side by side with the so-called Xibalbans, or Mayas. They, too, reached out from Tulan in Chiapas towards Anahuac, where they encountered the Quinames, or giants. Under the leadership of Cukulcan, they penetrated into Yucatan, where they came in contact with the Comes and Itzas. Gradually the Nahuas became strong in numbers and influence, and united with the Xibalbans on terms of equality. But some time before the fifth century of our era, there was a political upheaval. The various tribes were scattered, and the valley of Mexico became the center of the Nahua government. The Mayas and Nahuas became two separate peoples.

Geographical Extent. The language of the Nahuas at one time extended from the State of Sinaloa in northwestern Mexico on the Pacific, to the domain of the Mayas in Yucatan, a distance of about 1,500 miles; then down into Nicaragua, 500 miles more. It ruled supreme on the Mexican table lands. Its only real rivals were the Maya and Quiche languages.

Three Historical Periods. It is customary to speak of three periods of the later history of the Nahuas, viz., the Toltec, the Chichimec, and the Aztec. These and other Indian nations were closely related, and they were all Nahuas. According to some chroniclers, the Toltecs arrived in the valley in the year 648 A.D., and disappeared in 1031. The Chichimecs rose to power in 1170. The Aztecs arrived in Tula in 1196, founded Tenochtitlan (the City of Mexico) in 1325, and were the masters of the country when Cortez arrived in 1519.

Divided Opinions Concerning the Toltecs. The Toltecs are supposed to have been, at one times, at the head of a strong confederacy, with Tollan as its capital. Mr. Fiske[10] is of the opinion that, while there was a tribe of Toltecs at Tollan, at one time, the notion of a "Toltec empire" is misleading, and Brinton identifies them with the Aztecs. But all authorities agree that they were well advanced in culture, and many ascribe to them the buildings in Mexico and Central America, the ruins of which still testify of the greatness of an age that is past.

According to Galatin,[11] the Toltecs came to a country called Huehue Tlapallan in the year 387 A.D. This country is believed to have been situated somewhere in the northeast. Tradition has it that the southward migration of the Toltecs was occasioned by attacks of the Chichimecs and that the strife lasted for thirteen years, after which the remnant fled and finally reached Mexico. It is further stated that they displaced a people that had come in ships from South America, called, Colhuas.[12]

It is well to bear in mind the date of the last battle at Cumorah, 385 A.D., after which many Lamanites, undoubtedly, began a migration from the land of the same name as the hill.

Ixtlilxochitl also relates a Toltec tradition concerning a Huehue Tlapallan,[13] to which they had migrated 520 years after the flood. This may be a Toltec version of the Jaredite exodus from the home in the Old World.

The Toltecs are described by Nadaillac[14] as tall, well-proportioned, with clear, yellow complexions, dark eyes and hair, aquiline noses, and receding foreheads. They constructed roads and aqueducts, and knew how to work metals, such as gold, silver, copper, tin, and lead. They could spin, weave, and dye cloth, and cut precious stones. They built houses of rock, cemented with lime mortar, and they constructed mounds. In fact, Dr. Foster considers them as identical with the mound builders of the Ohio and Mississippi Valleys. They knew the medical value of some plants, and they used vapor baths. They even had hospitals where patients received free treatment. They made implements of flint, porphyry, basalt, and obsidian, and jewelry of emeralds, turquoises, and amethysts. They were great sculptors, and they adorned their temples and monuments with glyphs, and

[10]*Discovery of America*, Vol. 2, pp. 217-220.
[11]Schoolcraft's *Arch.*, Vol. 5, p. 96.
[12]James C. Southall, *Recent Origin of Man*, p. 532.
[13]Bancroft, *Native Races*, Vol. 5, pp. 18 and 209.
[14]*Prehistoric America*, p. 275.

their pottery was famous. Pestilence and famine, and civil strife, arising from dissensions of rival religious factions, undermined the Toltec regime. Other tribes became powerful, and many of the Toltecs fled to Guatemala, Tehuantepec, Campeche, and the distant coasts of the Isthmus.

The Pyramid of the Sun. This architectural marvel, which has only recently been completely unearthed at Teotihuacan, is a truncated mound 216 feet high and 760 feet around its base. It was, undoubtedly at first intended as an altar in honor of the Creator, whose splendor is revealed in the sun and the other heavenly luminaries. But in course of time, as the light of revelation grew dim and darkness fell upon the minds of men, the place was used for human sacrifices. According to accounts, the fairest and strongest boy or girl that could be found was selected for this sacrifice. They were feted in luxury for three weeks. The boy was given the finest of wines and food and the fairest daughters of the tribe. He was dressed in splendid gowns. The people poured their gifts on him. He was almost worshiped. Then on the sacrificial day he was led, with all the others selected for the rite, along what is called "The Highway of the Dead" to the top of the pyramid, and after certain ceremonies were observed was cast over the side to death.

This pyramid is only one of a great many. It is supposed to be from the Toltec period.

The Chichimecs. The Chichimec rule next claims our attention. Mr. Bancroft considers it probable that the great, original Nahua empire, whether it be called Huehue Tlapallan, Tamoanchan, Tulan, or Amaquemecan, was the Chichimec empire, from which the Toltecs migrated first, only to be followed by other Chichimec tribes.[15] All agree that the two were of one blood and language. They appear in the vicinity of Anahuac, after having wandered about for a whole year, but tradition can give us no clue to whether the country whence they came and which they called Amaquemecan, was to the north or south of Anahuac. All that is known with any degree of certainty is that during the 6th and 7th centuries Anahuac and adjoining territory north and west were settled by several Nahua nations. Some settled in the fertile valleys and became the standard bearers of the most advanced culture. They were known as Toltecs. Others were hunters, rude and barbarous. They were the "chichimecs," the "dogs" of their age; or as we should say, the "riff-raff," the "canaille."

The Aztecs. Among the warrior nations that rose to power in Anahuac were the Aztecs. They, too, were Nahuas, and the traditions

---

[15]*Native Races,* Vol. 5, p. 219.

THE BOOK OF ALMA

relating to their origin must be understood as covering the traditional infancy of all the kindred tribes or nations.

The Aztecs are said to have come from Aztlan. That name has been translated "the place of cranes," or "the place of salt water," or "the white country," the last rendition assuming that "aztlan" is from "iztac" which means "white." There may have been an Aztlan in New Mexico (Mr. Morgan), or in the Mississippi Valley (as held by some), as well as in Mexico, and Aztecs may have inhabited either or all of them, at one time or another; but the original Aztlan was, probably, in Asia. Mr. Denison[16] is inclined to this view. But he also makes this suggestion: "They worshiped towards the east, whence the sun rose, and that may be the true origin of the word"— Eastland.[17] It has also been suggested that it may mean, "The home of the gods." That would be the Scandinavian Asaland or Asaheim, the home of the Aesir," the chief city of which was Asgard, which means a castle on the hill, from *as*, "hill," "ridge," and *gard*, "castle," "burgh." Can it be, that Aztec tradition and Scandinavian mythology originally grew up in the same soil?

Tenochtitlan. On their arrival on the Mexican plateau, the Aztecs found the most favorable locations already occupied, but they established themselves on a spot protected by the marshes of lake Tezcuco, where, in due time, they built the famous pueblo of Tenochtitlan, so called, possibly after their great ancestor, Tenuch, one of six sons of Iztax Mixcohuatl.

Their power began to be felt in 1375 A.D., when Acamapichtli, having been elected to the position of *tlacatecuhtli*, or chief of men, made improvements that gave the city a standing among its neighbors.

Two Cities Combine. During the administration of *Itzcoatzin*, "Obsidian Snake," Tenochtitlan and Tezcuco joined forces and destroyed the city of the Tecpanecas, and butchered the inhabitants. After this "victory" the two cities mentioned and Tlacopan formed a federation for the express purpose of plundering other communities and dividing the spoils. This was the famous Aztec confederation which existed when Cortez arrived.

Montezuma a Despot. Montezuma II, a son of Axayacatl, was at the head of affairs then, having been elected *tlacatecutli*, or "chief of men" in 1502 A.D.[18] At that time the incumbent of that office was a despot with, broadly speaking, unlimited powers. He was re-

---

[16]*Primitive Aryans in America*, pp. 134-50.

[17]Another explanation is that the first settlers found there a rock upon which grew a cactus, in which an eagle with a serpent in its beak was perched, and that the word means, "place of the cactus rock."

[18]This position may be compared to that held by the tribal chief of Israel in the days of Moses and Joshua. These were "princes," which means "first" of men. (Num. 1:16) They were

vered as the representative of God, as were the Incas of Peru. He was so sacred that only five mortals were permitted to see his face.

Class Distinction. Next to the ruler stood a privileged class, each individual of which was a despot in his limited circle. When Cortez arrived upon the scene, a class war raged between this "nobility" and the merchant class, the latter being powerful because of their wealth. Montezuma sided with the nobles, and these were often guilty of extortion and violence.

The People were Slaves. A considerable portion of the people were slaves. Prisoners of war, criminals condemned to servitude, and persons who had sold themselves, or children sold, were in this class. Prisoners of war were kept for sacrifices, but the captor could dispose of them in the market, if he preferred to do so. Human beings were, therefore, always for sale. Slaves in the hands of good masters were treated well, as were those of the Hebrews anciently. (Deut. 15:15; 16:11, 12) They were permitted to marry, to raise families, to work for themselves at stated intervals, and even to keep slaves for their own convenience, if they could obtain them. Refractory slaves, however, were punished severely. If they persisted, they were sacrificed as cattle. If, however, a slave succeeded in escaping and reaching the courtyard of the palace, he was set free. To that extent the Aztecs had preserved the principle of the Hebrew law of refuge. (Num. 35:6) Compare Psalm 48:3: "God is known in his palaces for a refuge."

Children and Parents. Aztec children were taught to obey their parents and to honor aged persons. This is in accord with the Mosaic law. Pricking with thorns seems to have been a common educational punishment. The Jews, too, had a proverb about "kicking against the pricks." (Acts 9:5) Liars were punished severely. Sometimes their lips were split open. To work and to perform religious duties formed part of the education of the children.

Marriages. Among the Aztecs the age of marriage was about twenty years for men and between eighteen and twenty for women. As customary among Orientals, brides were selected by the parents. If these were tardy, the priest would hasten the matter. Those who refused to marry were taken for the temple service. Union between blood relations was not permitted. A brother was expected to marry his deceased brother's widow, as in the Mosaic law; but with this

judges. (Ex. 18:21) They took the lead in forwarding the offerings of the people for the support of the sanctuary (Num. 7:10, 84), and they acted as scouts for the camp. (Num. 13:1-16) The Aztec "chiefs of men," in addition to other duties, were commanders-in-chief of the military forces, and performed priestly functions. At first they were elected by popular vote, women as well as men exercising the franchise. Then a council of electors cast the vote for the people, the oldest brother or near relative of the deceased being chosen, thus making the office, virtually, hereditary.

difference: Under the Aztec code he was under obligation to do so, only if there were children to take care of, not otherwise provided for. Under the Mosaic law the Levirate marriage was instituted for the express purpose of perpetuating the name of the deceased. (Deut. 25: 5, 6) The marriage was completed in the temple[19] and ended with a banquet and dancing. Immediately after the wedding the newly-weds fasted for four days. This ordeal completed, they retired to a specially prepared couch, which the following day was brought to the temple as a thanks offering.

A Baptismal Rite. A kind of baptismal rite was performed as part of the marriage ceremony. The bridal pair was placed on green reed mats, and a priest poured water on them. Nobles who could afford the extravagance had four ablutions of water and as many of wine.

The arrival of a child was a great event among the Aztecs, as everywhere. But, strange to say, they called the time of the birth "the hour of death." The early Christians looked forward toward the day of death as their birthday.

Infant Baptism. The washing of the infant by the midwife was a ceremony of a solemn importance — a veritable infant "baptism." The lady took water, breathed upon it, and then touched the head and chest of the infant with it. Then, placing the little one in it, she said: "Enter thou into the water called *metlalac* and *tuspalac;* may it wash thee, and may the Omnipotent cleanse from thee all ill that is inherent in thee from the beginning of the world and from before the beginning. Begone, all evil imparted to thee by thy father and thy mother."

On the fifth day after the birth another "baptism" was administered, if the signs were favorable; if not, the ceremony was postponed. When applying the water this time, the midwife said: "Evil, wheresoever thou art, begone, avaunt! For the child liveth anew and is born again; once more it is purified: a second time it is renewed by our mother, *Chalchichuitlicue.*" Then, lifting up the infant toward heaven, she prayed to *Ometachtli* and *Omecioatl:* "Behold, O

---

[19]"Accompanied by the dancers and musicians, the newly wedded pair was conducted to the temple, at the door of which the tlamacazques, or priests, appeared to receive them. While the company remained below, the wedded couple with their sponsors and parents ascended the steps of the temple. The priest wore his robe of ceremony, and carried in his hand an incensory filled with incense, with which he proceeded to perfume them. He then placed himself between the two, with the man on his right and the woman on his left, and taking them by the hands led them to the altar of the idol, muttering prayers as he went. The altar reached, he placed a fine and showy shawl woven and variegated with many colors, in the center of which was painted a skeleton, as a symbol that death only could now separate them from each other. He then perfumed them again, and with the incensory, led them back to the door of the temple, where they were received by the assemblage and accompanied to their home with dancing and music." (Bancroft, *Native Races,* Vol. 2, pp. 257-8)

Lord, the creature which thou hast sent to this place of sorrow, affliction, and anguish; give it, O Lord, of they gifts and inspiration, for
thou art the great God and the great Goddess."

It is evident from this that the Aztecs had infant "baptism,"
whatever the explanation of the strange fact may be.[20] It is also evident that the Aztecs believed in inherited sin and pre-existence, and
the cleansing virtue of consecrated water.

In the eleventh month all women who had become mothers
during the year were "purified,"[21] and the children presented before
the Lord. Circumcision was practiced by some, but was not generally
observed.

Temple Services. The Aztecs held daily services in their temples.
The priests fasted often, and sometimes tortured themselves, and the
people imitated them, drawing blood from their arms, legs, tongues,
and other parts of the body. Offerings were brought to the sanctuaries at the festivals. Some of the people had, perhaps, only a flower
to give, or a cake of bread; others donated labor, robes, jewels, gold,
or even slaves. Sometimes children were carried to their death on
litters gorgeously ornamented with plumes and jewels. Bodies of
human victims were cut up and eaten, partly at least. At the festival
of the winter solstice a number of captives were slain, one of whom
represented the sun and another the moon. At harvest time the
first fruits of the season were offered to the sun, and a criminal was
sacrificed by being ground to death between two large stones. Every
eighth year the so-called festival of bread and water was observed,
and every fifty-second year, which completed the cycle, the festival
of the "binding up of the years" was celebrated.

Food Resources. Hunting, fishing, and agriculture furnished the
people with the means of subsistence. On the main land few fertile
spots were left uncultivated, and on the lakes were "floating gardens,"
as famous as the "hanging gardens" of ancient Babylonia. They were
built either on rafts or on the bottom of the lake where the water
was shallow. Among the domesticated animals were turkeys, quails,
geese, ducks, etc., and an animal, *techichi*, resembling a dog. The
nobles kept also deer, hares, and rabbits. Cannibalism was practiced
as a religious rite.

A Perfect Language. The Aztec language has been regarded as
the most perfect of all the American languages. It lacks the sounds
represented by *b, d, f, r, g,* and *s,* but it is nevertheless, rich and elegant. It compares favorably with Latin. It was spoken over a wide

---

[20]Infant baptism was one of the errors condemned by the prophet Moroni. See Moroni 8:
9-26.

[21]Compare Lev. 15:19. For the idea of consecrated water see Num. 19:2-9.

area, extending from the Valley of Mexico eastward to the Gulf of Mexico and westward to the Pacific. It was spoken in Salvador, Nicaragua, and in Guatemala, and traces of it have been found in Tabasco, and even in Yucatan. To the north, traces have been discovered in Sonora, Sinaloa, Durango, Chihuahua, Texas, Arizona, California, Utah, Nevada, Idaho, Montana, and Oregon.[22] "It is even possible," says Bancroft,[23] "that it may at one time have been used even east of the Mississippi." Sahagun, quoted by Bancroft, says the Apalaches were "Nahoas" speaking the Mexican language, and that they had highroads along which they traveled far into Mexico for purposes of barter and commerce. Dr. Brinton, who does not recognize the Toltecs and Chichimecs as separate tribes, places the Nahuas in the large group which he calls "the Uto-Aztecan tribes."[24] The principal members of this stock, he says, are the Utes, Shoshonees, and Comanches in the north; various tribes in Sonora, Chihuahua, Sinola, and Durango in the center, and the Nahuas and the Aztecs in the south. Tribes speaking these related dialects have been found from the Isthmus of Panama to the banks of the Columbia River. The relationship of these numerous bands, he adds, is unquestionable, although many of them have adopted words from other stocks. Besides the Nahuas, or Aztecs, numerous other tribes are known to have flourished in territory where they had settlements. Among these were the Otomis who preceded the Aztecs in Mexico; the Tarascans west of the Valley of Mexico; the Totonacos, who claimed they had come from the north and northwest; the Zapotecs and Mixtecs; the Zoques and Mixes, who had traditions of a migration from the south; the Chinantecs, and the Chapanecs. Many of these were highly civilized and valiant, and had enjoyed independence for centuries, when they came under Aztec rule.

Legends and Traditions. Nahua legends and traditions, as preserved by the native, Fernando deAlva Ixtlilxochitl, begin with an account of the flood and the building of a tower.[25] For many years after these events a few families kept together and wandered over wide expanses of land, and crossed waters, arriving, finally, at a place called Huehue Tlapallan.

Then came a great hurricane which swept away trees, rocks, houses, people. Only those who took refuge in caves were saved. When they emerged, they found a multitude of apes in the land.[26]

Next we hear of an earthquake which swallowed up the Qui-

---

[22]Bancroft, *Native Races*, Vol. 3, p. 557.
[23]*Ibid.*, p. 726.
[24]*The American Race*, Vol. 3, pp. 118-34.
[25]Bancroft, *Native Races*, Vol. 5, pp. 209-14.
[26]This is exactly how a legendary account of a voyage like that of the Jaredites, for instance, might be expected to read.

names in the coast regions, together with many of the Toltecs and Chichimecs. After that catastrophe there was peace, and the wise men came together and decided to make an historical record and to revise the calendar.

Convulsions in Nature. One hundred and sixteen years after this gathering of scribes and astronomers "the sun and moon were eclipsed, the earth shook, and the rocks were rent asunder, and many other things and signs happened, though there was no loss of life." This, we are told, happened in the year 33 A.D., the year of the crucifixion.[27]

Then follows an account of an exodus, which began with a revolt in the year 338 A.D., and ended with the entrance of the wanderers in Anahuac in the 6th century of our era.

This legendary account of the history of the Nahuas is in some essentials so similar to the Book of Mormon story of the Nephites and Lamanites, as to warrant the conclusion that the Nahuas were the descendants of those very nations, with, probably, a liberal element of Jaredite blood.

This conclusion is strengthened by the fact that the name *Nahua* is, both in form and meaning, the same as *Nephi.* I hope to enter into this proposition more fully in another place. Here I will only say that the Nahuas did not have a letter for our *f* or *ph* sound. Their *u* is equivalent to our *f*, so that the name may be pronounced, *Nah-fa.* That is *Nephi* almost without any change.

Anahuac is generally explained to mean, "any country situated about a lake or large sheet of water" (Nadaillac), or "country by the waters" (Bancroft), or "lake country" (Fiske); all on the authority of Brasseur de Bourbourg. I do not deny the correctness of this explanation, but somehow it does not appear satisfactory. As in the case of *Tenochtitlan,* which generally is said to be derived from two words meaning "rock" and "cactus," but which also has been regarded, with more probability, as immortalizing the name of a great leader, Tenoch, so there may be a simpler and more probable explanation of *Anahuac* than that proposed by the learned Abbé.

If, as I believe, *Nahua* is the Book of Mormon name *Nephi,* then *A-Nahua-c,* or *Ah-Nahua-ac* might be Maya for "the Land of Nephi."

That the Nephites at some time settled on the Mexican plateau is certain; or reasonably so; for they were by treaty given the land north of the "narrow passage," (at Tehuantepec?) "which led into the land southward." (Mormon 2:29)

We have already noted that some authors on prehistoric America

---

[27]Compare this with III Nephi 8:5-25.

hold that the Aztecs came to Anahuac from the north. Among modern writers who reject this view is Mr. John D. Baldwin. He examines
briefly the various theories offered to explain the origin of the Nahuas
— the lost-tribe theory; the Malay, the Phœnician, and the Atlantis
theories, and, after having rejected them all, he says:[28]

"It has sometimes been assumed that the Aztecs came to Mexico from the North,
but there is nothing to warrant this assumption, nothing to make it probable, nothing
even to explain the fact that some persons have entertained it. People of the ancient
Mexican and Central American race are not found father north than New Mexico and
Arizona, where they are known as Pueblos or Village Indians. In the old time that was
a frontier region, and the Pueblos seem to represent ancient settlers who went there
from the South. * * * Investigation has made it probable that the Mexicans or Aztecs
went to the Valley of Mexico from the South. Mr. Squier says: 'The hypothesis of
a Migration from Nicaragua and Cuscutlan to Anahuac is altogether more consonant
with probabilities and with tradition than that which derives the Mexicans from the
North.'"

In answer to the question whence they came into Nicaragua,
Mr. Baldwin gives this remarkable opinion:[29]

"The civilized life of the ancient Mexicans and Central Americans may have had
its original beginning somewhere in South America, for they seem more closely related
to the ancient South Americans than to the wild Indians north of the Mexican border;
but the peculiar development of it represented by the ruins must have begun in the
region where they are found. I find myself more inclined to the opinion that the
aboriginal South Americans are the oldest people on this continent; that they are
distant in race; and that the wild Indians of the North came originally from Asia."

---

[28]*Ancient America*, p. 217.
[29]*Ancient America*, p. 185.

RELIGIOUS CONCEPTS, TRADITIONS, MYTHS, LEGENDS AND INDIAN TRAITS

"There is no Gentile nation that refers to primitive events with such certainty as the Indians do. They give us an account of the creation of the world, of the deluge, of the confusion of languages at the Tower of Babel, and of all other periods and ages of the world, and of the long peregrinations which their people had in Asia." —Boturini, quoted by Dr. James E. Talmage, *Articles of Faith*, p. 287.

"The religious myths of antiquity and the fireside legends of ancient and modern times have their common root in the mental habits of primeval humanity. They are the earliest utterances of men concerning the visible phenomena of the world into which they were born."—John Fiske.

If, as the Book of Mormon teaches, people of Semitic, and, more especially, Hebrew lineage came over and settled in America; people who, as in the case of Lehi and his kindred, were reared in the Mosaic cultural atmosphere and were well versed in Egyptian theology and history, there should be unmistakable evidence of those Old-World civilizations in the moral and religious concepts, the traditions, myths, and legends of the Indians who are their descendants, no matter how far these may have gone astray, owing to the loss of the light of revelation and the written word, during centuries of unceasing struggle for existence and the consequent neglect of arts and sciences with which they may at one time have been familiar.

Indian Conception of God. The best authorities agree that the Indians, with whom the early explorers and conquerors became acquainted, concentrated their belief in a great Creator, and that they pictured him in their minds as a person, clothed in glory, comparable to that of the siderial heavens, as a magnificent rayment, and surrounded with sublime atmospheric phenomena, such as the rainbow, thunder, lightning, etc.

There may have been exceptions. All Indians may not have had this grand concept of the Deity. It has even been asserted that Indian tribes on the shores and islands of Terra del Fuego, notably the Yahgans and Onas, had no idea at all of a supreme Being. But the Rev. Despard thinks otherwise. He says the Yahgans believed that the sun and the moon were very old, and that they had a tradition to the effect that an aged man who knew their Maker had died without leaving any information about their creation. As for the Onas, they have, we are told, a native word which has been translated "medicine man," but which Father Beauvoir regarded as akin to the Hebrew Jehovah.[1]

---

[1] That word is *Jhow'n*. See John M. Cooper's *Tribes of Tierra del Fuego*, printed as Bul. 63, Bur. of Am. Ethn., Smith. Inst, Wash., 1917, pp. 148-9.

However, the Indians that had any culture certainly had a re-markably clear idea of the Creator and Ruler of the world as revealed in the visible creation. And in this respect, their concepts seem to have been identical with those of Hebrew poet-prophets. For these, also, speak of the heavens as the "vesture," the "garment," of the Almighty. See, for instance, Psalm 102:25, 26, quoted by Paul in Hebrews 1:10-12. See also Psalm 97, where the inspired poet, refer-ring to the awe-inspiring storm, sings:

"The Lord reigneth; let the earth rejoice; let the multitude of isles be glad thereof. Clouds and darkness are round about him: righteousness and judgment are the habitation of his throne. A fire goeth before him, and burneth up his enemies round about. His lightnings enlightened the world: the earth saw and trembled. The hills melted like wax at the presence of the Lord, at the presence of the Lord of the whole earth. The heavens declare his righteousness, and all the people see his glory."

This song about the presence of the Lord in the flashing light-nings and the rolling thunders, the sea heaving and roaring and wind shaking its drenched wings, express exactly the Indian idea of God and the world. How did they obtain it? From the same source as the Hebrews.

Rafinesque states that the Haytians believed in the existence of a Supreme Being, eternal, infinite, omnipotent, and invisible. They thought of him, according to the authority mentioned, as the father or mother, of Iocahuna or, the name is also spelled, Yocahuna, or Io-vana, who dwelt in the sun and was the "Lord of the world," as was the Jehovah of the Hebrews.[2]

Indian Belief in Pre-Existence. The Indian idea of the pre-exist-ence of man is noteworthy. The traditions and myths of the Iriquois may be regarded as representative. They tell us that, previous to the appearance of humans on earth, there were beings in existence which are called "the first people," or simply, "the people."

That, by the way, is the term that many of the Indians apply to themselves. The Eskimos call thmeselves *Innuit*, "men," the Iri-quois were "superior men," just as the Teutons at one time claimed to be *Ala-mana*, "all men," or, preferably, *Gher-mon*, "war-men." Some of the Indians called themselves *Unishin-aba*, a word which has been translated "common people," but which seems to mean "men-fathers," assuming that it is akin to the Hebrew *enosh*, "man," and *ab*, "father."

Those first people, in Indian tradition, lived for ages in peace

[2]The Egyptians, too, believed in a deity whom they called *Neter*, and who was self-existing, living, a generator and preserver of life. Some have compared the Egyptian *Neter* with the Roman *Natura* and the Greek *Physis*—our *Nature*. This Egyptian idea seems to have pervaded the Indian theocosmogony. In all Indian creation stories God is the Creator. The origin of the world is divine.

and harmony. At length there was a terrible conflict. The gods—for these first people are also called gods—warred against each other. During this struggle social and religious institutions were formed. The souls of the gods, finally, entered into material bodies, and that is how all things now existing, animate and inanimate, came into being. The religious and social institutions of the gods were bequeathed to man.[3]

"Human in form and feeling, and yet most divine, were the gods and deities of the ancient Seneca and the other Iroquoian peoples. While the divine social and political organization was necessarily, for psychological reasons, a close reflex or replica of the human, and although both gods and man derived descent from an original first parent, yet the first divine Ancestor was a self-existing God, and the first man was the creature of one of these divine Powers."[4]

I quote this, not because it proves that the Indians were absolutely orthodox in their theology, but to show how remarkably close they were to the Semitic conception of God and the creation. (Comp. II Nephi 2:14-24)

The Indwelling Spirit. The idea that every existing thing is the abode of a spirit, and that the spirits of the "first people" gave themselves up and took bodies, in order to sustain the life of man is, certainly, remarkable.[5] It should be compared with the doctrine of Paul, Romans 8:19-23:

"For the earnest expectation of the creature waiteth for the manifestations of the sons of God. For the creature was made subject to vanity, not willingly, but by reason of him who hath subjected the same in hope, because the creature itself also shall be delivered from the bondage of corruption into the glorious liberty of the children of God. For we know that the whole creation groaneth and travaileth in pain together until now."

In addition to the creation myths, the Indians had their versions of the story of the flood, related in allegories, in which a raft, a tree, a mountain, figured. They had traditions concerning the building of a tower; they knew something about the doctrine of the antonement, as evidenced by their sacrifices, though they were far from the present Christian conception of it. They believed in immortality and rewards, or punishments, in the hereafter. Many of them expected the coming of a divine ruler, a Messiah, who would establish a reign of peace.

---

[3]Curtin, *Hero Tales,* quoted in the Thirty-Second Annual Report of the Bureau of Am. Eth., on the Seneca Indians, Wash., 1918, p. 54.

[4]*Ibid.,* p. 62.

[5]"Vegetable gods, so called, have been scoffed at by writers on mythology. The scoff is baseless, for the first people were turned, or turned themselves, into trees and various plants as frequently as into beasts and other creatures. Maize, or Indian corn, is a transformed god who gave himself to be eaten, to save man from hunger and death." The Spaniards could not understand this theology. So, when they saw the natives eating little cakes and were told they were eating "gods," they concluded that Satan had taught them to mock and to blaspheme.—Curtin, quoted in the 32nd Ann. Rep., Bur. of Am. Ethn., p. 58.

A few extracts from Indian folk-lore should be of interest to the student of the Book of Mormon.

CREATION

The Chichés of Guatemala had a creation story, somewhat like this:

Behold the first word and the first discourse. There was no man, nor animal, nor bird, nor fish, nor crayfish, nòr any pit, nor ravine, nor green herb, nor any tree; nothing was but the firmament. The face of the earth had not appeared—only the peaceful sea, and all the space of heaven. There was nothing yet joined together, nothing that clung to anything else; nothing that balanced itself, that made the least rustling, that made a sound in the heaven. There was nothing but the sea, calm and alone in its boundaries; nothing existed; nothing but immobility and silence, in the darkness, in the night.

Then, the Creator, the Former, the Dominator, the Feathered Serpent—those that engender, those that give being, appear upon the water, like a growing light. They are enveloped in green and blue and are therefore called *Gucumatz*.[6] Then heaven and the Heart of Heaven come into existence. The Heart of Heaven is God. And they spoke; they consulted, and then they created. Earth, they said, and it was formed, like a cloud or a fog was its beginning. Then mountains rose over the water. The mountains and the plains were visible, and the cypress and the pine appeared. Then Gucumatz was filled with joy and shouted: Blessed be thy coming, O Heart of Heaven, Hurakan, Thunderbolt. Our work and our labor has accomplished its end.

After the earth had been thus prepared, various forms of animal life appeared. And the Makers said to the animals: Speak our name, honor us, your mother and father. Invoke Hurakan, the Heart of Heaven, the Heart of Earth, the Creator, the Former, Him who begets, Him who gives being—Speak, call on us, salute us! But the animals could not answer, they could not speak after the manner of men. Therefore the Creators decreed that the animals should be eaten.

Again the gods counseled together, and decided to make man. Accordingly, they made man of clay. But they did not succeed at first, wherefore the imperfect being which they had created was destroyed by water.

Again there was a council in heaven. "Let us make an intelligent being who shall adore and invoke us." The second attempt also was a failure. They lacked gratitude to their Maker and lived like beasts. They were therefore exterminated, all except a few who now live in the woods as little apes.

Again the gods consulted, whereupon the Creator made four perfect men; and wholly of yellow and white maize was their flesh composed. The names of the four men were, Balam-Quitze, Balam-Agab, Mahucutah and Iqi-Balam. They had neither father nor mother; they were wrought by the special intervention of the Creator. Now the gods could look on beings who could see with their eyes, and handle with their hands, and understand with their hearts. They gave thanks to the Creator for their existence.

But the Maker soon discovered that man's vision was too clear and his understanding too comprehensive. He aimed to become equal with God. The Heart of Heaven, therefore, breathed a cloud over the pupil of the eyes of men, and a veil came over it.

While the four men slept, the Creators made four women, Caha-Paluma for Balam-Quitze; Chomiha for Balam-Agab; Tzununiha for Mahucutah, and Cakixaha for Iqi-Balam. The women were exceedingly fair, and the men rejoiced over them.

---

[6]"The Feathered Serpent," supposed to be adorned with brilliantly colored plumage—green and blue, the colors of the sky and the vegetation.

Then other men were created, ancestors of other races than the Quiches in their various branches. At first these and the new-comers lived in peace together. They were filled with love and obedience. They had no religion, no altar. They lifted their eyes to heaven, where the bright morning star gave light, but they knew not why they had come to earth. But they prayed:

"Hail, O Creator, O Former! Thou that hearest and understandest us! Abandon us not, forsake us not! O God, thou that art in heaven and on the earth! Give us descendants and a posterity as long as the light endures. Give us to walk always in an open road, in the path without snares; to lead happy, quiet, and peaceable lives, free of all reproach."

Presently, the four men and their descendants set out for Tulan-Zuiva, also called the Seven Caves, and there each man as head of a family recieved a god. But Iqi-Balam had no children and founded no family, wherefore his god is not counted. Balam-Quitzes' god, Tohil, was the chief of all.

The journey to Tulan had been long, and the climate was cold there, but Tohil gave them fire. At Tulan the language was confused so that the people could not understand each other. Therefore they left Tulan under the guardianship of Tohil. They continued their journey amid the greatest hardships for want of food. They had to go through forests, to cross mountains, and to make a long voyage on the water. At length they came to a mountain which they called Hacavitz. Here they were given to understand that they were to see the sun. They rejoiced exceedingly, and danced and burned incense. A last the sun began to become visible. Then all creation rejoiced. Animals came to see the new wonder. The lion and the tiger roared. And the first bird that sang was Queletzu. All the animals rejoiced, and men prostrated themselves on the ground.

And now, when the sun rose, the three gods Tohil, Avilix, and Hacavitz were turned into stone, as were also other divinities connected with the lion, the tiger, and the viper. And thus the sun, by conquering inimical powers, prepared the earth for man.

Thus the story goes on, until the death of the four "first men," Balam-Quitze, Balam-Agab, Mahucutah, and Iqi-Balam, these men, "who came from the east, from the other side of the sea. Long had they been here when they died; and they were very old, and surnamed the Venerated and the Sacrificers."[7]

According to an old manuscript in the possession of Brasseur de Bourbourg, some of the Mexicans taught that the Creator produced his works in successive epochs. Man was made of dust on the seventh day, Ehecatl, but he was finished and perfected by Quetzalcoatl. The present age is said to be the fourth. It is called the Sun of Fire, and it is to be ended by a universal conflagration.

According to Another Legend. The Good Mind, when he had made the world, formed two images of the dust of the ground, in his own likeness, male and female, and by his breathing into their nostrils gave them the living souls, and named them, *Ea-gwe-howe,* "real people"; and he gave the great island and all the animals of game for their maintenance. * * * The bad mind, while his brother was making the universe, went throughout the island and made numerous high mountains and falls of water and great steps, and also created

[7]Bancroft, *Native Races,* Vol. 3, pp. 42-54.

various reptiles which would be injurious to mankind; but the Good Mind restored the island to its former condition. The bad mind proceeded further and made two images of clay in the form of mankind; but, while he was giving them existence, they became apes. * * * Another race was created which became highly civilized and made their residence in the southern parts of the island. But afterwards they were destroyed by barbarous nations, and their fortifications were ruined.

The story goes on to relate that there was a conflict between the Good Mind and the bad mind, in which the latter was defeated, whereupon he sank into the ground and said, as he disappeared, that he would have power over the spirits of men after death.

THE FLOOD

In addition to the creation story, the story of the Flood has been preserved almost all over the American continents.

The Mexican version says that during the age of water a great flood covered all the face of the earth, and the inhabitants were turned into fishes. Only one man, Coxcox, and his wife, Vochiquetzal, escaped. They saved themselves in the hollow trunk of a tree. They landed on the peak Colhuacan, where they increased and multiplied, but the children were all dumb, until a dove came and gave them innumerable tongues. Only fifteen of the descendants of Coxcox spoke the same language, and from these fifteen did the Toltecs, and the Acolhuas descend.

THE TOWER

The inhabitants of the Gila Valley believed that the Great Spirit made the earth and all living things. The first days of the world were happy and peaceful. Men and beasts talked together; a common language made all men brethren. But a flood came, in which all living beings perished, except Montezuma and his friend the coyote. They had made themselves boats and floated to dry land when the waters of the flood had subsided. The place where they landed is thus referred to in the legend: Montezuma sent the coyote out to find exactly where the sea lay. He went on four journeys. From the west and from the south, the answer swiftly came: The sea is near. A longer search was made towards the east. On the north no water was found, although the messenger wearied himself out, searching for it.

Montezuma was now the new ancestor of the race, but he did not remain faithful. Wickedness increased. Montezuma gathered the tribes together and began building a house which should reach up to heaven. Already it had attained great height. There were many apartments lined with gold and silver and precious stones. Then the Great Spirit let loose his thunder and laid the building in ruins.

A TRADITION OF THE ZUNI INDIANS[8]

The Zuni Indians in the western part of New Mexico are said to have a tradition to the effect that their ancestors journeyed from the northwest in quest of the "middle part of the world." Having found it, they settled down, until they were driven by a great flood that covered the earth. They, finally, located at Corn Mountain. These Indians, we are told, are believed to be composite people, some having come from the north and some from the south, just as the Book of Mormon leads us to believe concerning the descendants of Lehi, viz., that there first was a trek northward, when the Nephites retreated before the Lamanites; and then a southward movement after the battle of Cumorah.

THE TOTEM LEGEND

The word *totem* is, I understand, an Ojibway, or Chipeway Indian term meaning "friend." It is properly pronounced *do-daim*[9] and seems to be akin to the Hebrew *dod*, meaning "love," and also the object of love, such as a friend, a relative. A familiar form of the word is the name *David*, Arab., *Daod*, "beloved." It occurs in 1 Chron. 27:4 as *Dodai*, meaning one who loves the Lord.

To the Indians the totem is the symbol of the name of his progenitor. It is the name that is recorded on his grave stone, or whatever it is that marks his last resting place, and which identifies him and connects him, genealogically, with his ancestors. It, possibly, has some connection with his resurrection, for many Indians have the idea that the pronunciation of the name of the dead will resurrect them, and the Navajos do not permit the mentioning of a dead man's name.

A NAVAJO INDIAN'S STORY

Very many years ago the Grandmother brought from her home in the distant west nine races of men in the following forms: (1) The deer race; (2) the sand race; (3) the water race; (4) the bear race; (5) the hare race; (6) the wolf race; (7) the rattle snake race; (8) the tobacco plant race; (9) the reed grass race.

Having placed them on the spot where the village stands, she transformed them into men, who built the pueblos, and the distinction of the tribes have been kept up ever since.

The Indian narrator belonged to the deer race. That is, the

---

[8]*Ethnobotany of the Zuni Indians*, by Matilda Coxe Stevenson, 30th Ann. Rep. of Bur. of Am. Ethn., Smith. Inst., p. 35.

[9]*Neen dodaim*, "my totem friend." Ellen R. Emerson, *Indian Myths*, p. 238.

deer was his totem and the image of that animal indicated the identity of his tribal ancestor.[10]

A STRIKING COMPARISON

It is exceedingly interesting to compare these nine totem signs with the blessings pronounced by Jacob upon his sons, Gen. 49:3-27. Six of the nine are identical with the characteristics which the Patriarch appends to six of the names of his sons. These are:

(1) Deer race—Naphtali is a *hind*.
(2) Sand race—Zebulon shall dwell at the haven of the sea.[11]
(3) Water race—Reuben * * * unstable as *water*.
(6) Wolf race—Benjamin shall ravin as a *wolf*.
(7) Snake race—Dan shall be a *serpent*.
(9) Reed grass race—Issachar is a strong ass * * * and he saw that * * * the land was pleasant.[12]

The remaining three are not so obvious. But consider, for instance, the fifth. The totem is the hare.

The hare is an animal always hunted. But among the Indians it was also a representative of the Deity, as it was in Egypt, where it was the symbol of Osiris. "Among the Algonquins," says Prof. Fiske, "the sun god, Michabo, was represented as a hare, his name being compound of *nichi*, "great," and *wabos*, "hare." And Dr. Brinton tells us that the Powhatans of Virginia, the Lenni Lenapes of Delaware, the tribes of New England, the Ottawas of the far North, and the western tribes—all spoke of the great hare as their common ancestor, and the clan that had a right to this name, or rather the symbol of it, the totem, was looked up to with reverence. The hare, then, although an animal weak and hunted, was a symbol of the name of God.

Now, Jacob says of Joseph that the archers shot at him, but his bow abode in strength; hence is the Shepherd. That is to say, although he was hunted he became a savior, a shepherd. The Indian totem of the hare expresses these two ideas strikingly.

Who can escape the conclusion that some of the Indians, even if they themselves did not know it, preserved in their totem, a sort of record of their descent from Joseph, the greatest son of Jacob?

Concerning Simeon and Levi, Jacob said, in their anger they slew a man and in their self-will they "houghed oxen"; an exploit which might well have been performed by an angry brute with the strength of a *bear*. Finally, he said, Asher shall yield royal dainties. The *tobacco plant*, to the Indian, was just that. Smoking was part

---

[10]Ellen R. Emerson, *Indian Myths*, p. 238.
[11]Almost the entire coast line of Egypt and Palestine is vast *sand* beach.
[12]The simile is that of a donkey feeding in luxuriant *grass*.

of royal banquets, after feasts on tortillas, fish, tamales, ragouts, frog spawn, stewed ants, and sometimes human flesh. Smoking was a kind of religious ceremony, a burning of incense. "The nicotiana," says Schoolcraft, "was smoked and offered as incense to the Great Spirit, by all northern tribes."[13] The comparison between the tobacco plant totem and Asher, the son of Jacob, may, therefore, not be very inept.

AN INDIAN FUNERAL SERMON

That the Indians had about as clear ideas of a life hereafter, as most of us, who live now, have, may be gathered from the following excerpt from a funeral sermon:

"You are about to go to that land where our forefathers have gone. You have finished your journey here before us. We shall follow you and rejoin the happy groups which you will meet."[14]

INDIAN ELOQUENCE
(Sahagun, Book 6, Chapt. 25)

The following is an admonition of a father to his daughter:

"My dear daughter, precious as a gem and as sapphire, who art good and noble. It is now certain that our Lord, who is everywhere and shows kindness to whom he will, has remembered you. Perhaps your sighs and tears and the lifting of your hands before the Lord God, and the prayers and supplications which you have offered in the presence of our Lord, whose name is *Obscurity* and *Density,* in watches at midnight, have merited his favor; perhaps you have watched, perhaps you have employed yourself in weeping and in offering incense in his presence; perhaps for the sake of these things, our Lord hath dealt mercifully with you; perhaps on this very account it was determined before the beginning of the world in heaven and hell, that his kindness should be shown to you; perhaps it is true that our Lord Quetzalcoatl, who is the Maker and Former, has shown you his grace. Perhaps it had been decreed by the man and woman divinely named *Ometicutli and Ometicoatl.* Take care, my daughter, not to allow yourself to feel proud on account of the favor which has been shown to you: take care that you say not within yourself, *I* have conceived. Take care that you attribute not this favor to your own deserts, for should you do so, you will not be able to hide your inward thoughts from our Lord, for nothing is hidden from him, be it even within rock or tree; and thus you would excite his displeasure against you, and he would send some chastisement upon you, slaying your child in the womb, or causing it to be born an idiot, or to die in tender infancy; or perhaps our Lord would visit you with some disease of which you would die. For the fulfilment of our wish to have children depends upon the sole mercy of God, and if our thoughts are at variance with this truth, we defraud ourselves of the boon which he has vouchsafed us."[15]

ATAHUALPA'S DEFENSE

(From Com. Real., Garcilasso de la Vega, Transl. by Sir Paul Rycaut.)

When Pizarro had arranged for an audience with Atahualpa,

---

[13]*Hist. of the Indian Tribes,* Vol. 1, p. 109.
[14]*Ibid.,* Vol. 2, p. 68.
[15]Mrs. Simon, *The Ten Tribes of Israel,* p. 599.

at Caxamarca, in Peru, he sent to him an interpreter who explained to the Inca that the pope, who was the vice-gerent of Christ, had granted the newly discovered world to the Spanish monarch, wherefore it was the duty of the Inca to yield obedience to him and embrace his religion.

Atahualpa, who was in rebellion against his brother, Huascar, the real Inca, and plotted against his life, did not have a clear conscience, probably, but the reply he made to the challenge of Pizarro is, nevertheless, a classic, though the beauty of it, no doubt, is partly lost in the translation. He said, in part:

"And now, as far as I understand, methinks the discourse seems much different to that which your ambassadors propounded, for they treated of nothing but peace and friendship, of alliance and consanguinity; but now all the words of this Indian are nothing but menaces of wars, and death, and fire, and sword, with the extirpation and banishment of the Incas and their progeny; and that I must, voluntarily or by force, renounce all right to my kingdom and become tributary to another. From whence I collect one of these two things: That either you or your prince are tyrants and rove about to plunder the world, and to dispossess others of their kingdoms, killing and spoiling those who owe you nothing and never offered you injury or violence; or, otherwise you are the ministers of God (called by us *Pachamac*) whom he hath sent to visit us with vengeance and destruction. And if it be so, both I and my vassals do offer ourselves to death and to what punishment so ever you will inflict upon us; not for fear or out of any dread we have of your menaces or arms, but in compliance with the commands enjoined us by my father, Huayna Capac, at the time of his death; which was, that we should serve and honor a nation with beards like yourselves, which were to enter into these parts after his days and of which he prophesied some years before your ships coasted about our country, and whom he declared to be men with better laws, of more refined customs, more wise, and more valiant than ourselves. Wherefore, to fulfil the prophecy and testament of my father, we style you, *Viracochas,* understanding thereby that you are the messengers of the great god, Viracocha, whose will and pleasure, just indignation, arms and power, we are unable to resist; and yet, we are assured that he is all goodness and mercy. And for that reason you, who are his ministers and executioners of his will, ought to abstain from such robberies, slaughter, and violence as you committed in Tumpiz and the adjacent countries.

"In the next place, your interpreter acquaints me of five great personages whom I am to acknowledge. The first is God, who is three and one; that is, four, whom you call the Creator of this universe; which may, perhaps, be the same whom we call *Pachacamac* and *Viracocha*. The second is the father of all mankind, on whom all other men have heaped their sins. The third you call Jesus Christ, who was the only person who did not cast his sins on the first man, but that he died. The fourth you name is the pope. The fifth is Charles, whom, in comparison with others you call the most powerful monarch of the universe and the supreme lord of all."

Finally, the bewildered Inca said he could not understand why he should pay homage to any but God, who had created all things; to the man who was the father of all men, to Jesus Christ, who had no sins to "impute to him." As for Charles, he owed nothing to him. He never was the lord over Peru; he had never seen the country. But he, the Inca, would welcome further information.[16]

MIGRATION OF THE NAHUAS
(Fernando de Ixtlilxochitl)[17]

According to this writer, at the end of the "first age of the world, the earth was covered by water. A few families survived, and their descendants built a tower as a protection against future floods. The human race was scattered and the languages confounded, but seven families kept together and wandered about for years, crossing land and seas. Finally, they arrived at a place they called Huehue Tlapallan, which was a beautiful and desirable country.

At the end of the "second age" there was a great hurricane that swept away rocks and trees and houses. The people took refuge in caves. During the storm darkness prevailed. When the people emerged from the caves, they found a multitude of apes in the land.

Among the legends in the record is one concerning the arrest of the sun in his course and the part a humble mosquito played in starting it going again.

Next comes a legend concerning an earthquake in which many of the Quinames, many Chichimecs and Toltecs perished.

After this a period of peace came to the world, and during this time the wise Toltecs, both astrologers and other sages, gathered at a city called Huehue Tlapallan, "where they treated of many things, the calamities they had suffered and the movements of the heavens since the creation of the world, and of many other things," including the adjustment of their calendar to the actual solar year, and the arrangement of astronomical tables showing "years, months, weeks, days, signs, and planets, as they understood them." This was necessary because the records had all been destroyed.

One hundred and sixteen years after this event, there was another convulsion in nature. The sun and the moon were darkened, the earth shook, rocks were rent asunder, and many other things happened. "This," we are told, "was in the year *Ce Calli*, which, the chronology being reduced to our system, proves to be the same date when Christ, our Lord, suffered."

Three hundred and five years later there was a rebellion in the country against the legitimate rulers of the Toltecs. After long wars and conflicts the rebels were driven out of their stronghold in Huehue Tlapallan whereupon they settled in a place they called Tlapallan-

[16]Part II, Book 1, chapter 24.

[17]A Chichimec historian of the 16th century, who is supposed to have derived his information from documents that escaped the vandalism of the Spaniards.

conco, "Little Tlapallan." This is supposed to have happened in the fifth or sixth century, A. D.

Three years after the settlement in Little Tlapallan, the seven chiefs held council as to whether they should remain there permanently or go on. Then one of their great chiefs, named *Hueman*, or *Huematzin*, pointed out that they had suffered greatly, but that their sufferings had always been followed by great blessings. Their trouble, he said, "was a great evil immediately preceding the dawn of a greater good." He had, moreover, knowledge of a "broad and happy land" where the Quinames had lived for many years. This was situated towards the rising sun and was now depopulated. His counsel was that some of the people go there while others remain, who might, in time, become strong enough to recover their native land from the enemy. According to this counsel, a number of colonists left Little Tlapallan, eleven years after the exodus from Huehue Tlapallan.

Their stopping places, distances traveled, days occupied in travel, and general direction taken, as far as indicated, may be gathered from the subjoined table:

Stopping Places	Leagues Traveled	Days	Direction
Hueyzalan (Great Sandy)	70	12	near shore, east or west
Xalisco	100	20	near shore
Chimalhuacan Atenco	100	20	on the coast
Toxpan	80	18	east
Quiyahuitztlan Anahuac	100	20	east (in boats)
Zacatlan	80	18	
Tozapan	80	(18?)	
Tepetla	140	28	
Mazatepec	80	18	
Ziuhcohuatl	80	18	
Yztachuexucha	100	20	north
Tulancingo	80	18	
	1090 lgs.	228 days	

At Tulancingo they built a "house" — a pueblo, probably, — large enough to contain all the people. They lived there eighteen years before they moved to Tollan, farther east. They are thought to have reached Anahuac in the 6th or 7th century, A. D. They were, according to Ixtlilxochitl, 108 years on the road from Huehue Tlapallan, having halted generally serveral years in each place mentioned, and as much as 26 years in one place, Yztachuexucha.

It is not possible to understand all the details of this strange record. But this seems clear: There was a Tlapallan in the Old World, from which the Nahuas came, driven by convulsions of nature, or, more probably, by political upheavals which in Oriental phraseology often are represented as "earthquakes" and the darkening of the luminaries in the sky. Then there was a Huehue Tlapallan in the new country, from which they were expelled during a time of civil war, whereupon they undertook a migration of 1,090 leagues.

The recollection of the various migration traditions says Bancroft,[18] assumed different forms in the traditions of tribes until each nation claimed, or was deemed to claim, by the Spaniards, a distinct migration from its former home.

LENAPE ANNALS

The Book of Mormon is the only now known inspired record of the ancient Americans, and as such it has a value and an importance beyond calculation. But it is not the only early American record ever made. In Mexico and Central America, particularly, literature was flourishing. Writings, generally called hieroglyphics, adorn monuments and temples at Chiapas, Palenque, Copan, Chichen-Itza and Quirigua, to mention only a few places. A kind of hieratic writing, known to the initiated only, was, according to Nadaillac, made by the priests, specimens of which have come down to us in the Dresden manuscript, the Thoano manuscript, and a few others.

Bishop Landa thought he had discovered an alphabet of thirty-three signs, or letters, but these seem to have proved of no value to student of the monuments and the manuscripts. The hieroglyphs, as far as read, refer to astronomical dates and calculations.

According to a tradition recorded by Bancroft, during the reign of a Toltec king, Ixtlilcuechalmac, toward the end of the seventh century a meeting of the wise men was held under the direction of one Hueman. At this congress all Toltec records were brought together, and after careful study a volume was compiled which they called the *Teomorxtli*, or "The Book of God." This book is said to have contained a history of the world from the deluge, or even from the creation, together with the rites, laws and social customs of the people. It ended with prophecies concerning the future. Hueman, we are told, died shortly after the completion of this work, at the age of 300 years.

The books were made of cotton cloth, or of skins specially prepared, or of a composition of silk and gum, but more generally from the leaves of the aloe plant, called by the natives the *maguey*, from which a kind of paper was made, resembling the Egyptian papyrus. Sometimes they were made up in rolls, as Hebrew parchments, but sometimes folded like a folding screen, with a tablet of wood at each end, and when a manuscript was thus folded and closed, it resembled somewhat a modern bound volume. At the time of the arrival of

---

[18]See Bancroft, *Native Races*, Vol. 5, pp. 209-218.

the Spaniards, there were large quantities of such records in the country. There were numerous scribes, whose skill in drawing hieroglyphs astonished the new-comers.

Picture writing was more generally practiced. It is found in South America, in Central America, and North America. Some drawings are, no doubt, only the inspirations of primitive artists, but others are true writings, intended to convey information, or to record events, as a matter of tradition or history.

Such writings are sometimes symbolical. That is one picture may stand for a complex idea, one that we express by a sentence, or even several sentences. In such a case the meaning of the picture is unknown except as it is accompanied by the sentence it represents. The Lenapes had such writings, which have been preserved. The figures were engraved or painted on bark or slabs of wood, as the Norse runes. One of these came into the possession of Professor Rafinesque, who published a translation of it in 1836, in Philadelphia. Later it became the property of Dr. Brinton who, in 1885, published a facsimile of the symbols, together with the explanatory Indian text, and a translation of his own. The priceless North American record contains the traditions of the Lenapes and related tribes. It begins with the creation. It mentions the flood, and then the crossing of their forefathers over some large water on the ice, and continues with a history of the wanderings and wars of the people. It records the coming of the Europeans from the east, and closes about the year 1820, with the statement that Kithtilkund and Lapanibi, chiefs of two tribes, had agreed to return to the region beyond the *Masispek* (Mississippi). "Shall we be free and happy there?" the chronicler asks. "We want," he adds, "rest, and peace, and wisdom."

These records, Rafinesque observes, seem to be but adbridgments of more copious annals, or the bases of their traditions. "The Niniwas or Chippewas, the Ottowas, the Sakis and Shawanis, all Lenape tribes, have such painted tales and annals, called *Neobagun* by the former."

The Delawares, too, had records. Loskiel says: "The Delawares keep genealogies, with the character of each man, if wise, rich, renowned, or a mighty warrior. They use hieroglyphs on wood, trees and stones, to give caution, information, communicate events, achievements, keep records. Sometimes the hero has at his feet men, heads, or weapons. They have also paintings on skins of deeds, hunts, feats, etc."

A few extracts from the Lenape records or songs are here offered the reader.

I. THE CREATION

At first there was nothing but seawater on the top of the land.

There was much water, and much fog over the land, and there was also the God-creator.

And this God-creator was the first Being, an eternal Being and invisible, although everywhere.

It was he who caused much water, much land, much cloud, much heaven.

It was he who caused the sun, the moon, the stars.

And all these he caused to move well.

By his action it blew hard, it clear up, and the deep water ran off.

It looks bright, and islands stood there.

It was then, when again the God-creator made the makers, or spirits.

And also the first beings, and also the angels, and also the souls, all of them he made.

And afterwards he made the man-being, ancestor of the men.

He gave him the first mother, mother of the first beings.

And fishes he gave him, turtles he gave him, beasts he gave him, birds he gave him.

II. SNAKE WORSHIP

But there was a bad spirit who caused the bad beings, black snakes, and monsters or large reptiles.

And caused also flies, and caused also gnats.

All the beings were then friends and stood there.

Thou being *Kiwis,* good God *Wunand,* and the good makers, or spirits, were such.

With the jins *Nijini,* the first men, and the first mother, their wives, which were Fairies.

The first food of the jins and Fairies was a fat fruit.

All were willingly pleased, all were easy-thinking, and all were well-happified.

But after awhile a snake priest brings on earth seceretly the snake worship of the god of the snakes.

And there came wickedness, crime and unhappiness.

And bad weather was coming, distemper was coming, with death was coming.

All this happened very long ago, at the first land beyond the great ocean.

III. THE FLOOD

There was long ago a powerful Snake, when the men had become bad beings.

This strong Snake had become the foe of the jins, and they became troubled, hating each other.

Both were fighting, both were spoiling, both were never peaceful.

And they were fighting, least man with dead-keeper.

And the strong Snake readily resolved to destroy or fight the beings of the men.

The dark Snake he brought, the monster he brought, snake rushing-water he brought.

Much water is rushing, much go to hills, much penetrate, much destroying.

Meantime at *Tula,* at that island, *Nanabush* became the ancestor of beings and men.

Being born creeping, he is ready to move and dwell at *Tula.*

The beings and men, all go forth from the flood, creeping in shallow water, or swimming afloat, asking which is the way to the turtle back.

But there were many monsters in the way, and some men were devoured by them.

But the daughter of a spirit helped them in a boat, saying, Come, come; they were coming and were helped.

Nanabush, Nanabush became the grandfather of all, the grandfather of the beings, the grandfather of the men, and the grandfather of the turtles.

The men were there, they turtle there, they were turtling all together.

He was frightened, he the turtle, he was praying, he the turtle, let it be to make well.

Water running off, it is drying in the plains and the mountains, at the path of the cave, elsewhere went the powerful action.

IV. THE CROSSING OF THE WATER

After the flood, the manly men (Lenapes) with the manly turtle beings dwelt close together at the cave house and dwellings at *Talli.*

It freezes was there, it snows was there, it is cold was there.

To possess mild coldness and much game, they go to the northerly plain; to hunt cattle they go.

To be strong and to be rich, the comers divided into tillers and hunters.

The most strong, the most good, the most holy, the hunters they are.

And the hunters spread themselves, becoming Northerlings, Easterlings, Southerlings, Westerlings.

Thus the White country (Lumonaki), north of the Turtle country, became the hunting country of the turtling true men.

Meantime, all the Snakes were afraid in their huts, and the Snake priest said to all, let us go.

Easterly they go forth at Snakeland, and they went away earnestly grieving.

Thus escaping by going so far, and by trembling the burnt land is torn and is broken from the Snake fortified land.

Being free, having no trouble, the Northerlings all go out separating at the Land of Snow.

The fish resort to the shores of the gaping sea, where tarried the fathers of White Eagle and White Wolf.

While our fathers were always boating and navigating, they say in the east that the Snakeland was bright and wealthy.

The Head-beaver and the Big-bird were saying to all, let us go to the Snake island. By going with us, we shall annihilate all the Snaking people.

Having all agreed, the Northerlings and Easterlings went over the water of the frozen sea, to possess that land.

It was wonderful when they all went over the smooth deep water of the frozen sea, at the gap of the snake sea in the great ocean.

They were ten thousand in the dark, who all go forth in a single night in the dark, to the Snake island of the eastern land in the dark, by walking all the people.

They were the manly north, the manly east, the manly south; with manly Eagle, manly Beaver, manly Wolf; with manly hunter, manly priest, manly rich; with manly wife, manly daughter, manly dog.

All coming there, they tarry at Firland. But the Western men, doubtful of the passage, preferred to remain at the old Turtle land.

NOTES[19]

The translation of these Indian annals was completed in 1833, three years after the Book of Mormon had been published. It took

---

[19]From the *Improvement Era* for September, 1926.

the translator thirteen years, from the time he obtained the manuscript, to accomplish the task. He had to learn the language first.

The story of the creation in this record is remarkably like the account in Genesis. In both, the land is covered with water and vapor. The divine Creator, in Genesis, caused his Spirit to move upon the waters; in the Indian record he causes a wind to blow, and then the land appears.

In both accounts the Creator is the Originator of the heavens and the earth, and all that is in them, including spirits, the first beings, souls and the progenitors of the human race. In both, man is given dominion over the fishes in the sea, the animals of the field, the birds in the air, and all creeping things.

The accounts are so strikingly similar as to force us to conclude that they have come from the same source, and for that reason these annals are a remarkable confirmation of Genesis.

To one familiar with the language of the record the similarity between this narrative and that of Genesis would be more striking. The ancestor of men, for instance, is *Jinwis,* which word, Professor Rafinesque says, is identic with the Hebrew *ish* man the "w" being the masculine article "h."

In the story of the Snake worship we are told that peace and harmony prevailed in all nature, until a "Snake-priest" secretly introduced the Snake worship of the god of the Snakes. That caused a total change.

These Snakes evidently were, or were supposed to be "the black Snakes," a class of people which, the record says, were originated by a "bad spirit." The reference is not to the transgression of Adam, but rather to the fall of Cain, of whom we read in the Pearl of Great Price (p. 12 and 13, new edition) that he entered into secret compacts with Satan, to murder and get gain, and that Lamech succeeded him. As Satan is the "dragon" "the old Serpent," so Cain may well be referred to as the Snake priest who introduced Snake worship and its abominable secrets.

Beyond the Great Ocean. If the story was originally told to the children and descendants of Noah in the Old World, then, "beyond the great ocean" would, of course, mean on the American continents.

The story of the deluge is very much similar to the account in Genesis. A "powerful Snake" predominates on earth — that is, some follower of Cain and Lamech — and, as a consequence, there is strife and war everywhere. Then the "black Snake," Satan, undertakes to destroy the human race and all living creatures by a deluge. The waters rush and accomplish destruction. But Nanabush, the Noah of

Genesis, who was "born creeping" — that is to say humble — was willing to dwell in *Tula,* and there he was saved, and became the second ancestor of the race.

Tula. The word Tula is the name of the place from which the Toltecs and other nations in Mexico, according to their traditions, came. But in the Lenape, Professor Rafinesque says, it means "turtle" or "tortoise." It is the same as the Hebrew *Tor,* meaning strong. The Tula in the narrative is, therefore, the ark — the "tebah" of Genesis.

The story of the crossing of the water deserves close study.

According to the records, "Men" and "Turtles" dwell together near the cave house. They are, undoubtedly, two different tribes. The "Men" may be supposed to refer to some particularly prominent group, and the "Turtles" may have been so called from some special connection with the ark.

The Cave House. Many Indians have tradtiions of a cove, or several caves, from which their ancestors emerged. Many refer to ships in which they came across the deep.

It was cold in that place, and, consequently, the people decided to go to a plain to the north, where the climate was more congenial and the game more plentiful.

On this plain they divided into "tillers and hunters."

The hunters spread out over a wide area and became Northerlings, Easterlings, Southerlings, and Westerlings. And thus the White country (*Lumonaki*), north of the Turtle country, became the hunting ground of the valiant Turtles.

But in this new country there was another race, referred to in the record as "Snakes." These were trembling in their huts because of the invasion, wherefore their priest induced them to evacuate the country. They obeyed regretfully, and emigrated in an easterly direction. At the same time, some catasrophe in Nature devastated the old country by fire, and separated it in some way from the new Snakeland. The Northerlings were now free to roam, and they reached out as far as the Land of Snow.

We are now told of a place by the "gaping sea," where fish (perhaps shell fish) is abundant, and where the progenitors of White Eagle and White Wolf once had lived. Here, while the men were boating and sailing, they discovered Snakeland in the east, and found it to be a bright and wealthy country. Two great chiefs then persuade the people to invade Snakeland and exterminate the Snakes. The Northerlings and Easterlings crossed the water on smooth ice, to the number of 10,000, in one dark night. Having arrived in Snakeland, they settled in a country called Firland.

It is supposed that this refers to the crossing of the Bering Strait by Indian ancestors. But that notion must be given up as too fanciful. Ten thousand people could not be marched across 50 miles of frozen sea in one dark night. The Arctic ice is by no means smooth and even. When drifting cakes freeze together, they form ridges and obstacles of such a formidable nature that Arctic explorers sometimes have not been able to progress more than half a mile a day, and one authority has said that Commander Peary could not possibly have traveled 57 miles a day, though he had the advantage of broad daylight. Besides, the rocky, barren shores of the American side of the strait would hardly have attracted settlers from a country with plenty of game and an abundance of fish. If the tradition has an historical basis, as it, no doubt, has, that must be sought in some other crossing. Some river or narrow strait might be crossed in boats in one night, as Washington crossed the Delaware. Charles X, of Sweden, it is true, with his army, crossed the Little Belt on the ice, between the mainland and the island of Fyen, in 1658, but that strait is only a mile across at its narrowest point, and yet that is regarded as quite a feat in the grim history of war.

But if this was not a passage over Bering Strait, where could it have happened? Possibly it was not a march on the ice at all. The translators may have misunderstood the symbolic pictures, especially if they have been at all influenced by pre-conceived theories, as sometimes will happen. In the story of Deganawida it is said, that after he left his home he crossed the water in a "white canoe," which was perhaps a canoe of white birch. This, tradition has made first an "ice canoe," that is an ice flake, and finally a "flint" or "stone" canoe.[20] Whether some such mistake has happened in this record is a question. The "ice" may have been white canoes. But that is a question that must be left to scholars to clear up. If the ice feature is eliminated, there are many places that might fit the narrative.

The records follow the wanderings and divisions and conflicts of the people. At the Fish River (Nemasipi), which "separated the land," they settled for some time. Professor Rafinesque remarks that, according to Hekewelder, this river is the Mississippi, but the professor thinks it is the Illinois River. But here, he says, began the wars with the *Talegas*, the northern *Toltecs* or *Atlantes*, circa 48 generations before 1600, or near the beginning of our era, which continued for four generations, over 130 years, till about 150 after Christ. The allies, *Talamatans*, which are the Hurons and Iroquois, then united. They are since called *Delamanatans* and *Lamantans*.

---

[20]J. N. B. Hewitt, Smiths. Rep. for 1918, p. 537.

Laman. In these names, as in the geographical name *Lumonaki* (the White Country), the name of Laman seems to be perpetuated.

Sidon. That name means Fishing River. It is the name of a famous river in the Book of Mormon. The name Mississippi has the same meaning. The famous river in the Book of Mormon and the famous North American river have, if the meaning is considered, identically the same name.

Two lessons are brought home to us, when we compare the Book of Mormon and other ancient American records.

One is the absolute originality of the Book of Mormon. It is an independent document, with not the slightest trace of plagiarism.

The material on which it is written is neither cotton, nor silk, nor the maguey leaves, nor even stone slabs, but metal plates, the very best material for the purpose of the compilers of the book.

The script used is neither the hieroglyphs of the Mayas, nor the picture writing of other aborigines, but a simplification of "reformed Egyptian," which I suppose to be the "Old Israelitic," with which Lehi must have been familiar, and which actually was a "reformed Egyptian" alphabet, adapted to the needs of practical businessmen, like the Phœnicians.

The subject and scope of the Book are equally original. It is not, and it does not profess to be, a universal history of the American race, its origin, its development, its degeneration and wanderings and vicissitudes. It is neither a Maya record, nor an Aztec, nor an Inca, nor an Algonquin, but a Nephite record. It is one of the several original American records, with its own field. It tells us in broad outlines something of the history of the Jaredites, or rather a small portion of them; of the colonists of Lehi, with its two main divisions, and of the Mulekites. But it does not give us to understand that these are the only people that ever inhabited or ever settled on the American continents.

Another lesson is the agreement in the main features of the Book of Mormon history and other records. American ancient history is the history of retrogression from a very high cultural level to a lower one, due to disintegration and strife, with notable efforts here and there to regain the lost heights. This fact is written all over the American continents. And the agreement of the Book of Mormon with these facts is one of the strong evidences of the truth of the sacred volume, and this evidence is strengthened by every new discovery in the wonderful domain of American archæology.

A Book from Heaven.[21] In 1832 four Indians appeared on the streets of St. Louis and asked for food. They were wan and haggard, for they had come a journey of several hundred miles from the wilds of the far west. Two of them were from the Nez Perces, while the others were of the tribe of Flatheads, who roamed the country on the headwaters of the Missouri and Columbia rivers. They explained that they had heard of the "White Man's Book From Heaven" and they had come to find it.

General George Clark, the commander of the military post at St. Louis, entertained the visitors. They were shown about the frontier town, which to them was the "civilization of the palefaces." Two of the Indians soon died and then it was the others decided to return to the land of their fathers. Before their departure General Clark gave them a feast, to which a number of officers and citizens of St. Louis were invited.

The two Indians, whose names were Rabbit-Skin-Legings and No-Horns-on-His-Head, respectively, listened to the speeches of the Americans, and particularly were they told about the Bible and the desire of the whites to treat the Indians with justice. One of the Indians then arose and addressed the assembly in words humble yet dignified:

"I came to you over a trail of many moons from the setting sun. You were the friend of my fathers who have all gone the long way. I came with one eye open for more light for my people who sit in darkness. I go back with both eyes closed. How can I go back blind to my people? I made my way to you with strong arms, through many enemies and strange lands, that I might carry much back to them. I go back with both arms broken and empty. The two fathers who came with me— the braves of many winters and wars—we leave asleep here by your great water. They were tired in many moons and their moccasins worn out.

"My people sent me to get the white man's Book from Heaven. You took me where you allow your women to dance, as we do not ours, and the Book was not there. You took me where they worship the Great Spirit with candles, as we do not ours. The Book was not there. You showed me images of the Great Spirit and pictures of the good and the beyond, but the Book was not among them. I am going back the long trail and sad trail to my people of the dark land. You make my feet heavy with burdens of gifts, and my moccasins will grow old in carrying them, but the Book is not among them. When I tell my poor people, after one more snow, in the Council, that I did not bring the Book, no word will be spoken by our old men and our young people will die in darkness, and they will go on the long path to other hunting grounds. No white man will go with them and no white man's book to make the way plain. I have no more words."

In the paper from which this remarkable story is copied, there are several incidents told by Prof. Young, which are interesting in connection with their religious concepts, myths, legends and practices. For they show us the noble character of the race — the fruit of their

---

[21]This, and the rest of this chapter is from an article by Prof. Levi Edgar Young in the *Salt Lake Tribune,* Dec. 31, 1922.

faith, or their inheritance from great ancestors. And the tree must be judged by the fruit.

Columbus and the Indians. One of the first instances we have, if it is not the first, of Indian hospitality and good-will is the story told of the great chief Guacanagari, who entertained Christopher Columbus when the discoverer of America reached Cuba in 1492. So impressed was the admiral with the chief and his people that he was led to write:

"So loving, so tractable, so peaceable are these people that I swear to your majesties there is not in the world a better nation nor a better land. They love their neighbors as themselves, and their discourse is ever sweet and gentle and, accompanied with a smile; and though it is true that they are naked, yet their manners are decorous and praiseworthy."

When Columbus was shipwrecked off the coast of Cuba, Guacanagari "immediately sent all his people with all the canoes, large and small, that could be mustered. The cacique himself and his brothers and relatives rendered all the aid in their power, both on sea and land. From time to time he sent some one of his family, or some principal person of his attendants, to console and cheer the admiral, assuring him that everything he possessed should be at his disposal."

Washington Irving, in his *Life of Columbus,* says "That never in a civilized country were the vaunted rights of hospitality more scrupulously observed than by this uncultivated savage."

Governor Brigham Young Among the Indians. In 1854 Governor Young, with a party of horsemen and others in wagons, left Salt Lake City to visit the settlements in the southern part of the territory and to hold peace meetings if possible with Wakara and others who were carrying on a well developed plan of warfare against the settlements of Sanpete, Sevier and villages farther south. Captain Gunnison, with his companions, had been massacred by the Parvian Indians, and there was great excitement among the inhabitants of the villages. The people withdrew within the walls of their towns for protection and vigilant watchers, well armed, patrolled them all night.

Major Bidwell, the Indian agent, made arrangements for Governor Young to meet Wakara and the other Indian chiefs that a treaty of peace might be made. An imposing party of men on horses and under Governor Young went out to the camping grounds of the Utah chief, who had sent out word that "If Governor Young wanted to see him, he must come to him at his camp, as he did not intend to leave it to see anybody."

The governor realized that Wakara was a king and great chief, and, taking with him sixteen head of cattle, some blankets and clothing, as well as trinkets, arms and ammunition to give to the Indians, he approached the Wakara camp, which was protected by a number of chiefs on guard. Wakara sat on his buffalo robe, wrapped in his blanket, with the old chiefs around him. He did not rise, but held out his hand to Governor Young, and made room for him by his side. They shook hands, and for a number of minutes there was intense silence.

Finally the chief of the Sanpete Indians arose, and with tears rolling down his furrowed cheeks he gave utterance to his grievances.

"My son," he said, "was a brave chief. He was good to his old father and mother. One day, Wa-yo-sha was hunting rabbits as food for his old parents, when the rifle of the white man killed him. When the night came and he was still absent, his old mother· went to look for her son. She walked a long way through the thick bushes. At the dawn of day, the mother and son were both away, and the infirm and aged warrior was lonely. He followed the trail of his wife in the bush, and there he found the mother of his child lying over the body of Wa-yo-sha, both dead from the same bullet. The old woman met her son, and while they were returning home a bullet from the rifle of Americans shot them both down. Old Sanpete can fight no more. His hands tremble, his eyes are dim, the murderer of his wife and brave Wa-yo-sha is still living. San Pete no make peace with Americats."

The old warrior sank down exhausted on his blanket, and all remained silent. Governor Young asked Wakara to speak, but he refused. "Wakara got no heart to speak," said he, "no can talk today. Tonight, Wakara talk with Great Spirit. Tomorrow, Wakara talk with governor."

Walkara Speaks. The next morning the council assembled again. Governor Young brought cattle and other presents to the camp of Wakara, and sat down to hear what the old chief had to say. Wakara, who is a man of imposing appearance, was attired in only a deerskin hunting shirt, although it was very cold. His blue blanket lay at his side. He looked careworn and haggard, and spoke as follows:

"Wakara has heard all the talk of the good Mormon chief. Wakara no like to go to war with him. Sometimes, Wakara take his men and go long way off to sell horses. When he is absent, then Mericats come and kill his wife and children. Why not come and fight Wakara when he is at home? Wakara is accused of killing Captain Gunnison. Wakara did not. Wakara was three hundred miles away when the Mericat was slain. Mericat soldiers hunt Wakara to kill him, but no find him. Wakara hear it. Wakara come home. Wakara's heart very sore. Mericats kill Parvian Indian chief, and Parvian woman. Parvian young men watch for Mericats, and kill them, because Great Spirit says 'Mericats kill Indians; Indians kill Mericats.' Wakara talk with Great Spirit, Great Spirit say 'Make peace.' Wakara love Mormon chief. He is good man. When Mormon came to live on Wakara's land, Wakara gave him welcome. He gave Wakara plenty bread and clothing for wife and children. Wakara talked last night to Kahutah, Sanpete, Parvian—all Indian say 'No fight Mericats more.' If Indian kill white man again, Wakara make Indian howl."

The calumet of peace was again handed round, and all the party smoked. The council was then dismissed. Peace was made and Wakara and his braves acted as a guard to the governor and his party on much of the remaining journey.

SOME OF THE FUNDAMENTAL DOCTRINES
OF THE BOOK OF MORMON

This attempt at an introduction to the study of the Book of Mormon would be incomplete without a brief statement of some of the fundamental doctrines of this wonderful record.

CONCERNING GOD

The Cosmological Argument. The Book of Mormon resembles the Bible in this respect that it takes the existence of God for granted. Handbooks on theology generally begin by stating the philosophical arguments supposed to *prove* that there is a supreme Being, but God's books do not argue that question. "In the beginning God created the heavens and the earth" is the sublime opening statement of the Bible. One of the first incidents told in the Book of Mormon is that of a vision of the Prophet Lehi, in which he sees "God sitting upon his throne, surrounded by numerous concourses of angels in the attitude of singing and praising their God." (I Nephi 1:8) There is no attempt at argument; no appeal to the reasoning faculty of man; only a plain statement of a sublime fact, in the simplest possible language: *God Is.*

And yet, when the inspired writer has occasion to rebuke, he applies the cosmological argument with the greatest possible force. He says:

"If there be no God, we are not, for there could have been no creation." (II Nephi 11:7.)

That argument is unanswerable.

Philosophers have, indeed, asserted that God is not needed to accounts for the existence of worlds. Matter itself, they have told us, possesses all the potency necessary for all established facts. In this conclusion vast numbers in our superficial age concur and, at least pretend to, find satisfaction. If published accounts are true,[1] atheism is spreading with astonishing rapidity, not only among the illiterate but in our schools, colleges and universities, as well as outside our institutions of learning, as a result of intense propaganda of a strong association for the advancement of atheism.

The aims of this association are freely stated: Do away with chaplains in congress, legislatures, and in the army and navy. Recognize no religious festivals. Stop "bootlegging" Bible and religion in

---

[1]*Literary Digest,* July 2, 1927.

the schools. Use no Bibles to take an oath on. Do away with Christian morality. Take "In God We Trust" off the coins.

This program has been adopted by numerous organizations, calling themselves the society of "Damned Souls," "The Society of Godless," "God's Black Sheep," "The Devil's Angels," and other similar names. One of their publications has the following blasphemous paragraph:

"The Greek Zeus used to strike fear into the hearts of all but the most courageous. Today he is a harmless, powerless relic. Jupiter made the Romans hit the sawdust trail, but today even a Christian Fundamentalist isn't afraid to thumb his nose at this scepterless God. If history repeats itself—and they say it does—perhaps some day the bewhiskered Jewish—[let us leave the sacred name out]—will no longer be 'Big Bad Bill.' "[2]

Against such ignorant, blasphemous, arrogant atheism, the writers of the Book of Mormon stand up, as it were from their graves, in righteous rebuke. They say, in substance: You atheists, you materialists, you monists, etc., do not go far enough in your negation. You deny the existence of God, but, in order to be consistent, you must also deny the existence of the land in which you live, and the mountains, the islands, the forests, the animals, the plants, the earth, the sea, the sun, the stars, and, above all, your own existence, and say that the whole creation is only imagination. To admit the reality of the creation and then deny the existence of the Creator is an inconsistency, a self-contradiction, impossible in the reasoning of any intelligent being.

The Book of Mormon testifies to the existence of God (II Nephi 2:13, 14; 11:7; Moroni 9:19) against all forms of atheism, and gives us as complete a picture of the Godhead as we in our mortal state, can perceive.

Three Persons in the Godhead. According to the Book of Mormon, as well as the Bible, there are three glorious, exalted, sovereign persons in the Dodhead: The Father, the Son and the Holy Ghost.

Originally the term *God* included the entire plurality of divine personages, and even archangels and angels. The divine name, *Elohim* (the plural form) proves the plurality, but gradually that form of the word became the name of the supreme Ruler of the universe. He is the Elohim, the mighty One, also called the Father,[3] and the name is retained to denote the greatness of his majesty, power

[2]*Literary Digest,* July 2, 1927.

[3]The words "Yahweh our Gods," which show that Yahweh was identified with the Gods, *Elohim,* of the polytheistic period of the ancient Hebrew religion; it is, however, possible that when the verse in Deuteronomy was written the word Elohim had come to mean that Great God of the Hebrews, although originally it had meant a collection of sacred divine beings. (E. A. Wallis Budge, *The Gods of the Egyptians,* Vol. 1, p. 141.)

and glory. Generally, when the name is used without any qualification, it stands for the first *Person* in the Godhead.

The Father: Two Theories. There are two main theories concerning the relationship of God, the Father, to the children of men.

One conceives chiefly in cold juridic terms. He is an absolute sovereign, an avenger of sin for his own glory, meeting out punishment in an eternal fire, merely to satisfy his hunger and thirst for justice. In this concept of God, man comes in as a corrupt, diseased or otherwise defective being, utterly helpless. Some have even gone so far as to assert that God decreed that a certain number of human beings were created for the purpose of sinning, in order that the Creator might have a chance to send them to eternal torment and thereby display his own power and glory.

Christ taught the doctrine of the Fatherhood of God and the brotherhood of man, and that is the other conception of the relationship between God and man. It is as old as mankind. Christ revived it. His disciples proclaimed it and endeavored to put it into practice. It was almost lost sight of again until the Reformation, when it was brought to the attention of those who yearned for human liberty, and it contributed greatly to the success of the world struggles which culminated in the form of government upon which our republic rests. For this government recognizes human rights as between man and man, rulers and ruled, and it has become clear that God Himself, who raised up men to institute this government, surely respects the rights and privileges He has given His children, which are the very foundation of their responsibility as free agents.

With the attention thus turned to the doctrine of the Fatherhood of God, the life of Christ has been studied more closely than ever, since it is in Christ that God, the Father, is most clearly revealed.

In the Book of Mormon God is revealed as the Eternal Father, the Creator, Omnipotent, Infinite in perfection, in wisdom, goodness, in love and mercy, as well as justice. He reigns supreme and he proclaims His Son to the children of men: "Behold my beloved Son, in whom I have glorified my name—hear ye him."

References: I Nephi 11:21; 13:40; Mosiah 15:4; I Nephi 17:36; II Nephi 2:14; Jacob 4:9; I Nephi 1:14; Mosiah 3:5; III Nephi 12:48; II Nephi 1:10; II Nephi 1:15; 4:21; 26:24; Mosiah 4:11; Jacob 3:2; Mosiah 13:14; I Nephi 16:35; II Nephi 9:17, 26, 46; Mosiah 3:38; I Nephi 22:26; Mosiah 3:5; 12:21; III Nephi 11:3-7.

It is perfectly clear from this, that God, in the Book of Mormon, is revealed as a sovereign, but who rules as a wise, good, loving, and just Father in the midst of his family; not as an Eastern despot in the midst of slaves and sycophants. He is the supreme Ruler of beings to whom he has given free agency, and he rules under the celestial law of Common Consent. In his sovereignty he controls even that which seems accidental. Even seemingly trifling means and sometimes the wicked, serve, unknown to themselves, his purposes. He forgives the repentant sinner. He hears and answers prayers, and he takes care of those who put their trust in him, as loving, obedient children.

References: I Nephi 16:20; Alma 19:36; 26:37; 29:8; Jacob 7:22; Alma 33:4-6; Mosiah 27:14; III Nephi 17:15-21.

The Son. There is a tendency among modern professors of Christianity to accept the doctrine of the divinity of Jesus, on the slippery ground that every human is divine. This, they argue, follows from the fact that all nature is permeated by the divine, supreme essence. In one sense, thy say, all men are divine, and Christ is no more divine than we all are, or than all existing creatures are, for that matter. The only difference between him and us is, in their view, this, that he realized that he was divine, while we hope to be able to realize our divinity — some day.

It is not denied that there is some truth in the conception of a universal divinity. We are all God's children. But Christ is much more than a child among children. He is the Creator, our Savior, our Redeemer, the Captain of our Salvation, the Mediator between the Father and the rest of God's children. And that is a great difference.

The Book of Mormon is a mighty witness for the divine character and mission of our Lord.

This record states expressly that He is God: "There is a God, and he is Christ." He is "the Eternal God," and "God Omnipotent." He who died for us is the "Creator," the "Father of heaven and of earth, the Creator of all things." He is "the Father," the "Eternal Father," the *"Beginning* and the *End, the First* and the *Last."* He is so intimately associated with God, the Father, that, in his relation to the children of men, he is both the Father and the Son. He stands in God's stead. God has delegated to him all power in heaven and on earth, and he is one member of the great, divine, presiding and governing Council of Three, the Father, Son and the Holy Ghost, to whose communion baptism in his name and by his authority admits the redeemed child of God. He is, furthermore, "without beginning of days or end of years."

References: II Nephi 11:7; 26:12; Mosiah 5:15; II Nephi 9:5; Helaman 14:12; Mosiah 7:27; Alma 11:38, 39; III Nephi 11:27; Mosiah 15:2; Ether 3:14; Alma 13:9.

But although he is, in this sense, God, the Father, God, clothed in majesty and power and glory, he is also the Son of God; he is the "Beloved Son," in whom the Father has glorified his name; he is the "Only Begotten Son," and also the "Redeemer" and the "Lamb of God," and the only "Savior" of mankind.

References: I Nephi 10:17; 11:17; Alma 13:16; Helaman 3:28; III Nephi 9:15; III Nephi 11:7; Jacob 4:5, 11; Alma 12:33, 34; Helaman 5:12; Alma 34:7, 14; Mosiah 16:13; Alma 38:9; Moroni 3:3; Mosiah 15:1-4; Ether 3:14.

It may be seen from these references that in the Book of Mormon Christ is, as already stated, revealed as "being the Father and the Son." This is explained thus: "Because he dwelleth in the flesh, he shall be called the Son of God," and the Father "because he was conceived by the power of God," thus becoming the Father and the Son.

The miraculous birth of Christ is clearly stated in this Record. He was born of a virgin, conceived "by the power of the Holy Ghost."

References: I Nephi 11:14-23; Alma 7:9, 10.

The doctrine of the virgin birth of our Lord has been assailed even by some who profess to believe in his divine mission. But alas! for the inconsistency of skepticism. Our Savior either began his mission on earth as Matthew and Luke state, or else Christianity is a fraud *in toto.* The evidence for this stupendous miracle is of a different nature from the evidence for the miraculous life and the resurrection of our Lord. The latter is of a public character, resting on his public administration and teachings; the former is of an entirely private character, originally known to the few, most intimate friends of the mother. It could not, clearly, have been a subject of public discourses during her life time. And yet, the account must have come from Mary herself, who, as Luke informs us, "kept all these things and pondered them in her heart" (Luke 2:19), as she, naturally, would do her most sacred experience in life. In rejecting, then, the virgin birth of Christ, the testimony of his own mother is set aside as false. Can a *Christian* do that? No, a true Christian will contemplate the character as well as the work of his Savior and exclaim with Paul: "Thanks be unto God for his unspeakable gift."

The Holy Ghost. The third person in the great divine Council of Three is the Holy Ghost, also called the Holy Spirit, and the Spirit of the Lord. In I Nephi 11:11, if I read the passage correctly, Nephi in his prophetic vision sees him as a personage of spirit, in the form of man. He sees him coming down out of heaven at the baptism of our Lord. He represents him as the exalted Person who confers divine authority on the servants of God; who sanctifies those that, through faith and repentance, enter the High Priesthood; who imparts knowledge, faith, the gift to speak, power to ordain to the Priesthood, and "many" other gifts of God, enumerated in Moroni 10:9-19.

References: I Nephi 11:27; II Nephi 31:8; I Nephi 10:22; Alma 13:12; Ether 12:33; III Nephi 16:4; Jacob 7:12; Moroni 19:7; II Nephi 26:13; II Nephi 32:3; 33:1; Moroni 3:4; 10:8-19.

It is the Holy Ghost that "bears record," or testifies, of the Father and of the Son. He manifests, or expounds, the word of God. It is therefore, a great sin to deny him, or to contend against him.

References: Ether 11:36; I Nephi 10:11; Moroni 8:9; II Nephi 28:4; Alma 34:38; 39:5, 6.

The three are *one*, but not one individual person. They are three persons, in one great divine council.

"The Godhead is a type of unity in the attributes, powers, and purposes of its members. Jesus, while on earth, and in manifesting himself to his Nephite servants, repeatedly testified of the unity existing between himself and the Father, and between them both and the Holy Ghost. This cannot rationally be construed to mean that the Father, the Son, and the Holy Ghost are one in person, nor that the names represent the same individual under different aspects. * * * Immediately before his betrayal, Christ prayed for his disciples, the Twelve, and other converts, that they should be preserved in unity, 'that they all may be one' as the Father and the Son are one. We cannot assume that Christ prayed that his followers lose their individuality and become one person, even if a change so directly opposed to nature were possible." (Dr. James E. Talmage, *Articles of Faith*, p. 40.)

References: III Nephi 11:27, 36; 28:10; Alma 11:44; Mormon 7:7.

The doctrine of some modern philosophers that the Father, the Son, and the Spirit are merely terms expressing three modes in which the all-permeating divine essence relates itself to the experience of man finds no support in the Book of Mormon. Nor does this Book teach that in the Father we see "the Absolute in its original oneness"; in the Son its "self-objectification," and in the Spirit "the reunion of the two" — a set of phrases, the uselessness of which is their most conspicuous feature. On the contrary, the Book of Mormon, as the Bible, teaches, I repeat, that there are three distinct persons, perfectly united in their divine council, in their plans and purposes; united into one in the same sense, as Dr. Talmage reminds us, that Jesus, our Lord, was, and is, one with the Twelve.

The doctrine is exceedingly clear in the Book of Mormon:

"And now, behold, this is the doctrine of Christ, and the only and true doctrine of the Father, and of the Son, and of the Holy Ghost, which is one God without end." (II Nephi 31:21.)

Again:

"Christ the Son, and God the Father, and the Holy Spirit, which is one Eternal God." (Alma 11:44.)[4]

---

[4]"Let me tell you, the Holy Ghost is a man; he is one of the sons of our Father and our God; and he is that man that stood next to Jesus Christ, just as I stand by Brother Brigham." (Heber C. Kimball, Aug. 23, 1857; *Jour. of Dis.*, Vol. 5, p. 179. Compare I Nephi 11:11.)

The Holy Spirit. But, according to the Book of Mormon, as well as other scripture, there is also a Holy Spirit, sometimes called the Holy Ghost, which is not a person, but rather a divine essence, a force, or fluid — for want of a better term — which permeates all that exists. It is the medium through which God communicates with the world, and more especially with his children. It is through the presence of this holy, divine spirit that order is preserved in the universe. Were this mighty force withdrawn, the world would return to chaos. The planets would stop revolving in their wonted courses. The fountains of the great deep would again break its fetters and overflow; and even human society would fall into ruins. It is that Spirit, in whom "we live, and move, and have our being." It is through his Spirit that Christ gives light to all and all things. It "proceedeth forth from the presence of God to fill the immensity of space; it is the light which is in all things; which giveth life to all things; which is the law by which all things are governed; even the power of God who sitteth upon his throne, who is in the bosom of eternity, who is in the midst of all things." (Doc. and Cov. 88:4-13) It is through this Spirit that God "is above all things, and in all things, and is through all things, and is round about all things." (Doc. and Cov. 88: 41)

It is this Spirit that is imparted to the repentant believer who receives baptism and the laying on of hands by an authorized servant of the Lord. And it is through this Spirit that the spiritual gifts are distributed.

References: I Nephi 3:20; 13:12; Alma 5:47; Helaman 5:45; Moroni 10:8, 9; III Nephi 19:9-23.

CONCERNING MAN

Origin. In the Book of Mormon, as in the other inspired scriptures, the two-fold nature of man — body and spirit— is clearly recognized. The spirit "possesses" the body. At death there is a separation between the two, and at the time of resurrection they are again united. These two, the spirit and the body united, is Man, and man thus constituted is of divine origin.

References: II Nephi 9:6; 9:22; Alma 11:41-45; II Nephi 26:4, 5; Moroni 7:41.

Adam, the progenitor of the race, is the son of God. He was the first man. And he obtained existence on this earth, in a body, by a special act of creation. And not only that, but he was created in the image of God; that is to say, the man was created after the body of the spirit of Jesus Christ.[5] His spiritual body was the pattern for our mortal bodies.

---

[5]"All men in the beginning have I created after the body of my spirit. (Ether 3:14-17) This is the only place in the Book of Mormon where pre-existence is clearly spoken of, and

References: Alma 34:34; 18:34, 36; 22:10; Mosiah 7:27; I Nephi 17:36; II Nephi 2:12, 15; 29:7; Mosiah 2:20; Mormon 3:20; 9:12; Ether 1:3.

The doctrine of creation is contrary to any other explanation of the origin of man. It is particularly opposed to the evolutionary theories of Darwin and Lamarck and their various and diverse schools of disciples — theories that have been facetiously characterized as "the gospel of dirt." By recognizing the Fatherhood of God, it sets aside the speculations of philosophers, whose indisputable aim it is to account for the existence of the world without God.

Man a Free Agent. According to the Book of Mormon, man is a free agent. He is capable of discerning between good and evil, light and darkness, sin and righteousness, and to choose one thing and reject the other.

References: II Nephi 2:27-29; 17:15; Helaman 14:30.

On this point modern thought generally agrees with the Book of Mormon. The old, fatalistic conception that man is merely, as it were, a stone thrown by a supreme Being from the precipice of time into the abyss of eternity, necessarily describing a certain arc in its course and stopping in a predetermined place at a predetermined time, is no longer held. The very existence of a consciousness in man of his duty to do certain things and to avoid others presupposes, it is admitted, free agency. For none can feel it a duty to do what is known to be impossible.

But why, then, did Adam fall?

The Fall. On that question the Book of Mormon is explicit.

The old orthodox view has been that although our first parents were created innocent and holy, they were deceived by the fallen angel, sinned and fell from the original state of moral perfection, and thereby brought death, sin, and endless misery upon their children and all creation.

Modern thought has tried to get rid of the story of the fall entirely, explaining it as a venerable myth. Evolutionists have seen in the story a proof of their theory of the descent of man from a brute ancestry; forgetting the apparent fact that there is not a brute that does not stand higher than the moral level of a great many depraved, debased human beings, thus furnishing no starting point there for a supposed upward evolution.

According to the Book of Mormon, the fall was a necessary part of the "great plan." "Adam and Eve were in the beginning eternal

this was revealed before the organization of the Church." (Orson Pratt, *Jour. of Dis.,* Vol. 3, p. 352.)

beings, and were not under the ban of mortal death. Subject to death they must become, however, if their posterity should inherit corruptible bodies. The fall, then, was a deliberate use of law, by which act Adam and Eve became mortal, and could beget mortal children."[6]

The story of the fall is not a myth. It is a record, in poetic, highly figurative language, of an actual occurrence. It is a record of the transition of man from a state of innocent, childlike purity, to that of a more mature age, when, the immediate divine tutelage having been completed, Adam was prepared to begin for himself the struggle for existence and progress. And so, "Adam fell that man might be."

All the particulars of the story are not clear. That Adam and Eve, were, literally, our ancestors, and that the "serpent" was Lucifer, the rebellious outcast from heaven, is certain. Just what facts are represented by the symbolism of the tree, the fruit, the eating, etc., is not obvious. The tree of life, which Lehi saw in his dream, the angel explains, was "a representation of the love of God," as manifested in the earthly mission of his only begotten Son. (I Nephi 11:20-33; 15:33) In Indian legends, a tree with four roots represents the brotherhood of man.

In the same way, we may be sure, the tree of knowledge and the tree of life, in the narrative of the fall, represents important realities in the experience of our first ancestors.

The consequences of the partaking of the forbidden tree by our first parents were that they came in possession of knowledge of good and evil but were "cut off both temporally and spiritually from the presence of the Lord." This was "death." And in this condition they became self-willed, "carnal, sensual and devilish." (Alma 42:3-10) That was a "fall" which called for a plan of salvation. God supplied that plan, and thereby the fall became a "fall upward."

The Atonement. A plan of salvation, as has just been stated, had already been prepared. On this subject the Book of Mormon is exceedingly clear. But for the atonement all mankind would perish. The atonement was effected through the sufferings and death of the Son of God. He took upon himself the transgressions of his people, and atoned for the sins of the world. His atonement is specially for those "who have fallen by the transgression of Adam, who have died not knowing the will of God concerning them, or who have ignorantly sinned." That includes all who have died outside the light of revelation. The atonement satisfies the demands of justice. Mercy comes because of the atonement, and it bring about the resurrection

---

[6]Dr. John A. Widtsoe, *Rational Theology,* p. 47.

and makes it possible for the children of Adam to return to the presence of God.

References: Mosiah 4:7; 13:28; Alma 34:9; Alma 33:22; 34:8; 36:17; Mosiah 3:11; II Nephi 25:16; II Nephi 9:26; Alma 42:23.

The modern spirit of co-called enlightenment is entirely out of sympathy with the Christian doctrine of atonement. It has placed man on a pedestal of independence, where he seems to have no need of the divine plan of salvation. But the fact remains: Outside this plan the world is "dead." Through Christ alone can man regain "paradise lost."

"The inference that the Church of Jesus Christ of Latter-day Saints is not a Christian organization is too absurd to require any extended comment. The foundation upon which the Church rests is faith in God the eternal Father, his Son Jesus Christ, and the Holy Ghost, which constitute the Godhead. The Church teaches and its members testify that Jesus Christ is the Son of God, that by him the worlds were created, and that through the redemption wrought out, because of the atonement which he made, all mankind are redeemed from death, the penalty which was pronounced upon our father Adam because of transgression, and that through obedience to the doctrines which he taught we may be redeemed from personal sin. We bear witness to the world that there is no other name under heaven, nor is there any other means by which man can attain to glory, exaltation and eternal life except through the medium of Christ our Lord."[7]

CONCERNING THE CHURCH

Two Opinions. There are two widely differing opinions concerning the nature, characteristics and mission of the Church. One is that it is a kind of religious-political world organization, existing for the purpose of keeping the "masses" in subjection and providing them with bliss hereafter, on condition that they do their duties here patiently and comply with the rules of the Church. Outside this organization, according to this view, there is no salvation. The other opinion, held by many Protestants, is that the church is no organization at all, but merely the sum total of all believers in our Lord, whom he, and none else, knows as his. According to this opinion, one visible church organization is about as good as another. They are all aiming at the same goal, and the members of the many churches, if they are honest and sincere, will reach the one blissful abode by different routes. It is like traveling to the same Rome by a hundred converging roads.

In the Book of Mormon, both these views are met.

The Church of God. Already about 147 years before our era, the Prophet Alma founded a church that was called "The Church of God" or, "The Church of Christ," in the land of Mormon. The

---

[7]From a conference sermon by Pres. Anthony W. Ivins, April 3, 1927.

prophet held meetings at the Waters of Mormon. Multitudes gathered to hear him, and those who believed were united as members of the church. They had repented of their sins and by faith embraced the redemption that God had provided. But this was not enough. (1) They were desirous of coming into the fold of God. (2) They wanted to be called his people. (3) They were willing to bear one another's burdens, to make them lighter. (4) They were willing to mourn with those that mourned and comfort those that needed comfort. (5) They were willing to be witnesses for God in all places and at all times, in order that they might be numbered with the redeemed in the first resurrection, and have eternal life. Such being their desire, they were qualified to enter the church by baptism. None else could be a worthy member.

The church was, as it still is, a tangible organization, and the members covenanted with God, in their baptism, that they would serve him and keep his commandments.

References: Mosiah 18:1-17.

Officers. As an organization the church had officials, whose mission it was to watch over the members as shepherds. These were to be "men of God." Alma says: "Trust no one to be your teacher nor your miinster, except he be a man of God, walking in his ways and keeping his commandments."

Alma, the founder of the Church, was its High Priest. By the authority of the Lord he appointed priests and teachers and consecrated them, and none received authority to officiate in these callings except through him. The calling of a priest was to preach and teach the people concerning the kingdom of God, and in the church founded by Alma there was one priest for every 50 members. The order of the High Priesthood is "after the order of the Son of God," without beginning and without end. Those who held it were to labor with their own hands for their support.

In addition to the High Priest and priests there were elders and teachers. Nephihah was an elder, who, with the consent of the people, was by Alma, the High Priest, appointed both lawgiver, judge and executive, in order that he himself might have more time to preach. This was an emergency measure, at a time when pride, prosperity and iniquity threatened the community with destruction.

The special functions of these ministers may be gathered from Mosiah 26:1-7, where we read that when it became necessary to admonish unbelievers on behalf of the church, they were delivered, by the teachers to the priests, and by these they were brought before the High Priest.

References: Mosiah 18:18, 24; 23:14-16, 17, 18; Alma 4:18; 5:3; 8:23; 13:2-9; 10:19; Alma 1:7; 4:11-20.

In his vision, Nephi saw the Twelve Apostles of the Lamb, that were to be appointed in due time, and especially the Apostle John, who has left his imprint upon the gospel message of the Redeemer in the latter days as well as formerly. When our Savior came to his people in the Land of Bountiful he called twelve disciples and endowed them with authority to teach and to baptize. The names of the Twelve were, Nephi, Timothy, Jonas, Mathoni, Mathonihah, Kumen, Kumenonhi, Jeremiah, Shemnon, Jonas, Zedekiah and Isaiah.

Nephi and Timothy were brothers and Jonas I, was the son of Nephi. Timothy had been raised from the dead. Mathoni and Mathoniha were brothers. Nephi was baptized first. Then he baptized the others who had been chosen. After their baptism the Holy Ghost (or Spirit) fell upon them, and they were encircled by fire; angels administered to them and Jesus came and stood in their midst.

References: I Nephi 11:35, 36; 12:7-10; 14:20, 24, 25, 27; III Nephi 12:1; 13:25; 15:11; 19:4-36; 20:1-6; 26:17-21.

In addition to the disciples, who also were called elders, there were priests and teachers. These were ordained by the Twelve by the power of the Holy Ghost.

References: Moroni 3:1-4; 6:1.

The Priesthood. The officers of the church in all ages and dispensations are the bearers of the Priesthood and, as such, the servants of the Lord and his people.

"Some people ask, 'What is Priesthood?' I answer, 'It is the legitimate rule of God, whether in the heavens or on the earth; and it is the only legitimate power that has a right to rule upon the earth; and when the will of God is done on earth as it is in the heavens, no other power will bear rule.'" (John Taylor, *Jour. of Dis.,* Vol. 5, p. 187.)

Two Churches. According to the Book of Mormon, there are two, and only two, churches, the church of the Lamb of God, and the church of the devil.

If I understand the solemn truth, here revealed, correctly, it refers more particularly to the two kingdoms, the kingdom of God (also called the kingdom of Christ), and the kingdom of the adversary. This view seems to be justified by the fact that the church is sometimes referred to as the "kingdom." (I Nephi 22:22-26) These two kingdoms are both upon the earth among the children of men. Each has its own form of government, diametrically contrary to that of the other. The government of the kingdom of God is founded on the celestial principles of righteousness, common consent and equality.

The government of the adversary is founded on principles of iniquity, compulsion and despotism. These two kinds of government originated in the spiritual world before the foundations of the earth were laid; they came to the earth with the conflict between the Son of God and Lucifer. They are the only two kinds of government that exist, or can exist.

References: Kingdom of God: I Nephi 14:10; Alma 5:50; 7:9; III Nephi 3:10; 20; Jacob 1:6; Alma 34:36; Kingdom of the Devil: I Nephi 14:3; 22:22; Alma 5:25, 39; Ether 8:24, 25.

Sacred Institutions. The church, according to the Book of Mormon, has the sacred institutions, or ordinances,[8] with which readers of the New Testament are familiar. These ordinances ar especially baptism, the laying on of hands, the breaking of the bread, prayer, and the "fellowship." (Acts 2:41-47)

Baptism. Lehi spoke to his sons of the baptism of John the Baptist, of whom the Old Testament prophets had prophesied, and explained to them that the promised Messiah would be baptized by him, at Bethabara, a place, the location of which, no doubt, was known to Lehi, although it is unknown now. Faith and repentance are the first necessary conditions of baptism; without these the ceremony would be null and void. Repentance and baptism are the "gate" to the straight and narrow path. By baptism the believer takes upon him the name of Christ and makes a covenant that he will keep his commandments and serve him. Baptism must be performed by divine authority and in the name of Jesus Christ. The manner in which baptism is to be performed is expressly stated by our Savior: "Behold, ye shall go down and stand in the water, and in my name shall ye baptize them. And now behold, these are the words which ye shall say, calling them by name, saying: Having authority given me of Jesus Christ, I baptize you in the name of the Father, and of the Son, and of the Holy Ghost. Amen. And then shall ye immerse them in water, and come forth again out of the water."

This decides forever the question of the mode of baptism. There is only one mode — immersion, by one having the authority from God; no other form is Christian baptism.

It follows from this that baptism of infants is not part of the ordinance instituted by Christ. Little children are "without the law"; they are "alive in Christ" through the power of his redemption, and they cannot repent; to baptize them is, therefore, "mockery."

The following records of baptisms should be read carefully: By

---

[8]I use the term ordinances in the same sense that Paul uses it (Heb. 9:1), viz., as divine requirements in addition to the demands of the moral law, which are "commandments."

Alma in the Waters of Mormon. (Mosiah 18:7-17) Alma in the Land of Melek. (Alma 8:3-6) Baptism of Zeezrom (Alma 15:1-4) in the Land of Sidon. Baptism of 8,000 Lamanites in Zarahemla (Helaman 5:17-19) by Nephi, the son of Helaman, and his brother Lehi. The baptism by Nephi, the disciple of Christ. (III Nephi 19:10-13)

References: I Nephi 10:9, 10; II Nephi 31:5; 9:22-24; 31:13, 14, 17, 18; Moroni 8:25, 26; Moroni 6:3, 4; Mosiah 18:17; III Nephi 1:23; 11:22-28; Moroni 8:8-26.

Baptism of Fire and of the Holy Ghost. Intimately connected with baptism in water is baptism in that sacred "fire," which gives spiritual power and light, and which is called the Holy Ghost, or, if the other term is preferred, the Holy Spirit. It is the promise of the Son to whomsoever is baptized in his name, after true repentance, that the Father will give to him the Holy Ghost, as it was given to the Son. It is through this Spirit that the Father bears record, or testifies, of his beloved Son; and, on the other hand, the Holy Ghost, by the same Spirit, bears record of the Father and the Son. The promise of the Lord is, that after the believer has been baptized in water, he himself will administer the baptism with "fire and with the Holy Ghost." But the means by which he imparts his Spirit, with all the power and authority that it implies, is the laying on of hands, for so he instructed his disciples, at the time of his first appearance. (Moroni 2:2)

References: II Nephi 31:8, 12, 13; III Nephi 11:35, 36; 12:1; 19:11-14; 26:17, 18; III Nephi 18:37; Moroni 2:1-3; 3:1-4.

It is necessary to have clearly before our minds the difference between the Holy Ghost as a divine person, one with the Father and the Son, and the Holy Ghost or Spirit, which is the medium of communication between God and his creation, his children, as previously explained. The Prophet Joseph says: "There is a difference between the Holy Ghost and the gift of the Holy Ghost. Cornelius received the Holy Ghost before he was baptized, which was the convincing power of God unto him of the truth of the gospel; but he could not receive the gift of the Holy Ghost until after he was baptized. Had he not taken this sign, or ordinance, upon him, the Holy Ghost, which convinced him of the truth of God, would have left him." (*Hist. of the Church,* Vol. 4, p. 555)

The Holy Ghost opened personally, as it were, the door of the gospel to the gentile world, by pouring out upon those in the house of Cornelius a portion of the power and influence which enabled them to accept truth, speak with tongues, and magnify God. But the full measure of this divine gift came after baptism and the laying on of hands; otherwise, baptism in water would have been superfluous, as many in our day regard it. Until Cornelius observed the ordinances and received the Holy Ghost by the laying on of hands, he could not have healed the sick or commanded an evil spirit in the name of the Lord.

Dr. Talmage makes this distinction between the Holy Ghost as a person and a divine element: "The term Holy Ghost and its common synonyms, Spirit of God, Spirit of the Lord, or simply Spirit, Comforter, and Spirit of Truth occur in the Scriptures with plainly different meanings, referring in some cases to the person of God, the Holy Ghost, and in other instances to the power or authority of this great Being."

Orson Pratt: "When I speak of the Holy Spirit, I speak of it as being a substance that is precisely the same in its attributes as those of the Father and Son. I speak of it as being a substance that is diffused throughout space, the same as oxygen is in pure water or air. * * * This light, recollect, is so universally diffused, that it giveth light to all things. This is the same light that governs all things, and it is called 'The Power of God.' "

In the Book of Mormon the distinction as we have seen, is made between the Holy Ghost, the person, and "Fire and the Holy Ghost," the divine element or essence. This is a significant distinction.

Human language is but imperfect, and it is doubtful whether there is a word fully expressive of the true nature of this divine person and the medium through which God operates. In the Doctrine and Covenants, the divine element is called "the light which now shineth." (Sec. 88:11-33) Orson Pratt calls it a "substance." We may, with Dr. Talmage, refer to it as a "power," or an influence, or couple it with the term "fire." And it is all that. But it is more. It is "Holy Spirit," — a substance, an influence, a power, a light, a fire that proceeds from the Father and the Son and permeates everything. It is the Glory of God, the manifestation of the divine presence; the fire and smoke, which made Sinai tremble; the glory which rested on the mercy seat in the tabernacle and the temple; the wind which filled the house on the day of Pentecost. It is divine intelligence, since "the glory of God is intelligence." It is the force before which mountains flee and worlds perish, for "the presence of the Lord shall be as the melting fire that burneth, and as the fire which causeth the waters to boil." (Doc. and Cov. 133:41)

The Breaking of the Bread. This ordinance, which is also called the Sacrament, was instituted by our Lord himself, during his appearance in the Land of Bountiful, for the spiritual benefit of those who believed in him and had been baptized in his name in this part of the world. The broken bread in this ordinance was to be eaten in remembrance of the body of Jesus, as a testimony to the Father that his Son is remembered. The cup was, similarly, partaken of in remembrance of the blood of our Savior, which was shed for us, and a testimony to the Father that we are willing to keep the commandments which the Father has commissioned his Son to give us.

On one occasion our Lord provided bread and wine miraculously and explained the great truth that, "He that eateth this bread eateth of my body to his soul; and he that drinketh of this wine drinketh of my blood to his soul; and his soul shall never hunger nor thirst, but shall be filled." From which remarkable expression it is clear, that the eating of the material bread and the drinking of the material wine is the visible representation of the inward process by which the believer on Jesus partakes of the fruits of his atoning sacrifice of himself. The participants in this sacred meal, we read, "were filled with the Spirit"; that was the essence of which the bread and cup were the emblems; "and they did cry out with one voice, and gave glory to Jesus, whom they both saw and heard."

It is necessary, then, that no unworthy should partake of these sacred emblems. "For whosoever eateth and drinketh my flesh and blood unworthily eateth and drinketh damnation to his soul."

The Church made it a point to meet often to partake of the bread and wine in remembrance of the Lord Jesus.

References: III Nephi 18:5-12, 14; 20:1-9; 26:13; III Nephi 18:28; Mormon 9:29; Moroni 6:6.

The following account of *The Institution of the Sacrament by our Lord in Jerusalem* may be of interest to the student of the Book of Mormon.

In the New Testament there are at least five texts directly bearing on the Lord's Supper. They are:

"And as they were eating, Jesus took bread, and blessed it, and brake it, and gave it to the disciples, and said, Take, eat; this is my body. And he took the cup, and gave thanks, and gave it to them, saying, Drink ye all of it; for this is my blood of the new testament, which is shed for many for the remission of sins." (Matt. 26:26-28.)

"And as they did eat, Jesus took bread, and blessed, and brake it, and gave to them, and said, Take, eat; this is my body. And he took the cup, and when he had given thanks, he gave it to them: and they all drank of it. And he said unto them, This is my blood of the new testament, which is shed for many." (Mark 14:22-24.)

"And he took bread, and gave thanks, and brake it, and gave unto them, saying, This is my body which is given for you: this do in remembrance of me. Likewise also the cup after supper, saying, This cup is the new testament in my blood, which is shed for you." (Luke 22:19, 20.)

"I speak as to wise men; judge ye what I say. The cup of blessing which we bless, is it not the communion of the blood of Christ? The bread which we break, is it not the communion of the body of Christ? For we being many are one bread, and one body: for we are all partakers of that one bread." (I Cor. 10:15-17.)

"For I have received of the Lord that which also I delivered unto you, That the Lord Jesus the same night in which he was betrayed took bread: and when he had given thanks, he brake it, and said, Take, eat: this is my body, which is broken for you: this do in remembrance of me. After the same manner also he took the cup, when he had supped, saying, This cup is the new testament in my blood: this do ye, as oft as ye drink it, in remembrance of me. For as often as ye eat this bread, and drink this cup, ye do shew the Lord's death till he come. Wherefore whosoever shall eat this bread, and drink this cup of the Lord, unworthily, shall be guilty of the body and blood of the Lord. But let a man examine himself, and so let him eat of that bread, and drink of that cup. For he that eateth and drinketh unworthily, eateth and drinketh damnation to himself, not discerning the Lord's body." (I Cor. 11:23-39.)

The ordinance was instituted on the occasion of the last celebration of the Passover, by our Lord and his disciples. It may be necessary to recall the Jewish method of observing this commemorative and typical ceremony at that time.

It was customary for the males of the family to meet in the evening of the appointed day to partake of that sacred meal. After having washed their hands and feet, they placed themselves at the table, reclining on couches. In earlier days the passover was eaten by the participants standing, as if they were about to begin a journey (Ex. 12:11), but later the reclining position was chosen, because the people had entered the land of rest. There was, however, no divine authority for this change.

A cup containing wine, well diluted with water, over which this blessing was pronounced, "Blessed be he that created the fruit of the vine," was first passed round to each guest. The roasted lamb, unleavened bread, and bitter herbs, as prescribed in the law, and other kinds of food were then placed on the table. He who presided distributed pieces of the lamb and the bread. All the meat had to be eaten.

After this first course they again washed their feet. They were then ready for the second course. This consisted of bitter herbs, with a kind of sauce made of bruised palm branches, berries and vinegar. This sauce was called *haroseth*. It represented the bitter experience of the Israelites in Egypt. After this course the cup of wine was passed for the second time. Then the head of the family, who presided, divided a cake of bread into two parts. One he covered with a napkin; the other he distributed, saying, "Blessed be thou, O Lord, our God, the King of the whole world, in the eating of unleavened bread." When this part of the bread was eaten, he took the part that had been reserved and broke it into as many pieces as there were persons present. At this time someone of the company asked for an explanation of this service, and the head of the family replied, "This is the bread of affliction, which our fathers ate in the land of affliction. Let him that is hungry come and eat the passover; let him that hath need come and eat the passover; for this passover is our savior and our refuge." Or, he expounded Deuteronomy 26:5-9:

"And thou shalt speak and say before the Lord thy God, A Syrian ready to perish was my father, and he went down into Egypt, and sojourned there with a few, and became there a nation, great, mighty, and populous; and the Egyptians evil entreated us, and afflicted us, and laid upon us hard bondage: and when we cried unto the Lord God of our fathers, the Lord heard our voice, and looked on our affliction, and our labour, and our oppression: and the Lord brought us forth out of Egypt with a mighty hand, and with an outstretched arm, and with great terribleness, and with signs, and with wonders; and he hath brought us into this place, and hath given us this land, even a land that floweth with milk and honey."

Then he took the cup again, tasted it, and presented it to each, saying, "Blessed be thou, O Lord, our God, King of the world, who hast created the fruit of the vine." This third cup was known as "the cup of blessing." (Psalm 116:13; I Corinthians 10:16)

Before the company separated, the cup was passed round once more, and the great Hallel, or Hallelujah (Psalms 113-118), was sung.

Hale and other Biblical scholars consider that the institution of the sacrament was as follows:

When the roasted lamb and other dishes had been placed on the table, our Lord and the Twelve, took their appointed places, whereupon he remarked that he had earnestly desired to eat this passover before his departure. (Luke 22:15) Then he passed the cup the first time, having pronounced the usual blessing. The lamb was eaten next. This course finished, Jesus washed the feet of the disciples and explained the meaning of that sacred ordinance, and warned them against vain ambition. He also told them they were not all clean (John 13:11), alluding to Judas, and spoke of the kingdom which he had appointed to them. (Luke 22:28-38)

After the washing of feet and this discourse, they took their places at the table again, for the second course, and our Lord said, with unmistakable plainness, that one of those present should betray him. This caused consternation, and all the disciples, including Judas, asked, "Is it I?" To Judas he said, "It is" (Matthew 26:25), but this answer escaped the rest of the Twelve. Peter then beckoned to John, who had the place immediately in front of the Lord, to ask him who was meant. He did so, and the Master replied, that it was he to whom he should give a sop, whereupon he dipped a piece of bread in the *haroseth*, or sauce, and gave it to Judas. John says, "And after the sop Satan entered into him," and Jesus said, "That thou doest, do quickly." (John 13:27) Judas now left the room.

The Master then took the bread which had been put away in a napkin, blessed it, brake it, and gave the disciples. He likewise took the cup of blessing, and passed it, after having given thanks. When all had partaken thereof, he explained, perhaps in answer to the usual question, What does this mean? the symbolical meaning which, from now on, should be attached to the eating of the broken bread and drinking of the consecrated cup. Hitherto that broken bread had been, or represented, "the bread of affliction, which our fathers ate in the land of affliction"; henceforth it was to be the symbol of his body, as he said, "This is my body, which is broken for you." Up to this time the cup of blessing had been a reminder of the goodness and mercy of God, who in accordance with his covenant of old, had brought his people to the promised land; now it was to be a symbol of a new covenant: "This cup is the new testament in my blood." And thus our Lord indicated the completion of the old dispensation and the beginning of a new.

After this ordinance had been instituted, Jesus delivered the affectionate and deeply fascinating discourse, recorded by John (13: 31 to 16:33), and offered the prayer (John 17) which has been called the *Prayer of the High Priest,* in which he asks for himself: that he may be glorified and thereby glorify his Father; for his disciples: that they may be kept from falling and become one, as the Father and the Son are one; for the converts in all ages: that "the love wherewith thou hast loved me may be in them, and I in them." After this prayer they sang the great Hallelujah(Matt. 26:30), and then the Master took his disciples over the brook Cedron to the slope of the Mount of Olives, where they entered a grove called Gethsemane.

At first the followers of our Lord observed the ordinance daily; they met every day in the courts of the Temple, where they listened to the teachings of the Twelve, and then they partook of the Lord's supper and prayed in the private houses. (Acts 2:41-47) But soon the sacrament was distributed only on the first day of the week, when the disciples held their regular meetings. (Acts 20:7; I Cor. 16:2) This day was called the Lord's day (Rev. 1:10), and it was observed by his followers as such.

Love Feasts. In the earliest days of the primitive church, a so-called love-feast, *agape,* was held in connection with the celebration of the sacrament, analogous to the passover. To these meals all the members were invited, and the poor were provided for by those who had means. At these gatherings contributions of money were also made and placed in the hands of the presiding elder, or bishop, for the maintenance of widows and orphans, for the care of the sick, and for such aid of prisoners and strangers as might be required and could be rendered. Money was also freely spent on the purchase of the freedom of slaves. Tertullian says of these love-feasts:

"However much it may cost us, it is real gain to incur such expense in the cause of piety: for we aid the poor by this refreshment; we do not sit down to it till we have first tasted of prayer to God; we eat to satisfy our hunger; we drink no more than befits the temperate; we feast as those who recollect that they are to spend the night in devotion; we converse as those who know that the Lord is an ear-witness. After water for washing hands, and lights have been brought in, every one is required to sing something to the praise of God, either from the Scriptures or from his own thoughts: by this means, if any one has indulged in excess, he is detected. The feast is closed with prayer."

From I Cor. 11:21, II Peter 2:13, and Jude 12, it appears that the love-feasts very early became occasions of revelry. The rich consumed their own food and let the poor go away hungry. Some of them drank to excess, and, as a consequence, indulged in sensuality. The Roman authorities suspected that these love-feasts were held for political purposes. About the middle of the second century they were, for these reasons, separated from the sacrament.

The Universality of the Church. Nephi saw the Saints "scattered upon all the face of the earth," "armed with righteousness and the power of God."

References: I Nephi 14:14; II Nephi 30:8-18.

"Scattered everywhere is this people, building churches, as has been pointed out, in the East, in the West, and on the islands of the sea. It means permanency for the Saints. There will be branches of the Church throughout the world. In 1906 I had the pleasure of visiting the Old Country, in company with our beloved President Joseph F. Smith. In the city of Bern, in Switzerland, we held a Priesthood meeting one night, at which the power of God was richly and truly manifest. President Serge F. Ballif was there and is a witness to what I say. Joseph F. Smith said: 'Not only will we have churches here, but in this land of Europe we will have temples of the Lord built here and there, all over the land.' That was his prediction. I believe it. I believe in this vision of Nephi; that he saw our people scattered in small communities all over the face of the earth. The Church of God is permanent." (President Charles W. Nibley, Conference Sermon, Oct. 5, 1924.)

Prayer. Prayer is one of the great institutions of the Church of Christ, as is clear from the Acts 2:42, where we read that the converts "continued steadfastly" in prayers, as well as in the breaking of bread. The same is said of the church on this continent. (Moroni 6:5)

In the Book of Mormon we have many remarkable instances of prayer and answers to prayer.

Lehi, prayed, and in answer to his supplications, he had a glorious vision of the Almighty, and was commanded in a dream to depart from Jerusalem. And thus began the journey that was the beginning of a new era in American history, in prayer. See also the last words of Lehi.

References: I Nephi 1:6; 2:1-3; 8:8, 9; II Nephi 4:3-12.

Nephi cried unto the Lord, when his brothers Laman and Lemuel were rebellious and the Lord answered him and gave him instructions and promises.

I Nephi 2:16-24; 7:17-20.

He prayed, when the storms raged and his brothers sought his life. See his prayer after the death of his father Lehi.

I Nephi 18:21-23; II Nephi 4:20-35.

God hears the prayers of the faithful.

II Nephi 6:11; 26:15; 33:4; Alma 10:22, 23.

Jacob. The prayer of Jacob and the answer.

Jacob 7:20-23.

Enos' prayer answered.

Enos 11, 12.

Soldiers Pray. God hears and answers prayers on the day of conflict.

Mosiah 9:16-19; Alma 2:28; 58:10.

Alma. His prayers and answer thereto.

Mosiah 23:10; 27:14; Alma 5:46; 8:10.

Spirit of *prophecy* and revelation through prayer.

Alma 17:3; 26:22.

Ammon prays.

Alma 19:14.

Moroni prayed when he had raised the standard of liberty. He dedicated this land by prayer.

Alma 46:11-17.

Community Prayer. The followers of our Lord are instructed to pray in their public meetings of worship as well as in private.

Alma 6:6; 28:6; 30:2; 31:10; 45:1; Helaman 3:55; III Nephi 27:1; Moroni 6:5.

Pray Always. The injunction is: "Cry unto him when you are in your fields, yes, over all your flocks. Cry unto him in your houses, yea, over all your household, both morning, mid-day, and evening. Yea, cry unto him against the devil, who is an enemy to all righteousness. Cry unto him over the crops of your fields, that ye may prosper in them. Cry over the flocks of your fields, that they may increase.

But this is not all; ye must pour out your souls in your closets, and your secret places, and in your wilderness, yea, and when you do not cry unto the Lord, let your hearts be full, drawn out in prayer unto him continually for your welfare, and also for the welfare of those who are around you."

Alma 34:17-27.

Zenos on prayer.

Alma 33:3-11.

How Not to Pray. The people of God are warned not to use stereotyped prayers; they must let the Spirit of the Lord dictate their petitions. The Zoramites are held up as a warning.

Alma 31:12-18; 38:13.

The Lord's Prayer. Our Lord taught the people to whom he appeared in Bountiful the same prayer which he had given his disciples in Palestine as a pattern.

III Nephi 13:9-13.

Jesus himself prayed, humbly bowing himself down to the earth, although, or perhaps just because, his disciples had in their prayers acknowledged him to be their Lord and God.

III Nephi 19:18-36.

From the New Testament we learn that Jesus our Lord, while on his earthly mission, prayed continually. He prayed in order to obtain power to do his mighty works. He prayed when his day's work was ended. He prayed when the waves of sorrow and anguish passed over his soul. He commenced his work by fasting and praying for forty days, and he ended his work on earth by commending his spirit to his heavenly Father's care.

Here, in the Book of Mormon, we learn that he also prayed as a resurrected being, although he had conquered death and the grave, and been given all power, in heaven and in earth. (Matt. 28:18)

Let us remember that the institution of the Church, and the church itself, are patterned after the order that obtains in the celestial realms of God. They are given us in order that we may have the spiritual training needed for our lives in the presence of God hereafter. That is the great object for which we have been given membership in the Church, and the holy Priesthood. It is by the faithful performance of the duties and obligations connected with these institutions that we prepare ourselves for the activity hereafter, which is eternal progress.

In the Name of Jesus. Our prayers, in order to be acceptable, must be offered up in the name of Jesus; that is to say, what we desire we must ask for by his authority and because of his merit, as our Father, the head of the human family in all that pertains to salvation, the "last Adam." (I Cor. 15:45)

III Nephi 19:6, 7; Moroni 7:26.

Prayer and Thanksgiving. The followers of our Lord need hardly be reminded that it is their privilege and natural duty to render thanks to the Lord for all his mercies and blessings, whenever they pray. Thanksgiving and prayer should go hand in hand. "Bless the Lord, O my soul: and all that is within me, bless his holy name. Bless the Lord, O my soul, and forget not all his benefits." (Psalm 103:1-2) That is the only frame of mind in which to approach the Lord in prayer.

Alma 19:14; 26:37; Helaman 13:22; III Nephi 10:10; Moroni 7:6-10.

CONCERNING THE FELLOWSHIP

This is an important institution of the Church of Christ, which will be established when the Lord finds the conditions favorable. It is a form of society, too perfect for most of us, but one for which we are being educated and trained, slowly but surely. In the Book of Mormon we read: "And it came to pass that the disciples whom Jesus had chosen began from that time forth to baptize and to teach as many as did come unto them; and as many as were baptized in the name of Jesus were filled with the Holy Ghost. And many of them saw and heard unspeakable things, which are not lawful to be written. And they taught, and did minister one to another; and they had all things common among them, every man dealing justly, one with another. And it came to pass that they did do all things even as Jesus had commanded them." (III Nephi 26:17-20)

The united order was, as we see here, one of the fruits of the outpouring of the Holy Spirit, and it was in accordance with the commandments of our Lord.

For an explanation of and quotations on the united order, see *Doctrine and Covenants Commentary,* pp. 290, 322, 417, 492, 724, 826.

A CLOSING WORD

The Book of Mormon Needed. A radical change has come to the religious world during the last century, affecting both doctrine and practice. The idea of the authority of God, as set forth by revelation, has been laid aside as obsolete. The Bible, as an infallible source of truth, has been discarded, and thereby the entire foundation of Christian worship has violently been destroyed. The defenders of the Bible were, in their timidity, first driven to the position that the Bible was unreliable when dealing with subjects belonging to geology, biology, ethnology, astronomy, and history, but infallible on matters relating to ethics and religion. But criticism did not confine itself to that which pertains to the sciences. It soon attacked the moral precepts of the Bible as impossible, or impractical. Then the defenders retreated and suggested that the Bible is not Christianity, and that whatever may be said against the Bible, does not concern Christianity. And this Christianity, without revelation and divine authority, without the word of God as the final arbiter between truth and error, is now being lauded to the skies by many modern theologians, and their followers who do not know what their leaders are talking about. All is therefore confusion. All is like the fury of empty drums being beaten only for noise, not for harmony.

In the meantime, waves of atheism, anarchy and crime are sweeping Christian countries. Homes are being broken up by desertions and divorces, and children, left without the support of a father's and mother's combined care, are falling by the wayside in ever growing numbers. In our own country there is now one divorce for every seven marriages, and 90 per cent of delinquent children are from such destroyed homes. The Sabbath of the Lord is being desecrated. Crimes of violence and dishonesty are increasing, until, if the present condition continues, neither life nor property will be safe.

But far from the din of modern Babel, the effulgence of celestial glory broke through the clouds and illumined the earth, and in the light a heavenly messenger appeared who proclaimed the everlasting gospel, which neither the criticism nor the skepticism nor the atheism of apostate ages can touch, because the Lord has had it in safe keeping especially for this age. Now, it is needed for the salvation of man, just as the New Testament was needed at the close of the Mosiac dispensation. And this glorious, everlasting gospel was ushered in by the angel who, in pursuance of his divine commission, gave the Prophet Joseph Smith charge of the venerable record, for publication to the world. And the substance of this message is: "Fear God, and give glory to him; for the hour of his judgment is come; and worship him that made heaven, and earth, and the sea, and the fountains of water."

THEORIES AND FACTS

When the conquerors and explorers entered this newly redis-covered world in the 16th century, they found themselves face to face with strange types of culture, for which they could not account. And I do not know but that the mystery is as deep now as it was then. Except for the solution offered in the Book of Mormon, we would be forced to exclaim with Schoolcraft: "The Indian, an enigma at first, is a much greater enigma the more his history and character are examined."

The Theory of the Lost Tribes. One of the earliest opinions advanced was that the Indians were the descendants of the so-called "lost" ten tribes of Israel. Among those who are quoted as having advocated this view are Las Casas, Montesinos, Sahagun, Boturini, and Garcia, whose testimony is of the greatest importance.

Las Casas, an intimate friend of Columbus, spent the greater part of his life among the natives of America,[1] studying their institu-tions. Prof. Fiske, in his *The Discovery of America,* pays a most glow-ing tribute to his knowledge and judgment. Speaking of the origin of the Indians from a Hebrew source, he is quoted as having said: *Loquela tua manifestum te fecit* — "Thy speech bewrayeth thee."

Fernando Montesinos is one of the early writers on Peruvian history, but he is not considered an authority, except as far as he copies other writers, especially Blas Valera, which he is said to do frequently. He records the theory that Ophir, a "grandson of Noah" settled "Hamerica," as he spells the name, 340 years after the deluge, and that "Peru," the name, is derived from "Ophir."

According to Montesinos, the first settlers to arrive in the neigh-borhood of Cuzco were four brothers and four sisters. The oldest brother climbed a hill and from there proclaimed that he took pos-session of the land for himself and in the name of his brothers and their wives. Montesinos' chronological tables have been critically examined and amended by Philip Ainsworth Means in his edition of *Memorias Antiquas,* London, 1920.

Sahagun, a member of the brotherhood of St. Francis, came to Mexico in 1529. For years he gathered all the information he could obtain in the new country. He would submit questions to a number of well-informed Indians, and they would paint their answers in their hieroglyphic writing. These answers were then submitted to others

---

[1]The last position he held was that of Bishop of Chiapas, which he accepted in 1544 and left in 1547.

for interpretation, without the questions. When a final revision was made, he embodied the result in his great work, *A Universal History of New Spain,* a transcript of which Lord Kingsborough preserved in his monumental work.

Boturini, the Italian traveler, in 1736 fell under the suspicion of the Spanish government and was sent to Madrid, a prisoner, after years of research in the new world. In Spain he was declared innocent and set free, but his priceless collections of antiquities and manuscripts had been scattered, and the greater part was lost. However, enough has since been recovered, to show the value of his labors and of his opinion on the origin of the prehistoric Americans.

Garcia is the most voluminous of the early writers on the subject. He deals very largely with the laws, customs, ceremonies, sacrifices, and early history of the people. He states that the Spaniards generally who reside in the "Indies" believe that the Indians are the descendants of the ten tribes, and that this opinion is founded on their disposition, nature and customs.

Among the later writers on the subject may be mentioned a Rev. Thorowgood, who wrote a work on "Jews in America," London, 1650; William Penn, who expressed his views in a letter, dated 1683; James Adair, who spent forty years among the North American Indians, and published his observations in London, 1775; and, above all, Lord Kingsborough, who, in 1831-48, published his *Mexican Antiquities,* in nine magnificent volumes, at a cost of 30,000 pounds.

Schoolcraft. The great archeological work of Henry R. Schoolcraft, published by authority of Congress, may be mentioned in this connection, as an indirect source of information on this subject; for in the fourth volume,[2] he inserts a "Memoir on the Inflections of the Chippewa Tongue," by Rev. Thomas Hurlburt, in which that author says:

"The idea that our Indians were the descendants of the Jews, I always considered merely a poetic one, and fit only for works of fiction. But in spite of my prejudices to the contrary, parts have developed themselves, and shown a resemblance between the Hebrew and Indian languages in general which I cannot find between the Indian and any other language. I have no inferences, but let the facts speak for themselves."

On another page of the same volume,[3] we find this, from the pen of one Rev. William Hamilton, on the Iowa language:

"The principles of the language correspond more with the ancient than with the modern class of languages; with the Hebrew, so far as my knowledge of it extends, more than with any other, particularly in the conjugation of verbs, which is done by

---

[2]Philadelphia, 1854, p. 387.
[3]Vol. 4, p. 397.

the help of pronouns, or fragments of pronouns. They also have some modes of expression which, I believe, are peculiar to the people of the East. Anything great is said to be like God (see Job 1:16), 'the fire of God' meaning a 'great fire,' and similar expressions."

Schoolcraft himself did not claim to have found among the Indians any striking evidence of kinship with the Hebrews, but he makes this observation:[4]

"One of the most striking traits of resemblance in the sound, orthography, and definition of words of the aboriginal languages to the Hebrew is that of the verb denoting existence."

In speaking of the verb denoting existence, Mr. Schoolcraft refers to the Hebrew *hajah*, to be, to exist. The "h," he says, is not always pronounced in Indian speech, the combination of the two long vowels "I" and "A" as in "I-au" more perfectly representing the sound; but the aspirant, he adds, is often distinctly heard from Indian lips.

A summary of the reasons why so many of the early students of prehistoric Americans believed they had found the remnant of the ten tribes may be attempted here:[5]

1. The affinity of languages, as already pointed out.
2. The belief of the Indians in the symbolical purification of water—the "water of regeneration."
3. The practice of circumcision. The earliest Spanish writers on America, such as Peter Martyr, Gomara, Bernal Diaz, Garcia, and Torquemada, all have declared that that rite was practiced by various American nations.
4. The expectation of the coming of a Messiah. But for that fact, neither Cortez nor Pizarro could have made themselves masters of the natives.
5. The use of Hebrew words such as *hallel*, for instance, in connection with religious celebrations.
6. The resemblance of many Indian ceremonies to those of the Hebrews.
7. The similarity between Indian and Hebrew moral laws.
8. Traditions proving that both the Mexicans and the Peruvians had knowledge of the story of the Pentateuch, relating to the creation, the flood, the tower, etc. The Mexicans had a tradition regarding a book called *Teo-amoxtli*, the "divine book."
9. The traditions of the Mexicans concerning the migrations of their ancestors.
10. The frequency of sacrifices.
11. Finally, the acceptance by learned men, such as Las Casas, and of learned Hebrews, even, such as Rabbi Ben Israel and Montesinos, of the view that the Indians are of Hebrew descent.

Christianity in Prehistoric America. So weighty did the analogies bearing upon this question appear to many, that they were not content with the theory of a Hebrew origin for the Indians, but felt

---

[4]Vol. 3, p. 61.
[5]*History of America Before Columbus*, Lippincott Co., 1900, pp. 204-232.

convinced that Christianity had been preached in America at some time in the dim past, probably by one of the apostles of our Lord. P. de Roo, an able exponent of this opinion, refers to Las Casas, Oviedo, and many others, as authority for it, and he quotes Sahagun to the effect that Quetzalcoatl was only one of several prophets who at various times reminded the people of the teachings of St. Thomas, who, he thinks, had preached the gospel here. Sahagun is also referred to as authority for the statement that the *coatl* in *Quetzalcoatl* means "twin" or "Thomas," and not "serpent," as generally believed, and that he, therefore, was none other than the apostle of the New Testament.

This is interesting, and also important. For it proves that in the judgment of some of the ablest students of prehistoric America, some of the Indian beliefs and rites could be accounted for on no other supposition than acquaintance, in a long ago forgotten past, with the religion of our Lord.

The Satanic Theory. To be sure, others, as Torquemada, Acosta, etc., had another solution to offer. They held that Satan had, by some means managed to teach the Indians false doctrines, to prevent them from accepting the true gospel the Spaniards had to offer! D'Acosta considered it admirable in "Sathan" that he counterfeited the sacraments as well as the "idolatry and sacrifices." Herera and Ondegardo felt sure that the devil had counterfeited the "sacrament of confession."[6] Cortez and Bernal Diaz held similar views.

Only Two Alternatives. As far as this question is concerned, then, the early writers on America offer only this solution: Either the Indians had at some time heard and become familiar with Christianity; or, the little light, the little truth they had at the time of the discovery was given to them by Satan!

Only Few Adherents of the Hebrew Theory. Mr. Bancroft makes the remark that the advocates of the theory of Jewish descent, or, at least, those of them who have made original research, "are comparatively few." Perhaps so. But that is easily accounted for.

The early writers on America were not at liberty to record facts and give opinions for public information, unless the facts and opinions happened to be approved by the censors. And so it came to pass that important works on America were either suppressed or mutilated.[7]

---

[6]Prescott, *Peru*, New York, 1898, Vol. I, p. 97.

[7]The *Bibliotheca*, in Pinelo, a work the object of which was to illustrate the history of America by extracts from, and references to, valuable and unpublished manuscripts preserved in the most famous libraries of Spain and the public archives, especially those of Simancos, to which the author, through the interest of the duke of Medina de las Torres, obtained access, exists only in an epitome, and of the larger work, a learned writer has observed. "Not a leaf has been found." Garcia's *History of the Peruvian Monarchy* is also unknown. * * * The

And this kind of consorship was exercised in America as well as in Europe. Spanish prelates, such as Zumarraga and Landa, made bonfires in the public squares, of priceless carvings, paintings, and picture writings on wood, native paper, and deer skin, and so thorough was the infernal work of destruction, that only a few fragments of the native literature of Yucatan have ever been found since,[8] and it is probable that but for the plates of the Book of Mormon, the past of the inhabitants of the New World would be an unsolvable riddle — a sphinx wrapped in eternal silence.[9]

The Reason for Opposition. The reason for the warfare on American literary treasures is not hard to discover. In the first place, the Jews were bitterly persecuted in Spain at that time. It is claimed that 600,000 of them had been expelled about the time of the discovery of America by Columbus, and that they were perishing in great numbers on their way to unknown destinations. It would never do to admit that the Indians of the New World were Jews. Might not the exiled fugitives have hastened to America and perpetrated who knows what mischief, by the aid of the Indians, if they thought these were their brethren in martyrdom? To suppress the truth concerning the Indians was, clearly, part of the general warfare on the Jewish race.

In the meantime, lately it has been claimed that Columbus was a Jew, but that he hid the fact, because of the persecution of Ferdinand and Isabella.[10]

---

council of the Indies took cognizance of all writers treating on America, requiring that they should be, previous to publication, submitted to a strict censorship, with the power of recalling, even after the publication, any work they thought fit."—From Kingsborough's *Mex. Ant.*, quoted by Mrs. Simon, *The Ten Tribes*, p. 8.

[8]At this distance of time, when the state of the world is so different from what it was in the sixteenth century, it may not be readily conceived how easy it was for the Council of the Indies, through the power vested in it, of permitting or prohibiting the general circulation of all writing relative to America, to keep the rest of Europe in a state of darkness respecting the history of the new continent. For three centuries those who successively composed that Council exercised their function as censors with the gratest vigilance. If powerful patronage or inadvertence on their part suffered in the first instance any obnoxious work to appear in print, it was sure to be soon recalled. Thus the *History of the Indies*, by Gomara, dedicated to Charles V, and the *Conquest of Mexico*, by the same author, dedicated to Don Martin Cortez, son of the celebrated conqueror, became prohibited books soon after their publication. But there were other works against which a silent war was waged in Spain.—*Ibid.*, p. 10.

[9]There is a famous manuscript, known as the *Codex Dresdensis*, preserved between glass plates, in the Royal Library at Dresden. It was discovered by Goetz in Vienna, in 1873. There is another Maya chronicle, the *Codex Prezianus*, in the Imperial Library, Paris. In Madrid there are two manuscripts, the *Codex Cortezianus*, which is supposed to have been brought to Spain by Cortez; and the *Codex Troano*, discovered in a Spanish library. The *Popul Vuh* was found by Karl Scherzer in the University library at Guatemala, where it had rested in oblivion for 150 years, since its first discovery by Francisco Ximenes, who made a translation of it. This is the "Bible" of the Quiches. It has also been translated by Brasseur de Bourbourg. The *Chilam Balam* books were found by Dr. Berendt, in Yucatan. They were partly hieroglyph and partly Spanish. See Dr. Brinton's *Library of Aboriginal American Literature*, Vol. 6, and his *Essays of an Americanist*, pp. 255-273.

[10]See a Lisbon Dispatch, *Deseret News*, Jan. 14, 1922, p. 7. "Associated with Columbus in the voyage were at least five Jews: Luis de Torres, interpreter; Marco, the surgeon; Bernal, the physician; Alonzo de la Calle, and Gabriel Sanchez. * * * Luis de Torres was the first man ashore. * * * He settled in Cuba."—*The International Jew*, Dearborn, Mich., 1820, p. 33.

Nor would it do to admit that the Indians were in any sense, or ever so remotely, Christians, as might have been contended, if it were admitted that the apostles of our Lord had preached among them. The Spanish policy was one of spoliation. When Las Casas pleaded the Indian cause before Bishop Fonesca, a member of the Council for the Indies, and told him that 7,000 children had perished in Hispaniola, the prelate exclaimed, "Look here, you droll fool, what is all this to me, and what is it to the king?"[11] Exactly! The Spaniards, with a very few noble, individual exceptions, were in America, to rob and to enrich themselves. It was necessary, therefore, to represent the Indians as "heathens," the worshipers of Satan, and to suppress everything contrary to that assumption. Hence the censorship, and especially the effort to cover up all reliable and intelligible information regarding, for instance, Quetzalcoatl, the Mexican Messiah.

Not the Ten Tribes. But, notwithstanding all this, neither the affinity of languages, nor the similarity in customs, religious conceptions and rites, nor the traditions, etc., prove that the American Indians are the Ten Tribes, or their descendants. The theory is not broad enough. It takes in only one set of facts, and leaves many other facts unexplained. It is perfectly true that the Indian languages have many Semitic words, but it is equally true that they are not Hebrew languages.

Rafinesque, who made a special study of the subject, divided the American languages into twenty-five groups. He placed the Haytian language in one group with the Arawak, Peruvian, and Chilean languages of the South, and the Darien, Maya, Mexican, Nachez, etc., of the North. He found in that group affinities with the Libyan, Egyptian, Bask, Persian, and Sanskrit. His conclusion was that the Haytians are of Pelasgic origin, and he derives the word *pelagic* from *Peleg*, the son of Eber. (Gen. 10:25) Another branch of the Pelasgians, he thinks, settled the shores of the Mediterranean.[12]

A more recent writer, T. S. Denison, comes to an almost similar conclusion.[13] He says:

"The Mexican language is Aryan in vocabulary and in verb construction. Its post-positive system suggests Turanian (Accadian) kinship, but it is analogous to that of the Indo-Iranian dialects descended from Old Aryan. In antiquity Mexican appears to lie between Sanskrit and Greek as indicated by both vowels and consonants. Mexican mythology partakes of the Aryan, Turanian, and Semitic."[14]

11Fiske, *The Discovery of America,* Vol. 2, p. 452.

12*American Nations,* Vol. 1, p. 217-219.

13*Primitive Aryans of America,* Chicago, 1908, p. 9.

14*Aryan* is from a Sanskrit word meaning "excellent." It is akin to *Iran,* and probably, *Erin.* It is the name of a prehistoric people that inhabited the region east of the Caspian Sea. The Aryan language is supposed to be the source of Hindoo, Persian, Greek, Latin, Celtic, Teutonic, and Slavonic languages, known as the Indo-European group. The *Semitic* languages

The Autochthonic Origin. Some of the foremost students of prehistoric America refuse to admit the Semitic or other analogies here pointed out. They regard them as mere accidental similarities. The Indians, they maintain, grew on American soil, and their culture developed here independently of any accession from abroad. Marquis Nadaillac puts the theory in the form of a question:[15]

"Must we admit different centers of creation? Were the primeval Americans born on American soil? Could evolution and natural selection * * * have produced on the shores of the Atlantic and the Pacific a type of man resembling the European and the Asiatic, alike in the structure of his frame and in his intellectual development?"

Mr. Bancroft rather thinks evolution and natural selection have produced such a man. The theory, although not proved, he says, "is, nevertheless, worthy of the gravest consideration."[16]

Dr. Brinton arrives at the conclusion that man came to America from western Europe, at a time when there must have been a land bridge between the two continents, of which Iceland and Greenland formed a part.[17] This migration happened so far back — "into a past for which we have no time measure."

Dr. W. H. Holmes[18] asserts that "no evidence has been found that man existed in this part of the world before or during the glacial period," and he favors Bering Strait as the possible gateway to America.

All agree that the American race, no matter what its origin was, is, if not "autochthonous," at least so modified and specialized as to be a race by itself, the *American race.* And this is, I think, indisputable. But the equally indisputable fact that both the Indian languages and other characteristic features of Indian culture show unmistakable Semitic and Aryan imprints also demands an explanation. It cannot be disposed of by laying it on a shelf and forgetting it. The Book of Mormon furnishes the explanation — the only possible explanation — and that without denying one single fact, scientifically established.

What the Book of Mormon Claims. The Book of Mormon tells us, as we have seen, that, let us say, four thousand years ago a small colony, under the leadership of the Brother of Jared, came to this hemisphere from Asia, from the very region of the original home of mankind after the flood. These colonists flourished here for perhaps

comprise the Hebrew, Aramœan, Assyrian, Syrian, Phonician, Arabic, Abyssinian, and Ethiopian. The Egyptian is classed as Hamitic.

[15]*Prehistoric America,* p. 15.
[16]*Native Races,* Vol. 5, p. 129.
[17]*The American Race,* pp. 28-32.
[18]*Handbook of Aboriginal American Antiquities,* Vol. 1, p. 35.

eighteen or nineteen centuries, during which time they branched out in every direction, built cities and established "kingdoms." This accounts for the Aryan, or Asiatic, characteristics of the Indian languages and religious ideas.

The Book of Mormon tells us that about 600 B. C., two companies of colonists from Jerusalem, one later known as Mulekites, and the other as Nephites and Lamanites, came over and settled, the first in a northern country and the second in a southern. It also tells us that, about 200 B. C., the Mulekites united with a portion of the Nephites, and the two became one people. This accounts for the strong Semitic element in the languages and the culture of the Indians.

The Book of Mormon, further, relates that the Jaredites were decimated by savage warfare, accompanied by famine and pestilence, and that they were harrassed by murdering and plundering bands of outlaws. Under these conditions their civilization, naturally, suffered, and the people degenerated.

The Book of Mormon describes, also, how the Nephites and Lamanites, through internal strife and bloodshed, suffered a similar fate. In that book we read that the Nephites were driven from place to place and, consequently, were scattered in all directions. Some of them must have amalgamated with such remnants of Jaredites as may have been found in out-of-the-way places, while the main body retreated and was, finally, crushed at Cumorah, about A. D. 385. War and bloodshed continued among the Lamanites. All records had been destroyed, or hidden, to escape destruction. The voice of prophets was not heard. The wheels of civilization were turned backwards for a long time.

Such are always the consequences of long-continued warfare. We need only look at Europe today,[19] to see an illustration of the frightful rapidity of the descent of nations by the route of militarism, from the high positions of civilization to the depths below, from which the upward climb has been long and wearisome. And Europe's war lasted only five years. What would the ruin wrought have been in a hundred years?

From the Book of Mormon we also learn that our Lord himself visited this country, after his resurrection, and preached to the people, and, through his chosen apostles, established churches, and eventually, a reign of unity and peace, which lasted for about one hundred fifty years.

These facts explain the originality that is, undeniably, a characteristic of the Indian languages and culture. These grew and developed, as soon as circumstances permitted, with the battered rem-

---

[19]This was written in 1959.

nants of Jaredite-Nephite-Lamanite achievements as their starting point. In that sense they are American — "autochthonous," if that term is preferred, while they retain unmistakable features of an Asiatic, both Semitic and Aryan, origin.

Book of Mormon Supported by Scientific Opinion. Scientific opinion, it seems to me, supports this view, as I read it in the Book of Mormon. Mr. Bancroft[20] says:

"Brasseur de Bourbourg, although he rejects Kingsborough's theory, thinks that some Jews may have reached America; he recognizes a Jewish type on certain ruins, and calls attention to the perfectly Jewish dress of the women at Palin on the shores of Lake Amatitlan."

Mr. Bancroft admits the possibility of the landing of "stray ships" in America, or even the landing of adventurous spirits, and then he says:[21]

"The result of such desultory visits would be exactly what has been noticed, erroneously attributed to immigration en masse.[22] * * * This, then, would account for many Old World ideas and customs that have been detected here and there in America, while at the same time the difficulty which arises from the fact that the resemblances, though striking, are yet very few[23] would be satisfactorily avoided."

J. Catlin[24] says:

"I believe, with many others, that the North American Indians are a mixed people—that they have Jewish blood in their veins, though I would not assert, as some have undertaken to prove, *that they are Jews,* or that they are 'the Ten Lost Tribes of Israel.' "

"The first and most striking fact among the North American Indians that refers us to the Jews, is that of their worshiping, in all parts, the Great Spirit, or Jehovah, as the Hebrews were ordered to do by Divine precept. * * * The North American Indians are nowhere idolaters—they appeal at once to the Great Spirit, and know of no mediator either personal or symbolical."

J. W. Foster expresses the opinion that the Central Americans must have had, at one time, a more perfect language than those that have been preserved. He says:[25]

"While thus, then, the Indian spoken language has all the elements of a primitive character and of a high antiquity, there must have been another language, the vehicle of more exact expression and of more refined ideas, spoken by the inhabitants of Central America, which has become irrevocably lost."

Mr. John Fiske, who verily believes that the aboriginal American,

---

[20]*Native Races,* Vol. 5, p. 95.
[21]*Native Races,* Vol. 5, p. 130.
[22]Note that the Book of Mormon says nothing of an "immigration en masse at any time.
[23]That they are not "very few" I hope has been shown in another chapter.
[24]*North American Indians,* pp. 261 and 263.
[25]*Prehistoric Races of the United States,* pp. 321-322.

as we know him, came from the Old World at a time when land connection existed, nevertheless has this to say:[26]

"Whether the Indians are descended from this ancient population or not, is a question with which we have as yet no satisfactory method of dealing. It is not unlikely that these glacial men[27] may have perished from off the face of the earth, having been crushed and supplanted by stronger races. There may have been several successive waves of migration, of which the Indians were the latest."

It seems to me that this conclusion is one that a student of the Book of Mormon must arrive at, as far as it deals with "successive waves of immigration."

Concerning the question of the comparative antiquity of the Central American and South American civilizations, the opinion of the authorities differ. Mr. Philip Ainsworth Means, in his notes of Montesinos' list of Peruvian rulers, observes that the trend of modern historico-anthropological research, and our growing geographical knowledge alike make it impossible to believe that the South American cultures were of greater antiquity than those of the north of them in Central America. Everything, he says, indicates that the earliest ethnic shifts were from north to south.

Mr. John Fiske has arrived at a dffierent view. He says that although the historic period for Peru dates no farther back than for Mexico, there are some reasons for supposing that the story of the Incas would carry us much father into the past than anything to be found in Mexico. According to Sir Clements Markham, an extensive and consolidated empire was at one time governed from Tiahuanacu. Peruvian tradition has preserved the names of 65 rulers of the Pirua dynasty. Allowing 25 years for each, then they would cover thirteen centuries. But as there was at least 400 years of disintegration between this dynasty and the time of Manco Capac, the Pirua dynasty would have begun in the fifth century before our era. (John Fiske, *The Discovery of America*, Vol. 2, p. 302-303)

The fact is, as Mr. Fiske also observes, that the entire American continents, from the table lands of New Mexico and Arizona [and we may just as well include the Ohio and Mississippi valleys and the Rocky Mountain states], down to the fastnesses of Bolivia and the region of the Cordilleras was the field of culture of a high order, and that the South American level in some respects, notably in religious concepts and practices, surpassed that of Central America, and further, that the little province of Chiriqui in Panama still gives evidence, in the numerous antique works of art there found, of its position as part of the connecting link between the northern and southern continents.

---

[26]*The Discovery of America*, Vol. 1, p. 15.
[27]Of the existence of which Dr. Holmes says we have no evidence.

A Mixed Race. As stated, many scholars believe that the Indians are a mixed race. Rafinesque thought it highly probable that all the nearest nations of the Atlantic and Pacific coasts had either visited or colonized the Americas. He refers especially to the Phœnicians, the Etruscans, the Tartars, the Chinese, and the Polynesians. There is a story to the effect that Buddhist missionaries, in the fifth century of our era, came to Mexico by way of Kamtchatcha, and, according to newspaper reports, ancient Chinese glyphs have been found on the temple walls at San Juan Teotihuacan, near the City of Mexico, and this report, if authentic, would seem to lend support to that story. There are also reports of voyages of the Welsh and the Irish, to the American shores. Needless to say, the Book of Mormon neither affirms nor denies such reports. It confines itself entirely to the history of the Jaredites and the descendants of Mulek and Lehi. Whether other colonists did or did not appear in America at any time, scientists must find out from other sources. The word of revelation is not given on that question.

Another question discussed is whether the fossil remains found in early geological strata, both in South America and North America, do not prove the existence of man in this hemisphere way back in the early tertiary age, and the probability that the Indian is the descendant of this early man.

That is another question with which the Book of Mormon does not deal. It confines itself to what happened to a very small portion of mankind after the building of the Tower. Nothing that scientists can find regarding man before, or even after, that event can come in conflict with what the Book of Mormon reveals concerning the descendants of the brother of Jared and Lehi, provided the men of science confine themselves to facts.

Pre-Adamites. A great many young students are uneasy because unable to reconcile the scriptures with the findings of scientists regarding the age of the human race on earth. The scriptures, it seems, allow only 6,000 years from Adam, while the scientistis believe they have found evidences of man on earth many thousands, or even millions, of years further back than that. "No scientist," they tell us, "will admit for a moment that human evolution has proceeded as rapidly as the story in Genesis necessarily supports." They tell us that the Cro-Magnon man lived 25,000 years ago; that the Cro-Magnon man was preceded by the Neanderthal man; before him the Heidelberg man existed; and then the Trinil man, and the Foxhall man — all named from the localities in which their supposed remains have been unearthed. The Foxhall man, we are assured, lived in England about 500,000 years ago. Many are at a loss to find even a possible way to reconciliation between the seemingly irreconcilable statements of the sacred record and the findings of the sciences, and the apparent contradiction is a great trial of their faith in the inspiration of the divine word.

The common argument by which it is sought to explain the discrepancy is, that the scriptures are precious manuals of religion, but not text-books on science. As books on religion, they lay down rules of conduct, and inspire faith and hope. They reveal God in Jesus Christ, but they do not pretend to state facts concerning the creation of the world.

But this reasoning is no way out of the difficulty. It takes for granted that the scriptures are partly true and partly not true, and it virtually leaves the reader free to accept what he thinks is true and reject the rest. The word of God cannot be "edited" and blue-pencilled in that way. It must either be accepted as we have received it, barring errors of transmission and translation; or it must be rejected *in toto*.

There is a better explanation. Competent Bible students have thought it probable that this world was inhabited before the days of Adam, who was the first "man," by a race which perished long before his advent. If this should prove to be the case, the remains found in the earlier geological formations may have belonged to that race, and furnish no basis for conclusions regarding a high antiquity of any part of the now living human family.[28]

A Theory That May Have Merit. But how could a race be destroyed, without the destruction of the earth?

An interesting theory was advanced a few years ago by Prof.

---

[28]Dr. R. A. Torrey, in *Difficulties in the Bible*, p. 31, says: "There is grave reason to doubt if anything in Genesis 1, after verse 1, relates to the original creation of the universe. All the verses, after the first, seem rather to refer to a refitting of the world that had been created and afterwards plunged into chaos by the sin of some pre-Adamic race, to be the abode of the present race that inhabits it, the Adamic race."

Orson Hyde also believed that this earth had been inhabited by a race that had lived and died here before Adam came, and that it, consequently, was refitted for him, as a house may be rebuilt and refurnished when a new family is about to move in. He says: "The world was peopled before the days of Adam, as much so as it was before the days of Noah. * * * When God said, Go forth and replenish the earth, it was to replenish the inhabitants or the human species, and make it as it was before." (*Jour. of Dis.*, Vol. 2, p. 79.) This statement was made in a sermon in Salt Lake City, Oct. 6, 1854, and it received the endorsement of President Brigham Young in the following words: "We have had a splendid address from Brother Hyde, for which I am grateful."

Without discussing the merits, or demerits, of this hypothesis, let me say that the other theory, according to which man, ages and ages ago, evolved from the most advanced beasts, is contradicted both by history and archaeology. As far as history goes back, it presents to our view some highly developed civilization, in some parts of the world with lower stages in other parts, just as is the case today. And, beyond the reach of written history, the earliest human skull ever found shows no marks of inferiority. It may, for aught we know, have, as Huxley puts it, "belonged to a philosopher." Barbary and savagery are, most probably, due to degeneration.

LeRoi Tobey, which, if proved, would satisfactorily explain the periodical destruction of the higher life forms upon the earth, through alternating glacial periods and seasons of intense heat. The theory is briefly stated in an article in *Smith's Magazine* for July, 1906, and seems to me to be worthy of consideration.

According to this theory, our solar system describes a circuit around the star Arcturus in 104,000 years. We are now about midway between the perihelion and aphelion in this orbit, as the nearest point to and the farthest point from the central star is called, and we are being rushed toward the perihelion at the rate of 184,000 miles an hour.

That is to say, we have just arrived at the beginning of the beautiful solar spring. Behind us is the winter, the evidence of which is still with us in the form of melting polar ice caps and diminishing glaciers, while before us is the spring and the summer of our solar system.

Our solar spring began March 21, 1905, we are told, and it will last 18,000 of our years. Then comes the summer, also 18,000 years, beginning June 21, 19,905. During this time Arcturus will appear from the earth as a sun, larger than the moon, and artificial light will not be needed night or day. But, probably, every living higher organism will be destroyed by light and heat. The autumn will begin Sept. 23, 37,905, and this season will merge into a winter that will last 50,000 years, beginning Dec. 22, 55,905. Arcturus will then appear as a mere point in the sky. The earth's winters will grow colder and colder. The ice will again form, and in January, in the year 82,905 the earth will be enveloped in ice, unless, indeed the temperature of the solar winter is modified by the sun's drawing near to some other immense star in the Milky Way.

It was, we are assured, during the winter from which our sun has just emerged — the coldest "day" of which must have been about the year 23,095 B. C. — that the earth passed through its last glacial period.[29]

What appears to be slightly corroborative of this theory came in April, 1923, from the American consul in Bergen, Norway, in the form of a report to the Department of Commerce in Washington. The consul stated, as reported, that the Arctic Ocean had become much warmer that winter. Seals were retiring far north to the ice field much beyond their usual grounds. Ice fields were disappearing, glaciers were melting in Greenland, leaving bare ravines and moraines

[29]"If the close of the glacial period in the Ohio and Delaware valleys for example, should be placed at 20,000 years ago, it might in the region of the Great Lakes have been 10,000 years ago."—Holmes, *Abor. Am. Antiquities*, Vol. 1, p. 73.

never seen before. The white-fish have vanished and herring and smelt have gone north to take their places. Dr. Hoel, geologist of the University of Norway, had just returned from an arctic expedition and reported that he found very little ice and that his soundings to a depth of more than two miles showed the north arm of the Gulf Stream very warm as far up as 81 degrees 21 minutes, nearly 14 degrees inside the arctic circle. An arctic fisherman, he stated, said that it has been growing warmer in the arctic since 1918.

The Value of This Theory. I am not stating this as a demonstrated proposition, but as a possible explanation of certain facts. The scientists tell us that they find remains of human beings and human handicraft in certain geographical strata which date back from twenty-five to five hundred thousand years. It follows, they argue, that the present human race must be that old. The answer is, not necessarily. Those remains may, possibly, belong to a race that lived and died before the present race came to this earth. And that is a sufficient answer to the theory advanced for the purpose of discrediting a word of God.

"Believe in God; believe that he is, and that he created all things; both in heaven and in earth; believe that he has all wisdom, and all power, both in heaven and in earth; believe that man doth not comprehend all the things which the Lord can comprehend * * * retain in remembrance the greatness of God and your own nothingness, and his goodness and long-suffering towards you, unworthy creatures, and humble yourselves even in the depths of humility, calling on the name of the Lord daily, and standing steadfastly in the faith of that which is to come, which was spoken by the mouth of the Angel."—(King Benjamin, Mosiah 4:9, 11.)

THE MANUSCRIPT FOUND
or
THE SPAULDING STORY

The many writings of the teachers and leaders of Israel in these last days consist largely of the personal narratives of these men of God in which it is shown how the Lord preserves, guides, inspires, and directs, His servants in this dispensation, and reveals His word and will to them after the same manner and by like methods as those by which He manifested Himself to the righteous in every former generation of Israel.

With feelings of intense joy, deep devotion, and profound gratitude to Him, these experiences have been read by thousands of Latter-day Saints. We now take a somewhat new departure. We treat of a book — a divine record, the true story of its discovery and translation, and of the falsehoods that have been invented, nourished, and sown broadcast throughout Christendom to blind men's eyes to its real import. For this book (the Book of Mormon) being true then Joseph Smith is a prophet of God and *Mormonism* is the Everlasting Gospel of our Lord Jesus Christ; but if it is a forgery, as our enemies assert, then would all our hopes be vain and our faith worthless.

The so-called *Spaulding Story* for many years has been the last refuge of those who have undertaken to prove that the Book of Mormon is not what it claims to be. All other hypotheses have long since been committed to limbo as too silly, too outragious, or too inconsistent, even for a gullable anti-Mormon public. In this short treatise we have endeavored to prove the utter untenability of this theory. We have shown that the upholders of this myth are not only at varience with each other, but that all their assertions are inconsistent with the well-known facts associated with its discovery; and when we proceed further to examine the internal evidence of the Book we very soon discover that the conglomeration of conjectures, guesses, suppositions, etc., of which this "Spaulding Story" is formed is as "unstable as water," and utterly unworthy of belief.

THE HISTORY OF THE MANUSCRIPT

Time and again, at recurring intervals of unequal length, the Church of Jesus Christ of Latter-day Saints is assailed with a rehash of the notorious "Spaulding story," which from frequent repetition as become as familiar in the mouths of many of the Saints as household words. True, the story in its details is not always identical, it is altered, re-arranged, or "cooked" to suit the necessities of the story teller, but in its essential particulars it remains the same. Its burden is that a certain "reverend" gentleman of Conneaut, Ohio, named Solomon Spaulding, in the early part of the last century, wrote a historical romance which he entitled the "Manuscript Found," that in some unexplained and unexplainable way, but generally imagined to have been through Sidney Rigdon, the youthful Joseph Smith obtained accoss to this manuscript and from its canty pages elaborated the Book of Mormon, which he afterwards palmed upon the world as a divine revelation.

This is the substance of the "Spaulding story." It is a frantic effort to prove the Book of Mormon a forgery and a fraud, for it is very evident that if the Book of Mormon is not of God then the whole superstructure of "Mormonism" is of necessity a gross imposture, the cruelest of religious deception that for many centuries has misled humanity. All other theories advanced to prove this record false having long since failed, the "Spaulding story" is the last and only resort of those who oppose the divine mission of Joseph Smith, and though many a time refuted and proved an impossibility, yet, it is that or nothing; and the malignant hatred of the wicked not permitting the Book of Mormon to stand on its own intrinsic merits, or be judged by its own internal evidences, this story has to be again and again revamped as the last hope of a hopeless cause which perceives in the triumph of "Mormonism" the seal of its own destruction. To consider this story, its origination and history, its claims on the credulity of mankind, and the weight of evidence for and against it, will be the topic of the following pages.

Attention has been drawn and interest created anew in Mr. Spaulding and his unpublished romance by the appearance in the public prints of articles and affidavits by members of his family, in which the story of the "Manuscript Found" is given, and efforts made to connect it with the Book of Mormon. Among the most important of these papers is an affidavit of Mrs. McKinstry the daughter of Mr. Spaulding, which gives a history of the manuscript from the time it was written until it passed out of the hands of the family. We will first draw attention to the various points made by Mrs. McKinstry from her actual knowledge, leaving out those reflections, suppositions and vain imaginings in which she indulges when she wanders from the path of her actual knowledge; but lest it should be asserted that we have not fairly represented her statements, we insert the affidavit in full as an appendix to this little thesis.

According to Mrs. McKinstry's affidavit she resided with her father, Mr. Solomon Spaulding, at Conneaut, Ohio, in 1812, she then being a child in her sixth year.

About this time her father was very much interested in the antiquities of this continent, and wrote a romance on the subject, which he called the "Manuscript Found," in which she believes the names of Mormon, Moroni, Nephi and Lamanite appear.

This was not the only work of Mr. Spaulding, he was a man of literary tastes and wrote a number of tales, etc., which he was in the habit of reading to his family, to his little daughter, now Mrs. McKinstry, among the rest.

From Conneaut the family removed to Pittsburg, Pennsylvania, where they had a friend named Patterson, a bookseller. To this gentleman, her mother states, the "Manuscript Found" was loaned and by him read, admired and returned to the author.

The stay of the family in Pittsburg was very brief, for they shortly removed to Amity, Pennsylvania, where Mr. Spaulding died in 1816. Immediately afterwards she and her widowed mother paid a visit to the latter's brother Mr. William H. Sabine, at Onondaga Valley, Onondaga Co., New York. A trunk containing all the writings of the deceased clergyman was taken with them and in this trunk was the "Manuscript Found." While here Mrs. McKinstry saw and handled the manuscript and describes it as closely written and about an inch thick.

Afterwards her mother went to reside with her father (Mrs. McKinstry's grandfather) at Pomfret, Connecticut, but she did not take the trunk of manuscript with her. In 1820 she again married and became the wife of a Mr. Davison, of Hardwicks, near Coopertown, New York. After her marriage she sent for her things left at her brother's, among the rest the old trunk of manuscript. These reached her in safety.

In 1828, Mrs. McKinstry was herself married, and resided in Monson, Hampton Co., Mass. Very soon after her marriage her mother joined her there, and was with her most of the time until the latter's death, which took place in 1844.

Mrs. Davison when she went to reside with her daughter left the trunk of manuscript at Hardwicks, in care of Mr. Jerome Clark.

In 1834, one Hurlburt visited her. He bore a letter from her brother, Mr. Sabine, and requested the loan of the "Manuscript Found." She reluctantly gave him a letter addressed to Mr. Clark, at Hardwicks, to deliver him the manuscript; Hurlburt having made repeated promises to return it.

The family afterwards heard that Hurlburt received the manuscript from Mr. Clark, but from that time the Spaulding family never again had it in their possession, though they repeatedly wrote to Hurlburt about the matter.

In the above we have the history of the notorious manuscript from the time it was written until it fell into the hands of D. P. Hurlburt, who was the first man who endeavored to connect it with the Book of Mormon. Its history may be thus summed up:

Written in 1812 at Conneaut, Ohio.

Taken to Pittsburg shortly after. (1814.)

Thence to Amity, where it was in the possession of its author when he died in 1816.

In 1816 taken to Onondaga Valley, New York.

In 1820 removed to Hardwicks, New York, where it remained until 1834, when it was handed to Hurlburt.

Here we have an unbroken history of its wanderings until years after the Book of Mormon was published.

How then is it presumed that Joseph Smith obtained possession of it? This is an unanswered question. Was Joseph in any of those places at the time the manuscript was there? No, there is not the least proof that he ever was, all the testimony and evidence is directly to the contrary. Was Sidney Rigdon ever in these places? Not at the same time as the "Manuscript Found," as we shall presently show.

The Prophet Joseph Smith was born in Vermont, December 23rd, 1805, and was consequently in his sixth year when the romance was written. He was only fifteen when it was taken to Hardwicks. It would be preposterous to imagine that before that age any such labor as the changing of the "Manuscript Found" into the Book of Mormon could be accomplished by one so young, so inexperienced, and withal so ignorant. For all admit, both friend and foe, that his education at that time was very limited. In 1820, he received his first vision, and began his prophetic work, being then a resident of Manchester, New York.

In 1823 he still resided with his parents at Manchester, and it was in that year that he first began bearing testimony with regard to the coming forth of what we now call the Book of Mormon, and that he had seen the plates from which it would be translated. Manchester is from 80 to 100 miles from Hardwicks in a direct line, and in the last named place the "Manuscript" still remained hidden in an old trunk in a garret, no one knowing or expecting that recourse would be had to it for such a base purpose.

Joseph continued to live with his father's family. It is not until 1825, that we have any account of his leaving home for any length of time; until then, when not employed on the farm, he hired out by the day to his neighbors in Manchester and vicinity.

THE ORIGINATOR OF THE SPAULDING
STORY

Doctor Philastus Hurlburt was the originator or inventor of the "Spaulding Story."

He was not a doctor by profession, but his mother gave him that name because he was the seventh son, a very common custom in some parts at the time he was born.

Those who adopt his fabrication with regard to the authorship of the Book of Mormon would have people believe that he really was a doctor. It gives an air of respectability to their tale, and tends to make the public think that he must have been a man of good education, though he really was not.

We will now give some statements with regard to his life, and the causes that led to the invention of the desperate lie, regarding the Book of Mormon, which has tended to deceive so many people. These statements are, for the most part, abridged from the writings of one who was intimately acquainted with him.

Hurlburt embraced the gospel in 1832. Previous to this he had been a local preacher in the Methodist church, but had been expelled therefrom for unchaste conduct. Soon after his baptism he went to Kirtland, where he was ordained an Elder. In the Spring of 1833, he labored and preached in Pennsylvania. Here his self-importance, pride and other undesirable traits of conduct soon shook the confidence of the members of the Church in him as a man of God; and before long his unvirtuous habits were so plainly manifested that he was cast off from the Church, and his license taken from him by the conference.

Some may here ask, "How is it that men who leave the Church of Christ and come out in opposition to its truths are so often proven to have previously been men of immoral lives?" The answer is plain and simple: pure, honest, virtuous men do not apostatize and turn against the principles of the gospel. They remain faithful. But men who have been wicked and who do not sincerely repent when they enter the Church, though they may profess to do so, are very apt to turn aside and fight against God's cause. It is for this reason that so many men of Hurlburt's stamp have, unfortunately for them, been proven to have led very wicked lives before their baptism. Had their repentance been sincere, their after lives would have been different.

Hurlburt went to Kirtland, the seat of the government of the Church, and appealed to the general conference. His case was there reconsidered, and because of his confession and apparent repentance his license was restored to him.

On his way back to Pennsylvania he stopped in Ohio. There he attempted to seduce a young lady, but his design was frustrated. For this crime he was expelled from the Church. Finding he would be tolerated by the Saints no longer, he determined to be revenged by injuring them to the utmost extent of his power. He went to Springfield, Pennsylvania, and commenced to preach against "Mormonism." Here he was received with open arms by those who were vainly endeavoring to stay the progress of God's work in that region, and churches, chapels and meeting houses were crowded to hear him.

He was now dubbed the Rev. Mr. Hurlburt, and was petted and patronized by priest and people; but for all that he did very little in staying the progress of the truth. As an anti-"Mormon" lecturer he was a failure.

During his stay in Pennsylvania, Hurlburt formed many acquaintances, and mingled with all sorts of people. While in a small settlement called Jackson, he became familiar with a family of the same name, (possibly the persons who had given the name to the settlement). Some of this family had been acquainted with the now widely-known Mr. Solomon Spaulding, and from them Hurlburt learned that that gentleman had once written a romance called the "Manuscript Found," which professed to recount the history of the ancient inhabitants of this continent.

Hurlburt had now given himself up to the work of opposing "Mormonism." He quickly perceived that this romance could be used as a weapon to carry on the warfare. If he could obtain possession of it and find any points in common between it and the Book of Mormon he could exaggerate those seeming resemblances and falsify other statements. If he found no agreement between the two he could contrive to have the "Manuscript Found" accidentally (?) destroyed and then claim that its contents were almost identical with the record of Mormon. He found it necessary to pursue the latter course.

In carrying out his design he repaired to Kirtland, and there made an appointment to deliver a lecture, calling upon all who were opposed to "Mormonism" to attend. They did so in force. At this lecture Hurlburt told his audience that in his travels in the State of Pennsylvania, lecturing against "Mormonism," he had learned that one Mr. Spaulding had written a romance, and the probability was that it had by some means fallen into the hands of Sidney Rigdon, and that he had transformed it into the Book of Mormon. Hurlburt further stated that he intended to write a book, and call it "Mormonism Unveiled," in which he would reveal the whole secret.

His anti-Mormon" hearers were delighted. One mobocrat, a Campbellite, advanced the sum of $300 towards the prosecution of the work. Others contributed for the same purpose, and Hurlburt, being thus provided with funds, at once proceeded to hunt up the manuscript.

With this view he journeyed to New Salem or Conneaut Ohio, the place where Mr. Spaulding formerly resided. There he called a meeting and made known his intentions. His harangues created quite a stir. He told the same story about the manuscript and Sidney Rigdon that he had told in Kirtland. The idea was new to his hearers, but as it was something which was to destroy "Mormonism," they did not object to it, and some helped him with more money. He was here advised to visit Mrs. Davison, formerly the wife of Mr. Spaulding, who now resided at Monson, Massachusetts. This he determined to do.

It should here be mentioned that the gospel had already been preached with considerable success in the neighborhood of New Salem; and though it was the place where the "Manuscript Found" was written, the Spaulding story was never dreamed of there until Hurlburt mentioned it. But it was too good a thing for those who had rejected the truth to let pass. It afforded them some slight excuse for not receiving the doctrines of "Mormonism." Such persons clutched at it eagerly, as drowning men are said to grasp at straws. Nevertheless the work of the Lord did not stand still in those parts. Numbers were afterwards baptized in that very section, so little effect had Hurlburt's fabrication upon the minds of the people.

Hurlburt at once carried out the advice given to him by his New Salem acquaintances. He proceeded to Monson, called on Mrs. Davison, and by representing his wishes in his own unscrupulous and untruthful manner obtained from her the writings of her former husband. Further she told him that there was a trunk somewhere in the state of New York that also contained papers which he might have, if they were found to suit his purpose, and according to the latest version of the story it was from that trunk that Hurlburt obtained the "Manuscript Found."

Mrs. Davison positively asserts that she gave Hurlburt the original of the "Manuscript Found," either directly, or through her order to Mr. Clark, and that he promised to publish it, which however he never did. He claimed that *it did not read as he expected,* or he found nothing that *would suit his purpose.* In this he for once undoubtedly told the truth. Quite lately, however, he has made the following affidavit.

"Gibsonburg, Ohio,
January 10th, 1881.

"To all whom it may concern:

"In the year eighteen hundred and thirty-four (1834), I went from Geauga county, Ohio, to Monson, Hampden county, Mass., where I found Mrs. Davison, late widow of the Rev. Solomon Spaulding, late of Conneaut, Ashtabula county, Ohio. Of her I obtained a manuscript, supposing it to be the manuscript of the romance written by the said Solomon Spaulding, called the 'Manuscript Found,' which was reported to be the foundation of the 'Book of Mormon.' I did not examine the manuscript till I got home, when upon examination I found it to contain nothing of the kind, but being a manuscript upon an entirely different subject. This manuscript I left with E. D. Howe, of Painsville, Geauga county, Ohio, now Lake county, Ohio, with the understanding that when he had examined it he should return it to the widow. Said Howe says the manuscript was destroyed by fire, and further the deponent saith not.

(Signed)   "D. P. Hurlburt."

Mrs. Davison says Hurlburt obtained the "Manuscript Found." He, in the above, says it was nothing of the kind, but *was a manuscript upon an entirely different subject.* What was that subject? Hurlburt in his original statement says, (these are his own words,) "It is a romance, purporting to have been translated from the Latin, found on twenty-four rolls of parchment, in a cave, but written in modern style—giving a fabulous account of a ship being driven upon the American coast, while proceeding from Rome to Britain, a short time previous to the Christian era; this country then being inhabited by the Indians."

Such is his description of the manuscript he received. No wonder it did not suit his purpose. No work treating on the ancient inhabitants of America could be more unlike the Book of Mormon than this. But Mrs. Davison says this was the original of the "Manuscript Found." We regard it altogether more probable that this was the plot of Mr. Spaulding's romance than the ten tribe version, which we consider to be a latter invention, manufactured by some ignorant anti-"Mormon," who really imagined that the Book of Mormon conveyed that idea. We have nothing more than unauthenticated gossip for the assertion that Mr. Spaulding ever believed that the American Indians were of Israelitish descent. In fact, it is stated that during the later years of that gentleman's life he was strongly inclined to infidelity.

If the papers given to Hurlburt contained the "Manuscript Found," as stated by Mrs. Davison, we know what became of it, if we can believe D. P. Hurlburt. It was burned so that it might never be brought up to confront those who claim that in it is to be found the origin of the Book of Mormon. If Hurlburt did not receive it, Mrs. Davison must have retained it. Then what became of it? Solomon Spaulding's family could have no possible motive for not publishing it. To them it would have been a mine of wealth; at least they thought so, as evidenced by the agreement between Mrs. Davison and Hurlburt, that she was to have half of the profits accruing from its publication, as hereafter shown in her interview with Mr. Haven.

There is another fact that strongly bears out Mrs. Davison's statement. It is this, that it is highly improbable that Mr. Spaulding would write two entirely distinct and varying romances on the ancient inhabitants of America. We never hear of him writing more than one on this subject. If then the Roman story was not the "Manuscript," what was it? It certainly in many particulars agrees with the statements of those who profess to know something about Mr. Spaulding's writings. Both (if there were two) are said to have been written in the Latin language; both were found, supposedly, in a cave near Conneaut, Ohio. This is altogether unlikely. The evidence, we believe, to be overwhelming that Hurlbut did receive the "Manuscript Found," and not finding it what he wanted, he destroyed it or had it destroyed.

We have previously referred to the Jacksons of Jackson settlement, Pennsylvania, from whom Hurlbut first heard of Mr. Spaulding's writings. In justice to Mr. Jackson it must be stated that on one occasion Hurlbut called on him and asked him to sign a document which testified to the probability of Mr. Spaulding's manuscript having been converted into the Book of Mormon. This he indignantly refused to do. He had read both books and knew there was no likeness between them. He then and there stated that there was no agreement between the two; adding that Mr. Spaulding's manuscript was a very small work in the form of a novel, which said not one word about the children of Israel, but professed to give an account of a race of people who originated from the Romans, which Mr. Spaulding said he had translated from a Latin parchment that he had found. The Book of Mormon, Mr. Jackson continued, purports to be written by a branch of the house of Israel; it is written in a different style, and is altogether different. For this reason he refused to lend his name to the lie, and expressed his indignation and contempt at Hurlburt's base and wicked project to deceive the public.

Mr. Jackson's recollection of the plot of the "Manuscript Found" tallies exactly with Hurlburt's description of the contents of the manuscript he received from Mrs. Davison, and is confirmatory evidence of the truth of her statement, that she gave the work to Hurlburt. It is also the strongest kind of testimony in favor of the theory that Spaulding's romance had nothing Israelitish in its narrative, but was Roman from beginning to end, in detail, incident, language, writing, parchment and all.

To return to Hurlburt's work; those who were anxious that it should be published, discovered that it would be better that it should not appear in his name, his reputation having grown too bad. The manuscript was therefore sold to Mr. Howe of Painesville, Ohio, for $500 and was published by him. It did not prove a financial success, its circulation was but small. Mr. Howe eventually offered the copies at half price, but they would not sell even at that reduction. Hurlburt rapidly spent his ill-gotten gains in drink, and for many years bore a most undesirable reputation. He is now an old man, residing at Gibsonburg, Ohio.

The following remarks regarding D. P. Hurlburt, are from the writings of the late Elder Joseph E. Johnson.

"In the year A. D. 1833, then living in Kirtland, Ohio, I became acquainted with a man subsequently known as Dr. Hurlburt. He was a man of fine physique, very pompous, good looking and very ambitious, with some energy, though of poor education. Soon after his arrival he came to my mother's house to board, where he remained for nearly a year. While there he made an effort to get into a good practice of medicine, sought position in the Church, and was ever striving to make marital connection with any of the 'first families.'

"Finally in 1834, he was charged with illicit intercourse with the other sex; was tried and cut off the Church. He denied, expostulated, threatened, but of no use, the facts were too apparent, and he at once vowed himself the enemy of the Church—threatened to write a book that would annihilate 'Mormonism,' and went to Painesville, ten miles, and allied himself to a publisher there, who agreed to print his book if he would furnish the matter. A fund was raised by the anti-"Mormons" in the village around, and enough means raised to send Hurlburt east to hunt up and obtain the writings of Solomon Spaulding, called the 'Manuscript Found,' which had already become famous as the alleged matter from which the Book of Mormon was written.

"Hurlburt went east and was absent some two or three months—and on his return publicly declared that *he could not obtain it*, but instead brought several affidavits from persons who claimed to have heard Solomon Spaulding read his 'Manuscript Found' in 1812, and believed, as well as they could remember, that the matter and story were the same as printed in the Book of Mormon. And these were published in his book of 'Mormonism Exposed,' in that or the subsequent year, but not a sentence from the 'Manuscript Found,' which it appears that *he did really obtain*, but finding no similarity between the two, suppressed the Spaulding manuscript, while he publicly announced in his book that he had entirely failed to obtain it. Hurlburt proved himself to be a man of gross immorality and was untruthful and unreliable."

THE BOGUS AFFIDAVIT

The next noteworthy person who entered upon the crusade against the Book of Mormon was a Congregationalist minister of Holliston, Massachusetts, named Storrs.

This man was greatly annoyed at the loss of some of the best members of his congregation through the preaching of the everlasting gospel, and in his anger published to the world what he asserted was the affidavit of the widow Solomon Spaulding, but which she afterwards repudiated, as shown from the following article published in the Quincy (Illinois) *Whig* shortly after the appearance of the bogus affidavit:

"A Cunning Device Detected.

"It will be recollected that a few months since an article appeared in several of the papers, purporting to give an account of the origin of the Book of Mormon. How far the writer of the piece has effected his purposes, or what his purposes were in pursuing the course he has, I shall not attempt to say at this time, but shall call upon every candid man to judge in this matter for himself, and shall content myself by presenting before the public the other side of the question in the form of a letter, as follows:

"Copy of a letter written by Mr. John Haven, of Holliston, Middlesey Co., Massachusetts, to his daughter, Elizabeth Haven, of Quincy, Adams Co., Illinois.

"Your brother Jesse passed through Monson, where he saw Mrs. Davison and her daughter, Mrs. McKinstry, and also Dr. Ely, and spent several hours with them, during which time he asked them the following questions, viz.:

Question.—'Did you, Mrs. Davison, write a letter to John Storrs, giving an account of the origin of the Book of Mormon?'

Answer.—'I did not.'

Q.—'Did you sign your name to it?'

A.—'I did not, neither did I ever see the letter until I saw it in the *Boston Recorder*, the letter was never brought to me to sign.'

Q.—'What agency had you in having this letter sent to Mr. Storrs?'

A.—'D. R. Austin came to my house and asked me some questions, took some minutes on paper, and from these minutes wrote that letter.'

Q.—'Have you read the Book of Mormon?'

A.—'I have read some in it.'

Q.—'Does Mr. Spaulding's manuscript and the Book of Mormon agree?'

A.—'I think some few of the names are alike.'

Q.—'Does the manuscript describe an idolatrous or a religious people?'

Q.—'An idolatrous people.'

A.—'Where is the manuscript?'

A.—'D. P. Hurlburt came here and took it, said he would get it printed and let me have one half of the profits.'

Q.—'Has D. P. Hurlburt got the manuscript printed?'

A.—'I received a ietter stating that it did not read as he expected, and he should not print it.'

Q.—'How large is Mr. Spaulding's manuscript?'

A.—'About one-third as large as the Book of Mormon.'

Q.—To Mrs. McKinstry: 'How old were you when your father wrote the manuscript?'

A.—'About five years of age.'

Q.—'Did you ever read the manuscript?'

A.—'When I was about twelve years old I used to read it for diversion.'

Q.—'Did the manuscript describe an idolatrous or a religious people?'

A.—'An idolatrous people.'

Q.—'Does the manuscript and the Book of Mormon agree?'

A.—'I think some of the names agree.'

Q.—'Are you certain that some of the names agree?'

A.—'I am not.'

Q.—'Have you read any in the Book of Mormon?'

A.—'I have not.'

Q.—'Was your name attached to that letter, which was sent to Mr. John Storrs, by your order?'

A.—'No, I never meant that my name should be there.'

'You see by the above questions and answers, that Mr. Austin, in his great zeal to destroy the Latter-day Saints, has asked Mrs. Davison a few questions, then wrote a letter to Mr. Storrs in his own language. I do not say that the above questions and answers were given in the form that I have written them, but these questions were asked, and these answers given. Mrs. Davison is about seventy years of age, and somewhat broke.'

"This may certify that I am personally acquainted with Mr. Haven, his son and daughter, and am satisfied they are persons of truth. I have also read Mr. Haven's letter to his daughter which has induced me to copy it for publication, and I further say, the above is a correct copy of Mr. Haven's letter.

A. Badlam."

Notwithstanding the above refutation and *expose* the opponents of "Mormonism" have continually from the time of its publication, copied, re-published and harped upon this forged affidavit of Mrs. Davison. Their ears have been ever deaf and their eyes blind when the refutation of the slander has been presented to them. They did not then, and do not now want it; they prefer the lie which one of their number has concocted and spread broad-cast through the world.

We must now turn to Sidney Rigdon who by many is regarded as the agent or go-between by and through whom Joseph Smith came into possession of the "Manuscript Found," and who was, in fact, the chief instrument in converting that romance into the Book of Mormon. It is urged that Joseph had neither the learning, ability nor industry to perform so arduous a literary work, but that Rigdon had the audacity, cunning and education necessary to perpetrate such a fraud, and that Joseph Smith was his willing tool, whom he used as a screen to protect himself from public observation and through whom he palmed his imposture on the world. None of those who accept this theory have yet been able to explain what possible motive Rigdon could have had in taking such a course, were such an arrangement possible; but we have most trustworthy and reliable testimony that it could not be so for two altogether sufficient reasons:

First: Sidney Rigdon never was at Pittsburg or any other place at the same time as Mr. Spaulding's manuscript was there and therefore he could not have seen or read it, it being remembered that it never was out of the possession of the author's family only during the short time it is said to have been in the hands of Mr. Patterson.

Second: Sidney Rigdon never saw Joseph Smith until years after the latter received the sacred plates, indeed, not until after the Book of Mormon had been printed and the Church of Jesus Christ organized.

Let us consider the first of the above propositions. Mr. Spaulding resided in Pittsburg only for a short time between 1812, when he lived at Conneaut, and 1816 when he died at Amity. The general opinion is that he moved to the last named place in 1814. It was then, between 1812 and 1814, that, if ever, the manuscript was in the hands of Mr. Patterson; Sidney Rigdon was then a youth of not more than twenty years of age, residing on and working his deceased father's farm at St. Clair, Pennsylvania. To make this point more clear, we will here give a short sketch of Rigdon's early life:

Sidney Rigdon was born in St. Clair township, Alleghany Co., Pa., on the 19th of February, 1793. In his twenty-fifth year he connected himself with a society, which in that country was called Regular Baptists. In March, 1819, he received a license to preach in that society, and in the following May he left Pennsylvania and went to Trumbull Co., Ohio, where he was afterwards married. In 1821 he was called to the pastoral charge of the first Baptist church of Pittsburg, which invitation he accepted early in the following year, and soon became a popular minister. After ministering in that position for two and a half years he withdrew from that sect, because he considered its doctrines were not altogether in accord with the scriptures. With Mr. Alexander Campbell he founded the "Campbellite" or "Disciples" church; but having retired from the ministry he for two years worked as a day laborer in a tannery; after which he removed to Bainbridge, Geauga Co., Ohio, where the people solicited him to preach. He complied with their request and soon grew quite popular. He advocated the doctrines of repentance and baptism for the remission of sins, and baptized numbers from all the country round. During this time he removed from Bainbridge to Mentor, some thirty miles distant, and it was there that Parley P. Pratt and other Elders found him, in the Fall of 1830.

We will now give the testimony of a number of persons who were most intimately acquainted with Sidney Rigdon during his youth. These testimonies we copy from a work lately published by Mr. Robert Patterson, of Pittsburg, son of Mr. Patterson, the printer, to whom the Spaulding romance is said to have been taken. He is the person called "the present writer" in these extracts, which in his work follow a short account of Sidney's early life:

"1. Rigdon's relatives at Library, Pa. Carvil Rigdon (his brother) and Peter Boyer (his brother-in-law), in a written statement dated Jan. 27, 1843, certify to the facts and dates as above stated in regard to his birth, schooling, uniting with the church, licensure, ordination and settlement in Pittsburg in 1822. Mr. Boyer also in a personal interview with the present writer in 1879 positively affirmed that Rigdon had never lived in Pittsburg previous to 1822, adding that they were boys together and he ought to know. Mr. Boyer had for a short time embraced Mormonism, but became convinced that it was a delusion and returned to his membership in the Baptist church.

"2. Isaac King, a highly-respected citizen of Library, Pa., and an old neighbor of Rigdon, states in a letter to the present writer, dated June 14th, 1879, that Sidney lived on the farm of his father until the death of the latter, in May, 1810, and for a number of years afterwards, farming with very indifferent success; "it was said he was too lazy and proud to make a good farmer;' received his education in a log school-house in the vicinity; 'began to talk in public on religion soon after his admission to the church, probably at his own instance, as there is no record of his licensure;' went to Sharon, Pa., for a time, and was there ordained as a preacher, but soon returned to his farm, which he sold (June 28th, 1823) to James Means, and about the time of sale removed to Pittsburg.

"3. Samuel Cooper, of Saltsburg, Pa., a veteran of three wars, in a letter to the present writer, dated June 14, 1879, stated as follows: 'I was acquainted with Mr. Lambdin, was often in the printing-office; was acquainted with Silas Engles, the foreman of the printing-office; he never mentioned Sidney Rigdon's name to me, so I am satisfied he was never engaged there as a printer. I was introduced to Sidney Rigdon in 1843; he stated to me that he was a Mormon preacher or lecturer; I was acquainted with him during 1843-45; never knew him before, and never knew him as a printer; never saw him in the book-store or printing-office; your father's office was in the celebrated Molly Murphy's Row."

"4. Rev. Robert P. DuBois, of New London, Pa., under date of Jan. 9th, 1879, writes: 'I entered the book-store of R. Patterson & Lambdin in March, 1818, when about twelve years old, and remained there until the Summer of 1820. The firm had under its control a book-store on Fourth Street, a book-bindery, a printing-office (not newspaper, but job-office, under the name of Butler & Lambdin), entrance on Diamond Alley, and a steam paper-mill on the Allegheny (under the name of R. & J. Patterson). I knew nothing of Spaulding (then dead) or of his book, or of Sidney Rigdon."

"5. Mrs. R. W. Lambdin, of Irvington, N. Y., widow of the late J. Harrison Lambdin, in response to some inquiries as to her recollection of Rigdon and others, writes under date of Jan. 15th, 1882: "I am sorry to say I shall not be able to give you any information relative to the persons you name. They certainly could not have been friends of Mr. Lambdin.' Mrs. Lambdin resided in Pittsburg from her marriage in 1819, to the death of her husband, Aug. 1st, 1825. Mr. Lambdin was born Sep. 1st, 1798."

In addition to this we have the testimony of Sidney Rigdon's mother. She informed one gentleman, who published her statement years ago, long before the Spaulding story was concocted, and therefore with no design to mislead on that matter, that her son lived at home and worked on the farm until the twenty-sixth year of his age and was never engaged in public life until after that period, either politically or religiously. Thus, according to his mother's statement which is sustained by these other testimonies, he did not leave home until 1819. He did not go to Pittsburg until 1822; eight or nine years after the manuscript of Spaulding's romance had been returned to its author (if, indeed, it had ever been out of his hands), and that author had removed from Pittsburg and died.

Again it is asserted that Sidney Rigdon was associated with the printing-office of Patterson and Lambdin during his stay in Pittsburg. The testimony above given is very strong evidence to the contrary. In addition to which we have Rigdon's own refutation of the falsehood, made at the time that Mrs. Davison's bogus affidavit was first given to the world. He asserts in effect, most positively, that when he went to Pittsburg he did so as a minister of the gospel at the call of a religious congregation, and was never in any way directly or indirectly connected with any printing office during his stay there; and if he had been associated with a Pittsburg printing office nobody claims that the "Manuscript Found" was in that city at that late date (1822). According to Mrs. McKinstry's already quoted affidavit it was then hid up in an old trunk at a small village called Hardwicks, in the state of New York, hundreds of miles from Pittsburg. To tide over this difficulty some one has suggested that probably Spaulding made a copy of his romance for the printer, and it was this copy that Rigdon afterwards found. But this a baseless supposition; until lately such an idea was never thought of, and it loses all its force from the fact that those best acquainted with the history of that manuscript say that the copy Spaulding gave to Patterson was returned to him; it was not left in the office to be found by Rigdon, or any one else in after years.

It may be asked, is there no conflicting testimony? Do not some persons assert that Rigdon was in Pittsburg and acquainted with Patterson and Lambdin years before 1822? Yes, but their testimony is of little value for many reasons. It is, in the first place, almost invariably second hand. They do not testify of what they themselves actually knew on these points, but of what somebody else knew, or said, or told them. In the second place, they are made, as a rule, by very aged persons, whose memory, when we consider the mass of trash that has been published on this subject, cannot be trusted. They, where desiring to be truthful, have mixed up what they really knew and what they have since heard and read. A third class are "divines," men with "reverend" tacked on their names, whose testimony, it is a sad fact but it is a truth, can scarcely ever be trusted on anything pertaining to "Mormonism." One very aged lady, whose father and husband kept the post office from 1804 to 1833, says that Rigdon and Lambdin used to come together to the post office for mail matter as early as 1815, if not earlier, and that as youths they were intimate. But it must be remembered that there was a difference of six or seven years in the ages of these two young men, Rigdon being the elder, and Mr. Lambdin's wife asserts of him and others that "they certainly could not have been friends of Mr. Lambdin." Again it is altogether inconsistent to believe that a young man of Rigdon's ambition would associate with a boy so many years his junior; the supposition is altogether more consistent that this lady has mixed her names and dates, and that young Lambdin having a companion who came with him for letters, she has in the course of many years confused this companion with Rigdon who doubtless often visited the post office at a later period, and at a time when his name would be well known through all Pittsburg.

But it is an open question whether Mr. Patterson ever had the "Manuscript Found" in his possession. The Spaulding family say that he had, he asserts that he had not. On being interrogated on the subject, soon after the publication of Mrs. Davison's bogus affidavit, he said that he knew nothing of any such manuscript.* Even Hurlburt states that "he called on Mr. Patterson who affirmed *his entire ignorance of the whole matter.*" Here is evidently a grand mistake or a gross falsehood. To us, it seems from the evidence, that the story of Mr. Patterson having received the manuscript was first invented by Priest Storrs on purpose to connect Sidney Rigdon with the "Manuscript Found" and the ladies of the Spaulding family have heard it so often reiterated that in their old age they have imagined that they have some recollection of such an incident, when, in truth, it is only the confused remembrance of what has been ding-donged into their ears by over-anxious opponents of "Mormonism" for the last forty years. It is a well-known fact that the human mind is so constituted that after brooding over imaginary circumstances for a lengthened period it will frequently grow to regard such fables as facts. This peculiarity of the human mind has often been commented upon. A laughable incident in this connection is related regarding King George IV., of England. He got it into his head that he was present at the battle of Waterloo, and was especially fond of referring to the circumstance in the presence of the Duke of Wellington, and then requiring the aged warrior to back up his statement. It is said that the duke, with the true instinct of the courtier, would reply on such occasions, "I have heard your majesty mention that circumstance before." So Mrs. Davison and her daughter have so frequently heard the statement that the Book of Mormon was taken from the "Manuscript Found," that the "Manuscript Found" related to the lost ten tribes, that Mr. Patterson borrowed it in Pittsburg, and that Sidney Rigdon had something inexplicable to do with it, that these ladies actually came to believe that these assertions were all truths, and in their old age were willing to make affidavit to their belief in many things about which in earlier days they were nothing like so sure.

With regard to the second point, as to when Joseph Smith first saw Sidney

*——The gentleman to whom he made this statement is understood to have been Mr. Ephraim S. Green, of Philadelphia.

Rigdon, we draw attention to the two following extracts from the writings of Elder Parley P. Pratt:

"The Mormonites.

"To the Editor of the New York Era:

"Sir.—In yours of the 20th inst., there is an article copied from the *Boston Recorder*, headed, 'Mormon Bible,' and signed, 'Matilda Davison,' which, justice to our society and to the public requires me to answer, and I trust that a sense of justice will induce you, sir, to give your readers both sides of the question.

"I am one of the society who believe the Book of Mormon, and as such I am assailed in the statement professing to come from Matilda Davison.

"In the first place, there is no such thing in existence as the 'Mormon Bible.' The 'Mormons,' as they are vulgarly called, believe in the same Bible that all Christendom profess to believe in, viz.: the common version of the Old and New Testament. The Book of Mormon is not entitled a Bible, except by those who misrepresent it. It is entitled the 'Book of Mormon.'

"The religious sect alluded to in your paper, are there accused of knavery and superstition. Now we are not sensible of being guilty of knavery, and we do not know wherein we are superstitious, but very much desire to know in order that we may reform. If some good minister or editor will condescend to particulars and point out our superstitions, we will take it as a great kindness, for we are the declared enemies to knavery and superstition.

"If a firm believer in the gospel of a crucified and risen Redeemer, as manifested to all nations, and as recorded in their sacred books, amounts to superstition, then we are superstitious. If preaching that system to others and calling them to repentance is superstition, then we are superstitious. If refusing to fellowship the modern systems of sectarianism which are contrary to the pure doctrines of the Bible be superstition, then we are superstitious, for we hereby declare our withdrawal from all the mysticism, priestcraft and superstitions, and from all the creeds, doctrines, commandments, traditions and precepts of men, as far as they are contrary to the ancient faith and doctrine of the Saints; and we hereby bear our testimony against them.

"We do not believe that God ever instituted more than one religious system under the same dispensation, therefore we do not admit that two different sects can possibly be right. The Churches of Jesus Christ, in any age or country, must be all built upon the same faith, the same baptism, the same Lord, the same Holy Spirit, which would guide them into all truth, and consequently from all error and superstition. The Book of Mormon has never been placed by us in the place of the sacred scriptures, but, as before said, the sacred scriptures stand in their own place, and the Book of Mormon abundantly corroborates and bears testimony of the truth of the Bible. Indeed there is no society, within our knowledge, whose members adhere more closely to the Bible than ours. For proof of this we appeal to the multitudes who attend our religious meetings in this city and in all other places.

"The piece in your paper states that 'Sidney Rigdon was connected in the printing office of Mr. Patterson' (in Pittsburg), and that 'this is a fact well known in that region, and as Rigdon himself has frequently stated. Here he had ample opportunity to become acquainted with Mr. Spaulding's manuscript (romance) and to copy it if he chose.' This statement is utterly and entirely false. Mr. Rigdon was never connected with the said printing establishment, either directly or indirectly, and we defy the world to bring proof of any such connection. Now the person or persons who fabricated that falsehood would do well to repent and become persons of truth and veracity before they express such acute sensibility concerning the religious pretensions of others. The statement that Sidney Rigdon is one of the founders of the said religious sect is also incorrect.

"The sect was founded in the state of New York, while Mr. Ridgon resided in Ohio, several hundred miles distant. Mr. Rigdon embraced the doctrine through my instrumentality. I first presented the Book of Mormon to him. I stood upon the bank of the stream while he was baptized, and assisted to officiate in his ordination, and I myself was unacquainted with the system until some months after its organization, which was on the 6th of April, 1830, and I embraced it in September following.

"The piece further states that 'a woman preacher appointed a meeting at New Salem, Ohio, and in the meeting read and repeated copious extracts from the Book of Mormon.' Now, it is a fact well known, that we have not had a female preacher in our connection, for we do not believe in a female priesthood. It further says that the excitement in New Salem became so great that the inhabitants had a meeting and deputed Doctor Philastus Hurlburt, one of their members, to repair to Spaulding's widow, and obtain from her the original manuscript of the romance, etc. But the statement does not say whether he obtained the manuscript, but still leaves the impression that he did, and that it was compared with the Book of Mormon. Now who ever will read the work got up by said Hulburt, entitled: 'Mormonism Unveiled,' will find that he there states that the said manuscript of Spaulding's romance was lost and could nowhere be found. But the widow is here made to say that it is carefully preserved. Here seems to be some knavery or crooked work; and no wonder, for this said Hulburt is one of the most notorious rascals in the western country. He was first cut off from our society for an attempt at seduction and crime, and secondly he was laid under bond in Geauga county, Ohio, for threatening to murder Joseph Smith, Jr., after which he laid a deep design of the Spaulding romance imposition, in which he has been backed by evil and designing men in different parts of the country, and sometimes by those who do not wish to do wrong, but who are ignorant on the subject. Now what but falsehood could be expected from such a person? Now if there is such a manuscript in existence, let it come forward at once and not be kept in the dark. Again, if the public will be patient, they will doubtless find that the piece signed 'Matilda Davison' (Spaulding's widow) is a base fabrication by Priest Storrs, of Holliston, Mass., in order to save his craft, after losing the deacon of his church, and several of its most pious and intelligent members, who left his society to embrace what they considered to be truth. At any rate, a judge of literary productions, who can swallow that piece of writing as the production of a women in private life, can be made to believe that the Book of Mormon is a romance. For the one is as much like a romance as the other is like a woman's composition.

"The production signed 'Matilda Davison,' is evidently the work of a man accustomed to public address, and the Book of Mormon I know to be true, and the Spaulding story, as far as the Book of Mormon is connected with it, I know to be false.

"I now leave the subject with a candid public, with a sincere desire that those who have been deluded with such vain and foolish lies, may be undeceived.

"Editors, who have given publicity to the Spaulding story, will do an act of justice by giving publicity to the foregoing.

"P. P. Pratt.

"New York, Nov. 27th, 1839."

The following explicit statement is also copied from the earlier writings of Elder Parley P. Pratt:

"About A.D. 1827, Messrs. A. Campbell, W. Scott, and S. Rigdon, with some others, residing in Virginia, Ohio, etc., came off from the Baptist, and established a new order, under the name of Reformed Baptist, or Disciples. And they were termed by their enemies, Campbellites, Rigdonites, etc. This reformation as to its doctrine, consisted principally of the baptism of repentance, for the remission of sins, etc. And Mr. Rigdon in particular held to a literal fulfilment, and application of the written word, and by this means he was an instrument to turn many from the false notions of sectarianism, to an understanding of the prophecies, touching the great restoration of Israel, and the mighty revolutions of the last days. Many hundred disciples were gathered by his ministry, throughout the lake country of Ohio, and many other preachers stood in connection with him in these principles. I was then pursuing agricultural life, and mostly occupied in converting the wilderness into a fruitful field. But being a member of the Baptist church, and a lover of truth, I became acquainted with Mr. Rigdon, and a believer in, and teacher of the same doctrine. After proclaiming those principles in my own neighborhood, and the adjoining country, I at length took a journey to the state of New York, partly on a visit to Columbia county, N. Y., my native place, and partly for the purpose of ministering the word. This journey was undertaken in August, 1830; I had no sooner reached Ontario county, N. Y., than I came in contact with the Book of Mormon, which had then been published about six months, and had gathered about fifty disciples, which were all who then constituted the church of Latter-day Saints. I was greatly prejudiced against the book, but remembering the caution of Paul, 'Prove all things, hold fast that which is good,' I sat down to read it, and after carefully comparing it with the other scriptures, and praying to God, He gave me the knowledge of its truth, by the power of the Holy Ghost, and what was I, that I could withstand God? I accordingly obeyed the ordinances and was commissioned by revelation, and the laying on of hands, to preach the fulness of the gospel. Then, after finishing my visit to Columbia county, I returned to the brethren in Ontario county, where, for the first time, I saw Mr. Joseph Smith, Jr., who had just returned from Pennsylvania to his father's house in Manchester. About the 15th of October, 1830, I took my journey in company with Elders O. Cowdery and Peter Whitmer, to Ohio. We called on Elder S. Rigdon, and then for the first time his eyes beheld the Book of Mormon. I, myself, had the happiness to present it to him in person. He was much surprised, and it was with much persuasion and argument, that he was prevailed on to read it, and after he had read it, he had a great struggle of mind, before he fully believed, and embraced it; and when finally convinced of its truth, he called together a large congregation of his friends, neighbors and brethren, and then addressed them very affectionately for nearly two hours during most of which time, both himself and nearly all the congregation were melted into tears. He asked forgiveness of everybody who might have had occasion to be offended with any part of his former life; he forgave all who had persecuted or injured him in any manner, and the next morning, himself and wife were baptized by Elder O. Cowdery. I was present, it was a solemn scene, most of the people were greatly affected, they came out of the water overwhelmed in tears. Many others were baptized by us in that vicinity, both before and after his baptism, insomuch that during the Fall of 1830, and the following Winter and Spring, the number of the disciples was increased to about one thousand, the Holy Ghost was mightily poured out, and the word of God grew and multiplied, and many priests were obedient to the faith. Early in 1831, Mr. Rigdon having been ordained under our hands, visited Elder J. Smith, Jr., in the state of New York, for the first time, and from that time forth rumor began to circulate that he, Rigdon, was the author of the Book of Mormon.

"The Spaulding story never was dreamed of until several years afterwards, when it appeared in 'Mormonism Unveiled'—a base forgery, by D. P. Hurlburt and others of similar character, who strove to account for the Book of Mormon in some other way than the truth. In the west, whole neighborhoods embraced Mormonism, after this fable of the Spaulding story had been circulated among them: indeed, we never considered it worthy of an answer, until it was converted, by the ignorant and impudent religious editors of this city, into something said to be positively certain, and not to be disputed. Now, I testify that the forgers of the Spaulding lie (concerning S. Rigdon and others), are of the same description as those who forged the lie against the disciples of old, accusing them of stealing the body of Jesus, etc."

We also insert, at this point, the affidavit of the only surviving sister of Joseph Smith, which conclusively shows that Sidney Rigdon had no communication with the Prophet or any other of the family until months after the Book of Mormon was published.

"STATE OF ILLINOIS, ⎱ ss.
Kendall county. ⎰

"I, Katherine Salisbury, being duly sworn, depose and say, that I am a resident of the state of Illinois, and have been for forty years last past; that I will be sixty-eight years of age, July 28th, 1881.

That I am a daughter of Joseph Smith, Senior, and sister to Joseph Smith, Jr., the translator of the Book of Mormon. That at the time the said book was published, I was seventeen years of age; that at the time of the publication of said book, my brother, Joseph Smith, Jr., lived in the family of my father, in the town of Manchester, Ontario county, New York, and that he had, all of his life to this time made his home with the family.

"That at the time, and for years prior thereto, I lived in and was a member of such family, and personally knowing to the things transacted in said family, and those who visited at my father's house, and the friends of the family, and the friends and acquaintances of my brother, Joseph Smith, Jr., who visited at or came to my father's house.

"That prior to the latter part of the year A.D. 1830, there was no person who visited with, or was an acquaintance of, or called upon the said family, or any member thereof to my knowledge, by the name of Sidney Rigdon; nor was such person known to the family, or any member thereof, to my knowledge, until the last part of the year A.D. 1830, or the first part of the year 1831, and some time after the organization of the Church of Jesus Christ, by Joseph Smith, Jr., and several months after the publication of the Book of Mormon.

"That I remember the time when Sidney Rigdon came to my father's place, and that it was after the removal of my father from Waterloo, N. Y., to Kirtland, Ohio. That this was in the year 1831, and some months after the publication of the Book of Mormon, and fully one year after the Church was organized, as before stated herein.

"That I make this statement, not on account of fear, favor, or hope of reward of any kind; but simply that the truth may be known with reference to said matter, and that the foregoing statements made by me are true, as I verily believe.

"Katherine Salisbury.

"Sworn before me, and subscribed in my presence, by the said Katherine Salisbury, this 15th day of April, A.D. 1881.

"J. H. Jenks, *Notary Public.*"

Has it ever entered into the thoughts of our opponents that if Sidney Rigdon was the author or adapter of the Book of Mormon how vast and widespread must have been the conspiracy that foisted it upon the world! Whole families must have been engaged in it. Men of all ages and various conditions in life, and living in widely separate portions of the country must have been connected with it. First we must include in the catalogue of conspirators the whole of the Smith family, then the Whitmer's, Martin Harris and Oliver Cowdery; further, to carry on this absurd idea, Sidney Rigdon and Parley P. Pratt must have been their active fellow-conspirators in arranging, carrying out and consummating their iniquitous fraud. To do this they must have traveled thousands of miles and spent months, perhaps years, to accomplish —what? That is the unsolved problem. Was it for the purpose of duping the world? They, at any rate the great majority of them, were of all men most unlikely to be engaged in such a folly. Their habits, surroundings, station in life, youth and inexperience all forbid such a thought. What could they gain, in any light that could be then presented to their minds, by palming such a deception upon the world? This is another unanswerable question. Then comes the staggering fact, if the Book be a falsity, that all these families, all these diverse characters, in all the trouble, perplexity, persecution and suffering through which they passed, never wavered in their testimony, never changed their statements, never "went back" on their original declarations, but continued unto death (and they have all passed away save a very few), proclaiming that the Book of Mormon was a divine revelation, and that its record was true. Was there ever such an exhibition in the history of the world of such continued, such unabating, such undeviating falsehood? if falsehood it was. We cannot find a place in the annals of their lives where they wavered, and what makes the matter more remarkable is that it can be said of most of them, as is elsewhere said of the three witnesses, they became offended with the Prophet Joseph, and a number of them openly rebelled against him; but they never retracted one word with regard to the genuineness of Mormon's inspired record. Whether they were friends or foes to Joseph, whether they regarded him as God's continued mouthpiece or as a fallen Prophet, they still persisted in their statements with regard to the book and the veracity of their earlier testimonies. How can we possibly with our knowledge of human nature make this undeviating, unchanging, unwavering course, continuing over fifty years consistent with a deliberate, premeditated and cunningly-devised and executed fraud!

MRS. DICKENSON'S SPECULATIONS

We next invite attention to one of the latest versions of the "Spaulding story." It appeared in *Scribner's Magazine* for August, 1880, and purports to be written by Mrs. Ellen E. Dickenson, a grand-niece of Mr. Spaulding. It is conspicuous for its inexactness, but is valuable as containing the affidavit of Mrs. M. S. McKinstry already considered.

Referring to the discovery by Mr. Spaulding of bows and other relics in a mound near his home at Conneaut, Mrs. Dickenson writes:

"This discovery suggested to him the subject for a new romance, which he called a translation from some *hieroglyphical writing* exhumed from the mound. This romance purported to be a history of the peopling of America by the *lost tribes of Israel,* the tribes and their leaders *having very singular names,* among them Mormon, Moroni, Lamanite, Nephi. The romance the author called 'Manuscript Found.' This all occurred in 1812, when to write a book was a distinction, and Mr. Spaulding read his manuscript from time to time to a circle of *admiring friends.* He determined finally to publish it and for that purpose carried it to Pittsburg, Pennsylvania, to a printer by the name of Patterson. After keeping it awhile, Mr. Patterson returned it, declining to print it. *There was at this time in this printing office a young man named Sidney Rigdon,* who twenty years later figured as a preacher among the Saints."

In the above extract we have printed in italics those statements to which we wish to draw special attention.

Mrs. Dickenson says Mr. Spaulding called his romance "a translation from some hieroglyphical writing." This is an entirely new version of the old fiction. According to the original story it was written in Latin, but now after fifty years the writing is changed to hieroglyphics to make the theory agree better with the Book of Mormon which was translated from plates engraved in reformed Egyptian. We are told by earlier writers, before the matter was so entirely befogged as it is now by anti-"Mormon" speculations, assumptions and hypothesis, that the author's idea was to palm off his romance as a reality, and when he wrote it he expected the masses would believe it when published. Now it would be quite consistent for a graduate of Dartmouth College (as was Mr. Spaulding) to translate a Latin parchment—that would appear to be an every-day matter for a recognized clergyman of an orthodox sect, but to translate hieroglyphics would be entirely another thing; for it must not be forgotten that it was not until nearly thirty years after Mr. Spaulding wrote his "Manuscript Found" that the first dictionary and first grammar of Egyptian hieroglyphics were published.* Egyptiology being now a science, Mrs. Dickenson has outraged all consistency by claiming that Mr. Spaulding pretended to translate from hieroglyphics of which none at that time had any definite understanding. Mr. Spaulding as an educated man who wished his work to receive credence would know better than to start off with an evident tell-tale impossibility.

_____
*Those of M. Champolleon published between 1836 and 1844.

Mrs. Dickenson calls the names in the Book of Mormon "very singular." This is because she has not read the book. A large number of the names in Mormon's sacred record are also found in the Holy Bible; as examples: Jacob, Joseph, Aaron, Noah, Jeremiah, Isaiah, Ishmael, Lemuel, Timothy, Shem, etc. Are these singular? Another large percentage finish with the Hebrew termination: iah (Jah) an abbreviation of Jehovah. One scribbler asserts that "the real author of the Book of Mormon was well acquainted with the classics; the names of most of his heroes have the Latin termination of i, such as Nephi, Lehi, Moroni." This ignoramus was evidently not himself acquainted with the classics or he would have known that the most frequent termination of the masculine singular in the Latin language is us not i; and of names ending in us there are but very few in the Book of Mormon, probably half a dozen. Mrs. Dickenson gives an example of some of these "singular names": "Mormon, Moroni, Lamanite and Nephi." Surely neither Laman or Moroni are singular names. There are, at any rate, more than one river of this name in South America running through the region where, according to Book of Mormon history, the Nephite general, Moroni, carried on his campaigns and held military control. Nephi is an ancient Egyptian name, and a title of Osiris, one of the gods of that people; its meaning is "the benevolent one." That it was common among the Israelites of the age of Nephi (B.C. 600) is shown from the fact that the word Nephites in the original Hebrew plural form occurs twice in the Bible, in Ezra 2:50, and Nehemiah 7:52. Lehi is also a Bible proper name.

Regarding the circle of "admiring friends" who heard the "Manuscript Found" read by its author, is it not a little singular that they so loudly praised it when the Book of Mormon, which is said to have been copied from it "word for word," is berated as uninteresting, dull, dry, stupid and everything else that is not commended or admired in literary productions? Neither is the style of the Book of Mormon that of a man educated in modern English; it is incomprehensible that a student in the literature of this age would express himself in the phraseology and style of this record. And again it is not written in the language of either Joseph Smith or Sidney Rigdon. If we compare the revelations given through Joseph Smith at the time the plates were being translated, we find altogether different diction; or let us compare it with the Lectures on Faith in the Book of Doctrine and Covenants and then with the acknowledged writings of Sidney Rigdon, and we shall find there is nothing common in any of these with the peculiarities of grammatical construction and verbal idiosyncracies of the Book of Mormon. Judging then by the usual and accepted methods of criticism on which some rely so strongly, and throwing out the direct evidence as to its origin, this book could not be the creation of either Solomon Spaulding, Sidney Rigdon or Joseph Smith. Again, how is it that when the manuscript of the Book of Mormon was presented to the printer (see Mr. Gilbert's statement) it was misspelled and without punctuation. Did neither the graduate of Dartmouth College nor the minister of a flourishing religious congregation, who, by the way, according to some accounts, had formerly worked in a printing office, know anything of punctuation? This is the extreme of folly. But if they did, what conceivable reason could there be for leaving the punctuation out of the copy taken to the printer. Mr. Gilbert's statement of the great care shown by Hyrum Smith to have the book printed exactly as written, his extreme solicitude regarding the manuscript, his ignorance of the use of commas, colons, etc., and his one unwavering and unchanging testimony regarding the discovery and translation of the plates are all strong corroborative evidence that no educated man had anything to do with the production of the book; and how inconsistent with the stories of Joseph Smith's confirmed laziness is the idea that he would go to the trouble of copying out a manuscript which makes more than six hundred pages of closely printed matter! The promoters of the "Spaulding story" are terribly inconsistent in the various parts of their theory.

The statement that Mr. Spaulding took his romance to Mr. Patterson may be true or it may not, individually we do not believe it, but the assertion that Sidney Rigdon worked in that gentleman's printing office we have elsewhere shown to be utterly false. We will let Mr. Howe, who purchased Hurlburt's manuscript, give his version of this affair; simply reminding our readers that his book, "Mormonism Unveiled," was published in 1834, when the exact facts would be much fresher in the memory of the participants than in 1880. Speaking of the "Manuscript Found," he writes:

"It was inferred at once that some light might be shed upon this subject and the mystery revealed by applying to Patterson and Lambdin, in Pittsburg. But here again death had interposed a barrier. That establishment was dissolved and broken up many years since, and Lambdin died about eight years ago. Mr. Patterson says he has no recollection of any such manuscript being brought there for publication, neither would he have been likely to have seen it, as the business of printing was conducted wholly by Lambdin at that time. He says, however, that many manuscript books and pamphlets were brought to the office about that time, which remained upon the shelves for years without being printed or even examined."

Mark how strangely this statement disagrees with the assertions of the ladies of the Spaulding family with regard to Mr. Patterson's friendship and intimate acquaintance with Mr. Spaulding, and the latter's admiration of the "Manuscript Found."

Now notice the insincerity and actual dishonesty of the next passages, in view of the fact that Hurlburt had received the "Manuscript Found" from the Spaulding family, and according to his account had given the document that he had received to Howe, the publisher of the work from which we are quoting:

"Now as Spaulding's book can nowhere be found, or anything heard of it after being carried to this establishment, there is the strongest presumption that it remained there in seclusion till about the year 1823 or 1824, at which time Sidney Rigdon located himself in that city. We have been credibly informed that he was on terms of intimacy with Lambdin, being seen frequently at his shop."

Here is a desperate attempt to connect Rigdon with the affair. Lambdin was dead so he could not contradict any statement about his intimacy with Rigdon; but the whole hypothesis amounts to nothing in view of the positive statements of the Spaulding family that the "Manuscript Found" was in their undisturbed possession, hundreds of miles from Pittsburg, from 1814 to 1834. One thing, however, it shows that in those days Sidney Rigdon's life was too well known for Howe to write other than the truth regarding the time he first visited Pittsburg, for when Mrs. Dickenson wildly imagines and falsely asserts he was working in the office of Patterson and Lambdin, all trustworthy authorities, including his mother, assert that he was laboring upon his father's farm at St. Clair, Alleghany Co., Pennsylvania, which he did not leave until he was in his twenty-sixth year, when he went to Ohio and afterwards to Pittsburg.

Possibly doubting the Spaulding story herself Mrs. Dickenson suggests another solution, yet still more ridiculous. She writes: "Smith, however, could easily have possessed himself of the manuscript if he had fancied it suitable to his purpose, for it is understood that he was a servant on the farm, or teamster for Mr. Sabine (Mrs. Spaulding's brother) in whose house the package of manuscript lay exposed in an unlocked trunk for several years."

Prodigious! Let us examine this wonderful suggestion. According to Mrs. Mc-Kinstry's affidavit the "Manuscript Found" was at Mr. Sabine's from 1816 to 1820. Joseph Smith was born in the latter part of December 1805, consequently he was not fifteen years old when the manuscript was removed from Mr. Sabine's. A boy of his age would make a rather youthful teamster or farm-hand. And then how preposterous the thought that an illiterate boy of eleven, twelve, or thirteen should conceive the idea of converting that old romance into something very like the Bible, and of founding a religious society on its principles! Then again calculate how much spare time a hired man or boy had on a farm in western New York fifty years ago; from sun up to sun down he was kept at work, often with chores to do after dark. How long would it take an ignorant boy under these circumstances, and lazy in the bargain, to transcribe a book that makes more than 600 pages of printed matter and contains, at a rough estimate, more than 300,000 words? Oh consistency! whither art thou fled!

But unfortunately for Mrs. Dickenson's very original theory, the testimony of all, friends and enemies alike, is positive that during this time Joseph was living with his father's family at Palmyra and other places. It is during this period of his life that the foes of divine revelation falsely charge him with confirmed idleness, vagabond habits, etc., and on this charge base their arguments that such a youth would never have been chosen by the Almighty as His servant. But should there be any doubt on this matter we extract a few lines from the already quoted affidavit of his sister, Mrs. Katherine Salisbury. When speaking of the publication of the Book of Mormon, she avers: "At the time the said book was published, I was seventeen years of age; that at the time of the publication of said book, my brother, Joseph Smith, Jr., lived in the family of my father, in the town of Manchester, Ontario county, New York, and that he had, all of his life to this time made his home with the family." To which we may add during the latter years of this period occasionally hiring out for short intervals, but never at the early age and for the lengthened period necessary to give consistency to Mrs. Dickenson's suppositions. We shall pass by several other outrageous misstatements of this lady, and simply refer to one which purports to be from the veteran journalist, Thurlow Weed, simply to show how utterly unreliable many persons' memories become where "Mormonism" is concerned.

Mr. Weed states that Joseph Smith called on him in 1825, desiring to get his manuscript printed, and spoke of finding the plates (Joseph did not obtain the plates until September, 1827, and the translation was not finished until June or July, 1829). That in a few days he brought Martin Harris (Harris was not associated with Joseph until after the plates were found). Seemed about thirty years of age (Joseph was not twenty until December 23rd of that year). Was about 5 feet 8 inches high (Joseph was fully 6 feet). Thus it appears in every detail Mr. Weed's memory was at fault; dates, age, height, etc., are all wrong, very wrong, and his statement is untrustworthy from beginning to end.

In passing we draw attention to the difference between the size of the "Manuscript Found" and the Book of Mormon. The former, according to Mrs. McKinstry, was about one inch thick of *written,* not printed, matter. According to Hurlburt, the manuscript which he obtained from Mrs. Davison's chest, which she states was the "Manuscript Found," contained *about one quire of paper.* And this was the only manuscript book in the trunk. Mrs. Davison stated in her interview with Mr. Haven that the manuscript was about *one third* the size of the Book of Mormon; while Mr. Jackson said the romance was a very small work. All agree that it was much smaller than the Book of Mormon, while Hurlburt had evidently a motive in making out that it was less than it really was. He desired to make it appear that there must have been some other writings than the one he obtained. In any case it is a consistent question, who manufactured all the rest of the Book of Mormon?

WHAT THE BOOK OF MORMON REALLY IS

The Book of Mormon is the record of God's dealings with the people of ancient America from the era of the building of the Tower of Babel to four hundred and twenty-one years after the birth of Christ. It is the stick of Ephraim spoken of by

Ezekiel—the Bible of the western continent. Not that it supersedes, or in any way interferes with the Bible, any more than the history of Mexico supersedes or interferes with the history of Rome; but on the other hand, in many places it confirms Bible history, demonstrates Bible truths, sustains Bible doctrine, and fulfils Bible prophecy.

The Book of Mormon contains the history of two distinct races. The first came from the Tower of Babel and was destroyed a little less than six hundred years before Christ. The story of their national life is given very briefly, but sufficient is said to prove that they were one of the mightiest nations of antiquity, and in the days of their righteousness a people highly blessed of the Lord. Their fall and final destruction were the result of their gross wickedness and rejection of God's prophets. These people were called the Jaradites, their history in the Book of Mormon is contained in "the Book of Ether." Ether was one of their last prophets who wrote his account on twenty-four plates of gold. Moroni, the last prophet of the Nephites, abridged Ether's history and it is his abridgment that has been translated and published in this generation, and which forms a portion of the Book of Mormon.

The next race that inhabited this continent were of Israelitish origin, the descendants of Joseph and Judah. The Nephites, the ruling branch, were principally the descendants of Manasseh. By divine guidance their first prophet and ruler, Lehi, was brought out of Jerusalem with a small company of his relatives and friends, eleven years before the Babylonian captivity (B.C. 600). They sailed from southeastern Arabia across the Indian and Pacific oceans, and landed on the American shore not far from where the city of Valparaiso now stands. In the first year of the captivity another small colony was led out from Jerusalem, Mulek, one of the sons of King Zedekiah, being their nominal leader. This party landed in North America some distance north of the Isthmus of Darien, and soon after migrated into the northern portion of the southern continent, where for nearly four centuries they grew in numbers, but not in true civilization.

In the meantime the descendants of the colonists under Lehi had also grown numerous. Early in their history they had separated into two nationalities; the first, called Nephites, observing the laws of Moses, the teachings of the prophets, and developing in the decencies and comforts of civilized life; the others, called Lamanites (after the cruel, rebellious elder brother of Nephi), sank into barbarism and idolatry. These latter gradually crowded the Nephites northward until the latter reached the land occupied by the descendants of Mulek's colony, now called the people of Zarahemla, with whom they coalesced and formed one nation. From their national birth to B.C. 91, the Nephites had been ruled by kings, but at that time the form of government was changed and a republic founded. The nation was then ruled by judges elected by the people. This portion of the history of the Nephites is a very varied one. One third of their time they were engaged in actual war with the Lamanites, and at other times they were distracted with internal convulsions and rebellions. About A.D. 30, the republic was overthrown and the people split up into numerous independent tribes. At the crucifixion of the Savior this continent was the scene of terrible natural convulsions, which resulted in a great change in the face of nature and an immense loss of human life. Shortly after these days of terror the Redeemer appeared to the surviving remnants, taught them His gospel and organized His Church. A lengthened period of blessed peace followed in which all men served the Lord. Gradually, however, the old evils again crept in, many returned to the sins of their forefathers, the spirit of darkness and bloodshed again held sway, and finally the whole Nephite race was overpowered and destroyed (A.D. 384) by the other faction who had assumed the old name of Lamanites. The descendants of these Lamanites are found in the American Indians, not of the United States alone, but as the aborigines of the whole continent from Patagonia to the Arctic ocean.

The records of this people, engraved on various plates were hid by the last of the Nephite prophets, Mormon, and his son Moroni. A portion thereof has, by God's grace, been restored to the knowledge of mankind in this age, and translated into many languages, that the truths contained therein, whether they be history, doctrine, or prophecy, may be known by all men.

UTTER DISAGREEMENT OF THE TWO HISTORIES

It is our purpose in this chapter to demonstrate, from the Book of Mormon itself, the absurdity of the "Spaulding Story," and the utter impossibility of the Prophet Joseph Smith ever having used Mr. Spaulding's reputed romance, the "Manuscript Found," as the groundwork for that divine record.

At different times since the publication of the Book of Mormon various writers have undertaken to explain the plot and contents of the "Manuscript Found," and to show how remarkable is the resemblance between it and the Book of Mormon.

We are told by one clerical author that when the Book of Mormon was read to Solomon Spaulding's widow, brother and six other persons, all well acquainted with Mr. Spaulding's writings, they immediately recognized in the Book of Mormon the same historical matter and names as composed the romance, although this reading took place some years after they had read the latter work. The writer further states that they affirmed that the Book of Mormon was with the exception of the religious matter, copied almost *word for word* from Spaulding's manuscript.

Another writer affirms that the romance of Spaulding was *similar in all its leading features* to the historical portions of the Book of Mormon. A third writer maintains that the historical part of the Book of Mormon was immediately recognized by all the older inhabitants of New Salem, Ohio, as *the identical* work of Mr. Spaulding, in which they had been so interested twenty years before.

Those who claim to have been acquainted with the writings of Mr. Spaulding, differ materially as to the incidents and plot of the "Manuscript Found." According to their widely different statements, his romance was based upon one of two theories. The first on the idea of the landing of a Roman colony on the Atlantic seaboard shortly before the Christian era. The second (now the most generally known and accepted) on the supposition that the present American Indians are the descendants of the ten tribes of Israel, who were led away captive out of their own land into Media, where historically the world loses sight of them, but where Mr. Spaulding's romance finds them and transports them to America. It is upon this idea of the transportation of his great and numerous people from the land of their captivity to the western world that this gentleman's novel is generally said to have been founded.

We will examine this statement first, and strive to discover how nearly it agrees with the historical narrative of the Book of Mormon, which we are told was immediately recognized as being *identical and copied almost word for word* from the pages of the "Manuscript Found."

In the first place, it is well to remark that the Book of Mormon makes but very few references to the ten tribes, and in those few, it directly, plainly and unequivocally states that the American Indians are not the descendants of the ten tribes, and further, that the ten tribes never were in America, or any part of it, during any portion of their existence as a nation.* On the other hand, the Book of Mormon as directly informs

---

*Our crucified Redeemer, in His teachings to the Nephites, thus refers to the ten tribes of the house of Israel:

"And behold this is the land of your inheritance, and the Father hath given it unto you. And not at any time hath the Father given me commandment that I should tell it unto your brethren at Jerusalem; neither at any time hath the Father given me commandment, that I

us from whom the aborigines, or natives, of this continent are descended. This being the case, how is it possible for the two works to be identical?

But admitting, for the sake of argument, that Joseph Smith might have changed the statement of the author of the "Manuscript Found" in this one particular, we will proceed to show that such a supposition is utterly impossible; for to have retained the unities of the work and the consistencies of the story (for the story of the Book of Mormon is consistent with itself), he must have altered not only the leading features but also the minor details of the whole historical narrative. He must have altered the place of departure, the circumstances of the journey, the route taken by the emigrants, the time of the emigration and every other particular connected with such a great movement. We must recollect that the Book of Mormon gives the account of a small colony (perhaps of about thirty or forty souls) being led by the Lord from the city of Jerusalem through the wilderness south and east of that city, to the borders of the Red Sea, thence for some distance in the same direction near its coast, and then across the Arabian peninsula to the sea eastward. What insanity could have induced Mr. Spaulding to propose such a route for the ten tribes? For of all out-of-the-way methods of reaching the American continent from Media, this would be one of the most inaccessible, difficult, round-about and improbable, and would carry them along the two sides of an acute angle by the time they reached the shore where the ship was built. It would almost certainly have taken these tribes close to, if not through a portion of their own ancient homes, where it is reasonable to suppose nearly all would have desired to tarry, when we consider how great was the love that ancient Israel bore for that rich land given to them by divine power.

Mr. Spaulding, as a student of the Bible, would have made no such blunder. But even supposing that he was foolish enough in his romance to transport the hosts of Israel from the south-western borders of the Caspian Sea (where history loses them) by the nearest route, most probably over the Armenian mountains, across the Syrian desert, and by way of Damascus through the lands of Gilead, Moab and Edom into the wilderness of the Red Sea, where, we ask, is there an account of such a journey in any portion of the Book of Mormon? There is none, for the Book of Mormon opens with the description of Lehi's departure from Jerusalem, with the causes that led thereto, he having been a resident of that city all his days, and never a captive in Media. Therefore we are justified in asking, at the very outset of this inquiry, where, from the opening pages onward, is there any identity between the two books?

Then, again, is it not obvious to every thinking person that the moving of a nation, such as the ten tribes were, must have had associated with it events and circumstances entirely inconsistent and at variance with the simple story of the journey of Lehi and his family as given, frequently with minute detail, in the Book of Mormon? How numerous were the host of the captive Israelites we have no means of definitely ascertaining. We learn, however, that in one invasion alone, Shalmaneser, king of Assyria, carried off two hundred thousand captives form the kingdom of Israel. Even admitting that in their captivity these two hundred thousand did not increase in numbers, and entirely ignoring all the other thousands that were led away captives in other invasions, we should necessarily expect that Spaulding, in his account of the moving of this mass of humanity—men, women and children, with their flocks, herds

should tell unto them concerning the other tribes of the house of Israel, whom the Father hath led away out of the land" (III Nephi 15:13-15).

"That they" (the Jews) "may receive a knowledge of you by the Holy Ghost, and also of the other tribes whom they know not of" (III Nephi 16.4).

"The other tribes hath the Father separated from them" (III Nephi 15:20).

"But now I go unto the Father, and also to show myself unto the lost tribes of Israel, for they are not lost unto the Father, for He knoweth whither He hath taken them" (III Nephi 17:4).

and supplies—would write a narrative consistent with the subject and not one such as the Book of Mormon contains. But whether he did or did not, the Book of Mormon contains nothing whatever of the kind. In that work no vast armies are led out of Media by any route whatever to the American continent.

We have there an entirely different story, more dissimilar indeed from Spaulding's supposed narrative than the history of the deliverance of Israel out of Egypt, under Moses, is from the story of the departure from the old world, the voyage across the Atlantic and the landing on this continent of the Pilgrim Fathers, of revered memory. In the narrative that the Book of Mormon gives of the journeyings of Lehi and his little colony, all the incidents related are consistent with the idea of a small people and entirely inconsistent with that of a vast moving mulitude.

For instance, let us take as an example, the story of Nephi breaking his bow by which the little caravan was placed in danger of starvation. If there had been a vast host, numbering nearly a quarter of a million souls, such an incident could have had no weight; for surely Mr. Spaulding never wrote that one hunter alone supplied such a multitude with all the necessary food, and it would be equally absurd to imagine that that gentleman would tell such an improbable story as that all the hunters broke all their bows at the same time. Again, the Book of Mormon tells us that Lehi and his companions depended on the chase for their entire food. Where, we would ask, in the midst of the Arabian desert, could game enough be found to supply the entire wants of the migrating ten tribes? And further, what would they do for water for such a company in the trackless Arabian desert without divine interposition and the manifestation of miraculous power? But the Book of Mormon hints at no such contingency.

Again, the story of the building of the ship by Nephi must have been entirely altered, for no one ship, though it had been twenty times as large as the *Great Eastern*, could have carried Mr. Spaulding's imaginary company and their effects across the wide waters of the Indian and Pacific oceans.

We must now draw attention to the time when the Book of Mormon states Lehi and his company were led out of Jerusalem. There is no ambiguity on this point. It is repeatedly stated that this event took place six hundred years before the advent of our Savior; that is, it was previous to the Babylonian captivity. The ten tribes were not lost sight of at that time; they were undoubtedly still in the land of their captivity, and if Mr. Spaulding was foolish enough in his romance to set a date to his exodus, he certainly would not have placed it during the lifetime of Jeremiah, the prophet, and of Nebuchadnezzar, king of Babylon; for not only would such a date have marred the consistency of the story, but it is also utterly impossible for us to conceive, as an historical probability, that the mighty king of Babylon would have permitted the ten tribes to escape from their captivity at that time, and above all things to have taken such a route as would have brought them near the borders of the Red Sea. If they escaped at all, it necessarily would have been to the uninhabited regions northward. From a political standpoint it would have been suicidal and utterly inconsistent with the polity of the king of Babylon to allow the captive Israelites to march forth in the supposed direction; for it would have placed them in immediate contact with the kingdom of Judah and enabled them to have formed an alliance with their former brethren antagonistic to his interest and policy.

To pursue the subject still further: when the colony reached the land of promise, which we call America, the incidents related in the Book of Mormon are entirely consistent with the story of the voyage and of the peopling of the land by a small colony and not by a vast host. If Joseph Smith, as some claim, had changed Mr. Spaulding's romance, he must have still continued to alter the narrative throughout the entire volume, for the story still maintains its consistency, and through it from beginning to end there runs a thread, possible only on the theory that it was a single family with their immediate connections through marriage that first founded the nations of the Nephites and Lamanites. The entire history hinges on the quarrels of the sons of Lehi and the results growing therefrom; for from the division of this family into two separate and distinct peoples grew all the wars, contentions, blood-shed, troubles and disasters that fill the pages of this sacred record; while on the other hand, the blessings flowing to both nations almost always resulted from the reconciliation of the two opposing peoples and the inauguration of a united and amicable policy beneficial alike to both. Had the American continent been peopled at the commencement by a vast host, the whole current of the story must have been vastly different, not only in the events that took place, but also in the motives that controlled the hearts of the actors who took part in those events, and in the traditions of the masses. In the case of the Nephites and Lamanites, these traditions had an overwhelming influence in the shaping of public affairs, which shape they never could have received by any set of traditions incidental to Mr. Spaulding's story.

What, too, shall we say of the Jaredites? From whence did Joseph Smith beg, borrow or steal their history? Did Mr. Spaulding bring his ten tribes from the tower of Babel, and give them an existence ages anterior to the lifetime of their great progenitor, Jacob? If not, will somebody inform us how this portion of the Book of Mormon was manufactured?

From the above it is evident that if Mr. Spaulding's story was what its friends claim, then it never could have formed the groundwork of the Book of Mormon, for the whole historical narrative is different from beginning to end. And further, the story that certain old inhabitants of New Salem, who, it is said, recognized the Book of Mormon, either never made such a statement, or they let their imagination run away with their memory into the endorsement of a falsehood and an impossibility. Either way there is a lie; if they asserted that the Book of Mormon is identical with the "Spaulding story," then they are guilty of having violated the truth; if they did not make this statement, then the falsehood is with those who, in their hatred to modern revelation, have invented their testimony. The same statement applies to those who assert that the Book of Mormon was copied almost word for word from the "Manuscript Found." A book that is entirely dissimilar in its narrative cannot be exact in its wording. As well might we say, and be just as consistent and every way as truthful, that the history of England was copied from the adventures of Robinson Crusoe. So it is with the Book of Mormon and the Spaulding romance.

If then the resemblance is so small between the Book of Mormon and the "Manu-script Found," when we consider the ten tribe version of the latter work, where is it possible there can be the shadow of similarity when we examine the Roman colony theory? For instance:

Lehi left Jerusalem; Spaulding's heroes sailed from Rome.

Lehi started on his journey not knowing whither the Lord would lead him; the Romans were bound for Britain.

Lehi and his companions wandered for several years on land; the Roman party made the entire journey by water.

Lehi traveled by way of the Arabian peninsula and the Indian and Pacific oecans; Spaulding's imaginary characters sailed by way of the Mediterranean sea and the Atlantic ocean.

The travels of one party were considerably south of east; the voyage of the others west or north-west.

One party landed on the South Pacific shore;* the other on the North Atlantic.

Mormon's record was written in reformed Egyptian; the imaginary "Manuscript Found" in Latin.

Mormon's record was engraved on plates of metal; Spaulding's pretended manuscript was written on parchment.

The original of the Book of Mormon was hid in the hill Cumorah, state of New York; Mr. Spaulding's manuscript is claimed to have been discovered in a cave near Conneaut, state of Ohio.

The Book of Mormon gives an account of a religious people, God's dealings with whom is the central dominant idea; Spaulding's romance tells the story of an idolatrous people. Such is the positive statement of his widow and daughter.

There is another point worthy of our thought: If Joseph Smith did make use of the "Manuscript Found," it must have been for one of two reasons: Either because he was not able to write such a work himself, or that he might save himself trouble and labor. In the first place he could not have done this for the lack of ability; for anyone who could have so adroitly altered a history of the ten tribes so that it now reads as a distinct, detailed and consistent history of a small company of the tribe of Joseph, most assuredly could have written such a history for himself if he had felt so disposed. Then again, he could not have done it to save himself work, for to so change a long history from one end to the other, until it contradicted all it had previously asserted, and became the harmonious history of another people, would save no man trouble. Then, again, in considering these points, we must remember what an "idle vagabond" Joseph was, according to some people's stories. What could have possibly possessed him to do such an enormous amount of copying, when, as illiterate as he was, such an operation would have been immensely hard work? Though it must be remembered all this time he was loafing round the street corners, telling fortunes and doing everything but honest toil—that is, if some people's tales are to be believed.

And, again, to show the weakness of our opponents' arguments, supposing for a moment that Joseph was an impostor, than he ran the risk of detection by copying another man's work, he ran that risk without a single motive, except it was the privilege of toiling for nothing, or the pleasure of being exposed, when by writing it himself he need have no risk at all.

JOSEPH SMITH'S EARLY LIFE

The supposed bad character of Joseph Smith when a youth has been made the text for many a tirade against the gospel that he, by God's grace, restored to the earth. How is it possible, it is asked, that we can believe that God would choose such an instrument for His work? We answer in the first place, God's ways are not as man's ways, and He has a perfect right to choose whomsoever He will. But further we assert, knowing we speak the truth, that the stories about Joseph Smith's bad character are false, and were never whispered until after God called him, and he had commenced the work that heaven assigned him. Until that time he and his parents with their entire family enjoyed a good reputation among their neighbors.

No sooner had Joseph borne his simple testimony of angelic visitations, than the evil one commenced to vilify his character, to destroy the effect of his testimony. Evil reports spread far and wide, growing as they went, as lies always do, until the days of

---

*Regarding the route taken by Lehi and his company, the Prophet Joseph Smith states:

"They traveled nearly a south, south-east direction until they came to the nineteenth degree of north latitude; then, nearly east to the sea of Arabia, then sailed in a south-east direction, and landed on the continent of South America, in Chili, thirty degrees south latitude."

D. P. Hurlburt, who, when going east to obtain the "Manuscript Found," made it his business to visit the neighborhood of Joseph's early home, and gather for publication all the floating scandal that had been in circulation from the beginning. He also procured an affidavit, or affidavits, which he asserted numbers of the old neighbors of the Smith family signed. Some of the persons who names were attached to those papers have since repudiated all knowledge thereof, and make statements with regard to Joseph Smith's character entirely at variance with the tenor of the affidavits. Others signed from hearsay and rumor and not from actual knowledge. Others are said to have been themselves men of such disreputable character that to be traduced by them was a compliment. The names of entire strangers were also added to swell the list. These fraudulent and untruthful affidavits have been reprinted time and again, and others have followed in Hurlburt's footsteps, inventing other statements with regard to Joseph Smith, and attached the names of well-known residents of Palmyra, Manchester, etc., thereto without their knowledge and consent, and putting into their mouths statements entirely at variance with their sentiments and expressions. We regret to have to say that this dirty work has generally been done by professed ministers of the gospel.

The affidavits gathered by Hurlburt make the signers thereto complain that the Smith family, especially Joseph, was indolent, intemperate, untruthful, "entirely destitute of moral character and addicted to vicious habits." These charges are not only false, but they also manifest all the bitter hatred of religious bigotry and all the exaggeration of envy and revenge.

Joseph was undoubtedly not perfect—none of us are—but he was far superior in almost every respect to his neighbors and associates. In his own account of his youth, between the time of his first vision and the visit of the angel Moroni, he in the humility of his repentance fully confesses his youthful follies, and, as is natural with sensitive and consciencious natures, such as his, evidently applies the strongest language to his shortcomings, and exaggerates rather than extenuates his youthful misdeeds.

He writes:

"During the space of time which intervened between the time I had the vision and the year eighteen hundred and twenty-three (having been forbidden to join any of the religious sects of the day, and being of very tender years, and persecuted by those who ought to have been my friends, and to have treated me kindly, and if they supposed me to be deluded to have endeavored, in a proper and affectionate manner, to have reclaimed me), I was left to all kinds of temptations, and mingled with all kinds of society. I frequently fell into many foolish errors, and displayed the weakness of youth, and the corruption of human nature, which, I am sorry to say, led me into divers temptations, to the gratification of many appetites offensive in the sight of God. In consequence of these things I often felt condemned for my weakness and imperfections; when on the evening of the twenty-first of September, after I had retired to my bed for the night, I betook myself to prayer and supplication to Almighty God, for forgiveness of all my sins and follies, and also for a manifestation to me, that I might know of my state and standing before Him; for I had full confidence in obtaining a divine manifestation, as I had previously done."

The above is a simple, straightforward, artless statement of his condition, in which he seeks to hide nothing, but at the same time shows that the rebuffs he received, the persecutions he suffered from those who should have been his guides and friends had sufficient influence to cause him occasionally to give way to the weakness of youth incidental to association with the rough and unrestrained society he from his lowly position in life was naturally compelled to mingle with.

When comparing the before-mentioned vile charges with the testimony of those who knew the future Prophet's family best, we learn that instead of being indolent, the family were "good workers"; instead of being untruthful and vicious, they were honest, upright, religious and veracious, good neighbors, kind in sickness, but very poor, and with but little of the knowledge of this world. Their poverty, which some uncharitable souls have transformed into "shiftlessness," or lack of management, is one of the heaviest charges brought against them.

The charge of intemperance can be simmered down to the fact that on one or two occasions, in the harvest field, Joseph drank rather more cider than did him good. All the witnesses declare that "everybody drank in those days." It was before the age of temperance societies, and all classes of poeple considered it perfectly right to take a little strong drink occasionally. Drunkenness was the besetting sin of that era among the English race. Joseph was not a "teetotaler," because there were none. He was also very fond of wrestling, as many of his friends of later years know, and doubtless when stimulated with cider was on hand for a bout, or for any other athletic game or trial of strength that might be suggested. From this exuberance of animal spirits, the enemies of God's latter-day work have built up the story of Joseph's inebriety and vagabond character.

Again, he is charged with the grave offense of being a "money-digger." In one sense this is true. The whole country round about western New York was in those days affected with a mania to discover hidden treasures in the earth. Most marvelous stories are told of the interposition of unseen beings when some of these treasures were disturbed. The public mind was greatly troubled on this subject, and Joseph Smith was employed by a man at one time to dig for him in the hope of discovering some of these buried riches, or an ancient Spanish mine. Joseph worked for him as he would for any other man, or for the same man if he engaged him to plant potatoes or hoe corn. From this grew the story of Joseph being a money-digger. Even if he dug for treasure on his own responsibility, we do not know that there is anything degrading, dishonest or criminal in such an action.

The following is Joseph's own account of the manner in which he became saddled with the title of "Money-digger":

"As my father's worldly circumstances were very limited, we were under the necessity of laboring with our hands, hiring by day's work and otherwise as we could get opportunity; sometimes we were at home and sometimes abroad, and by continued labor we were enabled to get a comfortable maintenance.

"In the year 1824, my father's family met with a great affliction, by the death of my eldest brother, Alvin. In the month of October, 1825, I hired with an old gentleman by the name of Josiah Stoal, who lived in Chenango county, State of New York. He had heard something of a silver mine having been opened by the Spaniards, in Harmony, Susquehanna county, state of Pennsylvania, and had, previous to my hiring with him, been digging, in order, if possible, to discover the mine. After I went to live with him he took me among the rest of his hands to dig for the silver mine, at which I continued to work for nearly a month without success in our undertaking, and finally I prevailed with the old gentleman to cease digging after it. Hence arose the very prevalent story of my having been a money-digger."

Somewhere about this time, or possibly rather later, Joseph worked for Mr. Joseph Knight, of Colesville, New York.

Of Josepn, Mr. Knight's son, Newel writes in his private manuscript journal, as follows:

"The business my father was engaged in, often required him to have hired help, and among the many he, from time to time, employed was a young man by the name of Joseph Smith, Jun., to whom I was particularly attached. His noble deportment, his faithfulness, and his kind address could not fail to win the esteem of those who had the pleasure of his acquaintance. One thing I will mention which seemed to be a peculiar characteristic with him in all his boyish sports and amusements: I never knew anyone to gain advantage over him, and yet he was always kind and kept the good will of his playmates."

In March, 1881, two gentlemen, named Kelley, residing in Michigan, for their own satisfaction, visited the neighborhood where Joseph spent his youth, and questioned the older residents who were acquainted with the Smith family as to their knowledge of the character of Joseph, his parents and his brothers and sisters. Their interviews with numerous parties who claim to have known Joseph were afterwards published. Among those visited were the families, and sometimes the identical persons whose names had been appended, often without their knowledge, to former scurrilous affidavits regarding the reputation of the Smith family. In several cases these parties stated that they did not so much as know that any statement of theirs had ever been published; that they never uttered the sentiments or made the assertions attributed to them, and in some instances that they had been abused because they would not make the damaging statements regarding Joseph character that those who visited them required. In many cases where they spoke disparagingly of the Prophet's family to the Messrs. Kelley, these gentlemen found that they spoke *from hearsay,* and *not from actual knowledge;* while those who knew Joseph best spoke of him the most highly. We here append a few extracts from these interviews, at the same time remarking (to put the feeling in the mildest language), that some of these gentlemen were no friends of the Smith family.

"What did you know about the Smiths, Mr. Gilbert?"

"I knew nothing myself; have seen Joseph Smith a few times, but not acquainted with him. Saw Hyrum quite often. I am the party that set the type from the original manuscript for the Book of Mormon. They translated it in a cave. I would know that manuscript to-day if I should see it. The most of it was in Oliver Cowdery's handwriting. Some in Joseph's wife's; a small part though. Hyrum Smith always brought the manuscript to the office; he would have it under his coat, and all buttoned up as carefully as though it was so much gold. He said at the time that it was translated from plates by the power of God, and they were very particular about it. We had a great deal of trouble with it. It was not punctuated at all. They did not know anything about punctuation, and we had to do that ourselves."

"Well; did you change any part of it when you were setting the type?"

"No, sir; we never changed it at all."

"Why did you not change it and correct it?

"Because they would not allow us to; they were very particular about that. We never changed it in the least. Oh, well; there might have been one or two words that I changed the spelling of; I believe I did change the spelling of one, and perhaps two, but no more."

"Did you set all the type, or did some one help you?"

"I did the whole of it myself, and helped to read the proof, too; there was no one who worked at that but myself. Did you ever see one of the first copies? I have one here that was never bound. Mr. Grandin, the printer, gave it to me. If you ever saw a Book of Mormon you will see that they changed it afterwards."

"They did! Well, let us see your copy; that is a good point. How is it changed now?"

"I will show you (bringing out his copy). Here on the title page it says (reading), 'Joseph Smith, Jr., author and proprietor.' Afterwards, in getting out other editions they left that out, and only claimed that Joseph Smith translated it."

"Well, did they claim anything else than that he was the translator when they brought the manuscript to you?"

"Oh, no; they claimed that he was translating by means of some instruments he got at the same time he did the plates, and that the Lord helped him."

The Messrs. Kelley also called upon Dr. John Stafford, at Rochester, N. Y. He is now a retired physician, being too aged and infirm to practice. Answering a question as to the character of Joseph Smith, he said:

"He was a real clever, jovial boy. What Tucker said about them" (the Smith family) "was false, absolutely. My father, William Stafford, was never connected with them in any way. The Smiths, with others, were digging for money before Joe got the plates. My father had a stone, which some thought they could look through, and old Mrs. Smith came there for it one day, but never got it. Saw them digging one time for money; (this was three or four years before the Book of Mormon was found) the Smiths and others. The old man and Hyrum were there, I think, but Joseph was not there. The neighbors used to claim Sally Chase could look at a stone she had, and see money. Willard Chase used to dig when she found where the money was. Don't know as anybody ever found any money."

"What was the character of Smith, as to his drinking?"

"It was common then for everybody to drink, and to have drink in the field; one time Joe, while working for some one after he was married, drank too much boiled cider. He came in with his shirt torn; his wife felt bad about it, and when they went home, she put her shawl on him."

"Had he been fighting and drunk?"

"No; he had been scuffling with some of the boys. Never saw him fight; have known him to scuffle; would do a fair day's work if hired out to a man; but were poor managers," (the Smiths.)

"What about that black sheep your father let them have?"

"I have heard that story, but don't think my father was there at the time they say Smith got the sheep. I don't know anything about it."

"You were living at home at the time, and it seems you ought to know if they got a sheep, or stole one, from your father?"

"They never stole one, I am sure; they may have got one sometime."

"Well, doctor, you know pretty well whether that story is true or not, that Tucker tells. What do you think of it?"

"I don't think it is true. I would have heard more about it, that is true. I lived a mile from Smith's; am seventy-six years old. They were peaceable among themselves. The old woman had a great deal of faith that their children were going to do something great. Joe was quite illiterate. After they began to have school at their house, he improved greatly."

"Did they have school in their own house?"

"Yes, sir; they had school in their house, and studied the Bible."

"Who was their teacher?"

"They did not have any teacher; they taught themselves." * * *

"If young Smith was illiterate as you say, doctor, how do you account for the Book of Mormon?"

"Well, I can't; except that Sidney Rigdon was connected with them."

"What makes you think he was connected with them?"

"Because I can't account for the Book of Mormon any other way."

"Was Rigdon ever around there before the Book of Mormon was published?"

"No; not as we could ever find out. Sidney Rigdon was never there, that Hurlburt, or Howe, or Tucker could find out."

"Well; you have been looking out for the facts a long time have you not, doctor?"

"Yes; I have been thinking and hearing about it for the last fifty years, and lived right among all their old neighbors there most of the time."

"And no one has ever been able to trace the acquaintance of Rigdon and Smith, until after the Book of Mormon was published, and Rigdon proselyted by Pratt, in Ohio?"

"Not that I know of." * * *

"Were you acquainted with them" (the Smiths) "Mr. Saunders?"

"Yes, sir, I knew all of the Smith family well; there were six boys: Alvin, Hyrum, Joseph, Harrison, William and Carlos, and there were two girls; the old man was a cooper; they have all worked for me many a day; they were very good people.

Young Joe (as we called him then), has worked for me, and he was a good worker; they all were. I did not consider them good managers about business, but they were poor people; the old man had a large family."

"In what respect did they differ from other people, if at all?"

"I never noticed that they were different from other neighbors; they were the best family in the neighborhood in case of sickness; one was at my house nearly all the time when my father died; I always thought them honest; they were owing me some money when they left here: that is, the old man and Hyrum did, and Martin Harris. One of them came back in about a year and paid me."

"How were they as to habits of drinking and getting drunk?"

"Everybody drank a little in those days, and the Smiths with the rest; they never got drunk to my knowledge." * * *

"How well did you know young Joseph Smith?"

"Oh! just as well as one could very well; he has worked for me many a time, and been about my place a great deal. He stopped with me many a time, when through here, after they went west to Kirtland; he was always a gentleman when about my place."

"What did you know about his finding that book, or plates in the hill over here?"

"He always claimed that he saw the angel and received the book; but I don't know anything about it. Have seen it, but never read it as I know of; didn't care anything about it."

"Well; you seem to differ a little from a good many of the stories told about these people."

"I have told you just what I know about them, and you will have to go somewhere else for a different story." * * *

"To our inquiries if he, Mr. Thos. H. Taylor, was acquainted with the Smiths, and the early settlers throughout that part, sometimes called Mormons, he said":

"Yes; I knew them very well; they were very nice men, too; the only trouble was they were ahead of the people; and the people, as in every such case, turned out to abuse them, because they had the manhood to stand for their own convictions. I have seen such work all through life, and when I was working with John Brown for the freedom of my fellowman, I often got in tight places; and if it had not been for Gerritt Smith, Wendell Phillips and some others, who gave me their influence and money, I don't know how I would ever have got through."

"What did the Smiths do that the people abused them so?"

"They did not do anything. Why! these rascals at one time took Joseph Smith and ducked him in the pond that you see over there, just because he preached what he believed, and for nothing else. And if Jesus Christ had been there, they would have done the same to Him. Now I don't believe like he did; but every man has a right to his religious opinions, and to advocate his views, too; if people don't like it, let them come out and meet him on the stand, and show his error. Smith was always ready to exchange views with the best men they had."

"Why didn't they like Smith?"

"To tell the truth, there was something about him they could not understand; some way he knew more than they did, and it made them mad."

"But a good many tell terrible stories, about them being low people, rogues and liars, and such things. How is that?"

"Oh! they are a set of d——d liars. I have had a home here, and been here, except when on business, all my life—ever since I came to this country, and I know these fellows, they make these lies on Smith, because they love a lie better than the truth . I can take you to a great many old settlers here who will substantiate what I say, and if you want to go, just come around to my place across the street here, and I'll go with you."

"Well, that is very kind, Mr. Taylor, and fair; and if we have time we will call around and give you the chance; but we are first going to see these fellows who, so rumor says, know so much against them."

"All right; but you will find they don't know anything against those men when you put them down to it; they could never sustain anything against Smith."

"Do you think Smith ever got any plates out of the hill he claimed to?"

"Yes; I rather think he did. Why not he find something as well as anybody else? Right over here, in Illinois and Ohio, in mounds there, they have discovered copper plates since, with hieroglyphics all over them; and quite a number of the old settlers around here testified that Smith showed the plates to them—they were good, honest men, and what is the sense in saying they lied? Now, I never saw the Book of Mormon —don't know anything about it, nor care; and don't know as it was ever translated from the plates. You have heard about the Spaulding romance; and some claim that it is nothing but the books of the Bible that were rejected by the compilers of the Bible; but all this don't prove that Smith never got any plates."

We close this chapter with an extract from the writings of Elder Oliver Cowdery, published in a very early day of the Church's history:

"But in consequence of certain false and slanderous reports which have been circulated, justice would require me to say something upon the private life of one whose character has been so shamefully traduced. By some he is said to have been a lazy, idle, vicious, profligate fellow. These I am prepared to contradict, and that, too, by the testimony of *many* persons with whom I have been intimately acquainted, and know to be individuals of the strictest veracity and unquestionable integrity. All these strictly and virtually agree in saying, that he was an honest, upright, virtuous and faithfully industrious young man. And those who say to the contrary can be influenced by no other motive than to destroy the reputation of one who never injured any man in either property or person."

JOSEPH'S ACCOUNT OF THE DISCOVERY OF THE PLATES

We will now give the Prophet Joseph's own narrative of the finding of the plates from which he, by divine aid, translated the Book of Mormon, with the causes that led thereto. It is a simple, unvarnished statement of facts that bears on its face the evidence of its truth.

On the evening of September 21st, 1823, Joseph went to bed with a strong feeling of regret for his youthful follies, and with a determination to seek the Lord for forgiveness and for a manifestation of his standing before heaven. With this desire, in strong faith, he betook himself to prayer and supplication. He then says:

"While I was thus in the act of calling upon God, I discovered a light appearing in the room, which continued to increase until the room was lighter than at noonday, when immediately a personage appeared at my bedside, standing in the air, for his feet did not touch the floor. He had on a loose robe of most exquisite whiteness. It was a whiteness beyond anything earthly I had ever seen; nor do I believe that any earthly thing could be made to appear so exceedingly white and brilliant; his hands were naked, and his arms also, a little above the wrist; so, also, were his feet naked, as were his legs, a little above the ankles. His head and neck were also bare. I could discover that he had no other clothing on but this robe, as it was open, so that I could see into his bosom.

"Not only was his robe exceedingly white, but his whole person was glorious beyond description, and his countenance truly like lightning. The room was exceedingly light, but not so very bright as immediately around his person. When I first looked upon him I was afraid, but the fear soon left me. He called me by name and said unto me that he was a messenger sent from the presence of God to me, and that his name was Moroni. That God had a work for me to do, and that my name should be had for good and evil among all nations, kindreds, and tongues; or that it should be both good and evil spoken of among all people. He said there was a book deposited, written upon gold plates, giving an account of the former inhabitants of this continent, and the source from whence they sprang. He also said that the fulness of the everlasting gospel was contained in it, as delivered by the Savior to the ancient inhabitants. Also, that there were two stones in silver bows (and these stones, fastened to a breastplate, constituted what is called the Urim and Thummim) deposited with the plates, and the possession and use of these stones were what constituted Seers in ancient or former times, and that God had prepared them for the purpose of translating the book.

"Again, he told me that when I got those plates of which he had spoken (for the time that they should be obtained was not yet fulfilled) I should not show them to any person, neither the breastplate with the Urim and Thummim, only to those to whom I should be commanded to show them; if I did, I should be destroyed. While he was conversing with me about the plates, the vision was opened to my mind that I could see the place where the plates were deposited, and that so clearly and distinctly, that I knew the place again when I visited it.

"After this communication, I saw the light in the room begin to gather immediately around the person of him who had been speaking to me, and it continued to do so, until the room was again left dark, except just around him, when instantly I saw, as it were, a conduit open right up into heaven, and he ascended up till he entirely disappeared, and the room was left as it had been before this heavenly light had made its appearance.

"I lay musing on the singularity of the scene, and marveling greatly at what had been told me by this extraordinary messenger, when, in the midst of my meditation, I suddenly discovered that my room was again beginning to get lighted and in an instant, as it were, the same heavenly messenger was again by my bedside. He commenced, and again related the very same things which he had done at his first visit, without the least variation, which having done, he informed me of great judgments which were coming upon the earth, with great desolations by famine, sword, and pestilence, and that these grievous judgments would come on the earth in this generation. Having related these things, he again ascended as he had done before.

"By this time, so deep were the impressions made on my mind, that sleep had fled from my eyes, and I lay overwhelmed in astonishment at what I had both seen and heard, but what was my surprise when again I beheld the same messenger at my bedside, and heard him rehearse or repeat over again to me the same things as before, and added a caution to me, telling me that Satan would try to tempt me (in consequence of the indigent circumstances of my father's family) to get the plates for the purpose of getting rich. This he forbid me, saying that I must have no other object in view in getting the plates but to glorify God, and must not be influenced by any other motive but that of building His kingdom, otherwise I could not get them. After this third visit, he again ascended up into heaven as before, and I was again left to ponder on the strangeness of what I had just experienced, when almost immediately after the heavenly messenger had ascended from me the third time, the cock crowed, and I found that day was approaching, so that our interviews must have occupied the whole of that night. I shortly after arose from my bed, and, as usual, went to the necessary labors of the day, but, in attempting to labor as at other time, I found my strength so exhausted as rendered me entirely unable. My father, who was laboring along with me, discovered something to be wrong with me, and told me to go home. I started with the intention of going to the house, but, in attempting to cross the fence out of the field where we were, my strength entirely failed me, and I fell helpless on the ground, and for a time was quite unconscious of anything. The first thing that I can recollect, was a voice speaking unto me calling me by name; I looked up and beheld the same messenger standing over my head, surrounded by light, as before. He then again related unto me all that he had related to me the previous night, and commanded me to go to my father, and tell him of the vision and commandments which I had received.

"I obeyed, I returned back to my father in the field and rehearsed the whole matter to him. He replied to me that it was of God, and to go and do as commanded by the messenger. I left the field and went to the place where the messenger had told me the plates were deposited, and owing to the distinctness of the vision which I had had concerning it, I knew the place the instant that I arrived there. Convenient to the village of Manchester, Ontario county, New York, stands a hill of considerable size, and the most elevated of any in the neighborhood. On the west side of this hill, not far from the top, under a stone of considerable size, lay the plates, deposited in a stone box; this stone was thick and rounding in the middle on the upper side, and thinner towards the edges, so that the middle part of it was visible above the ground, but the edge all round was covered with earth. Having removed the earth and obtained a lever which I got fixed under the edge of the stone, and with a little exertion raised it up; I looked in, and there indeed did I behold the plates, the Urim and Thummim, and the breastplate as stated by the messenger. The box in which they lay was formed by laying stones together in some kind of cement. In the bottom of the box were laid two stones crossways of the box, and on these stones lay the plates and the other things with them. I made an attempt to take them out, but was forbidden by the messenger, and was again informed that the time for bringing them forth had not yet arrived, neither would arrive until four years from that time; but he told me that I should come to that place precisely in one year from that time, and that he would there meet with me, and that I should continue to do so until the time should come for obtaining the plates.

"Accordingly as I had been commanded, I went at the end of each year, and at each time I found the same messenger there, and received instruction and intelligence from him at each of our interviews, respecting what the Lord was going to do, and how and in what manner His kingdom was to be conducted in the last days.

"At length the time arrived for obtaining the plates, the Urim and Thummim, and the breastplate. On the 22nd day of September, 1827, having gone, as usual, at the end of another year, to the place where they were deposited, the same heavenly messenger delivered them up to me with this charge, that I should be responsible for them; that if I should let them go carelessly or through any neglect of mine, I should be cut off; but that if I would use all my endeavors to preserve them, until he, the messenger, should call for them, they should be protected.

"I soon found out the reason why I had received such strict charges to keep them safe, and why it was the messenger had said, that when I had done what was required at my hand, he would call for them; for no sooner was it known that I had them, than the most strenuous exertions were used to get them from me; every stratagem that could be invented was resorted to for that purpose; the persecution became more bitter and severe than before, and multitudes were on the alert continually to get them from me if possible; but, by the wisdom of God, they remained safe in my hands, until I had accomplished by them what was required at my hand; when according to arrangements, the messenger called for them, I delivered them up to him, and he has them in his charge until this day, being the 2nd day of May, 1838.

"The excitement, however, still continued, and rumor, with her thousand tongues, was all the time employed in circulating tales about my father's family, and about myself. If I were to relate a thousandth part of them, it would fill up volumes. The persecution, however, became so intolerable that I was under the necessity of leaving Manchester, and going with my wife to Susquehanna county, in the state of Pennsylvania. While preparing to start (being very poor, and the persecution so heavy upon us, that there was no probability that we would ever be otherwise), in the midst of our afflictions we found a friend in a gentleman, by the name of Martin Harris, who came to us and gave me fifty dollars to assist us in our afflictions. Mr. Harris was a resident of Palmyra township, Wayne county, in the state of New York, and a farmer of respectability. By this timely aid was I enabled to reach the place of my destination in Pennsylvania, and immediately after my arrival there, I commenced copying the characters of the plates. I copied a considerable number of them, and by means of the Urim and Thummim I translated some of them, which I did between the time I arrived at the house of my wife's father in the month of December, and the February following.

"Some time in this month of February, the afore-mentioned Mr. Martin Harris came to our place, got the characters which I had drawn off the plates, and started with them to the city of New York. For what took place relative to him and the characters, I refer to his own account of the circumstances as he related them to me after his return, which was as follows:

" 'I went to the city of New York, and presented the characters which had been translated, with the translation thereof, to Professor Anthon, a gentleman celebrated for his literary attainments. Professor Anthon stated that the translation was correct, more so than any he had before seen translated from the Egyptian. I then showed him those which were not yet translated, and he said that they were Egyptian, Chaldaic, Assyraic, and Arabic, and he said that they were the true characters. He gave me a certificate, certifying to the people of Palmyra that they were true characters, and that the translation of such of them as had been translated was also correct. I took the certificate and put it into my pocket, and was just leaving the house, when Mr. Anthon called me back and asked me how the young man found out that there were gold plates in the place where he found them. I answered that an angel of God had revealed it unto him.

" 'He then said unto me, 'Let me see that certificate.' I accordingly took it out of my pocket and gave it to him, when he took it and tore it to pieces, saying that there was no such thing now as ministering of angels, and that if I would bring the plates to him, he would translate them. I informed him that part of the plates were sealed, and that I was forbidden to bring them; he replied, 'I cannot read a sealed book.' I left him and went to Dr. Mitchell, who sanctioned what Professor Anthon had said respecting both the characters and the translation.'

"On the 15th [5th] day of April, 1829, Oliver Cowdery came to my house, until then I had never seen him. He stated to me that having been teaching school in the neighborhood where my father resided, and my father being one of those who sent to the school, he went to board for a season at his house, and while there, the family related to him the circumstance of my having the plates, and accordingly he had come to make inquiries of me.

"Two days after the arrival of Mr. Cowdery (being the 17th [7th] of April), I commenced to translate the Book of Mormon, and he commenced to write for me."

The foregoing is the Prophet Joseph's own account of the discovery of the plates, with some details as to the manner of their translation. We will now insert the testimony of the witnesses, who, by divine permission, saw, handled and examined these sacred records, and afterwards draw attention to the value of this testimony, more especially to that of the three witnesses, whose lives for so long a period were estranged from the Church and people to whom their words are of most value.

THE TESTIMONY OF THREE WITNESSES

Be it known unto all nations, kindreds, tongues and people unto whom this work shall come, that we, through the grace of God the Father, and our Lord Jesus Christ, have seen the plates which contain this record, which is a record of the people of Nephi, and also of the Lamanites, their brethren, and also of the people of Jared, who came from the tower of which hath been spoken; and we also know that they have been translated by the gift and power of God, for His voice hath declared it unto us; wherefore we know of a surety that the work is true. And we also testify that we have seen the engravings which are upon the plates; and they have been shown unto us by the power of God, and not of man. And we declare with words of soberness, that an angel of God came down from heaven, and He brought and laid before our eyes, that we beheld and saw the plates, and the engravings thereon; and we know that it is by the grace of God the Father, and our Lord Jesus Christ, that we beheld and bear record that these things are true; and it is marvelous in our eyes, nevertheless the voice of the Lord commanded us that we should bear record of it; wherefore, to be obedient unto the commandments of God, we bear testimony of these things. And we know that if we are faithful in Christ, we shall rid our garments of the blood of all men, and be found spotless before the judgment-seat of Christ, and shall dwell with Him eternally in the heavens. And the honor be to the Father, and to the Son, and to the Holy Ghost, which is one God. Amen.

Oliver Cowdery,
David Whitmer,
Martin Harris.

AND ALSO THE TESTIMONY OF EIGHT WITNESSES

Be it known unto all nations, kindreds, tongues and people unto whom this work shall come, that Joseph Smith, Jun., the translator of this work, has shown unto us the plates of which hath been spoken, which have the appearance of gold; and as many of the leaves as the said Smith has translated, we did handle with our hands; and we also saw the engravings thereon, all of which has the appearance of ancient work, and of curious workmanship. And this we bear record with words of soberness, that the said Smith has shown unto us, for we have seen and hefted, and know of a surety that the said Smith has got the plates of which we have spoken. And we give our names unto the world, to witness unto the world, that which we have seen; and we lie not, God bearing witness of it.

> Christian Whitmer,
> Jacob Whitmer,
> Peter Whitmer, Jun.
> John Whitmer,
> Hiram Page,
> Joseph Smith, Sen.
> Hyrum Smith
> Samuel H. Smith

TIME OCCUPIED IN TRANSLATING THE BOOK OF MORMON

Objection has been made to the divinity of the Book of Mormon on the ground that the account given in the publications of the Church, of the time occupied in the work of translation is far too short for the accomplishment of such a labor, and consequently it must have been copied or transcribed from some work written in the English language, most probably from Spaulding's "Manuscript Found." But at the outset it must be recollected that the translation was accomplished by no common method, by no ordinary means. It was done by divine aid. There were no delays over obscure passages, no difficulties over the choice of words, no stoppages from the ignorance of the translator; no time was wasted in investigation or argument over the value, intent or meaning of certain characters, and there were no references to authorities. These difficulties to human work were removed. All was as simple as when a clerk writes from dictation. The translation of the characters appeared on the Urim and Thummim, sentence by sentence, and as soon as one was correctly transcribed the next would appear. So the enquiry narrows down to the consideration of this simple question, how much could Oliver Cowdery write in a day? How many of the printed pages of the Book of Mormon could an ordinary clerk transcribe from dictation in a day? When that is determined, divide the total number of pages in the Book of Mormon by that number and you have the answer in days.

It now becomes important to discover when the translation was commenced and when it was finished. This cannot be determined to a day, but enough is known for our purpose.

When Oliver first visited Joseph some little had been translated, exactly how much is not known. The next question is: When did that visit occur? We will let Oliver answer. He writes (*Times and Seasons Vol. I*, page 201): "Near the time of the setting of the sun, Sabbath evening, April 5th, 1829, my natural eyes, for the first time, beheld this brother. He then resided in Harmony, Susquehanna county, Pennsylvania. On Monday, the 6th, I assisted him in arranging some business of a temporal nature, and on Tuesday, the 7th, commenced to write the Book of Mormon."

In the history of Joseph Smith, we read: "During the month of April I continued to translate and he (Oliver) to write with little cessation, during which time we received several revelations." And again: "We still continued the work of translation, when, in the ensuing month (May 1829) we, on a certain day went into the woods to pray." Oliver also states: "These were days never to be forgotten—to sit under the sound of a voice dictated by the inspiration of heaven awakened the utmost gratitude of this bosom! Day after day I continued, uninterrupted, to write from his mouth, as he translated with the Urim and Thummim, or, as the Nephites would have said, 'Interpreters,' the history or record called the Book of Mormon."

Thus we see these two young men bent the whole energy of their souls towards the accomplishment of this most important work. They united their youthful zeal "day after day, uninterrupted" and "with little cessation" to the labor of translation. It requires very little imagination to understand how diligently and earnestly they toiled, how they permitted nothing to interfere with their labor of love, how they devoted every hour, until fatigue overcame them, to the divinely imposed task (and young and vigorous as they were it was not a little that would tire them out), while curiosity and other far worthier feelings would give zest and inspiration to their labors; as they progressed we can well imagine how their interest in the narrative increased until they could scarcely tear themselves away from their inspired labors even when their minds and bodies called for food and rest. The enthusiasm with which Oliver speaks of those days shows plainly that this was the case, and we cannot reasonably think that Joseph was any less interested than he.

Now let us examine when these two brethren commenced their marvelous work. Two series of dates have been given. Oliver's given above, and another in the history of Joseph Smith, which gives the dates as the 15th and 17th of April, or ten days later. Oliver's has this evidence of its correctness, that, as he states, the 5th, 6th and 7th of April, 1829, fell on Sunday, Monday and Tuesday, which, of course, those ten days later would not. Again, the event being of more importance in his life than in Joseph's, he was more likely to recollect the details, besides, being a better scholar and penman, it is more probable that if any record of the circumstance was made at that time he made it. But really there is no discrepancy. The dates 15th and 17th in the Pearl of Great Price in Joseph's history, etc., are unfortunately typographical errors, or mistakes in printing. In the original manuscript in the Historian's Office— the dates are the same as those of Oliver Cowdery—the 5th and 7th. But the mistake having once been printed it has been copied out of one journal or book into another until nearly all our works have perpetuated the blunder. Of course it is impossible to tell now whether the mistake was first made by a copyist in the Historian's Office or by a compositor at the printer's.

From Joseph's and Oliver's narrative we learn how far they had progressed in the work of translation at the time of the visit of the angel, John the Baptist, and their baptism. This took place on May 15th of the same year. It was because they found in the teachings of the risen Redeemer to the Nephites certain instructions regarding baptism that they were led to enquire of the Lord regarding this ordinance, and their inquiry led to the angel's visit. Where are these teachings found? In the third book of Nephi; some, probably the very ones that so deeply impressed the minds of these young men, on pages 422 and 437 of the Book of Mormon (latest edition). Then it is evident that between April 7th and May 15th they had translated as much as makes 422 or 437 pages of the printed Book of Mormon. How much is this a day? Between these two dates, including April 7th but not May 15th, there are thirty-eight days, which would make almost twelve pages a day, if we allow nothing for what was previously transcribed. A swift writer copying from dictation could write four such pages in an hour, as we have demonstrated experimentally, an ordinary writer about three. But allowing that Oliver Cowdery might be a very slow writer, and that he only copied at the rate of a page in half an hour, even then he would only have had to work six or seven hours each day to accomplish the task; and if they rested entirely on Sundays about one hour more. So we see, making no allowance for the work already done, allowing Oliver Cowdery to be a slow penman for his profession—a schoolmaster—and admitting that they ceased from their labor on the Sabbath, still it was only necessary for them to do a short day's work, especially for two young men in the prime and vigor of life; and yet allow ample time for the reception of revelations (which were given through the Urim and Thummim) and the performance of other duties that possibly called for their attention.

To show how easy such an effort would be we will state that President George Q. Cannon has informed us that when he translated the Book of Mormon into the language of the Sandwich Islanders, he frequently translated as many as eight or ten pages a day. This was far heavier work to do alone and without the assistance of the Urim and Thummim, than it was for Joseph and Oliver together to translate from twelve to fifteen pages with the all-important assistance of the "Interpreters."

After the date of their baptism, the brethren appear to have worked more leisurely. Early in June they moved to Mr. Peter Whitmer's, at Fayette, Seneca county, New York, who had kindly offered them a house. Here the work was continued, John Whitmer, one of the sons, assisting them very much by writing. Joseph states: "Meanwhile our translation was drawing to a close, we went to Palmyra, Wayne county, New York, secured the copyright and agreed with Mr. Egbert Grandin to print five thousand copies for the sum of three thousand dollars." The copyright was secured on June 11th, so it appears that between May 15th and the last-named date, or twenty-six days, they had translated ninety-nine pages—not four pages a day—or they would have finished their work sooner. The exact date the translation was entirely completed is not known, at least we have not been able to discover it.

Thus we see between the dates given, Joseph and Oliver had ample time to do the work claimed by and for them, the objection falls to the ground, and the truth is again vindicated.

THE THREE WITNESSES

In the investigation of the genuineness of the Book of Mormon we must consider the nature of the direct evidence that we have with regard to its origin. And in this respect the testimony is strong, clear, complete and unimpeachable. The existence of the plates is testified to in a most solemn and sacred manner by eleven witnesses in addition to Joseph Smith. Eight of these witnesses actually handled, lifted, and carefully examined the plates, satisfying themselves in a manner beyond all dispute that the plates were real and tangible. It is altogether unlikely that Joseph Smith could have imposed upon these eight witnesses by giving into their hands something different from metallic plates. So, at any rate, we have the evidence of eight men that they handled certain plates and that they had the appearance of very ancient workmanship. If these plates were not the plates from which the Book of Mormon was translated, what were they? where did Joseph Smith get them? and what did he do with them? are all pertinent inquiries. That he had plates in his possession of the kind and description from which he states he translated the Book of Mormon is strong *prima facie* evidence in favor of his story. And the fact that he only showed them to certain few individuals is another evidence of the truthfulness of his statement; for if he, as is claimed, was an ignorant impostor, he would have naturally argued that to the more persons he showed his spurious plates, the wider would grow his influence and the greater would be the number of believers in his story. To keep the plates hidden from the multitude would naturally appear in the average mind to be the surest way of retarding his success and blocking his own progress; and assuredly if Joseph Smith had the cunning and dexterity to invent the story of the discovery of the plates and to manufacture a set of plates to agree with the story, he would have had cunning enough to present them to the public, surrounded by so much mystery and glamour that while they saw them they would not be able to examine them critically.

But we have greater and stronger evidence than that of these eight witnesses.

We have the testimony of three other men that the plates from which the Book of Mormon was translated were shown to them by an angel of the Lord, and not the plates only, but the engravings upon them; and still further they declare that they know that these plates were translated by the gift and power of God, for His voice had declared it unto them. Here, then, we not only have testimony of the existence of the plates, but also to their genuineness and to the truhfulness of the translation, which translation we have in the shape of the Book of Mormon. And it must be remembered that not one of these three witnesses has ever denied his testimony, or contradicted it in the least particular, but under all circumstances and upon every occasion all have in the strongest and most decided language declared that their testimony was true. Again, there is one very noteworthy fact with regard to these three men. They were all severed from the communion of the Church during the lifetime of the Prophet Joseph. If Joseph Smith had been an impostor, he was in the power of each of these "three witnesses"; for any one of them, whenever he pleased, could have exposed the conspiracy, if conspiracy there had been, and shown to the world how the testimony had been manufactured; but none of them have ever done so. Although, at certain periods of their lives, they smarted under the denunciation and reproofs they received from the Prophet and entertained towards him the most bitter feelings for the course he took towards them, going so far as to denounce him as a fallen prophet, yet with all their acrimony and hatred they never once deviated from the testimony that is printed above their names at the commencement of the Book of Mormon. We appeal to all reasonable minds, and ask if it is possible to suppose that, if the Book of Mormon were a fraud, Joseph Smith would have dared to have treated these men in the resolute and uncompromising manner that he did. To use a common expression, he would have been under their thumb and would have had to conciliate them and retain their silence by concessions, by flattery and by trimming his course to their requirements. This the Prophet never did; he was as independent of them as of any other men. He rebuked unrighteousness in them as strongly as he did in others; and when their conduct could no longer be tolerated in the Church of God, he and the Saints withdrew fellowship from them. This is not the way of an impostor, but of an honest, fearless man, who knows his cause is just and puts his trust in God. Neither did any of the eight witnesses ever turn from his testimony and deny its truthfulness. They ever maintained that their statement was the truth and nothing but the truth. They have all gone beyond the veil now, to receive their reward; and all but one died faithful members of the Church of Jesus Christ of Latter-day Saints.

In considering the nature and value of the testimony of the Prophet Joseph and the three witnesses, the following remarks by Elder Orson Pratt are most pertinent: "No reasonable person will say that these four persons were themselves deceived; the nature of their testimony is such that they must either be bold, daring impostors, or else the Book of Mormon is true. They testify that they saw the angel descend, they heard his voice, they saw the plates in his hand, they saw the engravings upon them as the angel turned them over leaf after leaf, at the same time they heard the voice of the Lord out of the heavens. What greater evidence could they have? They could have had nothing that would have given them greater assurance. If they were deceived there is no certainty in anything. If these four men could be deceived in seeing an angel descend from heaven, on the same grounds the apostles may have been deceived in seeing the Savior ascend up to heaven."

Then in answer to the suggestion that it is probable that these four men had conspired together to deceive mankind, Brother Pratt asks:

"Is it probable that four men who were, for the most of their days, strangers to each other, residing in three or four different counties, should combine together to testify that they had seen an angel and heard his voice, and also the voice of God, bearing testimony to the truth of the Book of Mormon, when no such thing had happened? Three of these witnesses, namely, Joseph Smith, Oliver Cowdery and David Whitmer, were young men from twenty to twenty-five years of age; they were men who had been accustomed from their childhood to the peaceful vocations of a farmer's life. Unacquainted with the deceptions, which are more or less practiced in large towns and cities, they possessed the open honesty and simplicity so generally characteristic of country people. Is it, in the least degree, probable that men so young and inexperienced, accustomed to a country life, and unacquainted with the world at large, would be so utterly abandoned to every thing that was good, so perfectly reckless as to their own future welfare, so heaven-daring and blasphemous as to testify to all nations that which, if false, would forever seal their damnation? * * * We are not aware that there ever were three, or four, or five impostors who originated an imposition, and succeeded in palming it upon the world as a message of God. Such a thing might barely be possible, but such a thing would be highly improbable."*

OLIVER COWDERY

Oliver Cowdery is the first of the three witnesses. He was severed from the Church for immoral conduct during the time that the Saints were in Missouri. Often after his separation from the Church efforts were made to prevail upon him to deny his testimony, but always without effect. At all times, in all places, before all people he continually bore record when the subject of the Book of Mormon was introduced, "Gentlemen, I saw an angel, and I know who that angel was." No amount of cross-questioning could weaken his testimony or confuse his statements on this point. We now copy from the *Deseret News,* a very interesting episode that occurred during the last few months of his life:

"At a special conference at Council Bluffs, Iowa, held on the 21st of October, in the year 1848, Brother Oliver Cowdery, one of the three important witnesses to the truth of the Book of Mormon, and who had been absent from the Church, through disaffection, for a number of years, and had been engaged in the practice of law, was present and made the remarks here annexed. Brother Orson Hyde presided at the said conference. Brother Reuben Miller, now Bishop of Mill Creek Ward [since deceased] was also present at the time and noted what he said, and has furnished us, what he believes to be a verbatim report of his remarks, which we take pleasure in laying before our readers:

"'Friends and brethren, my name is Cowdery—Oliver Cowdery. In the early history of this Church I stood identified with her, and one in her councils. True it is that the gifts and callings of God are not without repentance. Not because I was better than the rest of mankind was I called; but, to fulfill the purposes of God, He called me to a high and holy calling. I wrote, with my own pen, the entire Book of Mormon (save a few pages), as it fell from the lips of the Prophet Joseph Smith, as he translated it by the gift and power of God, by the means of the Urim and Thummim, or, as it is called by that book, 'holy interpreters.' *I beheld with my eyes and handled with my hands the gold plates from which it was translated.* I also saw with my eyes and handled with my hands the 'holy interpreters.' That book is *true.* Sidney Rigdon did not write it. Mr. Spaulding did not write it. I wrote it myself as it fell from the lips of the Prophet. It contains the everlasting gospel, and came forth to the children of men in fulfillment of the revelation of John, where he says he saw an angel come with the everlasting gospel to preach to every nation, kindred, and people. It contains principles of salvation; and if you, my hearers, will walk by its light and obey its precepts, you will be saved with an everlasting salvation in the kingdom of God on high. Brother Hyde has just said that it is very important that we keep and walk in the true channel, in order to avoid sand-bars. This is true.

---

*From "Divine Authenticity of the Book of Mormon."

The channel is here. The holy Priesthood is here. I was present with Joseph when an holy angel from God came down from heaven and conferred on us or restored the lesser or Aaronic Priesthood, and said to us, at the same time, that it should remain upon the earth while the earth stands. I was also present with Joseph when the higher or Melchisedek Priesthood was conferred by the holy angel from on high. This Priesthood was then conferred on each other, by the will and commandment of God. This Priesthood, as was then declared, is also to remain upon the earth until the last remnant of time. This holy Priesthood or authority we then conferred upon many, and is just as good and valid as though God had done it in person. I laid my hands upon that man—yes, I laid my right hand upon his head (pointing to Brother Hyde), and I conferred upon him this Priesthood, and he holds that Priesthood now. He was also called through me, by the prayer of faith, an Apostle of the Lord Jesus Christ.' "

DAVID WHITMER

David Whitmer, the second of the three witnesses, still lives. His home is in Richmond, Ray Co., Missouri. He left the Church during the dark days of persecution in Missouri and has never returned to the communion of the Saints. He even to this day holds some very bitter feelings toward the Prophet Joseph Smith, whom he wrongfully imagines endeavored to injure him. But notwithstanding these feelings and the fact that he is not a member of the Church he has all the days of his life testified to the divine origin of the Book of Mormon. His word in this respect has never wavered.

Of late various testimonies given to visitors or written by David Whitmer have been widely published in the public newspapers. We subjoin extracts from one or two of these. The first is a portion of a statement signed by himself and dated at Richmond, March 19th, 1881:

"Unto all Nations, Kindreds, Tongues and People, unto whom these presents shall come:

"It having been represented by one John Murphy, of Polo, Caldwell county, Missouri, that I, in a conversation with him last Summer, denied my testimony as one of the three witnesses of the 'Book of Mormon':

"To the end, therefore, that he may understand me now, if he did not then; and that the world may know the truth, I wish now, standing as it were, in the very sunset of life, and in the fear of God, once for all to make this public statement:

"That I have never at any time, denied that testimony or any part thereof, which has so long since been published with that book, as one of the three witnesses. Those who know me best well know that I have always adhered to that testimony. And that no man may be misled or doubt my present views in regard to the same, I do again affirm the truth of all my statements as then made and published.

" 'He that hath an ear to hear, let him hear'; it was no delusion; what is written, is written, and he that readeth, let him understand."

The following are portions of a letter to the Chicago *Times*, detailing the visit of one of its correspondents to Mr. Whitmer, on October 14th, 1881. The statements are given as those of David Whitmer, and though exceedingly correct as a whole, sometimes, owing to the correspondent's want of familiarity with the subject, they make the speaker fall into slight blunders on historical and other points. He writes:

"The plates from which the book was translated, supposed to be gold, were found in the latter part of the year 1827 or 1828, prior to the acquaintance on Mr. Whitmer's part, with Joseph Smith, and he was loath to believe in their actuality, notwithstanding the community in which he lived (Ontario county, New York), was alive with excitement in regard to Smith's finding a great treasure, and they informed him that they knew that Smith had the plates, as they had seen the place that he had taken them from, on the hill Cumorah, about two miles from Palmyra, N. Y. It was not until June, 1828, that he met the future Prophet, who visited at his father's house, and while there completed the translation of the Book of Mormon, and thus he became conversant with its history, having witnessed Smith dictate to Oliver Cowdery the translation of the characters that were inscribed on the plates, said by Mr. Anthon, our Egyptian scholar, to resemble the characters of that ancient people. Christian Whitmer, his brother, occasionally assisted Cowdery in writing, as did Mrs. Joseph Smith, who was a Miss Hale before she was married.

"In regard to finding the plates, he was told by Smith that they were in a stone casket, and the place where it was deposited, in the hill Cumorah, was pointed out to him by a celestial personage, clad in a dazzling white robe, and he was informed by it that it was the history of the Nephites, a nation that had passed away, whose founders belonged to the days of the tower of Babel. The plates which Mr. Whitmer saw were in the shape of a tablet, fastened with three rings, about one-third of which appeared to be loose, in plates, the other solid, but with perceptible marks where the plates seemed to be sealed, and the guide that pointed it out to Smith very impressively reminded him that the loose plates alone were to be used, the sealed portion was not to be tampered with.

"After the plates had been translated, which process required about six months, the same heavenly visitant appeared and reclaimed the gold tablets of the ancient people informing Smith that he would replace them with other records of the lost tribes that had been brought with them during their wanderings from Asia, which would be forthcoming when the world was ready to receive them. At that time Mr. Whitmer saw the tablets, gazed with awe on the celestial messenger, heard him speak and say: "Blessed is the Lord and he that keeps His commandments"; and then, as he held the plates and turned them over with his hands, so that they could be plainly visible, a voice that seemed to fill all space, musical as the sighing of a wind through the forest, was heard, saying: "What you see is true; testify to the same." And Oliver Cowdery and David Whitmer, standing there, felt, as the white garments of the angel faded from their vision and the heavenly voice still rang in their ears, that it was no delusion—that it was a fact, and they so recorded it. In a day or two after, the same spirit appeared to Martin Harris while he was in company with Smith, and told him also to bear witness to its truth, which he did, as can be seen in the book. Harris described the visitant to Whitmer, who recognized it as the same that he and Cowdery had seen.

"The tablets or plates were translated by Smith, who used a small oval or kidney-shaped stone, called Urim and Thummim, that seemed endowed with the marvelous power of converting the characters on the plates, when used by Smith, into English, who would then dictate to Cowdery what to write. Frequently one character would make two lines of manuscript while others made but a word or two words. Mr. Whitmer emphatically asserts, as did Harris and Cowdery, that while Smith was dictating the translation he had *no manuscript notes or other means of knowledge,* save the Seer stone and the characters as shown on the plates, he being present and cognizant how it was done.

"In regard to the statement that Sidney Rigdon had purloined the work of one Spaulding, a Presbyterian preacher, who had written a romance entitled the 'Manuscript Found,' Mr. Whitmer says there is no foundation for such an assertion. The 'Book of Mormon' was translated in the Summer of 1829, and printed that Winter at Palmyra, New York, and was in circulation before Sidney Rigdon knew anything concerning the Church of Christ, as it was known then. His attention was specially brought to it by the appearance at his church, near Kirtland, Ohio, in the Fall of 1830, of Parley Pratt and Oliver Cowdery, he being at that time a Reformed or Christian preacher, they having been sent west by the Church in New York during that Summer as evangelists, and they carried with them the printed book, the first time that he knew such a thing was in existence. * * *

Mr. Whitmer emphatically asserts that he has heard Rigdon, in the pulpit, and in private conversation, declare that the 'Spaulding story,' that he had used a book called the 'Manuscript Found' for the purpose of preparing the 'Book of Mormon,' was as false as were many other charges that were then being made against the infant Church, and he assures me that the story is as untruthful as it is ridiculous.

"In his youth Joseph Smith was quite illiterate, knew nothing of grammar or composition, but obtained quite a good education after he came west; was a man of great magnetism, made friends easily, was liberal and noble in his impulses, tall, finely-formed and full of animal life, but sprang from the most humble circumstances. The first good suit of clothes he had ever worn was presented to him by Christian Whitmer, brother of David. * * *

"Mr. Whitmer's beliefs have undergone no change since his early manhood; he has refused to affiliate with any of the various branches that have sprung up through false teachings, and rests his hopes of the future 'in the teachings of Christ, the apostles and the prophets, and the morals and principles enunciated in the scriptures; that the Book of Mormon is but the testimony of another nation concerning the truth and divinity of Christ and the Bible, and that is his rock, his gospel and his salvation.' Seeing, with him, is believing. He is now as firm in the faith of the divinity of the book that he saw translated as he was when the glory of the celestial visitant almost blinded him with the gleam of his glowing presence, fresh from the Godhead; and the voice, majestic, ringing out from the earth to the mighty dome of space, still lingers in his ears like a chime of silver bells."

The *Deseret Evening News* at the time of the publication of his letter corrected some of the errors of this correspondent. We cannot do better than use its language:

"The first [error] is that the founders of the Nephites 'belonged to the tower of Babel.' The Nephites sprang from Nephi, the son of Lehi, who came to this land from Judea, in the reign of King Zedekiah. The Jaredites, whose history is briefly given in the Book of Mormon, were a distinct and preceding race; they descended from a colony that peopled this country after the dispersion from Babel. The term 'lost tribes' is also incorrect, as the Nephites had no identity with the lost tribes of Israel, being descendants of Joseph, the son of Jacob.

"The next mistake is that 'In a day or two after David Whitmer and Oliver Cowdery saw the angel and the plates the same spirit appeared to Martin Harris.' The truth is that it was shortly after, on the same day. Martin Harris was with Joseph, Oliver and David, but there was no answer to their prayers, until Martin, who felt that his lack of faith was a hindrance, withdrew. Then the angel appeared, and after the vision closed, Joseph Smith went to the place where Martin Harris was, a little distance off, and joined with him in prayer, when the angel again appeared, and Martin rejoicingly bore testimony that he had seen and heard as the others.

"The next error is that the seer stone which Joseph used in the translation 'was called Urim and Thummim.' The instrument thus denominated was composed of two crystal stones 'set in the two rims of a bow.' The seer stone was separate and distinct from the Urim and Thummim. The latter was delivered to the angel as well as the plates after the translation was completed; the former remained with the Church and is now in the possession of the President."

A still later interviewer gives the following as David Whitmer's testimony to the party of visitors of which the writer was one:

"We asked him if his testimony was the same now as it was at the time the Book of Mormon was published, regarding seeing the plates and the angel. He rose to his feet, stretched out his hands and said: 'These hands handled the plates, these eyes saw the angel, and these ears heard His voice; and I know it was of God.'"

Our concluding extract is a statement made by David Whitmer to Elders Orson Pratt and Joseph F. Smith, when these brethren visited him at his home in September, 1878.

In answer to Elder Pratt's question, if he remembered the date he saw the plates, he answered:

"It was in June, 1829—the latter part of the month, and the eight witnesses saw them, I think, the next day or the day after. Joseph showed them the plates himself, but the angel showed us [the three witnesses] the plates, as I suppose to fulfill the words of the book itself. Martin Harris was not with us at this time; he obtained a view of them afterwards [the same day]. Joseph, Oliver, and myself were together when I saw them. We not only saw the plates of the Book of Mormon but also the brass plates, the plates of the Book of Ether, the plates containing the records of the wickedness and secret combinations of the people of the world down to the time of their being engraved and many other plates. The fact is, it was just as though Joseph, Oliver and I were sitting just here on a log when we were overshadowed by a light. It was not like the light of the sun nor like that of a fire, but more glorious and beautiful. It extended away around us, I cannot tell how far, but in the midst of this light about as far off as he sits (pointing to John C. Whitmer, sitting a few feet from him), there appeared, as it were, a table with many records or plates upon it besides the plates of the Book of Mormon; also the sword of Laban, the directors —i.e. the ball which Lehi had, and the Interpreters. I saw them just as plain as I see this bed (striking the bed beside him with his hand), and I heard the voice of the Lord as distinctly as I ever heard anything in my life, declaring that the records of the plates of the Book of Mormon were translated by the gift and power of God.'

"Elder Pratt then asked, 'Did you see the angel at this time?'

"David Whitmer answered, 'Yes; he stood before us. Our testimony as recorded in the Book of Mormon is strictly and absolutely true, just as it is there written.' "

MARTIN HARRIS

It is probable that many of our readers have seen Martin Harris.* It is but a few years since he died in our midst. Though his name is signed last to the testimony of the three witnesses he was considerably older than the other two.

Martin Harris was the instrument used by the Lord to enable Joseph to print the Book of Mormon. He supplied the funds necessary to pay the printer. All of this was repaid to him, by Joseph, and as he said, "more too." We mention this because it has been falsely asserted that Joseph made Martin Harris his dupe and never paid back the money he borrowed of him.

Brother Harris was a well-to-do farmer at the time he became acquainted with the Prophet Joseph. He was respected and esteemed by his neighbors, but like all the others who had anything to do with the publication of the Book of Mormon, he was assailed with savage bitterness, and accused of numerous sins as soon as it was known that he was a believer in that holy book. He was charged with being visionary, cruel and untruthful, and with having beaten his wife and turned her out of doors.

We will now refer to the testimony of the Kelley brothers, which we quoted when we considered the character of Joseph the Prophet. We found they asked the old residents of Manchester some questions with regard to the reputation of Martin Harris. Those who knew him, invariably spoke well of him. One said, "He was an honorable farmer; he was not very religious before the Book of Mormon was published." Another stated "Harris was an industrious, honest man." A third affirmed "He was an honorable man. He was one of the first men of the town." And so on, one after another denied the calumnies that had been heaped upon the head of this inoffensive, though somewhat peculiar gentleman, whose worst act in the eyes of these neighbors was that he helped Joseph Smith to give the Book of Mormon to the world.

It will be remembered that the testimony of the three witnesses, with regard to the plates from which the Book of Mormon was translated, is to the effect that "We also know that they have been translated by the gift and power of God, for His voice hath declared it unto us; wherefore we know of a surety that the work is true. And we also testify that we have seen the engravings which are upon the plates;

---

*Brother M. Harris, accompanied by Elder E. Stevenson reached Ogden on the 29th of August, 1870; he afterwards resided until his death at the home of his son in Smithfield, Cache county.

and they have been shown unto us by the power of God and not of man. And we declare with words of soberness, that an angel of God came down from heaven, and He brought and laid before our eyes, that we beheld and saw the plates and the engravings thereon.' But it must be remembered that this was not the only time that Martin Harris saw the plates. He states that on one occasion he held them on his knee for an hour and a half, and also affirms that "as many of the plates as Joseph Smith translated I handled with my hands, plate after plate." This testimony was given when Harris was not a member of the Church.

Early in the history of the Latter-day Saints Martin Harris became disaffected. He committed grave errors and gave way to a very unchristian-like spirit. The communion of the Saints was withdrawn from him and he became an outcast to the blessings of the gospel. Thus he remained many years, or more than a third of a century, but in his old age he returned as a wandering sheep to the true fold, and again became a partaker of the gifts and blessings of the everlasting gospel. We will now insert an interview had with him when he was not a member of the Church (in 1853?) and two letters written by him nearly twenty years afterwards, after he had renewed his covenant with the Lord at the waters of baptism.

September 15th, 1853

"Be it known to all whom this may concern that I, David B. Dille, of Ogden City, Weber county, Salt Lake, *en route* to Great Britain, having business with one Martin Harris, formerly of the Church of Latter-day Saints, and residing at Kirtland, Lake county, Ohio, did personally wait upon him at his residence, and found him sick in bed; and was informed by the said Martin Harris that he had not been able to take any nourishment for the space of three days. This, together with his advanced age, had completely prostrated him. After making my business known to Mr. Harris, and some little conversation with him, the said Martin Harris started up in bed, and, after particularly inquiring concerning the prosperity of the Church, made the following declaration:

" 'I feel that a spirit has come across me—the old spirit of Mormonism; and I begin to feel as I used to feel; and I will not say—'I won't go to the valley.' Then addressing himself to his wife, he said—'I don't know but that, if you will get me some breakfast, I will get up and eat it.'

"I then addressed Mr. Harris relative to his once high and exalted station in the Church, and his then fallen and afflicted condition. I afterwards put the following questions to Mr. Harris, to which he severally replied with the greatest cheerfulness: 'What do you think of the Book of Mormon? Is it a divine record?"

"Mr. Harris replied: 'I was the right hand man of Joseph Smith, and I know that he was a prophet of God. I know the Book of Mormon is true—*and you know that I know that it is true.* I know that the plates have been translated by the gift and power of God, for His voice declared it unto us; therefore I know of a surety that the work is true; *for did I not at one time hold the plates on my knee an hour and a half,* while in conversation with Joseph, when we went to bury them in the woods, that the enemy might not obtain them? Yes, I did. *And as many of the plates as Joseph Smith translated, I handled with my hands, plate after plate.'* Then, describing their dimensions, he pointed with one of the fingers of his left hand to the back of his right hand and said: 'I should think they were so long,' or about eight inches, 'and about so thick,' or about four inches; 'and each of the plates was thicker than the thickest tin.'

"I then asked Mr. Harris if he ever lost 3,000 dollars by the publishing of the Book of Mormon?

"Mr. Harris said, 'I never lost one cent. Mr. Smith paid me all that I advanced, and more too.' As much as to say he received a portion of the profits accruing from the sale of the books.

"Mr. Harris further said: 'I took a transcript of the characters of the plates to Dr. Anthon, of New York. When I arrived at the house of Professor Anthon, I found him in his office and alone, and presented the transcript to him, and asked him to read it. He said if I would bring the plates, he would assist in the translation. I told him I could not, for they were sealed. Professor Anthon then gave me a certificate certifying that the characters were Arabic, Chaldaic and Egyptian. I then left Dr. Anthon, and was near the door, when he said, 'How did the young man know the plates were there?' I said an angel had shown them to him. Professor Anthon then said, 'Let me see the certificate!' Upon which, I took it from my waistcoat pocket and unsuspectingly gave it to him. He then tore it up in anger, saying, there was no such things as angels now, it was all a hoax. I then went to Dr. Mitchell with the transcript, and he confirmed what Professor Anthon had said.'

"Mr. Harris is about fifty-eight years old, and is on a valuable farm of ninety acres, beautifully situated at Kirtland, Lake county, Ohio."—*Millennial Star.*

"Smithfield, Utah,

"Nov. 23, 1870.

"Mr. Emerson,

Sir:—I received your favor. In reply I will say concerning the plates, I do say that the angel did show to me the plates containing the Book of Mormon. Further, the translation that I carried to Professor Anthon was copied from these same plates; also, that the professor did testify to it being a correct translation. I do firmly believe and do know that Joseph Smith was a prophet of God; for without, I know he could not had that gift; neither could he have translated the same. I can give, if you require it, one hundred witnesses to the proof of the Book of Mormon. I defy any man to show me any passage of scripture that I am not posted on or familiar with. I will answer any question you feel like asking to the best of my knowledge, if you can rely on my testimony of the same. In conclusion, I can say that I arrived in Utah safe, in good health and spirits, considering the long journey. I am quite well at present, and have been, generally speaking, since I arrived. With many respects,

"I remain your humble friend,

"Martin Harris."

"Smithfield, Cache Co., Utah,

"January, 1871.

"To H. Emerson,

Dear Sir:—Your second letter, dated December, 1870, came duly to hand. I am truly glad to see a spirit of inquiry manifested therein. I reply by a borrowed hand, as my sight has failed me too much to write myself. Your questions:

"Question 1. "Did you go to England to lecture against Mormonism?"

"Answer. I answer emphatically, No, I did not. No man ever heard me in any way deny the truth of the Book of Mormon, the administration of the angel that showed me the plates; nor the organization of the Church of Jesus Christ of Latterday Saints, under the administration of Joseph Smith, Jun., the prophet whom the Lord raised up for that purpose in these latter days, that He may show forth His power and glory. The Lord has shown me these things by His Spirit, by the administration of holy angels, and confirmed the same with signs following, step by step, as the work has progressed, for the space of fifty-three years.

The Lord showed me there was no true church upon the face of the earth, none built upon the foundation designed by the Savior, the rock of revelation, as declared to Peter. (See Matt. 16:16-18.) He also showed me that an angel should come and restore the holy Priesthood again to the earth, and commission His servants again with the holy gospel to preach to them that dwell on the earth. (See Revelation 14:6, 7.) He further showed me that the time was nigh when He would 'set His hand again the second time to restore the kingdom of Israel, when He would gather the outcasts of Israel and the dispersed of Judah from the four corners of the earth,' when He would bring the record of Joseph which was in the hand of Ephraim, and join with the record of Judah, when the two records should become one in the hand of the Lord to accomplish His great work of the last days. (See Ezekiel 36, 37; also Isaiah 29; also Isaiah 58 to the end of the book; also Psalms.)

"Question 2. 'What became of the plates from which the Book of Mormon was translated?'

"Answer. They were returned to the angel, Moroni, from whom they were received, to be brought forth again in the due time of the Lord; for they contain many things pertaining to the gathering of Israel, which gathering will take place in this generation, and shall be testified of among all nations according to the old prophets; as the Lord will set His ensign to the people, and gather the outcasts of Israel. (See Isaiah 11.)

"Now, dear sir, examine these scriptures carefully; and should there still be any ambiguity relative to this great work of the last days, write again and we will endeavor to enlighten you on any point relative to this doctrine.

"I am, very respectfully,
"Martin Harris, Sen."

The following interesting statement is an extract from a letter written to the *Deseret News,* by Elder Edward Stevenson:

"Martin Harris related an instance that occurred during the time that he wrote that portion of the translation of the Book of Mormon, which he was favored to write direct from the mouth of the Prophet Joseph Smith. He said that the Prophet possessed a seer stone, by which he was enabled to translate as well as from the Urim and Thummim, and for convenience he then used the seer stone. Martin explained the translation as follows: By aid of the seer stone, sentences would appear and were read by the prophet and written by Martin, and when finished he would say, 'Written,' and if correctly written, that sentence would disappear and another appear in its place, but if not written correctly it remained until corrected, so that the translation was just as it was engraven on the plates, precisely in the language then used. Martin said, after continued translation they would become weary and would go down to the river and exercise by throwing stones out on the river, etc. While so doing on one occasion, Martin found a stone very much resembling the one used for translating, and on resuming their labor of translation, Martin put in place the stone that he had found. He said that the Prophet remained silent unusually and intently gazing in darkness, no traces of the usual sentences appearing. Much surprised, Joseph exclaimed, 'Martin! What is the matter? All is as dark as Egypt.' Martin's countenance betrayed him, and the prophet asked Martin why he had done so. Martin said, to stop the mouths of fools, who had told him that the Prophet had learned those sentences and was merely repeating them, etc.

Martin said further that the seer stone differed in appearance entirely from the Urim and Thummim that was obtained with the plates, which were two clear stones set in two rims, very much resembled spectacles, only they were larger. Martin said there were not many pages translated while he wrote; after which Oliver Cowdery did the writing.

In concluding this portion of our subject we desire to draw attention to the entire agreement between the witness as to the manner in which the plates were translated. If any fraud had been practiced, or there had been a conspiracy to deceive, these witnesses in the lapse of so many years would doubtless have told conflicting stories, especially in regard to minor details. But as it is their statements are harmonious one with the other, their testimony unchangeable and the whole consistent with the narrative of the Prophet Joseph and the condition of things by which they were then surrounded.

INTERNAL EVIDENCES OF THE BOOK OF MORMON

We will now consider for a short time a few of the internal evidences of the genuineness of the Book of Mormon, or the proofs in itself that it is what it claims to be, a record of God's dealings with the former inhabitants of this continent.

Among the more prominent internal evidences of its genuineness may be mentioned:

1. Its historical consistency.

2. The entire absence of all anachronisms, or confusion in its chronology, and of conflicting statements with regard to history, doctrine or prophecy.

3. The purity of its doctrines, and their entire harmony with the teachings of our Savior and His inspired servants as recorded in the Bible.

4. Its already fulfilled prophecies.

5. Its harmony with the traditions of the Indian races.

6. Its entire accord with scientific truth; none of its geographical, astronomical or other statements being contrary to what is positively known in these sciences.

There is nothing in the entire historical narrative of the Book of Mormon that is inconsistent with the dealings of the Almighty with mankind, or conflicting with history as far as the history which has been handed down to us in other records deals with events referred to in the Book of Mormon. On the other hand, the whole scheme of human salvation, as developed in the dealings of the Lord with the Jaredites, Nephites and Lamanites, gives us the most exalted ideas of His love for His mortal children and His condescension towards the erring   sons and daughters of Adam. Even if the Book of Mormon were not true, it deserves to be so, from the sublimity of the ideas that it conveys with regard to God's providences and His ways and methods of leading, directing and preserving His children. No nobler monument to the glory, the mercy and the long-suffering of our Heavenly Father than this wonderful book was ever presented for the consideration of mankind.

It requires a great deal more credulity to believe it possible that any author, ignorant or learned, be he Joseph Smith, Sidney Rigdon or Solomon Spaulding, could, without the inspiration of the Almighty, bring forth such a work as the Book of Mormon, than to believe that it is a revelation from the Almighty.

Hengstenberg, in his work on the Pentateuch, says:

"It is the unavoidable fate of a spurious historical work of any length to be involved in contradictions." This is obviously true. No thinking person will deny that it would be one of the most difficult of all literary feats to compose a historical work extending over thousands of years and dealing with hundreds of individuals without introducing some blunders as to time, place or circumstance, or permitting egregious contradictions to pass unnoticed. But the Book of Mormon is entirely free from all blunders of such a kind. This alone stamps it as of more than human origin. For more than fifty years, the bigoted and skeptical have been endeavoring to find errors, inconsistencies or impossibilities within its contents. But in this they have utterly failed. Not one of all their pretended discoveries of errors has stood the test of investigation. It has been found, without exception, that in such cases the objector has either dishonestly garbled the text, put an impossible construction on good, plain English, or presented his own private interpretation of the words of the book instead of the words themselves. The writer of this having perused the Book of Mormon many times, confidently asserts that there is no conflict of dates, no contradiction of details, no discordant doctrine, no historical inconsistency, from the commencement of the first Book of Nephi to the end of Moroni. All is a plain, simple narrative, occasionally somewhat unpolished in its style, and here and there at variance with the strict rules of grammar, but throughout maintaining its unities and harmonies, and bearing upon its face indelible marks of its divine origin.

We now come to the doctrinal portions of the work:

It is readily admitted on all hands that no sectarian preacher like Mr. Spaulding would write doctrines, such as the Book of Mormon contains, these doctrines being at variance with the creed that he professed; and, indeed, in many respects different to those of every creed then extant upon the face of the earth. The Book of Mormon, be it human or divine, is a new revelation on religious matters to this generation, and its entire accord with the revelations of the Almighty contained in the Bible is a proof so strong of its divinity that none have been able to gainsay it. It is utterly ridiculous to imagine that Joseph Smith, unlettered as he was, could have written a work in such entire harmony with the holy scriptures and entering into many new particulars, as it frequently does, with regard to doctrines only slightly touched upon in the Old or New Testaments: it not only harmonizes with the scriptures, but it explains them, makes clear the meaning of many an obscure passage, and while it never conflicts with, it often develops, truths of the utmost importance to humanity.

How wonderful a miracle!—much greater than the discovery of the records in the hill Cumorah—that an uneducated youth, (and neither friend nor foe claims he was educated), could produce a work pregnant with principles connected with the most vital interests of the human family, and treating on subjects that concern man's temporal and eternal welfare, which cannot be refuted by all the learned of the world. Would not this be much more wonderful, calling for a much greater strain on our credulity than to believe that God had again spoken and brought to light this long-hidden treasure? And if it be inconsistent to believe that neither Joseph Smith nor Solomon Spaulding was the author of the religious portions of the Book of Mormon, wherein is it more consistent to ascribe the authorship to Sidney Rigdon? He was as utterly ignorant of many of the doctrines and principles made plain in the Book of Mormon as was Solomon Spaulding or any other uninspired priest of fifty or more years ago. There was no system of philosophy, ethics or religion then known to mankind from which he could have drawn the inspiration to write many of the doctrinal precepts in the Book of Mormon.

To tide over this difficulty, persons unacquainted with the contents of the Book of Mormon (which unfortunately the greater portion of mankind are) have suggested that Solomon Spaulding wrote the historical portion (an impossibility, as we have heretofore shown) and that Joseph Smith or somebody else added the religious portion. To those who have read the Book of Mormon, this hypothesis is supremely ridiculous.

An objector to the Bible might, with equal consistency, assert that somebody wrote the historical portion of the Old and New Testaments, and somebody else, after the historical portion was all written, introduced the religious teachings. One is as impossible as the other. Every one who knows anything of the Book of Mormon knows that the narrative of events grows out of and is inseparably connected with the religious idea. The book opens with the statement that Lehi was a prophet, bearing Jehovah's unwelcome message of destruction to the inhabitants of the sin-seared city of Jerusalem. They rejected and persecuted him. By divine command he fled with his family into the wilderness and was led by that same inspiration to the American continent. The reason why the Lord thus delivered him was, that he might raise up to Himself a people that would serve Him. He covenanted to give Lehi and his posterity this most precious land as their inheritance if they kept His commandments. How they fulfilled His law, how they prospered when obedient, how they suffered when disobedient, is the burden of the story of the writers of the Book of Mormon. It is the main idea to which all others are incidental, the controlling thought around which all others concentrate; it is the life of the whole record, the golden thread running through all its pages, which gives consistency to all its parts. A man might just as well attempt to write the gospel of St. Matthew and leave out all references to the Lord Jesus Christ, as write the Book of Mormon without its religious theory and teachings.

The creature who invented the idea of the dual authorship of this book must have imagined that the doctrinal portion was dropped in by lumps or clumsily inserted between different historical epochs. It is true there are places where liberal extracts from the Bible are quoted, and if these were all, there might be some semblance of consistency in the supposition. But it is not so, the doctrinal and historical portions are, as a general thing, so intermingled and blended that neither could be withdrawn without destroying the sense of the other. If it were possible to conceive of the amalgamation of two separate documents—one religious and the other historical—it would be much easier to believe that the doctrinal portions were written first and that the historical ideas were afterwards filled in; for, as before mentioned, the historical narrative is but secondary and tributary to the religious idea. But this would not support the theory of the Spauldingites; it would, in fact, entirely upset all their arguments for the reason that they claim that the "Manuscript Found," a historical romance of an idolatrous people, be it remembered, was written by Spaulding not later than 1812, while the Book of Mormon was not published by Joseph Smith until 1830, consequently such an arrangement would be fatal to their hypothesis.

We next glance at the prophecies of the Book of Mormon, a number of which are already fulfilled. These are among the most irrefutable evidences of the divinity of the work; the facts are patent to all the world, they are within the reach of all mankind. Ever since the year 1830, men have had the opportunity of testing the contents of the Book of Mormon, as it has not been hidden in a corner, but has been published in all the dominant languages of Christendom. To say that many of its prophecies have not been fulfilled is to deny history. And it cannot be asserted that these prophecies are happy guesses, as, at the time when the Book of Mormon was published, they appeared most improbable, none more so than those which foretell the results that would follow its own publication. For it must be remembered that when it was published there was no Church of Jesus Christ organized upon the earth, and there was no remote probability of the then non-existent church producing the results in itself and to the world that the Book of Mormon declares should follow its establishment, which have been fulfilled, year by year, from the time of its publication to the present. If the Book of Mormon be not true, then these prophecies originated with Joseph Smith, and, as they have been fulfilled, he was a true prophet; further, as they were declared in the name of the Lord and the Lord has recognized them by permitting their fulfillment in so many wondrous ways and by such direct manifestations of His divine power, therefore the conclusion is inevitable that the Lord owned and acknowledged Joseph Smith as His servant. On the other hand, if they did not originate with Joseph Smith, then the record is genuine, for the prophecies are true, and they were uttered by the men to whom they are ascribed. If so, Joseph's account of his discovery of the plates is true and he was a seer and a revelator, especially called of God to lay the foundation of the mighty work of the last days.

Those who are so strongly opposed to "Mormonism" can accept whichever horn of the dilemma they choose. But to our mind the first supposition is utterly untenable, as it is impossible for us to conceive that God, who hateth a lie, would choose for His servant a man who made such a science of falsehood; or that the Divine One would add the seal of His approbation to a forgery and an imposture, such as the Book of Mormon would be under these circumstances. To believe such a thing, would be as consistent as to believe that if there were prophecies contained in "Gulliver's Travels" the Lord would move heaven and earth to bring about their fulfillment; for if the Book of Mormon be not what it claims, then it is as much a romance as the celebrated work of Dean Swift, and one is as worthy of credence as the other.

THE PROPHECIES OF THE BOOK OF MORMON

Let us now consider a few of the fulfilled prophecies of the Book of Mormon. On page 487 it is stated: "And behold ye [the translator] may be privileged that ye may shew the plates unto those who shall assist to bring forth his work; and *unto three shall they be shewn by the power of God;* wherefore they shall know of a surety that these things are true. And in the mouth of three witnesses shall these things be established; and the testimony of three and this work * * * shall stand as a testimony against the world at the last day." (Ether 5:2-4.)

In the above we have the statement that three witnesses are to be raised up by the power of God to testify to the truth and genuineness of the book. At the commencement of the Book of Mormon we have the testimony of these three witnesses—Oliver Cowdery, David Whitmer and Martin Harris—to the fulfillment of the above prophecy. They declare that an angel of God came down from heaven, who brought the plates and laid them before their eyes. "Ah, but," says our opponent, "what an easy matter it would be for an impostor like Joseph Smith to conspire with three other men to fulfill the prophecy?" Such a thing is quite supposable to ignorant persons unacquainted with the matter, but very improbable under the circumstances as already shown. Or Joseph Smith might even have deceived three men had he shown them the plates himself; but not all the impostors in the world could bring an angel down from heaven, or cause the Lord to declare with His own voice that the plates were translated by His gift and power. In this is the utter impossibility. As we have before shown these three men under all circumstances have borne one continuous, undeviating testimony that they saw the angel and heard the voice, and that their testimony in the Book of Mormon is true. No amount of sophistry can persuade the sincere investigator into these matters that Joseph Smith had sufficient cunning and dexterity, even if he had appliances, to deceive these three men into the belief that they had acually seen an angel descend from heaven and present them the plates for their examination. This is altogether too great a stretch for the imagination of an ordinary sane person.

It is more difficult to select isolated passages from the prophecies of the Book of Mormon than from those of the Bible; for as a general thing they are so intimately associated with the context that their force, power and meaning are surprisingly weakened when quoted alone. Among the prophecies of Mormon's record that are partially fulfilled or are now in process of fulfillment may be mentioned those relating to—

The carrying of the Book itself to the Indians, and their acceptance of its truths.

The beginning of the gathering of the Jews to their ancient home in Canaan.

The establishment of Christ's Church, and the spilling of the blood of the Saints by the wicked.

The great increase of corruption among those who reject the gospel message.

The formation of numerous powerful secret societies for the purpose of murder, plunder and gain, and for the overthrowal of governments and nations.

We append a few of these prophecies:

"And now behold, I say unto you, that when the Lord shall see fit, in His wisdom, that these sayings shall come forth unto the Gentiles, according to His word then ye may know that the covenant which the Father hath made with the children of Israel, concerning their restoration to the lands of their inheritance is already beginning to be fulfilled." (III Nephi 29:1.)

"And then shall the work of the Father commence at that day, even when this gospel shall be preached among the remnant of this people [the Indians]. Verily I say unto you, at that day shall the work of the Father commence among all the dispersed of my people; yea, even the tribes which have been lost, which the Father hath led away out of Jerusalem. Yea, the work shall commence among all the dispersed of my people, with the Father, to prepare the way whereby they may come unto me, that they may call on the Father in my name. Yea, and then shall the work commence, with the Father among all nations, in preparing the way whereby His people may be gathered home to the land of their inheritance. And they shall go out from all nations; and they shall not go out in haste, nor go by flight, for I will go before them, saith the Father, and I will be their rearward." (III Nephi 21:26-29.)

"And there are also secret combinations, even as in times of old, according to the combinations of the devil, for he is the foundation of all these things; yea, the foundation of murder, and works of darkness, yea, and he leadeth them by the neck with a flaxen cord, until he bindeth them with his strong cords for ever." (II Nephi 26:22.)

"And whatsoever nation shall uphold such secret combinations, to get power and gain, until they shall spread over the nation, behold, they shall be destroyed, for the Lord will not suffer that the blood of His Saints, which shall be shed by them, shall always cry unto Him from the ground for vengeance upon them, and yet He avenge them not;

"Wherefore, O ye Gentiles, it is wisdom in God that these things should be shewn unto you, that thereby ye may repent of your sins, and suffer not that these murderous combinations shall get above you, which are built up to get power and gain, and the work, yea, even the work of destruction come upon you, yea, even the sword of the justice of the eternal God shall fall upon you, to your overthrow and destruction, if ye shall suffer these things to be;

"Wherefore the Lord commandeth you, when ye shall see these things come among you, that ye shall awake to a sense of your awful situation, because of this secret combination which shall be among you, or wo be unto it, because of the blood of them who have been slain; for they cry from the dust for vengeance upon it, and also upon those who built it up.

"For it cometh to pass that whoso buildeth it up, seeketh to overthrow the freedom of all lands, nations, and countries; and bringeth to pass the destruction of all people, for it is built up by the devil, who is the father of all lies; even that same liar who beguiled our first parents; yea, even that same liar who hath caused man to commit murder from the beginning; who hath hardened the hearts of men, that they have murdered the prophets, and stoned them, and cast them out from the beginning." (Ether 8:22-25.)

"And no one need say, They shall not come, for they surely shall, for the Lord hath spoken it; for out of the earth shall they come, by the hand of the Lord, and none can stay it; and it shall come in a day when it shall be said that miracles are done away; and it shall come even as if one should speak from the dead.

"And it shall come in a day when the blood of the Saints shall cry unto the Lord, because of secret combinations and the works of darkness;

"Yea, it shall come in a day when the power of God shall be denied, and churches become defiled, and shall be lifted up in the pride of their hearts; yea, even in a day when leaders of churches, and teachers, in the pride of their hearts, even to the envying of them who belong to their churches." (Mormon 8:26-28.)

"Yea, why do you build up your secret abominations to get gain, and cause that widows should mourn before the Lord, and also orphans to mourn before the Lord; and also the blood of their fathers and their husbands to cry unto the Lord from the ground, for vengeance upon your heads?

"Behold, the sword of vengeance hangeth over you; and the time soon cometh that He avengeth the blood of the Saints upon you, for He will not suffer their cries any longer." (Mormon 8:40, 41.)

For further information on this subject we refer our readers to President George Q. Cannon's admirable "Life of Nephi," wherein the prophecies of that ancient worthy are considered in much detail, and with great care and plainness.

In conclusion to sum up the internal evidence, we will adopt the words of Elder Orson Pratt:

"If the historical parts of the Book of Mormon be compared with what little is known from other sources concerning the history of ancient America, there will be found much evidence to substantiate its truth; but there cannot be found one truth among all the gleanings of antiquity that clashes with the historical truth of the Book of Mormon.

"If the prophetical part of this wonderful book be compared with the prophetical declarations of the Bible, there will be found much evidence in the latter to establish the truth of the former. But though there are many predictions in the Book of Mormon, relating to the great events of the last days, which the Bible gives us no information about, yet there is nothing in the predictions of the Bible that contradict in the least, the predictions in the Book of Mormon.

"If the doctrinal part of the Book of Mormon be compared with the doctrines of the Bible, there will be found the same perfect harmony which we find on the comparison of the prophetical parts of the two books. Although there are many points of the doctrine of Christ that are far more plain and definite in the Book of Mormon than in the Bible, and many things revealed in relation to doctrine that never could be fully learned from the Bible, yet there are not any items of doctrine in the two sacred books that contradict each other or clash in the least.

"If the various books which enter into the collection, called the Book of Mormon, be carefully compared with each other, there will be found nothing contradicting in history, in prophecy, or in doctrine.

"If the miracles of the Book of Mormon be compared with the miracles of the Bible, there cannot be found in the former any thing that would be more difficult to believe, than what we find in the latter.

"If we compare the historical, prophetical and doctrinal parts of the Book of Mormon with the great truths of science and nature, we find no contradictions, no absurdities, nothing unreasonable. The most perfect harmony therefore exists between the great truths revealed in the Book of Mormon and all known truths, whether religious, historical, or scientific."

APPENDIX

MRS. MATILDA SPAULDING McKINSTRY'S STATEMENT REGARDING THE "MANUSCRIPT FOUND"

Washington, D. C., April 3, 1880.

So much has been published that is erroneous concerning the "Manuscript Found," written by my father, the Rev. Solomon Spaulding, and its supposed connection with the book called the Mormon Bible, I have willingly consented to make the following statement regarding it, repeating all that I remember personally of this manuscript, and all that is of importance which my mother related to me in connection with it, at the same time affirming that I am in tolerable health and vigor, and that my memory, in common with elderly people, is clearer in regard to the events of my earlier years, rather than those of my maturer life.

During the war of 1812, I was residing with my parents in a little town in Ohio called Conneaut. I was then in my sixth year. My father was in business there, and I remember his iron foundry and the men he had at work, but that he remained at home most of the time, and was reading and writing a great deal. He frequently wrote little stories, which he read to me. There were some round mounds of earth near our house which greatly interested him, and he said a tree on the top of one of them was a thousand years old. He set some of his men to work digging into one of these mounds, and I vividly remember how excited he became when he heard that they had exhumed some human bones, portions of gigantic skeletons, and various relics. He talked with my mother of these discoveries in the mound, and was writing every day as the work progressed. Afterward he read the manuscript which I had seen him writing, to the neighbors, and to a clergyman, a friend of his who came to see him. Some of the names that he mentioned while reading to these people I have never forgotten. They are as fresh to me to-day as though I heard them yesterday. They were *Mormon, Maroni, Lamenite, Nephi.*

We removed from Conneaut to Pittsburg while I was still very young, but every circumstance of this removal is distinct in my memory. In that city my father had an intimate friend named Patterson, and I frequently visited Mr. Patterson's library with him, and heard my father talk about books with him. In 1816 my father died at Amity, Pennsylvania, and directly after his death my mother and myself went to visit at the residence of my mother's brother, William H. Sabine, at Onondaga Valley, Onondaga county, New York. Mr. Sabine was a lawyer of distinction and wealth, and greatly respected. We carried all our personal effects with us, and one of these was an old trunk, in which my mother had placed all my father's writings which had been preserved. I perfectly remember the appearance of this trunk, and of looking at its contents. There were sermons and other papers, and I saw a manuscript about an inch thick, closely written, tied with some of the stories my father had written for me, one of which he called "The Frogs of Wyndham." On the outside of this manuscript were written the words, "Manuscript Found." I did not read it, but looked through it and had it in my hands many times, and saw the names I had heard at Conneaut, when my father read it to his friends. I was about eleven years of age at this time.

After we had been at my uncle's for some time, my mother left me there and went to her father's house at Pomfret, Connecticut, but did not take her furniture nor the old trunk of manuscript with her. In 1820 she married Mr. Davison, of Hartwicks, a village near Cooperstown, New York, and sent for the things she had left at Onondaga Valley, and I remember that the old trunk, with its contents, reached her in safety. In 1828, I was married to Dr. A. McKinstry, of Hampden county, Massachusetts, and went there to reside. Very soon after my mother joined me there, and was with me most of the time until her death in 1844. We heard, not long after she came to live with me—I do not remember just how long—something of Mormonism, and the report that it had been taken from my father's "Manuscript Found"; and then came to us direct an account of the Mormon meeting at Conneaut, Ohio, and that, on one occasion, when the Mormon Bible was read there in public, my father's brother, John Spaulding, Mr. Lake and many other persons who were present, at once recognized its similarity to the "Manuscript Found," which they had heard read years before by my father in the same town.* There was a great deal of talk and a great deal published at this time about Mormonism all over the country. I believe it was in 1834 that a man named Hurlburt came to my house at Monson to see my mother, who told us that he had been sent by a committee to procure the "Manuscript Found" written by the Rev. Solomon Spaulding, so as to compare it with the Mormon Bible. He presented a letter to my mother from my uncle, Wm. H. Sabine, of Onondaga Valley, in which he requested her to loan this manuscript to Hurlburt, as he (my uncle) was desirous "to uproot" (as he expressed it) "this Mormon fraud." Hurlburt represented that he had been a convert to Mormonism, but had given it up, and through the "Manuscript Found" wished to expose its wickedness. My mother was careful to have me with her in all the conversations she had with Hurlburt, who spent a day at my house. She did not like his appearance, and mistrusted his motives, but having great respect for her brother's wishes and opinions, she reluctantly consented to his request. The old trunk, containing the desired "Manuscript Found," she had placed in the care of Mr. Jerome Clark, of Hartwicks, when she came to Monson, intending to send for it. On the repeated promise of Hurlburt to return the manuscript to us, she gave him a letter to Mr. Clark to open the trunk and deliver it to him. We afterward heard that he had received it from Mr. Clark, at Hartwicks, but from that time we have never had it in our possession, and I have no present knowledge of its existence, Hurlburt never returning it or answering letters requesting him to do so. Two years ago I heard he was still living in Ohio, and with my consent he was asked for the "Manuscript Found." He made no response, although we have evidence that he received the letter containing the request. So far I have stated facts within my knowledge. My mother mentioned many other circumstances to me in connection with this subject which are interesting, of my father's literary tastes, his fine education and peculiar temperament. She stated to me that she had heard the manuscript alluded to read by my father, was familiar with its contents, and she deeply regretted that her husband, as she believed, had innocently been the means of furnishing matter for a religious delusion. She said that my father loaned this "Manuscript Found" to Mr. Patterson, of Pittsburg, and that when he returned it to my father, he said: "Polish it up, finish it, and you will make money out of it." My mother confirmed

---

*A gentleman who resided near Conneaut at that time stated, soon after the first publication of this story regarding Mr. John Spaulding, that he (J. S.) never lived in Conneaut to the writer's most positive knowledge.

my remembrances of my father's fondness for history, and told me of his frequent conversations regarding a theory which he had of a prehistoric race which had inhabited this continent, etc., all showing that his mind dwelt on this subject. The "Manuscript Found," she said, was a romance written in Biblical style, and that while she heard it read she had no special admiration for it more than other romances he wrote and read to her. We never, either of us, ever saw, or in any way communicated with the Mormons, save Hurlburt, as above described; and while we have no personal knowledge that the Mormon Bible was taken from the "Manuscript Found," there are many evidences to us that it was and that Hurlburt and others at the time thought so. A convincing proof to us of this belief was that my uncle, William H. Sabine, had undoubtedly read the manuscript while it was in his house, and his faith that its production would show to the world that the Mormon Bible had been taken from it, or was the same with slight alterations. I have frequently answered questions that have been asked by different persons regarding the "Manuscript Found," but until now have never made a statement at length for publication.

(Signed)   M. S. McKinstry.

Sworn and subscribed to before me this 3rd day of April, A.D. 1880, at the city of Washington, D.C.

Charles Walter, Notary Public.

INDEX